The Secret Expedition
The Anglo-Russian Invasion of North Holland 1799

Geert van Uythoven

Helion & Company

Helion & Company Limited
Unit 8 Amherst Business Centre
Budbrooke Road
Warwick
CV34 5WE
England
Tel. 0121 705 3393
Email: info@helion.co.uk
Website: www.helion.co.uk
Twitter: @helionbooks
Visit our blog at http://blog.helion.co.uk/

Published by Helion & Company 2018. Reprinted in paperback 2021
Designed and typeset by Mach 3 Solutions Ltd (www.mach3solutions.co.uk)
Cover designed by Paul Hewitt, Battlefield Design (www.battlefield-design.co.uk)

Text © Geert van Uythoven 2018
Maps drawn by George Anderson © Helion & Company 2018
Cover: "Capture of Hermann", by Jacob Ernst Marcus after Dirk Langendijk. (Rijksmuseum, RP-P-OB-67.852)

Every reasonable effort has been made to trace copyright holders and to obtain their permission for the use of copyright material. The author and publisher apologise for any errors or omissions in this work, and would be grateful if notified of any corrections that should be incorporated in future reprints or editions of this book.

ISBN 978-1-914059-13-1

British Library Cataloguing-in-Publication Data.
A catalogue record for this book is available from the British Library.

All rights reserved. No part of this publication may be reproduced, stored in a retrieval system, or transmitted, in any form, or by any means, electronic, mechanical, photocopying, recording or otherwise, without the express written consent of Helion & Company Limited.

For details of other military history titles published by Helion & Company Limited, contact the above address, or visit our website: http://www.helion.co.uk

We always welcome receiving book proposals from prospective authors.

Contents

List of Plates		v
List of Maps		vii
Introduction		viii
1	The Batavian Republic – Patriots and Orangists	9
2	The Second Coalition and Plans to Invade the Batavian Republic	23
3	Batavian and French Military Forces	36
4	The British and Russian Military Forces	55
5	Preparations for the Secret Expedition	70
6	The Franco-Batavian Response to the Threat	98
7	The British Landing: Battle of Calandsoog 27 August	119
8	Building up Forces and the Surrender of the Batavian Fleet	143
9	The Orangist Incursion into the Batavian Republic	162
10	The Battle of Zijpe, 10 September	177
11	The Russians Arrive	197
12	The Battle of Bergen, 19 September	212
13	Distrust and Doubt	247
14	The Battle of Alkmaar, Egmont op Zee, or 2nd Battle of Bergen 2 October	270
15	The Battle of Castricum (or 2nd Battle of Egmond op Zee) 6 October	293
16	The Armistice	321
17	The End of the Campaign	349

Appendices

I	Convention closed between Great Britain and Russia on 22 June 1799	374
II	The Escort Squadron under the Command of Vice Admiral Andrew Mitchell	379
III	Ships Transporting the Russian Army from the Baltic	381
IV	British Invasion Force under the Command of Abercromby, 27 August 1799	384
V	French troops stationed in the Batavian Republic (4 July 1799)	386
VI	The Batavian Fleet at the Roads of Texel, 27 August 1799	388
VII	Composition of the 1e Bataafsche Divisie (Daendels) before the British landing	389
VIII	Composition of the Anglo-Russian North Sea fleet, commanded by Admiral Adam Duncan	391
IX	Order of Battle of the Anglo-Russian Fleet engaging the Dutch Fleet, 30 August 1799	392

X	Composition of the Franco-Batavian Army in Holland on 9 September 1799	393
XI	Composition of the Anglo-Russian army on 18 September 1799	396
XII	Anglo-Russian Order of Battle, 19 September 1799	400
XIII	Dispositions of the Franco-Batavian Army on 18 September 1799	403
XIV	British ships present on the Zuiderzee on 23 September 1799	406
XV	Anglo-Russian Order of Battle, 2 October 1799	408
XVI	French Troops Present in Holland, 1 and 3 October 1799	411
XVII	Order of Battle of the French troops present in the Batavian Republic, 22 November 1799	412
XVIII	Officers sent to Holland to raise the 1st and 2nd Dutch Regiments	414
XIX	Plans for the Orangist Invasion of the Batavian Republic	416
XX	Letter of 7 October 1799 to the Duke of York, proposing the retreat to the Zijpe	419

Bibliography	421
Index	432

List of Plates

"British landing at Calandsoog", by Reinier Vinkeles after a drawing of Dirk Langendijk. (Rijksmuseum, RP-P-OB-64.536)	133
"British landing at Calandsoog", by Cornelis Brouwer after a drawing of Jan Anthonie Langendijk. (Rijksmuseum, RP-P-OB-86.723)	135
"Anglo-Russian army camp near Calandsoog", by Dirk Langendijk. (Rijksmuseum, RP-T-1900-A-4380)	155
"Batavian *jager* ambush a British patrol near Schoorldam", by Cornelis Brouwer after a drawing of Dirk Langendijk. (Rijksmuseum, RP-P-OB-86.721)	161
"Defeat of a British outpost near Schoorldam", anonymous. (Noord-Hollands Archief, NL-HlmNHA_480_000500_M)	161
"Skirmish between the *Gewapende Burgermacht* of Arnhem and the Orangists in Westervoort", by Reinier Vinkeles after a drawing of Dirk Langendijk. (Rijksmuseum RP-P-1944-694)	170
"The execution of the Freule van Dorth", by Reinier Vinkeles. (Rijksmuseum RP-P-OB-86.761)	174
Approaches of Krabbendam from the direction of Schoorldam. (Author photo)	178
The crossroads at Krabbendam: Schoorlsche Zeedijk – Westfriesche Zeedijk – road to Schoorldam. (Author photo)	186
Krabbendam. Schoorlsche Zeedijk facing the direction of Zijpe Sluices. (Author photo)	191
Zijpe Sluices. (Author photo)	193
"Field bakery", by Joannes Bemme after a drawing of Dirk Langendijk. (Rijksmuseum, RP-P-1912-306)	200
"View of the Ij", anonymous. (Noord-Hollands Archief, NL-HlmNHA_359_000369_M)	202
Zijpe polder seen from the Westfriesche Zeedijk between Eenigenburg and St. Maarten. (Author photo)	206
Approaching lane from Schoorl to Bergen at the curve near the dunes. (Author photo)	213
Bergen, church ruins 1. (Author photo)	215
Bergen, church ruins 2. (Author photo)	215
Straight avenue from the curve at the dunes to Bergen. (Photo by John Grooteman)	216
Bergen, town hall. (Author photo)	220
Bergen, Sterkenhuis, the oldest house of Bergen. (Author photo)	221
Wooded dunes north of Bergen. (Author photo)	225
Wooded area east of Bergen. Close to the manor house Het Hof. (Author photo)	227
"Battle of Bergen", by Pieter Gerardus van Os. (Rijksmuseum, RP-P-1914-4345)	227
"Bitter close quarter combat", by Jacob de Vos after a drawing of Dirk Langendijk. (Noord-Hollands Archief,NL-HlmNHA_480_000429_M)	229

"Capture of Hermann", by Jacob Ernst Marcus after Dirk Langendijk. (Rijksmuseum, RP-P-OB-67.852) 230
"The Franco-Batavians attacking the Anglo-Russians near Schoorl", C. v.d. Voort van Zijp. (Noord-Hollands Archief, NL-HlmNHA_480_000497_K) 235
Old farmhouse in Dirkshorn, a model to be found in the whole of North Holland in 1799. (Author photo) 249
"Anglo-Russian prisoners brought in", anonymous. (Noord-Hollands Archief, NL-HlmNHA_53001376_K) 253
"Russian Cossacks". (Noord-Hollands Archief, NL-HlmNHA_53001377_K) 257
"British attack on Lemmer", by Reinier Vinkeles after a drawing of Dirk Langendijk. (Rijksmuseum, NL-HlmNHA_53001377_K) 263
Location of the French positions on the beach at Egmond aan Zee facing north. (Author photo) 271
High dunes along the beach at Egmond aan Zee facing north. (Author photo) 275
"French infantry defending a farm", by Dirk Langendijk. (Noord-Hollands Archief, NL-HlmNHA_480_000636_K) 280
Dunes north of Egmond aan Zee. (Author photo) 281
Typical terrain north of Bakkum. (Author photo) 297
"Battle of Castricum", by Joannes Bemme after a drawing of Dirk Langendijk. (Rijksmuseum, RP-P-OB-86.744) 303
"Cavalry engagement", by Dirk Langendijk. (Noord-Hollands Archief, NL-HlmNHA_480_000902_M) 306
"Cavalry fight", by Dirk Langendijk. (Noord-Hollands Archief, NL-HlmNHA_480_000597_G) 309
Aartswoude facing south-east. (Author photo) 332
Aartswoude facing in the direction of Kolhorn. (Author photo) 332
"Re-embarkation of the Anglo-Russian army", by Dirk Langendijk. (Rijksmuseum, RP-P-1908-2473) 343
Russian memorial at Bergen. (Author photo) 356
Plaque on the Russian memorial at Bergen. (Author photo) 357
"The Bond Street Battalion" (imposters impersonating wounded soldiers of the 1799 campaign in Holland), by John Cawse. (Rijksmuseum, RP-P-1911-747) 371
"Opening the Sluices or the Secret Expedition" (depicting the unexpected Franco-Batavian resistance) by John Cawse. (Rijksmuseum, RP-P-1981-43) 372

List of Maps

1	The Dutch Republic until 1795.	11
2	The Batavian Republic in 1799.	73
3	The Batavian fleet at the Roads of Texel.	104
4	The defences at Den Helder.	117
5	Daendels' dispositions to resist the British landing.	130
6	The Battle of the Zijpe.	181
7a	The fighting around Bergen Phase 1, c. 8:00-9:00 .am.	222
7b	The fighting around Bergen Phase 2, c. 9:00-10:00 a.m.	228
7c	The fighting around Bergen Phase 3, c. 10:00-11:00 a.m.	231
7d	The fighting around Bergen Phase 4, c. 11:00 a.m.-2:00 p.m.	236
8	The Battle of Alkmaar.	277
9a	The Battle of Castricum: positions before the battle.	295
9b	The Battle of Castricum, Phase 1: c.7:00-12:00 a.m.	304
9c	The Battle of Castricum, Phase 2: c.12:00-5:00 p.m.	305
9d	The Battle of Castricum, Phase 3: c.5:00-7:00 p.m.	311

Introduction

In 1799, as a result of an intriguing alliance forming part of the Second Coalition against France, an Anglo-Russian army landed in Holland to overthrow the Batavian Republic and to reinstate the Stadtholder Willem V of Orange. Five major battles were fought between the armies of four different nations. When I read about it, it quickly became clear that all existing accounts, as well as contemporary ones, were biased and providing an incomplete picture. Therefore I decided to do more research in an effort to get a clearer and complete picture of the campaign. This resulted in the publication of a seven-part series about the campaign for 'First Empire' magazine in 1992-1993. The series was well received and resulted in an offer from a British publisher to write a book about the campaign. More years of research followed, but when the script was ready in 1998 the publisher did not exist anymore. A Dutch publisher instead was quickly found and just before the bicentennial of the campaign in 1999 my book *Voorwaarts, Bataven!* appeared, although the text had to be compressed extensively and much had to be left out. Nevertheless the book received a warm welcome and managed to create a broader interest in the campaign, by (local) historians, students, wargamers as well as board gamers. Still I continued my research, aided over the years by correspondence with many persons also interested in the campaign, finally leading to this book, the product of all those years.

The book is based on source material from all participating countries, including numerous firsthand accounts of eye-witnesses and contemporaries. The aim is to give a balanced, detailed, and complete account of the events taking place during the invasion: the preparations on both sides, detailed descriptions of the battles as well as the events taking place on sea and in the eastern provinces of the Batavian Republic. Providing answers on questions like: What were the causes of 'The Secret Expedition'? Did Brune indeed delay reinforcing the Batavians? What caused the frequent panics in the participating armies? Were the French veteran troops and the Batavians soldiers unreliable? How was the treaty closed? Many quotes are added to the text, providing the reader with a mirror to the past.

As already stated, throughout the years my research was supported by many: some more, some less, and it is difficult to mention names without missing out someone. Nevertheless I would like to make an exception for Andrew Bamford, for editing and proofreading this book. And of course for my wife Marjan, for her patience and understanding during all those years dedicated to the creation of this work.

Geert van Uythoven, July 2018

1

The Batavian Republic – Patriots and Orangists

To understand the situation in the Netherlands in 1799 and what would finally lead to an uneasy Anglo-Russian alliance and the so-called 'Secret Invasion' of the Batavian Republic, it is necessary to provide a short history to describe the origin of the differences between the Patriots and Orangists, and how the Batavian Republic was created as a French satellite.

The Republic of the United Provinces, hereafter called the 'Dutch Republic', was a late participant in the fighting against Revolutionary France. However on 1 February 1793 France declared war both to the Stadtholder of the Dutch Republic and the King of England. In January 1795, the Dutch Republic ceased to exist and the Batavian Republic, a satellite of France, was created. To understand how it is possible that Revolutionary France defeated the once so powerful Dutch Republic, it is necessary to look at what happened in the years before to appreciate how this quick downfall could happen.

Many see the American and French Revolutions as the cradle of modern democracy, but in fact they were preceded by the rising of the Low Countries against their lawful King, Philip II of Spain (1555-1598). Philip II became King of Spain and her colonies and of the Netherlands (roughly nowadays Belgium and the Netherlands). During his reign, the Dutch became very discontented, mainly about the fact that the Dutch had less and less influence in politics; the presence of Spanish troops in the Netherlands (because of the war with France); the brutal persecution of heretics by the Spanish Inquisition; and, last but not least, taxes. Resistance started with the higher nobility and was taken over by the lower nobility and later the common people. The tension culminated in 1566 in the *beeldenstorm*, the plundering of Catholic churches. The answer of Philip II was the dispatch of the Duke of Alba with 10,000 Spanish soldiers. The rebelling inhabitants reacted by forming small armies, but Dutch government forces subdued these. From 1568 on the rebellion gathered pace, with military resistance concentrating around Willem 'the Silent', Count of Nassau, Prince of Orange. The war against Spain lasted 80 years. Only in 1648, the separation was formalised by the Peace of Munster (Peace of Westphalia): seven Dutch provinces formed a republic. The southern provinces of the Netherlands, roughly nowadays Belgium, remained Spanish.

The Constitution of the Dutch Republic

The Republic consisted of seven independent provinces, each governed by its own States, in which the cities in Holland and Zeeland held the majority of the votes. In Gelre and Overijssel the votes were equally divided between the cities and the nobility, in Friesland the countryside held the majority of votes, and in Groningen the votes were equally divided between the city and the countryside. Finally in Utrecht the cities, church, and nobility had each a vote. These seven provinces had allied themselves in the Union of Utrecht (1579), which was principally an agreement of military co-operation. The army of the Dutch Republic consisted of mercenaries. In particular many Germans served in the Dutch army, but there were also complete foreign Swiss and English battalions. In fact, there was no Dutch army, because every province had its own army and without approval of the States, these troops could not be used outside their own province.

Holland was the most important and powerful province, with Amsterdam as the most important city. The province Holland paid 58 percent of the expenses of the Republic, so its influence was huge. In most cases, commercial interest was decisive. The provinces had each one vote in the States-General, sited at The Hague in the province Holland, which took care of all joint cases. There were also three so-called *generaliteitslanden*, the provinces Brabant, Limburg, and Zeeuws Vlaanderen. These were treated as conquered territories and were governed directly by the States-General. Finally there was Drenthe, not regarded to be an equal province like the others but also not a *generaliteitsland*. It had its own government but no vote in the States-General.

The States of each province could each appoint a Stadtholder, so theoretically there could be seven at the same time. In reality, by virtue of multiple provinces appointing the same individual, after 1600 there were no more than two Stadtholders and from 1747 only one. The States of a province chose a Stadtholder, but they always choose one out of the House of Nassau, so practically the position was hereditary to this House. From 1747 on, the position of Stadtholder became hereditary by law. The Stadtholder was Captain-General of the army and Admiral-General of the fleet. In this role he had to report to the States-General and these took the important decisions. Most of the time, the States-General attached representatives to the field army, to watch over the actions of the Stadtholder, not unlike the representatives attached to the French armies during the Revolutionary Wars. In addition, the Stadtholder appointed the municipalities of the cities.

Relations between the Stadtholder and the States-General were difficult. Because of the balance of votes in the States, the cities had most of the power, but this did not mean that there was common democracy. Power was with the regents, the wealthy merchants, and these took the decisions, always taking good care of their own personal commercial interests. The one thing they were afraid of was a Stadtholder with too much power. Further, a Stadtholder was a very useful scapegoat if things went wrong. There was always discussion about who had more power: the States-General or the States of the separate provinces. The Stadtholder advocated a strong central government, to conduct strong foreign politics. The regents tried to prevent this, because they were afraid of their commercial interests. So two parties arose: the 'Pro-States', consisting of the regents, and the 'Orangists', consisting of the nobility and common people.

Map 1 The Dutch Republic until 1795.

The Rise of the Patriots

Stadtholder Willem III became in 1688 King of England. The regents used his absence to strengthen their own power. When Willem III died in 1702 without any children, the States decided to appoint no Stadtholder in his place. Up to 1747, there was no Stadtholder in the Dutch Republic. During this period government was bad and the regents considered power as their own property; government and common people grew apart. In 1747, the French invaded the south of the Dutch Republic. The country was panicking and the common people wanted an Orange back as Stadtholder. The regents became afraid of the popular movement and quickly appointed Stadtholder Willem IV, Count of Nassau, Prince of Orange. Willem IV however was much too weak to be able to influence the complex situation, disappointing his followers. Soon the regents noticed that they were able to maintain power and fell back in their old habits.

Except for the common people, wealthy citizens also had no influence on (local) politics. These were educated people and were now influenced by the ideas of men of their time, such as Voltaire and Locke. At first, these citizens also hoped that Willem IV would change things, but now it was clear they could not count on him; if it was possible to change things at all. So beside the 'Pro-States' and 'Orangists' a third party arose: the 'Patriots'. Willem IV died in 1751, leaving a three-year-old son. Because the position of Stadtholder was now hereditary, the widow of Willem IV, Princess Anna of England, was installed as 'governance'. Because she was English and had no understanding of the Dutch language and Dutch politics, the regents again met no resistance. When she died in 1759, the Prince was still under age and now a 'guardian' was installed: the German Duke Ernst von Braunschweich-Wolfenbüttel (Duke of Brunswick), at that moment serving in the Dutch army. As a guardian, officially he had no real power, but behind the curtains he managed to make himself indispensable both with the young hereditary Stadtholder and with the regents.

In 1766, Stadtholder Willem V was declared of age, but he was also much too weak to influence things. He was strongly influenced by the Duke of Brunswick (Willem V promised to do nothing without his approval) and by his own wife, the Prussian Frederika Sophia Wilhelmina von Hohenzollern, sister of the future King of Prussia. Again, the regents ruled without opposition. However, the Patriots gained more and more influence. They opposed the Duke of Brunswick, who in their opinion had a bad influence on Stadtholder Willem V. In 1780, the Dutch Republic found itself at war with England, lasting till 1784. Overseas trade was impossible and the merchants' losses were huge. The Duke of Brunswick was blamed and the Patriots acted so strongly against him that he was forced to leave the Dutch Republic. The Patriots were in high spirits because of this victory. Of course, problems were not solved overnight and next they blamed the Stadtholder for their loss. More dangerously, they started to arm themselves and formed their own armies, called *exercitiegenootschappen* (Free Corps). It was said that the Free Corps were created against the threat of the Austrian Emperor Josef II, who, the Southern Netherlands then being part of the Austrian Empire, wanted the River Scheldt reopened for shipping, something the Dutch Republic naturally opposed to. After some 'border incidents' and a provocation (a ship tried to use the river to leave Antwerp for Dunkirk) Joseph II declared war to the Dutch Republic, at the end of the year 1784. Joseph II was not prepared for the steadfastness the Dutch showed and France sided with the Dutch. Without any fighting, during 1785 peace was signed again. However, seeds of distrust were sown and the results would show later. Because of this 'war', the Dutch Republic closed a defensive alliance with France in November 1785. In reality, however, the Free Corps were created as a protection against the army and as a counterpoise against the militia, which were in general composed of Orangists. Especially in the province of Holland, the Patriots had much influence. The Patriots and regents competed in gaining as many followers as possible.

During 1784, the Patriots became more daring. The Free Corps were the cause of many riots, especially in the city of Utrecht, all in the name of freedom and justice. The situation was explosive, only a spark was needed. On 4 September 1785, a member of the *exercitiegenootschap* of the city of Leiden called Harteveld was, in his uniform with black cockade, insulted in the presence of some of his friends. A riot resulted and the States of Holland ordered that the garrison of The Hague had to patrol the streets in the future, to prevent the same thing happening again in their city. The Stadtholder Willem V judged that he was the only one who had the right, in his function as Captain-General of the army, to give orders of this kind to the garrison. However, the States did not budge and repeated their order to the garrison. Willem V, by this act practically removed from his 'command' in The Hague, decided to leave and relocated his court to the city of Nijmegen, in Gelre. The insult done to his son-in-law caused the Prussian King to protest, but the States of Holland not surprisingly ignored this protest completely. The Patriots smelled victory and everything that reminded of Orange had to be removed. Wearing orange was forbidden. A grocer was flogged because he wrapped something in orange paper. However, in other cities the Orangists still had the upper hand and the situation became very confusing, with riots taking place in many cities. Only in the provinces of Friesland, Gelre, and Zeeland were the States still on the side of the Stadtholder; in the other provinces the Patriots had the upper hand.

The situation escalated quickly. Two cities, Hattem and Elburg in the province of Gelre, were openly patriotic and gathering places of Patriots from the province. On 21 August 1786, the States of Gelre ordered the Stadtholder, in his quality as Captain-General of the army, to send troops to these cities to restore order. In Hattem the Patriots, led by Herman Willem Daendels, received news of this order and were busy strengthening the defences. Members of the Free Corps of other cities reinforced them. Daendels even managed to obtain from the city of Zwolle some guns with ammunition. The task of restoring order in Hattem was given to *Generaal-Major* Spengler. After some skirmishing his troops stormed the gate and took Hattem without loss, most of the Patriots having already taken flight. After taking the city the troops started to plunder and it took some time before their officers could restore order. Everywhere the Patriots called out for revenge. Although the Stadtholder only followed the orders given to him by the States, the Patriots called him a tyrant and an oppressor. On 22 September, the States of Holland removed him from his position as Captain-General and formed a defensive army corps commanded by the *Rheingraf* von Salm. He was ordered to protect the provinces of Holland and Utrecht. In addition, the Patriots believed that they could count on support from France, because of the defensive alliance that existed.

In the province of Utrecht the people were divided. Part of the States of Utrecht had moved to the city of Amersfoort, were they still kept in close contact with Willem V, while most cities sided with the Patriots. During May 1787, the Patriots received news that the States residing at Amersfoort had sent for troops from the province Gelre. The Patriots decided to advance on them with about three hundred members of the Free Corps of the city of

Utrecht. Near the village of Vreeswijk they clashed and the troops from Gelre were routed. Nevertheless a few Patriots were killed and became martyrs, and again the Stadtholder took the blame. The States of Holland acted by sending their own troops to Utrecht. The Dutch Republic was at the brink of civil war.

The Prussian Invasion of 1787

Then, however, the Patriots made a big mistake. The wife of Willem V was, as we have seen, the Prussian Wilhelmina von Hohenzollern, sister of the now Prussian King Friedrich Wilhelm III. Princess Wilhelmina wanted to try to save the nation in person and, only accompanied by some servants, moved from Nijmegen to The Hague. On 28 June 1787 the Patriots at Goejanverwellensluis, near the border of the province of Holland, stopped her and refused passage. The States of Holland approved the action, but the States of the provinces Gelre, Zeeland, Utrecht, and Friesland condemned it. When the King of Prussia received news of the insult done to his sister, he demanded satisfaction and punishment for the guilty ones. However, the Patriots felt themselves safe, with their Free Corps, militia and their field army commanded by the *Rheingraf* von Salm. The city of Gorkum, the key of Holland, was strongly fortified. The city of Utrecht was believed unassailable. In addition, in case of a Prussian attack, the Patriots counted on French support.

In August, the Prussians started massing troops in the Duchy of Cleve, commanded by Karl Wilhelm Ferdinand, *Herzog* von Braunschweig und Lüneburg, to reinforce the Prussian claim for satisfaction. Still the States of Holland did not give way. On 8 September, a Prussian ultimatum followed: the Prussians would attack the province Holland if their States did not give satisfaction, punish the guilty ones, and give Princess Wilhelmina free passage. Again the States of Holland refused. On 13 September the Prussians crossed the Dutch border. They made it very clear from the beginning that they only fought against the province Holland and not against the other provinces and the *generaliteitslanden*. The Prussian advance was swift, in cooperation with the loyal Orangist troops. The *Rheingraf* von Salm abandoned the Patriot army before any fighting occurred and his troops dispersed. No French support materialised. Many Patriots now believed that they fought for a lost cause and deserted. Whole units abandoned their defensive positions and dispersed, returning home. Utrecht was captured on 16 September by Orangist troops without any opposition. The remaining Patriots retreated to Amsterdam, but any resistance became futile with the Prussians closing in. After some skirmishing, on 10 October the city capitulated. The capitulation of Amsterdam signalled the end of the Prussian campaign and now the balance could be made up. In spite of many combats and skirmishes the Prussians lost only 211 men killed out of a total of over 26,000 men taking part in the campaign. Only 15 men deserted – also a remarkably low number for this period in history. These losses were more than made up by Prussian recruiting in the Dutch Republic during the campaign and persuading prisoners of war to enlist.

As can be imagined, the disarming and disbanding of the Free Corps proved difficult and it also took a few weeks before riots between Orangists and Patriots ceased. The reliability of the depleted Dutch army was doubtful with so many units also having fought on Patriot side. It would take time before the Dutch army would have been brought up to strength again. The Dutch Republic was very vulnerable, especially with so many Patriots within its borders. Although many Dutch sources state that about 40,000 Patriots had left the country to seek refuge in the Austrian Netherlands and France, the historian Colenbrander has convincingly reasoned that their number was not more than 5,000 or 6,000 at the most, most of them remaining in the Dutch Republic.[1] Many Patriots went to France and joined the Revolutionary French armies, later enlisting in a Batavian Legion under the command of the Patriot Daendels.

In order to maintain a firm grip on the Dutch Republic, the States-General asked for 3,000-4,000 Prussian soldiers to remain in Holland, until sufficient German troops could be hired to improve the reliability of the army and become available to garrison the most important fortresses. The King of Prussia agreed and even offered to pay the troops himself, if the States-General would take care of their provisions. These troops stayed until the following year when, on 6 May 1788, the last Prussian soldiers left the Dutch Republic, after the German troops that had been hired arrived: 2,906 men from the Duke of Brunswick, 1,389 men from the Count of Anspach, and 1,000 men from the Duke of Mecklenburg-Schwerin.

The Prussian invasion of Holland in 1787 put for the time being an end to the power of the Patriots. Willem V of Orange was again Stadtholder of the restless provinces of the Dutch Republic. To strengthen the position of Willem V even more, on 15 April 1788 treaties were concluded between the Dutch Republic and respectively Great Britain and Prussia. These treaties stipulated mutual assistance in case of an attack and that the latter countries guaranteed the hereditary rights of the House of Orange in the Dutch Republic. This was followed on 13 August 1788 by an alliance concluded between Prussia and the Dutch Republic, to support each other in case of an attack. The side effect of all this was that in international affairs, the Dutch Republic was highly dependent on both countries and, because of this and the fact that France had promised the Patriots their assistance (that as shown above failed to materialise), relations with France deteriorated.

The behaviour of the Dutch Republic was rather dualistic. Inside the Republic, care was taken that the Patriots lost all their power and that they were removed from important political positions. On the other hand, Belgian or Brabantian Patriots, resisting Joseph II, ruler of the Austrian Empire – which included present-day Belgium, then known as the Austrian Netherlands – found refuge on Dutch soil. The Belgian Patriots were admitted because of two reasons. First, to prevent them taking refuge in France. Secondly, out of revenge, because the Dutch Patriots found refuge in the Austrian Netherlands. In addition, relations with Joseph II were already bad, because the Austrian emperor wanted free passage on the River Scheldt (in which he did not succeed) and the evacuation of the so called 'barrier cities' by the Dutch army (in which he did succeed). With respect to these latter, to guarantee safety against a French surprise attack, the Dutch Republic occupied a whole chain of fortress-cities in the Austrian Netherlands, along the French border. Joseph II chose to see this as an encroachment on his rights as ruler of the Austrian Empire. The fortresses were also in decline and the garrisons were much too weak. When Joseph II demanded their evacuation, the Dutch Republic agreed, taking in account that it would

---

1 H.T. Colenbrander, *Gedenkstukken der Algemeene Geschiedenis van Nederland van 1795 tot 1840* ('s-Gravenhage: Martinus Nijhoff, 1907), Vol.I, pp.XXXI–XXXIII. A recent in-depth study of the Patriot refugees has been done by Joost Rosendaal, *Bataven! Nederlandse vluchtelingen in Frankrijk 1787-1795* (Nijmegen: Uitgeverij Vantilt, 2003).

save money and that the Austrian Netherlands would already provide a safe buffer between France and the Dutch Republic. Time would prove that this was a mistake.

The Belgian Patriots formed a committee in Breda, led by Van der Noot and they even formed their own army under Colonel van der Mersch, armed with Dutch weapons. On 24 October 1789, the Austrian Emperor was declared to be extinct from his rights as Duke of Brabant and Count of Henegouwen and, as a result, an Austrian army invaded the Austrian Netherlands. The Austrian troops under General d'Alton lost the war and had to capitulate. On 17 December Van der Noot entered Brussels and the independent Vereenigde Belgische Staten ('United Belgian States') were declared. However, during 1790 the Austrians, now under their Emperor Leopold II, counterattacked and Marshal Bender defeated the Belgian Patriots and retook the Austrian Netherlands. The exiled Belgian Patriots, including many men who would make name for themselves in the following years, such as Dumonceau, Ghigny, and Lahure, joined the Dutch Patriots already present in France. They now all had a common cause to fight for.

The French Revolution

In the meantime, in France the Revolution was taking place and as a result Prussia, Saxony, and Austria allied themselves on 7 August 1791 at Pillnitz to bring back Louis XVI to the French throne. Later that year and during 1792, other countries joined the coalition, but their contribution was insignificant. With the Dutch invasion of 1787 still fresh in his mind, King Friedrich Wilhelm III of Prussia was confident he could pull off the same in France without any trouble. Again, the Duke of Brunswick, 'experienced' in these matters, would lead the attack. Things would have a different outcome this time. The Prussians were not very active and Austrian strength in Belgium was less than a third of that of the Prussians.

Great Britain as well as the Dutch Republic stayed neutral initially. After the events of 10 August 1792, during which King Louis XVI was taken prisoner and his Swiss Guard slaughtered, both countries recalled their ambassadors from Paris, however still declaring they had no desire to meddle themselves with the internal affairs of France. The retreat of the Prussian army after the Battle of Valmy (20 September) and the defeat of the Austrian army at Jemappes (6 November), leading to the conquest of most of the Austrian Netherlands, made however a huge impression on the French Revolutionaries. Until now, most of the French leaders did not really believe it would be possible for them to defeat the regular armies of Prussia and Austria. *Lieutenant-Général* Charles-François de Perrier, known by the name Dumouriez, conquered the whole of the Austrian Netherlands within three weeks. The French lines were pushed forward as far as the border of the Dutch Republic and the cities Venlo and Achen, while the government of the Austrian Netherlands found refuge in the cities Roermond and Maastricht. If the French had followed up their advance into the Dutch Republic, military resistance would have been virtually impossible. However, the sorry state the Revolutionary armies were in prevented any further advance for the moment. However much desired by the Dutch Patriots that had taken refuge in France, the order to attack the Dutch Republic was not given and to be realistic, if it had been given it could most probably not have been carried out successfully. The French soldiers lacked everything, even muskets and supplies were non-existing. The Dutch Patriots formed a *Comité Revolutionair*, a 'revolutionary committee' and called on their brethren in the Dutch Republic to rise against Willem V. However, the time was not yet right.

Not surprisingly, tension between France and the Dutch Republic was rising. The States-General still felt themselves safe, with the promised support of Great Britain and Prussia, and no preparations were made for the eventuality of a war. Great Britain itself did nothing, sitting on the fence, safe on the other side of the Channel and watching their arch-enemy France becoming weaker every day. The British even felt some sympathy for the French. The French, however, were much less careful in their relations with the neighbouring countries. By now, they had promised their support to all suppressed nations that would want to free themselves from their oppressors. In Belgium, Dumouriez demanded free passage across Dutch territory through the fortress-city of Maastricht. Next, the French claimed free passage on the River Scheldt, closed by the Dutch to prevent all shipping to Antwerp, a right internationally recognised after the Treaty of Westphalia in 1648. The British were not happy with the capture of Antwerp by the French, the 'pistol on the breast of Great Britain' and its capture, combined with free passage on the Scheldt, was a direct threat to Britain's security.

British Prime Minister William Pitt told the French ambassador in London that the British never would allow the one-sided breach of an agreed treaty. A British squadron set sail for Zeeland. The Dutch Republic was made clear that the British would fulfil their obligations deriving from the alliance of 1788. The Prussians declared the same. In spite of this, the Dutch chose the easiest way out and opened secret negotiations with Dumouriez in order to prevent, or at least slow down, a French attack on the Dutch Republic. They were even prepared to recognise the French Revolutionary government. However, events in Paris prevented all this. On 21 January 1793, Louis XVI met his death on the Place de la Révolution. Europe was struck with horror. On 24 January Great Britain ordered the French ambassador to leave the country within eight days. The French National Convention took this move as an affront without any grounds. As a result, and also to lay their hands on the huge amounts of money supposed to exist in the very wealthy Dutch Republic, on 1 February 1793 France declared war. In Revolutionary style, war was declared against the King of Great Britain and the Stadtholder of the Dutch Republic, not against the countries themselves. The National Convention forgot in their ignorance that Willem V was not, as a Stadtholder, head of state, but only the first servant of the Republic.

Dutch Preparations for War

The Dutch Republic was a seafaring nation. Land armies had less interest for the government, and the people as a whole, for as long as the Republic had existed. Conscription did not exist. The Dutch army was neglected. In spite of the dangerous situation in Europe and the bad relations with their neighbour Austria, the Dutch were only interested in making money and not spending it on defence. Nothing was done to strengthen the army or to maintain the fortresses in good condition. The units of the Dutch army were paid by, and officially in the service of, a particular province, not by the Dutch Republic itself. Because of this arrangement, a unit had to swear first an oath to the province in which service it was and an additional one to the Stadtholder. The States-General representing the provinces were, unlike the Stadtholder and his sons, of the opinion that the Republic would have to remain neutral at all times, so a strong army was not necessary. Even during the spring of 1792 when tension was rising, and despite the strongest remonstrance by Prince Willem of Orange, the oldest son of Willem V and commander in chief of the Dutch field army, the States-General only agreed with the introduction of new drill-regulations for the infantry and the abolition of the parade-step! Only on 7 September 1792, after long deliberations, an agreement was reached about a resolution that laid down the strength for the Dutch army at 44,823 men. A large part of this Dutch army consisted of foreigners. For example of the infantry, only 26 out of 40 regiments were national. Even in these national regiments, many foreigners were enlisted with Dutch recruiters active in most countries in Europe.

The events in the south, where Dumouriez quickly defeated the Austrians and advanced up to the borders of the Dutch Republic, caused the Dutch to believe that maybe it would not be possible after all to remain neutral any longer. Therefore, plans for an augmentation of the army were laid down before the States, on 31 December 1792 and 9 January 1793. The proposal was to strengthen the army with an additional 13,260 men. When the augmentation was finally approved, on 6 and 21 February, war had already begun. Where to find the men was the next problem; the infantry, for example, was already before the augmentation 2,500 men short! The cavalry was 1,000 horses short. The units lacked sufficient cartridges, cartridge boxes, and even muskets. Recruitment was made even more difficult because a 'fifth column' consisting of Patriots and foreigners tried to talk soldiers out of Dutch service by promising them better pay. This practice was quickly forbidden by penalty of death. The same occurred with horses. These were bought and sold in foreign countries, until huge fines countered this practice.[2]

The field army would be led by the son of Willem V: Willem Frederik, Hereditary Prince of Orange and Nassau, the future King Willem I. The following measures were taken to create a field army from scratch. The grenadier companies were taken away from their parent units and converged into grenadier battalions. The musketeer companies of each regiment were combined into a battalion of eight companies and a weak depot. However, in practice most of these battalions were no stronger than six companies. Problems were so huge that bounties were offered to captains who could bring their companies up to war footing at a certain date! Especially because of the lack of horses, the cavalry regiments in the field were initially not stronger than two squadrons each. The number of horses and also vehicles were completely inadequate. Command of the artillery and the cavalry was given to the other son of Willem V: Willem George Frederik, Prince of Orange and Nassau (Prince Frederick of Orange).

Despite all measures, the Dutch army never came even close to its full establishment strength of 3,230 officers, 54,853 others and 6,557 horses. At the end of February 1793, strength of the field army did not exceed 16,000 men and 3,000 horses, insufficiently armed and equipped! Experience of these troops was low. Without counting the Prussian invasion of 1787, during which hardly or no real fighting took place, the army had not taken the field for 45 years. Practice had been limited to drill and parades, but no real preparation for war.

---

2   Cornelis van der Aa, *Geschiedenis van den Jongst-geëindigden Oorlog, tot op het Sluiten van den Vrede te Amiëns. Bijzonder met Betrekking tot de Bataafsche Republiek* (Amsterdam: Johannes Allart, 1802 & 1806), Vol.I, p.331

Long marches were also not practised, so when the army took the field in 1793, every two or three days a resting day had to be held to allow the many stragglers to catch up with their parent units. Some regiments even forgot to take their colours into battle! Further, as we have already seen, especially with the infantry, many foreign units were part of the Dutch army. The most experienced were those foreigners who had not much stomach to fight for the Dutch Republic, at least not without better payment. For these reasons, the States-General thought it much more efficient to use these for garrison duty and to let the inexperienced national troops do the fighting. Perhaps surprisingly, the morale of the soldiers was not as bad as might be expected. Most soldiers serving involuntarily had already found one way or another to desert the Dutch army. Regarding the senior officers, most of them were of advanced age, with no experience in the 'modern' French way of doing battle. They were surprised by the ferocity of the French attacks, by their unorthodox tactics and their quick – according to the standards of this time – advance. Therefore they would be no match in the upcoming war until they could regain their posture.

The First Coalition

On 26 June 1792, Prussia and Austria had formed the First Coalition. After the execution of Louis XVI and the French declaration of war against Great Britain and the Dutch Republic, these countries joined the First Coalition, followed by Spain and later also Russia, the German Empire, Portugal, the Two Sicilies, and Tuscany. Real military support from the latter countries however would be minor or even non-existent.

After the declaration of war, a council of war was held at The Hague to prepare for the defence of the Dutch Republic. It was – correctly – assessed that the southern part of the Dutch Republic was under the circumstances not defensible against a determined French attack. The decision was made to yield this terrain, except for some fortresses, which would be defended to hamper French movement and to force the enemy to use troops to blockade or besiege these. For this purpose the most important fortress-cities in the south were reinforced. Other fortress-cities in the south were believed to be strong enough for the moment, or of less importance and only their garrisons received some reinforcements. The main defence line would be formed behind the Rivers Meuse and Waal where the French would have to use boats or bridges to cross. This would give the Dutch time to concentrate their troops at the threatened location and give the Dutch a chance to inflict heavy casualties with their batteries and superior naval forces.

Luckily, the Dutch would not have to fight alone. Of course, the Austrians and Prussians were already present in force along the Rhine. On the last day of February 1793 the first British troops arrived in the Dutch Republic. The British were fully aware of the dangers that a French capture of the Netherlands would bring for the safety of Britain, therefore, there was no hesitation in sending troops. With them came the Duke of York, who would command the British expeditionary force. This was a calculated choice. Command in the field of the Dutch army was held by both sons of the Stadtholder Willem V, the Hereditary Prince Willem of Orange and Prince Frederic of Orange. Both sons were young and inexperienced. Lord Auckland, British Ambassador in the Dutch Republic, wrote on 15 February 1793 to Lord Grenville:

> I have a farther motive for wishing to see His Royal Highness [i.e. the Duke of York] here. The young Princes of Orange are high-spirited; but I will not be answerable for the steadiness of the father when the hour of danger approaches.[3]

So what was needed was a British commander who would be acceptable to the Dutch, to lead also the Dutch army under both the two princes. Only one person could meet this demand: the Duke of York. On 20 February orders were given to the three first battalions of the British Foot Guards to make themselves ready for foreign service. These three battalions would form a brigade, commanded by Major General Gerard Lake. The brigade would be augmented with a composite Guards Grenadier Battalion of four companies, created from two grenadiers companies of the 1st Foot Guards and one from both other regiments. On the 25th the Guards Brigade, nearly 2,000 men, embarked in Greenwich, the King himself present at their embarkation. York's instructions were unclear though. He was to support the Dutch in their defence and to guide both princes. At the same time it was made perfectly clear to him that he would have to husband his guards. They would have to stay within immediate reach of their transports, 'in case their services should be required elsewhere'.[4] In time he would be reinforced by more British, Hanoverian, and Hessian troops, but it was unclear when these would arrive. Further, it was still to be seen if the Dutch Republic would be able to defend itself against the French at all. So York decided not to undertake risky operations and to restrict himself mainly to garrison duty until he had sufficient forces at his disposal and the situation would be more clear.

Diplomatically, in The Hague there were still secret negotiations going on between the French and the Dutch. These were broken off on 13 February 1793. The French National Convention ordered Dumouriez to attack immediately. In the Dutch Republic, on 15 February the Dutch guard left The Hague for the front in the south. These troops had just enough time to reach their destination before the French attack came. However, the concentration of the field army would not even start until eight days later. Prince Willem of Orange, who at the moment was in Frankfurt to confer with the Prussians, hurried back to take command of the field army. It was clear that the Dutch were much too late with their preparations. Now the only thing they could do was try to buy time.

The French Attacks on the Dutch Republic

Dumouriez planned to move with his Armée de Hollande along an advance line that would leave the fortress-cities of Breda and Geertruidenberg on his right and the fortress-cities of Bergen-op-Zoom, Steenbergen, and Willemstad on his left. These cities would be covered by sufficient forces to prevent any sorties, while Dumouriez would try to cross the swampy estuary called the Biesbosch, near Dordrecht. In this way he hoped to avoid a crossing of the probably heavily defended rivers and this advance would place him directly in the heart of the Dutch Republic. He would continue his advance by capturing the cities of Rotterdam,

---

3   H.T. Colenbrander, *Gedenkstukken der Algemeene Geschiedenis van Nederland van 1795 tot 1840* ('s-Gravenhage: Martinus Nijhoff, 1907), Vol.I, p.294.
4   J.W. Fortescue, *A History of the British Army* (London: MacMillan and Co. Limited, 1906), Vol.IV Part 1, p.80.

Delft, The Hague, Leiden, Haarlem, and finally Amsterdam, not expecting much resistance because of his bold advance from an unexpected direction. Dumouriez' whole plan was further based on the assumption that the Dutch army would present no real threat and that the Dutch inhabitants, according to his view mainly Patriots, would give extensive help to his troops in any way they could. This view was strengthened by the Patriot exiles fighting in the French ranks, especially by *Colonel* Daendels. Dumouriez expected to augment his army with 25,000 to 30,000 Batavian volunteers. His flank would be covered by *Lieutenant-Général* Francisco de Miranda, commanding the Armée du Nord, advancing to Nijmegen to prevent the Prussians coming to the aid of the Dutch.

On 17 February 1793 the Armée de Hollande crossed the Dutch border and concentrated in the area between the fortress-cities of Bergen-op-Zoom and Breda. Among its light troops were three Batavian (Patriot) battalions under the command of *Colonel* Daendels. The French troops brought no provisions and had to live of the land. Every village where the French came had to deliver not only billets for the soldiers but also food, guides, labourers, horses, cattle and wagons, without any payment at all. Also many villages had to provide for a 'loan' in cash. Therefore, not surprisingly, the inhabitants had more and more the idea of being plundered instead of being 'freed' from the oppression of the House of Orange. As a result, only few volunteers joined the French. The Dutch did nothing to hamper the advance of the French, at the moment the French weakness was unknown to them. Meeting no real resistance until now, Dumouriez decided to bombard and try to take one or more of the fortress-cities in the western part of Brabant. Success would enable him to capture the much-needed cannon and ammunition, while more boats were being gathered for a crossing of the rivers. In addition, Breda was ideally located as a base for further operations. On 25 February, after a siege lasting five days, the city surrendered to the French. Geertruidenberg also surrendered, even before a proper siege had begun. The weakly defended fortress-city of Klundert was taken by storm, but Willemstad managed to hold out, despite a fierce bombardment and various French attacks. This city was strategically important. French possession of the fortress would prevent all Dutch shipping on the Hollandsch Diep and would give a useful harbour from which a crossing of the river could be undertaken. After the siege was lifted, Willemstad became the symbol of Dutch resistance against the French invasion.

Luckily for the Dutch, the Austrians moved to recapture the Austrian Netherlands. When hearing of the Austrian advance in the east, Dumouriez had to give up his plans for the conquest of the Dutch Republic to oppose the Austrians and defend Belgium. On 18 March, Dumouriez lost the Battle of Neerwinden. In order not to be cut off, the French troops in the south of the Dutch Republic had to retreat. A British expeditionary force landed in Flanders and Dumouriez defected to the Allies. Again the situation looked very bad for France, but this time the lack of co-operation between the allies saved them. The French National Convention in August ordered the *levée en masse* and the French armies became bigger and bigger. Already the First Coalition began to crumble and in the Battle of Fleurus (26 June 1794) the French under Jourdan succeeded in defeating the Allies. The Austrians now retreated to Germany behind the River Meuse, while the Anglo-Dutch troops retreated into the Dutch Republic followed by the French under Pichegru. Again, the French had conquered the Austrian Netherlands. A very cold winter helped them to conquer also the Dutch Republic: the main protection of Holland, the rivers and inundations were worthless now and even the Dutch fleet at the roads of Texel was captured by a regiment of French cavalry! The Orange family took refuge in Great Britain and the Patriots proclaimed the Batavian Republic.

The new Batavian government had to accept the Treaty of The Hague (16 May 1795), containing the following conditions, to stay 'independent':

1. Payment of 100 million guilders to the French Republic;
2. Renunciation of Dutch Flanders and Dutch Limburg with the cities of Venlo and Maastricht to the French Republic;
3. Tax free French shipping on the Rivers the Scheldt, Meuse, and Rhine;
4. Exclusively a French garrison inside the fortress city and naval harbour of Flushing, in war as well in peace time;
5. In case the Batavian or French Republic would be attacked by an enemy power from the direction of the Rhine or Zeeland, French garrisons would be placed in the fortress-cities Bergen op Zoom, 's Hertogenbosch, and Grave;
6. To place at the disposal of the French Republic, 12 ships of the line and 18 frigates;
7. To place at the disposal of the French Republic, half of the Batavian army;
8. For the defence of both republics, the French Republic will continue the occupation of the Batavian Republic by a number of soldiers agreed between both countries;
9. To feed, clothe and pay 25,000 French soldiers stationed in the Batavian Republic.

The Batavian Republic now was nothing more than a French satellite and the result was a British declaration of war to the Batavian Republic on 15 September 1795.

2

The Second Coalition and Plans to Invade the Batavian Republic

The Armistice of Leoben on 18 April 1797, followed by the Treaty of Campo Formio on 18 October, ended the war of the First Coalition. Great Britain stood now alone against France, its ally Spain, and its satellite state the Batavian Republic. Between these countries the war continued, outside the European mainland. At sea the British won a number of naval battles important for the safety of Great Britain, its colonies and international interests. On 14 February 1797, Admiral Sir John Jervis defeated a much larger Spanish fleet off Cape St Vincent. In the Mediterranean, Rear Admiral Horatio Nelson defeated the French fleet that had brought Napoleon Bonaparte to Egypt at the Battle of the Nile or Aboukir on 1 August 1798. On 11 October 1797, the Batavian *Vice-Admiraal* de Winter was defeated by Admiral Duncan in the Battle of Camperdown, the Batavians losing 10 ships of the line and four frigates. Especially this battle, just after the mutiny at the Nore, restored confidence in the British navy. A French attempt to invade Ireland or Great Britain was thwarted. The French Republic was considered vulnerable again for a number of reasons:

- Napoleon Bonaparte with 35,000 of the best French troops was bottled up in Egypt after the defeat of the French fleet in the Nile;
- Early 1799 the Austrian army recovered most of Germany and Italy. The French were heavily engaged in Switzerland by an Austro-Russian army, losing much territory in Italy;
- The French Republic was again divided. The rule of the *Directoire* was despotic, there was tightened press censorship, people were persecuted, the Vendée was again rebellious;
- Uprisings took place in Italy and in the southern Netherlands the population rose against the French in the *Boerenoorlog* (Peasants' War). The population in Switzerland and the Batavian Republic were openly dissatisfied with French influence;
- France had huge financial problems, mainly because of the huge armies she had to maintain;
- Britain was master of the seas blockading French overseas trade. The French fleet formed no threat after their loss in the Mediterranean, the remains of the Spanish fleet were blockaded at Cadiz and the Batavian fleet was blockaded at the roadstead of Texel.

The Treaty of Campo Formio had given extensive territorial gains to the French Republic: the Republic of Venice was dissolved, with Istria and Dalmatia going to Austria, the Ionian Islands with Corfu to France. The Austrian Netherlands became part of the French Republic. In northern Italy, Genoa ceased to exist as an independent power, Austria had to recognise the Cisalpine and Ligurian Republics, both nothing more than French satellite states. Rather interestingly, *Général de Division* Guillaume Brune attempted a *coup d'état* in the Cisalpine Republic in the autumn of 1798. The *coup* failed and as a result Brune was transferred to the Batavian Republic, to resume command of the Armée de Hollande:

> On 15 October, Brune was appointed *général en chef* of the Army of Holland, but he had been detained in Paris on account of his conduct in the Cisalpine Republic. The march of the Russians put an end to the scruples of the Directory, which, on the 28th of December, permitted Brune to take possession of his command. Arriving on 8 January 1799, Brune immediately succeeded Hatry.[1]

In additional clauses of the Treaty of Campo Formio, the borders of the French Republic would be extended to the Rhine, while they would also have free navigation on the Rhine, Meuse, and Moselle Rivers. The details of these territorial issues would be solved at the Congress of Rastatt but negotiations proved to be difficult. The great powers remained suspicious of each other. The Austrians were reluctant to hand over regions they ought to have given up according to the Treaty of Campo Formio; the French came with additional claims. In February 1798 the French occupied the Papal States and declared the Roman Republic, yet another French satellite state. Switzerland suffered the same fate in March, becoming the Helvetic Republic. Closing a military alliance with the Helvetic Republic in August 1798, the French gained free passage across the strategically important Alpine passes.

Until March 1799, the main adversaries on the European mainland avoided armed conflict. However, on the first day of that month, *Général de Division* Jourdan crossed the Rhine at Kehl and Basel, despite no war being declared. Austria regarded this as a breach of the Treaty of Campio Formio and the Archduke Karl was ordered to react but for the moment not to attack. On 12 March the French officially declared war and the fighting commenced. Jourdan was defeated by the Austrian Archduke Karl at Ostrach (21 March) and again at Stockach (25 March) and was forced to fall back over the Rhine. That summer a Russian army also arrived on the scene, with Suvorov making name as a fine commander for his campaign in Switzerland, but due to bad political and strategic decisions he was finally defeated. The Russians were also ready to send their navy to the Mediterranean, but initially they were not allowed by the Turks to pass the Dardanelles, despite Napoleon having invaded Egypt. Reluctant as the Turks were, Nelson's defeat of the French fleet at Aboukir changed everything. With the French naval threat to the Turks removed, on 9 September the Turks declared war on France. An unlikely naval cooperation between Russia and Turkey against the French was the result. On 24 August 1798, Admiral Ushakov left Sebastopol with a fleet of six ships of the line and additional frigates. After having been joined by a

---

1 Charles Dolly, 'Chronologie historique des armées de la République et de l'Empire', in *Le Spectateur Militaire*, Vol. XLIX, p.25.

Turkish squadron consisting of four ships of the line and some smaller ships, he entered the Mediterranean on 1 October. In January 1799 he was joined by another two ships of the line. He soon captured all the Ionian Islands occupied by the French and also took Corfu, capturing the last French position in March. Then he turned his attention to the Italian coastal fortress of Ancona, also occupied by a French garrison, but failed in capturing it. For the remainder of their presences in the Mediterranean the Russians participated in the blockade of the Italian coast and Ushakov would return to the Black Sea in October 1800.

Creating the Second Coalition

In Great Britain it was believed time was ripe to align the major powers against France again. British diplomats were active in forging a new coalition. Although Great Britain was safe in doing so, protected as it was by the power of its naval forces, the great powers on the European mainland were more reluctant. They had met with the full force of the French armies, bringing chaos and destruction to great parts of Europe and were still recovering from their losses. There was a dispute between Great Britain and Austria about the repayment of Austrian loans closed in 1795 and then there was the historical distrust between Austria and Prussia. Both countries feared Revolutionary France, but they feared each other even more. Each saw the possibility of a bargain with the French at the expense of their German rival and feared that the rival would make the bargain first.[2] Great Britain had of course its own reasons to form a Second Coalition against France.

In 1798 Napoleon Bonaparte took more than 35,000 soldiers to Egypt, officially to block Great Britain's access to India, for scientific research and to protect French trade interests. It also seems that the *Directoire* saw Napoleon as a threat and were glad to have him out of the way. The capture of Malta by Napoleon, on his way to Egypt, had infuriated the Tsar of Russia, Paul I. The Tsar was protector of the Knights Hospitallers who had their seat on Malta and its capture was one of the reasons Tsar Paul I would join the Second Coalition, although Russian cooperation with the British was not new. As long ago as June 1795, when the French overran the Dutch Republic and the Batavian Republic was created, a Russian naval squadron consisting of 12 ships of the line and eight frigates under Rear-Admiral Chanykov joined the British North Sea fleet blockading the Batavian ports. They remained during the winter in English ports. During 1796 their presence did not influence the war, various Russian ships cruising with the British North Sea fleet. Early October Chanykov returned to Kronstadt and next month Rear-Admiral Makarov sailed for the North Sea with a fresh Russian squadron consisting of three ships of the line and three frigates. Again wintering in English ports, the Russian warships joined Duncan again in June 1797 but were almost immediately ordered back to Kronstadt, so the Russians were not present at the Battle of Camperdown.

On 2 June 1798, Vice Admiral Makarov sailed from Kronstadt for the North Sea again, with a third Russian squadron consisting of five ships of the line and a frigate. At the

---

2   Piers Mackesy, *Statesmen at War: the Strategy of Overthrow, 1798–1799* (London and New York: Longman Group Ltd., 1974), p.8.

beginning of July they joined the British fleet cruising off the Texel. In September he was joined by an additional five ships of the line and in November five more ships of the line and some frigates arrived. Their presence enabled the British to reinforce their Mediterranean fleet. After again wintering in English ports, two of the Russian ships of the line and a frigate returned to the Baltic during July while three ships of the line and a frigate were ordered to join Admiral Ushakov in the Mediterranean in June. This left Makarov with a squadron consisting of eight ships of the line, two frigates and a brig.[3] During July, the Russian Rear-Admiral George Tate was despatched with three ships of the line and two frigates to keep an eye on the Batavian ships in Hellevoetsluis. Not surprisingly, the British navy had no high opinion of their Russian allies and, despite the fact that a lot of foreign naval officers were serving on the Russian warships, there still was a lot of mistrust and squabbling over precedence. Still, their presence enabled the British to deploy their ships on other more critical stations.

The British plans for a coalition of the four great powers, taking in account the views and goals of Austria and Prussia, are clearly outlined in a letter from Lord Grenville, British Foreign Secretary, to Sir Charles Whitworth, British envoy in St. Petersburg:

> The views of Austria appear now to be principally directed towards Italy, where her success would certainly afford least ground of jealousy to Prussia. No objection could reasonably be made at Berlin to the effect of any measures which should lead to the recovery of all the former dominions of Austria in Lombardy; provided it were distinctly understood that no further encroachment should be made on the possessions of the other powers of Italy. And the reconquest of the Milanese, added to the acquisitions already made by Austria in Italy would, it is conceived, furnish a sufficient indemnity to that power for those exertions which indeed her own safety indispensably requires her to make both on the side of Italy and Switzerland. It might therefore on this ground, and in conformity to the principles of the negotiation already established between Austria and Prussia, be expressly stipulated that no indemnity should be sought by Austria in Germany.
>
> The disposition of the King of Prussia to act eventually on the side of Holland for the restoration of the House of Orange and for the reestablishment of a solid and efficient government in that country, have been intimated to H. M., and nothing could more effectually tend to consolidate the tranquillity of Europe than the success of measures to be taken for this purpose, in which H. M. would willingly cooperate in so far as could in any manner depend on him. It is uncertain whether the court of Berlin has in view any, and what, objects of separate advantage in addition to that general benefit which would result from the restoration of the tranquillity and security of Europe. It seems therefore very important that the King of Prussia should, on the present occasion, be invited to explain himself confidentially and fully on this head, and to define and limit by precise stipulation the nature and extent of any such advantages, if any such are in his contemplation.

---

3   For the composition of the combined Anglo-Russian North Sea fleet, see Appendix VIII.

> From the establishment of the general basis of treaty already laid down, the independence of Switzerland and Holland will necessarily follow; as well as the restoring to the German Empire those parts which were to be ceded to France by the negotiation of Rastadt, and the compelling the French to renounce the possession of Savoy and the Netherlands. But as these last provinces cannot probably under all the circumstances which have occurred be replaced under the dominion of Austria, and as it may well be doubted whether these acquisitions would be an object of ambition to either of the two great German powers, it will remain to be considered what plan will be most effectual to provide for the defence of this highly important barrier against the future encroachment of France. None has here occurred which is thought equally effectual and practicable as the uniting those provinces to the Dutch Republic under the administration of a Stadtholder, and with such provisions as may be best adapted to the maintenance of their respective civil and religious constitutions. But on this head H. M. would willingly receive the suggestions of his ally, directed as he is confident they would be to the same object to which H. M. looks, that of securing those provinces as far as possible from falling again a prey to the restless ambition of France; a point the accomplishment of which must always be regarded by H. M. as being at least equally important with any other objet in the whole range of the extensive interests which would be to be adjusted in such a negotiation.[4]

Beside the restoration of the House of Orange and the Dutch Republic, for the first time the merging of Belgium with the Dutch Republic was mentioned. The road to a coalition of the four great powers turned out to be difficult though. During December 1798, the Second Coalition was created, but it was again a very loose and unstable alliance, based on bilateral treaties between Naples and Austria (20 May 1798), Britain and Russia (the provisional 'Treaty of alliance and subsidies', 29 December 1798), and Russia and Turkey (3 January 1799). It lacked agreed political aims and an overall strategic plan. In the absence of this, the allies would follow their own political and strategic aims, making a concerted execution of the war against France impossible. Negotiations for this treaty had started August 1798; the treaty which formally created the Second Coalition was closed on 22 June 1799. There was no new treaty closed between Austria and Russia (an existing one, dating 28 September 1795, remained in force) but British diplomats finally succeeded in persuading the reluctant Austrians to request to Tsar Paul to send General Suvorov, to lead an Austro-Russian army against France.

The goal of the provisional 'Treaty of alliance and subsidies' between Great Britain and Russia was 'to oppose the successes of the French arms and the extension of the principles of anarchy, and to bring about a solid peace, together with the re-establishment of the balance of Europe'.[5] The treaty was based on the assumption that Prussia would join the coalition against France as well: Tsar Paul would support the Prussians with an army corps of 45,000

---

4 Letter in English of 16 November 1798 from Grenville to Whitworth, in Colenbrander, *Gedenkstukken*, Vol.III, pp.889-890.
5 Anon., *A Collection of State Papers Relative to the War against France. Now carrying on by Great Britain and the Several other European Powers* (London: S. Gosnell, 1800), p.vi.

men. The British would subsidise this with £225,000 followed by monthly payments of £75,000. In case the Prussians would not join, an additional agreement would decide to send the Russians to a theatre were their presence would be the most effective. Based on this treaty, the Russian envoy in Berlin, Count Panin, was ordered to ask the King of Prussia to join the treaty, offering him this corps of 45,000 Russians. On 17 February he was joined by Mr. Thomas Grenville, who was delayed on his journey by bad weather. In fact, Thomas Grenville nearly lost his life when the frigate he was on (*Proserpine*, 6th Rate 24) grounded in the Elbe estuary 1 February.

Again a proposal was made to the Prussian government to join Great Britain and Russia in an effort to liberate the Dutch Republic and the southern Netherlands. Prussia would receive British subsidies and territory at the expense of France. The Prussians however still held off. For a number of reasons they were not ready to join the war against France but on the other hand they also could not ignore the possibility of a French attack against Prussian territory. Therefore a blunt refusal to negotiate with the British and Russians was no option either. The Prussian minister Haugwitz was ordered to reject the proposals made by Grenville and Panin, at the same time stating that Prussia was prepared to negotiate a defensive agreement. According to Count Finckenstein, the Prussian King:

> Rejected an offensive war, and would confine himself to preserving the peace of northern Germany as long as possible. But he would be happy to form a defensive concert with Britain and Russia for the security of northern Germany and the Empire, and in certain circumstances would not hesitate to change from the defensive to the offensive. Panin and Thomas Grenville replied that a defensive alliance was incompatible with the intentions of England and Russia; nor did they see any value in the hint of a possible change to the offensive unless the precise circumstances and time were fixed beyond the possibility of a disputed interpretation.[6]

As a result, negotiations were finally broken off. The Batavian diplomat Pierre Bourdeaux in Berlin reported on 20 April that the Prussian position was based on the poor financial position of Prussia, because of the expenses of the previous king, forcing his successor to aim at correcting this deficit. Whilst this could not be done by being at war, Prussian strategy was based on maintaining neutrality and restoring the financial situation, while other countries would exhaust themselves by going to war.[7] Despite this formal Prussian position, the Batavians were still not sure the Prussians would indeed remain neutral. On 17 April, Minister of Foreign Affairs Maarten van der Goes wrote to the Minister of War Gerrit Pijman, that he had received a letter from the Batavian agent Johan Reinhold in Hamburg containing the strength of the so-called 'Army of Neutrality' in Lower Saxony and Westphalia: Prussian troops; 29 infantry battalions, 5 cavalry regiments and a substantial artillery train – Brunswick; 2 infantry battalions and two cavalry squadrons – Hanoverian; 14 infantry battalions, 2 *jager* companies, 14 cavalry squadrons and an artillery train. Remarking: 'Their dislocation will confirm, what you already know very well, that the

---

6   Quoted in Mackesy, *Statesmen at War*, pp.65-66.
7   Quoted in G.J.W. Koolemans Beijnen, 'Krijgsgeschiedkundige studie over de verdediging der Bataafsche Republiek in 1799', in *Militaire Spectator*, 1893, p.6.

Prussian part of this army is cantoned close to our borders in such a way that they would be able to concentrate close to our borders in only a few days'.[8]

In May, Grenville and Panin made a new proposal to Prussia. Great Britain offered a million pounds sterling if the Prussians would join the coalition. This time the offer was supported by the Prussian Foreign Minister Christian Haugwitz, advising his King Friedrich Wilhelm III to accept the proposal. Despite the huge amount of money offered, Friedrich Wilhelm still hesitated. Most of his advisors opposed joining the Second Coalition or had the opinion it was still too early for Prussia to go to war with the French Republic. Especially the influence of Jean Lombard, private secretary of the King, was crucial in this matter. Lombard acknowledged that the growing power of the French Republic was endangering Prussia's safety, but at the same time he pointed out the dangers that would arise if Prussia was to enter a war against the French. This proved to be decisive for Friedrich Wilhelm's decision and on 12 May the King declared that he would not join an undertaking against the Batavian Republic. At the same time he allowed negotiations to continue with Great Britain and Russia in an effort to close a 'Treaty of Guarantee' and an agreement for peace. Negotiations continued but time and again Friedrich Wilhelm refused to join the Second Coalition.

Slowly, events began to prove that the Prussians would not join the Second Coalition despite all the generous proposals made to them. This was also again quickly noticed by the Batavians:

> A certain Count Van Luning [an Orangist], which I already mentioned in previous letters, is in Munster with some kind of adjutant. He declares to have been charged with raising a new corps. General Blücher has told him that, if he would recruit only a single man, he would arrest him and transport him to the fortress of Wesel… A few days ago, General Blücher has stopped a transport of Austrian recruits, marching from Steinforth to Rheda and brought to Munster ten of these as deserters of Prussia and Munster. From this all, Citizen Minister, can be concluded that General Blücher has received instructions not to have any preference for the enemies of the French Republic.[9]

Nevertheless, despite continuous refusals, the British were still not giving up hope that Prussia could be persuaded to join together with other countries. At this time the British mentioned to the Russians for the first time a possible landing at the Dutch coast. As the distance to cover was too great for the Russian army to arrive in time, with the Prussian territory in its way, it was proposed to transport the troops overseas. The Batavian Republic was of special interest for Great Britain. Not only because of its geographical location, close to the British coast with good ports, that could be used to launch expeditions to Great Britain, but also because of its relatively large navy, its extensive trade and its large and rich overseas colonies. By 'liberating' the Batavian Republic from the French, France would receive a serious blow in losing a substantial auxiliary army and a financial source. It would

---

8   Koolemans Beijnen, 'Krijgsgeschiedkundige studie', 1893, pp.7-8.
9   Letter of 22 June 1799 from *Minister Plenipotentiaris* (ambassador) Clemens de Raet van Bögelscamp to the Minister of Foreign Affairs Maarten van der Goes, in Koolemans Beijnen, 'Krijgsgeschiedkundige studie', 1893, p.447.

also free Britain's North Sea fleet from the need for blockading the Batavian ports. Finally, it was widely believed that the Batavian Republic was ripe for a counter-revolution, providing additional troops to fight against France. These amounted to more than enough reasons for the British to propose an invasion of the Batavian Republic, although diplomatically the liberation of the Dutch Republic and the reinstatement of the House of Orange was pointed out as the main goal of the expedition. Tsar Paul quickly accepted although there was some discussion about the amount of troops the Russians would provide for. The 45,000 men initially proposed to support the Prussians was reduced to 26,000, the Tsar wanting to hold back troops for possible joint operations with Prussia if, against all odds, an agreement was made after all. This was further reduced to 17,000 when Sweden offered to join the Second Coalition, the King of Sweden openly declaring that every German ruler would be bound to provide a contingent and that he would provide for 8,000 men at his own expense, although Great Britain was prepared to pay subsidies for these troops as well. It was further hoped that Denmark would join also, for, as a trading country, it suffered much from the continuous blockade of the Dutch, French, and Spanish ports.

An ambitious plan for the campaign was drawn up, based on the participation of a 100,000-strong Prusso-German corps which would invade the Batavian Republic. The main army of North Germany would cross the Rhine near Wesel and occupy the whole area up to the River Meuse. A second German corps of 20,000 men would advance into the north eastern part of the Dutch Republic and occupy the cities Zwolle, Zutphen, and Deventer and the provinces on the right bank of the River Ijssel. A third German corps of 10,000 men would embark at Emden, enter the Zuiderzee, and land near Muiden, close to Amsterdam. A fourth German reserve army would be placed between Kassel, Wetzlar, and Frankfurt to tie up a substantial part of the French troops around Mainz. The Anglo-Russian troops would land on the islands of Goeree and Voorne, and in Zeeland. These operations would force the French troops in the Batavian Republic, threatened from all sides, to evacuate the Batavian Republic and to retreat south. Regarding the Batavian fleet, it was believed to be preferable to destroy it so that it would not have to be returned when peace would be made.[10]

The hoped for involvement of Sweden, Denmark and other German territories did not materialise in the end though and Prussia would not join as well. So on 22 June a convention was concluded between Great Britain and Russia, by which it was agreed that Russia would provide an army of 17 infantry battalions, two artillery companies, a pioneer company, and a hussar squadron, a total of 17,593 men. For providing these troops, Great Britain would pay Russia the sum of £88,000: one half to be paid when they should be ready to embark at Reval, the other half three months later; also a subsidy of £44,000 a month, to be computed from the day the troops were ready. Horses were to be furnished by the British for their officers, artillery, and baggage. In case the Russian troops should be unable to return to their own country before the ensuing winter season, Great Britain was to find them good quarters on British territory.[11]

---

10 Oberst Miliutin, *Geschichte des Krieges Russlands mit Frankreich unter der Regierung Kaiser Paul's I. im Jahre 1799* (München: Jos. Lindauer'schen Buchhandlung, 1857-1858), Vol.III, pp.107, 329.
11 See Appendix I for the full text of the convention that was closed between Great Britain and Russia on 22 June 1799.

Plans and Preparations for the 'Secret Expedition'

Chances for a successful invasion of the Batavian Republic looked good. The people were divided and the population suffered under the constant French demands and Britain's coastal blockade. Military resistance was expected to be minimal. The Batavian army was weak and badly trained. The same was believed of the French troops present in the Batavian Republic of which there were about 18,500 instead of the intended 25,000 as part of them were employed along the Upper Rhine and Flanders, because of the enemy threats and uprisings.[12] The British however believed there were far less French troops present and that the Batavians would support an invasion. As the Orangist Charles Bentinck, correspondent of the British government on the mainland, reported to George Hammond, British under secretary of state for foreign affairs on 4 November 1798:

> Among the Directors, I have reason to think Hoeth, van Hooff and Haersolte may be brought to take a part against the French, if they are not all of them so disposed. Hoeth is under obligations to, and I believe strongly influenced by, Mr. Engelhard of Groningen. Of the agents or ministers, La Pierre the agent of police is the only one who seems very violent. Spoors, Tadama, van der Goes, and perhaps the two others may be found useful, if applied to by persons who will not betray them. Their power however is so precarious, and their apprehensions of a discovery so great, that hitherto no very decided measures can be expected from them. You will know what use to make of these hints. But whatever may be their intentions, you may depend upon our friends entering into no compromise with them, unless they take a most unequivocal part towards bringing about a restoration, the absolute necessity of which is felt more and more every day by all descriptions of men.
>
> All our accounts agree in stating, that there are only 5 or 6,000 French in the United Provinces, besides those who may be in Zealand. There are movements in the Prussian army; we do not know the object of them. I cannot help flattering myself some secret concert subsists between England and Prussia respecting the United Provinces, and that should it be thought expedient to attempt a landing on the coasts of these provinces, it will be combined with the march of a powerful army into the heart of the Netherlands. Our friends are very impatient to be called upon to give proofs of their zeal.
>
> P. S. I am going to Holland with an Oldenburg passport as a subject of the Duke of Oldenburg, and with his express leave.[13]

He confirmed again his beliefs in his next letter on 11 December 1798:

> I mentioned in my last, that I was going to Holland. I set out on the 5th of last month, and returned to this place on the 8th instant. I have been at Utrecht, at Amsterdam, at the Hague, and at Woerden, without being obliged (thanks to my

---

12   See Appendix V for the French troops present in the Batavian Republic on 4 July 1799.
13   Letter in English of 4 November 1798 from Charles Bentinck to Hammond, in Colenbrander, *Gedenkstukken*, Vol.III, pp.352-353.

Oldenburg pass) to make a single application to those who govern the Republic at this moment, excepting asking of the mayor of Woerden (Costerus) the permission of seeing my brother. In all the different places I have been at, I found the same disposition pervading all ranks of people with few exceptions, which we have often stated to prevail so generally in those parts of the country to which we have chiefly directed our attention. I am happy to say that in the provinces of Holland and Utrecht I found as great a number of persons old and young, whose support would be an honor to any cause, who have shewn the same spirit and constancy as our Groningen and Friesland friends in resisting, as far as was practicable in their situation, the views and machinations of those who have been acting more or less openly for these last four years, and most likely from an earlier period, under the influence of or in concert with France.

There were very few French troops in the United Provinces at the time of my stay there, and at this moment the number of these troops quartered in different parts of the country, including even Zealand, is not supposed to exceed 6,000 men. During above a fortnight I passed at Utrecht, which, at one time, was stated to be more infected with the spirit of the times, than any other place in the country. We were several days without French troops. At Amsterdam the garrison was very weak, and there were no French troops whilst I was there; at the Hague very few; not a man, I believe, in the provinces on this side the Issel, and only weak French garrisons in a few places in the Republic, and yet the well intentioned, and those in particular who are most noted for their unshaken and avowed attachment to the House of Orange, were perfectly secure, and even very much courted by all parties. Nay, I am convinced that it is in a great measure to their steady and wise conduct, and to the well judged use they make at this moment of their wealth and influence, that the profound tranquillity, which now prevails, is chiefly to be ascribed. I was informed that at the Hague there were above 5,000 poor maintained at this time by the charities of the rich; at Amsterdam and its environs my brother, who is well informed, though in confinement, told me there were above 50,000 persons supported in the same manner, and great pains are taken by those, who have most influence amongst the poorer classes (the more affluent are not so ready to run any risks), to impress them with the necessity of not giving way to their impatience till assurances can be given them of effectual support from without. The same is the case at Utrecht, and in most populous places.

I have every reason to think, that without some similar plan of conduct, the Batavian soldiers would not pay much attention to the orders of their commanders. General Daendels was, as I am told, consulted lately as to the expediency of sending a force to the frontiers of Brabant to watch the motions of the insurgents on that side. He said in answer that the government ought not to rely on the troops, who would most likely join the insurgents, and that for that reason he was against the measure, and not very much inclined to take the command, if so employed. The disposition of the Batavian fleet is no less doubtful, to say no more, and it is to that cause, that in a great measure is to be ascribed the wish of many of the officers, and of the members of the present government, that it should retire to the Nieuwediep, and that all further naval expeditions should be given up for the present, notwithstanding the repeated applications and threats of the French minister at the Hague… During the time I was at the Hague, I heard Lombard used every art of intimidation to obtain further sums of money from the Batavian government. Speaking on the subject with general Daendels, he (Lombard) said: "what will you do, if we set up the Jacobins again"? Daendels, it is said, replied: "what will you do, if we put on the Orange cockade"?

But to return for a moment to the state of the fleet, I should not forget saying, I had an opportunity of conversing for some time with one of the principal officers of the Batavian fleet, who was absent on leave. He told me he was one of those, who advised in the strongest manner to give up all idea of any further expeditions, or of attending to the applications of the French on that subject. He had said to his employers, that it was in vain to expect from the navy any cordial cooperation with the French; that as to the idea of manning the ship partly with Frenchmen, it would only hasten their capture, if the men did not, as he expected, absolutely refuse in the most decided manner to serve with them. With respect to the frigates lately taken with French troops on board, he had forewarned them of what happened. He told me he had the prints of Lords Duncan and Nelson and other English naval officers in his own cabin, and that the same disposition, which prevailed on board his ship, existed more or less on board the whole fleet. He said it was a folly to send out the fleet: as well might the government order them to sail into an English port. All this, and a great deal more, he told the agent of the marine Spoors and others. To all this Spoors lent a willing ear, being heartily tired of the French, who besides have offended him personally, and of being the instrument of any further follies.

In the course of conversation, I deplored in the strongest terms the wretched state the country was reduced to. I avowed as usual my attachment for England, the care I took not to lose my connections there, and my looking to that country to put an end to so many calamities, and added , the best thing his employers could do would be to use their naval and military force to expel the French from the country, and for the restauration of the House of Orange, as soon as an opportunity offers.[14]

Prospects looked good for the Orangists. The Stadtholder was especially in high spirits about the possible addition of the former Austrian Netherlands to his rule: the inhabitants had never been satisfied with Austrian rule and during the First Coalition, according to the British, the Austrians could have done much more in its defence. As already described, at Campo Formio the Austrians willingly handed over the Austrian Netherlands to France, for territorial gains in Venice. So for the British returning these territories to Austria again was no secure option, whereas uniting them with the Dutch Republic was much more advantageous as in addition to strengthening the Dutch it created a firmer bastion against France. However, everything was not as it seemed. As described, it was widely believed the Dutch population would rise en masse in favour of the allies, although in reality there was not much support for an overthrow of the Batavian government. There was especially

---

14 Letter in English of 11 December 1798 from Charles Bentinck to Hammond, in Colenbrander, *Gedenkstukken*, Vol. III, pp.355-358.

widespread discontent with the House of Orange, historically already the cause of frequent friction with inhabitants and government officials and factions as well, as described in the previous chapter. After the capture of the Dutch Republic by Revolutionary France in 1795, it was the exiled Stadtholder who authorised the British occupation of the Dutch colonies to prevent them falling in the hands of the French as well, thereby doing much harm to Dutch trade.

In June, Anglo-Russian preparations started for the invasion referred to as 'Secret Expedition'. Finding enough ships, in addition enough sailors, to transport all the troops to the Batavian Republic was a problem, as the amount needed was enormous. To provide enough transports for the Russians, Captain Home Popham was sent to St. Petersburg to make arrangements and it was agreed that the British would provide transports for 10,000 Russians; the remaining 8,000 would embark in Russian transports for which the British would pay as well. To this purpose separate articles were added to the treaty.[15] The British would provide all horses necessary for the Russians, to save on transport. Fetching enough transports was still a major problem, also illustrated by the following paragraph from the *Naval Chronicle*:

> We understand that the Petition of the Russian Merchants in England, for leave to import the produce of Russia into this Kingdom in Neutral Vessels, has been granted for a limited time. The reason for this application is said to be that Captain Popham was gone to Russia, with powers to engage all the British ships he possibly could. for the purpose of bringing from Russia the Troops in the pay of England; it was therefore thought proper to grant the Petition, fearing there might not be English Ships sufficient in the Baltic to bring the hemp, flax, deals, &c. that are requisite for the consumption of this Country.[16]

Captain Popham did his job well, receiving much gratitude from the Tsar:

> Our Countrymen who have been employed at Revel, in conducting the Embarkation of the Russian Troops. have been honoured with great marks of attention from the Emperor and his Family.
>
> His Imperial Majesty requested the Nile Lugger, in which Captain Popham went to Petersburgh, to be brought up close to his Palace of Peterhoff, where he went on board, accompanied only by one Nobleman. The Lugger was immediately got under weigh; and there being a fine breeze of Wind, His Majesty was highly surprised and gratified at the swiftness of her sailing. After a two hours' Cruise, he was landed again at the Palace, when the Lugger gave him a Royal Salute.
>
> It appears the account he gave of the English Vessel had greatly excited the curiosity of the rest of the Imperial Family, as next day Captain Popham was honoured with the company of the Emperor, the Empress, four Princesses and three Princes, with their Retinue, when they were of course treated with a sail, at which they

---

15 See Appendix I for the full text of the convention that was closed between Great Britain and Russia on 22 June 1799, including the separate articles mentioned.
16 *Naval Chronicle*, Vol.II, p.256.

were highly delighted and with great condescension partook of some Ship beef and biscuit. The Emperor was particularly attentive to every thing on board the Lugger, visiting every part of her; and when the Sailors ware hoisting the sails, he insisted on helping for once to set the sails of a Vessel belonging to his gracious Ally and actually hauled the rope with the Men. The Empress begged that the Crew would sing "God save the King," which was instantly complied with to Her Majesty's entire satisfaction.

Captain Popham was presented by the Emperor with an elegant Snuff box set with diamonds and with a valuable Ring from Her Imperial Majesty. His Majesty has likewise knighted Captain Popham, conferring on him the Order of St. John of Jerusalem. Lieutenant Pratt, Captain Popham's Assistant in this business, has also been presented with a gold Snuff-box from the Emperor and a handsome gold Watch and Chain from the Empress.[17]

Opinion of the qualities of the Russian soldier was high in Britain and Western Europe. The actions of the Russians under Field Marshal Suvorov, who fought in Italy and Switzerland and won battle after battle, did much to strengthen this opinion. The erratic behaviour of the Tsar was a point of concern for the British though: 'How much under the influence of passion and sometimes of caprice is the first moment in which he decides… Such is the irritability of the Emperor, and so violent the first effect of his displeasure, that there is no knowing to what lengths this particular point may carry him.'[18] Nevertheless, Tsar Paul and his Russian armies were regarded as saviours of Europe. The contrary was the opinion of the British troops; according to the French and Batavians their quality was very bad, as shown in the 1794-1795 debacle in the Dutch Republic. Britain's army was small, but Parliament was prepared to commit a large part of it for the 'Secret Expedition' because in 1798 the much-feared French invasion of Ireland had been repelled and the French were not able to use troops for another invasion at the moment because all available forces were tied up along the eastern borders.

---

17 *Naval Chronicle*, Vol.II, p.262.
18 British ambassador Whitworth to Grenville on 5 April 1799, quoted in Mackesy, *Statesmen at War*, pp.34, 60.

3

Batavian and French Military Forces

The Batavian Army

The Batavian field army consisted of two divisions: the 1e Bataafsche Divisie was commanded by *Lieutenant-Generaal* Daendels and the 2e Bataafsche Divisie by *Lieutenant-Generaal* Dumonceau. Daendels was the senior commander. Commander-in-chief would be the French *Général de Division* Brune. The characters of Daendels as well as Brune are described by a Batavian civil servant:

> The promptness and mad courage of Daendels, which had already recommended him in the French army. Also respected for this with the soldiers, the more while usually, when his temper was not provoked, he was amicable with them. However, he was very variable in that respect, and in his rising temper he neither spared officers nor soldiers, did not fear to lay his hands to them, and behave like a true madman. When he gave orders, he usually said: "It has to happen" … In the meantime, it was fortunate that Brune appeared soon to bring about any order in the military operations. For even though he was regarded to be a moderate commander, he had more experience and was less ferocious. However, he was charged with the fact that he was too much attached to the brandy, and to his comfort, leaving too much matters to his chief of staff. Moreover, having a fierce male appearance, good-natured to everyone, he was very loved by the officers as well as the soldiers.[1]

The Batavian army was a raw army consisting for the greater part of men with very little or no battle experience. When in 1795 the Dutch Republic was occupied by the French, the ancient army was regarded by the population as a tool of the former government and as such they had much to endure and even had to be protected by the French. Reorganising and bringing up to strength a new Batavian army and navy was one of the first goals of the new government. Senior command would be formed of officers originating from the Dutch Republic or the Austrian Netherlands, formerly in French service, the *Lieutenant-Generaals*

---

1 A.W. Engelen, *Uit de Gedenkschriften van een Voornaam Nederlandsch Beambte* (Tiel: H.C.A. Campagne & zoon, 1882), p.209.

Daendels and Dumonceau and *Vice-Admiraal* de Winter being the most senior ones. Both army generals had combat experience, fighting for the French during the war of 1792-1795. Further, it was decided to concentrate the remainder of the Dutch army in the vicinity of the French occupying forces: a third of the infantry between Bergen op Zoom and Breda; another third between Breda and 's Hertogenbosch; the remaining third of the infantry around Utrecht; the cavalry and artillery in Holland; the German and Swiss regiments in Dutch service in the provinces Friesland and Groningen.

On 8 July 1795, the organisation of the new Batavian army was established, based on roughly the following key elements:

1. The ownership of the companies to be taken away from the officers and passed over to the government of the Batavian Republic;
2. The commanders of battalions, *halve brigades* (regiments), brigades, and divisions to have the responsibility for their units. To each brigade, a commissioner of war to be assigned. Payment of the military to take place out of the general treasury;
3. A health office to be established, to take care of the health of the military and their families;
4. Four military or artillery schools to be established in Delft, Zutphen, Groningen, and Breda;
5. The inspectors of the cannon foundry, arsenals and construction warehouses to no longer be connected to the artillery battalions;
6. The senior officers, not being the owner of companies anymore, to receive payment from the government. The national infantry to be formed into six halve brigades, of three battalions each. There will be four *jager* battalions. The artillery to consist of four battalions of six companies each, including some horse artillery for the defences along the dikes and the coast. In case of war, strength to be raised. The cavalry to be formed into four regiments; two of ordinary cavalry, a dragoon and a hussar regiment. The miners corps to be two companies strong. There will also be a pioneer company and an engineer corps. A decision about the foreign troops in former Dutch service to be made later by the government.

The Batavian army was to become a regular army of about 25,000 strong, including the garrisons. The field army was divided in two divisions, each of two brigades. Each brigade ideally consisted of two halve brigades of infantry and a *jager* battalion. Each division received one or two cavalry regiments and a horse artillery battery. The foot artillery was not incorporated into these divisions, it was allotted by the commander in chief to a division whenever the tactical situation, task, or terrain, made it necessary. One of the first measures was to appoint the necessary officers, as about seven to eight hundred officers of the former Dutch army had resigned. Additional officers had been pensioned out of the army, regarded as not being reliable. As a result, the few officers present with military experience received a commission which was often several ranks higher than the rank they held previously. To illustrate this, the officers of the 1e Halve Brigade, part of the 1e Bataafsche Divisie and having a major role in the upcoming campaign, have been checked on their previous experience and ranks held:

- *Colonel* Jacobus Rietvelt had served as a captain in the 2e Batalion van Byland and the 1e Batalion van Suljard de Leefdaal, dismissed after the events in 1787.
- *Adjudant Major* Daniel Clark had served as lieutenant and adjutant in the Regiment van Nyvenheim.
- *Lieutenant-Colonel* James Nicolson, commander of the 1/1e Halve Brigade, had served as a captain in the 1e Batalion van Dundas, taken prisoner by the Prussians in 1787.
- *Lieutenant-Colonel* Nicolaas Step, commander of the 2/1e Halve Brigade, had served as a captain in the Regiment Pallardy. Taken prisoner by the Prussians in 1787 and paroled, he had entered French service.
- *Lieutenant-Colonel* Gerhard van Till, commander of the 3/1e Halve Brigade, had served as a captain in the Regiment Hardenbroek, dismissed after the events in 1787.
- Of the 27 captains present, 24 had seen active service in the former Dutch army as an ensign or lieutenant; one had served in the Dutch navy and two had seen no previous active service.
- Of the 27 1st lieutenants present, 17 had seen active service in the former Dutch army as a cadet or ensign; one had been a sergeant; two had served as a private and seven had seen no previous active service.
- Of the 27 2nd lieutenants present, two had seen active service in the former army as a cadet or ensign; seven had been a corporal or sergeant; one had been a private and 17 had seen no previous active service.[2]

As can be seen, the senior officers all had combat experience and in fact would do very well during the upcoming campaign. That was not the case with the captains and especially the lieutenants. Various letters report junior officers who in no case should be promoted, or who even should be dismissed. Another problem was to bring the units up to strength. Of the units in the former Dutch army, the guard units were abolished, as they were regarded to contain too many men in favour of the House of Orange and thus unreliable. This is except for the Compagnie Friesche Gardes, the Compagnie Groninger Gardes and both companies of the Amsterdamsche Stadssoldaten. The six Swiss regiments, 7,200 strong, also remained in Batavian service initially but their contracts were ended in 1796 and 1797. To replace these regiments, in 1797 a seventh halve brigade was raised. The German Regiment Saxen-Gotha as well as both Waldeck regiments and the 5e Bataljon Waldeck all remained in Batavian Service. Finally there were the remains of the Scots Brigade in Dutch service. This brigade, consisting of three regiments (Stuart, Bentinck and Van Nyvenheim), was absorbed into the Batavian army, forming the core of the 2/ and 3/6e Halve Brigade and the 2/7e Halve Brigade. In 1795, though, the remaining Scottish officers had already left service or were dismissed later by the Batavian government for being unreliable, although a few officers of Scottish origin would serve in the Batavian army in 1799: notably *Colonel* Stuart Bruce, *Major* David Bruce, *Adjudant-Major* Clark, *Capitein* Thomson, and *Eerste Lieutenant* Aberson. Already during the later years of Dutch service all three Scottish

---

2   Based on the information listed in Anon., *Naamlyst der Militaire Officieren, in Dienst van de Bataafsche Republiek* (Den Haag: 's Lands Drukkery, 1797), pp.1-9.

regiments recruited in the Dutch Republic and neighbouring regions, so there were probably few soldiers of Scottish origin left in 1799.

The Batavian army would be built on the remains of the army of the former Dutch Republic and the Walloon and remaining German units to which Batavian volunteers as well as foreign recruits were to be added. To recruit new soldiers, recruiters were sent to the neighbouring regions, which would be cause for conflict with the French trying to get conscripts from the greater part of the same areas. The correspondence of the chief of staff of the French army in the Batavian Republic, *Général de Brigade* Dardenne, contains several letters to Batavian senior officers and to the Batavian minister of war, urging them to guard against recruiting French conscripts, threatening to arrest and punish the recruiters when caught. Still, it was difficult to recruit enough men to enlist in the Batavian army. On 25 June 1797, *Colonel* Gelderman proudly reported from Lille that he managed to 'persuade' 1,462 deserters, held prisoner by the French in the citadel, to enlist in the Batavian army. *Generaal-Major* Bonhomme reported to *Lieutenant-Generaal* Dumonceau on 11 June 1799: 'In the battalion of Antingh [i.e. 2/6e Halve Brigade] many Prussian deserters and privates born in Nassau have enlisted'.[3] On 27 April 1799, with the threat of a landing becoming more and more concrete, a decree was issued to augment the army with 9,545 men. All units which would be on full strength before 1 August would receive a gratification of 3,000 Dutch guilders, or 2,000 guilders if they were at full strength on 1 September. To meet this number, everything was tried to attract recruits, including recruiting far into Germany:

> In reply to your request of the 19th this month, I have the honour to report to you that I have verified as best as I could if conscripts were enlisted in my battalion; I am pleased to say that I found none among my recruits… My recruiting outside the Batavian Republic was in Aachen; but after the arrest of two of my recruiters, which have been arrested by the French with ten recruits taken away from them, nobody liked to go there again. However after 32 days of arrest my recruiters were released again, having arrived with the battalion without any recruits.
>
> My German recruiters are in Ichstein in the Usingen region, on this side of the Main river, in Nieder-Hadamar and in Mannheim. *Lieutenant* Keiser has received permission from the French general commanding in and around Worms, to remain there as long as he will not recruit any French, recruiting many imperial [i.e. Austrian] deserters.[4]

As a result, at the moment of the invasion, a quarter of the army had only been in service for about three months. Later, on 22 June 1799, a general pardon was decreed for all deserters who would re-enlist. But this did not make the situation better as the desertion rate remained high. The low pay and the empty treasury of the government, combined with the constant lack of necessities, were one of the reasons for the high desertion rate. 'The real way to prevent desertion is to feed your troops; do not look for other… Feed your troops, take care

---

3 Koolemans Beijnen, 'Krijgsgeschiedkundige studie', 1891, pp.365-366.
4 Letter of 25 August 1799 by *Lieutenant Colonel* Johan Abbema to the minister of war, in Koolemans Beijnen, 'Krijgsgeschiedkundige studie', 1891, pp.370-371.

they are well kept; pay them well, you will keep the bravest people':[5] A remark made in 1796 by *Lieutenant-Général* Beurnonville; unfortunately not much had changed for the better in 1799.

After *Général de Division* Brune had received command of the Batavian army on 15 July 1799, on the 30th a letter was written to him by his chief of staff *Général de Brigade* Dardenne, outlining the importance to encourage the cooperation between the French and Batavian troops and his opinion on how to improve this:

> My general! The Batavian army placed under your command must compete with the French army in defending the Republic. Do not doubt that it is expected by the Government that you will make efforts to improve their lot and their inspiring love of glory by making the enjoyment of that consideration that they must be ready to pay with their blood for the country. If you can manage to do this, you will do a big favour to the Republic, you will necessarily attract the confidence of the soldier and can rely on him in war.
>
> A generally accepted truth is that in combined armies jealousy often bothers the best terms; it takes as much as possible to prevent this defect. I will provide some observations to suggest to you to use the necessary means to establish perfect harmony between the French and Batavian troops.
>
> The [Batavian] officer helps to lower the expense of the state like other citizens; he also makes a restraint of a twentieth of his annual salary, whereas at the organization of the army these salaries were fixed with such economy that this restraint is extremely discomforting. I saw officers from the 2nd Battalion of the 2e Halve Brigade at Alkmaar without servants. Such a state of degradation deprives them of any energy, and is the cause of malcontent; they are aware that France, which for several years has made so many sacrifices for the cause of freedom, never wanted to deprive the defenders of the smallest part of their pay.
>
> The Batavian troops on the march are usually lodged in churches or barracks, lying on the straw, while the French soldier is among the citizens; this difference in treatment discontents and makes them object of scorn from the locals.
>
> The fodder is now so overpriced and the chests of the cavalry regiments are so exhausted that commanders are forced to put some horses in the meadows, far from their garrisons; it follows from this if we will spontaneously need these troops, they would be unable to serve, and that the honour of the unit would be compromised, because this resource is not allowed, but merely tolerated.
>
> I would like to propose to remedy these abuses with the Batavian Government and as quickly as possible declaring the army on a war footing. That very soon the troops on the march will be treated like the French regarding lodging; that they will receive bread and meat without restraint; the fodder that will be distributed for cavalry and artillery horses, the officer will enjoy its unrestrained treatment.

---

5   Letter of 16 June 1796 by *Lieutenant-Général* Beurnonville, *général en chef de l'armée du Nord et des troupes stationnées en Batavie*, to the *Comité te Lande*, in Dr I. Mendels, *Herman Willem Daendels, vóór zijne Benoeming tot Gouverneur-Generaal van Oost-Indië (1762-1807)* ('s-Gravenhage: Martinus Nijhoff, 1890), p.104.

Probably the economy of the Government will delay putting the army on a war footing; it is nonetheless of interest that the requests you make, my General, are granted in advance and that you may announce the army that it will be put on a war footing, that it shall enjoy the same benefits as the French army; it will take away a means to enemies of the public to sow discontent amongst the soldiers and paralyze our means of defence.[6]

The letter above shows the problems the Batavian army had to cope with and one can easily imagine the effect it had on morale. It was the cause of men deserting the Batavian army only to re-enlist in the French army again, receiving much better payment and necessities, to be paid by the same Batavian government, as illustrated by the letter from a deserter to his former comrades:

I take my friend the opportunity to give you knowledge of my present situation. Since I left you, I arrived in Utrecht where I had the good fortune to enter the 5e Régiment de Chasseurs à Cheval, where I am very happy because my fate is much happier than I had before; but that of Gibart is not as pleasant, as he spent here about 4 weeks with one of his comrades in a deplorable state, devoid of everything and almost without clothes. They have cut their hair; I could hardly recognize them. They entered the 16e Régiment de Chasseurs à Cheval which is garrisoned in Breda… Many compliments to *Sergent-Major* Ouban, and all comrades, not to mention Manget and friend Franquiniol joining me as has Quisidor, who are also *Chasseurs* in the same regiment will tell you honest things.[7]

An additional problem was the fact that many soldiers were married, causing trouble in many cases. All marching orders limited the amount of women allowed to accompany the troops to two, sometimes four women per company. However, many more remained, seriously hampering military operations on the terrain the campaign was fought over in 1799: 'Despite the most precise orders of *Général* Brune, it was impossible to compel the Batavians corps to get rid of the huge amount of women and carts that are attached to each battalion. Also on 24 Fructidor [10 September 1799] found one much hampered'.[8] About the events referred to, taking place on 10 September, more detail will follow later. On that same day in the evening, a huge panic occurred at Daendels' division, causing Brune to issue the following order to Daendels and Dumonceau:

I demand that you do burn all baggage that is in your corps, beside that what is strictly necessary for every man, officer or soldier, and all that is not three hours away from the position of the army; and that you ignominiously chase away any

---

6 Quoted in Koolemans Beijnen, 'Krijgsgeschiedkundige studie', 1891, pp.146-147.
7 Letter of 27 February 1799 from H. Rolle to a comrade in Koolemans Beijnen, 'Krijgsgeschiedkundige studie', 1891, p.370.
8 Anon., *Mémoires Historiques sur la Campagne du Général en Chef Brune en Batavie, Du 5 Fructudor an 7, au 9 Frimaire an 8 ; Rédigés par un Officier de son État-Major* (Paris : Chez Favre, An IX), p.24.

woman who is not a *vivandière* or washer-woman, whose numbers must not exceed four with each battalion.[9]

The Batavian line infantry consisted of seven halve brigades (demi-brigades), each of three battalions with a grenadier company and eight fusilier companies. The grenadier companies were usually detached and operated combined with the grenadier companies from the same halve brigade, brigade, or division. In wartime each halve brigade formed a depot from the artisans, the untrained recruits and all unfit for duty, commanded by an officer. After the augmentation of April 1799, on paper, a halve brigade consisted of 2,997 men, a battalion 998 men and a company 109 men. In addition, the following German troops remained in Batavian service:

- Regiment Saxen-Gotha, consisting of two battalions each with a life company, a grenadier company, and six musketeer companies. Paper strength was 1,022 men, each battalion 504 men strong.
- 1e and 2e Regiments Waldeck, each consisting of two battalions with each a life company, a grenadier company and six musketeer companies. Paper strength was 1,023 men, each battalion 504 men strong.
- 5e Bataljon Waldeck, consisting of a grenadier company, six musketeer companies and a *jager* company. Paper strength was 563 men.

The German troops were however very under strength. The cause of this was a resolution of the *Comité te Lande* on 20 March 1795, not to recruit for these units any more. To illustrate this: on 31 March 1799, the 1/1e Regiment Waldeck had only 285 instead of the necessary 504 men; the 2nd battalion only 279. In the 5e Bataljon Waldeck the situation was even worse, with only 99 men under arms and 22 unfit for service in the grenadier and musketeer companies together; 11 under arms and 3 unfit for service in the *jager* company.[10] Not surprisingly, the German troops were not incorporated in the field army but instead did garrison duty.

The infantry was armed with a smoothbore musket, a bayonet and a short infantry sabre. They wore their long hair in a tail at the back. The grenadiers could wear a moustache; this was forbidden for the fusiliers.

There were also four *jager* battalions in the Batavian army. A battalion consisted after the augmentation of 1,001 men in six companies, each company 164 men strong. The *jagers* were divided in three platoons. The 1st platoon (1st Class *Jager*) was armed with rifles and a cutlass. The remaining platoons were armed with a rifled musket and a bayonet. In addition, the *jager* had a short infantry sabre. Only the *jager* had skirmisher training. As the upcoming campaign would prove, the *jager* turned out to be among the best trained men in the Batavian field army, inflicting serious loss on the Anglo-Russians with their fire. Finally, there were the Compagnie Friesche Gardes (200), the Compagnie Groninger Gardes (75) and both companies of the Amsterdamsche Stadssoldaten (400). The two first companies

---

9   Koolemans Beijnen, 'Krijgsgeschiedkundige studie', 1891, p.365.
10 Koolemans Beijnen, 'Krijgsgeschiedkundige studie', 1891, pp.416-417.

would be used to defend the provinces of Groningen and Friesland after the departure of the greater part of Dumonceau's division to Holland; the Amsterdamsche Stadssoldaten were during the campaign placed at disposal of Brune, who used them to counter the Orangist incursions in the eastern provinces of the Batavian Republic (see Chapter 9).

The Batavian cavalry consisted of four regiments:

1e Regiment Zware Cavalerie
2e Regiment Zware Cavalerie
Regiment Dragonders
Regiment Huzaren

Each regiment consisted of four squadrons of two companies each. In wartime, a depot was formed from the non-combatants. A regiment consisted of 630 men, a company of 77 men. There was no augmentation for the cavalry decreed in April 1799. The heavy cavalry had no carbines. They were armed with a straight-bladed sword and two pistols. The dragoons were armed with a carbine with bayonet, a curved sabre and two pistols. The hussars had a curved light cavalry sabre, a carbine, and a pistol.

The foot artillery of the Batavian army consisted of four battalions of six companies each. A battalion consisted of 33 officers and 964 NCOs and gunners; each company consisted of 5 officers and 160 NCOs and gunners. These battalions had to provide for the field artillery, which was organised only in wartime, as well as for the fortress artillery. The train serving the field artillery was also formed in wartime only and consisted of civilian drivers and requisitioned horses. In the Batavian army the train was not a proper part of the field army. If a train was necessary, each *departement* had to provide a contingent of 800 civilian drivers. Understandably, these were the worst elements the *departementen* could find. As a result, most of them had to be sent back on their arrival. Of the remainder, many deserted, taking with them the horses or selling them. Instead of feeding the horses, the hay and wheat was sold also. As a result, during this campaign, lasting only two months, over a thousand horses were lost! In many cases the gunners had to serve as a driver. Even officers appear to have acted in this way.[11]

Each company operated six guns. The foot artillery companies in the field were divided in 'brigade-artillery' and an 'Artillery Train' The 'brigade-artillery' was equipped with 6pdr guns and these were attached to the halve brigades; each infantry battalion received a section of two guns, which had to follow the movements of the battalion. The 'Artillery Train' formed the position-batteries and the reserve and ideally consisted of six 'train-brigades':

1st Brigade: eight 12pdr cannon
2nd Brigade: 12 6pdr cannon
3rd Brigade: four 3pdr cannon
4th Brigade: 10 24pdr howitzers, two 16pdr mortars
5th Brigade: 12 wagons with infantry cartridges
6th Brigade: 31 transport wagons

---

11 Anon., *Landungsgeschichte der Engländer und Russen in Holland, im Herbst 1799. Nebst Anekdoten über die Anführer, Verfaßt von einem Officier im Gefolge des Generals Brüne* (Hamburg: August Campe, 1800), pp.18-19.

Beside these wagons, every unit had its own, roughly 15 for each infantry battalion and 10 for each cavalry regiment.

The gunners were armed with a short infantry sabre, officers with a sword. The *rijdende artillerie* (horse artillery) consisted of a brigade of two companies. The brigade was commanded by the senior captain of one of the companies and received the rank of *2de lieutenant-colonel*. Each company had a strength of 106 men and 110 horses and served six guns; four 6pdr cannon and two 24pdr howitzers. The companies were divided in divisions of two guns when the situation required it. The gunners were armed with a curved sabre, officers had a sword.

The Batavian engineers consisted of a corps Mineurs en Sappeurs, two companies of 79 men each; a pontoneer company (60) and a Corps der Genie (engineers, 74 men). The Mineurs en Sappeurs did not take part in the campaign. The pontoneers were armed with a musket and a pistol.

All the infantry battalions had colours which were carried by the most senior cadet. The colours were of white silk, with the painted inscription '#.e Bataillon' and '#.e Halve Brigade' in gold (where # indicates the number). In the centre was a large green oak leaf wreath, with inside it an arm holding a curved sword with silver blade, coming from a grey cloud. The armour on the arm, and the hilt of the sword, were brass. The pole of the colour was brown with a brass spearhead with red, white, and blue cords. In addition, every company had a kind of guide pennon, with the battalion number on it. The cavalry and artillery had no colours.

The army also had to provide a bodyguard to protect the government in The Hague against *coup d'états* etc. On 29 November 1798, by ballot, the 2/3e Halve Brigade and the 1/2e Regiment Zware Cavalerie were appointed for this task for a term of two years. For that period, these units were removed from the strength of the Batavian army.

There was also a Batavian militia: Article 43 of the constitution of 23 April 1798, known as *Staatsregeling 1798*, stipulated: 'The Batavian people desire a *Gewapende Burgermacht* ('Armed Citizen's Force') to defend its freedom and independence, both inside and outside'. A committee was ordered to prepare a proposal to this purpose which on 4 May 1799 was approved by the 2nd Chamber with a majority of only two votes. Three days later the creation of the *Gewapende Burgermacht* was proclaimed by the *Uitvoerend Bewind* (Executive Administration)[12] It would consist of eight halve brigades of infantry (a halve brigade for each of the eight departments), four *jager* battalions and four artillery battalions, totalling 32,000 men. Initially all males between 18 and 29 (married) or 36 (unmarried) had to sign up; the colonels would select the suitable and most reliable to enlist. It proved to be difficult, for a number of reasons, to bring the *Gewapende Burgermacht* up to strength. The population in many places resisted signing up, and regular troops had to maintain order. In any case, time before the British landings took place was much too short to create and train its men into combat-ready troops, although a whole range of measures was taken to raise its numbers. A new proclamation urged the population to enlist voluntarily, but the result was not more than two companies of badly armed and untrained men. *Vice-Admiraal* de

---

12 *Proclamatie van het Uitvoerend Bewind der Bataafsche Republiek; Betreffende de invoering van het Reglement voor de Gewapende Burgermacht. Den 7. Mey 1799.*

Winter, made prisoner of war in the Battle of Camperdown in 1797 and released on parole, was appointed inspector of the *Gewapende Burgermacht*.

After the landings, several companies from all across the Batavian Republic were declared mobile and ordered to collect in Haarlem to form a Bataafsch Mobiel Burger Corps. In all, 10 grenadier companies, seven fusilier companies, and three *jager* companies were sent to Haarlem. However of these most proved to be a burden instead of a support. The men received no payment, no uniforms, and not enough food. As a result discipline was bad and in order to get some money for food some of them even sold the few uniform items they had. Many deserted and returned to their homesteads. Most men that remained under arms were used for auxiliary tasks, did garrison duty or guarded prisoners.

However, on 17 September, the Bataafsch Legioen or Légion Batave was formed. On paper it would have a strength of 3,000, and beside men of the *Gewapende Burgermacht*, every city was urged to send a specified amount of additional citizens. Of course nothing came of it and it never consisted of more than two weak battalions commanded by *Lieutenant-Colonel* van Oosterom. Already on that same day though, its 1st battalion composed of citizens of the *Gewapende Burgermacht* marched to Ouddorp just north of Alkmaar. From there, during the night, they marched east to Ooterleek, losing many deserters and stragglers in the process. Arriving at this village the articles of war were read to them, after which the grenadier and *jager* companies marched further west to the village of Rustenburg. There they joined four companies of the 1/4e Halve Brigade and were placed under the command of *Capitein* Kamps of that unit. A grenadier of the Bataafsch Legioen describes the situation he found himself in:

> Here it was that I was able to obtain a new pair of shoes. Only to those who never, as we at that time, had such a lack of these, can I describe how happy I was!!! I was so light from the bottom that I believed I could jump across the highest house; the shoes however were far from the best quality: one even says that no military quartermaster would have accepted them; the shoes were mostly too small, not reinforced at the heels, so after having been worn for a day they would become flat; the stockings were so small that they did not reach above the calves, but we were forced to use them because of our great shortage. Educated by the soldiers, we dug holes into the dike to light fires. We borrowed copper tripods (as we had none) from the soldiers or the inhabitants (there are about twenty houses) and boiled soup: but from what? We had some flesh, although old. In the hamlet we were able to find one pound of pearl barley, which out of pity the inhabitants sold to us for three pennies; a small bush of carrots and some beans thickened our soup: we ate supper, and lay to rest in the straw in the cow sheds.[13]

The 1/Bataafsch Legioen would remain here doing guard duty and only few men would take part in the fighting during the battle of 19 September. Some legionnaires, a company mainly from the city of Rotterdam, commanded by *Capitein* W. Teijssen, took part in the Battles of

---

13   Anon., *Eenige Berichten Omtrent den Veldtocht der Gewapende Groningers, naar Noord Holland. Behelzende; Een meenigte vreemde lotgevallen; armoede; gebrek aan klederen; onthouding van traktement en vyvres; slegte cazernering en weinige troost van huis enz. Door een Grenadier* (Groningen: A.F. Vos, 1799), pp.35-36.

Bergen and Castricum and gave a good account of themselves, being particularly mentioned in Brune's letter of 7 October to the Batavian Government. A letter of a volunteer captain in the 2/Bataafsch Legioen describes his participation in the Battle of Bergen:

> I got an order to escort a wagon in the midst of the firing and we managed to deliver it to its destination. On this occasion, I and one of our Rotterdammers overpowered a Russian Colonel, whom I took prisoner, his blooded spontoon I took as keepsake. Cleem Kugenius has distinguished himself; he shot two Russians from their horses and although wounded took their horses. Among others we have lost a sergeant, whom I knew very well, being Joost van Dijk a Rotterdammer who worked with me the past winter in The Hague. He has been killed with honour. Several were wounded and four men with an NCO, being citizen *jager* from Zwolle, have been made prisoners of war.[14]

On 15 October all members of the *Gewapende Burgermacht* were gathered at the exercise grounds just outside Haarlem and again an effort was made forming a proper combat battalion, commanded by *Colonel* van Lochteren Stakebrand. As desertion had taken its toll, it was necessary to force a number of grenadiers to become fusiliers in the centre companies, which of course was met with protest. Nevertheless, with more formal organisation and strongly enforced discipline, from now on the battalion became a more effective military force. The unit was short-lived. With the campaign in Holland already ended, on 26 October the battalion marched south to Leiden. On 20 November, the Bataafsch Legioen was disbanded and its members returned to their homesteads.

The Batavian navy had suffered much from the departure of many experienced officers when the Batavian Republic was created. The greater part of the sailors and officers who remained, were secretly Orangist or just opportunistic, just as many were foreigners, knowing all too well they would be no match for the British. This would have serious consequences in the upcoming campaign. Quality of the sailors was low, desertion high. Even a substantial number were French, about whom the French chief of staff Dardenne wrote:

> I have the honour to request you to look at the included communication; it will give you an idea of the French subjects enlisted in the Batavian navy. The four in question are part of the 14 claimed by citizen Girault, *vice-commissaire* in Rotterdam. I am not afraid to assure you that after having received accurate information I am certain that of the 800 claimed, 750 are bad people who have enlisted voluntarily after having deserted and other crimes. There are some among them who came from the Armée de Sambre et Meuse: can we be convinced that the Dutch lead them to this country by force. Finally they will poison the corps in which they will be admitted.[15]

---

14 Letter from J.C.C. den Beer Poortugael to his wife, 21 September 1799, in 'Levensbericht van Diederic Jacob den Beer Poortugael' in *Jaarboek van de Maatschappij der Nederlandsche Letterkunde, 1880 – Bijlage tot de handelingen van 1880*, p.38.
15 Letter by chief of staff Charles Dardenne to the French extraordinary envoy on 16 March 1799, in Koolemans Beijnen, 'Krijgsgeschiedkundige studie', 1892, p.69.

Vice-Admiraal de Winter had been appointed commander in chief of the Batavian fleet. De Winter had been a naval lieutenant in 1787, when he was forced to emigrate and entered French service as member of the Légion Franche Étrangère, in 1794 he was promoted to *général de brigade*. Losing the Battle of Camperdown and paroled, as already described, de Winter was ordered to organise the *Gewapende Burgermacht*. The Batavian fleet had suffered heavy losses, especially in 1796 when nine ships surrendered in Saldanha Bay (South Africa) and at Camperdown in 1797. Nevertheless, in the following years huge sums were used to build up the fleet again: During 1797 and 1798, twelve ships of the line, four frigates, three corvettes, a brig, five schooners, a yacht and eight gunboats were added to the fleet. Despite that, the Batavians were never a match for the British navy, and were blockaded inside the Batavian ports, with the main fleet at the roads of Texel under the command of *Schout bij Nacht* Story.[16] They were even unable to prevent the British blockading all Batavian inlets and ports.

The French Troops in the Batavian Republic

As already outlined, by treaty the French should have had 25,000 soldiers in the Batavian Republic, supplied and paid by the Batavians. The organisation of this corps was laid down in article 1 of the '*Règlement pour la formation, la subsistance & l'administration du Corps de 25000 hommes de Troupes Françaises, détaché de l'Armée du Nord, pour demeurer dans la Hollande*'. The commander-in-chief would be a *general en chef* with a staff. The French army would be organised in three divisions, each of two brigades. It would be formed of 10 demi-brigades of three battalions each; four cavalry regiments; four line artillery companies (each with six cannon, 18 caissons and 62 horses), two horse artillery companies; a detachment of 50 *gendarmes* and 20 *guides*. Additional men were added for the hospitals, medical, postal services, judiciary system, and so forth.[17] The 1e Division was stationed in 's Hertogenbosch, Utrecht and their environs, the 2e Division in South Holland, and the 3e Division in Zeeland. The latter division was by far the strongest as an attack on Zeeland was regarded as the most obvious and threatening for the French Republic. The organisation for maintenance and supply was to be taken care of by the Batavian Republic.

In order to provide all that was needed for the French troops in the Batavian Republic, the *Commissariaat voor de Fransche troepen, in soldij van de Bataafsche Republiek* ('Administration for French troops in pay of the Batavian Republic') was formed, with Jan Janssens appointed as First Commissioner for the French troops in the Batavian Republic. The necessary transport was also provided by the Batavians, for which the Batavians would requisition the necessary carts and wagons that were needed, as was common practice for the Batavian army as well. To provide food supplies and fodder, suppliers were sought and the contract awarded to an entrepreneur for a defined period of time. For example on 21 May 1799, the firm G. Schoonhoven Gz. received a contract for 13 months to provide all

---

16 The rank of *schout bij nacht* equates to that of rear admiral.
17 *Articles convenus, pour régler le service, l'administration, l'équipement & la solde de 25000 hommes de Troupes Françaises, qui doivent rester dans les Provinces-Unies, conformément au traité de paix & d'alliance fait entre les deux Républiques* (27 July 1795).

supplies and fodder for the French troops in the Batavian Republic, not only in their garrisons but also on the march and in the field. When the British invasion had begun and French troops converged on Holland from all sides, this task became virtually impossible to fulfil, as illustrated by the letter of *Commissaire des Guerres* Drolenvaux to Jan Janssens:

> I warn you, citizen, that 2,000 men of the 54th 1/2 brigade depart tonight to continue their journey to Haarlem and I invite you to provide them with a bread ration for two days, and a ration of water and kindly give orders for everything to be transported at midnight at the bend in the road between Leiden and Delft; that is where the distribution will be made to the troop. I have given my word to the *général* Azémar and *commandant* Vavé that this provision would be executed exactly and I beg you to give in this respect the most precise orders.[18]

Of course Jan Janssens realised all too well the importance and difficulties in provisioning all those marching troops, not only the French but also Batavian forces. Municipalities were urged with regards to these problems, by means of a circular, to give all the help they could to the entrepreneur:

> Municipality! The troops are in motion from all sides; many travel to North Holland; Ordinary means, to feed them and to lodge them are certainly insufficient. It is for no administration, even much less for an entrepreneur possible, to have stocks everywhere, which may necessitate unforeseen movements, and the troops may meet at no time any constraints. How many doom did not frequently happen in the past to armies which lacked victuals and other urgent necessities? The soldiers have to occupy themselves with battle and others have to be bothered with their maintenance. I apply to all of you then, Citizens Municipal administrators! To give all possible help and assistance to the general entrepreneur of victuals and fodder G. SCHOONHOVEN Gz. or his agents to enable execution of their service, to obtain all necessities, as well as transporting it: When necessary to use all your authority.[19]

In practice, the French were constantly in breach of the stipulations of the treaty. According to this treaty, four line artillery companies would be present. In 1798 there were two companies and 15 *escouades*, totalling about five companies.[20] April-May 1798 the 4e and 6e Compagnies and one half-*escouade* of the 7e Artillerie a Pied arrived, bringing the foot artillery to a total of seven companies and one half-*escouade*. July-August 1797, the 3/7e Artillerie Légère was exchanged for the 4/4e Artillerie Légère. On 22 September 1797, the

---

18 Letter of 30 August 1799 from Drolenvaux to Jan Janssens in Koolemans Beijnen, 'Krijgsgeschiedkundige studie', 1891, pp.141-142. *Général* Azémar was in fact Jean Jacques Dazémar. He was *adjudant-général*, chief of staff of the 2nd French Division, holding the rank of *chef de brigade* [colonel]; '*commandant* Vavé' was in fact *Chef de Brigade* Louis-Prix Varé, commander of the 54e demi-brigade.
19 Koolemans Beijnen, 'Krijgsgeschiedkundige Studie', 1891, p.142.
20 The term *escouade* (squad) appears to have had different meanings, the amount of men forming an *escouade* varying. In a letter of Jan Janssens to the Batavian minister of war (13 June 1799), he states that each foot artillery company was divided into 5 *escouades*: Koolemans Beijnen, 'Krijgsgeschiedkundige studie', 1891, pp.186-188.

23e Chasseurs à Cheval returned to the French Republic and was not replaced. February-March 1798, four demi-brigades disappeared, to be replaced by three others. During the same period, two hussar regiments were replaced by two regiments of *chasseurs à cheval*. In September 1798, the 1er and 8e Demi-Brigades had left the Batavian Republic to join the Armée de Mayence, but the French still counted them with the 25,000 men in Batavian pay. They were followed March 1799 by *General de Brigade* Laroche-Dubouscat with the 1/ and 2/60e Demi-Brigade, 1/ and 2/72e Demi-Brigade, and the four field squadrons of each of the 5e and 11e Chasseurs à Cheval. Finally, the *gendarmes* had also been recalled, to replace them the number of *guides* was raised from 20 to 50. Other units were rotated to the southern Netherlands to aid in suppressing the uprisings there: July 1799, five companies of the 2/48e Demi-Brigade, 1/49e Demi-Brigade and half of the 4/4e Artillerie Légère were there, a total of 1,117 men. These troops were still absent when the British landing took place. As the third battalions, and of course the depots, usually had the lowest-quality troops, the departure of the above units had a major effect on the quality of the French troops.

It is understandable that the French would send troops from the Batavian Republic to their threatened borders and would use these to suppress uprisings in the southern Netherlands, however that did not mean that the threat against the Batavian Republic itself was completely ignored by them. On 3 February, the chief of staff *Général de Brigade* Dardenne reported to Brune:

> All defences are deployed at all points [i.e. in Zeeland]. The Minister has nothing more to be desired in this regard from the *Général en chef* [i.e. Brune], which for his part has a lot to be desired from the Minister: the return of the troops sent to Belgium, among which there are 5 companies drawn from the island of Walcheren. It was observed that one can rely for the defence of the islands of Zeeland on support from the mainland during a raid, however in case of favourable winds to the British to arrive there we are too late; therefore it is essential to deploy there at all times the necessary force for defence. It is impossible to increase these means, if the Minister does not gives orders for the return of the troops. It would be necessary that the *Général en chef* has the means to be informed in time about the direction of the movements that the English could make. These know exactly everything that happens in this country; they have supporters in the interior and we can say that the coastal dwellers, including fishermen, are in favour of the Stadtholder.
>
> The armament of the troop is in a worse shape, it would take about a thousand muskets for each *demi-brigade*, to arm the conscripts to replace those that have been unfit for service. The cavalry is about 900 horses short. Supplying the fortresses is still an essential subject. Despite repeated requests the Batavian Minister of War would not yet give a formal report on this issue.
>
> The *Général en chef* should expect endless and multiple delays, in all demands that will made from the Government, and should act with vigour against the natural slowness of the Batavians.[21]

---

21 Letter of 3 February 1799 from Dardenne to Brune in Koolemans Beijnen, 'Krijgsgeschiedkundige studie', 1891, pp.190-191.

This report is of much interest, giving information about the quality of the French troops in the Batavian Republic. Not only the lack of muskets, horses, and other provisions, but also of the ability to take the field. All conscripts were initially sent to Breda where the *depôt des conscrits* was located, led by *Chef de Bataillon* Massabeau. From here, the conscripts were divided amongst the various French units in the Batavian Republic. April 1799 a second depot was formed in Nijmegen to handle the increasing stream of conscripts. This stream would become substantial. On 6 February, Dardenne wrote to Massabeau that 6 or 7,000 conscripts would be send from the Armée de Mayence. On 1 May, Dardenne informed the Batavian Minister of War Gerrit Pijman that 9,750 conscripts would be send from the *Départments du Nord, de la Somme*, and *Pas de Calais*, to bring the French troops in the Batavian Republic up to strength again. Desertion rate was high though, as shown by many reports. So on 11 July, Dardenne had to report to the French Minister of War that only 2,993 of the 9,750 conscripts had arrived, less than a third, despite all measures taken. Even the conscripts that did arrive had their deficiencies:

> The commander of Breda informed me my dear fellows, that he found among the men that has been sent to our army by the *Département du Nord*, an old man of 64, with a certificate certifying that he is unable to serve for suffering a stroke 8 years ago and being almost deaf and blind.[22]

The situation is also illustrated by *Colonel* van Ampt, commissioner inspector for the French troops in pay of the Batavian Republic, who made an inspection tour to Grave, Nijmegen, Utrecht, Breda, and Woerden, reporting to the First Commissioner Jan Janssens:

> 28 July: The 3rd Battalion [42e demi-brigade] is very large, but it lacks a lot of clothes and weapons. Despite the fact that forty disabled people among the conscripts are unfit for service, there are still many more unable to serve. The hospitals in Nijmegen and Utrecht are in the best possible order, but full of sick patients from the conscripts, mostly suffering from lingering illnesses; many perish. From Utrecht I went to Breda, where I have arrived and are still expecting the transports of recruits, all former deserters, who were taken under escort and their further transport happens with armed detachments of the various units in which they must be incorporated.
>
> 5 August: The troops composing the garrison of Breda are the 16e Régiment de Chasseurs à Cheval and the 3rd Battalion of the 48e Demi-Brigade. These two bodies form a perfect contrast with regard to the individuals who make up these units regarding their clothing, weapons and equipment. The former is composed of elite men, all dressed and prepared, in perfect order and lacking only weapons and horses. As the latter are revolting, composed of disabled veterans poorly dressed and recruits whose dress are a motley combination; some wearing white jackets and pants, others having no uniform clothing piece,

---

22 Letter of 10 July 1799 from Dardenne to the chiefs of staff of the French divisions, in Koolemans Beijnen, 'Krijgsgeschiedkundige studie', 1891, p.197.

appearing at the review in ragged clothes, headgear of any form, even with nightcaps and almost without shoes. Moreover, despite the removal of those unfit for duty among the conscripts, there are still over one hundred that are deaf and dumb, blind and crippled or imbeciles. The average part is not armed and they lack especially a lot of pouches and packs. Desertion is very high. It is very probable that there are debauchers in town, so no soldier dares to leave without being provided with a signed and sealed pass by the commander of the place. Finally the lack of order has shown during the review.[23]

After the British had landed in Holland, at all ferries across the main rivers two reliable French soldiers had to be posted, to prevent the crossing of soldiers without passports. Another problem was self-mutilation, as illustrated by a letter from the French chief of staff Dardenne to *Chef de Division* Castagnier, commanding the French navy in Flushing:

The Citizen *general en chef* gave orders to his division generals to remove from their corps all conscripts and recruits who will be judged incapable of serving. I learned that many of these are on the verge of getting their removal by cutting nerves and cutting off a few fingers; as I have no doubt that part of these are cowards, who have mutilated themselves, I want to deprive them of the satisfaction of return. Please let me know if you can use them in the navy on the ships that are under your command and what would be the number that you would require; from your reply I will take steps to forward them to Flushing. I will form a first depot in Bergen op Zoom.[24]

To cope with the lack of weapons – according to the treaty the responsibility of the French themselves – the Batavian Government had to help out: 'The absolutely necessary number would be 1,000 carbines and 500 sabres, the Batavian Government recently ordered 600 in Solingen'.[25] But even than there were not enough of them, as shown above and also illustrated by a remark about the review of the 3/49e Demi-Brigade in Bergen op Zoom on 21 July: 'The weapons for the conscripts are borrowed from the whole force, it is very discomforting if one must lend muskets to exercise'.[26] It took time to remedy all the deficiencies. A memorandum by the French chief of staff *Général de Brigade* Dardenne on 29 July:

The compelling circumstances require that the troops in the Batavian Republic, with 18,702 effectives,[27] however having only present under arms 16,804 men, is promptly put into condition to take the field, that the fortresses are armed and

---

23 Reports in French of 28 July and 5 August 1799 from *Colonel* Ambt to Jan Janssens, in Koolemans Beijnen, 'Krijgsgeschiedkundige studie', 1891, p.198. During this period the third battalions were so-called 'garrison battalions' which held the lowest quality troops.
24 Quoted in Koolemans Beijnen, 'Krijgsgeschiedkundige studie', 1891, p.197.
25 Letter of 23 May from Dardenne to the French Minister of War, in Koolemans Beijnen, 'Krijgsgeschiedkundige studie', 1891, p.192.
26 Quoted in Koolemans Beijnen, 'Krijgsgeschiedkundige studie', 1891, pp.192-193.
27 For the composition of the French troops present in the Batavian Republic on 4 July 1799, see Appendix V.

supplied. The *Général en chef* has for a long time strongly made requests to that extent, but decisions are extremely slow. However the implementation of a state of defence of a number of places is an operation that will require even more time as the gun carriages are usually bad, and there are very little spare ones in the arsenals.

The armament and clothing of the infantry are in a state that leaves nothing to be desired. It is the same with the clothing of the 5e, 11e and 16e Régiments de Chasseurs à Cheval that are complete; but it would take 1,000 carbines, 500 sabres and 900 horses… The Batavian Government agrees to fully equip the 5e and 16e Régiments de Chasseurs à Cheval under the condition that the French Government will remove from their pay list the 11e Régiment of the same arm, and whose 4 squadrons are with the Armée du Danube; in this case there should be given another destination to its depot in Rotterdam… The artillery consists of 717 men under arms, with 836 effectives, including officers.[28]

After the capture of the Dutch Republic in 1795, on 5 April the left wing and centre of the Armée du Nord became the Armées du Nord et de Hollande while its right wing became part of the Armée de Sambre et Meuse. The troops in Batavian pay were then known as the *Troupe francaise dans la République Batave*, on 26 August 1799 renamed Armée de la République Batave. Of course after the British landings in Holland became known to Paris, efforts were made to send additional units to the Batavian Republic as soon as possible, as well as a number of experienced senior officers: *Généraux de Division* Boudet, Morlot and Vandamme; *Généraux de Brigade* David, Fuzier, Girod, d'Hinnisdal, Pacthod, and Simon. Although *Général de Division* Reubell, nominally commanding the 2e Division, was the most senior *général de division* he would not move to the frontline; it was Vandamme who would have a major role on the battlefield and *Adjudant-Géneral* Dazémar who would effectively command the 2e Division. Reubell was 57 years old, in bad health and would be pensioned out of the army on 30 December 1799. He would die in 1804.

In order to have, in case of defeat, a reserve to oppose the Anglo-Russians, the Directorate ordered, on 13 September, in the vicinity of Maastricht the concentration of an army corps called the Armée du Nord. It was placed under the command of Brune, who had to reunite it with his own army in the Batavian Republic in case of a retreat. The nucleus of the Armée du Nord would be formed of nine battalions, 10 squadrons and 10 artillery companies, commanded by *Général de Division* Tilly, appointed second-in-command to Brune, who at that time became commander of the Armée du Nord as well as the Franco-Batavian army; both armies together were renamed Armée de la Batavie on 23 September. After the closing of the treaty and the evacuation of the Anglo-Russian army the organisation of the Armée du Nord was suspended.[29]

The French army in the Batavian Republic was a young army, for the greater part consisting of young conscripts. Originally the veterans, volunteers, and conscripts served in separate companies, but during 1796 these were mixed with each other. In this way the inexperienced conscripts could learn from the experience and knowledge of the veterans. Led by

---

28 Quoted in Koolemans Beijnen, 'Krijgsgeschiedkundige studie', 1891, p.194.
29 Charles Dolly, 'Chronologie historique des armées de la République et de l'Empire' in *Le Spectateur Militaire*, XLIX, pp.26-27.

motivated and experienced officers and NCOs the conscripts were still capable of achieving unexpected results. In addition, the greater part of the men were capable of acting in a skirmishing role and especially the grenadier companies were often used as such. The quality of the French troops in the Batavian Republic was average. Veterans of earlier campaigns were present, but about one third consisted of fresh conscripts. Regarding the infantry, only line demi-brigades were present in this campaign, no light ones. Theoretically, two demi-brigades formed a brigade, with two brigades augmented with cavalry and artillery forming a division. A demi-brigade consisted of three battalions, each with eight fusilier companies (123), a grenadier company (83) and a depot. By decree of 8 October 1798, the 1st and 2nd battalions were the field battalions, the 3rd battalion the 'garrison battalion', often garrisoned at the same location as the depot. On 2 June 1799 this decree was withdrawn but of course it would take time to become effective. Therefore, the third battalions often had the lowest quality troops. A demi-brigade had on paper a full strength of 3,235 men (excluding the depot), with each battalion 1,084 men strong. In practice this number was seldom reached. The depot had no fixed strength. As already described many French units already present, or sent to the Batavian Republic during the campaign, were raw and newly raised. For example:

- 90e Demi-Brigade: raised 21 December 1798, out of detachments of the 89e and 96e Demi-Brigades augmented with conscripts;
- 98e Demi-Brigade: raised 20 January 1799, out of 150 men of various corps, 180 NCOs of the 68e Demi-Brigade and the 10e Demi-Brigade Légère, detachments of the 27e and 70e Demi-Brigades augmented with conscripts.[30]

Also present in Holland later during the campaign were the 1e Batallion des Ardennes and the 1e Batallion du Nord, both National Guard units. These saw no actual fighting. The French infantry wore the National Guard uniform introduced in 1793, but this was regulation only. In practice a variety of uniforms was worn, with many men still wearing the old white uniform and many more wearing non-regulation trousers or overalls. They were armed with a smoothbore musket and a bayonet. Part of the men, especially the grenadiers, had a short infantry sabre as well. Officers were armed with a sword. In this period, the French infantry had colours with over two hundred different patterns.

The French cavalry present in Holland consisted of dragoons and *chasseurs à cheval*. Each regiment consisted of four squadrons each of two companies (114) and a depot. A regiment therefore consisted of 35 officers and 532 others. Dragoons were armed with a straight bladed sword and a musket with bayonet. The musket was slightly shorter than the infantry pattern. The *chasseurs à cheval* were armed with a curved sabre and a short musketoon.

The foot artillery of the French army was organised into regiments of 20 companies each. A company at full strength had 93 men. Each company operated a battery of eight guns, consisting of six 4pdr, 8pdr and/or 12pdr field cannon and two 6-inch howitzers. In practice, regimental artillery was not used anymore, but in some cases the 4pdr cannon were

---

30 M. Brahaut, 'Organisation des demi-brigades, deuxième formation', in : Jules du Camp, *Histoire de l'armée et de tous les régiments* (Paris: A. Barbier, 1850), Vol.IV, pp.xii-xiii.

still supposed to follow the movements of the infantry. To serve these guns, to each artillery company thirty *auxiliares* drawn from the infantry could be attached. The train consisted of civilians. The gunners were armed with a straight artillery sword (*briquet*) and the artillery musket (shorter than an infantry musket). The French foot artillery in the Batavian Republic had a huge shortage of horses, which had to be provided by a French entrepreneur.

The horse artillery of the French army was also organised in regiments, of six companies each. A company at full strength had 75 men. Each company operated a battery of six guns, consisting of four 6pdr field guns and two 6-inch howitzers (with long barrels), or four 8pdr field guns and two 6-inch howitzers (with short barrels). The gunners were armed with a curved sabre.

In 1799, French naval presence in the Batavian Republic was limited to gunboats, of which a number were sent to Amsterdam and the Zuiderzee. They arrived too late to take part in the campaign.

4

The British and Russian Military Forces

The British Army in Holland

To provide the army for the invasion of Holland, Great Britain had a task of almost insuperable difficulty. Forming an army of even 8,000 troops would at the moment be nearly impossible. From 1793 to 1795, a large British army had fought in Flanders. The subsequent retreat to Hannover during a severe winter had taken its toll on the troops. At the conclusion of this campaign most regiments were shipped at once to the West Indies, to capture the French and Spanish possessions. This proved to be disastrous, the soldiers died by the thousands:

> From the 1st March, 1796, to the end of 1799, there died, in the Leeward Islands, 2 brigadier-generals, 19 lieutenant-colonels, 12 majors, 72 captains, 169 subalterns, 11 adjutants, 9 quartermasters, 14 surgeons, 19 assistant-surgeons, and 14,327 non-commissioned officers and men, besides about 187 of the latter belonging to draughted regiments, who were left, in July, 1796, in the different general hospitals. This frightful mortality was greatest in St. Lucia and Grenada.[1]

The state the British military was in at this time, is perfectly described as follows:

> Scattered over the habitable world by half-regiments, in different garrisons, or frittered away in detachments in Ireland, the soldier has no other study but to keep his arms and accoutrements in order, to recollect as much of his marchings and wheelings as may save him from being sent to drill, and to be sober when he is ordered for guard-mounting. Lodged in good barracks, and his daily food placed before him, he gives himself no further trouble, and neither knows nor cares how the serious game of war is to be carried on at some future day. The regiments are in "apple-pie" order; the General commanding the district tells them they are all he can wish; but, unless they happen to be in Dublin garrison, and witness a few sham fights in the Phoenix Park, they are utterly ignorant of the combined movements of a body of troops, even so large as a brigade.

---

1 Anon., *The Campaign in Holland, 1799. By a Subaltern* (London: W. Mitchell, 1861), p.3.

> If this is the case with the infantry, how much worse is it with the cavalry! Sometimes years elapse without even the whole of a regiment being brought together; they are dispersed all over the country in small detachments, doing the duty of gens d'armes and petty constables, and are only required to possess that degree of philosophy which enables a man to sit still in quiet self-possession under a shower of brick-bats. When ordered on service, although possessing the best materiel in the world, in men, horses, and equipments, they are decidedly inferior to their opponents; and it requires at least two campaigns to bring them to a knowledge of their duties in the field, entirely from want of practice.
>
> The Artillery is the only branch that, by being kept together, attain that knowledge requisite for immediate entrance on a campaign; and even then they have a great deal to learn when they go first on service.[2]

To fill the gap in manpower a system was introduced, by which one could obtain a rank by raising enough men. This had the effect that in no time there were no less than 135 infantry regiments. This was only on paper, though, as officers anxious to obtain rank enlisted almost anyone. Hundreds of men made a regular trade of enlisting to receive the bounty in one regiment and then deserting to the next one. The Duke of York put an end to this as soon as he received command. The new regiments, numbering the 101st to the 135th, were disbanded and the few men present added to the skeleton regiments returning from the West Indies. An attempt in 1796 to persuade men from the supplementary regiments of the militia to volunteer for the regular army was unsuccessful. Finally, in 1799, Pitt managed to pass a Bill through Parliament which permitted a quarter of the effective strength of every militia regiment to volunteer for the regular army:

> His Royal Highness the Commander in Chief directs it to be declared to the Militia Forces at large, that an Act of Parliament has passed with a view to enable his Majesty to provide for the vigorous prosecution of the war, in which, among other provisions, it is enacted, that it shall be lawful for one fourth of the private men of the embodied militia to enter as volunteers into such of his Majesty's regular regiments of infantry, as his Majesty shall, by any order under his Royal Sign Manual, think proper to appoint, and that his Majesty has in consequence been graciously pleased to assign the following regiments for the reception of volunteers from the Militia Forces, viz. [follows a list of the regiments].
>
> The Commander in Chief is well acquainted with the spirit which universally pervades every part of his Majesty's forces; and from the frequent opportunities he has had of observing the zeal and honourable exertions, which have particularly characterised the militia during this war, his Royal Highness entertains no doubt that many will embrace this opportunity of extending their services, and of adding fresh lustre to the British arms by aiding the efforts of our Allies, sharing their glory, and, by improving their late successes, of contributing, with them to secure

---

2 Anon., 'Recollections of the British army, in the early campaigns of the Revolutionary War' in *The United Service Journal and Naval and Military Magazine*, 1836, pp.181-182.

the first object of his Majesty's paternal anxiety, a speedy restoration of peace, on terms secure and honourable to this country.

The Commander in Chief is persuaded, few arguments will be necessary to animate the men to whom he is addressing himself; but his Royal Highness has directed that it should be explained to the Militia Forces, that the Legislature has not been unmindful of the interest of those who may choose to become volunteers for the regular service; for the Act of Parliament expressly declares, that every volunteer who shall enter from the Militia into any of the above-mentioned regiments, shall be enlisted to serve for five years or during the continuance of the present war, and for six months after the expiration thereof, and no longer; and shall not be liable to be sent or to serve out of Europe; and that every such person shall, in addition to the usual and accustomed oaths to be taken by every person enlisting as a soldier in his Majesty's forces, take the following oath, that is to say,

"I, A.B. do sincerely promise, and swear, that I will be faithful and bear true allegiance to his Majesty King George; and I do swear, that I will faithfully serve, in the regiment of his Majesty's regular forces, within any part of Europe, during the term of five years, or for the continuance of the war, and for six months after the expiration thereof, unless I shall be sooner discharged."

The Act of Parliament declares likewise, that every such volunteer shall serve in the regiment of which he may make choice, and that he shall not, on any account whatever, be drafted to serve in any other regiment. It further provides, that every volunteer so entering into any of the above-mentioned regiments shall receive a bounty of ten guineas, one third of this bounty to be paid to him, or to such person, or such of his family as he may direct, on his being attested; and one guinea to be laid out in providing immediate necessaries, if it shall be thought requisite by the Magistrate before whom he may be attested. The remainder of this sum of ten guineas to be paid to him, on his joining the regiment of which he may have made choice, or on his arrival at the place of assembly fixed on for the rendezvous of the volunteers from the militia of the district, where he will be received by proper Officers of the regiment in which he has chosen to serve, and by them will be conducted to the head-quarters. Every volunteer will be entitled to pay, subsistence, and clothing, as a private soldier in the regiment of which he may make choice, according to the regulations of the service, from the instant of his obtaining his discharge from the militia.

No man is to be allowed to claim the benefit of a volunteer under the said act, unless he shall be at least five feet four inches high, and free from bodily infirmity.[3]

This time the plan worked, for the militiamen volunteered in thousands, being greatly excited by the prospects of an expedition in Holland, which according to popular opinion would be a walk in the park and cover the participants with glory as one contemporary newspaper had it:

---

[3] 'By Order of his Royal Highness, The Commander in Chief, Harry Calvert, Adjutant General of the Forces', in the *London Chronicle*, 18 July 1799.

> It is confidently reported here that the projected expedition is for Holland, and that it is undertaken on the invitation of a very numerous and opulent body of the inhabitants of that Republic. Whatever truth may be in the rumour, it has had the effect of greatly increasing the Volunteers from the militia regiments.[4]

A later history reflected on the same optimism:

> The newspapers of the day say that very large numbers of Militiamen volunteered, and they describe the mode of volunteering. "The British Regiments of Militia are vying with one another in volunteering into the Line. The General orders of Field-Marshal the Duke of York are read on three parades, and on the fourth day after, every man volunteering is to appear in a certain cockade. On the fourth day after these orders had been read to the South Lincoln, the whole Regiment to a man appeared with a cockade, as well as several Subaltern Officers".[5]

Within three weeks, regiments which had scarcely 300 effectives were raised to 1,700 or 1,800, and six of these formed second battalions. The 4th and 9th Foot, being favourite regiments, were even able to form a 3rd battalion. Total number of volunteers from the militia that volunteered for the regular army was 24,977 men, more than enough to form an army for the invasion of Holland. How many volunteers of the militia were given to the regular army is shown by the following returns, although a substantial part of them would never embark for Holland for various reasons. The number between brackets after the regimental title is the number of battalions of the regiment that participated in the campaign. Of the regiments that absorbed militia but did not participate in the campaign the dislocations are given.

Regiment	Number	Location
1st Foot Guards (1)	454	
Coldstream Guards (1)	557	
3rd Foot Guards (1)	290	
4th (King's) Foot (3)	3,034	
5th Foot (2)	1,268	
9th Foot (2)	2,695	(3rd battalion in Ashford, Kent)
15th Foot (0)	1,548	(Canterbury)
16th Foot (0)	761	(Canterbury)
17th Foot (2)	1,558	
20th Foot (2)	1,647	
31st Foot (1)	955	
35th Foot (2)	1,764	
36th Foot (0)	769	(Cirencester)
40th Foot (2)	1,504	
46th Foot (0)	694	(Barham Downs)

---

4   *London Chronicle*, 20 July 1799.
5   Lt. Col. Sir John M. Burgoyne, *Regimental Records of the Bedfordshire Militia from 1759 to 1884* (London: W.H. Allen & Co., 1884), pp.49-50.

52nd Foot (0)	1,861	(Ashford, Kent)
56th Foot (1)	774	
62nd Foot (0)	1,043	(Canterbury)
63rd Foot (1)	755	
82nd Foot (0)	702	(Canterbury and Blandford)
Royal Artillery	344[6]	

Charles Steevens, lieutenant in the 20th Foot at that time, as well as the regimental history of this regiment, describes the condition of his regiment and how it was brought up to strength again:

> The regiment was at that time in the West Indies, but in the spring following (1796) they returned to England a complete skeleton. All that remained of the XX after four years of war and disease in St. Domingo, was six officers and seventy non-commissioned officers and men. From Bury I went to Derby, where I was for six months, until the summer of 1799, when I was ordered to Windsor to receive volunteers, for the XX Regiment, from the old Stafford Militia.
>
> The regiment remained but a short time at Manchester, and from thence they went to Preston in the same county. Recruiting was more successful at Preston than at any of the towns in which the corps had previously been quartered: three hundred recruits joined the colours, and continued at Preston till they were ordered on the expedition to Holland, and accordingly left Preston on July 22nd, 1799, for Canterbury, where it was joined by one thousand eight hundred volunteers from the militia battalions of the counties of York, Lancaster, Stafford, Derby, Chester, Devon, Cornwall, and Cambridge… on August 4th, 1799, it was formed into two battalions.[7]

In the newspapers, the flow of militiamen was joyfully welcomed, leading to exaggerated articles:

> A braver or more loyal army never yet assembled, nor in a nobler cause. The militia are entitled to be considered as volunteers in the expedition; and such has been their zeal and enthusiasm, that had not the Act of Parliament limited the number to one-fourth which could be drafted from them into the line, whole regiments would have passed ever into the regular service. It is impossible to detail this vigorous display of the national power, spirit, and resources, without some natural exultation and honest pride. Almost at the close of the seventh year of a war, unparalleled in its exertions, and in which the public hopes of the enemy have uniformly been founded in the exhausture of our resources, the ruin of our credit, and the

---

6 'Return of Volunteers given by the Embodied Militia to the Regular Army, between the 18th July and 15th November, 1799', in Anon., *The Campaign in Holland, 1799*, p.77.
7 Lieut.-Col. Chas. Steevens, *Reminiscences of my Military Life from 1795 to 1818* (Winchester: Warren & Son, 1878), pp.5 & 7 & Major B. Smyth, *A History of the Lancashire Fusiliers (Formerly XX Regiment)* (Dublin: The Sackville Press, 1903), pp.184-187.

bankruptcy of the public spirit, is there an English man that can behold the departure of this expedition without a devout gratitude to Heaven, and a pious pride in the country it deigns to visibly to protect and distinguish?[8]

The quality of these units however was in fact low; the militia had no experience and lacked good officers and discipline. Volunteers from the militia received a bounty of 10 guineas if they signed up, with the condition that they would not serve outside Europe – this condition was very important, because the worst thing that a soldier could befall was a posting in the West-Indies: the chances of survival were very small because of tropical diseases. This amount of money was enough for them to get drunk every day till the day of embarkation, exactly what many of them did. Bunbury wrote about them:

> An Act of Parliament was passed for this purpose in the month of July: and during August the Militiamen, allured by extravagant bounties, were drunk and rolling riotously into the ranks of various regiments of the line. Many thousands of stout fellows were obtained by this measure; but for the time, they ceased to be the well drilled orderly soldiers of our Militia regiments, without becoming men on whom their new officers could rely for the regular service. So numerous were the volunteers that many regiments, which in August could hardly muster one or two hundred wasted old soldiers, found itself 2000 strong; healthy, athletic young men, and well drilled, as far as mere drilling could go. But these men were hardly sobered from the riotous jollity of their volunteering; their minds were unsettled; to them their new officers and sergeants were utter strangers; every thing was new and bewildering… If only three months had been gained for them to know something of their officers and serjeants, and the ways of the regiment into which they had entered, the men would probably have done their duty well; but such was not the case, and one cannot be surprised that, with the exception of the 20th and the 40th regiments, these suddenly created battalions proved unfit to meet a brave and skilful enemy.[9]

The following incident also describes the problems that arose with the enlisted militia:

> It was on that day also notified that Mr. Pitt would visit the army the next evening, and a *feu de joie* was to be fired for our recent success. A general sweeping was made next day of Canterbury and all the adjacent villages; and by three o'clock in the day every man able to stand or walk was brought into camp. We were drawn out in single line, extending from near the race-course to the Half-way House; and in due time the Premier and Mr. Dundas appeared in front, and seemed much pleased to see so strong a muster. The ceremony of priming and loading was gone through very decently, and the *feu de joie* commenced; it might have been called a *feu d'ivresse* ['a fire of drunkenness'], for there were certainly not five hundred

---

8   *London Chronicle*, 20 July 1799.
9   Sir Henry Bunbury, *A Narrative of the Campaign in North Holland. 1799* (London: Richard Bentley, 1854), pp.32-33. Bunbury was aide-de-camp to York during the campaign in Holland.

men quite sober. It was thought prudent not to attempt marching past, and we were dismissed immediately.[10]

The battalions were even further weakened by taking away the grenadier and light companies from six regiments by forming these into an Advance Guard: 'By this measure the want of coherence amongst the component parts of a regiment was increased and there never was such a confusion of militia in the world'.[11]

In general, the British troops taking part in the campaign were very inexperienced. Only a few regiments, for example the 23rd Royal Welsh Fusiliers, had some experience. The infantry battalions that were to form the First Echelon were the best present in England at that moment. All three Foot Guards regiments were participating in the 1st echelon, with a battalion each. An additional 'Battalion of Grenadiers Companies of the Guards' was formed out of two companies each of the 1st and 2nd battalions of the 1st Foot Guards, and two companies each from the Coldstream and 3rd Foot Guards. These four Foot Guards battalions formed the 1st and 2nd (Guards) Brigades of two battalions each. Battalion strength was theoretically about 1,000 men. Three additional brigades were formed from line infantry battalions. These line battalions were brought up to strength with volunteers of other line regiments. From the battalions forming Major General Coote's 3rd Brigade, the 2nd and 29th Foot had served in Ireland:

> Plymouth, 26 July 1799: Arrived from Waterford the Nereide, 36 guns, Captain Watkins, with part of the 29th Regiment on board, from Waterford for the Downs. She parted company in the Channel with the Melpomene, 44 guns, and Proselyte, 36, with the remainder of the 29th Regiment on board. In the evening the Nereide sailed for the Downs and the latter Frigates passed this Port.[12]

The 27th had come home from Grenada; the 69th had served on board of the fleet as marines and had distinguished itself in the Battle of Cape St. Vincent; and the 85th, raised in 1793, had seen service in Flanders the next year and now came from Jersey. Major General Moore's 4th Brigade was composed of the 2/1st (Royal) Foot, coming from Portugal in June; the 25th had returned as a skeleton from the West Indies in September 1796 and since then was on Guernsey; the 49th had returned from Jamaica in March 1798 and had also stayed on Guernsey; as well as the 79th Highlanders which had returned from the West Indies in August 1797 and the 92nd Highlanders which came from Ireland together with the 2nd and 29th.

Initially Moore's Brigade had a somewhat different composition and would consist of the 2/1st, 25th, 49th, 79th, 92nd, 64th and 69th. He wrote about these battalions in his diary:

> The Guards are certainly a fine body of men. The regiments of the Line are in general but poor, and a few of them are formed or disciplined. The 92nd (Highlanders) are an exception. They are excellent; my next best are the Royals and 25th; the 79th are

---

10 Anon. 'Recollections of the British army', p.184.
11 Anon. 'Recollections of the British army', p.185.
12 *Naval Chronicle*, Vol. II, p.257.

weak, but not bad. The 49th have not been a sufficient time embodied; the 64th are not fit to be sent upon service.[13]

The 64th Regiment of Foot was indeed removed from the invasion force and was left behind, while the 69th was transferred to Coote's 3rd Brigade. Colonel MacDonalds' Reserve consisted of the 23rd Royal Welsh Fusiliers as well as the 55th, which had returned from the West Indies in 1797. The 23rd had returned as a skeleton from St. Domingo in 1796: in 1798, its flank companies had been taken prisoner in the failed expedition to Oostende and since then the 23rd had stayed on Jersey. The name 'Reserve' for this brigade was a misnomer, as this brigade would lead the attack in every action in which it was engaged.

The battalions of the Second and Third Echelon consisted of skeleton-regiments already mentioned filled with militia volunteers. Major General Don's 5th Brigade consisted of the 17th Foot (2 battalions) which had returned from St. Domingo in March 1799 and the 40th (2 battalions) which had returned from the Leeward Islands in the spring of 1799. Major General the Earl of Cavan's 6th Brigade consisted of the 20th (2 battalions) which had returned from Jamaica in March 1796 consisting of only 60 or 70 NCOs and men on its return, and the 63rd which had returned from Jamaica in May 1799.[14] Major General the Earl of Chatham's 7th Brigade consisted of the 4th (King's) Foot (3 battalions) which had returned from Canada in 1797 and the 31st which had returned from Barbados only 85 men strong. Major General Prince William of Gloucester's 8th Brigade consisted of the 5th Foot (2 battalions) which together with the 4th had returned from Canada in 1797 where the remaining soldiers had been drafted into the 24th; and the 35th (2 battalions), which was the sole line regiment taking part in the upcoming campaign to have served in England over the last years. Finally, Major General Manners' 9th Brigade consisted of the 9th Foot (2 battalions) which had returned from Grenada in the autumn of 1797 and the 56th which had returned from St. Domingo in January 1799. Before leaving Barham Downs, two flank battalions were formed from the flank companies of 4th, 5th, 9th, 31st, and 35th Foot, making up a battalion of grenadiers and a battalion of light infantry, each of 10 companies. Both battalions initially formed an advance guard commanded by Major General Knox and were later during the campaign added to Colonel MacDonald's Reserve.

A line infantry battalion consisted of a 'headquarters', eight battalion companies, a grenadier company and a light company. Strength of a battalion was on paper nearly 1,150 men, each company having a strength of 111 men. Armament was a smoothbore musket with bayonet. Sergeants had nine-foot-long pikes and a sabre, officers a straight sword. Each regiment was normally recognisable by its facings but this was not the case with the 'militia' – or 'skeleton' – regiments, as described in the regimental history of the 20th Regiment of Foot:

> Officers and men were of different corps – were strangers to each other; their uniforms were different, the only outward mark showing that they belonged to the XX was the breastplate. The facings, the militia badges on the cap and on the pack, remained; but this tended more to confusion than otherwise.[15]

13 J.F. Maurice (ed.), *The Diary of Sir John Moore* (London: Edward Arnold, 1904), Vol.I, p.339.
14 Anon., *The Campaign in Holland, 1799*, p.15.
15 Smyth, *Lancashire Fusiliers*, p.187.

This is confirmed by another source: 'The tailors worked "double tides" to get at least the facings of the regiments altered, but only succeeded in part'.[16] Bunbury wrote about them:

> These raw soldiers did not even bear the uniforms of the regiments whose colours they were expected to defend, and whose honour they were to uphold. There had not been even time enough to provide clothing for them. When the men were ranked in the 5th, or the 17th, or 35th, or others of these new swollen regiments, there they stood in the respective garbs of the various corps of Militia from which they had been drawn.[17]

Of the participating infantry regiments, two were Highland regiments: the 79th and 92nd in Moore's Brigade. These regiments wore the Highland uniform consisting of a short single-breasted jacket and a kilt in the regimental colours. Both officers and men could have worn tartan pantaloons as well though.

Each infantry battalion had two colours: First the 'King's Colour'; the Union Jack with in the centre the regimental number or the regimental badge. The second colour was the 'Regimental Colour'. This one had the regimental colour, a small Union Jack in the highest corner of the colour at the side of the staff and in the middle the regimental number of the regiment in Roman numerals and (possibly) a wreath and motto.

The British cavalry present in this campaign consisted of light dragoons. A regiment of light dragoons consisted of four active or service squadrons and a depot squadron, each squadron consisting of two troops of 91 men. On paper a regiment had a strength of 919 men. Armament was the curved light cavalry sabre, two pistols, and a carbine.

Although the British artillerymen did their best, the British senior officers were inexperienced in making good use of the powerful arm. Present in this campaign were eight companies of the 3rd and 4th 'marching battalions' or foot artillery. Combined with drivers, horses and guns a company was known as an artillery brigade, the equivalent of what today would be called a battery. A brigade consisted of 12 guns: 3pdr, 6pdr or 12pdr cannon and 5.5-inch howitzers. Strength of an artillery brigade was 231 men. Personal armament was a smoothbore musket, bayonet, and short infantry sabre. Officers had a straight sword. Also present was A Troop (later called the Chestnut Troop for the colour of their horses) of the 'flying' or horse artillery. In a horse artillery troop the gunners were mounted on horses or rode on the carriages. They were originally armed with five 6pdr cannon and two 5.5-inch howitzers, but in 1798 York had ordered two 6-pdr cannon to be replaced by the much heavier 12-pdr cannon in each troop of horse artillery. A second troop of horse artillery under Captain Scott was made ready but did not embark. Strength of A Troop was 185 men and 191 horses. Personal armament was a sabre of light cavalry pattern, and pistols. Finding the necessary horses proved to be difficult and as a result their quality was bad.[18]

Beside this there were the battalion guns, a system already doubted:

---

16 Anon. 'Recollections of the British army', p.184.
17 Bunbury, *Narrative*, pp.32-33.
18 Major Francis Duncan, *History of the Royal Regiment of Artillery* (London: John Murray, 1879), Vol. II, pp.90-94.

Militia regiments, which were embodied, were also sending daily petitions for battalion guns, followed by remonstrances and strongly-worded indignation. And Colonel Macleod, in spite of his personal opinions, was obliged to strain every nerve to meet a wish, which was still supported by our military system. His personal opinions, it has been said, and truly: for the correspondence of the period reveals the fact that Colonel Macleod had commenced to detest the existing system of battalion guns. He dared not say openly what he thought; but from a private letter written at this time his opinion may be easily learnt. Writing of some detachments which had been collected under an officer's command, he said: "I believe they are intended for the battalion guns of the Infantry Brigades, and I had some thoughts of drawing them to Chatham, where I would have them drilled to the duty expected of them, appointing 1 non-commissioned officer and 7 gunners to each 6-pounder, and accustoming them to make use of a horse to advance, instead of drag-rope men; a custom which weakens the battalions they are attached to without aiding the services of the Artillery. For, between you and I, six men are too few to drag guns, and too many to stand with ropes in their hands to be shot at".[19]

The heavy armament for the horse artillery in this campaign, as well as the use of the artillery overall, was the cause of discussion later:

The troop was partly armed with 12-pounders, a very heavy armament for Horse Artillery, and one never again used: and it seems all the more unsuitable, when we find that the battalion guns, which were merely 6-pounders, were in one instance brigaded into a battery under Captain Frazer, presenting the anomaly in the army, on this 2nd October, of a light field artillery, intended for rapid movements, being armed with guns of twice the calibre of those used by what should have been the medium field artillery, and only required to accommodate itself to the movements of infantry.[20]

The Corps of Royal Engineers consisted only of officers and was very small, the rank and file being provided by the Royal Military Artificers. Some engineers were present in the campaign, commanded initially by Lieutenant Colonel Hay, who was killed by a shot of the Batavian horse artillery on the day of the British landings. Armament was a straight sword.

A new element in the British army was the Royal Wagon Train. Raised on 12 August 1799, it consisted of five troops, in September increased to eight troops, of 76 men each. Their contribution to the campaign was only minor.

The British Navy

The British Royal Navy, the 'wooden wall' of Great Britain, was in this era the biggest and by far the best navy in the world. British warships were of excellent design and built for

---

19 Duncan, *Royal Regiment of Artillery*, Vol.II, pp.94-95.
20 Duncan, *Royal Regiment of Artillery*, Vol.II, p.99.

long voyages and long stays at sea. To these the many captured foreign, especially French and Batavian, ships were added when they were fit enough. The best quality ships were used at remote stations and in the Mediterranean, while for example Admiral Duncan's North Sea fleet consisted of older and lesser quality ships. The oldest and worst ships were used as troopships and transports, and finally became prisoner hulks. Many ships were needed: to protect Great Britain and its overseas possessions and trade routes; to raid enemy trade routes and capture enemy shipping and privateers; to blockade enemy ports and keep battle fleets at hand to fight the enemy. The already massive Royal Navy was increased even further: from 420 ships in June 1793 to 777 in June 1798: 188 ships of the line, 26 50-gun ships, 217 frigates and 345 sloops. Beside these, numerous schooners, luggers, and brigs were hired to guard the British coast, to patrol, and to fight off the French and Batavian privateers: at the beginning of the year 1799, 61 armed cutters, 15 luggers and 12 other armed vessels were hired.[21]

The term 'ship of the line' was usually applied to all warships armed with 60 guns or more. From this period on, though, 50-gun ships ought to be strong enough to be armed with the same heavy calibre guns as bigger ships and when necessary they were placed in the line. 74-gun ships of the line were regarded as particularly useful in the line of battle. Frigates were armed with 20 to 40 guns although some frigates captured from the French were armed with 46 guns. The frigate was the workhorse of the Royal Navy, big and fast enough for long voyages and strong enough to battle all enemy ships except for the heavy ships of the line. Sloops of war were one size less than frigates, generally armed with 10 to 14 guns, with three masts. They were commanded by commanders. Brigs were vessels with two masts, armed with 16 to 18 guns. They were also commanded by commanders, sometimes lieutenants. Cutters were small sloops with one mast, schooners had two small masts, and luggers three small masts, the main and mizzen leaning towards the stern. These vessels were armed with 6 to 14 guns. They were chiefly employed to carry dispatches, to attend on fleets and to convey small craft along the coasts.[22]

All enemy harbours and waterways, from the Mediterranean all the way north to the North Sea, were blockaded. With the Wadden Sea and the Zuiderzee, as well as the coastal waters around the Batavian Republic being shallow, many captured small vessels and fishing boats were armed with guns to serve in these waters during the campaign and to provision the army.

The Russian Army in Holland

It was generally believed that the Russians possessed a formidable army, as illustrated by Walsh in his description of the Russian contingent in Holland:

> The fame of the Russian arms had already filled every quarter of the habitable globe. The courage, vigour, and discipline of those invincible troops claimed and

---

21 *Naval Chronicle*, Vol.I, p.292 & Appendix.
22 Based on 'Observations of the present state of the Royal Navy' in: *Naval Chronicle*, Vol.I, Appendix II.

obtained universal commendation, and British soldiers, for the first time, were about to take lessons in the science of war from their redoubtable allies. It must, however, be confessed, that the Russian troops were little or nothing indebted to external appearance for their high reputation. Their clothing, arms, and accoutrements were certainly, at least, not superior to our own. Their uniform was green, with black, yellow, or red facings; yellow breeches, and long black leggings. The grenadiers were only distinguished by conical caps, with fronts of white or yellow latten metal. Many of the men had one, two, and, some few, three silver medals, appending by a short ribbon from the lapels of their coats. These medals, which were stamped either with the effigies of the emperor Paul, or of the late empress Catharine, with a Russian inscription on the reverse, were tokens of military merit, bestowed on account of some signal exploit. How far such rewards might contribute to excite military emulation in the breast of the soldier, deserves to be considered… The Russian officers wore no epaulets, but they were known by a very large silver gorget, which possibly might be intended as a defensive armour for the breast.

In their persons, the Russians, for the most part, were rather under the middle size, but broad-chested, robust, and muscular. Their countenances, however, could not be thought prepossessing; to those who were unaccustomed to view them, they seemed even repulsive and ferocious. The Russian grenadiers had not been selected on account of their height, but for their superior strength of form…

The only cavalry attached to the Russian army consisted of one troop of hussars, and two or three troops of Cossacks. The former was a part of the *gardes-du-corps* of the emperor, and was composed of picked men of the largest dimensions, and of the finest proportions, most superbly appointed. The Cossacks were of a slenderer make, and had better countenances than the Russians. Their arms were a carbine slung across the back in a kind of cradle-sling, a scimitar, pistols in the waist-belt, and a spear twelve feet long in the hand. This furniture, together with their oriental dresses, and fine bushy beards, produced an effect more picturesque and romantic than formidable. They were mounted on a wretched looking race of small ambling horses, with long tails and manes, and of different colours. Notwithstanding which, these animals were reported to be docile, sure-footed, and indefatigable.

The general appearance of the Russian army, when drawn up under arms, announced, at the first glance, that it was composed of troops formed altogether for service, and not for show. There appeared to have been established throughout all ranks the most absolute subordination. Several priests accompanied the army, to whom was yielded implicit and reverential obedience.[23]

The Russian infantry participating in this campaign consisted of grenadier regiments, musketeer regiments, and a jager regiment. These regiments consisted of two battalions. Grenadier battalions had a flank company and five fusilier companies; musketeer battalions consisted of a grenadier company and five musketeer companies. The *jégerski* battalions had

---

23 E. Walsh, *A Narrative of the Expedition to Holland, in the Autumn of the Year 1799* (London: G.G. and J. Robinson, 1800), pp.46-48.

five jager companies. Every regiment had a geographic name, but during the reign of Tsar Paul, since 31 October 1798, the regiments wore the name of its chef; a general officer who in name, but not in practice, commanded the regiment. After the reign of Tsar Paul, the regiments received their geographical name again. The names of the chefs of the regiments participating in the campaign of 1799 were as follows:

> Regiment Grenadiers of Zherebtsov (Phanagoria Grenadiers)
> Regiment Grenadiers of Benkendorf (Taurica Grenadiers)
> Regiment Grenadiers of Emmé (Pavlovsk Grenadiers)
> Regiment Musketeers of Sedmoratzki (Bélozersk Musketeers)
> Regiment Musketeers of Arbénev (Dnieper Musketeers)
> Regiment Musketeers of Fersen (Tobolsk Musketeers)

On 13 December 1796 the grenadier companies of the musketeer regiments and flank companies of the grenadier regiments were combined to form 'combined grenadier battalions' which received the names of their commanders. The following combined grenadier battalions participated in the 1799 campaign:

> Battalion of Lieutenant Colonel Ericsson (Arkharov and Yelets Musketeers)
> Battalion of Lieutenant Colonel Mitiouchin (Pavlovsk Grenadiers and Bélozersk Musketeers)
> Battalion of Lieutenant Colonel Ogarev (Kozlov and Schlüsselburg Musketeers)
> Battalion of Lieutenant Colonel Ossipov (Sofiya and Chernigov Musketeers)
> Battalion of Lieutenant Colonel Strick (Taurica and St. Petersburg Grenadiers)
> Battalion of Lieutenant Colonel Timofeyev (Dnieper and Tobolsk Musketeers)

On paper a line infantry regiment consisted of about 72 officers and 1,996 NCOs and soldiers. Each battalion consisted of a 1st company or grenadier company (184 men) and five musketeer or fusilier companies (170 men each). The battalions participating in the campaign were weaker, also because of the creation of the combined grenadier battalions from the grenadier and flank companies. Headdress was a mitre cap for the grenadiers, with a brass front plate. Fusiliers had a lower mitre cap, musketeers had a bicorn. Armament was a musket with bayonet. Grenadiers had a short sword as well. NCOs had a sabre and halberd, except for grenadier NCOs who had a rifled musket. Subaltern officers had a halberd, in the grenadiers as well.

Only one *jager* regiment took part in the campaign: the 1st *Jégerski* of Suthoff. On paper this regiment consisted of 34 officers and 1,385 NCOs and jagers. Composition was two battalions each of a 1st company (146 men) and four centre companies (141 men each). Headdress was the bicorn, the same as for the line infantry. Armament was a cutlass and the infantry musket; only twelve sharpshooters in each company had rifled muskets. In addition a sword bayonet. Officers had a sabre. The line infantry had one 'white flag' per regiment and one 'coloured flag' per musketeer or fusilier company, so that each regiment had one white and nine coloured flags. The centre of the colour showed an orange oval with the black Russian eagle, with above the eagle the Tsar's crown. The remainder of the colour was divided into eight quarters, four fields and four corners.

Only few Russian cavalry was present during the campaign:

Life Guard Hussars of Lieutenant Colonel Sladkov (1 squadron)	76 men
Life Guard Hussars of Colonel Gladkov (1 squadron)	45 men
Life Guard Don Cossacks (1 sotnia)	70 men
Life-Sotnia of the Ural Cossacks (1 sotnia)	62 men

The Life Guard Hussars were divided in two weak squadrons as shown above. They were armed with a carbine and a curved sabre. The Life Guard Don Cossacks wore a red demi-caftan. Armament was a curved sabre, a pistol and of course the Cossack lance with red shaft. NCOs had no pistol. The Life-Sotnia of the Ural Cossacks wore a red caftan edged white, and red breeches. Armament was the same; the Cossack lance however had a brown shaft.

During this campaign, two companies of field or 'campaign' artillery with 16 guns and 491 men, and regimental artillery with a total of 36 guns were present. The field artillery consisted of the Company Durnov and elements of the Battalion Kaptsevich. On paper, a battalion of campaign artillery consisted of five companies (224 men each). This strength includes the 92 *handlangers* (auxiliaries) in each company. With the strength of the company Durnov listed as 101 men, it appears that the *handlangers* were either not present or not added to this count. A company of 'campaign' artillery usually consisted of twelve guns: four medium 12pdr and four short 12pdr cannon and four 24pdr unicorns. A unicorn (or licorne) was a kind of howitzer which was able to fire howitzer shells as well as solid shot just like a cannon, as well as canister and grapeshot. During the campaign in Holland the field artillery operated 12pdr and 6pdr cannon and 24pdr unicorns. The gunners wore the infantry bicorn. Armament was the infantry sabre, officers had a straight sword. The regimental artillery consisted of four guns for the grenadier and musketeer regiments, two guns for the *jégerski* regiment and two guns each for the combined grenadier battalions. These guns were usually 3pdr cannon or 3pdr unicorns. During the campaign in Holland the regimental artillery consisted of 6pdr and 3pdr cannon and 12pdr and 8pdr unicorns.[24] At this period the regimental artillery was manned by foot artillerymen (i.e. field artillery). In practice the regimental guns received their directions from the commander of the brigade they were attached to.

A pioneer company of the Battalion Schwanebach took part in the campaign, under the command of Captain Dreyer. Headdress was a low mitre cap. Armament was a pistol in a white holster worn at the rear of the waist belt and a curved 'fascine knife'. NCOs were armed with a sabre. Officers wore the bicorn.

The Russian Navy

The quality of the Russian navy was nothing compared with the Royal Navy of their British allies. The warships were of a bad quality and the crews inexperienced, a fact that could not

---

24 Miliutin, *Geschichte des Krieges*, Vol.IV, p.290.

be remedied by the large-scale employment of foreign officers and captains. Not surprisingly, some ships transporting the Russian army to Holland were unable to make the voyage. Of the ships send to the North Sea, many lost their masts during stormy weather and had to be patched up in British ports. An article in the *Naval Chronicle* makes the following assessment of the Russian navy:

> The Navy of Russia, in the ports of the Baltic and Archangel, consisted, in the latter end of 1778, of 38 ships of the line, 15 frigates, 4 prames, 109 gallies. Of this number about twenty-eight ships of the line and ten frigates, including those built with larch wood, were fit for immediate service. In case, however, of necessity or danger, Russia producing all the materials for the construction and equipment of ships, her navy might soon be considerably increased. But though Russia, since the beginning of this century, has made surprising exertions in the marine, and rapidly become more powerful at sea than her neighbouring kingdoms in the North; yet, in naval affairs, she must be considered as still in her infancy, being in a great degree indebted to the English, as well for the construction of her ships, as for manoeuvring and disciplining her fleet. Many circumstances indeed concur in retarding the progress of her maritime strength: 1. The want of ports in the Ocean; 2. The small extent of her sea-coast, and that obstructed by ice; 3. A deficiency of experienced seamen… Government retains in its pay about 18,000 sailors, most of whom have never served: a few in time of peace make annual cruises into the Baltic, or perhaps as far as the English Channel; and others are employed in the summer season in navigating the vessels laden with merchandize from Cronstadt to Petersberg. But such nurseries as these are by no means sufficient to rear a large number of seamen; nor can the deficiency be supplied, in case of an immediate war, by the sailors from private vessels; for Russia has scarcely any merchant ships; which is chiefly owing to the state of vassalage, and the strict laws that prevent the natives from quitting their country without formal license… The Navy of Russia, however, with all these deficiencies, is sufficient to protect her coasts; to convoy her merchantmen; to make her respectable in the Baltic; or, in case of a Turkish war, to send a fleet into the Archipelago. It is her advantage to maintain a good correspondence with the great maritime powers, whom she supplies with naval stores; and who are, on that account, equally interested to respect and cultivate her friendship. The frontiers of her immense dominions border upon Sweden, Poland, Turkey, Persia, and China; and the security of her empire depends as much upon her Army as her Navy.[25]

---

[25] Coxe, 'The Russian Admiralty', in the *Naval Chronicle*, Vol.II, pp.286-287.

5

Preparations for the Secret Expedition

British Preparations

At the beginning of June 1799, British and Russian preparations started for the Secret Expedition as the undertaking was referred to. Commander in Chief was to be Frederick Augustus, Duke of York and Albany. In 1794 he had been Commander in Chief of the British forces in the Netherlands, where he did not show much talent: some military writers of that time even had the opinion that he was more dangerous as an ally then as an opponent. As stated by the biographer of Major General Moore:

> It was an unfortunate measure to send a young prince, though endowed with a warm and beneficent heart together with a good understanding, to take the chief command from Sir Ralph Abercrombie, who had been trained to arms from early life. The position of the army, on a hostile shore, opposed to a skilful French General, required a leader of consummate experience to foresee and overcome all the obstacles and stratagems which were to be expected. The King's partiality to his gallant son was natural; but the cabinet council being unprepossessed, instead of appointing this ambitious youth to the superintendance, ought assuredly to have placed him under the guidance of the veteran general.[1]

Nevertheless, being a member of the royal family, his appointment as commander in chief was deemed necessary to satisfy the Russian Tsar. Although York was an able administrator, this time he had to perform the difficult task of leading a combined Anglo-Russian army. Because the British had to scrape the bottom of their resources to be able to field and army in the first place, seriously weakening the land defences of Great Britain, York was told that to preserve the British army and that to be able to embark again was more important than the liberation of the Dutch Republic. So no risks were to be taken. The initial British plans for an invasion of the Batavian Republic were directed at Ameland or Delfzijl, to support the uprising of the population that had been prepared for in Friesland and Groningen. Although

---

1   James Carrick Moore, *The Life of Lieutenant-General Sir John Moore, K.B.* (London: John Murray, 1833), Vol.I, pp 236-240.

the Orangists were very optimistic about the results of such an uprising, the British were not: for them it was obvious that an Orangist uprising was only possible with foreign military aid. So already, on 23 June 1799, Lord Grenville remarked that: 'it is extremely desirable to prevent any premature explosion in the Eastern provinces till the force appears off the island of Ameland, which may be by the end of August at the latest. But that everything should be in readiness to break out then'.[2] On 22 June 1799, a letter was received in London from the British envoy-extraordinary in St. Petersburg, Sir Charles Whitworth, confirming that Tsar Paul I had agreed with the proposal for a campaign in the Batavian Republic. On 2 July, a meeting was held in the house of Lord Grenville, at which at least present were the Secretary of State for War Henry Dundas, Lieutenant General Sir Ralph Abercromby, and Hendrik Fagel, Dutch agent for the House of Orange. At this meeting, Abercromby proposed a new plan, this time to direct the main attack at the estuary of the River Meuse, laying his arguments down in a memorandum to Henry Dundas:

> It has been proposed to seize the island of Walcheren with a British force. This would have been a most important point, should any of the great armies now on foot have crossed the Rhine and the Meuse, and have penetrated into Brabant. The advantages are so obvious that they require no elucidation. Considered as unconnected with any cooperation, it could be of no use to Great Britain. It would have required a strong garrison and a considerable naval force, to have protected it; and in autumn it is extremely unhealthy. Another plan offered has been to occupy the islands of Walcheren, Goeree and Ameland, with a view to encourage and support an insurrection in Holland. It is apprehended that the support, which the possession of these islands would have given, would not have produced the desired effect, being too superficial. The intention of landing 15,000 men in the province of Groningen probably would have produced considerable consequences, if put in execution. We may fairly suppose that such a force might have rescued from the hands of the French not only Groningen, but Friesland and part of Overyssel. It is doubtful if Coevorden could have been taken during the short remains of the good season. It is probable that the operation of this body of troops must have been confined to the Northern part of the United Provinces.
>
> The last proposition which has been made has been, to concenter the whole force now assembling, and to attack Holland by the Meuse. The advantages resulting from this mode of attack, if fairly estimated, are very considerable. The possession of the island of Voorn will afford a safe port, and a free communication with Great Britain. An immediate passage into the province of Holland will be opened. And if the whole force should happily arrive before the middle of September, it is hoped that a very considerable progress will be made in the reduction of the provinces of Holland and Utrecht before the month of November. At any rate we shall be in such force as to form a corps of observation to act on the Waal and the Rhine, and to secure us from any attempt on the part of France. We should likewise be enabled to

---

2   Grenville Papers, V, in G.J.W. Koolemans Beijnen, *De Erfprins van Oranje in Noord-Holland in 1799*, overprint from *Bijdragen voor Vaderlandsche Geschiedenis en Oudheidkunde* ('s-Gravenhage: Martinus Nijhoff, 1910), p.29.

open a passage to any power on the Continent who should decide to enter Holland either on the side of Groningen or of Guelderland and of Overyssel: by depriving Holland of her defence on that side, of the lines of the Greb, which we should take in reverse, whilst at the same time we should be enabled to facilitate in a great degree the passage of the Yssel. The free navigation of the Rhine to Arnheim would afford a certain supply of provisions to the army, and would save the expense of a heavy transport by land.

On a fair comparison of the respective advantages attending each plan, it is apprehended that an attack by the Meuse is preferable under every point of view, whether the attempt is made by an army from this country, which is not expected to be supported by any of the continental powers on the Eastern frontiers of the Republic, or whether it is made with the expectation of such cooperation. Under this last idea indeed it is still more to be preferred to any of the others, for the assistance we should give to such an ally would be immediate, and even operate previously to their attack. We should open the way for them, by acting in the rear of the enemy which opposed them. In the farther prosecution of the war, should it be found expedient to carry our operations into Brabant, Great Britain, from the augmentation of her force and her naval power, would be able, in the beginning of the next campaign, to seize Walcheren in the first instance, and to open the communication by the Scheldt, and to reduce the remainder of the province of Zealand.[3]

To keep the French guessing about the destiny of the invasion troops, the concentration took place on Shirley Common, near Southampton, supervised by Abercromby. Because of this place, many objects for an invasion were possible: the French coast, Portugal, the Mediterranean, Flanders, or the Batavian Republic. At the end of July the troops moved to Barham Downs, four miles from Canterbury. By this time it was universally believed that the Secret Expedition was intended for the Batavian Republic. Finally on 8 August they moved to Deal, Ramsgate, and Margate, were the assembly of the transport ships took place. The available shipping was insufficient to move the army all at once, so the invasion army had to be divided into three echelons, and only the first echelon could be sent overseas immediately. This first echelon would consist of about 12,000 men, composed of the best units available, commanded by Abercromby.[4]

Abercromby was 65 years old, a cautious commander who initially opposed the expedition. His opinion was that the British army was not ready for such a big undertaking. Especially the transport capabilities of the army were in his eyes insufficient. His complaints led to the formation of the Royal Wagon Train on 12 August, consisting of five troops, in September increased to eight troops. Despite all this, the British government considered themselves strong enough to start the invasion without the Russians. It was anticipated that Abercromby, favoured by the nature of the terrain and supported by the Royal Navy, would be able to stand his ground until reinforcements arrived. Also, the invasion would have to

---

3 Memorandum from Abercromby to Henry Dundas on 20 July 1799, in English in Colenbrander, *Gedenkstukken*, Vol. III, pp.377-378.
4 See Appendix IV for the composition of the 1st echelon.

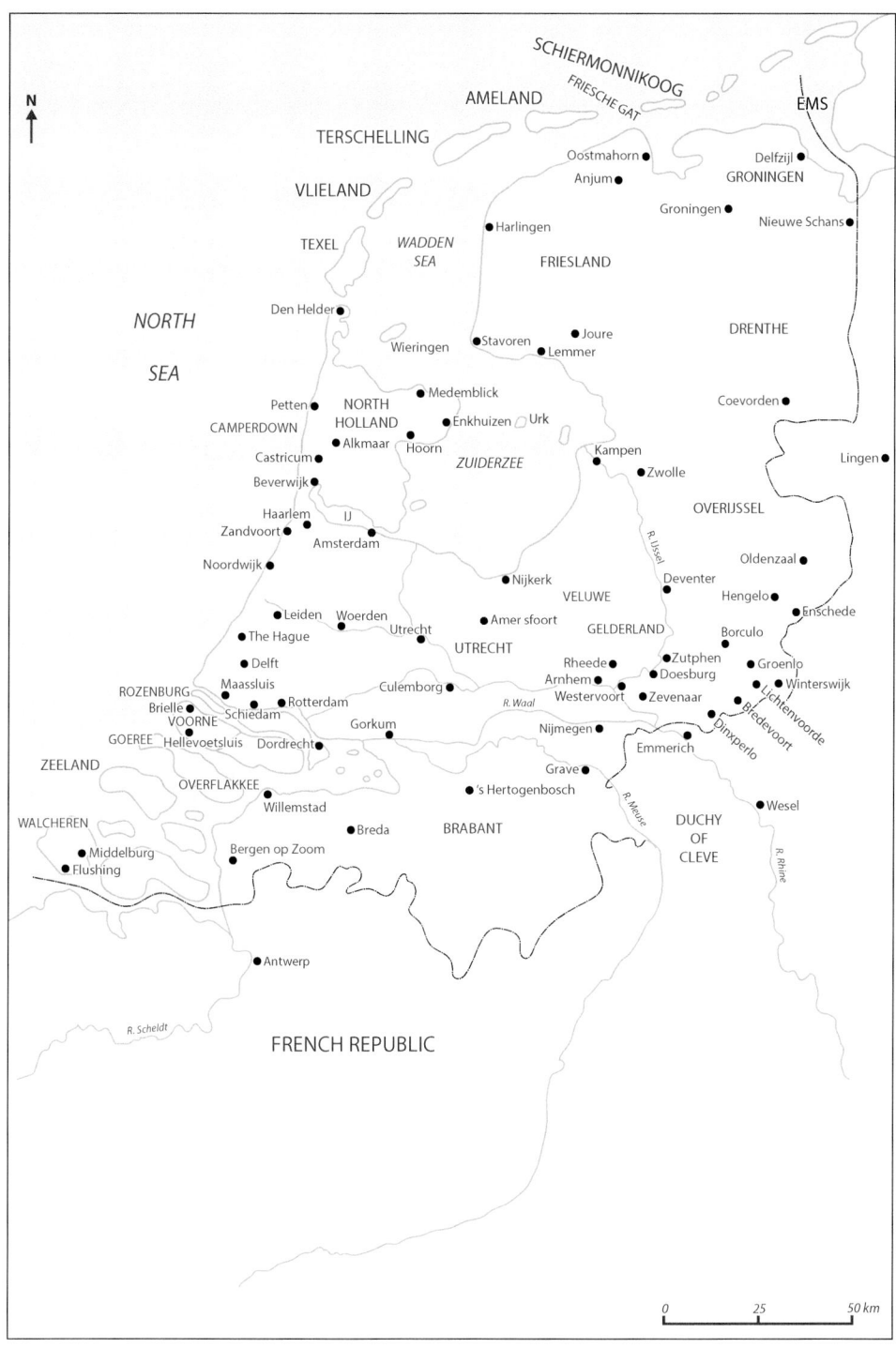

Map 2 The Batavian Republic in 1799.

take place as soon as possible because of the advanced season. Another reason was, that with the British and Russian transport fleets sailing from complete different directions, wind could never be favourable for both at the same time. This made a coordinated arrival of all troops at the same time improbable. For these reasons the British took the chance to send the first echelon of troops about two or three weeks ahead of the others. The danger was even greater because, with the use of sailing ships, with the need for favourable wind again no certainty could be given as to when the supporting echelons would arrive.

The British first echelon embarked between 8 and 12 August and the fleet set sail on 13 August. The troops were transported with 112 transport vessels and troop ships and protected by an escort squadron under the command of Vice Admiral Mitchell, who also commanded the transport fleet.[5] A number of Dutch officers would be present on the fleet with Abercromby. Lieutenant Colonel Sontag had in 1795 been an aide-de-camp of Abercromby. Beside English he spoke Dutch fluently and had much knowledge of the Netherlands. He would be appointed liaison to the Hereditary Prince of Orange after his arrival in Holland. Also very valuable was the aid of *Lieutenant ter Zee* Martinius. On 9 August, he received orders to sail to Chatham with Captain Winthrop, commander of the frigate *Circe*, together with three cutters and a lugger, to speak with the imprisoned Dutch sailors on the hulks lying there and to persuade them to join the invasion as voluntary sailors. Many Dutch sailors had been taken prisoner by the British during the Battle of Camperdown on 11 October 1797. In this battle, the British had captured eleven ships. These sailors had since that time been imprisoned on hulks at Chatham, partially on the same ships that had been captured at Camperdown. After two years of imprisonment, these sailors might have had other reasons than their Orangist inclination for accepting the proposal to join the invasion. Either way, 272 sailors agreed to this proposal and embarked on Captain Winthrop's ships.[6]

The British government made various plans for an attack on the Batavian Republic. By order of 3 August, Abercromby was directed to the mouth of the Meuse, to occupy the islands Goeree, Overflakkee, Rozenburg and Voorne in the Rhine-Meuse delta. After the arrival of the next echelons, the region north of the Waal would be occupied. To achieve this, a bridgehead on the mainland was needed. The choice was Abercromby's, but exceptionally useful for this purpose would have been the capture of Maaslandssluis, Schiedam, Rotterdam, or Dordrecht, in case of the need to maintain communications with the Prussians (if they could be persuaded to enter the Second Coalition). Finally Abercromby received a free hand to direct his attack to another part of the Batavian Republic:

> Supposing the attack to be resolved upon, it will rest with you and the naval commander to determine against which of the above mentioned places it should be directed, or to make choice of any other which a more exact knowledge of the state of affairs on the spot may suggest to you as preferable, bearing always in mind that the prospect of its affording by its local situation an easy and safe access to the province of Holland, and of its being carried and maintained (until reinforced) by

---

5 For its composition of the escort squadron see Appendix II. For the attack on the Batavian fleet at Texel, Duncan had temporarily detached 10 ships of the line from his North Sea Fleet to Mitchell.

6 Letter of Martinius to Fagel on 12 August 1799, in Koolemans Beijnen, *De Erfprins van Oranje in Noord-Holland*, pp.9, 113-115. This same lieutenant would drown when his ship the *Valk* foundered, as related in Chapter 16.

the troops you can allot for this purpose, are the leading considerations by which you are to be governed in this respect.[7]

Major General Moore had his own opinions about the orders given to Abercromby:

> On Sunday forenoon I went over to Deal, where I was invited to dine at Walmer Castle with Mr. Pitt and Dundas. They appeared to be in very good spirits, and only anxious for our departure. The original destination of the expedition was the island of Walcheren; this has since been altered; Goeree and Voorne are now the objects. The information with respect to the force upon these islands, their state of defence, &c., is extremely imperfect. The expedition has undoubtedly been hurried beyond reason, but the country having been put to the expense of assembling it, it is necessary that we should be sent to attempt something. We are now upon a voyage of adventure. The intention of Ministers is to get possession of Holland, for which 17,000 Russians and 17,000 British are assembling. Should this armament be able to establish itself the whole will then be under the Duke of York. There is a chance that the Dutch may rise in our favour; proclamations are ready to distribute both in the name of the Stadtholder and of the King of Great Britain. The island of Goeree, which commands the entrance of the Meuse, will first be attempted by General Coote's brigade. Should he succeed in landing he is to push forward to the island of Over-Flakkee and occupy the point opposite to Willemstad. Upon his success – and little opposition is expected – will depend, I believe, our future operations against Voorne, upon which are the fortified harbours of the Brielle and Hellevoetsluis.[8]

Although it was clear for the Franco-Batavians that the target of the 'Secret Expedition' would be the Batavian Republic, the place where the British would attack was still not. The British tried to keep this landing place a secret, but apparently they did not succeed for long, the French chief of staff Dardenne writing to *Général de Brigade* Gouvion on 13 August:

> I have the honour to inform you, my General, that by order of the *Général en chef* I have demanded General Dumonceau to assemble in Utrecht the Batavian Dragoon Regiment and two squadrons of the 2nd Cavalry Regiment of the same army, brigade of General Van Boecop. These troops are in the jurisdiction of your division and will be naturally under your orders, observing however that without extreme emergency you will not have them, because its assembly in Utrecht is ordered as quickly as possible which it is judged necessary by the *Général en chef*.

Again on 15 August:

> You can as you propose send a company of the 42e ½ brigade to Culemborg, I would prefer you send it to Woerden though, because it would be more within

---

[7] Letter of Henry Dundas to Abercromby, 3 August 1799, in English in Colenbrander, *Gedenkstukken*, Vol.III, p.385.
[8] Maurice (ed.), *Diary of Sir John Moore*, Vol.I, pp.340-341.

reach to get here [i.e. in The Hague] if needed, because we fear that the enemy has projects on the island of Voorn… please report me the arrival of the Batavian cavalry in Utrecht.[9]

The British Transport Fleet

Requests for transport shipping had to be forwarded to the Commissioners of Transports of the Transport Board, but actual execution of the requisition orders was the responsibility of the Transport Office, headquartered at Deptford on the Thames, near London. Its transport agents operated throughout the country, searching the ports for suitable shipping. For this Secret Expedition a large number of ships were needed. The Transport Office could make use of three sources to find the transports. Firstly there were the regular transports: the least important but the most reliable source, often converted old or captured naval war vessels. These ships, permanently fitted out for carrying troops, were never available in great numbers and were insufficient for the expedition ahead. There were different types of these, with the most common the troopships, artillery horse ships, artillery store ships and victualling or supply ships.

Secondly, there was the navy: frigates and ships of the line were not designed for carrying troops but could transport a substantial number of men when necessary. Smaller vessels could, because of their design, only be used over short distances and in times of extraordinary need. Given time some navy ships could be converted for transport purposes. A troopship was a 64-, 50-, or 44-gun two decker with its lower tier of guns removed to make room for men, supplies, or equipment. Such ships were said to be armed '*en flute*', derived from a Dutch term. These troopships were, especially for this expedition, prepared to land troops in shallow waters. As illustrated by a letter from the Batavian commissioner Van Aller in the Danish town Elsinore:

> On 31 July, another English ship passed, called the *Diadem*, commanded by Captain Danson, pierced 64 but according to their statement armed *en flute* with 250 men; I am told that all ships of the line that have passed are armed *en flute*, completely equipped as heavy frigates of 36 pieces and 44, having their upper tier, stern and bow chasers complete and 4 pieces in the lower tier, proportionally crewed, but the full complement of officers… They each have, beside their usual amount of small boats, a big flat bottomed vessel hanging over the side behind the main mast, with which 76 are able to land, in which they can manoeuvre a heavy cannon on a carriage, able to be served to the back and front as well as midships.[10]

Finally, the transport office could use civilian shipping to provide for the needs. Since regular transports and military troopships could not possibly provide the tonnage needed for this invasion, the transport agents had to negotiate individual contracts with private

---

9   Dardenne to Gouvion, in Koolemans Beijnen, 'Krijgsgeschiedkundige studie', 1892 , p.270.
10 Koolemans Beijnen, 'Krijgsgeschiedkundige studie', 1894, p.438.

owners. This involved several steps. Once a civilian ship was 'offered' or 'tendered' to the government, it had to be inspected or 'surveyed' by the transport agent in order to determine both its suitability for service and the measures required to have it converted or 'fitted out' for troops, horses, supplies, or equipment. The carrying capacity of these ships was stated in tons. Generally speaking, one to one-and-a-half tons was needed for each man, the exact calculation depending on the type of ship and the urgency of the service requested. Some smaller ships were simply not suited for carrying troops, even at a rate of several tons per man. Another source that was more readily available was the revenue cutters of the Treasury Department. However, although used, these were not very suitable, as they were so small and tightly built. After being inspected it was reported that these could be used for a short voyage, provided some precautions were taken: only one man for every two or three tons and even then each soldier should only carry his own pack and no other baggage. In addition, one third of the troops would have to be kept on deck at all times and the ships were only to sail in calm weather. For the 1799 invasion of Holland, 30 revenue cutters with a total displacement of 3,255 tons were used.

Except for the blockading squadron which would go after the Dutch fleet at Texel, the invasion fleet consisted of two components: the transport fleet, including ships of the sorts mentioned above and its escort squadron consisting of naval war ships, including supporting vessels like bomb vessels, etc. In addition, 39 flatboats were carried to be used as landing boats, as shown above. The First British Division sailed on 12 August 1799:

> 1st Guards Brigade (d'Oyly) 2 battalions, 2,119 men on 14 transports;
> 2nd Guards Brigade (Burrard) 2 battalions, 3,312 men on 13 transports;
> 3rd Brigade (Coote) 5 battalions, 3,442 men on 16 ships (13 transports & 3 troopships);
> 4th Brigade (Moore) 5 battalions, 3,571 men on 16 transports;
> Reserve (MacDonald) 2 battalions, 915 men on 5 transports;
> 18th Light Dragoons and staff horses (202 men and 409 horses) on 19 ships;
> Brigade and regimental artillery (241 men + 10 women) on 6 ships;
> Artillery store ships (215 men + 18 women); 14 ships;
> Artillery horse ships (218 horses, 192 men + 14 women); 9 ships.

So, excluding the artillery, for the infantry and a few hundred cavalry, a total of 12,359 men and 409 horses, already 83 transports were needed. With the artillery included, transport ships totalled 112. Added to the transport fleet were three hospital ships: the *Asia*, former 3rd Rate 64, the *Britannia*, and the *Friendship*. Also added were apparently 'two vessels totally laden with wide-barred hurdles, calculated to march our troops over the oozy shores of Holland, on which the transports might probably run aground'.[11] Abercromby, all general officers and their staffs were transported by the warships. Still missing were the 'victualling' or supply ships with one month's provisions for 12,000 men. This was however not an acute problem, as the warships and transports carried provisions for three and a half weeks. Still missing were also the transports carrying 40 commissary wagons and their 160 horses.

---

11   *London Chronicle*, Postscript, 24 August 1799. Although no mention has been found of the use of these 'hurdles' in contemporary accounts, several etchings of the landing show some kind of bridge, constructed by tying boats to each other, with soldiers marching over them.

The Embarkation

From mid-July, British newspapers openly published about the 'Secret Expedition' that would take place, which were copied by other European newspapers such as the *Hamburger Zeitung* and the *Gazette de Leyde*. They tell the story of the embarkation and the events leading up to it in astonishing detail, although sometimes the facts are a bit distorted, as illustrated by those in the *London Chronicle*:

> July 16. – Postscript: Yesterday a Military Council was held at the house of Mr. Dundas, at Wimbledon; when Field Marshal the Duke of York, Sir Ralph Abercrombie, and all the Commanders who are to be engaged in the secret expedition, were present. Various rumours were circulated with respect to this army. That the camp was immediately to be moved from Southampton to the Eastern Coast, and that Earl Moira was to have the chief command of a distinct expedition. It is certain that the Noble Earl came to town yesterday, and this may be enough to have given rise to the report, though certainly no Military Officer would be more qualified for such an enterprise. It has been said that a number of the larger transports, taken up by Government, are ordered to rendezvous at Yarmouth, in order to sail to the Baltic to bring round Russian troops to assist in the expedition which is meditating against some part of the territory of the French Republic. It is hardly possible to give credit to this report. If the Russian troops were destined to co-operate with the British in this adventure, it would hardly be left to the present moment to dispatch transports to convey them.
>
> Wednesday, July 17.: The secret expedition is now on the eve of taking place. The whole of the troops encamped on Shirley Common were to strike their tents, and march yesterday towards the Eastern coast, where they will shortly embark. A body of Russian troops, for the conveyance of which several ships sailed from Yarmouth on Sunday last, is to co-operate with this army; the plan has been so judiciously concerted, that the success of the enterprise (highly important and momentous in its nature) is deemed certain, as far as certainty can be ascertained from appearance, and reliance placed upon human effort.
>
> Saturday, July 20.: It is now said that there are to be two expeditions, for the second of which the very large ships are taken up. Certainly the East Indiamen are not adapted to any expedition to the coast of Flanders. Some more considerable object is in view; whatever it is, we trust it will be kept a profound secret, that the blow may be struck with effect. It is rumoured that Field Marshal the Duke of York will command in person… A braver or more loyal army never yet assembled, nor in a nobler cause. The militia are entitled to be considered as volunteers in the expedition; and such has been their zeal and enthusiasm, that had not the Act of Parliament limited the number to one-fourth which could be drafted from them into the line, whole regiments would have passed over into the regular service… Such is the urgency with which Government press the equipment of the ships at Woolwich and Deptford, that Admiral Mitchell, who is to have the maritime command of the expedition, has been

down at these dock-yards several times since last week, and visited the several ships in that quarter, in order to see that every possible expedition was used in forwarding them for sea.

Extract of a Letter from Portsmouth, July 17.: It is confidently reported here that the projected expedition is for Holland, and that it is undertaken on the invitation of a very numerous and opulent body of the inhabitants of that Republic. Whatever truth may be in the rumour, it has had the effect of greatly increasing the Volunteers from the militia regiments.

Thursday, Aug. 8. – Postscript: The expedition proceeds with the most earnest activity. Above 1000 vessels of various descriptions are taken for a time from our trade, and chiefly from our coasting trade, in favour of this enterprize, the van-guard of which is now completely ready for sea. From the smallness of many of the vessels employed, it is conceived that they cannot have a voyage of any length to make, and it is probable that the very nearest point of the opposite shore will be the place of destination. The guards began to embark on Tuesday last, and yesterday the embarkation continued with great activity. The troops were in the highest spirits… All the waggons and carts, without exception, were pressed on Tuesday and Wednesday last, on the Essex road, between Ingatestone and Colchester, to carry oats, and other forage, for the use of the cavalry, about to be embarked at Harwich on the grand expedition. The carriages were pressed, not in the usual mode, for limited stages, but to go right through to Harwich… Gen. Moore is employed in the secret expedition, at the particular request of Sir R. Abercrombie, who has often admired, particularly in the West Indies, the skill and gallantry of this excellent Officer, lately rendered conspicuous by his bold march upon Wexford, and unexpected capture of that city. Immense quantities of artillery, ammunition, and stores of every kind, have been forwarded from Woolwich Warren to the coast… The embargo has been extended along the Kent, Essex, Suffolk, and Norfolk coasts, and will probably continue till the troops have embarked and sailed. A fleet of victuallers sailed from Portsmouth on Wednesday, destined to the Downs, for the secret expedition.

Extract of a Letter from Margate, Aug. 8.: Three transports with troops are just arrived here: a pilot is just gone on board his boat to attend them. It is supposed they are going to the Downs. Fourteen thousand men are marching in several directions to encamp this day and to-morrow at Barham Downs, in place of those who left it yesterday. They are intended for the second general embarkation. The greater part of them marched on Monday, Tuesday, and Wednesday, from London to Canterbury. In consequence of the embargo, all the vessels of every kind, except transports, are stopped. The hoys, and even the fishing boats, are not permitted to go out.

Extract of a Letter from Canterbury, Aug. 8.: The greatest part, of the troops which were assembled at Barham Downs have been marched forward to the sea coast, and, it is laid, are embarking at Margate, Ramsgate, Dover, and Deal. This first embarkation is stated to be only the advanced guard of the expedition. Another camp is to be formed at Barham Downs, which it is said, will consist of 18 or

20,000 men, and will make a second embarkation. After this camp breaks up, a third, it is understood, will be formed of troops also destined for embarkation. Thus this formidable expedition will be composed of three divisions, which follow each other in succession. The first is doubtless intended to take possession of some important point on the enemy's coast, and thus open a port for the succeeding divisions, and whatever farther reinforcements or supplies may be necessary.

<u>Monday, Aug. 12.</u>: The embarkation took place under the most unfavourable circumstances, the troops drenched with wet during their march, and exposed to a rough sea on embarking; but the zeal they manifested, and the attention paid by Government to their comfort, were equally credible… Three of the transports, in going out on Thursday, struck on the mud, but without any other consequence than a little apprehension and delay. Ten women are allowed to go with each 100 men; but the state of the numerous women and children who were necessarily left behind is most distressing.

<u>Tuesday Aug. 13. – Postscript</u>: We have stated that the first division of the armament was embarked and ready to sail, and accordingly they yesterday morning sailed from the Downs with the wind at West; and we have no doubt but their first point of destination, is the Island of Walcheren. With all the publicity which the expedition has had, we have reason to believe that Sir Ralph Abercrombie and his army will find little or no resistance in their descent, and in a few days we shall have to announce the capture of the island. We have great pleasure in saying, that the Proclamation which the Commander in Chief is charged to distribute as soon as he shall have made good his landing in the Batavian territory is a State Paper recommended by its moderation, and calculated to conciliate the people of this country, as well as of Holland, to the object of the expedition… The sailing of the first division of the armament took place yesterday morning, in consequence of advice that the Russians had arrived at their destination, and were ready to co-operate with the British. We touch at length the moment when the grand scheme of the Confederacy, as well as its extent, will be developed. The King of Prussia can no longer maintain silence on the subject of the league. If the Russians are to disembark on any point which oblige them to traverse the line of demarcation that he has drawn for his Neutrality, he must declare himself. We confess we yet have our doubts concerning the part he will take, but whether he shall avow himself or not, we believe that there is a sufficient body of disaffection to the French in Holland and Brabant, to secure success to the Allies. The second or grand division of our armament, in which the cavalry are to be employed, will now be expedited with every possible speed; and Field Marshal the Duke of York will sail as soon as the footing is made, and the Scheldt opened. His scene of operations will be Brabant, and he will not have fewer than 16,000 men in the second embarkation. Every exertion within the last week has been made to forward this grand armament. On Friday 46 artillery waggons, with part of 2000 stand of arms, proceeded from the Tower, and yesterday 42 more, with the remainder of the arms and accoutrements for the troops at Dover, Margate and Ramsgate.

> From Chatham on Saturday and yesterday, the volunteers from the Militia were conveyed in every carriage that could be procured to their different places of resort. The most whimsical scenes were displayed by the impressing of carriages. Companies were left at inns on the road, and persons riding out for air, were forced to trudge home on foot… The Transport Board, as well as the Admiralty, used the greatest vigilance to forward the armament, and most of the troops, from the alacrity which has been used, are already embarked. The Dukes of York and Cumberland are expected to leave Windsor this morning, to join the General Officers who are to be employed on this occasion. Last night a general press took place on the River [Thames], and all the hands that could be spared were taken from every ship. Protections were disregarded.[12]

Spirits were high in Great Britain, popular believe was that the secret expedition would be an easy success, as also illustrated by the *London Chronicle*:

> The Secret Expedition, concerted for a year between our Cabinet and that of Russia, is evidently connected with all the military and diplomatic proceedings. It would be presumptuous to attempt to fix the precise point where the first division, which departed last week, will betake itself: but it is certain it has for its end the emancipation of Holland. The commotions which are at present agitating that country, the confidence which the Stadtholderian party is assuming, the flight of those of the Revolutionists who fear the restoration of the ancient order of things to Brussels, Hamburgh, Altona, &c. the unbounded trust which the Batavian Directory have reposed in the French Gen. Brune, prove that Holland is on the eve of a great commotion, and give ground for supposing that the British will be received by a great majority of the inhabitants, not as enemies, but as deliverers. The first division of 15 or 18,000 Russians, which is to concur in this enterprize, was not to leave Revel till the 31st of August. But the Emperor Paul is so extremely active in the execution of his plans, that it was made to sail on the 20th, under the command of Gen. Herman, a much esteemed Officer in the Russian army. The news of his departure was brought by the courier whom Lord Grenville received on Friday last.[13]

The Russian Army and its Transport

Despite the diplomatic failure persuading the Prussians to join the Second Coalition, the Tsar was more than willing to accept the British proposals, even ordering the composition of the Russian expedition force and the preparations of the ships before the treaty was signed. On 14 June, Rear-Admiral von Breyer was ordered to prepare six ships of the line, five frigates and two transport ships and to hold them ready for the secret expedition. For this purpose, part of a squadron already prepared by Admiral Chanykov was used: six ships

---

12 *London Chronicle* of the specified dates in 1799.
13 *London Chronicle*, 20 August 1799.

of the line and a frigate.[14] Another frigate came from Kronstadt and a frigate and both transport ships were already in Reval, were the squadron would collect and from where the Russian army would depart. Finally, from Rotschensalm, a Russian fortress in Finland, came two rowing frigates. On 7 July all assigned ships had arrived in Reval. As soon as they arrived they were prepared to serve as troop ships and armed *en flute*, the Russians being advised by Captain Popham. Yet another Russian squadron had gathered in Reval and sailed before the transport fleet left, commanded by Admiral Chanykov. This admiral with his squadron, consisting of seven ships of the line and three smaller warships, received the following order from Tsar Paul:

> In case the passage of the ships assigned to the secret expedition is unexpectedly blocked by the Danish war fleet or if the same is denying passage through the Sound, you will disembark landing troops and in cooperation with our war fleet take possession of Copenhagen.[15]

So Reval was the place where the Russian army destined for the secret expedition was assembled, commanded by Lieutenant General Hermann. By mid-July all units had arrived and on 20 July they started embarking. The first to embark was the 1st Division of Major General Essen, embarking on the Russian ships. It took them seven days before the 7,500 men had embarked and on 31 July the Russian squadron sailed under the command of Rear Admiral Chichagov who had taken over from Rear Admiral von Breyer. Almost immediately after their departure two ships, the *Panteleimon* and the *Revel*, had to return to Reval for not being seaworthy. The troops on these ships were transferred to British ships.

As at that moment it was unknown were the landing would really take place, the Russian squadron was to initially sail to Yarmouth, from there to sail again for the chosen point for the invasion. The British already having gained a foothold in Holland in the meantime, British vessels as well as the Russian brig *Dispatch* were send to intercept and to direct the Russians to the Texel directly. Unfortunately they missed the Russian squadron which for the major part sailed to Yarmouth as planned. There is not much known about the passage of this Russian squadron to England except for the mentioned ships that had to return to port. They arrived at the Sound on the 19th. Some ships had not managed to keep up, as on 24 August only five ships of the line, two frigates and a single transport with 6,000 men anchored at Elsinore.[16] The ships remained for some time at the roads of Elsinore and sailed again on the 28th, after having been joined there by a single ship and the second transport that had not managed to keep up. These ships arrived at Yarmouth on 7 September, again except for one ship and a transport which had reportedly departed from them four days before:

---

14 See Appendix III for the composition of the Russian transport squadron. The mentioned squadron of Admiral Chanykov had been formed in haste after the French Admiral Bruix had managed to slip out of Brest on 25 April with the French fleet and his whereabouts were still unknown. At one time it was rumoured that he would enter the Baltic to threaten the Russian coast: Miliutin, *Geschichte des Krieges*, Vol. III, pp.175-176, 329.

15 Order of 31 July 1799 from Tsar Paul to Admiral Chanykov, in Miliutin, *Geschichte des Krieges*, Vol.III, p.337.

16 These ships were the *Alexander Nevskii, Iona, Sviatoi Iannuarii, Mikhail, Emgeiten, Arkhangel Rafail, Svatoi Nikolai* and the transport *Neptune*, as listed in the *London Chronicle*, 10 September 1799.

> Yesterday morning four sail of Russian men of war, armed *en flute*, three frigates, and one transport, anchored in our roads [Yarmouth]. They have on board upwards of six thousand Russian troops, besides several companies of flying artillery. One line of battle ship and a transport parted company about four days before, and as they have not yet come in, it is supposed they have been spoke with by some cruiser, and gone to the Texel.[17]

The 2nd Division of Lieutenant General Zherebtsov, about 9,500 men strong, embarked on the British transport fleet. There was some substantial delay, as though the bulk of the British ships had arrived on 27 and 28 July in Reval, the remainder did not begin arriving until 10 and 11 August. They sailed on the 17th. The Russian commander in chief, Lieutenant General Hermann also embarked with this division on the British warship *Inflexible*. They arrived at the Sound on 31 August, continuing their journey from Elsinore on 7 September. Both fleets suffered from stormy weather making the journey for the soldiers very tough. The Russian Colonel Dubiansky, who had embarked on the *Diadem* with the Fersen Musketeers, relates:

> The muskets, the cartridge pouches as well as the ammunition had already been laid down on the quay and kept in proper order in the ship's hold. Each company marked its field equipment in haste with special signs; The English pressed on and hurried to set sail. On both steerages the soldiers lay in a double row, one beside the other, so that one could hardly move in the narrow space. In the middle between the rows of the feet a passage was left open. Above the heads of both rows hung the hammocks, one per man. The ship was like fish in a barrel. As long as a favourable wind carried the ship with full sails, we sang funny Russian songs, went up and down on the deck, and led the people from the steerages to the fresh air alternately. But when the wind grew more violent, swept the sea floor, threw the foaming waves over the deck, and at last turned in sight of Bornholm into a real storm, when the line of our fleet was broken by the unfavourable wind; and the hatches closed, then everyone crawled into his hammock, the songs fell silent, and made room for small-hearted sighs and sound sleep. The Russian warriors did not make much of their portions of pork with herbs, and the white biscuit vexed them. Everyone longed for Russian black bread, sauerkraut and corn spirits. The rum, which was distributed in portions, was scorned. The stormy winds soon led us back to the Swedish coast, and again to Bornholm; At last, on the morning of the 20th August, the island of Christiansö came in sight under torrential rain and violent thunder and lightning. Our squadron, which endured the oppressive winds full fifteen days and fifteen nights, finally sighted land and entered the Sound on the same day. The unaccustomed way of life and the first, if not long, sea-voyage had pretty affected our landing troops; everyone hastened to enjoy the pure air. The people had to be led to the deck in turn. The weather cleared, it became warmer and the soldiers hurried to bathe. In the meantime, the ship's steerages were smoked out and the whole ship was flushed. Our Russians helped the Englishmen with great zeal, which greatly

---

17 *London Chronicle*, 10 September 1799.

contributed to the strengthening of their health. There were no sick on our ship Diadem as well as on the whole squadron.[18]

On their way to England they were intercepted and redirected to Holland instead of Yarmouth and as a result arrived three days earlier then the Russians embarked on the Russian squadron which had sailed to Yarmouth first. There is also the account of Lieutenant Gardner of the *Blonde*:

> We had on board a Russian captain, two subs., a surgeon, and 296 privates, all hoffs, choffs, and koffs [referring to their Russian names]. The captain's name was Peter Glebhoff, who never pulled his boots off the whole time he was on board. The men were the most filthy I ever met with. They used to scrape the tallow out of the bottoms of the lanterns and make it up into balls, which they would swallow and wash down with a drink of train oil. They had bread made on purpose, of the coarsest flour mixed with vinegar, and their cookery it is impossible to describe; so that the Spartan black broth must have been a luxury (however unpalatable) to their abominable messes. I have positively seen them pick the vermin off one another's jackets, which they would eat without ceremony.[19]

Naval Operations

Great Britain was at war with the Batavian Republic since 1795 and a naval blockade of the Batavian ports and waterways was already in place for a long time. The devastating effect that this blockade had on Batavian economy will be treated in the next chapter. Much loss was inflicted on Batavian shipping but now and then the British lost ships as well. The war at sea was of much importance, before, during and after the 1799 campaign in Holland, also closely related to the defence of the Batavian Republic. Therefore the major incidents will be described here.

On 26 April 1798, the Batavian Brig *Courier*, according to the British being a privateer, was taken by the 16-gun sloop *Scorpion*:

> I have the honour of acquainting you, for the information of my Lords Commissioners of the Admiralty, that his Majesty's sloop Scorpion, under my command, Flamborough Head S.W. between two and three miles, fell in with, on the night of the 26th instant, and captured the Batavian republican brig Le Courier, pierced for 12, and mounting six four-pounders, and a number of swivels, commanded by Lieutenant John Ysbrands, and manned with 30 men, sailed eight

---

18 H.A. Ritter, *Een Russisch verhaal van den veldtocht in Noord-Holland in 1799* (Utrecht: A.W. Bruna & Zoon, 1914), pp.16-17, also quoted in Miliutin, *Geschichte des Krieges*, Vol.V, pp.276-277. The date mentioned is according to the Russian calendar.
19 Sir R. Vesey Hamilton & John Knox Laughton (eds.), *Recollections of James Anthony Gardner Commander R.N. (1775-1814)* (London: Navy Records Society, 1906), p.207.

days before from Helvoetsluys, and taken the Lark brig, of Whitby, coal laden, which the Scorpion retook.[20]

The *Courier* would see service in the Wadden Sea during the upcoming campaign, in the British Royal Navy this time. As we will see, more ships saw service on both sides during this war, being captured and recaptured again. On 14 June 1798, the lugger *Zeehond* was captured just north of Denmark by the 18-gun sloop *Hound*:

> I have to acquaint you, for the information of their Lordships, that at one A.M. on the 14th instant, Skaw bearing E.S.E. 10 leagues, I captured the Dutch lugger Sea Hound, pierced for fourteen guns, but having only seven mounted, and four swivels, manned with thirty men; she has been six weeks from Holland.[21]

On 26 August 1798, the British gun-vessel *Crash* (12 carronades, Lieutenant Praed) was taken by the Batavians on the coast of Holland: it would be retaken in the Wadden Sea by the British on 11 August 1799. A more serious engagement took place in October 1798. On the 23rd of that month, the *Sirius* (5th Rate 36, Captain King), was reconnoitring the naval force in the Texel and on the following morning encountered and pursued two Batavian frigates. Her captain reported:

> I parted company with the fleet on the evening of the 23d ult. to reconnoitre the force of the enemy in the Texel. At 8 A.M. on the following morning, the Texel bearing S. by E. 10 leagues, I fell in with two Dutch frigates* at that time about two miles distance from each other. Passing within gun-shot of the leewardmost of them, I stood on until I could (upon tacking) nearly fetch the weathermost (the Waakzaamheid), my object being to prevent their junction; and by this means, that being accomplished, I had the satisfaction to cut off the latter, and bring her to about 9 o'clock, when she hauled down her colours and fired a gun to leeward. As soon as the prisoners were exchanged, I made sail after the other, and, although nearly out of sight, I had the good fortune before 5 P.M. to bring her to a kind of running action, which continued about half an hour, within musket shot, at times, during which she kept a smart but ill-directed discharge of cannon and musketry, when she struck to his Majesty's ship. She is called the Furie, and under the orders of the captain of the Waakzaamheid, and had the commandant of the troops and a number of officers on board. I am happy to add, there was only one man wounded, by a musket-ball, and that his Majesty's ship suffered but little; one shot through her bowsprit, her rigging, &c. but little cut. The loss on board the Furie was 8 killed and 14 wounded: her hull masts, &c., have suffered much…
> * Waakzaamheid, Capt. Neitrop, senior captain, mounting 26 guns, 24-pounders, on the main-deck, 2 6-pounders on the forecastle, having 100 Dutch seamen and

---

20 Letter of 30 April 1798 from Captain Rodd to the Admiralty office, in Anon., *A Collection of State Papers Relative to the War against France. Now carrying on by Great Britain and the Several other European Powers* (London: S. Gosnell, 1800), Vol.VIII, Appendix, p.19.
21 Letter of 15 June 1798 from Captain Wood to the Admiralty office, in Anon., *State Papers*, Vol.VIII, Appendix, p.60.

122 French troops (total 222) on board, also 2000 stand of arms, besides ordnance stores.

Furie, Capt. Pletz, of 36 guns, 26 12-pounders on the main-deck, and 10 6-pounders on the forecastle, with 153 Dutch seamen, and 165 French troops (total 318 on board), also 4000 stand of arms, besides ordnance stores.[22]

Batavian sources give additional information: the French demanded that the Batavian Republic contributed to 'the Irish cause' as well. They 'invited' the Batavians to send two frigates to Ireland with as many soldiers, arms and other necessities as they could transport. Despite the presence of the British warships before Texel, the French insisting, the *Uitvoerend Bewind* agreed and the *Furie* (36, *Capitein-Lieutenant* Pletz) and *Waakzaamheid* (24, *Capitein* van Nierop) were ordered to sail with French soldiers, officers, arms, field artillery, powder, and other stores. They had orders to sail north in the direction of Denmark, close along the Wadden Islands in order to be able to retreat into the Wadden Sea when British warships were encountered. The Wadden Sea is shallow, with only few channels enabling bigger ships to sail here. Huge parts fall completely dry at low tide forming extensive sandbanks. After each storm, sand will displace and the position of the channels change constantly. Navigation is difficult for bigger ships and without pilots virtually impossible. From there they were to sail north of Scotland and to approach Ireland from the northeast. Despite these orders, after leaving Texel, *Capitein* van Nierop decided to sail directly north-north-west and naturally it did not take long before they were spotted by the *Sirius* as described, as well as a cutter also heading their way and an additional heavy warship at windward side. Both frigates tried to flee but were quickly overtaken by the much faster *Sirius*, manned with a much better crew.

On 7 January 1799 the *Apollo* (5th Rate 38) ran aground on the Haaks sandbank near Texel, when in chase of a Batavian ship and was totally lost through the ignorance of the pilot. The crew was saved by a Prussian ship passing by. Captain Halkett was tried by a court martial on board the *Monmouth* at Yarmouth, for the loss of his frigate but was honourably acquitted, 'but the pilot was broke and rendered incapable of ever serving his Majesty any more in the Navy'.[23] On 11 May 1799, the *Courier* (Lieutenant Searle), a hired armed brig which was captured from the Batavians the year before as described above, engaged near Texel a French privateer while on its way to the squadron at Texel:

> Having received orders from Captain Cobbe, of His Majesty's Ship Glatton, to proceed from Yarmouth Roads, and put myself under the Command of Captain Sotheron, of the Latona, I left Yarmouth on the 11th Instant, and on the morning of the 11th I observed a Brig in the act of capturing a Merchant Sloop, about eight or nine leagues off Winterton: I immediately made all sail, and at half past one brought her to close Action, proving to be a French Privateer of 16 guns, of six and nine pounders. We continued in close Action an hour and forty minutes, when, after every exertion being used, her superiority of sailing, together with having the

---

22 Letter of 1 November 1798 from Captain King to Admiral Duncan, in Sylvanus Urban (ed.), *The Gentleman's Magazine: and Historical Chronicle for the Year MDCCXCVIII*, Vol.LXVIII, November 1798, p.1070.
23 *Naval Chronicle*, Vol.I, p.168.

advantage of the Wind, she accomplished her escape, though, I flatter myself, in that shattered state as to render her incapable of continuing her Cruise. We continued in Chase of her till midnight when it came on thick and foggy weather, and we lost sight of her. At day-light in the morning, we perceived a Vessel in the north-east; supposing it to be the Brig we had previously engaged, again made sail: at eight came up with and captured the Ribotteur French Schooner, of six 3-pounders, two of which were thrown overboard in chase, and 26 Men, which we found to be in concert with the Brig above mentioned. I have to observe, that, at the time of my engaging the Brig, a Lugger Privateer was then laying at some distance on leeward, but showed no inclination to assist the Vessel we were then engaging… I am sorry to add, we had five Men wounded; but have every reason to believe the Enemy suffered considerably more.[24]

With the pending invasion, the British stepped up their activities along the coast. Warships of the North Sea fleet received orders to capture every vessel that could give the enemy warning of the movements of the fleet.[25] Before Texel, at all times a British fleet was present to blockade the Batavian fleet at its roadstead and to give early warning if this fleet would try to sail in force. This effectively prevented the Batavian navy from entering the North Sea. The British North Sea fleet was commanded by Admiral Duncan. Duncan was a man with experience but had problems with his health, which meant that he had to leave his post frequently. For example in January 1799 he had to be replaced by Vice Admiral Dickson, the *Naval Chronicle* even stating that 'the state of his Lordship's health rendering it very doubtful that he will go to sea again'. On 4 June, Duncan resumed command of the North Sea fleet again.

To understand the following reports it is needed to describe the situation in front of Texel. The Haaks is a huge sandbank west of the entrance from the North Sea to the roadstead of Texel. Since the beginning of April on the Breewijd, the channel just east of the Haaks, a small Batavian naval squadron was manoeuvring. It consisted of the *Amphitrite* (5th Rate 44, *Capitein* Schutter), *Embuscade* (5th Rate 32, *Capitein-Lieutenant* Rivery) and *Galathée* (Sloop 16, *Lieutenant* Droop), with orders to try to sail and cruise the North Sea to protect Batavian trade against the actions of single British warships. A series of reports kept the Batavian Ministry of Marine updated as to its activities:

> 19 April: The small squadron is still on the Breewijd and manoeuvres there continuously. Since the English have noted the sailing of these ships, and movement in our fleet, they are nine ships strong, among which are three ships of the line, continuously cruising along the coast and most of the time so close that one can recognise their flags. It is clear that during these circumstances the departure of the squadron is not favourable. Nevertheless it will remain under sail and *Capitein* van de Capellen remains on board of the *Amphitrite*.

---

24 Letter of 14 May 1799 from Lieutenant T. Searle of the *Courier* to Vice Admiral Dickson, in the *Naval Chronicle*, Vol. II, p.242.
25 Lieutenant-Generaal Baron Krayenhoff, *Geschiedkundige Beschouwing van den Oorlog op het Grondgebied der Bataafsche Republiek in 1799* (Nijmegen: J.C. Vieweg en Zoon, 1832), pp.44-46.

> 22 April: Since my last report an English fleet, thirteen ships strong, has showed itself, among which are several ships of the line; some of these constantly cruise along the Haaks, probably to observe all movement of the squadron on the Breewijd. This small squadron will therefore not depart.
>
> 29 April: The English fleet, which as it appears is reinforced from time to time, is constantly present in two divisions, one south, the other north of the Haaks before Texel. This way all opportunity to sail with a small force is completely taken away.
>
> 6 May: The English fleet, still before Texel is 15 ships strong, of which 9 or 10 are ships of the line, hold us closed in very tightly these days: during the whole day we are, when the weather is not too bad, in full view of each other; even this morning they had the courtesy to hoist the flag simultaneously.[26]

Also a number of incidents took place, for example *Lieutenant-Generaal* Jean Dumonceau reported on 22 March 1799 to the minister of war:

> I have the honour to report to you, that *Capitein* van Kaps, commanding on Vlieland, reported to me that on the 16th an English frigate appeared before the island, much closer than usual, its presence preventing a brig to be brought in; two pilot-boats which rowed out for this purpose, had to return. The garrison was ready to march to the beach at the first shot.[27]

More threatening for the Batavians was an incident taking place at Noordwijk on 2 and 3 April, illustrated by the messages to and from the Batavian senior officers and the *Uitvoerend Bewind*. Starting with an urgent message of J. Jansen, commanding officer of the *Gewapende Burgermacht* in Noordwijk to the Minister of War Pijman, received on the evening of the 2nd at 19:45 hours: 'The circumstances over here are unfavourable, as the English are making ready to land. Two warships are before the shoals. We resist with our two 12pdr cannon; more ships have come into view; we request assistance, with all haste'.[28] Immediately Pijman wrote to *Général de Division* Brune:

> The commander of the National Guard of Noordwijk Binnen tells me the instant that some enemy ships have shown off the coast and are threatening to raid. I immediately sent a copy of the report to *Général* Daendels with orders to take measures that are required by the urgent circumstances. The messenger that brought this report verbally added that a French frigate chased by an English ship was thrown on the coast and the enemy has launched sloops to make himself master of it; I hope, however, that the well-directed fire of two pieces of 12, which are stationed there, will force him to retreat and to abandon his project.[29]

---

26 Reports from *Schout-bij-Nacht* Samuel Story to the Batavian Naval Minister Jacobus Spoors in Koolemans Beijnen, 'Krijgsgeschiedkundige studie', 1893, pp.165-166.
27 Koolemans Beijnen, 'Krijgsgeschiedkundige studie', 1893, p.15.
28 Koolemans Beijnen, 'Krijgsgeschiedkundige studie', 1893, p.15.
29 Koolemans Beijnen, 'Krijgsgeschiedkundige studie', 1893, pp.15-16.

Before Daendels could respond to this threat, that same evening he received also a report from *Generaal-Major* Philip van Zuylen van Nyevelt in Leiden, commander of the 2e Brigade of Daendels' division:

> In this letter, an urgent call was made to send aid; apparently the English were preparing to land and the two 12pdrs, which they have there without any garrison the gunners that are with these pieces would not be able to protect them, etc. How unlikely this report of a threatening landing is, I prepared to go there in person, to be followed by part of the garrison and the corps citizen-artillery with their two 3pdr cannon. However the moment we were ready to depart, further information was received that a French privateer, chased by two English warships or frigates had to be put on the beach when it was fired upon, now being attacked by sloops. Until the moment the messenger that brought me this message had departed, the fire of our cannon on the beach had prevented these sloops to succeed.
>
> After receiving this report, I decided to limit my support to both pieces, a grenadier company and some cavalry, to prevent if possible the capture of the privateer and to reassure the citizens against a landing of the crews of the sloops, which you hopefully will approve of.[30]

The detachment dispatched to Noordwijk consisted of the grenadier company of the 3/1e Halve Brigade with some cavalry and both 3pdr cannon and was commanded by *Eerste Lieutenant* van Schack, who reported at half nine in the morning of the 3rd to *Generaal-Major* van Zuylen van Nyevelt:

> I stand on the beach with the corps under my orders. An English heavy frigate has anchored close to the coast and is heavily bombarding the village and the ship on the beach (being a Swedish coaster). I can do nothing against it. Both 12pdrs are demolished, as well as the battery. I have no ammunition, nor able gunners. Two English ships manoeuvre somewhat further from the coast, preparing to launch sloops. I have no resistance against the bombardment and request for supplies. If the enemy force will not become stronger, I believe I will be able to prevent a landing with sloops. But not knowing the intentions of the enemy, he will probably wait for nightfall. The 3pdrs that I brought with me are of no use at all; a few 24pdrs are needed, to drive off the enemy, without them nothing can be prevented.[31]

Before more measures could be taken by the Batavians the British ships sailed away. The beached French ship was in fact a Swedish coaster (Captain C. Geersch), which sailing from London to Hamburg had been taken by the French privateer *Le Barras* (schooner 14, *Capitaine* Fromentin) from Dunkirk. With a prize crew commanded by *Lieutenant* Thése the coaster had tried to reach a Batavian port, but after being intercepted by the British

---

30 Koolemans Beijnen, 'Krijgsgeschiedkundige studie', 1893, p.16.
31 Koolemans Beijnen, 'Krijgsgeschiedkundige studie', 1893, pp.16-17.

Thése decided to beach his prize on the Batavian coast near Noordwijk. After the departure of the British warships its cargo was salvaged.[32]

To protect Batavian shipping and taking in account the increasing threat of the British naval presence, it was decided to reinforce the gunboats at Delfzijl – *Lynx* (*Capitein-Lieutenant* Pool) and *Schorpioen* (*Capitein-Lieutenant* Prey) – with another three gunboats: *Crash* (former British gun-vessel, *Lieutenant ter Zee* Bybel), *Otter* (*Lieutenant ter Zee* van Ginkel) and *Adder* (*Capitein-Lieutenant* Goudakker). This did not prevent another incident taking place on the Wadden Sea, when the British captured two barges between the islands Ameland and Schiermonnikoog. These were captured by 15 British sailors in a sloop. A Batavian gunboat that was nearby appeared to have fired a single shot and then sailed away. As a result of this, the commanding officer of the gunboats was arrested.[33] On 20 May, a British lugger appeared in front of Zandvoort on the North Sea coast, launching a boat which started hunting the fishing boats. Some *jager* lodged in this village, together with some brave citizens, boarded a fishing boat and chased the British boat away.[34] Late in June, a squadron was detached by Admiral Duncan to cruise before Vlieland and the adjacent islands. This squadron of six ships was commanded by Captain Winthrop and consisted of the *Circe* (6th Rate 28, Captain Winthrop), *Tisiphone* (6th Rate 20, Captain Grant), *Jalouse* (Brig-sloop 18, Commander Temple), *Pylades* (Sloop 16, Commander Mackenzie), *Espiegle* (Brig-sloop 14, Commander Boorder) and the hired cutter *Nancy* (6, Lieutenant Kilkardy). On 28 June, the squadron anchored in the Friesche Gat, between the islands Ameland and Schiermonnikoog. After receiving information that some Batavian gunboats were sheltering behind Ameland, Winthrop planned to capture them:

> Having received information that several Dutch Gun-vessels were lying at the back of the Island of Ameland, and Captains Temple and Boorder, of His Majesty's Sloops Jalouse and Espeigle having very handsomely volunteered their services to cut them out, I ordered the Boats of His Majesty's Ships named in the margin [*Circe, Jalouse, Pylades, Espeigle, Tysiphone*] to proceed under their Command on the night of the 27th Inst. for that purpose, and anchored with the Ships as near the Shore as possible, in readiness to afford every assistance in my power. I am sorry to say it now appears that the Gun-vessels had previously shifted their birth with the ebb-tide, and were lying a-ground when the Boats got in, at a place where it was impossible to get near them. The Officers and Men were therefore ordered to cut out as many Vessels from the Wadde as it might be practicable to bring away; and I have the satisfaction to add, they succeeded in getting out twelve, without a Man being killed or wounded, though the Enemy annoyed them as much as possible from their Batteries. Six of the Vessels have valuable Cargoes, and were bound to Amsterdam; the others are in ballast.[35]

---

32 Anon., *Oeconomische Courant. Ter bevordering van nationale huishoudkunde, nyverheid, koophandel, zeevaart, fabrieken, trafieken, beoefenende konsten, landbouw, en alle andere middelen van bestaan* (Amsteldam: C. Covens, 1799), 10 April 1799 & 13 April 1799.
33 Report of *Lieutenant-Generaal* Jean Dumonceau in Koolemans Beijnen, 'Krijgsgeschiedkundige studie', 1893, p.338.
34 Koolemans Beijnen, 'Krijgsgeschiedkundige studie', 1893, p.341.
35 Letter of 29 June 1799 from Captain Winthrop of the *Circe* to Admiral Duncan, in the *Naval Chronicle*, Vol.II, p.249.

PREPARATIONS FOR THE SECRET EXPEDITION

After the presence of the British warships had been noted by the Batavians, signal shots were fired from the coastal battery at Oostmahorn. In response, *Capitein* van Dunne marched from Anjum to Oostmahorn with the 2e compagnie of the 1/6e Halve Brigade. Before he arrived the British boats already had retreated to the protection of their warships anchored in the Friesche gat. The report of *Eerste Lieutenant* Kerkhofs of the 3e Artillerie Bataljon, commander of the battery at Oostmahorn, says about the incident:

> This morning at half past seven, 8 armed English sloops appeared in front of my battery. We fired eleven shots to chase them away. These sloops have captured 4 loaded fishing boats and 6 merchant vessels. 6 other loaded fishing boats had been beached below my battery, but because of the high tide they were still in danger of being captured as well.[36]

The garrison on Schiermonnikoog also responded to the gunfire of the battery at Oostmahorn, moving a field gun to the western point of the island and firing at the British ships as well, being identified by them as three frigates and two brigs with their prizes. On 29 June, it was reported to the *Uitvoerend Bewind* that six fishing boats and as many barges had been captured, the amount matching with the British report, which, however, did not mention that half of these were fishing boats, although loaded with fish. *Capitein* van Dunne complained about the absence of the Batavian gunboats, but that was about to change. On 4 July, Naval Minister Spoors reported to the *Uitvoerend Bewind*:

> Citizen Directors! I have the honour to inform you, that on the 1st of this month, the country's gunboats the *Otter* and the *Vos*, commanded by *Lieutenant* Van Ginkel has fought for 1 ½ hour with four enemy sloops, each with a crew of 30, and with two fishing boats captured from us by the English earlier, each armed with two 8pdr guns. Van Ginkel succeeded in chasing away the English from the western part of the Wad and captured a sloop with five men, which has been brought to Delfzijl. The behaviour of the officers as well as the sailors deserves a lot of praise, they were despite their bravery however not able to prevent that the English, attacking with a much superior force of 13 armed sloops at all points of the Wadden simultaneously, captured some of our merchant vessels. To prevent this as much as possible, I am constantly busy to reinforce our force in the Ems and on the Wadden. The First Commissioner and commander of the fleet has already received orders, to send some armed barges over there, which I believe will have a good outcome. Four gunboat galleys, which have been build in Amsterdam, will soon leave for the Wadden as well, which will give our flotilla a respectable image.[37]

In the *Naval Chronicle* a letter was published which Captain Boorder had sent to the Batavians in Delfzijl at the Ems River, in an effort to free the five men taken prisoner:

---

36 Koolemans Beijnen, 'Krijgsgeschiedkundige studie', 1893, pp.563-565.
37 Koolemans Beijnen, 'Krijgsgeschiedkundige studie', 1893, p.565.

Sir, in consequence of the two Dutch gun-boats breaking the neutrality of this River on the 1st inst. in firing at three English boats, and detaining another with five men, which was sent as a Flag of Truce, and which, by the Laws of Nations, ought instantly to have been returned, I thought proper to act in the manner we did, on Friday last; and will have you and all the world to know that English seamen are not to be trifled with. I remain, Sir, your humble Servant, James Boorder.

P. S. I shall still expect that the officer and four men be delivered up to Admiral Lord Viscount Duncan, now blockading the Texel.[38]

On 9 July the newly built gunboat *Helhond* (*Eerste Lieutenant ter Zee* Eilbracht) arrived. The armed barges mentioned above arrived on 13 July on the Wadden Sea. On 15 July the gunboats *Hyena* (*Capitein-Lieutenant* Dusseau) and *Draak* (*Capitein-Lieutenant* de Veer) arrived from Zeeland, each with a crew of 30. On 19 July, the gunboat galleys *Breidel* (7 guns, *Capitein-Lieutenant* Frederiks) and *de Voorzorg* (7 guns, *Eerste Lieutenant ter Zee* Nooy), each with a crew of 80 men, were sent from Amsterdam to Texel. However, these Batavian reinforcements did not prevent the British ships from harassing the shipping on the Wadden Sea time and again. On 10 July, Winthrop again raided behind Ameland:

I feel great pleasure in acquainting your Lordship, that the boats of our little squadron [*Circe, Pylades, Espiegle, Courier* (Sloop 20, Lieutenant T. Searle), and the cutter *Nancy*] made another dash into the Watt, at the back of Ameland, last night, and brought out three valuable vessels deeply laden with sugar, wine, and brandy; they also burnt a large galliott, laden with brass ordnance and stores, which could not he brought off, notwithstanding the perseverance of Captain Mackenzie, to whom I am very much indebted for his coolness and judgment in the management of this affair; and also to Captain Boorder, whose local knowledge has been of great use to me. Lieutenant Searle, who commanded a schoot converted into a gun-boat, and Lieutenant Pawle who commanded the Circe's boats, upon this, as well as upon a former occasion, conducted themselves very much to my satisfaction, as did the honest fellows under their command, who were at their oars fifteen or sixteen hours in a very hot day opposed to an enemy of superior force, but I am happy to say not a man was hurt.[39]

The report of the Municipality of Ameland provides additional information about this incident:

It is our duty to report to you about what has happened here yesterday July 11th. During the night or the early morning, at the eastern end of the island six armed enemy sloops entered, while were anchored in front of our beach 2 frigates, 2 cutters and a brig as well as a *snik* [schoot] taken earlier. These sloops rowed inside in front of Nes village, with the objective of taking the armed barge anchored there,

---

38 Letter of 15 July 1799 from Captain Boorder, in the *Naval Chronicle*, Vol.II, p.349-350.
39 Letter of 11 July 1799 from Captain R. Winthrop of the *Circe* to Lord Viscount Duncan, in the *Naval Chronicle*, Vol. II, p.343.

shooting at it but the fire was returned in such a way that the sloops had to retire; however in the meantime they took 2 loaded vessels and 1 barge, as well as a brig destined for Embden, as well as a galliot near the Oosteinde with 3 telegraphs, which would be erected here; because the tide had passed, they could not take with them the ships mentioned; however in the afternoon with the flood they came in again, taking with them the 2 vessels and the barge already mentioned; however the galliot with the telegraphs had been scuttled by its commander, so the enemy set it on fire and it has completely burned with the telegraphs and all that was in it – the brig has been saved because it remained stuck – being the enemy sloops and the ships leaving from in front of our beach during the night again and at the moment out of our sight.[40]

Apparently, the British sailors did not recognise the telegraphs in the galliot. The continuous British raids in the Wadden Sea greatly disturbed and annoyed the Batavian government, blocking their last remaining trade route. However, by now it was too late, the Batavians completely being outgunned and outclassed by the British ships. For the purpose of keeping the Wadden Sea free from the British, all channels between the Wadden islands had to be defended, and the islands themselves guarded against enemy occupation. This was currently not the case at all, Ameland for example having only two 6pdr cannon with barely any ammunition for them. The garrisons of these islands came at this moment from the 2/4e Halve Brigade: two companies each on the islands Vlieland, Terschelling and Ameland; a detachment on Schiermonnikoog. The Batavian gunboats and armed sloops remained under cover of the battery of Oostmahorn, now and then sailing a bit further, only to return to safety quickly. This situation also meant that the threat of an Anglo-Russian invasion in Friesland or Groningen was very much real.[41]

In the meantime, the British continued bothering the Batavians. The following incident took place in neutral waters, the Prussian part of the Ems. *Lieutenant ter Zee* van Ginkel reported about the engagement:

Since your departure at this station and the crossroads near the Wadt buoy, as recommended to me by you, they enemy did not show themselves; until now, this morning about six o'clock I noticed an enemy brig (of 20 pieces), two cutters (each of 18 pieces), a fishing boat, a schuyt and six barges, all armed. I prepared everything with my small defence (the country's gunboats *Otter, Vos* and *Adder*), however, not expecting that the enemy would attack me at this neutral place. At half past six the above mentioned ships had approached within swivel gunshot; I received the broadside from the brig and both cutters; I cut the ropes as did the other ships at my signal and made sail, replying with my 8pdrs to the unexpected attack; the strong wind, and the strong inclination of the vessels was the cause that these shots were without effect; I retired to the grounds, hunted by this force, firing continuously at me; I was pursued by them to the Eemshorn, sailing through the

---

40 Letter of 12 July 1799 from the Municipality of Ameland, in Koolemans Beijnen, 'Krijgsgeschiedkundige studie', 1893, p.569.
41 Koolemans Beijnen, 'Krijgsgeschiedkundige studie', 1893, p.568.

Dokegat to Delfzijl; it is owing to this drought, which could not be crossed by these vessels, that I could escape this force. I regret to have to tell you that commander Goudakker of the *Adder*, his right leg shot off, died a few hours later.

Rest assured that I would not have left my post, so strongly recommended by you, except because of this major force.[42]

It seems the British indeed compromised the neutrality of Prussian territory, but no British report about this incident is known. On the 17th, Winthrop was relieved by Captain Sotheron with the frigate *Latona* (5th Rate 38). On 22 July Sotheron, aided by the *Espiegle* and *Nancy*, burned seven empty barges near Ameland. Again the ships' boats made the attack. On the 24th, a similar attack near Schiermonnikoog met with no result. On 11 August, two actions were fought. East of Schiermonnikoog, a large armed schooner was attacked in vain by boats from the *Pylades*. In addition, near Schiermonnikoog a force consisting of the boats of the *Pylades*, *Espiegle*, and *Courier*, which had entered the Wadden Sea through the Friessche Gat, attacked the *Crash*. Attacked from three sides, *Lieutenant ter Zee* Bybel defended himself for 50 minutes but finally had to strike his colours. The *Pylades* lost one sailor killed and two wounded. *De Weerwraak* (6, *Lieutenant ter Zee* van Maren), also present, abandoned the *Crash* and retreated to Schiermonnikoog. The *Crash* was immediately crewed and added to the British flotilla.

On the 12th this success was followed by an attack on two gunboats and an armed schuyt behind the island, made by boats from the *Juno* (5th Rate 32). The schuyt, armed with two 12pdr carronades, was captured, renamed *Undaunted* and also taken into service under the command of Lieutenant Humphreys of the *Juno*. On 13 August, Captain Mackenzie of the *Pylades* sent nine boats after the Batavian ships that had sought refuge in the tiny harbour of Schiermonnikoog, supported by the gunfire of the *Pylades*, *Courier*, *Crash* and *Undaunted*. Slowly making their way through the Friessche Gat, the *Courier* grounded and barely avoided capture. The boats made it into the harbour and attacked the Batavian ships. They captured a gunboat and 12 schuyts. The second gunboat, *De Weerwraak*, defended itself as long as possible. When the British closed in on him, *Lieutenant ter Zee* van Maren sent his crew, except three, to the island, with orders to maintain fire with muskets. With the remaining three sailors he spiked the cannon, threw the swivel guns overboard, and then set the ship on fire to avoid capture.[43]

The British followed up on their attack, landing sailors on the beach under cover of fire from the *Crash*. The defence of the island consisted of 26 men of the 1/6e Halve Brigade with two 3pdr guns commanded by *Lieutenant* Broers. He deployed his feeble force on the beach but, after the first shot of the *Crash*, the civilian drivers of the ammunition caissons took flight. Broers now retreated after spiking his guns and chose to make a stand in front of the village. The villagers, scared of the consequences of a combat, tried to persuade Broers to retreat, but they were answered that he would rather set the village on fire then to retreat any further. The British either believed Broers' position to be too strong or else they had already

---

42 Report of 13 July 1799 from *Lieutenant ter Zee* Ginkel to *Capitein-Lieutenant* Van Kervel, in Koolemans Beijnen, 'Krijgsgeschiedkundige studie', 1893, p.571. Goudakker was replaced by *Lieutenant ter Zee* Dingemans.
43 J.C. de Jonge, *Geschiedenis van het Nederlandsche Zeewezen*, Vol.V, p.448. British sources have translated the name of this ship as *Vengeance*.

reached their goal with the capture of the ships. In any case they evacuated the island again, taking with them nine captured vessels after sinking a tenth and both captured guns. The *Naval Chronicle* reported later:

> Yarmouth, July 24: Arrived the Courier cutter, with nine prizes, one of which was the Liberty, of Yarmouth, taken twelve months ago. These prizes were cut out of the Watt by L'Espiegle brig and the Courier cutter. The L'Espiegle landed a number of men, who went without any obstruction seven miles up the country, where they shot six bullocks, two of which they got on board the brig. In going for the rest they discovered some horsemen coming after them, which obliged them to abandon their design, and take to their boats and row on board.[44]

The British stated that they destroyed 'some batteries' on Schiermonnikoog, but that is a bit exaggerated. Anyway, Captain Mackenzie would be promoted post-captain for this action. The reports of Captains MacKenzie and Boorder about these engagements, beside giving a slightly different view of the engagements, contain additional information:

> We found the Navigation very difficult, from the wind being nearly right down; at times there was not two feet water more than this ship draws, and the channel is so narrow that there was not room to go more than twice our length. The service is much indebted to Mr. William Gray, Master of this ship, whom I had previously sent to sound, and who took charge of her up alongside of the Crash Dutch gun-vessel. Lieutenant Searle of the Courier cutter, from working fast to windward, I ordered to engage her until this ship or l'Espiegle should get up; which she did in the most gallant manner, considering she is five times the cutter's force. The Dutch officer fought the Crash a great deal longer than I imagined he would have done, as this ship and l'Espiegle were a great part of the time within half-pistol shot; both vessels have received considerable damage in their rigging and yards. The boats, previous to the ships getting into action, were sent to attack the large gun-schooner, which lay to the eastward of a sand, but she ran on shore, keeping up a heavy fire upon the boats, by which one man was killed in the Juno's cutter. This ship had one man killed and three wounded.
>
> The Crash's force is twelve carronades of thirty-two, twenty-four, and eighteen pounders, and sixty men. Thinking it for the good of His Majesty's service to fit and man the Crash, for the purpose of acting against the enemy's remaining force, I have appointed Lieutenant Slade, first of the Latona, to command her.
>
> One of the enemy's gun-schooners is hauled on shore on the Main; the other, called the Vengeance [*Weerwraak*], of six heavy guns, two of them long twenty-four

---

44 *London Chronicle*, 27 July 1799. Between 26 June and 1 August, at least the following merchant vessels were captured in the Wadden Sea by this British flotilla: *Twee Gebroeders, Jonge Evert, Vrouwe Regina, Anna Elizabeth, Vrouw Treintje, Marguarithat Sophia, Twee Gezusters, Juffrouw Maria Christiana, Vrouw Hendertje Marguaritha, Stad Oldenburg, Vrouw Antje, Vrouw Gesina, Eendracht* and *Frederik*: see Anon. *Steel's Prize Pay Lists, containing accounts of prize and head-money, paid, and now payable, for prizes taken or destroyed, during the last war*, new series corrected till 1805 (London: David Steel, 1805).

pounders, and seventy men, with a large row-boat, is under a battery of six heavy guns, on the Island of Schiermonikoog, where I am informed there are 300 armed men: if I can find water, you may depend upon my attacking them.[45]

In my letter to you of the 12th instant, I informed you of my intention to attack the enemy's force on Schiermonikoog; I sent Mr. Gray to sound, which he did with great diligence, and fortunately found a small channel; in the mean time, being in want of vessels for gun-boats, I dispatched the boats under the lieutenants Campbell and Humphreys at high water, to endeavour to cut out a schoot or two from under the protection of the schooner on the Main; they could only get at two; one of them was burnt, the other brought away, although the schooner kept up a well directed fire. I immediately had her fitted out with two twelve-pound carronades, called her the Undaunted, and gave the command of her to Lieut. Humphreys, of the Juno; at three o'clock yesterday afternoon I ordered the vessels to move on to the attack, viz.

The Crash. Lieut. Slade, and Mr. Moody, Master of the Juno, 12 carronades.

Undaunted, Lieut. Humphrey, two twelve-pound carronades, with Lieut. McDonald, of the marines.

Latona's launch, Lieut. Campbell, one twelve-pound carronade.

Pylades' launch, Lieut. Cowan, one twelve-pound carronade.

Pylades' Cutter, Mr. Ryan, acting lieutenant, and all the other small boats, some with swivels, others only small arms.

The Courier cutter was intended to cover them. But unfortunately grounded, and it was with great exertion she was saved; they went on till they grounded within half pistol shot of the shore, under a heavy fire from the schooner and battery, and latterly small arms; but when they got a little placed, their fire soon drove the enemy from their batteries, and the people of the schooner finding Lieutenants Humphreys and Campbell going to board her, all ran on shore; having set fire to her, which was found impossible to be extinguished, she was therefore burnt.

I am unable, as no person was taken belonging to her, to state her loss of men, but it must have been considerable. While that was doing, Lieutenant Cowan landed, and spiked the guns on the enemy's battery, and with getting more assistance from all that could land, brought off two brass field pieces, and spiked another twelve pounder. The row-boat and twelve schoots are taken. I have given orders for all the vessels to collect round this ship…What is most extraordinary, we have not lost one man killed or wounded… It would afford me great pleasure if I could, without a breach of delicacy, when mentioning an officer of equal rank, inform you of the abilities of Capt. Boorder, and the assistance I have received from him.[46]

During this engagement an incident took place on the *Pylades*. A seaman of Dutch origin, Garret Andrew Fauch, five years in British service, tried to take advantage of the absence of the best crew members being in the action on Schiermonnikoog. He excited some Batavian

---

45 Letter of 12 August 1799 from Captain A. MacKenzie of the *Pylades* to Admiral Lord Duncan, in the *Naval Chronicle*, Vol.II, pp.530-531.
46 Letter of 14 August 1799 from Captain A. MacKenzie of the *Pylades* to Admiral Lord Duncan, in the *Naval Chronicle*, Vol.II, pp.531-532.

prisoners on board to rise and to take possession of the ship. His plan failed and he was duly arrested and had to appear on front of a court martial on the *Seahorse* at Sheerness, where he was sentenced to death.[47] After the engagements, Captain Boorder sailed to Yarmouth with *l'Espiègle* and the *Crash*:

> I have to acquaint you of my arrival at this anchorage with His Majesty's sloop under my command, and of my having, in company with the Pylades Sloop and Courier cutter, cut out and took possession of, on the 11th inst. from Shiermonikoog, the Crash gun-brig, (formerly in our service) mounting twelve guns, eighteen twenty-four, and thirty-two pounders: as also having burnt a schooner, of 70 men; likewise took possession of a row boat, of 30 men; we then landed on the island (having previously drove the men from the battery), spiked four pieces of cannon, and brought off two brass field pieces, four pounders. The Crash made an obstinate resistance from forty to fifty minutes, and then struck. I am happy to add not more than two man were killed on our side, and three wounded, and recommend the Crash as an excellent vessel, well calculated for His Majesty's service, bring of a small draught of water. I cannot but express my satisfaction on our keeping the ships afloat, as in many places our soundings proved there to be not more than fourteen feet. the Espiègle drawing twelve.[48]

On 28 August the *Contest* gun-vessel (10 carronades, Lieutenant Short) was wrecked on the Batavian coast, having been driven onto a shoal during tempestuous weather. Two of her crew, eager to leave the wreck, in hopes of swimming to shore, threw themselves overboard and were drowned in the surf.[49]

---

47 *Naval Chronicle*, Vol. II, p.635.
48 Letter of 20 August 1799 from Captain J. Boorder of *l'Espiègle* to Vice Admiral Dickson, in the *Naval Chronicle*, Vol. II, pp.530-531.
49 *Naval Chronicle*, Vol.II, p.350.

6

The Franco-Batavian Response to the Threat

Although in 1795 the Batavian Republic had been proclaimed by the Patriots, it would take quite some time to organise a proper administration, copied from the French Republic. It took until 1 March 1796 before the first national assembly came together, but almost immediately two parties could be distinguished: the *Foederalisten* advocated an alliance of independent provinces, while the *Unitarissen* wanted an absolute union. It would take until 8 August 1797 before the first draft of a new constitution was submitted to the people for approval, but it was rejected by an absolute majority. This all led to a *coup d'état* on 22 January 1798, in which the French commander-in-chief in the republic, *Général de Division* Joubert, and *Lieutenant-Generaal* Daendels both participated. It appears that Daendels was the only Batavian senior officer participating in the *coup*. A provisional *Uitvoerend Bewind* (Executive Administration), comparable with the French *Directoire*, was appointed consisting of five Directors. The purified National Assembly named itself as the 'Constituent Assembly, representing the Batavian people' and on 17 March a new draft constitution was approved. In the meantime in the whole Batavian Republic, the people's assemblies were also been purified. So, not surprisingly, on 23 April the constitution known as *Staatsregeling 1798* was ratified by the majority of the voters. The Directors now however went too far. On 4 May they made the unconstitutional decision that the 1st, as well as the 2nd, Chamber of the *Vertegenwoordigend Lichaam* (the Parliament) would consist of two-thirds of members of the Constituent Assembly, with the remaining one-third chosen by the voters. In addition, they started to prosecute the opposition, sending them to jail or placing them under house arrest. This all caused much unrest. A group of people, again including Joubert and Daendels, planned another *coup* to stop this, but they first wanted to confer with the French. On 17 May Daendels left for Paris, receiving agreement by the French Minister of Foreign Affairs, Talleyrand. Returning on 12 June 1798 he removed the Directors and the 1st and 2nd Chambers of the Parliament by military force. On 31 July, a new, constitutionally chosen Parliament took their seats.

The *Staatsregeling 1798* of the Batavian Republic: Military Affairs

The *Staatsregeling 1798* was a product of the *Unitarissen*, advocating an absolute union. As a result of this constitution, absolute power was with the 1st and 2nd Chambers of the

Parliament. The 1st Chamber, consisting of 64 members, was solely responsible for designing and proposing all laws and decrees. The 2nd Chamber, consisting of 30 members, was responsible for ratifying these laws and decrees. The Parliament, residing in The Hague, was protected by a military guard consisting of at least 700 men, infantry and cavalry. Regarding military affairs, the Parliament was, inter alia, responsible for:

- Ratifying all agreements and alliances with foreign powers;
- Determining the strength, including recruitment and dismissal, of the army, including its payment;
- The employment and licensing of foreign troops;
- The equipment of the navy, the building of ships and the dismissal of crews;
- The permission of stay or passage of foreign troops on the territory of the Batavian Republic, if proposed by the *Uitvoerend Bewind*;
- The permission of foreign naval ships to enter the harbours of the Batavian Republic, if proposed by the *Uitvoerend Bewind*;
- Designing the necessary regulations for the creation of the *Gewapende Burgermacht*.

The *Uitvoerend Bewind* consisted of five directors, responsible for executing the laws and decrees of the Parliament. To assist them there were eight *Agenten* (ministers), for foreign affairs, navy, war, finance, justice, policy, education and economy. During the Anglo-Russian invasion, Gerrit Jan Pijman was minister of war. Additional commissaries could be appointed when deemed necessary in order to execute laws and decrees. Regarding military affairs, the *Uitvoerend Bewind* was responsible for the army and navy. They drafted proposals to be ratified by the Parliament, and appointed officers in the army and navy in service of the Batavian Republic. The appointment of commanders-in-chief and admirals had to be ratified by the Parliament. As shown here, in line with the ideas of the *Unitarissen*, the administration of the Batavian Republic was indeed completely centralised. As a result workload was enormously and it could take a long time before even important decisions were made. Soon there were laws for various issues. Again regarding military affairs, inter alia, it was established that in time of peace, all army units had fixed garrisons, the *Uitvoerend Bewind* was not allowed to transfer them, except by request of interior authorities in order to regain or maintain order. Also the *Uitvoerend Bewind* was prohibited to place or move any armed force inside the residency of the Parliament or within a three hours distance of this residency, except by authorisation or by order of the Parliament.

Financing all military measures was a heavy burden for the Batavian Republic. In accordance with the stipulations of the Treaty of The Hague of 1795, the Batavian Republic had to pay the French Republic 100 million guilders. Further, the Batavian Republic had to feed, clothe, and pay 25,000 French soldiers stationed in the Batavian Republic. This presence of French troops was a great financial burden, and the French had developed a special system for the 25,000 soldiers the Batavian Republic had to feed, clothe, and pay. Ragged troops from the front line armies were sent to the Batavian Republic. Here they were fed, paid, and clothed again. After some time, the troops returned to the front, fully equipped and rested and a new ragged and hungry contingent arrived. Vincent Lombard de Langres, who was the French extraordinary envoy in the Batavian Republic in 1798 and 1799, wrote about this matter in his memoirs:

In vain had the Dutch, aiding Pichegru's advance, promoted the capture of their own country. In vain they had received the fairest promises if they would offer little resistance, and let their territory be occupied by our troops. Hardly the seizure was done, or we behaved towards them as conquerors, and by the wealth that we presupposed by them, we measured our exactions. Had England recaptured them, they would have gained. Having already extracted them a large sum for starters; after having imposed on them annual levies, like the Turks do in their *pachaliks*, we still added more taunting torments, under a thousand pretexts. An article of the treaty stipulated, that their principal maritime city, until there was peace on the continent, would remain occupied by an equal number of French and Dutch soldiers. From this was concluded that half of that cities' full ownership belonged to France; and every time they wanted to wheedle new sums of money out of them, they made that claim equally shamelessly, as the poor Dutch, who wished to retain their port, paid submissively. If we had in our army some battalions that were totally emaciated, totally barren, one could be sure that they marched to Holland. After they were fed and fully equipped, one did not fail to recall them to make room for others. Looking just as miserable, and which by our good friends, were clothed all over again… In addition to a considerable salary, it was so much for the table of the General and Chief, so much for his special police, as much for his accommodations; it was again, as much for the chief inspector, as much for the deputy-inspectors and commissioners of any kind and colour; master, servant, big and small, each picked the loudest; all sought to have their share of the cake. It was believed that it was raining ducats in Holland.[1]

The fact that French units left the Batavian Republic did not mean that the Batavians did not have to take care and pay for them anymore. The French regarded these units still as part of the French contingent in the Batavian Republic and as such they remained on the Batavian payroll. As shown for example by a decision of the 2nd Chamber on 12 March 1799, to authorise the *Uitvoerend Bewind* to issue passports to export some goods, to cloth French troops in garrison in Dusseldorf, which were officially part of the 25,000 French troops in Batavian service.[2]

An additional financial disaster was the Battle of Camperdown on 11 October 1797, in which the Batavians lost 10 ships of the line and four frigates, with extensive damage to the remaining ships of the fleet. These losses had to be made good and the Parliament decided to raise a special levy of eight percent on the income of the people of the Batavian Republic. Not surprisingly, this measure met heavy resistance, but this was broken with the *coup d'état* of 22 January. In October 1798, another decree enforced a levy of five percent on everyone with an annual income of more than 600 Dutch Guilders to meet the great needs of the republic. Followed on 30 November by a general levy of 10 percent on all income and a levy of four

---

1   Lombard de Langres, *Bijzonderheden uit de tijden der Omwenteling, gedeeltelijk ten onderwerp hebbende den toestand en de betrekkingen van Nederland in het jaar 1798*, ('s Gravenhage & Amsterdam: De Gebroeders van Cleef, 1820), pp.258-260.
2   Anon., *Dagverhaal der handelingen van het Vertegenwoordigend Lichaam des Bataafschen volks* (De Haage: Swart en Comp., 1799), Vol.IV, p.146

percent on all possessions.³ The loss of Batavian warships was repaired with extraordinary speed, which did not go unnoticed by the British, as reported in the *London Chronicle*: 'The Dutch marine has, by uncommon exertions, repaired the losses which it sustained in the action of the 11th of October. The fleet in the Texel is in readiness for sea. To oppose it Lord Duncan is on his return from Scotland, to resume the Chief Command of the North Sea fleet'.⁴ However, the problems the Batavians had to prepare their fleet for battle again also did not pass unnoticed by the British. In December 1798, it was already noted that 'Enormous bounties for seamen, for the Dutch service, have lately been offered at Bremen, Lubeck, Hamburg and other places; but measures have been taken to put a stop to those proceedings'.⁵ A few months later: 'The Armament of the fleet in the Texel is delayed for want of sailors'.⁶

The Batavian economy also suffered heavily, especially because of the British naval blockade which brought overseas trade to a standstill and hampered fishing as well, also preventing the Batavian navy from putting out to sea. This was illustrated in the letter of a Prussian diplomat in The Hague: 'Admiral Duncan just reappeared before Texel with 15 ships of the line, eleven English and four Russian. So that it is impossible that the Batavian fleet can undertake the slightest attempt to get out during this blockade'.⁷ For example during the year 1798, 29 of the 31 Batavian whalers that sailed were captured by the British! Numerous merchant ships were captured. The blockade also meant that neutral ships were not allowed either: ignorance of a port being blockaded did not protect those neutral vessels that were bound to it and were captured by the British as well, and their cargoes were confiscated. The only shipping link still relatively safe was the one across the shallow Wadden Sea to Hamburg. However, it was not only the British who threatened Batavian trade; many French privateers were also active:

> Under the pretext of preventing trade with England, a throng of pirates who called themselves privateers, surround all ports. When, having escaped a thousand dangers at sea, a national ship loaded with the products of its colonies joyfully entered the harbour, it saw itself intercepted by these robbers; despite the rights of the owners, the mourning of Amsterdam, the fair complaints from the government, the cargo became prey of those vampires… The English ships cruising incessantly along the coast, fired occasionally at the fishing boats to pass the time; cannonballs flew into the dunes.⁸

Signs of the Forthcoming Invasion

As early as October 1798, reports were received about a possible invasion of the Batavian Republic. These became more concrete by the flow of reports from various sources, for

---

3 Koolemans Beijnen, 'Krijgsgeschiedkundige studie', 1891, pp.71-75.
4 *London Chronicle*, 18 March 1799.
5 *Naval Chronicle*, Vol.I, p.338.
6 *London Chronicle*, 22 March 1799.
7 Koolemans Beijnen, 'Krijgsgeschiedkundige studie', 1892, p.632.
8 Lombard de Langres, *Les souvenirs*, pp.259, 306.

example from *chargé d'affaires* Pierre Bourdeaux in Berlin, as illustrated by some of his letters:

> 15 January 1799: One speaks about a new combined undertaking by Russian and English troops against the Batavian Republic, rumours are still dark and undefined, nothing is certain at the moment.
> 18 January: Today we are assured that the Russian minister has declared last Saturday the intention of his Court to act jointly with England against France; even it is thought the Minister has demanded the passage of a corps of forty-five thousand Russian troops, which are intended to attack the Batavian borders, while this undertaking would be supported by an English fleet.
> 12 March: The Ministry has formally rejected all propositions of Russia; even those relating to the passage of a corps of Russian troops intended to attack us through the States of the King, and that the Minister had believed to obtain in any case.
> 28 May: The Lord of Stamford has left for Petersburg a few days ago, no one can know the real purpose of his journey.[9]

On 2 February 1799, the French Minister of Foreign Affairs Talleyrand send the following letter to Vincent Lombard de Langres:

> Citizen, the Naval Minister has informed me, according to information that he has received recently that the English Government is silently planning and preparing an attack against the territory of the Batavian Republic: he has every reason to believe that these preparations are against Zeeland and the island of Walcheren in particular, were are still many supporters of the late Stadtholder with which the English maintain intelligence and correspond daily. Already the Minister of War sent the General in Chief of the French troops in Holland orders to take measures at every point and especially to ensure that the port of Flushing is placed on a respectable defence and is safe from the enterprises of the enemy. You will take care to communicate these opinions to the Batavian Government and call its attention to ways to further thwart the hostile attempts of England.[10]

Lombard immediately forwarded this letter to the Batavian Minister of Foreign Affairs van der Goes, who on his turn forwarded it to the *Uitvoerend Bewind*. Initially this was without much effect: although the French took the threat very seriously apparently the Batavian government did not, or at least that was the French point of view. *Général de Division* Brune, who had become the French commander-in-chief on 14 January 1799, requested an audience with the *Uitvoerend Bewind* to talk about the British threat. On 4 February a secret meeting took place, in which Brune brought forward a number of his concerns regarding

---

9   G.W. Vreede, *Geschiedenis der Diplomatie van de Bataafsche Republiek* (Utrecht: J.G. Broese, 1863-4), 2nd part, 1st piece, pp.3, 43, 48. The reference in the last entry is to Henry de Stamford, envoy of the Hereditary Prince of Orange in Berlin.
10 Vreede, *Geschiedenis der Diplomatie,* 2nd part, 1st piece, Appendix I.

the defence of the Batavian Republic. Among the points discussed were the defence of Zeeland; the preparation of transport ships to be able to send troops to threatened islands quickly and to station gunboats there; adequate defence of Texel, as an enemy capture of this island would endanger the Batavian fleet; and to cloth, arm and provide for the 8 to 10,000 conscripts which would soon arrive from France. The answer that Brune received from the *Uitvoerend Bewind* was not satisfactory at all. The Batavians were of the opinion that already enough transport ships lay ready in Bergen op Zoom and that additional gunboats were not necessary; the defence of Texel was in perfect order; and the Batavian Republic would only provide for the 25,000 French troops stipulated in the treaty, excess troops would have to be negotiated first.

That the defence of Texel was in perfect order was not true. As observed by Dardenne as early as December 1797:

> The island of Texel is poorly defended; it is not even protected against a *coup de main*; The fort is located in an indent and in the worst condition and does not deserve as position in any defence. Battery *Horntje*, intended to form a crossfire with that of the *Union*, will always be unable to serve, as it is situated on sand which is not solid; the wind covers the sandy platform every day.[11]

In August 1799, regarding Texel not much had changed for the better. On 9 February, Van der Goes pointed out that the British attack could well be directed at the coast of Flanders, which according to him was badly defended, urging the French to give attention to its defence. On 10 March, *Général de Brigade* Osten, commanding the troops in Zeeland on Walcheren island, wrote that: 'I am informed directly that the British Government plans to attempt a landing on the coast of Flanders and Zealand'.[12] As a defensive measure some small and old vessels were prepared as gunboats and fire-ships. Brune wrote on 13 March to *Adjudant-Général* Durutte, chief of staff of the 3rd French Division in Bergen op Zoom: 'While it is true that our enemies are determined to attack us, I wish for our honour that the whole country is put in a state of siege; because the delays in our demands which we experience continuously could make us fail in our military operations'.[13] Also of interest is a letter of 6 April from Dardenne to the Batavian First Commissioner for the troops in the Batavian Republic Janssens:

> The *Général en chef*, having been informed that the English are planning an attack against Zeeland, believed it necessary to charge *Général* Osten to send someone to England to procure information. He asked me to send you herewith the state of expenses begging you to reimburse. It would be quite ridiculous, in charge of the defence of a country, if he was obliged to pay these kinds of charges at his own expense.[14]

11　Dardenne, *Notes sur l'état actuel des moyens de défense des côtes de la Nord Hollande vers la mer du Nord*, quoted in Koolemans Beijnen, 'Krijgsgeschiedkundige studie', 1892, p.636.
12　Koolemans Beijnen, 'Krijgsgeschiedkundige studie', 1892, p.640.
13　Koolemans Beijnen, 'Krijgsgeschiedkundige studie', 1891, p.78.
14　Koolemans Beijnen, 'Krijgsgeschiedkundige studie', 1892, p.641.

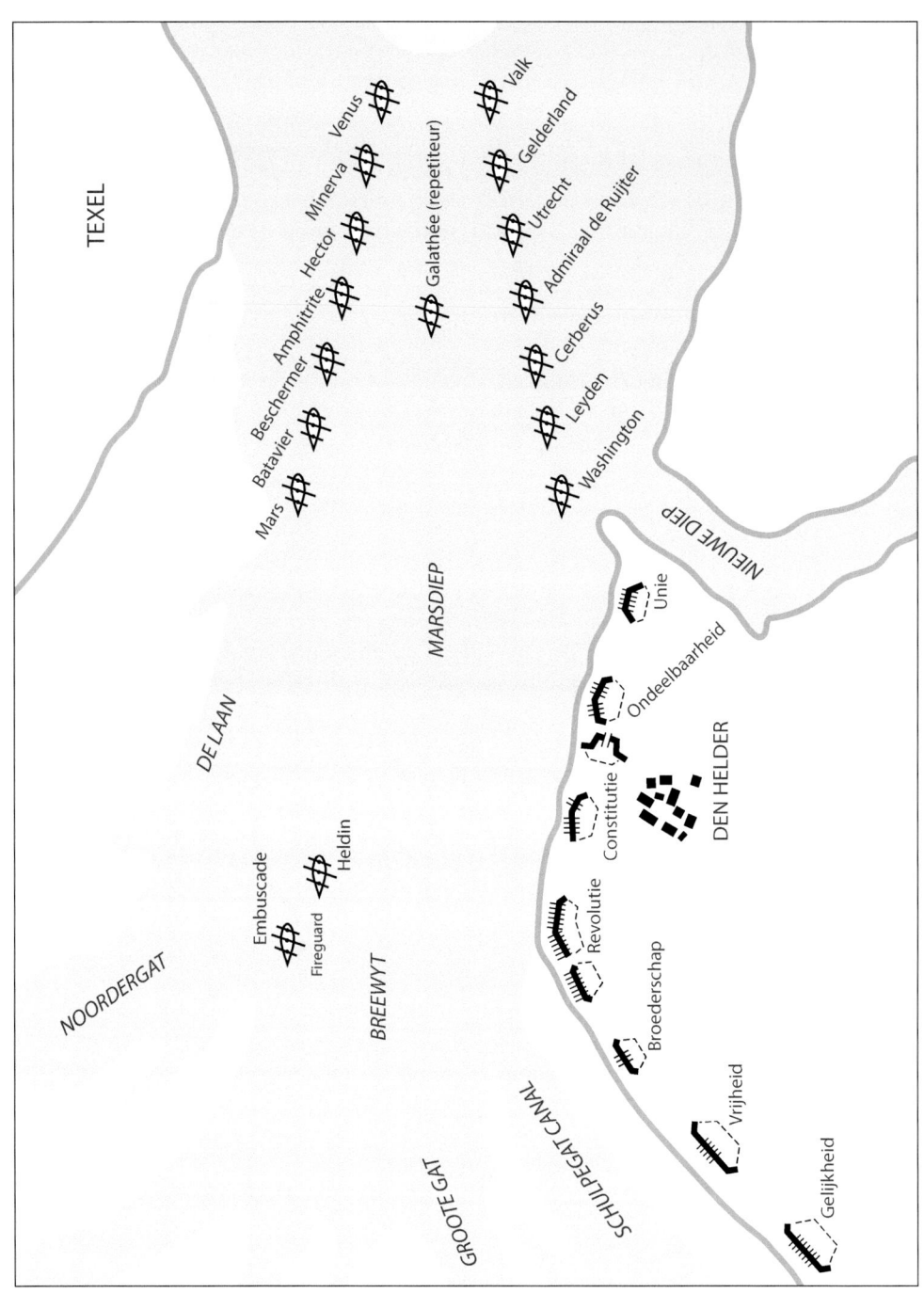

Map 3 The Batavian fleet at the Roads of Texel.

The result of this mission to Great Britain will be looked at later. Not only the French spied on the British, the Batavians also did, as illustrated by a secret report of the Batavian Naval Minister Spoors of 18 March:

> Citizen Laurens van Rij, charged with a mandate by the stakeholders of the fishing boats of Katwijk and Egmond, to promote the release of the fisherman still in England, is qualified by me to investigate and to receive all possible information about the English naval power and their objectives. And to provide me with reports from time to time about:
>
> 1. The force destined for the North Sea, its commanding officer, how the squadrons are distributed, when they sail and for how long they have victuals;
> 2. The convoys to the Baltic Sea and Archangel; the departure of the packet boats to Hamburg and the Weser, how they are escorted; expected ships and their convoy;
> 3. How many and which ships are at sea; especially to announce the date at which only few are at sea;
> 4. Outgoing expeditions, out of what ships they consist, especially if there are fire ships, and when cavalry, gunners and cannon are present to serve landing troops;
> 5. Reliable messages from Ireland, the state of mind of the nation in general.[15]

Lieutenant-Generaal Daendels also had his own spy in England who wrote to him on 25 March:

> The king has been pleased to cause it to be signified by the right honourable lord Grenville, His Majesty's principal secretary of state for foreign affairs, to the ministers of neutral powers residing at this court, that the necessary measures having been taken by His Majesty's commands for the blockade of the ports of the United Provinces. The said ports are declared to be in a state of blockade and that all vessels, which may attempt to enter any of them after this notice, will be dealt with according to the principles of the law of nations and to the stipulations of such treaties subsisting between His Majesty and foreign powers as may contain provisions applicable to the cases of towns, places or ports in a state of blockade.[16]

On 1 April, Daendels reported to the *Uitvoerend Bewind* that the gathering of troops on the Isle of Wight is not as significant as was reported and that the greater part had already embarked for the Mediterranean as well as to Portugal. Also that one still spoke about a landing in Zeeland and that no ostensible preparations had been noticed. It was also announced that his source would probably be able to provide an up-to-date overview of the British fleets. Indeed, three days later this overview was received and it is interesting to give

---

15 Koolemans Beijnen, 'Krijgsgeschiedkundige studie', 1893, pp.8-9.
16 The original letter in English, dated London 25 March 1799 and signed by one "A.B.C.", quoted in Koolemans Beijnen, 'Krijgsgeschiedkundige studie', 1893, p.9.

it here to illustrate the detail of information the Batavians received: On the North Sea, the fleet consisted of nine English and 10 Russian ships of the line. The former nine commanded by Vice Admiral Dickson were the *Ganges* (74 guns, Captain R. MacDonall), the *America, Ardent, Belliqueux, Director, Prince Frederick*, and *Veteran*, each of 64 guns and commanded by the Captains J. Smith, F. Bertie, J. Inglis, W. Bligh, J.G. Hall and J.R. Mosse; the *Madras* (54 guns, Captain J. Dilhes) and the *Isis* (50 guns, Captain W. Mitchell); and of the latter 10, commanded by Admiral Tet, were six 74s, two 66s and two 64s, while five smaller ships, carrying 44 and 40 guns are listed. Further is reported: one ship of the line at the Humber River, two with the squadron in the Downs, 14 with the fleet in the English and Irish channels, 31 in the harbours which are equipped, 15 in the Mediterranean, 16 before Cadiz, seven before Gibraltar, 13 at the Cape of Good Hope, in the East Indies and under sail, three in the West Indies under sail, eight at Jamaica and three in America and Newfoundland. A total of 132 ships of the line.[17]

On 10 April, Daendels sent another report to the *Uitvoerend Bewind*:

> Admiral Gardner has sailed on 2 March with 12 ships of the Channel Fleet, to patrol, and is reinforced on the 16th and 18th with another four ships. Admiral Duckworth will depart for the Mediterranean to take over command from Nelson. Vice-Admiral R. Curtis will depart for the Cape of Good Hope, to replace the deceased Rear Admiral H.W. Christian, accompanied by the new governor C. Yonge. Rear-Admiral Ch. Cotton will depart for Halifax, to replace Admiral van der Put who will come home. The Channel Fleet consists now of 19 ships of the line.[18]

Every few days or so Daendels was provided with new up-to-date reports of all British naval movements and preparations, with more than enough detail to prevent a surprise attack at the Batavian Republic, although the exact location of such an attack was never certain. At some time the situation became even more confusing, for example when on 6 April the Naval Minister Spoors reported to the *Uitvoerend Bewind* that he had been informed by most probable reports, that the Russians planned an attack on the Batavian Republic, especially on the coast of Friesland and Groningen. He used the occasion to point out the inferiority of the Batavian navy, as well as the lack of sufficient gunboats suitable to defend these coasts. In addition, that the gunboats that were present were leaving or had already left for Zeeland for the same purpose. This was causing the Batavians to limit themselves to a defence on land. He also pointed out that even if the land forces were able to fend off the enemy, the enemy naval presence would block all transport to Hamburg and on the Wadden Sea cutting off the last remaining trade route. A few days later he proposed to build six gunboat galleys and to hire and transform 30 to 40 barges into gunboats. The *Uitvoerend Bewind* however kept this proposal 'under advice' and no progress was made on this matter.[19]

---

17 Koolemans Beijnen, 'Krijgsgeschiedkundige studie', 1893, p.9-10.
18 Koolemans Beijnen, 'Krijgsgeschiedkundige studie', 1893, p.11.
19 Koolemans Beijnen, 'Krijgsgeschiedkundige studie',1893, p.13.

Of course it was not only the Franco-Batavians spying on the British. The other way round, British and Orangists did the same, causing Daendels to send a warning to Dumonceau on 29 June:

> I am informed, that officers of neutral powers are travelling around the Republic, probably with the intention to reconnoitre our fortresses and points of defence; I believe it necessary to inform you about this immediately, in case you would judge it necessary to give orders that, except for French or Batavian officers or well-known citizens, no one is allowed on the walls of the fortresses or inside the entrenched posts, situated in the arrondissement of *Generaal-Major* Bonhomme. I have notified *Generaal-Major* van Boecop about this matter yesterday. I believed this was necessary, because a Danish engineer-officer has to cross through his *arrondissement* and along the Ijssel in a couple of days.[20]

After a while the threat had become so real that the Batavians could not ignore it any longer. The British had decided not to make a secret out of it and even the newspapers in Great Britain openly wrote about the planned invasion and the preparations that were made. The British Ministry, never doubting of success, took no pains whatever to conceal it, although they still talked about the 'Secret Expedition', even in the newspapers. One of the first instances was a paragraph about a review of the British King which appeared in several newspapers:

> The restoration of the House of Orange will be attempted, and no doubt effected, under the British armament equipping for that purpose: transports for an army of not less than 20,000 men, with the necessary train of artillery, &c. are now preparing with all possible dispatch. The Prince Stadtholder will accompany this formidable armament in person. The King, during the review of the 1st Dragoon Guards on Wednesday, spoke to the Prince of Orange respecting the review of the Volunteers on the preceding day in terms of the warmest admiration; he declared it so have been the most gratifying and the proudest period of his life, adding, that he trusted in three months the Stadtholder would have the pleasure of witnessing in his own country a similar spectacle.[21]

It took eight days before this newspaper report reached the Batavian government. They took it very seriously this time and at a meeting on 20 June between the Minister of War Pijman, Brune and Daendels it was agreed upon that the French troops would concentrate on defending the southern part of the Batavian Republic while the Batavian army concentrated in the north. Only in the residence at The Hague would a French garrison remain. In case of an invasion, all forces would concentrate and support each other. The coastal batteries were assessed as being in good order. It was also deemed necessary to organise and bring up to strength the *Gewapende Burgermacht* as soon as possible to aid in the defence,

---

20 Koolemans Beijnen, 'Krijgsgeschiedkundige studie', 1893, p.562.
21 *London Chronicle*, 10 June 1799.

as well as maintaining order in the interior. On 28 June, the French chief of staff Dardenne forwarded a copy of a report from *Général de Brigade* Osten on Walcheren to the Batavian Minister of War Pijman, stating that: 'We cannot deny any longer that for a long time an embarkation is prepared in England and I believe it is urgent to increase the forces on the island of Walcheren. They consist of 2,157 French infantry only'. The contents of the report referred to are reflected in the letter that was immediately send by Pijman to Daendels and Dumonceau:

> Just has arrived a letter of the *adjutant-général* Dardenne, with inserted a report of *Général de Brigade* Osten, relating to the embarkation in two northern English harbours of 17,000 men on 300 transports, probably destined to undertake an expedition to this country. Therefore I forward this to you immediately.[22]

It was Brune himself who discussed this with the Batavian government, in a secret meeting with the *Uitvoerend Bewind* on 28 June. Brune expressed his opinion that the British expedition would be directed at Zeeland or Holland, urging all possible measure for defence. The *Uitvoerend Bewind* replied that all necessary measures had already been taken. Nevertheless Pijman was ordered to discuss with Daendels and Dumonceau all necessary means for defence against the expected enemy attack; to draw up an integrated plan and to complete and enhance all actions already taken; to arrange the dispositions of all French and Batavian troops; to make the most appropriate designs 'to defend the fatherland against the predatory Brit [*den roofzuchtigen Brit*]'; and finally to draw up a general plan, signed by all of them, to be approved by the Batavian government. Apparently the news of the British preparations and the urgings of Brune made an impression on the *Uitvoerend Bewind*. Already on 2 July, Pijman submitted a provisional general plan to the *Uitvoerend Bewind*, which was approved in a secret meeting the next day. Firstly, it was proposed to appoint Brune as commander-in-chief of the French army in the Batavian Republic as well as the Batavian army. Further the following was established:

> Art. 1. Because of the possibility that the enemy in an attack against the erstwhile province of Zeeland can win in the beginning some advantages and force our troops to withdraw for some time to be able to counterattack him with combined forces, it will be necessary to provide the places Breda, Bergen op Zoom, 's Hertogenbosch and Grave with sufficient ammunition for the cannon, and for a garrison of 2,500 men, at least for six weeks to avoid in case of such retirement the embarrassment which would follow a momentary shortage and not to upset the locals by unnecessary requisitions.
>
> Art. 2: The army of 16,000 French and 24,000 Batavians, not being strong enough to act on all the points against which an enterprise could be undertaken, will be divided and placed in such a way that prompt reinforcements may be sent to where the danger would be greatest. The undersigned imagine that even if the enemy suddenly was effecting a *coup* on a particular part of the coast

---

22 Koolemans Beijnen, 'Krijgsgeschiedkundige studie', 1893, p.449.

or if naval forces cannot push them back early enough, by the position that the army take, it would be attacked so swiftly that moving the government would not be urgent in case it is proved that this attack was not sufficient to dislodge the enemy. The plan for this disposition as well as that of the naval force with their measures taken will be presented to the *Uitvoerend Bewind* and submitted for approval.

Art. 3: The Naval Minister will take care that as soon as possible the Telegraph will be organized in a way that in a very short space of time you will be informed in The Hague about what happens along the coast.

Before signing, Brune added to the above:

> I believe that until the Batavian Government has completed the entire supplying of the places Breda, Bergen op Zoom, 's Hertogenbosch and Grave, it is probably necessary to send them provisional supplies for six weeks, and taking care of their armament and fortifications with all speed; it is also essential to link a good system of defence with forces that are not foreign to each other and that their points of communication are also favourable, so that the concentration of forces is done in no time. Unity of command leads to unity of action, as the Batavian Government will be busy, I believe it must be more than a desire to encounter the English in a way to disgust any other attempts.[23]

The above, especially the addition by Brune, is very interesting as it shows us the most important aim Brune had, being the protection of the northern frontier of the French Republic, including the departments of the annexed Austrian Netherlands. Brune now had justification to concentrate his French troops in the southern part of the Batavian Republic, as well as protecting the French borders with a line of well-provisioned fortresses behind the major River Meuse. Another interesting point is that the strength of the French troops in the Batavian Republic was set at 16,000; not the 25,000 which should have been present according to the treaty and for which the Batavian Republic was paying. In fact it appears that about 18,500 French were present at that moment, including non-combatants.[24] The provisioning of the four fortresses mentioned proved to be expensive: the *Uitvoerend Bewind* ordered Pijman to calculate the budget that was needed, which was forwarded to them on 6 July. It would cost 250,000 Dutch guilders and the *Uitvoerend Bewind* ordered Pijman initially to find the money in the budgets he already had at his disposal. As a result preparations were slow and resulted in weakening of other points of defence. On 10 July it was approved to transport cannon, ammunition and other necessities from Delft to Bergen op Zoom, as well as from Dordrecht to 's Hertogenbosch.

The finally active Batavian attitude changed the view Brune had of them, as shown in a letter he wrote on 19 July to the *Commissaire-Ordonnateur en Chef de l'Armée de Hollande*

---

23 *Arrangements préliminaires pour la défense de la République batave, concertés, par les Ministres de la Marine, de la Guerre, le Général en chef Brune et le Général Daendels, en conséquence de l'arrêté du Directoire Exécutif batave du 28 Juin 1799*, in Koolemans Beijnen, 'Krijgsgeschiedkundige studie', 1893, pp.450-451.
24 See Appendix V.

(Chief Intendant) Blanchard in Paris: 'I am glad that the Dutch are beginning to fear the enemy that threatens them; they take measures, awakening from their natural lethargy'.[25] On the other hand, the Batavian government was under no illusions about additional French support in case of an invasion; they knew all too well that the French Republic had it hands full, being attacked by major armies themselves which of course would always be French priority. One could conclude from the slow response of the Batavian government that they did not spend much money on defence before July, but that is not the case. With a population of about 1,880,000, annual expenses were nearly 80 million Dutch guilders. Of these, over 20 million was spent on the army and the fortifications; nearly 13 and a half million on the navy. Regarding the threat of an invasion, additional measures had been taken. By decree of 27 April, two million Dutch guilders were allocated to augment the army and to improve fortifications; by decree of 23 July, 500,000 Dutch guilders to organise the *Gewapende Burgermacht*; and by decree of 16 August 100,000 Dutch guilders for constructing new telegraphs along the coast. The day on which the invasion materialised (24 August), another five million Dutch guilders were allocated for the army.

Allocating money was one thing, but it had to be found first. The decrees on levies on income and possessions have already been lined out, but to obtain the money would take time, which was quickly running out by now. News of the upcoming invasion became more frequent and detailed. Although information about a possible participation of Russian troops was less concrete and sometimes contradictory, news about the British preparations was made public every day, as for example in the political newspaper *Nouvelles Politiques publiées à Leyde*, which is the continuation of the famous *Gazette de Leyde*:

> Letter of London of 18th June, about the labour with the utmost zeal, in Portsmouth & in other places, on the preparations for the expedition plans on the continent: It will be commanded by the Generals Ralph Abercrombie & Stuart; & embarkation must take place in the course of July. The equipment in Portsmouth consists of 4 large Frigates, 6 Flutes, 4 Cutters, and a huge number of Transports.[26]

On 4 July, a letter from the Batavian Commissioner van Aller in Elsinore to the Batavian ambassador Johnson in Copenhagen contained the following report:

> By two skippers, in 10 days from Petersburg, we received information that in Cronstadt is worked night and day to equip the fleet. Seven ships of the line should already be prepared; several small vessels are also being prepared and the English Captain Popham was with another officer in Cronstadt to make arrangements for the embarkation of the troops, of which is publicly said amount 41,000 men which will land in Lübeck.
>
> P.S. Yesterday evening another skipper arrived, telling that 10 ships of the line full of troops have sailed from Cronstadt. They had the lower layer of guns not on

---

25 Koolemans Beijnen, 'Krijgsgeschiedkundige studie', 1892, p.641.
26 *Nouvelles Politiques, publiées à Leyde* (Leyden : Abraham Blussé, 1799), 2 July 1799.

board, to be able to stow away the troops better. The amount is estimated at 8,000 men and more would quickly follow; it is believed their destination is Lübeck.[27]

On 9 July, a letter from B.E. Abbema in Hamburg:

> I received message from ambassador Johnson in Copenhagen, about the sailing of the Russian fleet from 10 ships of the line and 8,000 men troops, destined for Lübeck, which however according to information of the count van Bernsdorff in Lauenburg, from which a small point reaches to the Baltic Sea, would land near Travemünde, to march through that land and Hannover to their destination. This small army would for sure not be able to force the line of neutrality, and is also not agreed with the Prussians. In short I will have more important information.[28]

Also 9 July, again a letter from the Batavian Commissioner van Aller in Elsinore:

> Regarding the English, I believe more and more, that they will look for our northern islands, especially Ameland, the coasts of Groningen or Friesland, especially because here the Russian expedition will be easiest combined with the English ones; because however much and continuously in Lübeck the forthcoming arrival of the Russian fleet and transports with troops is disseminated, I believe this is only a ruse, to cover up the real intention.[29]

On 11 July, a letter from Naval Minister Spoors to the *Uitvoerend Bewind*:

> General Brune has informed me this morning about a report from general Desjardins, commanding in Zeeland, stating that the English are completing the particular embarkation in Southampton, an a report, in which is stated, that the fishermen of Schouwen are moving on board of armed English sloops from time to time, and that one of these has received information that the English would direct 40 of their warships against Texel and two, accompanied by four Russian warships, against Goeree.[30]

On 13 July news about the Russians also became more clear. On that day, Daendels wrote a letter to Dumonceau, ending with: 'About the rumours of a disembarkation of Russian troops in Lubeck, I can inform you that our resident in Hamburg knows with certainty from his correspondence, that in the port of Cronstadt only 11 ships of the line are equipped and that no preparations for embarking troops are made there, as well as no means for that purpose are present'. However, before sending off this letter, Daendels added: 'After writing this I learned that this morning official reports have arrived about the arrival of 11 Russian

---

27 Koolemans Beijnen, 'Krijgsgeschiedkundige studie', 1893, p.678.
28 Koolemans Beijnen, 'Krijgsgeschiedkundige studie', 1893, p.678.
29 Koolemans Beijnen, 'Krijgsgeschiedkundige studie', 1893, pp.678-679.
30 Koolemans Beijnen, 'Krijgsgeschiedkundige studie', 1893, p 677.

ships of the line in Reval with 8,000 men of troops, to sail west and south after having taking care of some business or maybe embarking more troops. *Gare la Bombe!*[31]

Then again a letter from Ambassador Johnson in Copenhagen:

> News from the Baltic, about the continuing extensive preparations, made in the Russian harbours for the known expedition. Then it is difficult to make from the stream of reports, which are very exaggerated, a just estimation of the correct number of ships and the strength of the troops, which will be used for this upcoming expedition. The result of the most matching information, which I incessantly try to gather, is this: The Russian fleet in Reval consists of not more than 12 ships of the line and a few frigates. About the number of transport ships to carry the troops one has whatsoever no conclusive information; the last reports from the Baltic say nothing about this matter, regardless that one estimated those at 30, and it is probable, that there will be no other ships to carry these troops, as which came from England a few days ago and passed the Sound. The strength of the troops is according to the most matching reports about 20,000 men. Last night the English ship *Coromandel* arrived in Elseneur, pierced for 54 pieces, but armed *en flute*. One says this vessel is a former East Indiaman, which has no other use then transporting troops, for which purpose it will join the English ships in Cronstadt or Reval.[32]

This was followed on the same day by a letter from the Batavian *chargé d'affaires* Bourdeaux in Berlin:

> The Hereditary Prince of Orange has these days made fruitless attempts for half an hour to persuade the King himself to adopt the interests of his House common with England and Russia. It is said that the prince wants to leave under the pretext of going to England to his father, but in fact to join the Russian Army, which is intended to act against us. The mission of Stamford to Petersburg must have related to this. It has not had the approbation of the king, which has declared these days, never to compete to oppress us; but on the contrary to make every effort to effectuate our most perfect independence and to confirm this. It is for this disposition that we owe, that the Russian troops would not be disembarked at Lubeck initially to march against us, these must now be picked up by British transport ships and taken to the North Sea.[33]

Preparations Against Invasion

It was by now certain that an invasion would take place, but it was not clear where the British really would land. Taking into account the ports where the British transport ships were gathering, a landing was expected in Zeeland near the mouth of the River Scheldt,

---

31 Koolemans Beijnen, 'Krijgsgeschiedkundige studie', 1893, pp.572-573. '*Gare la Bombe!*' signifies, 'Be on your guard!'
32 Letter of 27 July 1799 from Johnson to the Batavian Minister of Foreign Affairs van der Goes, in: Koolemans Beijnen, 'Krijgsgeschiedkundige studie', 1894, pp.552-553.
33 Vreede, *Geschiedenis der Diplomatie,* 2nd part, 1st piece, p.48.

THE FRANCO-BATAVIAN RESPONSE TO THE THREAT 113

or on the islands of Voorne or Goeree in the Rhine–Meuse delta. On the other hand, it was possible that the Russians would land in Friesland or Groningen. This was based on the fact that supplies were collected at Bremen and the Orangists gathering in Lingen, to invade the Batavian Republic in co-operation with the Russians. Instead of concentrating his troops, Brune spread them over the whole of the Batavian Republic, in order to defend all conspicuous landing places (Zeeland, Voorne/Goeree, North-Holland, and Groningen). This was also done to prevent possible Orangist uprisings. As already explained, the French 3e Division in Zeeland was by far the strongest, as an attack on Zeeland was regarded as the most obvious and threatening for the French Republic. The 2e Division was positioned around the mouth of the Meuse, while the weak 1er Division was positioned behind these divisions around Utrecht in order to provide quick support when necessary. Another measure that Brune took was to appoint French commanders to the strategic fortresses and cities in the Batavian Republic: *Chef de Brigade* Cantagrelle in Breda, *Adjudant-Général* Lejeune in Grave, *Chef de Bataillon* Soullain in Gorcum, *Chef de Bataillon* Charpignon in Hellevoetsluis, *Adjutant-Général Chef de Brigade* Malher in Nijmegen, *Chef d'Escadron* Villantrois in Rotterdam, *Chef de Bataillon* Pecheloche in 's Hertogenbosch and *Chef de Bataillon* Massabeau in The Hague.

In South Holland were also present both Waldeck regiments (of which the 2nd Regiment would move to Delfzijl later) and the Regiment Saxen-Gotha, German regiments in Batavian pay. Both divisions of the Batavian field army were positioned in the northern provinces. The 1e Bataafsche Divisie of 10,952 men, commanded by *Lieutenant-Generaal* Herman Daendels, defended Holland. The 2e Bataafsche Divisie of about 11,900 men, commanded by *Lieutenant-Generaal* Jean Dumonceau, was spread across the provinces Friesland, Groningen, Drenthe, Overijssel, and Gelderland. Apparently it was Daendels who already in May seriously counted on a landing in the north of Holland, supported in this thought by *Generaal-Major* van Guèricke and the senior naval officers:

> The *Generaal-Major* van Guèricke together with the heads of the fleet at Texel, are of the opinion that an enemy could complete a landing on our shores in one day during the impending favourable season. So it will be necessary to concentrate the brigade of this *generaal-major* more, and while this is so close to the coast and the places where a landing presupposed would be easiest, it cannot be done by lack of cantonments. So, as in the previous year, two infantry battalions at Den Helder will have to form camps, to which I have designated the 1st and 2nd battalion of the 7e Halve Brigade with your approval. But these battalions and the 3rd Battalion of the same halve brigade stationed at Den Helder will have to be provided with food and to that end, if approved by you, the Commissioner of War Rittner should be ordered to send tents and necessities to Den Helder for both battalions mentioned and to provide straw, wood, bread, meat and gin in order to take care of the three battalions of the 7e Halve Brigade and the 2e Bataljon Jagers, and to make the necessary arrangements for this purpose, in consultation with the *Generaal-Major* van Guèricke in Alkmaar. Furthermore, the 2e Bataljon Jagers will march from Hoorn to Schagen and the Zijpe, and from there detach two companies to occupy the observation posts along the coast. The 1e Bataljon Jagers and the 2e compagnie Rijdende Artillerie should move from Haarlem to Alkmaar to be garrisoned there;

if this transfer is approved by you, I request you to authorise the necessary orders to this purpose, as well as to instruct the commissioner of war and to delegate him to Alkmaar immediately.[34]

A letter from Daendels to Dumonceau of 10 August, explains the strategy the Franco-Batavians would use when the invasion had taken place:

> We are now, my dear general, almost certain that, the moment the Russian transport fleet has passed the Kattegat, the attack on our commonwealth will be executed with 40,000 men, and in order to be able to act with success against this force, it has been agreed to unite the French and Batavian forces into one mass, as soon as the enemy has succeeded to land the majority of his troops.[35]

For the purpose of moving the troops quickly to the landing site, inland waterway vessels lay prepared in Zeeland at the mouth of the River Meuse and in the ports of Hoorn, Enkhuizen, and Medemblik. For transport over land, wagons had been made available. Moving troops quickly to any threatened point was possible as long as the Franco-Batavians were masters of the Zuiderzee. They would remain masters as long as the Batavian fleet at Texel, along with the flat-bottomed vessels at Amsterdam, were present. On the 13th, while unknown to the Batavians the 1st British Division had already sailed, Daendels again wrote to Dumonceau, in compliance with the strategy outlined:

> [W]e strongly believe that one of the attacks of the enemy will be directed against Groningen, to become master of Delfzijl, in order to embark there the Artillery, horses and luggage with ease; if you will be able to hold up the enemy, I will come to your aid with 17 battalions, as soon as it is certain that no attack on North and South Holland will take place, and in case the enemy has disembarked his whole force, we will easily be capable of not only pushing him back, even with a bit of luck being able to prevent him to return.[36]

Of course all other defence measures that would be expected were taken: provisioning of fortresses, preparation of hospitals, preparing the train, provisioning the magazines, preparing inundations and so forth. The effect of all these measures will be related when they contribute to this account of the campaign. On 14 August, all unit commanders were ordered to recall all officers and men detached or on leave.

---

34   Letter of 18 May 1799 from *Lieutenant-Generaal* Herman Daendels to the minister of war, in: Koolemans Beijnen, 'Krijgsgeschiedkundige studie', 1891, p.363.
35   Koolemans Beijnen, 'Krijgsgeschiedkundige studie', 1894, p.436.
36   Koolemans Beijnen, 'Krijgsgeschiedkundige studie', 1894, p.437.

The Defence of Holland

To understand the way the battles and fighting took place, as well as the troubles the armies had to cope with, it is necessary to have a look at the landscape of North Holland. The beaches in Holland are sandy. No rocks or stones are found on Dutch beaches. The width of these beaches differs, not only with the tide. On the part of the coast where the British invasion took place, the width of the beach was not more than a hundred metres. However, especially on the part between Calandsoog and Petten, the beach was much wider, at places even more than one kilometre. Along these beaches there is a range of dunes. The Dutch dunes are best compared with the Sahara desert: hills consisting of loose sand. In some places there is some vegetation, especially inland, consisting of beach grass and thorny bushes. Height of the dunes is normally 15-25 metres, but at places, where the dunes are more extended, for example west of Schoorl and Bergen, the height of the dunes can be over 40 metres. Because the wind usually comes from the west, the eastern slopes are normally steep and the western slopes more flat. Movement through the dunes is difficult, fatiguing and very slow; for the artillery it was nearly impossible. Keeping the right direction is difficult, especially if the dunes are much extended. In addition, advancing troops would have to take special care for their flanks, because sight is limited and such troops could be attacked in their flank or rear very easily.

The only great marsh in this campaign was the Koegras. Because this is a salt marsh, tide had a direct influence on the water level and the accessibility of this terrain. In addition, because of the tide it was intersected by many streamlets. Beside this marsh some parts of the polders were also marshy, especially near the shores of the lakes, and some polders were inundated by the Franco-Batavians.

The polders are typical of the landscape in most parts of the Netherlands. In earlier times, this part of the country was looking much as the Koegras: parts were covered by the sea at high tide, or even constantly flooded. The first polders were made dry behind the dunes along the North Sea coast and gradually extended to the east by making dry new parts. How did a polder arise? First, a dike was thrown up, around the terrain that would be the polder. The earth from these dikes came from both sides of the dike. In this way on both sides of the dike, a canal was created. On these dikes, windmills were built. These mills pumped the water out of the canal inside the polder, into the canal at the outside. In this way, the polder was made dry. Now the whole polder was provided with parallel ditches, to lower the water level even more. Very fertile clay-ground became ready to be used for agriculture. The crops that grew in these polders were mainly potatoes, corn (growing to about two metres high at that time) and grass. In the vicinity of villages and cities, there were more different crops. Movement through the polders was very difficult. Especially in bad weather, the clay would hamper all movement and the situation would deteriorate rapidly if many men used the same part of the terrain. After some time, the trampling of all these feet would create a complete marsh that would suck the shoes of the feet of the soldiers. The fact that many ditches intersected the polders would hamper movement even more. However, normally these ditches would be fordable at most places. This could not be said of the canals on both sides of the dikes. These were five to 20 metres wide and not fordable. Movement of cavalry and especially artillery was restricted to the roads. Nearly all roads were on top of the dikes and if an army wanted to advance, these were the only ones to be used. Because there was a canal on both sides of the dike, it was impossible to deploy if contact with the enemy was made. Further, the defender could make an attack or advance even more difficult by making cuts in the dikes, destroying the windmills, and inundating the polders. Even if the water level in the polders would only be inches high, crossing the polders would become impossible because the clay would became soggy and the ditches invisible and non-fordable.

The villages in this part of the Netherlands were only a few hundred years old at the most. The villages consisted of ribbon development: houses along a road and some small and short side-roads. These houses were mainly made of wood and sometimes bricks were used. The gardens normally had no walls, but hedges, fences, or ditches as boundaries. The villages behind the dunes were on higher ground and much older. There were more roads and more and bigger gardens and orchards. Examples of such villages are the Egmond villages, Bergen and Schoorl.

The cities in North-Holland were in decline at this time. Medemblik, Hoorn, Alkmaar, Purmerend, Edam, Monnikendam, Haarlem, and Amsterdam were more or less fortified, but these fortifications were neglected and in a bad state. Because of this, it was for example impossible, but also tactically not very useful, for the Franco-Batavians to try to hold Alkmaar. Den Helder and Beverwijk were not fortified.

Den Helder was the major naval port of the Batavian Republic. Although there were ample defences for a naval attack, defences for an attack overland were inadequate. At the beginning of 1799 the roadstead of Texel and the Nieuwe Diep harbour were defended by seven coastal batteries:

- Battery *De Revolutie*, armed with 28 24pdr cannon and twelve 16pdr howitzers, all on coastal gun carriages, the biggest and main battery at the Kaaphoofd defending all the entrances from the North Sea to the Marsdiep. The cannon covered the canals preventing enemy ships from entering, while the howitzers had to protect the battery against an attack with sloops across the shallows. This battery was just in time closed at the reversed side and five 8pdr and 11 6pdr cannon had arrived, however these were still without ammunition on the day the British landing took place;
- Battery *De Gelijkheid*, between Kleine Keeten and Kijkduin, armed with seven 24pdr cannon to cover the Schulpegat canal;
- Battery *De Vrijheid*, southwest of Kijkduin, armed with five 24pdr cannon also to cover the Schulpegat canal;
- Battery *De Broederschap*, just north of Kijkduin, armed with three 24pdr cannon also to cover the Schulpegat canal;
- Battery *De Constitutie*, on the sea dike north of Den Helder, armed with six 24pdr cannon to cover the roadstead of Texel. This battery was completely open on the reversed side and vulnerable to an attack over land;
- Battery *De Ondeelbaarheid*, at the angle of the Barendskribbing, armed with seven 24pdr cannon, also covered the roadstead of Texel. This battery was protected from a land attack by a retrenchment, however it was not closed at the reversed side;
- Battery *De Unie*, at the entrance of the Nieuwe Diep and protecting the entrance of this harbour, was armed with five 24pdr cannon and six mortars. This battery was protected from a land attack by palisades, however it was also not closed at the reversed side.

THE FRANCO-BATAVIAN RESPONSE TO THE THREAT 117

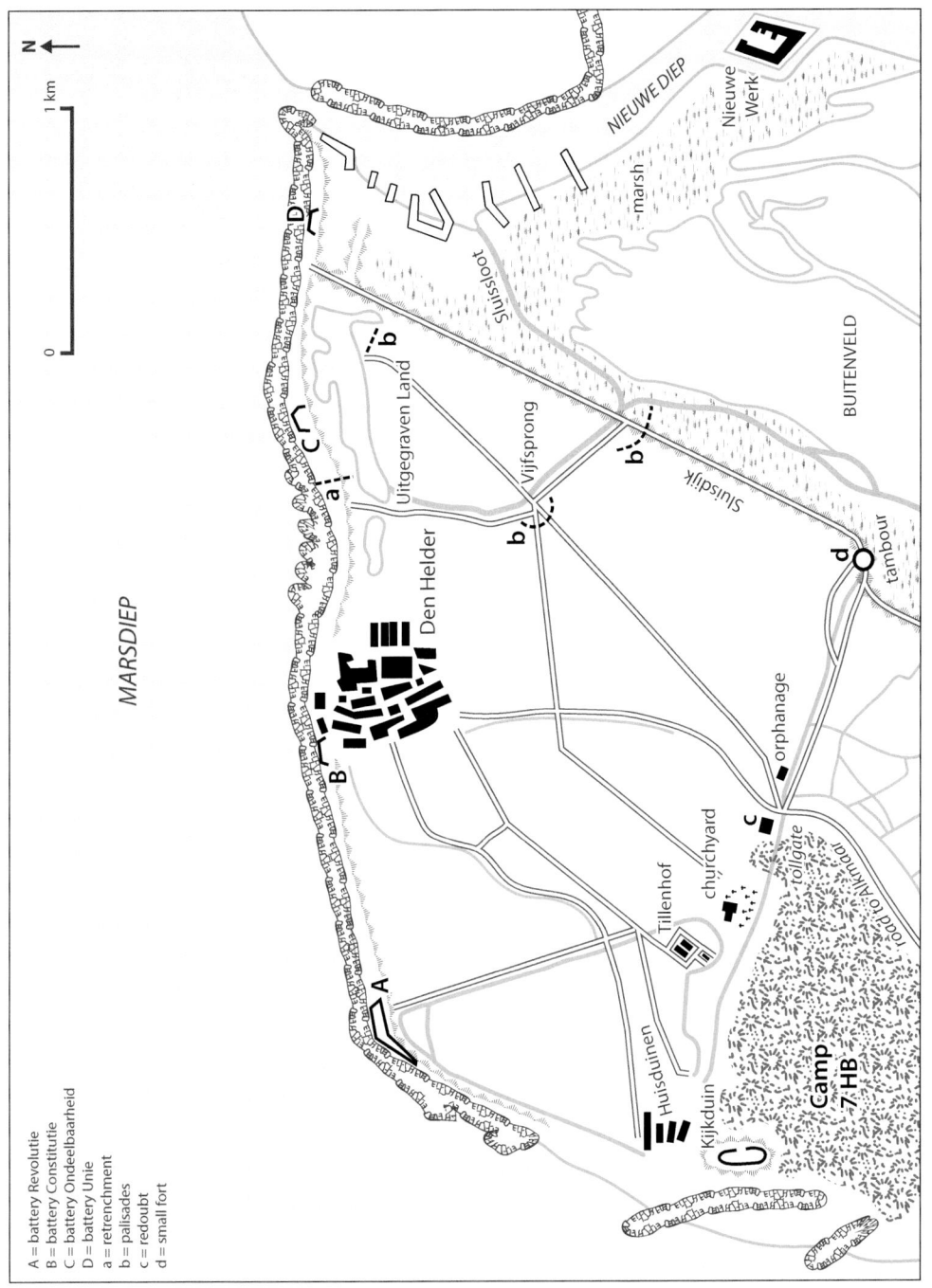

Map 4 The defences at Den Helder.

These batteries were carefully positioned and fully capable to fend off any naval attack directed at the Texel roadstead. At the moment of the invasion, the gunners at the batteries were commanded by *Lieutenant-Colonel* ten Cate of the artillery. There were however not enough gunners present. On 1 May there were only 151 gunners in Den Helder, too few to man the battery *De Revolutie* adequately, let alone all other batteries as well. As only smaller ships would be able to navigate the Schulpegat, on 8 May Daendels made the decision to dismantle the batteries *De Gelijkheid, De Vrijheid*, and *De Broederschap*. A great weakness of the remaining batteries, except for *De Revolutie*, was that they were not closed at the reversed side, making them vulnerable for an attack over land. This was what happened in 1799, causing Daendels to abandon Den Helder and its defences after the British landing had succeeded. Most historians point out that there were no defences at all against an attack over land, but this is not completely correct. There were some defence works, but these were totally inadequate against a full scale attack:

- To protect the Nieuwe Diep from an attack over land from the west, a retrenchment was constructed across the sea dike just west of the battery *De Ondeelbaarheid*, armed with four 8pdr cannon;
- Palisades had been constructed south of the Uitgegraven Land and along the Sluisdijk, behind a ditch 15 to 18 feet wide, the dike itself serving as a retrenchment this way. In front of the Sluissloot the dike was protected by a tamboer (a small fortification for direct defence of an entry) with a 3pdr field cannon;
- Palisades at the Vijfsprong;
- A redoubt at the tollgate near the orphanage, armed with four 8pdr cannon.

There were plans to strengthen the reinforcements on the land side substantially but the British landing took place too early for them to be executed.

7

The British Landing: Battle of Calandsoog 27 August

The Arrival of the British Invasion Fleet

On 13 August, after a gale had ceased, the transport fleet with Abercromby's division set sail under a favourable wind. A calm succeeded it and during the remainder of Tuesday the 13th and the whole of that night, the fleet covered about 50 miles. Then it became stormy again. During their journey the transport fleet encountered the Anglo-Russian North Sea fleet on the 15th and Admiral Duncan separated himself and joined the expedition with his flagship *Kent*, although Mitchell still remained in command of the expedition fleet. The day after setting sail a council of war was held. Although the council preferred an invasion at the mouth of the River Meuse, Abercromby and Mitchell made the decision to land at the Holland peninsula near Den Helder, in order to capture or destroy the Batavian fleet. This place was also chosen because coastal defences were virtually non-existent on this part of the coast and the cities were not fortified in this part of the Batavian Republic. Further, once ashore, Abercromby would possess a good harbour to disembark the remainder of his troops and the necessary supplies safely. In addition, he would find on the peninsula good positions to defend until the Russians and additional British troops arrived.[1] With the British navy being master of the seas, such positions could not be turned by the Franco-Batavians and would be easy to defend with the troops at his disposal. A disadvantage was the fact that Holland was a Patriot bulwark, so chances on co-operation by the population would be much smaller as would be the case if the invasion would have taken place at the Rhine-Meuse delta or in the northern provinces.

Major General Moore wrote in his diary on 21 August:

> The weather since the second day after we sailed has been so stormy and bad, that it has been impossible to approach the coast. The fleet continued to cruise off and on. Yesterday the weather cleared and was very fine, and this morning it became

---

[1] According to Reese, the decision to land in North Holland had already been made well before the fleet departed from Great Britain: Paul P. Reese, *"The Ablest Man in the British Army": The Life and Career of General Sir John Hope* (Florida State University, 2007), pp.38-43.

almost calm. A signal was made pretty early for the Generals and Captains of the fleet. When I went on board the Isis I found the original plan was changed. The difficulties attending the landing at Goeree and Voorne induced both the Admiral and Sir Ralph to give it up, and they determined to attack the Texel. The army lands, it is hoped, to-morrow. We are now standing for the shore, and shall anchor this night or to-morrow at daylight. The disposition is to land to the south of the Helder.[2]

From 15 to 20 August weather was stormy, with wind gusts and rain showers. The fleet was widely scattered and separated. Finally on 20 August the wind became favourable and the fleet collected again; although many ships were damaged none were lost. Mitchell received much praise for the way he managed to sail the huge fleet to the Batavian coast:

It is impossible to do too much justice to the manner in which our fleet has been conducted by Admiral Mitchell. He has brought us all safe through a very heavy tempest, which, when the number is considered, reflects great praise on his judgment and attention. Our fleet consists of one hundred and sixty-six sail, with troops; eleven luggers, and fifty flat-bottomed boats for the purpose of disembarking the troops. To these are to be added the Cynthia's convoy of twenty-four ships with cavalry, with the cutters, making in all two hundred sail; and yet… there is not one missing, nor out of her station, in the whole fleet![3]

The British Secretary of State for War Henry Dundas had also much praise for Mitchell, giving the following speech to the House of Commons on 16 September 1799:

The Armament destined for Holland sailed from hence with very fair weather, which continued for two or three days; but early on the morning of the third day there arose a very heavy, and, for the time of the year, a very uncommon storm. In this storm this gallant Admiral had the conduct of an armament of two hundred transports of various descriptions, subject to no military discipline, from the nature of things; and in this condition that Admiral conducted the whole of this mass for ten or twelve days; he kept them together, immense as they were, and brought them in safety to their place of landing – an event that could not have taken place, but from consummate skill, unremitting perseverance, and great exertion.[4]

On 20 August the first ships of the British transport fleet reached the Texel estuary. Of course the Batavians, expecting them somewhere on the Batavian coast, immediately raised the alarm. Next day, the majority of the ships had arrived. *Schout-bij-Nacht* Story, commanding the Batavian fleet at Texel, wrote to the Batavian Naval Minister Spoors:

2   Maurice (ed.), *Diary of Sir John Moore*, Vol.I, p.341.
3   Anonymous letter in the *Naval Chronicle*, Vol.II, p.348.
4   *Naval Chronicle*, Vol.II, p.435.

> Right at this moment I returned from Kijkduin, from where I observed the English fleet about which I already reported to you this noon, a very considerable transport fleet, 150 partially three-, partially two-masters. *Generaal-Major* van Guèricke, who I met there, assured me to have counted over a hundred; *Capitein* van de Capellen has even counted 140, while the signal men assure that there number is even bigger, if not 200. I myself was, because of their huge number, not able to count them more precise; nevertheless I certainly dare to report to you between 140 to 150, if not more. When we left Kijkduin, the fleet hoisted more sail and moved west, across the Texel.[5]

Although the exact destination was still unknown. The Batavian Minister of War Pijman wrote to *Lieutenant-Generaal* Dumonceau on 22 August:

> Tidings of an English fleet with a huge number of transport ships before our coasts have been confirmed from all sides. So we have to expect a landing. The *general en chef* has taken the necessary precautions in order to, too the place where it will take place in earnest, send the necessary reinforcements very quickly.[6]

That same day at daybreak the transport fleet was sighted lying at anchor, two miles west of the Haaks, a huge sandbank west of the Schulpegat channel which was the access to the Texel roadstead and Den Helder. A short while later the fleet set sail again, worked its way closer to the coast and again dropped anchor. Shortly before noon, Vice Admiral Mitchell dispatched a rowing boat under a flag of truce, which was taken in tow to the Batavian flagship *Washington* by the advice-vessel *Coburg* of the pilot Duinker. According to *Schout-bij-Nacht* Story's own account, he was surprised by its arrival but had no choice than to receive the officers on board of this boat: Lieutenant Colonel Maitland, who was Abercromby's secretary; Captain Winthrop, commander of the *Circe*, and Lieutenant Collier of the British flagship *Isis*. Story received these officers in his cabin, where they delivered to him a letter from Admiral Duncan:

> Sir, More than 20,000 men being at this moment disembarked at the Helder, who will be followed by many others; you have now a favourable opportunity of manifesting your zeal for your legitimate sovereign the Prince of Orange, by declaring for him, together with all the ships which may chuse [sic] to follow your example. All those who shall declare for him in like manner, hoisting the Orange flag, shall be considered as allies and friends. As soon as I shall have made Sir Ralph Abercromby, commander in chief of the British land forces, and Admiral Mitchell, who commands the naval part of the expedition under me, acquainted with this declaration; all the ships which are desirous of so doing, may come out and join me; they will be treated with the most sincere friendship as allies, and will be received in the bosom of the English fleet, with which they may remain until they shall

---

5 Letter of 21 August 6 o'clock in the evening, from *Schout-bij-Nacht* Story on the Vlieter on the flagship *Washington* to the Batavian Naval Minister Spoors, in Koolemans Beijnen, 'Krijgsgeschiedkundige studie', 1895, p.115.
6 Koolemans Beijnen, 'Krijgsgeschiedkundige studie', 1894, p.450.

receive the commands of the Prince of Orange, with respect to the conduct which they are to pursue.

P. S. The bearer of this letter, Captain Winthrop, is commissioned to assure the officers of the Batavian fleet of my esteem for them.[7]

The statement that 20,000 men had already been landed was clearly not correct. When the letter found its way in the newspapers, producing an 'unfavourable impression on the minds of the people in the United Provinces', the British hastened to state that the letter was a false copy, sending a statement to be published in the Hamburg newspaper.[8] True or not, Story's answer to the above was as to be expected:

Admiral, I should be unworthy of Lord Duncan, and should forfeit the esteem of every honest man, were I to accept the proposal you make me. I know the duty which I owe to the flag I obey, and to my country: were your force double, my sentiment would still remain the same. Your lordship may therefore expect from me a defence worthy of my nation, and of my honour. I shall however, immediately send your summons to my government, and if you please to await its determination, I will inform you of the result.[9]

Maitland additionally told Story that he also had a letter from Abercromby to the commander at Den Helder, which he ought to deliver personally. Story refused to give him permission to go to Den Helder, however he sent for the commander, *Colonel* Gilquin, to come on board of the *Washington*. While waiting for his arrival, the British officers were placed under care of the commanding officer of the *Washington*, *Capitein* van Capellen, who spoke English. This did not prevent Maitland from communicating with other officers of the ship, handing over a proclamation from Abercromby. About 2 o'clock, *Colonel* Gilquin, accompanied by *Lieutenant-Colonel* Verhorst, arrived on the *Washington*. They received a letter from Abercromby urging Gilquin to surrender immediately, accompanied by two proclamations from Abercromby (in Dutch and English) and the Stadtholder (in Dutch):

Lieutenant General Sir Ralph Abercromby being entrusted by his Majesty, the King of Great Britain, the ancient and good ally of the United Provinces, with the command of a body of British troops to be employed in delivering these provinces from the degrading tyranny of the French republic, has received his Majesty's command to make this public and explicit declaration of the intention of his Majesty, and of the august sovereigns who are united with him in this great work.

It is not as enemies, but as friends and deliverers, that the British troops enter the territory of the United Provinces. It is to rescue the inhabitants of this once free

---

7   Original letter in English in Isaac Schomberg, *Naval Chronology; or, an Historical Summary of Naval & Maritime Events, from the Time of The Romans to the Treaty of Peace 1802* (London: T. Egerton, 1802), Vol.III, p 225; Walsh, *Narrative*, pp.152-153.
8   Letter in English of 10 September 1799 from James Crawfurd to Grenville, in Colenbrander, *Gedenkstukken*, Vol.III, pp.396-397.
9   Schomberg, *Naval Chronology*, Vol.III, p.229; Walsh, *Narrative*, p.153.

and happy country from the oppression under which they now groan; to protect their religion from the intolerant and persecuting spirit of infidelity and atheism; to deliver their civil government from the despotism of a rapacious anarchy, and to re-establish their ancient liberty and independence, by restoring to them the benefits of that constitution, for which under the auspices of the illustrious house of Orange, their ancestors sought and conquered; and in the enjoyment of which they so long flourished in friendship and alliance with Great Britain.

For this object, and under the same auspices, his Majesty doubts not that the ancient valour and energy of the Dutch nation will be now exerted with the same spirit and success. The hand of Providence has already shewn itself in the deliverance of a great part of Europe, from those miseries in which the arms and principles of the French republicanism have for a time been permitted to involve it. The force which his Majesty has confided to Lieut. Gen. Abercromby, and those which his Majesty's allies have destined to the same object, are abundantly sufficient for the protection of those who shall stand forth in the cause of their country. It is principally by the efforts of the Dutch nation, that these sovereigns wish the deliverance of the republic to be accomplished. In the steps that are to lead to this salutary end, his Majesty earnestly recommends to all the inhabitants of provinces, union and concord. Forgiveness of the past, and a determined resolution to protect against every tumultuous and vindictive excess, the lives and properties of their fellow citizens, even those whose errors of misconduct have contributed to the calamities of their country; but whom the irresistible conviction of experience shall now unite in this great cause.

On these principles, and in this spirit, the British army will conduct itself among a people whom Englishmen have long been accustomed to regard as their friends and allies; but if from henceforth there shall be sound any Dutchmen, who by their adherence to the oppressors of their country, at the moment, when by the blessing of God, its deliverance is at hand, shall shew themselves unworthy of the blessings of tranquility, of lawful government, and of religious and civil liberty; those and those alone, his Majesty's troops will consider and treat as decided and irreconcilable enemies, not only to his Majesty, and his allies; but to the prosperity of their own country, and to the general interests and safety of Europe.[10]

We, William, by the Grace of God, Prince of Orange and Nassau, Hereditary Stadtholder, &c. &c. &c. to all those to whom these presents shall come greeting.

Dear Countrymen,
The long wished for moment when you are at last to be delivered from so many calamities under which you have suffered for more than four years past, is, we hope, arrived, and we enjoy the satisfaction again to address you under that pleating prospect. It would be superfluous to enumerate the different hardships under which you have groaned ever since the violence you suffered in consequence of the French

---

10 Schomberg, *Naval Chronology*, Vol.III, pp.226-227; Walsh, *Narrative*, pp.159-160.

invasion, and the events which have followed it. If cruel experience has made you feel them but too severely; and if our ardent wishes could have been sooner fulfilled, you would have been relieved long ago from that intolerable burthen. We have been but too long obliged to confine ourselves to deploring your fate in silence, without having it in our power to alter it; at last that time is come: His Majesty the King of Great Britain, moved by his affection and friendship towards the Republic of the United Provinces, and pitying your misfortunes, has taken the generous resolution, as soon as the general circumstances of Europe have allowed it, to employ in concert with the allies vigorous measures for your deliverance. The military force which is now sent for that purpose, is to be followed by still more numerous troops.

The object of this expedition is made known to you in the name of his Britannic Majesty, by the commander of the first body of troops, which is to open this glorious career. Those troops do not come to you as enemies, but as friends, and deliverers, in order to rescue you from the odious oppression under which you are held by the French government, and by the French troops; and to restore you to the enjoyment of your religion and liberty; those invaluable blessings for which with the divine assistance your and our own ancestors sought and conquered! Hesitate not, therefore brave inhabitants of the United Provinces, to meet and assist your deliverers; receive them among you as friends and protectors of the happiness and welfare of your country; let every difference of political sentiments and opinions vanish before this great object; do not suffer the spirit of party, nor even the sense of the wrongs you may have suffered, to induce you to commit any acts of revenge or persecution. Let your hands and your hearts be united, in order to repel the common enemy, and to re-establish the liberty and independence of our common country. Let your deliverance be as much as possible your own work: you see already, and you will experience it still more in suture, that you may depend on being vigorously and powerfully assisted. As soon as the first efforts which are making towards your delivery, shall have acquired some consistency, our dearly beloved son, the hereditary Prince of Orange, who is in possession of our entire confidence, and is deserving of yours, and who is perfectly well acquainted with our intentions, will join you, put himself at your head, and following the steps of our illustrious ancestors, spare neither his property nor his life, in order to assist you, and for your sake in bringing this great undertaking to a successful issue. We ourselves also, will then as soon as circumstances shall allow it, proceed to join you. And as we have always considered our own happiness as inseparably connected with that of our dear country; we will then, after seeing your laws and privileges restored, and yourselves re-established in the possession of those benefits which belong to a free people, under a lawful government, make our greatest and heartfelt satisfaction consist (under the divine blessing); in the advancement of the public, and of the prosperity and welfare which formerly made our once happy country an object of admiration to the surrounding nations.[11]

---

11 Schomberg, *Naval Chronology*, Vol.III, pp.227-229; Walsh, *Narrative*, pp.160-162.

THE BRITISH LANDING: BATTLE OF CALANDSOOG 27 AUGUST

Not surprisingly, *Colonel* Gilquin also replied in the strongest words that he would never surrender, awaiting the arrival of the British with all confidence in his troops. The Batavian Minister of War Pijman informed *Lieutenant-Generaal* Dumonceau in a letter on 23 August:

> General Daendels has left for Den Helder at one o'clock tonight. Tidings, written there about midnight and just received, only report that this morning before eight o'clock no attack has to be expected. In the meantime, the commander of the fleet Story has received a message from the English Admiral Duncan and Colonel Gilquin a similar one from the English General Abercromby with enclosed proclamations and a publication of the Prince of Orange. Both *chefs* have, as to be expected from officers with honour, answered… We all agree unanimously, that the enemy will not continue cruising along our coasts, but will try to occupy a post. This will be most probably Den Helder, Delfzijl or Walcheren.[12]

The events described, and the appearance of the British fleet before Texel, made it very clear to the Franco-Batavians were the landing would take place and would give them five days to reinforce the troops already in North-Holland. However, Brune was still of the belief that the British appearance was only a feint and that the real attack would take place elsewhere, writing:

> The appearance of the enemy before the Texel, a demonstration which does require you to move your entire division to North Holland. However as it is possible that the enemy wants us to make the change, forcing us to make the wrong move, it is prudent, to disposition your troops in echelons, to be able to shift the defence line quickly.[13]

Therefore, no French reinforcements were sent to North Holland and for the time being Daendels was on his own to await the inevitable attack. In all haste orders were given to concentrate his 1st Batavian Division in North Holland: The 1/ and 2/1e Halve Brigade, the 1/ and 2/1e Regiment Zware Cavalerie and the artillery train with six 6pdr cannon from The Hague to Haarlem; the 3/1e Halve Brigade moved from Leiden to Alkmaar; the 1/4e Halve Brigade and 3/6e Halve Brigade from Amsterdam to Alkmaar; the half company of the 2e Compagnie Rijdende Artillerie from Haarlem to Alkmaar; and the Regiment Dragonders from Utrecht to Haarlem and from there to Schagerbrug. Daendels himself arrived in Schagerbrug on the 23rd, setting up headquarters here.[14]

On the 24th, in the camp at Huisduinen, a conference was held at which were present Daendels, *Schout-bij-Nacht* Story, the *Capiteins ter Zee* van Capellen, de Jong van Rodenburgh, van Braam, and Kolff, and the commander of the engineers *Lieutenant-Colonel* Krayenhoff. It was judged by these that the means of defence on land were insufficient to act in co-operation with the greatly outnumbered Batavian fleet counting just eight ships of the line, three frigates, and a sloop. According to Krayenhoff the naval captains

---

12   Koolemans Beijnen, 'Krijgsgeschiedkundige studie', 1894, p.451.
13   Order from Brune to Daendels, 23 August 1799, in Koolemans Beijnen, 'Krijgsgeschiedkundige studie', 1895, p.120.
14   For the composition of Daendels' 1e Bataafsche Divisie see Appendix VII.

were discouraged but no one mentioned the unreliability of their crews.[15] Further it was proposed, and agreed on, to block the entrance to the Texel roadstead, the Schulpegat, by sinking ships with ballast. Krayenhoff was ordered to bring the order to the flagship *Washington*, were he was met by many objections from the naval captains and pilots present. Finally, *Capitein-Lieutenant ter Zee* Buiskes was ordered to execute the plan and by the afternoon of the 26th five ships had been prepared. Sinking these ships at the right spot was, however, made impossible by the increasing west-north-western wind and the plan had to be abandoned, the appearance of the British fleet making another attempt impossible. In the evening, a British frigate sailed into the Schulpegat, ascertaining the range of its guns to the military camp of Huisduinen.

As already has been outlined, Lieutenant Colonel Maitland was able to speak with a number of officers on board of the *Washington*. This gave the British valuable information about the disposition of Batavian officers and the crews of the ships, as well as about the Batavian defences. Maitland reported verbally about his findings, also making notes for Abercromby. These notes were later forwarded to the British Secretary of State for War, Henry Dundas:

> Colonel Brownrigg has informed me, that you desire to have a copy of the notes which I made for Sir Ralph Abercromby on my return from the Helder the 22 August; that I may not lose time, I have the honor to inclose the original.
>
> You will remark in the notes, that I pass over the conversations which took place on board the Washington, purposely that the opinions and sentiments expressed by captains van Capellen, van Braam and de Jong generally in the presence of admiral Story might not become public, and those officers thereby endangered. To you in this letter, I apprehend I do right to inform you, that the above mentioned captains did declare their attachment to the Stadtholder and the former government, and their disgust at the present government and their French connection. They are all family men, and assigned that reason for their conduct, as having induced them, from want, to enter the service, and as binding them, by that forcible tie, to the most considerate use of their commands: least the vengeance which they should excite by risking a different way of acting, should fall on those whom they left in the power of the opposite party. I believe that subsequent events have confirmed the truth of what I have said.
>
> I saw but little of the commandant of the Helder, colonel Gilquin. There was nothing in his words or conduct to lead me to infer that he was attached to the Orange family and government.
>
> [Enclosed]
>
> NOTES ON BOARD H.M.'s SHIP THE ISIS 24 AUGUST 1799.
> On the 21 August directed by general Sir Ralph Abercromby to proceed to the Texel with a summons from him to the commanding officer of the Dutch troops at the Helder.

---

15 Krayenhoff, *Geschiedkundige*, pp.59-60.

The 22nd about 7 a.m. boarded a Dutch pilot boat, which came to receive us (captain Winthrop R.N., lieutenant Collier R.N., lieutenant colonel Maitland), being then about 2 miles South of Kijkdune. In this position I observed the whole coast before us to be very favorable for landing in tolerable fine weather, and with the wind which then blew, South West (1).

We got on board the *Washington* a little after 8 a.m., we remained until past two: full six hours. It was impossible to come away sooner, the flood tide setting in with a strong S.W. wind. This time was spent in conversation with admiral Story, captains van Capellen, de Jong, and van Braam. I believe I need not here detail the substance of their declarations, having already fully done it verbally.

I learned that the garrison of the Helder was 1300 men, encamped immediately in the rear of Kijkdune. That in 3 days they could assemble 7000 men, which number would be increased daily afterwards. That the Texel island has a very small garrison: the skipper of the boat who is a pilot, and lives on the island, said only 100 men.

The distance from the Texel island to where the body of the Dutch fleet lays in the Marsdiep, is too great to drive them from their station, if we possessed that island, unless by the heaviest mortars. I believe a battery of the heaviest mortars would prevent any shipping using the anchorage of the Marsdiep, but they could retire up the Nieuwediep. When on board the *Washington*, a schuyt arrived from the Eastward with men for the admiral's ship.

They knew of no movement whatever made by the Prussians, and did not seem to look for any. The boatmen, seven in number, who belonged to the pilot boat which carried us in (2), were apparently all very zealous in our favor. They asked us, if the Prince of Orange was on board our fleet; they received with great satisfaction the Orange ribbands we gave them (3), and with still greater 7 guineas which I gave them to drink his health, which however I did not do until after they had given captain Winthrop and lieutenant Collier every necessary information about the entrance into the Texel. They said all the inhabitants of the Helder were Orange men; that their distress was great for want of employment, not even being allowed to fish.

It was remarked, why did we not go to Groningen, where all the country would join us, rather than try North-Holland, where we should meet with the greatest opposition.

[Notes from Maitland:]
(1) Captain de Jong said that with the wind N. Of West, particularly N.W., the coast was very dangerous, having a heavy surf.
(2) There was a Dutch lieutenant with us.
(3) This was in returning when there was no Dutch officer present.[16]

---

16 Letter in English of 9 September 1799 from Lieutenant Colonel Maitland to Henry Dundas, in Colenbrander, *Gedenkstukken*, Vol.III, pp.393-394.

Despite the information about the disposition of the Batavian population in Groningen and Holland, the decision had already been made to land in Holland. The landing was planned for the 22nd and preparations were made for the landing, but a sudden storm prevented this. Towards the evening the wind shifted from the east to the southwest and commenced to blow heavily, so that the transport fleet was forced to weigh anchor in all haste and stand out to sea again:

> Every arrangement was thus admirably made. The whole fleet on Wednesday evening were at an anchor within two miles of the shore off a place called Kickdown [Kijkduin], the boats were in readiness to receive the troops. In short, we thought we had nothing to do but to step into them. Every one in the highest spirits and eager for the common cement of the business. At three o'clock on Thursday morning the drums in every ship and vessel in the fleet were heard beating to arms, and in a few minutes every one was ready. At eight o'clock, A. M. the signal was made from the Kent for the transports to get under weigh, and to proceed within half a mile of the shore, the tide not serving our purpose sooner. At this moment, big with expectation to us all, a flag of truce was seen standing into the Texel from our fleet. Its purpose, we learnt, was to apprise the Dutch of the true motives of our expedition – to rescue them from the tyranny of France, and restore their ancient and legitimate Government. The gun boats and other small vessels had taken their stations between the transports and the shore, and the men of war were just making sail to stand in, in line of battle; when the wind, which had been easterly, blowing a fine gentle breeze, shifted to the S.W. with every appearance of blowing weather again coming on. Most fortunately the fleet was partly under way, and the rest got so immediately, for at noon it came on to blow with as much violence as before, and continued to do so all that day and yesterday. Happily, however, the whole fleet again escaped without accident or damage.[17]

The weather remained bad for the next few days and by this time all the fresh provisions had been consumed and water began to become scarce. Some transports had to return to Great Britain and the possibility of having to retreat with the whole expedition fleet became real. Then, however, the weather moderated and on the 26th the fleet again anchored before the coast of Holland. The delay had given the Batavians valuable time to send troops to Holland, but as outlined only Daendels concentrated his division in North-Holland; of all other Batavian and French troops in the Batavian Republic, dispositions remained mainly unchanged. The chosen site of the landing was the coastline between Groote Keeten and Huisduinen, a strip of dunes about seven kilometres of length, 650 metres wide and 15-20 metres high. In the east the dunes ended at the Zanddijk, with the road to Den Helder on it. East of this dike was the marshland called Koegras, separated from the dike by a ditch. The Koegras was intersected by ditches and creeks and flooded at high tide. The hamlets Groote Keeten and Kleine Keeten were of no tactical value; these were nothing more than two groups of shacks to give shelter and storage for tools for the workers of the dike-reeve.

---

17 Letter of 24 August 1799 'from an officer embarked in the Secret Expedition', in the *London Chronicle*, 27 August 1799.

THE BRITISH LANDING: BATTLE OF CALANDSOOG 27 AUGUST

The fleet was arranged as follows: on the outside in the centre the transports were anchored. Close to these were the ships of the line. Next to them the frigates, somewhat closer to the shore. Finally the brigs, sloops, bomb-vessels, and gunboats were anchored close along the shore to cover and support the landing. Of course the British fleet was immediately sighted by the Batavians off the coast between Huisduinen and Groote Keeten. Daendels sent three messages to Brune to keep him informed, of which the third is of interest because it contains Daendels' battle plan:

> I arrived this instant at the coast after I have travelled all over the front of the enemy fleet, which is arranged in line and anchored between Huisen [Huisduinen] and Groote Keeten. They are busy lowering the boats they have on board and prepare for a landing. This fleet that takes nearly a mile and a half wide, is anchored so close to shore that his cannon are protecting his landing, it is impossible to expose troops to dispute the beach; but after having effected a landing they have to cross the dunes occupied by *jagers* and lead into plains on which I made all my arrangements for receiving them. You will find enclosed a state of the positions of the various units that I command. The dunes are extremely difficult terrain, but the difficulty is greater for the enemy then for us. Prudence forces me to be very careful not to jeopardize my troops; but after they have crossed the dunes in the open, while enjoying the benefit of our cavalry and our artillery, two weapons they be deprived of, I will meet them with such vigour that I hope they will soon be forced to abandon the coast.[18]

Opinions differ if Daendels was right in protecting his troops from the effect of the naval gunfire. Some assume that the cannonballs would have buried themselves into the soft sand of the beach and dunes instead of ricocheting, and therefore have done minor damage to his troops. In addition, the dunes would have provided good cover if the Batavians had deployed behind the first row of dunes. If Daendels had deployed at this position with all the troops at his disposal, he probably would have managed to drive the British into the sea with his first charge the moment they landed and at the same moment these British would stand in the line of fire of their own naval covering fire. Instead of the above, Daendels chose to attack the enemy after they had landed, and drive them back into the sea. Even the execution of this plan would be difficult, because if the British could advance some hundreds of metres, the Batavians would have to fight in a bad position with the Koegras marsh at their backs. Therefore Daendels decided to defend in the centre with a weak force and to defend both flanks strongly to prevent a British advance in these directions. He then wanted to counterattack on both flanks simultaneously when the time was right. The 1e and 2e Bataljon Jagers would form the centre at the spot where the landing was supposed to take place. Their task was to engage the British and to lure them inland. Both commanders were urged to keep their battalions together and to retreat if the pressure became too heavy. To support their retreat the 2/5e Halve Brigade, commanded by *Lieutenant-Colonel* Herbig, was placed on their left flank near Groote Keeten.

---

18 Letter from Daendels to Brune on 26 August 1799, 10:00 p.m., in Koolemans Beijnen, 'Krijgsgeschiedkundige studie', 1895, pp.269-270.

130 THE SECRET EXPEDITION

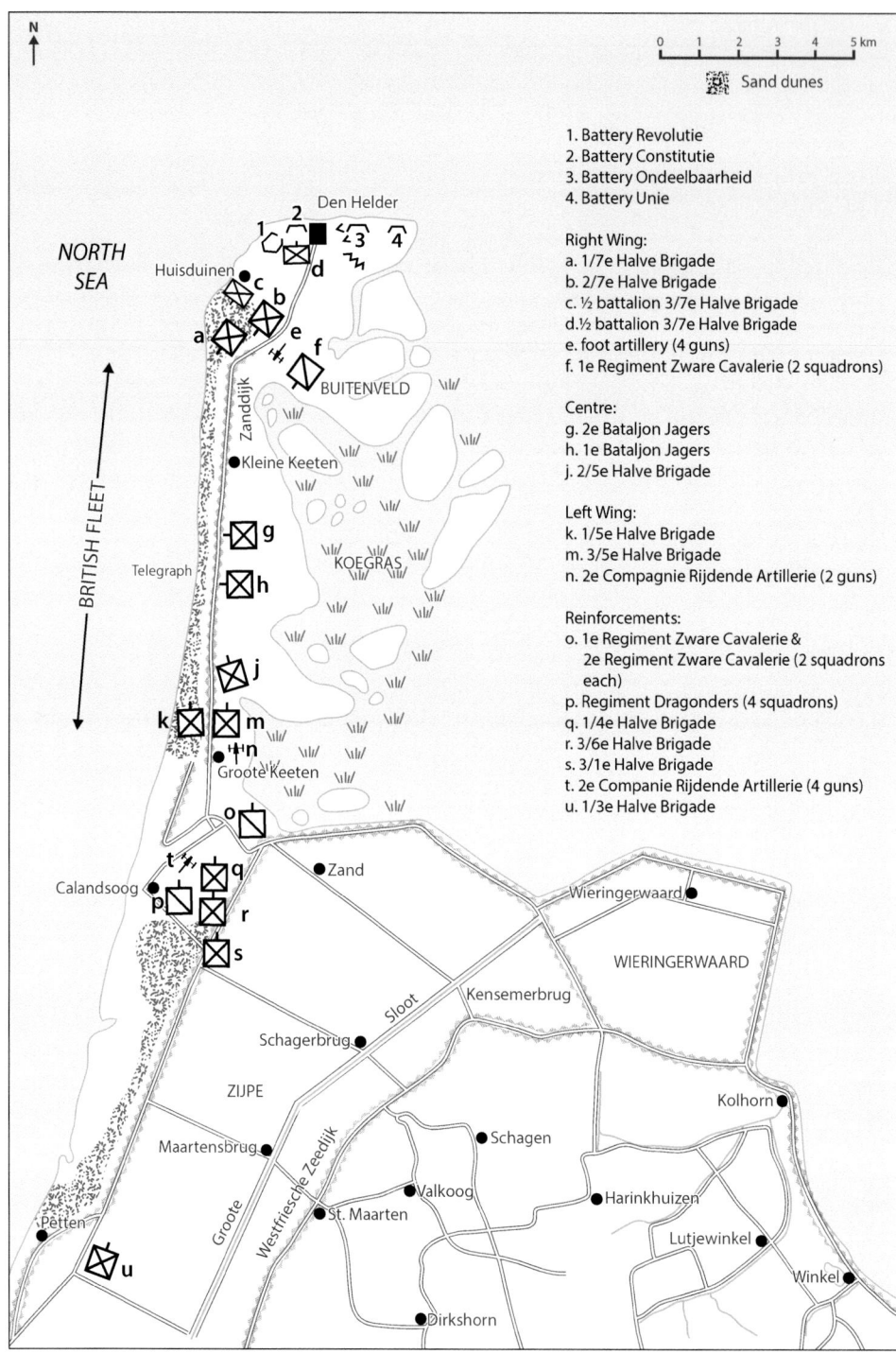

Map 5 Daendels' dispositions to resist the British landing.

The right wing was commanded by *Generaal-Major* van Guèricke and consisted of the 7e Halve Brigade (3 battalions), two squadrons of the 1e Regiment Zware Cavalerie, and four 6pdr cannon of the foot artillery. Of the 7e Halve Brigade, the 1e Battalion was deployed in the dunes facing south; of the 3e Battalion, five companies were deployed *en echelon* to the left of the 1e Battalion; on their left the 2e Battalion was positioned; the remaining four companies of the 3e Battalion occupied the coastal batteries *Revolutie* and *Unie*, to protect these and to aid the gunners. On the Buitenveld, the plain behind the dunes and south of Den Helder, on the left flank of the infantry, both cavalry squadrons were positioned. The four cannon were deployed to cover the roads leading from the dunes to Den Helder. Daendels ordered Van Guèricke not to leave this position before being ordered to do so and to maintain communications with the left wing of the army.

The left wing was commanded by *Colonel* Crass and consisted of the 2/ and 3/5e Halve Brigade and two guns of the 2e Compagnie Rijdende Artillerie. This wing would be reinforced by *Generaal-Major* van Zuylen van Nyevelt, who was force-marching during the night with his brigade from Alkmaar and Haarlem. The Batavian navy would do nothing to prevent the British landings:

> Three Dutch ships of war near Helder hoisted their sails and one frigate attempted to move out of the Mars Deep and threaten the flank of the British fleet as it deployed. Lord Duncan quickly moved two frigates to block the Dutch sortie. Once the Dutch saw the British reaction, all of their ships returned to their original positions and dropped their sails. The fleet was safe and the invasion preparations continued throughout the night.[19]

The landing was planned to start in the morning of 27 August at 3:00 a.m. For this purpose, the invasion force was divided into two: the Southern Division commanded by Lieutenant General Pulteney and the Northern Division commanded by Abercromby himself.[20] The Southern Division would be the first to land. Their mission was to drive the enemy from the dunes, to penetrate into the marshland of the Koegras and then to advance south. The Northern Division would embark in the designated smaller warships and boats immediately after the Southern Division had set off. These vessels would approach the beach as near as possible. The troops would then embark in the flatboats that had returned from landing the Southern Division, so that these did not have to go the whole way back to the transport vessels. The Northern Division would perform the main attack and therefore contained the best troops; both Guards brigades and Moore's 4th Brigade. Every soldier was supplied with 60 cartridges and food for two days.

---

19 Based on 'The Hope papers' in: Paul P. Reese, *"The Ablest Man in the British Army"*, pp.48-49.
20 For the composition of the British invasion force see Appendix IV.

The British Landing, 27 August

Around 3:00 a.m. the British soldiers started embarking the flatboats and sloops, supported by 550 Russian marines and two hundred armed Russian sailors with boats:[21]

> At 3 a.m. on the 27th instant, two flat-bottomed boats from the "Melpomene", together with the ship's boats, were filled with the Flank companies of the regiment, under the command of Captain D. White. The men had each been supplied with 60 rounds of ball ammunition, two days' provisions, and had their canteens filled with spirits and water. Major Ramsay, of the "Queen's", commanded the Flank companies of the brigade. When everything was ready, a gun fired from the admiral's ship, gave the signal for the simultaneous advance of the landing parties, whose approach covered by a heavy and incessant fire from all the men-of-war, and gunboats, met with but small opposition.[22]

Preceded by an intense artillery barrage from the warships starting about 3:30 a.m., at about 5:00 a.m. the first infantrymen of Coote's 3rd Brigade, accompanied by Lieutenant General Pulteney, were landed. MacDonald's Reserve quickly followed. The 27th Foot, commanded by Lieutenant Colonel Graham, was the first to set foot on land and quickly crossed the beach to the forward line of dunes. Here they waited for the other units to arrive. Weather was good, but the strong surf made the landing difficult. Many boats turned over, or were smashed against each other and sank, and 20 soldiers drowned. More boats were sent from the fleet to rescue soldiers from drowning. The *Naval Chronicle* relates about the landing: 'The surf in landing our troops was so great, that we are sorry to learn that several of our boats were swamped' and 'Came in the Ranger Cutter from the Texel. By her is learnt, numbers of our brave men were drowned in the surf near Helder, from too great impatience to get on shore'.[23] The landing of the British did not go completely according to plan, as Walsh relates:

> It was at first intended, and so ordered, that all the launches that carried troops from the transports should rendezvous under the stern of such frigates as lay nearest the landing-place; after which the army was to disembark in the following order: Major-general Coote's brigade, with a detachment of the light artillery, were to effect a landing on the right of the whole, under the command of Sir James Pulteney. After which, the rest of the army, under the commander in chief, was immediately to follow; major-general Doyley's brigade taking its position on the right; major-general Burrard's occupying the centre; and that of major-general Moore being posted on the left. This plan of operations, however, was not precisely executed, for the first boats that received the men from the transports, having been taken into tow by wherries and schooners, pushed on directly to the beach, under a press of sail,

---

21 Ritter, *Een Russisch verhaal*, p.10 & Krayenhoff, *Geschiedkundige*, Vol.III p.24.
22 Major H. Everard, *History of Tho's Farrington's Regiment, subsequently designated the 29th (Worcestershire) Foot 1694 to 1891* (Worcester: Littlebury & Company, 1891), pp.233-234.
23 *Naval Chronicle*, Vol.II, pp.349, 353.

THE BRITISH LANDING: BATTLE OF CALANDSOOG 27 AUGUST 133

"British landing at Calandsoog", by Reinier Vinkeles after a drawing of Dirk Langendijk. (Rijksmuseum, RP-P-OB-64.536)

without attending to the general rendezvous; whilst the soldiers, as soon as ever the boats took the ground, jumped out on the strand, and instantly formed under cover of the flotilla, which kept up an incessant and tremendous fire of shot and shells during the whole of the engagement that succeeded. Thus it was that the body of troops which attacked and defeated the enemy was composed of the reserve, and of detached parties of different regiments, chiefly of the third brigade.[24]

Major General Moore wrote in his diary about the landing: 'We landed with great confusion and irregularity. I was put on shore with not more than 300 men of my brigade and these a mixture of every different regiment; the ground was such as to render the fire from the shipping of no avail'.[25] The regimental history of the 29th Foot, which had been transported on the East Indiaman *Royal Admiral*, related:

In the meanwhile the remainder of the regiment was anxiously awaiting the arrival of the boats to take it ashore, for those of the "Royal William" [sic] had been detained near the beach. At length a lugger came alongside, and by means of it, the men were landed in detachments, which advanced until met by General Coote, who ordered them to halt, and await his further orders.[26]

---

24 Walsh, *Narrative*, pp.27-28.
25 Maurice, *Diary of Sir John Moore*, Vol.I, p.341.
26 Everard, *History*, p.235. The 29th Foot were in fact transported by the East Indiaman *Royal Admiral*, not the *Royal William*.

Nevertheless, the covering fire from the warships had forced the outposts from the Batavian *jager* battalions out of the forward dunes and the landing took place unopposed. On the beach, the British soldiers quickly formed into their units. The first six battalions ashore entered the dunes and, although still disordered and mixed with each other, fiercely attacked the Batavian *jager*. These, despite being in lose order and greatly outnumbered, managed to hold their ground for some time aided by the loose sand of the dunes. Eventually Major General Coote ordered Lieutenant Colonel Graham with two light companies and part of the 27th Foot to flank the Batavian *jager*.[27] The commander of the 1e Bataljon Jagers, *Lieutenant-Colonel* Luck, had already received two wounds and was killed in this attack and his battalion broke, British soldiers even throwing away their packs in the pursuit:

> The Grenadiers of the 29th regiment, finding themselves encumbered with their knapsacks, &c., whilst pursuing the enemy through the heavy sand, threw away both them and their provisions. After the battle, they petitioned to have these necessaries replaced, but, from a strict interpretation of the rules of military discipline, the request could not be granted.[28]

Lieutenant-Colonel Herbig, commanding the 2/5e Halve Brigade, observed the rout and tried to counter-attack the British, instead of providing the *jager* with support in order to help them rally as was ordered. His battalion also had no chance against the much superior British and retreated after Herbig had also been killed; the retreat was covered by the grenadier company. The survivors of the centre were thrown back to the south-east, into the Koegras marshes. Most *jager* rallied there and continued to harass the British with their fire for some time, while the survivors of the 2/5e Halve Brigade retreated in the direction of Kleine Keeten (to the North!) where they rallied on the 2/7e Halve Brigade. The centre of Daendels' division ceased to be a real threat for the British.

Some flank companies of Coote's 3rd Brigade captured a high dune with a telegraph on it:

> The right flank being unavoidably exposed to the whole force, and fire of the enemy, many casualties occurred. The first object of contention, was a signal station situated on a slight eminence, which, after a sharp contest, was carried by the Flank companies of the "Queen's", 27th, 29th, and 85th regiments. This position afterwards proved of great service in directing the fire from the fleet, and gunboats.[29]

Meanwhile the British landing continued smoothly. After three hours, 7,000 men and some sailors had been put ashore. Abercromby arrived with part of the Northern Division and, noticing that the biggest threat came from the Batavian troops in the south, he switched the roles of the Southern and Northern Division. The Southern Division had to face the troops near Den Helder while some troops were ordered to engage the *jager* that retreated

---

27 James J. Graham, *Memoir of General Graham with Notices of the Campaigns in which he was Engaged from 1779 to 1801* (Edinburgh: R. & R. Clark, 1862), p.231.
28 Anon., *Campaign in Holland*, p.11 & Walsh, *Narrative*, p.29.
29 Everard, *History*, p.234.

"British landing at Calandsoog", by Cornelis Brouwer after a drawing of Jan Anthonie Langendijk. (Rijksmuseum, RP-P-OB-86.723)

into the Koegras, while the Northern Division advanced south. Nevertheless, in the midst of the battle and because of the confusion, the greater part of the Southern Division already engaged would continue the fight.

Generaal-Major van Guèricke had observed the rout of the *jager*. He could do nothing but watch the British building up their forces and after some time his mere 2,100 men were facing nearly 5,000 British (Coote's and MacDonald's brigades). Every half-hour he dispatched a staff officer to Daendels, to ask permission to engage the British, but did not receive any answer.[30] After hours of waiting, he left his positions with part of his force on his own initiative and moved into the Koegras with the 2/7e Halve Brigade and both his squadrons of cavalry to support the *jager*. He left behind the 1/ and 3/7e Halve Brigade and the artillery, commanded by *Colonel* Gilquin, to defend Den Helder. Naturally, Van Guèricke could not do much in the marshy terrain of the Koegras. The British in the meanwhile had consolidated their positions and were already advancing in great force to the south in the direction of Groote Keeten. The 1st Guards Brigade had reinforced Pulteney. It was too late now for Daendels' counterattack. Instead of attacking immediately after the first landings, he had postponed it to 1:00 or 2:00 p.m.

When Daendels at last gave the order to attack, *Generaal-Major* van Guèricke , with half of his force in the marshes, could not take part anymore; *Colonel* Gilguin with the

---

30 J.W. Van Sypesteijn, 'Iets over den Veldtogt in Noord-Holland, in het jaar 1799', in *Militaire Spectator*, 1855, p.406.

remainder of the troops near Huisduinen, received no orders and remained standing idle. So the attack was only made by the left wing. Daendels deployed his troops to counterattack in the following order. The 1/ and 3/5e Halve Brigade formed the first line under *Colonel* Crass, on their left supported by two guns of the horse artillery (*Capitein* d'Anguerand), covered by the newly-arrived 4/Regiment Dragonders (*Capitein* van Heilman). The three remaining dragoon squadrons were placed on the right flank.[31] The remnants of both *jager* battalions were re-formed and also deployed on the right flank at the Zanddijk. A second and third line was formed with the battalions of the 2e Brigade (Nyevelt) as soon as they arrived.

Crass attacked vigorously and, despite the odds, succeeded in driving back the British some distance, although there are British sources stating that the Batavian attack coincided with a planned British retreat of troops that had to advanced too far ahead. Lieutenant General Pulteney was wounded in the arm and had to retreat from the battle, he was replaced by Major General Coote. The attacking Batavians at first drove back the British but were then stopped by the fire from the supporting ships, which were covering the open spaces between the dunes. In addition the British received continuous reinforcements – as fast as they landed from their boats, the British troops pushed forward and came into action by detachments. The Batavians were also shot at from the flanks by British infantry who were occupying some dunes near the beach under cover of the gunfire. Nevertheless, the Batavian horse artillery inflicted heavy loss on the British troops and a shot of its cannon badly wounded Lieutenant Colonel Hay, commander of the Royal Engineers, whose thigh was shattered by a round shot while watching the battle through his telescope and who would die under amputation.

Efforts to reinforce the Batavian infantry with cavalry failed, the horses sinking in the loose sand up to their bellies, Maule relating:

> Our loss at this period became serious. The enemy shewed some detachments of cavalry. But could not act. The light artillery and howitzers amply compensated them upon this point. A furious cannonade obliged the leading divisions of the English to pause. They were overwhelmed with a shower of grape-shot, as were also the troops which were advancing by the sea side. Many officers and soldiers here lost their lives… Howitzers, the best artillery which can be employed against an army seated on hills, were adopted by the enemy on this occasion. The large masses of the advancing brigades afforded an excellent mark, and by the elevation of the enemy's guns much loss was unavoidably sustained.[32]

The Batavian horse artillery tried to advance even closer but met the same fate as the cavalry, nearly losing their cannon to the British. Batavian losses were also heavy, despite that they managed to hold on against two successive bayonet attacks. In one of these attacks Lieutenant Colonel Graham, commanding the 27th Foot, was hit by a rifle ball in the left

---

31   Van Sypesteijn, 'Iets over den Veldtogt', p.201.
32   Francis Maule, *Memoirs of the Principal Events in the Campaigns of North Holland and Egypt* (London: F.C. and J. Rivington, 1816), pp.4-6.

temple, completely depriving him of the sight of his left eye.[33] The battle raged on with continuous British reinforcements arriving, but the Batavians were also reinforced by the arrival of the 1/4e Halve Brigade, 3/6e Halve Brigade and the 1/3e Halve Brigade. Some time later the 3/1e Halve Brigade also arrived at the battlefield. Nevertheless, without the simultaneous attack from the other wing a decision could never be reached. Daendels himself was in the front line all the time without any escort. Eyewitnesses recorded him 'standing in a rain of bullets'. The horse he sat on was shot dead under him.[34] It was very brave of him to stay in a dangerous position the whole afternoon, but also foolish. If he had been badly wounded or even killed, command and control would have become very difficult and his death would have had a bad effect on Batavian morale.

The Batavian Retreat

At about 3:00 or 4:00 p.m., Crass was forced to retreat and give up the captured terrain because of the heavy losses sustained and the continuous supporting fire from the British warships. At this time the British had disembarked two field cannon, manhandled by sailors, which were positioned on the crescent of a dune. Supported by their fire the 1st Guards Brigade attacked Crass and his troops along the beach. Crass re-formed his troops and received the attack, which was beaten back. Then he resumed his retreat to Groote Keeten. The fighting ended at about 6:00 p.m. after which the Batavian troops retreated further south to Calandsoog. *Generaal-Major* van Guèricke in the meanwhile had left his troops in the Koegras, to ask Daendels for orders in person. He found Daendels still alone in a 'rain of bullets'. Daendels was of the opinion that it was impossible to defend Den Helder against a general attack over land and ordered Van Guèricke to evacuate Den Helder after spiking the guns and throwing the powder in the water, and to join him. With Daendels still in danger of being killed, Van Guèricke insisted on receiving such a far-reaching order in writing and then returned to his troops still in the Koegras. Arriving there he ordered his aide-de-camp, *Capitein-Adjoint* Schober, to deliver, with an escort of 30 dragoons commanded by Lieutenant de Braconier, the above order to *Colonel* Gilquin. Gilquin wrote about this in his report:

> At half-past six in the afternoon of 27 August, I received by the *Capitein-Adjoint* Schober verbal order of the *Lieutenant-Generaal* Daendels, to spike the pieces on the batteries and to make the ammunition and further necessities of war unusable and withdraw with everything. I hesitated to comply with this verbal order, as being the matter of the utmost gravity, and decided to consult the senior officers, and some subalterns, which were with me at that time, being the *Lieutenant-Colonel* Verhorst, the *majors* Bruce and Van der Wyck, *Adjudant-Major* Visscher, the *capiteins* Van der Wiele, Favauge and Van Geen, and *Lieutenant* Arentz of the artillery, by way of court-martial, and seek their advice. The result was to request *Lieutenant-Generaal* Daendels to forward this order in writing, and in the

---

33 Graham, *Memoir of General Graham*, p.231.
34 Van Sypesteijn, 'Krijgskundige Beschouwingen over den Veldtogt van 1799 in Noord-Holland', in: *Nieuwe Spectator* (1853), p.680.

meantime to prepare everything to execute that order. Little while after I got my letter, which I have written for that purpose, back, and at the bottom of the same I was ordered by *Generaal-Major* van Guèricke, by order of *Lieutenant-Generaal* Daendels, to evacuate Den Helder and further posts as soon as possible, which order I have executed at once. Meanwhile, I have informed *Schout-bij-Nacht* Story, commanding the nation's fleet, about this order. Receiving report from *Lieutenant-Colonel* ten Cate that the batteries were spiked, I marched off both of my battalions, also taking with me three howitzers. Now I had, not wanting to risk being cut off by the enemy, remain far away from him, and so I decided to make a detour behind the Buitenveld, the men having to wade through the water and mud up to their belly, reason I had to abandon my three howitzers as it was impossible to get them out of the mire. Finally I arrived at Zand with a weary force, at two o'clock in the night.[35]

With the troops under his own command in the Koegras, *Generaal-Major* van Guèricke retreated south and joined Daendels. As described, *Colonel* Gilquin abandoned Den Helder as ordered, despite strong objections from *Schout-bij-Nacht* Story.[36] Favoured by darkness and led by the able *Capitein* van Geen with the advance guard they reached Zand, being not much more than a tavern in the north of the Zijpe. From there Gilquin retreated further to the new position chosen by Daendels. The right wing was at the Zuiderzee near Oude-Sluis; the left wing at the North Sea near Petten; the centre behind the Oost-Egalement-Sloot. Headquarters was to remain at Schagerbrug.[37] Although this position had some strength, it was too extended and Daendels had not enough infantry at his disposal to defend it properly, the cavalry being of not much use because of the intersected terrain. Daendels wrote the following after-action report to Brune, asking urgently for reinforcements:

As I expected, the enemy has attacked us at daybreak, effecting his disembarkation in front of the fleet, between the two Keeten. The nice weather and the calm sea enabled him to put much people on land; fiercely our two *jager* battalions, positioned in the dunes, were attacked by the enemy, behaving in this initial moment not as I had hoped; the superiority and the musket fire of the enemy soon forced them to leave the dunes. On this occasion it was that the brave *Lieutenant-Colonel* Luck, intending to encourage his *jager* with his own bravery, exposed himself with such an audacity that he lost his life. I had made my dispositions to drive the enemy out of the dunes; but this arid region benefits them entirely; I could not attack with cavalry, not even with my artillery The result was a violent and destructive musket fire with the only purpose of taking, abandoning and retaking the crescent of some dunes; I even dared not to engage our troops in a general attack, because once they would advance, the plains among the hills exposed their flanks to the fire of the enemy fleet; I have therefore limited myself to retain my position at the Groote Keeten, to keep the enemy in check, and to block any further advance. Next, as

---

35 Report from *Colonel* Gilquin, in: Krayenhoff, *Geschiedkundige Beschouwing*, Bijlage No. V, pp.30-31.
36 J.C. de Jonge, *Geschiedenis van het Nederlandsche Zeewezen* (Zwolle: Van Hoogstraten en Gorter, 1869), Vol.V, pp.362-363.
37 Krayenhoff, *Geschiedkundige Beschouwing*, pp.83-84. The Oost-Egalement-Sloot is a canal.

citizen *Lieutenant* Allemand reported to you, I ordered the division to take position in the Zijpe, both my wings resting on the Noord- and Zuiderzee, in the front covered by a country intersected with canals.

Except for the first mistake of the *jager*, which afterwards returned to the fighting with courage, I am very satisfied with the behaviour of the troops, and in particular those of *Colonel* Crass, who has done miracles of bravery with the two battalions under his command. On both sides no prisoners of war have been made; we have few dead; but suffered many wounded. In this uneven terrain one cannot hope to make a regular attack; Crass has undertaken one but it was fruitless.

The arrival of new ships is announced; during this night the enemy could bring a huge force on land, and now general! it is time to unite the important force about which I have spoken to you. As it is on this height that the enemy will unite all his forces, etc.[38]

Abercromby wrote the following in his after-action report to the Secretary of State for War Henry Dundas, also reporting about the capture of Den Helder which will be looked at further in the next chapter:

From the first day after our departure from England, we experienced such a series of bad weather, as is very uncommon at this season of the year. The ardour of admiral Mitchel for the service in which we were jointly engaged, left it only with me to follow his example of zeal and perseverance, in which I was encouraged by the manner that he kept a numerous convoy collected. It was our determination not to depart from the resolution of attacking the Helder, unless we should have been prevented by the want of water and provisions. On the forenoon of the 21st instant the weather proved so favourable, that we stood in upon the Dutch coast, and had made every preparation to land on the 22d, when we were forced to sea by a heavy gale of wind. It was not until the evening of the 25th that the weather began once more to clear up. On the 26th, we came to anchor near the shore of the Helder; and on the 27th, in the morning, the troops began to disembark at daylight. Although the enemy did not oppose our landing, yet the first division had scarcely begun to move forward before they got into action, which continued from five in the morning until three o'clock in the afternoon. The enemy had assembled a very considerable body of infantry, cavalry, and artillery, near Calandsoog, and made repeated attacks on our right with fresh troops.

Our position was on a ridge of sand-hills, stretching along the coast from north to south. Our right flank was unavoidably exposed to the whole force of the enemy. We had no-where sufficient ground on our right to form more than a battalion in line; yet, on the whole, the position, though singular, was not, in our situation, disadvantageous, having neither cavalry nor artillery. By the courage and perseverance of the troops, the enemy was fairly worn out, and obliged to retire in the evening to a position two leagues in his rear. The contest was arduous, and the loss

---

38 Krayenhoff, *Geschiedkundige Beschouwing*, Appendix IV, pp.17-19.

has been considerable. We have to regret many valuable officers lost to the service, who have either fallen, or been disabled by their wounds. The corps principally engaged were, the reserve under the command of colonel Macdonald, consisting of the 23d and 55th regiments. The regiments of major-general Coote's brigade, which have been much engaged; were the Queen's, the 27th, 29th, and 85th regiments. Major-general Doyley's brigade was brought into action towards the close of the day, and has sustained some loss.

As the enemy still held the Helder with a garrison of 2000 men, it was determined to attack it before day-break on the morning of the 28th; and the brigade under major-general Moore, supported by major-general Burrard's, were destined for this service; but about eight o'clock yesterday evening, the Dutch fleet in the Mars Diep got under weigh, and the garrison was withdrawn, taking their route through the marshes, towards Medemblick, having previously spiked the guns on the batteries, and destroyed some of the carriages. About nine at night, major-general Moore, with the 2d battalion of the royals, and the 92d regiment, under the command of lord Huntley, took possession of this important post, in which he found a numerous artillery of the best kind, both of heavy and field train. All that part of the Dutch fleet in the Nieuve Diep, together with their naval magazine at Nieuve Werk, fell into our hands this morning – a full detail of which it is not in my power to send. This day we have the satisfaction to see the British flag flying in the Mars Diep, and part of the 5000 men, under the command of major-general Don, disembarking under the batteries of the Helder.

During the course of the action, I had the misfortune to lose the service of lieutenant-general Sir James Pulteney, from a wound he received in his arm; but not before he had done himself the greatest honour; and I was fully sensible of the loss of him. Major-general Coote supplied his place with ability. Colonel Macdonald, who commanded the Reserve, and who was very much engaged during the course of the day, though wounded, did not quit the field.

Lieutenant-colonel Maitland returning to England, to go on another service, and major Kempt, my aide-du-camp, and bearer of this letter, whom I beg leave to recommend to your notice and protection, will be able to give any further information which may be required.

A list of the killed and wounded, as far as we have been able to as certain it, accompanies this letter.[39]

Then follows a return of killed and wounded, of which the following is the amount: total; 1 lieutenant colonel, 1 subaltern, 3 serjeants, 51 rank and file, killed; 1 colonel, 1 lieutenant colonel, 1 major, 9 captains, 6 subalterns, 18 serjeants, 1 drummer, 334 rank and file, wounded; 26 rank and file missing.

Abercromby's above return of killed and wounded is not correct though, defining the loss at 56 killed, 371 wounded and 26 missing. The official return gives a total loss of 57 killed, 376 wounded and 26 missing, a total of 459. Added to these must be the 20 men that

---

39   Walsh, *Narrative*, pp.96-99.

drowned during the landing: 1 NCO and 4 gunners of the Royal Artillery; 1 sergeant and 14 others of the 92nd Highlanders. Senior British officers killed were Lieutenant Colonel Smollet, 1st Guards, Brigade-Major of the 1st Guards Brigade, and Lieutenant Colonel Hay, commanding the Royal Engineers (Hay was initially replaced by Captain Bruyeres, Lieutenant Colonel Twiss was send to resume command). Wounded were Lieutenant General Pulteney; Colonel Hope, 25th Foot, Deputy Adjutant General; Colonel MacDonald, 55th Regiment, brigadier; Lieutenant Colonel Murray, 3rd Foot Guards, Assistant Quarter-Master-General; and Lieutenant-Colonel Graham, 27th Foot.[40] There were concerns about the huge number of officer casualties as described in the *London Chronicle*:

> The disproportionate loss of Officers to that of the private men, on our troops landing in Holland, proves that they were picked off by French riflemen stationed for that purpose on the lines of Helder: the calculated loss of Officers on general service, is 4 to 100 privates: in the late action the former exceeded double that proportion both in slain and wounded.[41]

The *Naval Chronicle* gives a similar explanation for the high loss of officers: 'The wounds of our officers are in general by no means dangerous, being simple gun-shot wounds. The Dutch had a corps of riflemen in their entrenchments, which may account for the very large proportion of officers that have been wounded'.[42] As described the riflemen were indeed not French but came from the two Batavian *jager* battalions. The losses inflicted by the Franco-Batavian riflemen and light infantry skirmishers, suffered during this and all subsequent battles, and the need to oppose them were apparently grounds for several requests of light infantry reinforcements. The first to arrive between 14 and 17 September were additional flank companies amounting to 1,730 men. It was also the reason for the creation of the 'Experimental Corps of Riflemen' in 1800, with Major General Moore regarded as their founding father.

The first day had been a disaster for the Batavians. 1,400 men were dead, wounded, or missing, including 57 officers.[43] Senior Batavian officers killed were *Lieutenant-Colonel* Luck, 1e Bataljon Jagers and *Lieutenant-Colonel* Herbig, 5e Halve Brigade. Wounded were the *Lieutenant-Colonels* Lycklama à Nijeholt and Van Sandick, both of the 5e Halve Brigade. Regarding these losses, an Orangist report states that 162 Batavians had deserted to join the Orangist cause. The 5e Halve Brigade suffered the most, having all three of its battalion commanders as casualties, illustrating the fierceness of the fighting. The British had succeeded in consolidating their positions and gained a strong bridgehead. They captured Den Helder and its harbour at little cost. Their losses were surprisingly small, especially for a landing on a defended hostile coast, although loss in officers was relatively high as described above. Giving up Den Helder was sensible from a tactical point of view as the

---

40 Anon., *Campaign in Holland*, Appendix No.3, pp.76-77.
41 *London Chronicle*, 7-10 September 1799.
42 *Naval Chronicle*, Vol.II, p.349.
43 Krayenhoff, *Geschiedkundige Beschouwing*, p.77. Note, though, that many missing soldiers who had fled into the Koegras would rejoin their units later.

troops still remaining there were heavily outnumbered with inadequate defences, but it was a heavy blow for Batavian morale.

Most Batavians believed that the defences of Den Helder were strong enough to withstand an attack, and giving it up without any fight was one of the reasons for the Batavian fleet to subsequently surrender to the British. Daendels' defence for his decision to evacuate Den Helder was:

> The officers of the navy having given repeated assurances that the battery *la révolution* was useless for the defence of the channel; also that this battery is not constructed in a way to hold a garrison, once isolated, making it impossible to defend. The Lieutenant General [i.e. Daendels himself] therefore did not want to expose fruitlessly two battalions of the 7th to the risk of losing them, which inevitably would have been captured if the enemy had cut off the only road left to them to retreat.[44]

Daendels' defence for the decisions he made do not completely remove the blame from him, as it was he who was ordered to defend Holland and he was responsible for strengthening these defences if they were inadequate. The more so as he had expressed several times his opinion that the British would land in Holland. In his defence, there are letters indicating that he indeed troubled himself strengthening the defences, especially the coastal batteries, but that it all came too late.

---

44 H.W. Daendels, *Rapport des Opérations de la Division du Lieutenant-Général Daendels; Depuis le 22 Août, jusqu'à la capitulation de l'Armée Angloise et Russe, le 18 Octobre 1799. An 5*, p.19. An English translation of this report can be found in Anon., *The History of the Campaign of 1799, in Holland* (London: J. Barfield, 1801), pp.429–479.

8

Building up Forces and the Surrender of the Batavian Fleet

The British Consolidate

Abercromby did not follow up on his successful landing and did not pursue Daendels. According to Krayenhoff, who states that he asked Abercromby himself about the reason for this, Abercromby explained that he believed it would be safer to capture Den Helder and the roadstead of Texel, to possess a safe harbour to disembark his supplies and cavalry. This was preferable to engaging in a battle with an uncertain result, as he supposed that the Batavians would have already received substantial reinforcements during the night. Even more, Abercromby feared that the Batavians would attack him again, so he was preparing for that case.[1] For the time being, the British troops had to camp in the barren dunes, lacking good shelter and food. The British advance south would have to wait until Den Helder was captured, the Batavian fleet neutralised, and the British fleet able to protect and support both flanks of his army, on the North Sea as well as on the Zuiderzee.

On 28 August before daybreak Major General Moore was ordered to attack Huisduinen and Den Helder with his brigade, with the brigade of Major General Burrard in support. During their march, word was received that the Batavians had evacuated these positions and had retreated south. The 2/1st Royal Regiment of Foot and the 92nd Highlanders of Moore's brigade occupied Den Helder and received a warm welcome by the citizens, wearing orange and hoisting orange flags. In the coastal batteries 74 guns were captured. The Nieuwe Diep harbour and navy magazines were also captured intact. Captain Winthrop of the *Circe* was send to take possession of it:

> Sir, I have the honour to inform you, that I this morning took possession of the New Diep, with the ships and vessels under mentioned, and also of the naval arsenal containing ninety-five pieces of ordnance. A copy of the naval stores I will transmit you as soon as it can be made out.

---

1   Krayenhoff, *Geschiedkundige*, p.83.

Names.	Guns.
Urwachten	66
Broederschop	54
Hector	44
Diuffee	44
Expedition	44
Constitutie	44
Belle Antoinette	44
Unie	49
Helder	32
Pollock	24
Minerva	24
Venus	24
Alarm	24

Dreighlerlahn, Howda, Vreedelust, Indiamen; and a Sheer Hulk.[2]

Abercromby was surprised by the strong resistance he had encountered when he landed and this made him cautious. However, he also had other concerns. The few civilians living in this part of Holland did not show the enthusiasm on the arrival of the British as had been assured to him. The Batavian troops were much more disciplined, determined, clothed, and armed than expected and did not desert *en masse*. In addition Abercromby believed, as was most probable, that the Batavians had received strong reinforcements. He had reached his main objective for now; to capture and consolidate a harbour to disembark the next echelons of British and Russians. So he did not want to take any risks. Some sources state that his decision to consolidate was also influenced by the hereditary Prince of Orange, who was of the opinion that most of the inhabitants were Orangist and would rise *en masse*. Therefore, he wanted to protect them against the damages of the fighting, for this reason for asking Abercromby not to advance. So Abercromby decided to wait.

On 28 August the next echelon of British troops arrived, 5,000 men disembarking more comfortably at Den Helder or at the Nieuwe Diep then on the open North Sea beach:

Major General Don's 5th Brigade (2,768)
    1/17th Foot (709)
    2/17th Foot (695)
    1/40th Foot (702)
    2/40th Foot (662)

---

2   Letter of 28 September 1799 from Captain Winthrop to Vice Admiral Mitchel, in the *Naval Chronicle*, Vol.II, pp.619-620. The correct names and types of the ships captured are: *Verwachting* 3rd Rate 66, *Broederschap* 4th Rate 54 (which was the guard ship), *Hector* 5th Rate 44, *Heldin* 5th Rate 32, *Alarm* 6th Rate 24, *Valk* 6th Rate 24, *Minerva* 6th Rate 24, *Venus* 6th Rate 24. The transport ships *Constitutie* (44), *'t Duifje* (13), *Expeditie* (44), *Sibilla Antoinetta* (44) and *Unie* (24). The former East Indiamen *Drechterland* (16), *Gouda* (12) and *Vreedelust*. A sheer hulk and about 13 merchant ships. Many of these ships were in bad shape or mere hulks and some of these would be used by the Anglo-Russian army to provide firewood.

> Major General the Earl of Cavan's 6th Brigade (2,387)
> 1/20th Foot (799)
> 2/20th Foot (795)
> 63rd Foot (793)

These regiments were all skeleton battalions brought up to strength with a huge number of militia. Because of this the quality of these regiments was substantially lower. They were lucky to be able to embark in a harbour, which was just as well because the wind had increased making disembarkation at the open beach impossible. Nevertheless it was not completely without discomfort, nor was their subsequent stay in the dunes, as the regimental history of the 20th Foot describes:

> At about four o'clock in the afternoon of August 28th, both battalions of the XX disembarked under the guns of the "Helder," and had to wade through the water, carrying the ammunition on the top of their knapsacks; in this way some of it was destroyed, and a few stand of arms lost… As soon as the disembarkation was completed, the XX bivouacked on the sandhills about four miles to the south of Helder town. It was a cold, rainy night, and the whole division was without baggage, food, or wood.[3]

Lieutenant Colborne of that same regiment relates:

> We landed without our baggage on a cold, rainy night, and were on the bare sands with no food and no wood. General Don had a nice little cart with his things in, in which he was to sleep, and I recollect envying him when he said: "Now gentlemen, we halt here; make yourselves comfortable!" An officer I recollect shot a wildfowl and roasted it himself, and gave us all some.[4]

The only means by which the soldiers could manage to protect themselves against the cold and the frequent showers of rain and gusts of wind, was by lying in trenches scooped out of the sandy soil. The supply by the fleet was also interrupted by the continual storms, so that the arrival of provisions was very irregular and uncertain right from the beginning. On the 30th also 180 cavalry and 10 field guns disembarked. Abercromby now had about 18,000 men at his disposal. So finally on 1 September, when Daendels had retreated even further, the British troops advanced to take up positions in the Zijpe polder, behind the Schoorlsche and Westfriesche Zeedijk. These dikes and the canal in front of them formed a formidable defensive position. At strategic points, entrenchments and parapets were thrown up and batteries positioned to cover all accesses. On 5 September the 11th Light Dragoons disembarked (530 men), the troopers swimming their horses to the beach.

Until the arrival of more army reinforcements British marines garrisoned Den Helder. Major Finlay of the Royal Engineers received orders to fortify Den Helder:

---

3   Smyth, *Lancashire Fusiliers*, pp.188-189.
4   G.C. Moore Smith, *The Life of John Colborne, Field-Marshal Lord Seaton, Compiled from his Letters, Records of his Conversations, and Other Sources* (London: John Murray, 1903), p.8.

> I am now sent to the Helder to fortify the old Position that Col. Moncrief & I examined in 1788… I have my Hands as full of Business as I can manage, and indeed rather more than I can well get through. I am on Horseback every Morning before Six, and seldom get off till dark, when my Writing Business begins… I have a most motley Crew under my direction, English Soldiers & Sailors, Dutch Carpenters & Peasants, and the whole of the Dutch Deserters a Body that are daily increasing in numbers. The Works I am carrying on are charged to the Extraordinaries of the Army, so that I am Paymaster as well as Commanding Engineer, and shall have the trouble of becoming a Public Accountant, probably without making Money by it like Neighbour Montresor. Sir Ralph is very anxious I should soon put this Place in a respectable state of Defence, writes to me in a very friendly Stile, and gives me ample powers.[5]

The soldiers were much better off in the Zijpe than during their stay in the dunes, as there were numerous large farmhouses, being surrounded by barns, making excellent and commodious barracks:

> We had no tents, but were lodged in the farm houses, which, in Holland, are large, and of a peculiar construction, having the byre, stable, hay-loft, and barn, under one large oblong square roof, made of thatch. A great number of these houses were ranged at such regular distances, along the banks of the canals, in the rear of the dyke, that they formed convenient cantonments; and each house contained from one to two hundred, who slept in a loft among the hay, without any other covering than their great coats and the hay. The fields are all divided by broad and deep ditches, in place of hedges, which are only to be seen up on parts of the road sides, and round the orchards at the farm houses and gentlemen's seats.[6]

Supplying the army became a huge problem though. It was quickly discovered that the Dutch countryside provided fresh provisions, cattle, and sheep, but as the army grew in numbers this source was quickly exhausted and so most provisions had to be brought over from England to Den Helder. From Den Helder it was difficult to get the supplies to the front. There was a great shortage of carts and wagons, because the British assumed that they could rely on local transport. However, that did not materialise; only about 60 wagons and 250 horses could be obtained. Most of the supplies had to be moved to the front by carrying parties. Rain had turned the roads into mud. To overcome this problem the navy had to come to the support of the army. With boats the supplies were brought from Den Helder to Oude-Sluis. From there they were distributed. However, even this supply route was frequently out of use because of the stormy weather.

The island of Texel was also occupied. Its Batavian garrison consisted of about 50 or 60 men of the 3/7e Halve Brigade commanded by *Capitein* Cornelisse. After the British landing and subsequent occupation of Den Helder and having only few men with which to

---

5 Letter of 5 September 1799 from John Finlay to his wife, in A.J.B. Wace, 'A British officer on active service, 1799' in *The Annual of the British School at Athens*, Vol.23, pp.131-132.
6 Anon., *Narrative of a Private Soldier in His Majesty's 92d Regiment of Foot* (Glasgow: University Press, 1820), p.40.

occupy the whole island, the garrison retreated to a redoubt. Consequently, the Orangists on the island took their chance and everywhere orange colours were hoisted until most of the islanders were wearing orange ribbons and cockades. Already that same evening (27 August) Cornelisse evacuated the island completely, which was occupied by the British on the 29th, in the name of their King and the Prince of Orange. The redoubt was garrisoned by a hundred British infantry of the 20th Foot, commanded by Captain Paddon. The island would be used to collect the Orangists and Batavian deserters as described later on.

The Surrender of the Batavian fleet

After *Colonel* Gilquin had abandoned his positions at Huisduinen and Den Helder, the Batavian fleet found itself in a vulnerable position at the roadstead of Texel and *Schout-bij-Nacht* Story had no other choice then to fall back to the Vlieter, south-east of Texel. Already that same evening of the 27th, pilots and other vessels were dispatched to the Vlieter and next morning at eight o'clock the Batavian fleet came under sail and arrived around noon at its new destination, anchoring in order of battle in line east-south-east.[7] Story's decision to retreat was in cooperation with an order he had received from the Batavian Naval Minister Spoors:

> Pending your further tidings, it seems to me, to give to you in consideration, and thus authorize you if necessary, for as long as Den Helder is in our power, to await the enemy on the roadstead of Texel, and let him, if he would attack the Batavian fleet, experience what love for the Fatherland, coupled with courage, even with inferior forces, might achieve; but when the enemy unexpectedly would become master of Den Helder, then to retire with all ships to the Vlieter; and pursued by the enemy, to defend yourself to the utmost. The passage to the Vlieter is so narrow that superiority is fruitless, providing you a nice occasion, to take up a good position with the nation's fleet.[8]

From here, the crews observed the arrival of the British redcoats on the captured coastal batteries, and a few moments later the hoisting of the orange flag on the church tower of the village of Oude Schild on Texel island. At dawn of the 29th, already great part of the British transports and warships had anchored at the roadstead of Texel or in the Nieuwe Diep. That same day, Orangist *Lieutenant ter Zee* Twent and the pilot Duinker placed beacons to enable Mitchell to reach the Batavian fleet on the Vlieter. On 30 August, Admiral Mitchell sailed to engage the Batavian fleet in the Vlieter in battle formation, with 11 ships of the line, five frigates and six smaller warships, including two Russian ships of the line.[9] These line of battle was followed by two fire-ships, eight bombs, and 10 brigs, all flying both British and Orange colours.

---

7 For the composition of the Batavian fleet at the roadstead of Texel see Appendix VI.
8 Order of 23 August 1799 from Spoors to Story in Krayenhoff, *Geschiedkundige*, Appendix VI, pp.32-33.
9 For the composition of Mitchell's Anglo-Russian squadron see Appendix IX.

The channel to the Vlieter was narrow and sailing it with such a large fleet was not without danger. Several ships grounded:

> To show the danger and difficulty of the passage into the Texel, we have only to observe, that in following the Dutch fleet, the America, of 64 guns, and Latona frigate, ran aground; and so did the Ratvisan, a Russian man of war. The former got off with the loss of her rudder, but has again grounded: the Ratvisan was in danger to be completely lost. But assisted by the crews of other ships, some of the guns were removed from the ship which became afloat, fit for service again the next day. The Latona rejoined the line.[10]

Mitchell's advance had a huge impact on the crews of the Batavian ships. The events that unfolded now are fairly accurately described in the after-action report written by *Schout-bij Nacht* Story:

> When this fleet approached, again disorders occurred on the Washington, and well as on many others ships as was reported later to me. This moment was the most difficult one that I ever experienced. An enemy fleet, almost once stronger than mine, coursed towards me dead running, and at that moment I was not sure if from all my ships, but a single shot would be fired. Forced by the unpleasant situation, I decided to send the *Capiteins* van de Capellen and De Jong, with a parliamentary sloop, to the quickly approaching English admiral. Ordering them to point out to him the situation that we find ourselves in our last retreat and had decided to defend our ships to the extreme. That he would therefore gain nothing with his attack, except, perhaps, to destroy a fleet, he had declared himself to want to spare, and treating friendly; and finally to propose him to anchor at a sufficient distance of us, to await further dispositions from my Government about my present situation. Of course I intended to use this meaningless message for nothing more than to gain time.
>
> In the meantime I signalled our ships to prepare themselves for battle; then, that moment decided completely, what awaited me.
>
> When the alarm was beaten at the Washington, the entire crew, except for the NCOs and a few men, instead of manning the guns, gathered on the forecastle, gangway and even on the quarterdeck, with deafening yells; declaring that no one was willing to fight for even one moment, or make any preparations to do so. I went to the quarterdeck with *Capitein* van Braam, who at that moment was on board of the Washington; we tried both, first with persuasive words, and then with most vehement threats, to bring the mutineers to the batteries and to their duty, but completely in vain. At once they ran under an incessant clamour of *Hoezee!* and the like, to the guns, removed the round shot of these, and threw them overboard together with a number of baskets with cartridges. Some brave men who had together rolled out two guns on the main deck, were pulled away with violence and

---

10 *Naval Chronicle*, Vol.II, pp.349, 616.

forbidden under the strongest threats to do something for defence; from some of the other ships I heard from time to time a rebellious cry.

At that moment the *Capiteins* van de Capellen and De Jong had arrived near the English fleet, which had anchored on a short distance. Both captains returned, bringing me a letter from the English admiral, of which I enclose a copy. Also reporting that they had obtained with difficulty one hour for council; furthermore, with them having two British officers who were ordered to receive my reply. I already had, in preparation, let all the commanding officers of the ships come aboard to me and held council of war about our situation and what we should do. Of the Washington, I had to express, was not a shot to expect; *Capitein* Kolff declared the same about the Utrecht. The *Capiteins* van Braam and De Jong declared that their crews refused to fight. The other captains were all the same, the more, the other with less objections except for the *Capitein* van Senden, who reported to me that his crew was in order up to this moment, but that there was not to expect anything from them in case the admiral's ship would not take part in the defence; the Batavier, the ship he commanded, was moreover positioned behind in the Vlieter. These being the circumstances, added to the certain conviction that we were up against double odds, nothing, or taken at best, would be able to do then to fire a few gun shots from our entire fleet, decided, which side we had to choose. By unanimous vote it was decided to remove the Batavian flag and to declare myself and my officers prisoner of war, without entering in detail regarding the protestations of friendship, or hoisting any other flag.[11]

Vice Admiral Mitchell's after-action report relates about the surrender of the Dutch fleet as follows:

> Sir, it blowing strong from the South-west, and also the flood tide, I could not send away my short letter of last night; I therefore have, in addition, to request you will lay before the Lords Commissioners of the Admiralty, that on the morning of yesterday I got the squadron under weigh at five o'clock, and immediately formed the line of battle, and to prepare for battle. In running in, two of the line of battle ships, Rattvisan and America, and the Latona frigate, took the ground. We passed the Helder Point and Mars Diep, and continued our course along the Texel, in the channel that leads to the Vleiter, the Dutch squadron lying at anchor in a line at the Red Buoy in the East South-east course. The Latona frigate got off and joined me, but as the two line of battle ships did not, I closed the line. About half past ten I sent Captain Rennie of the Victor, with a summons to the Dutch Admiral, as it was Lord Duncan's wish that I should do so; and in her way she picked up a flag of truce, with two Dutch Captains from the Dutch Admiral, to me. Captain Rennie very properly brought them on board, and from a conversation of a few minutes, I was induced to anchor in a line a short distance from the Dutch squadron, at their earnest request. They returned with my positive orders not to alter the position of the ships, nor do anything whatsoever to them, and in one

---

11 Report of 31 August 1799 from *Schout-bij-Nacht* Story to the Batavian Naval Minister Spoors, in: Krayenhoff, *Geschiedkundige*, Appendix VIIb, pp.43-51.

hour to submit or take the consequences. In less than the time they returned with a verbal answer, that they submitted according to the summons, and should consider themselves (the officers) on parole, until I heard from the Lords Commissioners of the Admiralty and the Prince of Orange for my farther proceedings.

I have now the honour to enclose you herewith the line of battle in which the squadron advanced, a copy of my summons to the Dutch Admiral, and also a list of the Dutch fleet. Admiral Story's flag is down, and I have sent an officer on board each of his ships to have an eye over and the charge of them, as they themselves requested that it should be so. I have also furnished them with the Prince of Orange's standard, many of them not having had it before, and they are now all under these colours. To maintain quiet among their crews, I issued a short manifesto, of which I also enclose a copy herewith.

The animated exertions and conduct of the whole squadron are far above any praise I can bestow on them, but I shall ever feel most sensibly impressed on my heart their spirited conduct during the whole of this business. We have all felt the same zeal for the honour of our Sovereign and our Country: and although the conclusion has not turned out as we expected, yet the merit I may say, in some measure, is still not the less due to my squadron: and if I had brought them to action, I trust it would have added another laurel to the Navy of England in this present war. The Dutch were astonished and thunderstruck at the approach of our squadron, never believing it possible that we could so soon have laid down the buoys, and led down to them in line of battle in a channel where they themselves go through but with one or two ships at a time.

I have sent Lieutenant Collier with these dispatches, who will give their Lordships every information, as he has been employed in the whole of the communication with the Dutch squadron, and was also on shore with me as my Aide-du-Camp on the day of landing.

P.S. Since writing the above I received the Dutch Admiral's answer in writing, which I enclose herewith.

LINE OF BATTLE.
At noon, August 30, 1799.
Glatton – Capt. Charles Cobb, 54 guns, 343 men.
Romney – Capt. John Lawford, 50 guns, 343 men.
Isis -Vice-Admiral Mitchell, Capt. James Oughton, 50 guns, 343 men.
Veteran – Captain A. C. Dickson, 64 guns, 491 men.
Ardent – Capt. T. Bertie, 64 guns, 491 men.
Belliqueux – Capt. R. Bulteel, 64 guns, 491 men.
Monmouth – Capt. Geo. Hart, 64 guns. 491 men.
Overijssel – Capt. J. Bazely, 64 guns, 491 men.
Mistisloff – Capt. A. Moller, 66 guns, 672 men.
Melpomene, Latona, Shannon, Juno, and *Lutine* frigates.[12]

---

12 After-action report of 31 August 1799 from Vice Admiral Mitchell to Evan Nepean, in the *Naval Chronicle*, Vol.II, pp.617-618.

BUILDING UP FORCES AND THE SURRENDER OF THE BATAVIAN FLEET

Then follows the correspondence leading to the surrender of the Batavian fleet, enclosed with Mitchell's after action report. Starting with his initial summons:

> Sir, I desire you will instantly hoist the flag of His Serene Highness the Prince of Orange. If you do, you will immediately be considered as friends of the King of Great Britain, my most gracious Sovereign, otherwise take the consequences. Painful it will be to me for the loss of blood it may occasion, but the guilt will be on your own head.[13]

Next the letter sent to Story after his surrender:

> The undersigned Vice-Admiral in the service of His Majesty, the King of Great Britain, charged with the execution of the naval part of the expedition to restore the Stadtholder and the old and lawful constitution of the Seven United Provinces, guaranteed by His Majesty, having agreed, that in consequence of the summons to Rear Admiral Story, the ships, after hoisting the ancient colours, will be considered as in the service of the allies of the British Crown, and under the orders of His Serene Highness the Hereditary Stadtholder, Captain and Admiral General of the Seven United Provinces, has thought it proper to give an account of this agreement to the brave crews of the different ships, and to summon them by the same to behave in a peaceable and orderly manner. so that no complaints may be represented by the officer, the undersigned will send on board each of the ships to keep proper order, until the intention of His Majesty, and His Serene Highness the Prince of Orange, as Admiral General, shall be known, for the further destination of these ships, on account of which dispatches will be immediately sent off. And to make them aware, that in case their conduct should not be so as may be expected from the known loyalty and attachment of the Dutch Navy to the Illustrious House of Orange on this occasion, any excess or irregularity will be punished with the severity which the disorders that may have been committed merit.[14]

Finally, Story's letter confirming his surrender:

> ADMIRAL, Neither your superiority, nor the threat that the spilling of human blood should be laid to my account, could prevent my showing you to the last moment what I could do for my Sovereign, whom I acknowledge to be no other than the Batavian People and its representatives, when your Prince's and the Orange flags have obtained their end. The traitors whom I commanded refused to fight; and nothing remains to me and my brave officers, but vain rage and the dreadful reflection of our present situation: I therefore deliver over to you the fleet which I commanded. From this moment it is your obligation to provide for the safety of my

---

13   Letter of 30 August 1799 from Mitchell to Story, in the *Naval Chronicle*, II, p.618.
14   Letter of 30 August 1799 from Mitchell to Story, in the *Naval Chronicle*, Vol.II, p.619.

officers, and the few brave men who are on board the Batavian ships, as I declare myself and my officers prisoners of war, and remain to be considered as such.[15]

The Batavian fleet remained in the Vlieter until 4 September, when it sailed to the roadstead of Texel anchoring there among the British ships.

The Prince of Orange in Holland

The hereditary Prince of Orange was in Lingen, at the eastern border of the Batavian Republic, preparing for the Orangist invasion from that side. On 2 September a letter came in (dated 28th August) for the Prince of Orange to join Abercromby in Holland. For that purpose, the British frigate *Cynthia* was waiting for him in Emden. Orangist command in Lingen passed over to *Lieutenant-Generaal* Prince Christiaan van Hessen-Darmstadt. After four days, on 7 September, the Prince of Orange arrived at Den Helder. Because of the strong wind and the tide the *Cynthia* could not enter the Marsdiep and a sloop had to bring the Prince to Huisduinen, from where he walked to Den Helder. He was welcomed by the citizens with orange flags on the houses and everyone wearing orange ribbons and cockades. It is questionable, however, if the citizens really meant it or were just showing the orange given the state of things. In any case, the Prince of Orange was very pleased by it, writing to his father the Stadtholder: 'I have the honour to report to you that I came here last night to the cheers of residents'. Also writing in the same letter: 'The roadstead of Texel, were the English and Dutch fleets have joined, provide a stunning sight'.[16] Few Orangists of any importance joined him though, the only exception being Mr. Hendrik van Stralen, who on 1 September came from Hoorn through the lines under the pretence that he was looking for the Patriot *Colonel* Gelderman, but having no problems of remaining with the British at Abercromby's request.[17]

The Prince of Orange was very optimistic about the state of things, as illustrated in the same letter. The same optimism is shown in the letter to his mother, Princess Wilhelmina, on the same date: 'Today I will go to the fleet and pay my respects to Admiral Mitchell, desiring to take much advantage of the crews, weapons and ammunition on board'.[18] More good news would arrive: *Lieutenant-Colonel* Panhuys handed over a list of 162 Batavian deserters since the British landings on 27 August: two cavalrymen, 142 line infantry, eight *jager* and 10 artillerymen. Every day deserters would come over to the British lines to declare

---

15 Letter of 30 August 1799 from Story to Mitchell, in the *Naval Chronicle*, Vol.II, p.619.
16 Letter of 8 September 1799 from the Heriditary Prince of Orange to the Stadtholder in Koolemans Beijnen, *De Erfprins van Oranje in Noord-Holland*, pp.2-3.
17 Hendrik van Stralen was an Orangist. He held various government positions until in 1795 the patriots came to power. This brought him some trouble but he managed to stay in Hoorn, although without holding an important position anymore. He joined the Prince of Orange in North Holland, although it would remain a mystery if he did that on purpose or was forced, after the failure of the invasion he refused to leave for England and returned to Hoorn. He was taken in custody but released after twelve days and rather surprisingly not bothered with any further.
18 Letter of 8 September 1799 from the Hereditary Prince of Orange to his mother, in Koolemans Beijnen, *De Erfprins van Oranje in Noord-Holland*, p.11.

for the Prince of Orange, although their number was by no means as considerable as had been expected.

That same day, Vice Admiral Mitchell picked up the Prince of Orange and both boarded the British flagship *Isis*. At its main mast the Dutch colour was hoisted, which was saluted by the British and Dutch fleet and the two Russian warships that were present. After that council was held, during which it was agreed that the Prince of Orange would try to convince the Dutch sailors to become volunteers and to form a corps for service on land or on the Zuiderzee. The Dutch ships would remain on the roadstead of Texel until orders would be received from the Stadtholder or the British Government. Next, the Prince of Orange boarded the *Washington*, the flagship of *Schout-bij-Nacht* Story. He was welcomed by the sailors, yelling *Hoezee!* three times. The sailors were addressed and requested to volunteer in the service of the State. The address was answered with cheers of joy. *Capitein ter Zee* Spengler was ordered to do the same on the other surrendered Batavian ships, after which the Prince of Orange returned to Den Helder. In total, 2,391 sailors volunteered. Added to these were the 162 Batavian deserters already mentioned and the 272 formerly imprisoned sailors that *Lieutenant ter Zee* Martinius had been able to win over for the Orangist cause from the prison hulks at Chatham as related in Chapter 5. This gave a corps of 2,825 men, for which at the moment only 14 officers were available, the ones that had been sent for from Germany still not having arrived from Britain.[19]

From Den Helder, the Prince of Orange went to Schagerbrug, to the headquarters of Abercromby. The Prince told about the arrangements made with Vice Admiral Mitchell, to which Abercromby could agree. It was arranged that the Dutch corps would be organised on Texel island and that a diversion to support the Orangist incursion in the east of the Batavian Republic could be made as soon as reinforcements would have arrived, enabling Abercromby to spare some detachments for this purpose. Although the Prince of Orange left Abercromby much satisfied, it seems that Abercromby in fact was not obliged to help at all. On the 11th, he wrote to the Secretary of State for War Henry Dundas: 'The Hereditary Prince of Orange arrived a few days ago; he has many projects to which I listen, but follow what to me appears for our interest.'[20]

Next day on the 9th, the Prince of Orange returned to Den Helder, making plans for diversions on the Zuiderzee, on the coast of Friesland at Harlingen and the coast of Gelderland at Nijkerk. Arrangements were made to embark the Dutch sailors and to transport them to Texel. Then Major General Don arrived with another proposal. He was of the opinion that Abercromby was too weak to defend the whole Westfriesche Zeedijk and that it was very important to reinforce him with a Dutch corps, if possible that same day. The Prince of Orange agreed immediately, sending the officers on board of the Batavian ships to prepare their disembarkation. However, Vice Admiral Mitchell convinced him that this would take time to prepare and that a proper disembarkation could not be executed before noon the next day. That same evening a message was send to Abercromby, asking him if he could approve the change. Nothing would come of it though. Early in the morning of the 10th, the Franco-Batavian army undertook a massive attack on the British positions along the

---

19 On 10 August it had been decided to send two thirds of the officers present at Lingen to Great Britain and from there to the Batavian Republic to form a Dutch corps: see Chapter 9 and Appendix XVIII.
20 Koolemans Beijnen, *De Erfprins van Oranje in Noord-Holland*, pp.11-13, 20. Abercromby's remark in English.

Schoorlsche and Westfriesche Zeedijk. Abercromby requested immediately Mitchell for all warships that could be spared, to clear the roadstead of Texel, to prevent disorder in the eventuality that a defeat would require a quick embarkation of his troops on the transport fleet. Almost at the same time, naval Lieutenant Collier returned from Great Britain, with orders of the British government and the Stadtholder to sail the Batavian ships to Great Britain. With all haste, the volunteers were disembarked and put on other vessels, without time to bring food or other necessities.[21]

Two days later, the ships arrived before the English coast:

> We have the satisfaction to announce the arrival in Ozely Bay, on the Suffolk Coast, of twelve sail of Dutch men of war, principally line of battle. These ships left the Texel on Tuesday last, bound to the Nore, under the command of Capt. Cobb, of the Glatton, accompanied by the Veteran, Ardent, Belliqueux, Monmouth, Overyssel, and two Russian ships. Previous to their departure many of the Dutch sailors were inclinable to be refractory, and absolutely refused to assist in getting up the ships anchors; however, a detachment of our gallant tars were soon distributed on board the respective ships, and Admiral Mitchell judged it necessary to send a sufficient force to see them safe to the Nore. The Washington is a remarkable fine ship, of 74 guns, was never before at sea, and sails faster than any ship in the fleet. The Ambuscade Dutch frigate, of 32 guns, came over with the above ships, but proceeded to Yarmouth Roads. Prior to the ships before mentioned leaving the Texel, the Marines were landed from all the English ships to do garrison duty, to enable the regular troops to join the main army. The Hereditary Prince of Orange has joined the army. His Highness visited the fleet on Sunday last, and was saluted by all the ships. Such of the Dutch sailors who declared for the Stadtholder, were drafted out of the respective ships before the fleet sailed.[22]

Daendels' Retreat

Daendels had retreated to a new position after the fighting of the 27th: The right wing was at the Zuiderzee near Oude-Sluis; the left wing at the North Sea near Petten; the centre behind the Oost-Egalement-Sloot. His position was vulnerable; much too extended and especially weak on the left wing at the North Sea where the British could advance along the beach protected by the cannon of their fleet and turn the Batavian positions. The Oost-Egalement-Sloot was not a major obstacle, as it had been filled with much sand over time. Daendels had under his command about 7,650 infantry, 1,000 cavalry, and 18 guns to hold a front-line of 16 kilometres. His ammunition supply was insufficient and there was no chance of quick support. Lastly, the British could support their attacks with gunfire from the fleet and execute an additional landing behind the Batavian positions. Daendels expected a British

---

21 Koolemans Beijnen, *De Erfprins van Oranje in Noord-Holland*, pp.13-15.
22 Extract of a letter from a correspondent in Harwich, 12 September 1799, in the *London Chronicle*, 14 September 1799.

"Anglo-Russian army camp near Calandsoog", by Dirk Langendijk. (Rijksmuseum, RP-T-1900-A-4380)

attack on the 28th but as described Abercromby was more interested in capturing Den Helder and taking possession of a safe harbour.

Again Daendels urged Brune to send reinforcements as soon as possible, but it would take time for the French to arrive at the front. It was observed that more British transports had arrived. The British front line was pushed forward, warships slowly made their way south along the coast in the direction of Petten. Batavian engineers had already begun constructing an entrenchment near Petten, batteries and parapets were thrown up. Nevertheless, thinking his position not strong enough and his opinion shared by many of his officers, Daendels ordered a retreat to a better line of defence, to prevent being his troops cut off and destroyed entirely. On the 30th at 3:00 a.m. the whole division started to retreat south. He took up new positions, initially temporarily, behind the northern canal of the Schermer polder with his left wing at Alkmaar, his right at the connection of the canals near Avenhorn. Arriving here, Daendels received word that French troops were in fact marching to his support, the first units being due to arrive in Alkmaar that same day. Ascertaining that these positions were strong enough to defend, especially the part behind the very deep circular canal of the Schermer polder, he decided to remain and to form a defence line here. The first French troops that arrived, led by *Général de Brigade* Gouvion, occupied the terrain between Alkmaar and the North Sea coast. They were the 2/ and 3/42e Demi-Brigade, the grenadier company of the 3/72e Demi-Brigade and an *escouade* of the 5/6e Artillerie à Pied with two 4pdr cannon, which had arrived in Haarlem on 29 September, by boat from Utrecht.[23] These units would be gradually reinforced by additional French troops as soon as they arrived.

Daendels placed his headquarters at Schermerhorn. The 31st was used to reinforce this defence line even more, throwing up parapets and constructing entrenchments and other field works. The commander of the Batavian engineers, *Lieutenant-Colonel* Krayenhoff, was sent to Amsterdam to strengthen its defences, on the seaside as well as on land. The behaviour of *Generaal-Major* van Guèricke on the 27th, marching his troops in the Koegras marsh contrary to his orders, unable to join the battle, caused him to be relieved from his brigade command and sent to Amsterdam to resume command of the city. In his place command of the 1e Brigade was given to *Colonel* Rietvelt, former commander of the 1e Halve Brigade which became the core of the 1e Brigade.

Daendels' defeat and the subsequent evacuation of Den Helder came as an unexpected shock for the Batavian government, as well as for Brune, as it was generally believed that the British would be defeated when they landed or at least would lose heavily. Evacuating Den Helder without a shot fired was impossible in their eyes. After this debacle, on the 29th, Brune had ordered Daendels: 'You must dispute the ground every inch of the way, defending Alkmaar. If you are forced out of the Zijpe, the only reason that you can abandon it, your retreat should take place at the last extremity.'[24] When hearing about Daendels' further retreat on the 30th, he is reported to have said: 'He is mad, or he is a traitor!' ('*Il est fou, ou il est traitre*').[25] Enraged and determined to force the Batavians to fight for their own country, he requested and obtained from the Batavian *Uitvoerend Bewind* the power to punish the cowards:

> On the proposal on this subject, having considered that the salvation of the country requires that no action will be overlooked and also everything from the Batavian army that could be suspect of cowardice, or bad faith, will be powerfully suppressed. Stopped. The *général en chef* Brune, although authorized by the very nature of his appointment and powers given to him, for all suspect military national units under his command, provided that it needs to be expressly stated an is actually declared by us, authorized and instructed to place under arrest all Batavian military officers, senior or subaltern, was it even *Lieutenant-Generaal* Daendels himself, if he judged it is necessary to hold such suspect officers in custody until they can placed on trial according to the law.[26]

On 1 September, the *Uitvoerend Bewind* ordered one of its members, Joannes van Hooff, together with the Minister of War Pijman, to go to Brune's headquarters in Alkmaar in order to:

---

23 Édourd Gachot, *Jourdan en Allemagne et Brune en Hollande* (Paris : Didier Perrin et Cie, 1906), p.228.
24 Letter of 29 August from Brune to Daendels, quoted in Gachot, *Brune en Hollande*, p.228.
25 Krayenhoff, *Geschiedkundige Beschouwing*, p.102. Daendel's retreat led to much discussion amongst historians, the best analysis given by G.J.W. Koolemans Beijnen, 'Het terugtrekken van Daendels in 1799 uit de Zijpe naar den Schermer' in *Jaarboek van de Maatschappij der Nederlandse Letterkunde* (Leiden: E.J. Brill, 1898), pp.211-220.
26 The *Uitvoerend Bewind* to Brune, 1 September 1799, quoted in Gachot, *Brune en Hollande*, pp.227-228.

Inform themselves about the current state of the Army, the inclination of senior and subaltern officers, and the reasons for the repeated retrograde marches. And to make, concerted with the *Generaal en Chef*, such preparations, to take an offensive posture when it is possible; to express that the Batavian Army and the men of honour, which command them, can all rely on the courage and steadfastness of the Batavian Government; to express strongly that orders are to be followed from the Government and of the *Generaal en Chef*; the Constituted Powers, in and around the Theatre of War, encouraging to do their duty and to maintain order and safety; at all occasions to express in the most convenient way the disposition and feelings of the Batavian Government; and to try to take away any adverse effect, which cowardice may have instilled either with the Batavian Army or the respective citizens inside the cities or in the countryside.[27]

Arriving 2 September at Brune's headquarters in Alkmaar and informing themselves about the situation, this commission judged that the decision of Daendels to retreat had been correct under the circumstances.[28] Brune also had to conclude that Daendels' previous positions were untenable, so no repercussions followed. French trust however would not be restored that quickly. French support, on the other hand, was high on the agenda of the Batavian Government. It was widely believed that the French would only care for the defence of their northern border and even on the 29th, the French *Directoire* had to send a letter to the Batavian Government to assure that: 'The French Government, as a faithful ally, would never allow that freedom would be suppressed on Batavian soil, and that the whole nation would haste to stand against the common enemy as one man!'[29] Still, when the British landing took place, it was rumoured that Brune was too slow in sending French troops to Holland. This supposition was taken over by a number of Dutch historians stating that Brune was still believing the landing in North-Holland to be a feint, expecting the real invasion elsewhere. This is not supported by the facts though. The location of the landing could only be sure when the actual landing took place, as the British fleet was already before the Batavian coast for a week. The first French troops that arrived in Holland, coming from Utrecht, had embarked there on inland barges on the evening of the 28th at nine o'clock, the day after the landing. Taking in account that time was needed to give the necessary orders, which then had to reach Utrecht, to assemble the troops and to prepare the embarkation, it could never have happened sooner.

The barges sailed on the inland waterways during the night, by the light of lanterns. They arrived in Haarlem on the 29th, were they found half of the 1/8e Artillerie Légère armed with a 4pdr and an 8pdr cannon and a howitzer. From there, starting on the 30th at first light, they force-marched by Beverwijk and Castricum to Alkmaar. Leaving behind part of the 2/42e Demi-Brigade in this city the remainder marched on, joining Daendels' Batavians at six o'clock in the evening. On the 30th, the 3/60e Demi-Brigade and a weak squadron

---

27 Letter of 1 September 1799 from the *Uitvoerend Bewind* to the Batavian *Vertegenwoordigend Lichaam* in *Besluiten der Eerste Kamer van het Vertegenwoordigend Lichaam des Bataafschen Volks. September 1799*, pp.8-10.
28 Krayenhoff, *Geschiedkundige*, p.103.
29 Letter from the French *directoire* to the Batavian *Uitvoerend Bewind*, quoted in *Besluiten der Eerste Kamer. September 1799*, pp.6-7.

of the 5e Chasseurs à Cheval arrived in Haarlem. So in just three days substantial French forces had joined Daendels. The next and following days more troops arrived, raising French strength quickly to about 7,000. On 2 September, Brune arrived in Alkmaar, establishing his headquarters there. On the 4th, he reconnoitred the terrain between Egmond aan Zee and Avenhorn.

On the 5th the French troops were organised in a division commanded by *Général de Division* Vandamme, consisting of three brigades commanded by *Généraux de Brigade* Gouvion, David, and Fuzier.[30] Vandamme occupied the terrain around the villages Schoorl and Groet, on the left flank of the Franco-Batavian army. At the village of Koedijk a bridge was built over the Kanaal van Alkmaar, in order to maintain communications with the centre.

From this moment on, also many measures for a defence in depth were carried out: gunboats were posted on the IJ and the Pampus; on the coast along the Zuiderzee batteries were prepared; the front line in North-Holland was strengthened with entrenchments and defences in depth were made ready. Redoubts were constructed in the line Haarlem-Amsterdam near Spaarndam, Penningsveer, and Liebrug. Inundations were prepared in the line Monnikendam–Purmerend–Knollendam–Krommenie–Beverwijk. In the approaches, entrenchments and batteries were constructed. This line would need few troops to defend it and would protect Amsterdam against an attack from the north. In the second line, inundations were made ready in the line Uitdam–Oost-Zanen. Both companies of the Amsterdamsche Stadssoldaten were sent to Leiden. The stores at Hoorn were emptied and brought south to safety, behind the Franco-Batavian lines. Daendels instructed his officers that:

> The commanders of detachments or patrols, on towers, or other public and also private buildings, finding and orange or princely flag, are ordered to set on fire the building and to let it burn down. They will arrest those persons wearing orange cockades or ribbons, or if they tried to escape shoot them dead; they will be responsible for all negligence or excess in such matters.[31]

In Haarlem the Municipality was ordered to prepare hospitals. In Amsterdam a French hospital was set up. Haarlem was also appointed concentration point for the companies of the *Gewapende Burgermacht*. On 29 August six hundred men of the *Gewapende Burgermacht* of Amsterdam arrived here, the next day followed by a corps of citizen artillery. On 1 September a grenadier, a *jager* and a fusilier company from Utrecht arrived. In all, 10 grenadier companies, seven fusilier companies and three *jager* companies were sent to Haarlem. Arriving besides the companies already mentioned were a company from Arnhem, one from Gorkum, one from Amersfoort, and one from Rotterdam; a fusilier and a grenadier company from Groningen commanded by *Capitein* Scholten; a *jager* company from Zwolle and a grenadier company from Zutphen. However of those that arrived, most proved to be a burden instead of a support. The men received no payment, no uniforms, and

---

30   Gachot, *Brune en Hollande*, pp.228-233. See Appendix X for the composition of the French troops.
31   Quoted in L.C. Vonk, *Geschiedenis der Landing van het Engelsch-Russisch leger in Noord-Holland* (Haarlem: François Bohn, 1801) Vol.I, pp.102-103.

not enough food. As a result discipline was bad and in order to get some money for food some of them even sold the few uniform parts they had. Many deserted and returned to their homesteads. On 7 September the greater part of the *Gewapende Burgermacht*, useless citizens 'including our heroes of Utrecht who were sent back for their heroism in gorging, drinking, partying, and whoring'[32] were sent back from Haarlem to Leiden. To make room for these, the Amsterdamsche Stadssoldaten went from Leiden to Utrecht. Most men that remained under arms were used for auxiliary tasks, did garrison duty or guarded prisoners.

On the 30th *Lieutenant-Generaal* Dumonceau, defending the north-eastern provinces with the 2e Bataafsche Divisie, received orders from Brune to assemble two thirds of his division and to proceed as quickly as possible to Amsterdam, to await further orders. With the Batavian fleet captured and the British navy free to roam the Zuiderzee, it was no longer safe to transport the soldiers by ship and they would have to march overland. The troops marched already the next day, leaving behind the following units:

- 2e Regiment Waldeck in Delfzijl and environs;
- 5e Bataljon Waldeck on the Nieuwe Schans and environs;

These units were composed of German soldiers in Batavian service, which had already been in service of the Dutch Republic. The officers of this regiment had declared to an Orangist agent, that they would submit to the British forces if summoned to do so. The British failed to use this to their advantage though. These units were so understrength that they were not fit for field service. Additionally left behind were:

- 2/4e Halve Brigade in Harlingen and other towns at the Zuiderzee coast, detachments on the islands Vlieland, Terschelling and Ameland;
- Detachment of the 3e Bataljon Jagers in Coevorden;
- Compagnie Friesche Gardes (200) in Coevorden;
- Compagnie Groninger Gardes (75) in Groningen.

Command of these troops was given to *Colonel* Boonacker. Brune took a risk to leave so few troops behind to defend the northern provinces but he had no choice because the troops were badly needed in Holland. Again, proof that Brune reacted as quickly as possible to concentrate all troops at his disposal against the British in Holland.

All regular Batavian units available were now present in Holland with the following exceptions: the above mentioned troops that remained in the north-eastern provinces; the Regiment Saxen-Gotha in garrison in Rotterdam and Schiedam; the 2e Regiment Waldeck in garrison in The Hague; the 2/3e Halve Brigade and the 1/2e Regiment Zware Cavalerie which formed the bodyguard of the Batavian Government in The Hague; the 3/3e Halve Brigade in garrison in Middelburg and the greater part of the foot artillery serving along the coast and in various fortresses. The 1/ and 2/5e Halve Brigade had suffered heavily on the 27th and had to be removed from the line temporarily.

---

32 Hendr. Keetell, 'Aanteekeningen betreffende de Bat. Omwenteling voornamelijk binnen Utrecht. Door een ooggetuige' in *De Navorscher* (Utrecht: C. Snoek Wz., 1902), p.460.

By 7 September, Dumonceau reached Amsterdam with his troops, some units marching up to 240 kilometres in seven days![33] From there the troops were embarked on inland barges to continue their journey to Holland. On the 8th and 9th they reached Alkmaar. The Batavian troops were reorganised to create two divisions of almost equal strength. Dumonceau received command of the centre of the Franco-Batavian army, Daendels commanding the right wing while Vandamme's French division was on the left.[34] Since the landing, only some skirmishing between outposts and patrols took place. Lieutenant Colborne of the 20th Foot, commanding at an outpost in front of Crabbendam at the road to Alkmaar, relates the following incidents:

> I was to remain with the picquets all night. At the grey of the morning the post was attacked, two men on my picquet were killed and some wounded… On another occasion I was visiting a distant picquet near a dyke when I heard a sound in the water which I thought at first was a dog, but on going with a sergeant to reconnoitre, we discovered a Dutch officer in uniform measuring the depth of the dyke with a stick, and we captured him. The dyke was about three feet deep in water and three in mud. It was thought he was measuring with a view to an attack, and the surmise proved to be correct, for we were attacked two days afterwards.[35]

In the morning of 9 September, a British force of 20 light dragoons tried to penetrate into the village Oud-Karspel. The Batavian *jagers* from the 1e Bataljon Jagers, who were in position behind some fascines, let them advance until they were only a few metres away. Then they fired a volley, killing or wounding 12 light dragoons and as many horses. The survivors routed instantly.

Finally, a curious incident must be mentioned which took place in the evening of 31 August, when the British Major General Don arrived at the Batavian outposts under a flag of truce. He stated he had a mission for the Batavian government and requested a passport for The Hague. Daendels decided to use this event to his advantage in buying time and refused the passport on the grounds that there was no order to provide one and that Don had to wait for the arrival of Brune, who was still in The Hague. When Brune arrived in Alkmaar on 2 September, Don's request was flatly refused and he had to return to the British headquarters without completing his mission. Daendels was glad he had bought a few days this way to reinforce his positions, without being disturbed by the British.[36]

---

33 A.F. Meyer, *Dagboek van den luitenant-generaal jonkheer Adriaan Frans Meyer, geboren 1768* (NIMH, Handschriften, 511, inv.58), p.17.
34 For the compositions and locations of the Franco-Batavian army on 9 September 1799, see Appendix X.
35 Moore Smith, *Life of John Colborne*, pp.10-11.
36 Krayenhoff, *Geschiedkundige*, pp.103-104.

"Batavian *jager* ambush a British patrol near Schoorldam", by Cornelis Brouwer after a drawing of Dirk Langendijk. (Rijksmuseum, RP-P-OB-86.721)

"Defeat of a British outpost near Schoorldam", anonymous. (Noord-Hollands Archief, NL-HlmNHA_480_000500_M)

9

The Orangist Incursion into the Batavian Republic

The Orangist incursion in the eastern provinces of the Batavian Republic would make a huge impression on the population, not in the last place because of the subsequent execution of the *freule* van Dorth tot Holthuizen. This was the first 'modern-time' execution of a woman by a military tribunal, to set an example and as such also a political one. The huge outcry caused by this execution led to a fair number of local publications about this subject. Outside the Netherlands however the Orangist incursion is more or less neglected, as is their whole participation in this campaign. Although from a military view the Orangists indeed did not contribute much, their actions however were significant from a political view.

Support for the Orangist cause had always been strong in the eastern provinces, especially amongst the peasants and the lower nobility, contrary to the western parts of the country where all the big cities were situated, bastions for the Patriots. As we have seen this divide culminated in an open Patriotic revolt when Prussian military support was needed to enable the House of Orange to maintain in power (see Chapter 1). After years of intense fighting in the southern Netherlands in 1793 and 1794, and despite extensive British military support, the curtain finally fell after the Austrian retreat and the subsequent French advance across the frozen rivers. Despite lenient treatment of the Orangists, with few being badly treated or punished by the Batavian government, many chose to leave the country. Especially and not surprisingly, many soldiers and officers of the former army emigrated to the German and Prussian areas east of the Batavian Republic, not wanting to ally with the French archenemy. Many gathered at Osnabruck in 1795, forming the so-called *Rassemblement*, waiting for the right chance to invade the Batavian Republic from the east, again with Prussian support. However, hope quickly faded away when Prussia closed the Peace of Basel with France, abandoning the First Coalition. Even more, the treaty stipulated that the Prussians would uphold a line of demarcation and therefore the *Rassemblement* had to be disbanded. The soldiers and NCOs received a gratification from Great Britain, the officers, however, received a British allowance. Not able to return to the Batavian Republic they settled along the eastern border of the Batavian Republic, ready to take up arms again whenever the opportunity would arise. Of course these were the officers and others persons which had the financial means to remain here; the common people in most cases had no choice as to return to the Batavian Republic and make the best of it, aided by the Patriot tolerance. In the months prior to the Anglo-Russian invasion, however, new emigrants had arrived from the Batavian republic, men who wanted to evade the conscription that was imposed by the

Batavian government and who now would otherwise have been sent to Holland to fight against the British. Not surprisingly though, not all of the latter were eager to take up arms against the Batavian Republic instead.

The Prince of Orange in Lingen

Despite the peace of Campo Formio of 17 October 1797, which left Great Britain standing alone in its war against France, the political situation in Europe remained unstable. During the whole of 1798, secret negations took place between Great Britain, Austria, Russia, and Prussia. Tsar Paul I of Russian was prepared to march his armies against France when subsidised by Great Britain. An attack on the Batavian Republic by a Prussian army supported by a Russian contingent paid for by the British, to support the reinstatement of the Stadtholder, William V of Orange, was one of the proposals that were made. Trustworthy Orangist officers made preparations to overthrow the Batavian government and contacted Orangists still living in the Batavian Republic. They even contacted the rebels in the Southern Netherlands who fought the French in the so called *Boerenkrijg* (Peasants' War).[1] The negotiations with Prussia were arduous and the outcome was still unsure. This was illustrated by Thomas Grenville in his letter of 12 March to London:

> I am occupied in pursuing with General Stamfort a project proposing to Petersburg the immediate march of a large Russian force towards Germany: It may in its march decide the doubtful conduct of Berlin; and it may encourage the Elector of Saxony who is well disposed to exertion. May not this be well assisted by a naval enterprise at the same time from the Baltic, to carry troops from Russia and Denmark to Holland? But time presses and we should be acting.[2]

Despite this, no progress was made with the Prussians, but in April 1799 the Austrians and Russians under Suvorov launched a successful attack on the French in Italy. The Anglo-Russian design for an attack on the Batavian Republic became more concrete as well, as already described. The House of Orange was in high spirits; even more when, in mid-June, a report came in that former *Captain-Lieutenant ter Zee* Ver Huell had been able to persuade *Capitein ter Zee* van Braam, commanding the ship of the line *Leyden* which was part of the Batavian fleet at the roads of Texel, to declare for the House of Orange when the British fleet would arrive, and to persuade the whole fleet to join the British.[3] On 22 July, the British asked the hereditary Prince of Orange to go to Lingen on the eastern Batavian border, to organise an invasion of the Batavian Republic. As before, he was instructed not to advance before

---

1   G.J.W. Koolemans Beijnen, *De Erfprins van Oranje te Lingen in 1799*, overprint from *Bijdragen voor Vaderlandsche Geschiedenis en Oudheidkunde* ('s-Gravenhage: Martinus Nijhoff, 1907), p.12.
2   G.J.W. Koolemans Beijnen, 'De invloed van de Oranje-partij in Gelderland op het voornemen tot de landing der Engelschen en Russen in Noord-Holland in 1799', *Jaarboek van de Maatschappij der Nederlandse Letterkunde* (Leiden: E.J. Brill, 1900), p.174.
3   A report from Ver Huell about his conversation with *Capitein ter Zee* van Braam is in Colenbrander, *Gedenkstukken*, Vol.III, pp.993-996.

foreign military aid was at hand; despite Orangist enthusiasm, the British were still very convinced that an Orangist invasion and uprising could not succeed without foreign support:

> About the same time that the English fleet sails, it would be advisable for the Hereditary Prince of Orange to approach the frontier. He will be ready to penetrate rapidly into the interior of the country as soon as he shall be informed of what has passed at The Hague, and will establish himself in the town where he may choose to fix his head-quarters; Arnheim perhaps would be to be preferred as centrical. If from any cause whatever he should arrive before the Prince his Father shall have landed, it will be advisable for him to take upon himself the administration ad interim, declaring at the same time that he will make no other use of his authority than to deposit it in his father's hands.
>
> As soon as he shall have arrived, the Directory will send orders to their troops to put themselves under his command. The Prince will send into each of the different towns an officer on whom he can depend to take the command provisionally and to introduce any fresh troops he may think proper to send. The English in the mean time having landed at the Texel, the Brill or whatever ports might be thought preferable, the few French troops now in Holland would find themselves under the necessity of making a precipitate retreat. Little resistance is to be expected from the Dutch fortresses, as the small French force in each would be under the necessity of following the impulse of the Dutch troops.[4]

The Prince of Orange arrived in Lingen on 3 August, in fact starting a new *Rassemblement*. Orangists gathered at several places, especially Lingen and Emmerich. The Orangists were for a long time convinced that their advance would be supported by a Prussian army corps, as a result of the negotiations between Great Britain and Prussia. That hope would become a big disappointment though. Negotiations with Prussia ended abruptly on 25 July when the Prussians stated that they wanted to continue negotiating with the French first. Events were unfolding quickly: on 31 July London was informed of the failed negotiations with Prussia, three days later Sir Ralph Abercromby received his instructions:

> An agreement having been entered into between H.M. and His ally the Emperor of Russia, to endeavour by their joint efforts to rescue the United Provinces of Holland from the degrading tyranny of the French Republic and to restore them to their independence under the authority of the Prince of Orange and their lawful government, H.M., anxious to contribute to the utmost of His power to the success of this great enterprise, has directed such preparations both naval and military as can be supplied from the resources of this country to be made with the utmost vigour and expedition… I have the satisfaction to inform you that H.M. has been graciously pleased to make choice of you to command the first division of troops which are to be sent from this country.[5]

---

4   Letter in English of 26 July 1799 from Munniks to Hammond in Colenbrander, *Gedenkstukken*, Vol.III, pp.380-381.
5   Letter in English of 3 August 1799 from Henry Dundas to Abercromby in Colenbrander, *Gedenkstukken*, Vol.III, p.383.

At Lingen on 10 August, the Prince of Orange received a message from the British government that he was authorised to raise three Dutch infantry regiments paid by the British, to be officered by the officers present at the *Rassemblement*. It was decided to ship two thirds of the officers needed for two regiments to Great Britain, from there to the Batavian Republic when needed to raise these regiments there.[6] The third regiment would be raised in the eastern part of the Batavian Republic.[7] In the meantime, every effort was made to persuade officers, Batavian units, peasants, everyone who could contribute, to join the Orangist cause, and to be ready to support the eastern advance into the Batavian Republic when news of the British invasion would be received. Despite many refusals, the general Orangist view still was that the eastern provinces would rise *en masse* to support their cause, aided by the fact that most of the Batavian regular troops would have been moved west to defend the coast against an anticipated British invasion. What was left in the eastern provinces were some small depots and the volunteers of the *Gewapende Burgermacht*, armed civilians with minor or no military training at all. However, even of the latter, the grenadiers of the *Gewapende Burgermacht* from Arnhem and Zutphen had marched to Holland.

That the inhabitants would join the Orangist cause in large numbers was not at all that certain however. Although many Patriots were by now disappointed by what the creation of the Batavian Republic and the intimate relation with France had brought, taking sides with the Orangists again was an entirely different matter. To make things worse, amongst other measures taken, on 23 August the Batavian government issued a decree that was, even for that time, far-reaching regarding the punishment for a whole range of activities in favour of the Orangists:

> That all persons, which after the date of this law, leave the country without proper passport, will be considered emigrants, and when caught will be punished by death! That those who have left with a proper passport, but of which is proven that they have one way or another, direct or indirect, have corresponded, collaborated, or participated in treasonous talks with enemies of the State, will be punished by death without any leniency! … That all expatriates, who are caught armed, will be punished by death, the verdict to be carried out without any trial within 24 hours; including all officers, natives of the State, which have been licensed or discharged … That all who resist against the lawful government, armed or in any other way, contrary to the order of things, which will participate in the restoration of any unlawful government, in what form or under what name whatsoever – All which will yell riot cries, will wear or raise signs or give signs, ring church bells, light fires or such kind of things, give motive for gatherings or riots – All which, without being a member of the *Gewapende Burgermacht*, will appear on the streets carrying any weapons, or are in secret possession of weapons – All who defect to the enemy, have contact with the enemy, or carry weapons to support the enemy – All leaders of looters or looting themselves ore have committed such kind of crimes, will be punished with death without the usual form of trial… Finally, the

---

6   See Appendix XVIII for a list of the officers.
7   Koolemans Beijnen, *De Erfprins van Oranje te Lingen*, p.39.

Executive Government is authorised to declare martial law when necessary for all cities, places or regions, and to withdraw martial law again when it is not necessary anymore. Any city, place or region were martial law is declared, is subject to the orders of the Military Power… A military tribunal will investigate and judge in all insurgent cases.[8]

This decree was the basis for a publication issued by the executive government, pointing out the consequences of the declaration of martial law, repeating the contents of the decree regarding the grounds for punishment and adding (as article 13) that all verdicts of the military tribunal had to be executed within 24 hours, without the possibility of appeal.[9] This publication was proclaimed throughout the Batavian Republic and had indeed the desired impact on the population.

The Orangist Plan

In all their enthusiasm, the Orangists completely forgot the British instruction to wait until foreign military support had arrived. The Orangist Baron van Lynden van Hoevelaken wrote on 19 August to the Prince of Orange: 'Things have now come so far, even if the British invasion would fail, it has to go through!'. The Prince of Orange replied on the 22nd:

I agree with U.H.W.G. [Your High Born] that the cause has advanced so far, that it should be put through. I believe that will happen shortly, as I received report that the first division of the expedition under the command of General Abercromby has departed on the 13th, with favourable winds; so that we could receive news every moment that the landing has taken place.[10]

At the same time and despite their enthusiasm, the Orangists were running out of time. On the 23rd, *Schout bij Nacht* Rietveld in Emmerich was ordered to buy four hundred muskets, including powder and ball, and if possible sabres and cartridge pouches. This was not only to arm the men that would join their cause; most Orangists themselves were without proper weapons. On 1 September, *Colonel* van Dongen wrote to the Prince of Orange:

Madame Van Voerst writes me from Zwolle that two Batavian battalions have arrived there, more to be expected… Luckily I received some powder, and this afternoon several hundreds of cartridges will be prepared, as well as a number of very heavy *moordslagen* [a kind of defensive hand grenade, used to defend breaches], to make up for the lack of cannon. No deserters arrive, so my corps consists, except for 8 to 10 privates, of officers only. *Capitein* Noblet commands my *jager*, numbering

---

8 *Besluiten van de Tweede Kamer en Decreeten van het Vertegenwoordigend Lichaam des Bataafschen Volks. Augustus 1799*, 23 August 1799.
9 *Publicatie van het Uitvoerend Bewind der Bataafsche Republiek, wegens het beleid der Justitie in plaatsen, in staat van beleg gesteld*.
10 Koolemans Beijnen, *De Erfprins van Oranje te Lingen*, pp 64-65.

twelve, all in green and armed with good muskets or double-barrelled hunting rifles.[11]

Two days later, the Orangists at Lingen learned that the British fleet had been sighted at Texel on the 22nd. On the 28th letters arrived dated 23 and 24 August, informing them firstly that the original plan to land on Voorne or Goeree had been abandoned and that the landing definitely would take place south of Den Helder, and then that because of bad weather, the fleet had put to sea again and had not been able to berth. On 31 August news arrived that the British had finally landed. Reports were exaggerated though: Batavian losses were supposed to be heavy, whole regiments had been destroyed or had defected to the British! This caused the Prince of Orange to send a letter to Abercromby, firstly to congratulate him with his success and secondly to request to him to send some vessels to the Zuiderzee to open communications and to send him a 1,000 to 1,500 British soldiers to reinforce the Orangists. There still was no news about the Batavian fleet, nevertheless former *Vice-Admiraal* van Braam was requested to take over command of this fleet as soon as it had defected, but in fact Van Braam would not show up. A proclamation was printed, urging the population to join the Orangist cause.

As we have seen, however, the Prince of Orange however would not remain in Lingen to see the outcome of the Orangist incursion in the east. On 2 September a letter arrived (dated the 28th) requesting the Prince of Orange to join Abercromby in Holland. For that purpose, the British frigate *Cynthia* was waiting for him in Embden. Orangist command in Lingen passed over to *Lieutenant-Generaal* Prince Christiaan van Hessen-Darmstadt.[12]

The Orangist Incursions

The Orangist invasion that was about to take place was badly coordinated and apparently no specific plan was followed. A number of incursions took place and at many towns and villages, Orangists gathered only to disperse when a threat came near. However, the events itself and their aftermath left a lasting impression and changed the way Patriots and Orangists until now had treated each other. To give an impression, a description of the major events taking place during these incursions follows.

On 2 September an Orangist force led by *Colonel* van Dongen entered Enschede at five o'clock in the morning. Van Dongen commanded 100 men, mainly Orangist officers, all wearing an orange cockade. They were partially armed with hunting rifles and muskets, others unarmed. Arriving in Enschede sentries were placed at the gates, in addition four men were posted at the church tower to prevent the bell being rung. Then *Colonel* van Dongen forced the commander of the *Gewapende Burgermacht*, a sergeant-major, to hand over all weapons, which were used to arm the men still without them. In the evening the Orangists retreated to Glaanderbrug at the border. In the afternoon of 3 September, the Orangists again occupied Enschede, only to retreat again to Glaanderbrug before darkness.

---

11   Koolemans Beijnen, *De Erfprins van Oranje te Lingen*, pp.72-73.
12   Koolemans Beijnen, *De Erfprins van Oranje te Lingen*, pp.73-74.

Next day it was autumn fair in Enschede and when the Orangists arrived here, for the third day on a row, they met many farmers from the neighbouring countryside. A fair number of them were persuaded to join the cause and joined the Orangists. In the afternoon a group of eight officers were ordered by *Colonel* van Dongen to go to Hengelo in order to capture all weapons that could be found there. Accomplishing this without any trouble, in the morning of the 5th they were joined by *Colonel* van Dongen with the remainder of the officers and the farmers.

The captured weapons were loaded on carts and the whole force moved on to the next town, Oldenzaal. Their strength was now about forty officers and the partially mounted farmers, the latter mostly armed with cudgels and scythes. Arriving at the gate they were met by the mayor, asking Van Dongen what his intentions were. Van Dongen replied that he came to occupy the city and to capture all weapons and ammunition present. The mayor answered that he would not prevent the Orangists entering the city, but would prevent the capture of the weapons by force. After this refusal, the Orangists formed a column and entered the city, marching to the town hall, believing that the weapons would be stored here. Arriving at the market place, they encountered members of the *Gewapende Burgermacht*, which resisted: some shots were fired, slightly wounding some Orangists. The Orangists charged and a some men of the *Gewapende Burgermacht* retreated into the town hall, barricading the doors. With a beam, the doors were forced open, and the Orangists disarmed those of the *Gewapende Burgermacht* that surrendered, throwing others out of the windows.

The occupation of Oldenzaal did not last long though; receiving news that regular troops were advancing, the Orangists retreated to the border again taking with them all captured weapons.[13] These regulars were soldiers from Deventer: here, an Orangist uprising had also taken place. On 4 September however, *Capitein* Vognitz managed to get into the city with two Batavian infantry companies and prevented further Orangist manifestations.

During the night of 2-3 September, a group of Orangists crossed the border and entered the town of Dinxperlo. Here they cut down the liberty tree, sign of freedom for the Patriots. Then the Orangists crossed the border leaving the Batavian Republic again. Next day again an Orangist troop arrived in Dinxperlo, this time *Lieutenant-Colonel* Spengler commanding a group of 40 officers wearing the ancient Dutch uniform. However, after having proclaimed the proclamation of the Prince of Orange already mentioned and hoisting an orange flag from the church tower, they also returned across the border. In the morning of the 5th, *Lieutenant-Colonel* van Heemskerck arrived in Dinxperlo with about 300 men. He requested quarters to be prepared for a cavalry regiment 1,000-strong and three infantry regiments, also of 1,000 men each. Then on the 6th they requisitioned 12 horses and some wagons, loaded them with their weapons and departed for the border.[14]

At Emmerich about 70 Orangist officers had gathered. Only a few had good muskets; most were armed with worn-out, nearly useless muskets that had been bought in Wesel. On 3 September in the evening, they were ordered to move in the direction of the border.

---

13 P.Q.R., 'Inval der Oranje-Emigranten in Overijssel', in *De Navorscher* (Amsterdam: Frederik Muller, 1854), pp.232-233; A.A. IJske, 'Inval der Oranje-Emigranten in Overijssel', in *De Navorscher* (Amsterdam: Frederik Muller, 1855), pp.33-35.
14 J.W. Staats Evers, *De Geldersche Achterhoek in 1799. Eene bijdrage tot den Patriottentijd* (Winterswijk: K.J.M. van Tiffelen, 1879), p.6.

They had no clue what their destination or what the purpose of their march was. Arriving in Zevenaar they remained for the night, trying to get some sleep in an inn, on the chairs and benches. In the morning they resumed their march, led by *Lieutenant-Colonel* Spengler who was executing his part of the plan. Arriving at the border they found two carts with muskets and cartridges, allowing everyone to be armed properly.[15] Apparently the original party of 70 men was reinforced with farmers armed with sticks, cudgels, and scythes, giving Spengler a force of 200 to 300 men, recognisable by their orange cockades. Reaching Westervoort they occupied the village and captured the floating bridge across the River IJssel, removing some of the pontoons. An orange flag was hoisted from the church tower and the proclamation read aloud. The Geldersoor entrenchment was also captured without any opposition as the only men present were a few labourers.

The arrival of the Orangists in Westervoort, one hour distance from Arnhem, caused dismay amongst the Patriots in that city: the troops garrisoned here had been send to Haarlem to confront the British invasion and the only military force left were about a hundred men of the *Gewapende Burgermacht*, led by *Colonel* Schoonman who commanded the *Gewapende Burgermacht* in the *Departement van den Rijn*. Because of the Orangist capture of the floating bridge, the strength of the Orangists was unknown and it was rumoured that they were accompanied by 3,000 Prussian and Hessian regulars. Further rumours had it that more than 10,000 Prussian troops were to follow. Drums were beaten and the *Gewapende Burgermacht* was called out, all gates closed and occupied by doubled guards. Messages were sent to the municipalities of all the villages along the river near Arnhem, to confiscate and fetch all boats and pontoons to this side of the river, to prevent any Orangist crossing. At about 11 o'clock a detachment, commanded by *Capitein* van der Sanden and *Lieutenant* Verwoert, left Arnhem and marched to the River Ijssel opposite Westervoort. It consisted of 50 volunteers, including some actors with their imitation-weapons(!), and a light field cannon under the command of *Eerste Lieutenant* Kniest. They halted at the Scheysprong, under cover of some trees, sending out an advance guard to reconnoitre. The ferries close by were occupied to prevent their use by the Orangists.

Arriving at the river, the advance guard was greeted with some irregular shots by Orangists who had taken up position along the riverside, yelling 'Oranje Boven!' and cursing at the Patriots.[16] Schoonman deployed the field cannon and a few shots drove back the Orangists from the riverside, which now took up position behind the dike and in nearby houses. A second light field cannon was brought up from Arnhem and *Lieutenant* Kniest deployed it in a flanking position, starting to fire at the roof tops. This was enough to force the Orangists to retreat, returning to Zevenaar. Sources differ about losses but these were minor: two to three wounded Patriots of which one would die of his wound; the Orangists suffered one or two wounded and a few dead.

---

15   J. Brauw, *Mijne emigratie in Duitschland, Engeland en Ierland, in de jaren 1799-1802* (Utrecht: N. van der Monde, 1837), pp.8-12.
16   *Oranje Boven*, 'Orange Top', relates to the Dutch national flag during the war against Spain in the 17th Century, which originally was orange over white over blue. The yell refers to the colour orange as well as to the Dutch leader at that time, Prince William of Orange. It remained that way when in later years the orange in the national flag was changed to red.

"Skirmish between the *Gewapende Burgermacht* of Arnhem and the Orangists in Westervoort", by Reinier Vinkeles after a drawing of Dirk Langendijk. (Rijksmuseum RP-P-1944-694)

The Patriots had no time to celebrate though: news came that in Rheede and other villages, Orangist farmers had taken up arms. A detachment of the *Gewapende Burgermacht* sent by *Colonel* Schoonman encountered about 300 armed farmers and had to lay down their arms. Schoonman decided to retreat to Arnhem in order not to be cut off. Next day, the colonel dispatched *Capitein* Conrady with 50 men and a 3pdr gun to Rheede. The armed farmers were quickly dispersed and the patriots returned to Arnhem, bringing in two or three prisoners.[17] News of this swift defeat caused other Orangist farmers, especially in Ede en Veenendaal, to disperse and return to their homes. The Orangists that had been at Westervoort were greatly disappointed and a request to march to Dinxperlo for another attack was ignored by them. It had been promised that the Prussians would allow Hanoverian forces to support the Orangists, but of course none came. The fear of falling into Batavian hands was also a cause for giving up.[18]

On 4 September, Orangists gained power in Borculo. The whole town was ornate with orange ribbons and orange flags were hoisted. While yelling *'Oranje Boven!'*, members of the Patriot municipality were insulted. Next day, *Lieutenant-Colonel* Schikhardt arrived in Borculo, stating that he had orders to prepare billets for 500 men of the army of Baron van Heeckeren van Suideras. He also declared the Patriot municipality was illegal and reinstated

---

17 L.C. Vonk, *Geschiedenis*, Vol.I, pp.116-118.
18 Brauw, *Mijne emigratie in Duitschland*, p.13.

the municipality from before 1795. With the statement that Van Heeckeren was on his way from Wesel to Borculo with a force of 10,000 men, *Lieutenant-Colonel* Schikhardt managed to gather a various armed band of Orangists. With these he moved to Groenlo to welcome Van Heeckeren, with drums beating and an Orange flag at their front. Not surprisingly at Groenlo they found no one. When somewhat later that day some dragoons appeared from Zutphen, the reinstated municipality and other Orangists took flight across the border, including Schikhardt.[19] Next day, 5 September, the municipality at Groenlo received word that many citizens of Winterswijk and Lichtenvoorde, decorated with Orange cockades, were on their way to Groenlo, Again to welcome Van Heeckeren who supposedly would arrive. In the afternoon three men arrived, wearing ancient Dutch uniforms, orange sashes and armed with sabres and pistols, followed by a mob of 30 armed Orangist citizens from Winterwijk also decorated with orange. The Patriot municipality was threatened and mistreated, the liberty tree cut down.[20] No Van Heeckeren showed up however.

Where was Baron van Heeckeren van Suideras? That same day, around 9 o'clock, he in person arrived in Winterswijk on horseback, with a group of about 40 persons, partially mounted and a few on carriages. He halted in front of the house of judge Willem Paschen, after which again the proclamation was read aloud, the liberty tree cut down, and orange flags ordered to be hoisted. All Patriots had to give up their muskets and rifles, horse were requisitioned. Judge Paschen, who we will meet again later, was also forced to give up his hunting rifles and sabre. With these weapons a mob of 30 citizens was armed and dispatched to Groenlo as described earlier. An additional 24 men were formed into a civilian guard to maintain order in Winterswijk. Then, just before noon, Van Heeckeren left for Bredevoort with a substantial group of Orangists, mostly armed with sticks, cudgels and scythes. Bredevoort had been a fortress in better times but the defences had been neglected and the city was occupied without any fighting. Again the orange flag was hoisted but this time the liberty tree was spared under the condition that it was decorated with orange ribbons. In the evening Van Heeckeren left again and crossed the border leaving the Batavian Republic. He would not return.[21]

The last incursion of any importance took place at Lichtenvoorde. Here, tax collector Huinink appeared in the morning of 5 September on the street with an orange cockade, spreading the word that the Hereditary Prince of Orange himself would pass through Groenlo this day. Believing this news, many Orangists gathered and, decorated with orange, they left for Groenlo. Amongst them were *freule* van Dorth tot Holthuizen and her brother, in a carriage decorated with orange ribbons.[22] This journey to Groenlo was in vain as already described. While they were gone, a stabbing took place in an inn just outside Lichtenvoorde. A well-known Patriot was stabbed to death by a whole mob, it was impossible to ascertain who were the offenders. After returning from Groenlo and hearing about

---

19   Staats Evers, *De Geldersche Achterhoek*, p.9.
20   Anon., *Geschiedenis van den Gewapenden Inval der Uitgeweeken Nederlanderen, in het Departement van den Rhyn, in de Maand September 1799* (Arnhem: J.H. Moeleman junior & Comp., 1801), pp.44-45.
21   Anon., *Geschiedenis van den Gewapenden Inval*, pp.46-54.
22   *Freule* (Lady) van Dorth tot Holthuizen, 52 years old and unmarried, was an ardent Orangist. An interesting biography has recently appeared although in Dutch: Hermine Manschot-Tijdink, *'Een allerneeteligst caracter' – Het leven van Judith van Dorth (1747-1799)* (Aalten: Fagus, 1999).

the murder, *freule* van Dorth tot Holthuizen yelled: *'Zoo moet het gaan! Er moeten er meer kapot; dat is er nu nog maar één!'* ('This is the way it should go! More should be destroyed, this is only one!'). Then, turning to her brother: *'Broer! Toon moet direct naar Grol, om vier of vijf honderd huzaren met scherp te halen: dan moeten ze allen kapot!'* ('Brother! Toon [the servant] should go to Groenlo immediately, to fetch four or five hundred hussars with live rounds: then they should all be destroyed!'). After her ranting, someone in the crowd yelled *'Vivat de Republiek!'*, after which the *freule* replied: *'Wacht maar manneke! Wij zullen u wel krijgen!'* ('Just you wait little man! We will get you!'). However, after an uneasy night it became clear that the Orangist invasion was virtually over and that no aid would come. The excitement was gone and so was the orange flag from the church tower. The ranting of *freule* van Dorth tot Holthuizen would however not remain without consequences.

Franco-Batavian Reinforcements

To further frustrate the Orangists intentions, the *Gewapende Burgermacht* served beyond expectation, which was much needed because of the lack of regular troops. Three hundred of them marched from Zwolle into the Twenthe region to suppress the Orangist uprisings. In Zutphen only a depot of 60 infantry and 17 dragoons had been left. The remainder of the garrison and most men of the *Gewapende Burgermacht* had marched to Holland.[23] The dragoons in particular were, despite their small number, very effective in suppressing Orangist activity, as shown in Groenlo. After the appearance of the Orangists at Westervoort the departmental administration of Arnhem had sent a request to the French commander in Nijmegen, *Adjutant-Général Chef de Brigade* Malher, for some companies of infantry and cartouches for the cannon. Malher however refused because two companies of French infantry was all he had and there were a known number of Orangist supporters inside the city. However he dispatched a courier to *Général de Brigade* Prévost in Grave for aid.[24] Prévost replied by sending a column of 120 French infantry with two guns from Grave. These joined a force of 200 men of the *Gewapende Burgermacht* and two guns from Utrecht, commanded by *Major* Schut, and advanced to the threatened provinces. Arriving in Arnhem on 5 September, small garrisons were send to Doesburg, Aalten and Borculo. After their arrival many Orangist supporters took flight across the border, even ones that were completely innocent, out of fear for harsh repercussions!

On 13 September, the departmental administration of Arnhem was order to take harsh measures to quell all Orangist activity and to punish those who had rebelled. To assist them, the four companies of the Amsterdamsche Stadssoldaten (400) and a French battalion of the 72e Demi-Brigade formed a flying column of 1,100 men under the command of the French *Général de Brigade* Girod, sealing the fate of the Orangists. In accordance to the decree of the Batavian government of 23 August, martial law was declared for the region and Girod was ordered to investigate what had happened, to disarm all Orangists that were found, to tear down all orange flags, and to erect new liberty trees.

---

23 Anon., *Geschiedenis van den Gewapenden Inval*, p.36.
24 Anon., *Geschiedenis van den Gewapenden Inval*, p.17.

On 16 September the last of the Orangists that had crossed the border had left the Batavian Republic again. This time, contrary to 1795, there was no tolerance for the Orangists supporters who had been involved in the incursion, punishment was harsh. A woman from Rheede, who had thrown two stones at militiamen of the *Gewapende Burgermacht*, was on 17 September condemned to severe flogging and five years *tuchthuis* (house of correction). An innkeeper from Borculo, who had welcomed the Orangists wearing an orange cockade and yelling *'Oranje Boven, Hoezee!'* was condemned to 10 years *tuchthuis* and banishment for life. There are verdicts known of civilians asking for a drink of *Oranje bitter* and yelling *'Oranje Boven!'* condemned to severe flogging and multiple years of *tuchthuis*.[25]

Freule van Dorth tot Holthuizen

Général de Brigade Girod also heard about the murder at the inn near Lichtenvoorde. He was informed by the sisters of the victim about the ranting of *freule* van Dorth tot Holthuizen, who had not fled and still was at her house, In addition it was rumoured that she hid the murderer. A few soldiers were dispatched to arrest him but a murderer was not found. *Freule* van Dorth was arrested instead and transported to Arnhem. In accordance with the decree of 23 August a military tribunal was formed, consisting of three civilians from the *Gewapende Burgermacht* of Utrecht and two of the Amsterdamsche Stadssoldaten: *Kapitein* H. Schaaps from Utrecht (a coppersmith) was president; the four other members were *1ste Luitenant* J. Van Reijsen from Utrecht (a tanner), *2de Luitenant* P.H. Peijpers from Amsterdam (a hatter), *Sergeant-majoor* R. Verburg from Utrecht (a barber's attendant) and *Sergeant* F. Van Bergen from Amsterdam (a fortune-hunter, no occupation). The commissioner was Willem Paschen who, as already described, was judge in Winterswijk. Judge advocate was G. Bom from Lichtenvoorde, a lawyer by profession. One of the first verdicts of this military trial was on 25 October, against the blacksmith Jan Barend Klein Hesselink of Dinxperlo, who had walked through the village on 2 October with a musket, supposedly only because of a wager with an emigrant. In accordance with the decree of 23 August verdict was clear: death by firing squad. Before the execution could take place however, the blacksmith managed to escape and fled across the border. Rather ironically on 2 June 1800 he got into a fight with some Batavian soldiers at the border and was shot dead as a result.

Freule van Dorth tot Holthuizen, to the surprise of many, was on 21 November 1799 sentenced to death as well. Of course there was more than enough evidence of her bad behaviour and statements during the Orangist incursion, but she never had been a real threat to the safety of the Batavian Republic. The members of the military tribunal however were determined to set an example and the fact that the *freule* was a woman, would make clear to all enemies of the state that no one would be safe. Of course, the military tribunal only acted according to the decree of 23 August of the Batavian government and after the publication on 28 August, no one could claim not to have been warned. According to article 13 of the publication, the execution would have to be carried out within 24 hours after the verdict. So on 22 November *freule* van Dorth was brought to the execution place, a muddy

---

25 Staats Evers, *De Geldersche Achterhoek*, pp.8-10.

"The execution of the Freule van Dorth", by Reinier Vinkeles. (Rijksmuseum RP-P-OB-86.761)

field near Winterswijk, on a farmer's cart. Much has been written about the execution and the event was used as propaganda by Orangists and Patriots who both changed the story and added 'facts' wherever convenient. Therefore it is impossible to ascertain what really took place but apparently this is what happened.

On the execution place two lines of Batavian soldiers had been formed, commanded by *Kapitein* van der Linden. Arriving at the execution place between these lines the *freule* put on a black silk dress and after having been blindfolded she had to kneel. Then she was executed by a firing squad consisting of 12 soldiers. Immediately her body, apparently hit by six musket balls, was laid into a coffin. Seemingly the body still moved; according to the Patriots these were only convulsions, according to the Orangists she was still alive. Anyway, a soldier shot here again from close range, the wadding of the shot setting fire to her silk dress, which was quickly put out by some soldiers carrying the water in their hats. Needless to say that this drama was a shock to many, Patriots as well as Orangists, and also outside the Batavian Republic: the King of Prussia, Princess Wilhelmina and the Prince of Orange amongst others, expressed their condolences to the brother of the *freule*. A heated argument took place after the Orangist author Cornelis van der Aa had written his *Geschiedenis van den jongst-geëindigden oorlog (1793-1802), tot op het sluiten van de Vrede van Amiens*, which told a one-sided story about the *freule*, badly wounded and bleeding from many wounds, thrown into the coffin alive and receiving the *coup de grâce*, blaming judge Willem Paschen for this murder. Paschen however replied by writing an extensive statement of defence.[26] To this, Van der Aa promptly replied with an even longer statement![27]

---

26 Willem Paschen, *Verdediging van Willem Paschen gtz. Drost van Breedevoort tegen Cornelis van der Aa, schrijver der geschiedenis van den jongst geeindigden oorlog* (Deventer: Gerrit Brouwer, 1807).
27 Cornelis van der Aa, *De zoogenaamde verdediging van Willem Paschen Gtz. Drossaard van het Ampt Bredevoort* (Utrecht: Cornelis van der Aa, 1807).

New Plans for an Orangist Invasion

The Prince of Orange in Holland was informed about the Orangist efforts to capture some of the cities in the eastern regions of the Batavian Republic. The initial report was so optimistic that the Prince of Orange told Abercromby on 9 September: 'I also received the positive news that part of Gelderland and Overijssel have risen'. On that same date however, the Prince of Hessen-Darmstadt wrote to the Prince of Orange about the outcome of the Orangist incursions: 'It seems that in leaving Lingen, eight days ago, the fortune of Your Highness also left us, since the expedition in question has not responded to our expectations'.[28] The population had not risen and after conferring with Van Lijnden and d'Yvoy, the Prince van Hessen-Darmstadt had decided to make a detailed plan to unite with the army in Holland.[29] A copy of this plan was send to the Prince of Orange, together with a report made by *Ritmeester* (Cavalry-Captain) van Tuyll van Serooskerken. This *ritmeester* had been send to the Veluwe region, to reconnoitre the inclination of the population and to look for favourable landing spots. Most of his information came from Jacob Baron Schimmelpenninck van der Oye, who had assured Van Tuyll van Serooskerken that he would be able to raise and lead a force of 6,000 farmers in the Veluwe region, and that the town of Nijkerk would be a very suitable place to land. So again the Prince of Orange went over to British headquarters, this time to speak with the Duke of York who had become commander-in-chief of the British army after his arrival on 13 September. York could not decide to detach two or three thousand man to support a possible uprising in the Veluwe or the eastern regions of the Batavian Republic, despite the fact that this was part of the original plan and that at the same time his whole army of 40,000 men was bottled up in Holland.

The Orangists in the east could not understand that the British did not send any aid. Many letters were written to the Prince of Orange, all with the same request. For example by the Prince van Hessen-Darmstadt on 13 September:

> The news that the revolution broke out in Gelderland is premature, but I hope it will not be long, provided that we can effectively support the well-intentioned. I trust that Your Highness soon provide us the opportunity to show our zeal for the good cause.[30]

Others wrote in a similar vein. *Colonel* Crause de Frens on 14 September: 'Hoping that Your Highness will make haste sending over to us the long expected English and even if it would be three hundred Russians, fear for the latter will perform miracles'. *Colonel* Bentinck on 19 September: 'We are still hoping that Your Highness will soon give us news that a corps of our allies will cross the Zuiderzee, to enable us somehow to come in action'. Also on 19 September, Jacob Fagel from Lingen: 'We impatiently look forward to news of a corps of troops being send to Gelderland or Overijssel, and we count the minutes to the moment we can go from here'. Finally Count Charles Bentinck on 23 September:

---

28 G.J.W. Koolemans Beijnen, *De Erfprins van Oranje in Noord-Holland in 1799*, p.27.
29 See Appendix XIX.
30 Quoted in Koolemans Beijnen, *De Erfprins van Oranje in Noord-Holland*, p.31.

> I urge Your Serene Highness to pressure as much as possible sending the troops we are waiting for such a long time, to act in the provinces of Friesland and Groningen. The English are expected for a long time with great impatience and everything is prepared for the uprising to operate in concert with them the moment they arrive.[31]

Yet time and again, the Duke of York refused to send any troops across the Zuiderzee, a fact for what he received much criticism, not only from the Orangists but even from Thomas Grenville in his letters on 1 and 7 October.[32] On 20 October, the Prince of Orange answered to Mr. van der Haer: 'The troops you wanted, with good reasons, to go to Friesland, were not received. It is not my fault, time and again I urged with the Duke of York to send them, but all in vain'.[33]

Although expectations were high by some of the Orangists their invasion was doomed to fail. The Orangists were just too weak, too badly armed and no foreign military aid would arrive. They initially acted without a clear plan and no clear command structure. Success was based on massive support from the inhabitants, which, as we have seen, never came. The Orangists who crossed the border never went far inland and preferred to cross back into safety for the night and to return next day. At the slightest idea of the approach of regular Batavian or French troops they ran. The whole invasion was nothing more than wishful thinking. The Orangist incursions in the east of the Batavian Republic were also of no military importance. The events however – the Patriot reaction to the threat and the decree of 23 August; the harsh verdicts and finally the execution of *freule* van Dorth tot Holthuizen – widened the gap between the Patriots and Orangists and even had an effect on the acceptation of Louis Bonaparte as King of Holland in 1806 as it was one of the reasons that many Orangist officers decided to return and to enter service into the army of Holland.

Internationally, the Orangist incursion was not completely without consequences. The Prussians, still engaged in peaceful negotiations with the French, were displeased with what had happened. Things became even worse when the Prussians found out that the Orangists had forged a letter, purportedly sent by General von Schladen, the Prussian military commander of the region, to the mayor of Zutphen stating that the Prussians would support the Orangists with a military force of 30,000 men.[34] As a result, General von Schladen declared that in case of another incursion, the Prussians would not allow the Orangists to retreat across the border again. This effectively put an end to all Orangist activity in this region. Later on, many of these officers left Germany and chose to go to Great Britain to join the Dutch Brigade.

---

31 All the above quotes in Koolemans Beijnen, *De Erfprins van Oranje in Noord-Holland*, pp.32-33, 128-131.
32 Grenville Papers, V, pp.446, 458, referenced in Koolemans Beijnen, *De Erfprins van Oranje in Noord-Holland*, p.34.
33 Koolemans Beijnen, *De Erfprins van Oranje in Noord-Holland*, p.34.
34 Correspondence relating to this incident in: Vonk, *Geschiedenis der Landing*, Vol. I, pp.130-135.

10

The Battle of Zijpe, 10 September

The British Defences at the Zijpe

On 1 September the British had advanced from the dunes at their landing spot to take up positions in the Zijpe polder, behind the Schoorlsche and Westfriesche Zeedijk. These dikes and the canal in front of them formed already a very strong defensive position from their nature. The dikes provided cover for the infantry, their height giving a perfect field of fire; the canal was about 40 metres wide and at most places not fordable. Additional defence works were constructed to transform the Zijpe into a formidable fortress. At strategic points entrenchments and parapets were thrown up, redoubts constructed, and batteries positioned to cover and enfilade all access. Two villages just in front of the Zijpe, Krabbendam and Eenigenburg, were fortified with redoubts, parapets and batteries. Outposts and pickets were at the villages of Kamp, Groet, Warmenhuizen, Haringkarspel, and Dirkshorn with a strong reserve at the village of Schagen. This reserve was placed there to prevent an attack on Oude-Sluis and to be able to execute a flank attack on enemy troops if they attacked the centre of the British positions.

The most vulnerable parts of the British lines were the North Sea beach and the village of Krabbendam. To defend the beach against an enemy attack, in front of the village of Petten a battery with 10 cannon was constructed. Petten itself was reinforced with entrenchments. Two gun-vessels were anchored near the coast to provide support with their cannon. Also the frigate *Shannon* (5th Rate 32) had orders to protect this part of the British lines.[1] At Krabbendam the British lines were vulnerable, because if captured by the Franco-Batavians the village could provide cover for them to advance close to the British defences at the dike. So holding on to this village was very important. On the left flank Oude-Sluis was also fortified, because this was the place where supplies from Den Helder arrived by boat. Many goods, carts, boats, and wood were requisitioned in the Wieringerwaard polder. Hundreds of men from the countryside were pressed to work on the entrenchments and batteries.

The positions at the Schoorlsche Zeedijk from Petten to the Zijpe Sluices were defended by about 3,400 men of the 1st and 2nd Guards Brigades, supported by a detachment of

---

1   Coleman Osborne Williams III, *The Role of the British Navy in the Helder Campaign, 1799* (Unpublished dissertation, UMI, 1985), p.220.

Approaches of Krabbendam from the direction of Schoorldam. (Author photo)

Marines. They were commanded by Lieutenant General Pulteney. Major General Moore had to defend the positions at the Westfriesche Zeedijk from the Zijpe Sluices to St. Maarten, with the 2/1st (Royal) Foot and the 92nd Highlanders. Both battalions were positioned along the dike at Eenigenburg. The remaining battalions of Moore's 4th Brigade (25th and 49th Foot, 79th Highlanders) were positioned at Oude-Sluis. To replace these battalions, Moore received command of both battalions of the 20th Foot. The 1st Battalion of this, the best of the skeleton-regiments, defended Krabbendam. Its 2nd Battalion occupied Eenigenburg. The Westfriesche Zeedijk from St. Maarten to the north-east was defended by Major General Don's 5th Brigade.

Brune's Plan of Attack

For now Brune had to fight with the troops at his disposal; about 14,000 Batavians and just over 7,000 French.[2] Reinforcements from France arrived slowly in the Batavian Republic, despite assurances from the French Minister of War Bernadotte, for example on 7 September:

> I have informed you, citizen general, by my letter dated the 9th of this month [French Republican Calendar; 26 August] that I had given orders to extract from

---

2   See Appendix X.

the auxiliary battalions which are being formed at the moment in the 1st, 2nd, 3rd, 4th, 15th and 16th Military divisions 3,500 conscripts destined to complete the cadres of the French troops now stationed in the territory of the Batavian Republic, and to have them directed on Breda without delay. I warn you that I have instructed the generals inspectors of the organization of these auxiliary battalions to make all the necessary arrangements for these 3,500 conscripts to be armed, dressed and equipped before their departure. If this operation will not be completed by the time they arrive under your command, I charge you to employ all the means in your power to provide for it and thus to enable these troops to be actively employed immediately after their arrival in Holland. I inform you that the 90e demi-brigade and the 10e régiment de dragons will arrive at Antwerp on the 24th of this month [10 September], I have given orders to direct them immediately to you as well as another demi-brigade and a regiment of chasseurs à cheval.[3]

Général de Division Tilly, who commanded the French troops in the Belgian departments, was however reluctant to send troops, afraid to weaken himself too much due to the need to suppress the local population. Nor did numbers tell the complete story, as the announced 90e Demi-Brigade had been raised in December 1798 and consisted mainly of raw French conscripts. Brune received however assurances from *Général de Division* Kellerman at Brussels that he would receive reinforcements from the garrisons in Flanders as soon as possible but these also would arrive slowly, as illustrated by a letter in the *London Chronicle*:

> The troops which were to proceed from our coasts to the Batavian Republic, have received counter orders, and some corps which were already on their march have returned. These new dispositions are rendered necessary by the appearance of several English ships, which were descried again the day before yesterday at the Mouth of the Scheldt. It has been determined that the coasts of Flanders shall not be left without troops to defend them, until the destination of the second expedition, preparing in the ports of England, be known, different reports stating it to be destined against the Islands of Zealand or Belgium. On the other hand all the places on the coast, from Nieuport to the Scheldt, are fortified with the greatest activity. The Minister of War has ordered considerable magazines of provisions and ammunition to be formed in the citadel of Antwerp. All persons who reside there are to quit it within a fortnight; none but the garrison will be allowed to remain. Orders have likewise been given to mount batteries on Fort Lillo, and to augment both its fortifications and garrison. It is certain that six battalions of infantry, a regiment of hussars, and a company of artillery, are on their march from the environs of Paris for the Batavian Republic; those troops will pass through here this week. More than 20,000 conscripts will also be sent to our departments, to be organized into battalions. Some battalions of infantry in garrison at Liege, Aix-la-Chapelle, or Limburg, or who are posted on the Meuse, have

---

3   Letter of 7 September 1799 from Bernadotte to Brune, in Colenbrander, *Gedenkstukken*, Vol.III, p.XXIII. For more correspondence to and from Brune about the French reinforcement, see *ibid*, pp.XVII-XXX.

received orders to proceed immediately to Bois-le-Duc and Nimwegen: they will be followed by several other corps from Givet and Namur.[4]

Brune knew that more enemy troops were on their way to the Batavian Republic and did not rule out the possibility of a second landing in Groningen or in South Holland, which would create an impossible situation as he had insufficient troops to fight on two fronts at the same time. In addition the Batavian Government pressured Brune to attack as soon as possible. With the promise of the arrival of more French reinforcements he decided to do so, trying to destroy Abercromby's army in the Zijpe before more enemy troops could arrive. His attack was planned for 10 September, although Dumonceau's Batavians were still much fatigued from their march to Holland, most of them only arriving at the front the day before. Although British strength was about 18,000, Brune estimated Abercromby's forces at about 20,000 men.

Brune would direct his attack at the British positions in the Zijpe between the villages Petten and Eenigenburg. The attack would take place in three columns, each of the three divisions of the Franco-Batavian army forming a column. The first column would be the right wing of the Franco-Batavian army, consisting of the 1e Bataafsche Divisie (Daendels). Its objective was the fortified village Eenigenburg and the Westfriesche Zeedijk behind it. They were then to turn right and to proceed in the direction of the village St. Maarten. The left wing of their advance would be protected by the demolition of the bridges across the Groote Sloot, a wide canal in the Zijpe running parallel to the Westfriesche Zeedijk, covered by the artillery. The second column would be formed of the centre of the Franco-Batavian army, consisting of the 2e Bataafsche Divisie (Dumonceau). Its objective would be the Westfriesche Zeedijk between the villages Eenigenburg and Krabbendam. After taking this objective they had to proceed to Krabbendam and to capture this strongly fortified village. The 1e Brigade (Bonhomme) reinforced by the Voorhoede [Advance Guard], would attack Warmenhuizen and Tuitgenhorn and attack the Westfriesche Zeedijk from there. The 2e Brigade (Bruce) and the Achterhoede [Rear Guard] would advance along the Kanaal van Alkmaar and attack Krabbendam and the Westfriesche Zeedijk next. In this case, the rear guard would operate as an advance guard for the 2e Brigade. The third column would be formed by the left wing of the Franco-Batavian army, consisting of the French division of Vandamme. This division would be led by Brune himself and had to attack the British defences at the Schoorlsche Zeedijk between Petten and Krabbendam and support the Batavian attack on Krabbendam. All three columns had to attack the British simultaneously at 2:45 a.m. The Franco-Batavian attack would be made on a relatively broad front but because of the darkness at that moment and the terrain, which was heavily intersected by canals and ditches, the attackers were forced to use the roads on the dikes leading to the British positions for their advance. After having given his marching orders and concentration points, Brune told Daendels that he had ordered *Général de Brigade* Barbou and *Adjudant-Général* Durutte to accompany him. This was explained as their being military advisors, but clearly Brune did not trust Daendels and wanted to keep him under close observation.

---

4   Letter of 5 September from Brussels, *London Chronicle*, 19 September 1799.

THE BATTLE OF ZIJPE, 10 SEPTEMBER 181

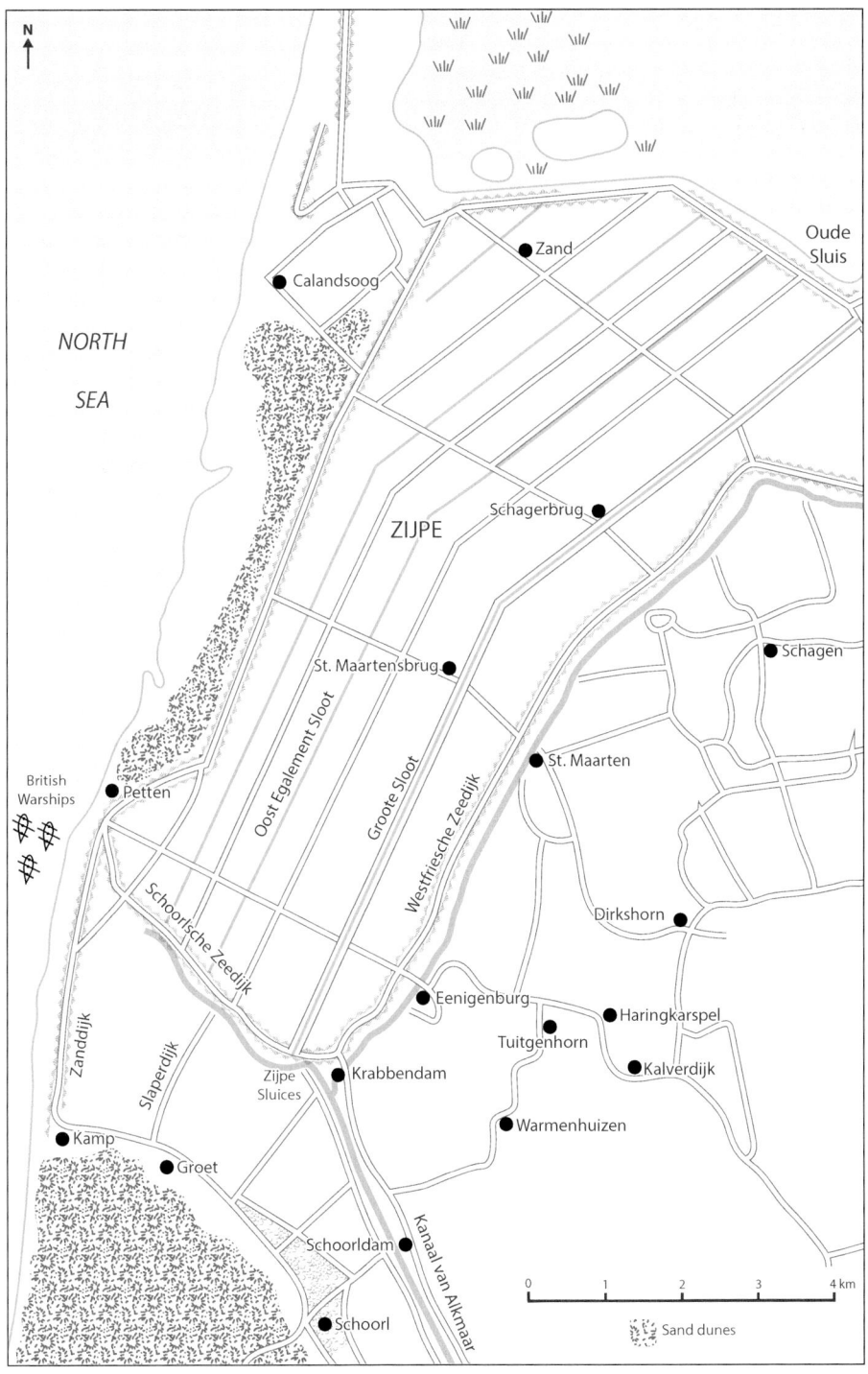

Map 6 The Battle of the Zijpe.

1e Bataafsche Divisie (Daendels)

At 2:00 a.m. Daendels left his starting positions and at 4:00 a.m. had already expelled the British pickets of the 92nd Highlanders from their forward positions at Haringkarspel and Dirkshorn, as Major General Moore related in his diary:

> A smart fire began at this moment at the picquets to which I had sent Captain Anderson. The confidence which I had in the strength of Krabbendam and in the good conduct of Lieutenant-Colonel Smith, who with the 20th Regiment was charged with the immediate defence of that post, made me less anxious about it: as yet it was not attacked. I was more anxious about that part of the dyke which was in rear of Haring's-Karspel and Ennigerburg, because a good road through those villages ran along it, and the impediments of the country made it extremely difficult for an enemy to advance except by roads. The manner in which the attack was being made on the outpost left me in no doubt as to the further intentions of the enemy. As I galloped towards that quarter which was the alarm post of the Royals and 92nd Regiments I was confirmed in my opinion that an attack was intended to be made there, as it was now sufficiently light for me to distinguish large bodies of the enemy marching towards Haring's-Karspel. By this time the regiments were nearly at their alarm posts. The picquets from the villages were falling back, but Captain Anderson had the presence of mind to get the different bridges on the canals lifted up. This gave them time to retire, and retarded the advance of the enemy.[5]

Moving from Haringkarspel towards his objective of Eenigenburg, Daendels found the assigned road blocked by Bonhomme's brigade from the second column. He reinforced this brigade with a *jager* battalion and directed the remainder of his troops to St. Maarten, defended by Colonel Spencer and the 40th Regiment Foot. Daendels attacked this village with two battalions of the 1e Halve Brigade, supported by two guns of 2e Compagnie Rijdende Artillerie (*Capitein* d'Anguerand) covered by a detachment of dragoons (*Eerste Lieutenant* Hoevenaar), and succeeded in capturing a redoubt. At that moment Daendels received news of the disorder in some of Bonhomme's battalions, whose attack was repulsed at Eenigenburg. Temporarily halting his advance, he left his division at its previous positions and went personally to join Bonhomme with part of the 2e Bataljon Jagers.[6]

After restoring order in Bonhomme's brigade, Daendels returned to his own troops. He was just renewing the attack when he received a message that Bonhomme's second attack also had been repulsed, as related by a private of the 92nd Highlanders:

> A strong party attacked the position entrusted to our regiment, which was the first time that we were in actual action with an enemy. The dyke sheltered us from their shot; for when they drew near, we stood on the top of it and fired a volley or two, which drove them back, and then we sheltered ourselves from the fire of their

---

5   Maurice (ed.), *Diary of Sir John Moore*, Vol.I, p.346.
6   N.J.A.P.H. van Es, *De Veldtocht in Noord-Holland 1799* (Arnhem: Coers & Roest – G.J. Thieme, 1898), p7.

artillery by sitting down on the near side of it. The shot whistled over our heads, and fell, when its strength was spent, on the ground in our rear. The enemy was repulsed at all points with loss. Our regiment's loss was small; one man killed and the captain of the grenadiers, and three men wounded.[7]

With a failed attack in the centre, any further advance on the right would be dangerous and expose Daendels' division. Therefore he decided that further attacks were fruitless. He limited his actions to maintaining his previous position until a strong British column advanced from Schagen in the direction of Dirkshorn. Becoming aware of this, Daendels retreated at 2:00 p.m. back to his own lines after sending again some reinforcements to Bonhomme, this time part of his horse artillery. The 2e Bataljon Jagers, two horse artillery guns, and some dragoons covered his retreat. He was pursued by the British until these arrived at Haringkarspel, were they could not advance any further because the bridge there had been burned by the Batavian rearguard. Daendels' losses were 10 men killed, 71 wounded and 82 missing. Daendels' report relates:

> On 9 September in the evening, the *général-en-chef* gave the whole army the order for a general attack; and the goal for the division was the village Eenigenburg, which she had to force and seize the dike. In order to execute these orders, the lieutenant-general went to his advance guard, which at 2:00 a.m. was put in motion, under the command of *Colonel* Crass. At 4:00 a.m., she was already master of Haringkarspel and Dirkshorn; advancing on Eenigenburg, to form up for the attack, but all roads were occupied by the division of *Lieutenant-Generaal* Dumonceau. The brigade of *Generaal-Major* Bonhomme, which was not on the assigned road, which actually did not exist, was forced to take the one on which the division of the lieutenant-general arrived. Unable then to develop his strength as his right was pressed, he was forced to give up attacking Eenigenburg and instead of that St. Maarten. The initial attack was fortunate; already the enemy had abandoned a redoubt he had at the entrance of the village; the lieutenant-general, after having silenced the enemy artillery fire, was about to take the rest of the position by force when he was informed by *Colonel* Crass that some battalions of the brigade of *Generaal-Major* Bonhomme had made an unfortunate attack on the dike at Eenigenburg, retreating in disorder. This event forced the lieutenant-general to delay his attack. He moved quickly to his left retaining the *jager* following the battalions of *Generaal-Major* Bonhomme: he rallied them a league behind the position and brought them back in the field. *Generaal-Major* Bonhomme would resume his attack: the lieutenant-general also returned to direct the one on St. Maarten; but he perceived from the direction the firing came from, and reports confirmed it, that on the left no progress was made. *Generaal-Major* Bonhomme, after a second attempt, could not penetrate to the dike near Eenigenburg; the lieutenant-general fearing to get too involved, stayed on the same height of the division of *Lieutenant-Generaal* Dumonceau, confining himself

---

7   Anon., Narrative of a Private Soldier, p.41.

to maintain his early advantages in the hope of receiving news of the success of the attack on Petten and new orders from the *général-en-chef*.

At 2:30 p.m., he noticed that the firing on his left had completely ceased and that the enemy had send a considerable column on the right to flank him; then certain that the battle had ended along the whole line, leaving him the only one still continuing his attack, he ordered a retreat. It was in great order, though the enemy sought to trouble him, attacking his rear and the right side of Dirkshorn; but all his efforts had no other result then burning the village with his howitzers. The loss of that day, both in killed, wounded or missing, was 150 men. The lieutenant-general is very pleased with the conduct of the 1e Halve Brigade, of which two battalions executed the attack on St. Maarten, with the greatest effect: he also needs to give the highest praise to the light artillery company, commanded by *Capitein* d'Anguerand, his *Adjudant* Maas, as well as the *Onder-Lieutenant* of the artillery Van Alphen. These officers as soon as the attack was ordered, maintained a very heavy fire and advanced their guns in battery only 100 yards from the enemy entrenchments.[8]

2e Bataafsche Divisie (Dumonceau)

Dumonceau's 1e Brigade (Bonhomme) was the first to attack. Its orders were to advance from Schoorldam to the villages Warmenhuizen and Tuitgenhorn and to attack the Westfriesche Zeedijk from there. Arriving at Warmenhuizen a strong British picket was pushed back but at Tuitgenhorn problems began. The road designated by Brune to Bonhomme was in fact not a road but a wide canal! Because of this mistake Bonhomme was unable to follow his orders. So on his own initiative, and not being acquainted with the terrain because of his arrival only days ago, he followed the only other narrow road in the direction of the enemy, the road to the village of Eenigenburg. There he blocked Daendels' advance as already described. The brigade continued its advance in the direction of Eenigenburg, coming under heavy fire. Only at 5:00 a.m. was Bonhomme in a position to attack the British positions at Eenigenburg. Arriving in front of this village, a 6pdr cannon and a howitzer of the horse artillery, commanded by *Onder-Lieutenant* Straube, were deployed across the road and opened fire, supporting the 4e Bataljon Jagers and the *jager* detached by Daendels to assist him.[9] The *jager* advanced within range in skirmish order and opened a brisk fire on the British in Eenigenburg, the 2/20th Foot. This battalion was relieved by Moore's Brigade and was sent to Krabbendam to reinforce its sister battalion there.

After a while Bonhomme ordered his battalions to attack. They charged in closed column and reached the canal in front of the Westfriesche Zeedijk, but were unable to cross because the bridge was destroyed by cannon fire. They were under heavy fire and suffered many casualties, to which they could not reply effectively by reason of room to deploy. The attacking battalions broke and retreated in disorder. After restoring order, aided by Daendels, and after reinforcing these troops with the 1/ and 2/7e Halve Brigade, the Batavians attacked

---

8   H.W. Daendels, *Rapport des Opérations de la Division du Lieutenant-Général Daendels; Depuis le 22 Août, jusqu'à la capitulation de l'Armée Angloise et Russe, le 18 Octobre 1799. An 5* (La Haye: I. van Cleef, 1799), pp.28-31.
9   van Es, De Veldtocht in Noord-Holland 1799, pp.7-8.

again. Again they were repulsed in disorder. Even the example of the *Lieutenant-Colonel* de Collaert of the hussars who, unable, to do anything with his cavalry because of the intersected terrain, went forward in person to lead the attacking infantry, had little effect. Realising that further attacks were fruitless Bonhomme ordered his troops somewhat back out of range of the British guns and took up positions there. He left his artillery and the *jager* at their current position, reinforced by another two guns of the 2e Compagnie Rijdende Artillerie sent by Daendels, to prevent a British counterattack or pursuit.[10] The brigade held this position until the retreat of Daendels, after which Bonhomme also drew back his troops at about 3:00 p.m. He was not pursued. His losses were 460 men, including 15 officers. Major General Moore related in his diary:

> A number of the enemy's Yagers and light troops, taking advantage of such cover as presented itself, commenced a fire. Some artillery also began to play upon us, and under cover of their fire a large column attempted, with shouts and drums and bugles, to charge us. Till now our men had remained concealed on the reverse of the dyke, except a few individuals who had been directed to fire upon the riflemen, but upon the column advancing the whole sprang up and threw in a fire so galling, that, being supported by some field artillery, which had been previously placed upon the dyke, it forced the enemy to give way and retire in confusion. The different attacks were repulsed nearly at the same time. The enemy appeared for some time to support a feint attack which they had begun upon the village of St. Martin, but it was merely designed to cover their retreat, which they had begun from all quarters.[11]

The 2e Brigade (Bruce) also saw their efforts come to nothing. They had to attack Krabbendam before 3:00 a.m. As most of this brigade was in fact still marching towards the front line, a number of units found their way at Alkmaar blocked by numerous vehicles and could only reach the battlefield much later. Dumonceau, knowing that the result of the whole battle depended on the capture of Krabbendam, had already started the attack at 6:00 a.m. with the few troops he had at his disposal; a hundred infantry from Bonhomme's brigade, a hussar company, and a howitzer: a feeble force, led by his adjutant, *Lieutenant-Colonel* Vichery. Moving along the road and the east bank of the Kanaal van Alkmaar and despite the fire of two cannon covering that road, the entrenchments in front of Krabbendam were attacked and some houses occupied. At 7:00 a.m. the first of Bruce's troops arrived. In his after action report to Dumonceau, *Colonel* Bruce reported:

> General, I have the honour to report to you that as soon as I arrived with the brigade to the height of Schoorldam, I have detached from the column the advance guard consisting of two hundred *jager* and three grenadier companies. These approached the enemy close to Crabbendam, where the fight has started. When the advance guard arrived, I gave orders to two infantry companies to go to the left of the canal

---

10 van Es, *De Veldtocht in Noord-Holland 1799*, pp.7-8.
11 Maurice (ed.), *Diary of Sir John Moore*, Vol.I, p.347.

The crossroads at Krabbendam: Schoorlsche Zeedijk – Westfriesche Zeedijk – road to Schoorldam. (Author photo)

to provide cover from there, and also sending the horse artillery. To support those troops, I detached also the 2e bataljon of the 6e Halve Brigade. Furthermore, with the remaining troops I marched to Crabbendam along the shortest route, leaving behind the 1e Regiment Cavalerie as the terrain did not permit to use it.

About half past six the battle started with the enemy advance guard and we had some advantages in the beginning, so that we made some prisoners. The troops having come to the height of Crabbendam, I immediately gave the 1st and 2nd battalion of the 2e Halve Brigade orders to expel the enemy from their advantageous position when possible. This was supported by a few pieces of artillery. We managed to get to the enemy battery, where the 1st battalion of the 2e Halve Brigade was placed underneath the colours. If we had been supported by the 2nd battalion of the 6e Halve Brigade, then I do not doubt that the battery would have been taken. Which was not difficult as there was a bridge at this point. But to my regret, General, I must report to you that the aforementioned battalion was the first to retire, although there was no need for it. This retreat was the cause that the troops on the right wing also retired. In order to prevent this, I ordered the 3rd battalion of the 2e Halve Brigade, which had remained in reserve, to support the two battalions in the advance guard, but doing so we were all forced to retreat, which happened with as much order as in such cases can take place.[12]

When the *jager* received the order to attack and join the infantry in Krabbendam, they did so with such vigour that they captured the battery of two guns covering the road. With the way to Krabbendam cleared, Bruce reinforced the 3e Bataljon Jagers and the 2/6e Halve Brigade with the 1/ and 2/2e Halve Brigade and attacked the entrenchments in front of Krabbendam and the village itself, supported by two 6pdr guns and a howitzer. In reserve were the 3/2e Halve Brigade and the 1e Regiment Zware Cavalerie, of which the latter was of no further use since, because of all the canals and ditches, movement was restricted to the road on the dike. Bruce succeeded in capturing the entrenchments in front of Krabbendam and part of the village, taking some prisoners of the 20th Foot. Then he reinforced the infantry with 3/2e Halve Brigade and resumed the attack.[13]

On the British side Lieutenant General Abercromby, who was present here in person, knew this was the decisive moment of the battle: if the Batavians were to succeed in penetrating his defences his whole position in the Zijpe would become untenable. He even sent a message to Vice Admiral Mitchell for all battleships that could be spared, including the captured Batavian fleet, to clear the roadstead of Texel in order to prevent disorder in case of a British defeat requiring quick embarkation of his troops aboard the transport fleet. He ordered his reserve, positioned behind the British left wing, to march to Krabbendam. Then he dismounted and personally took over command of five companies of 2/20th Foot, the only troops available at that moment and encouraged them to hold their position as long as possible. They received the Batavians with heavy musketry and cannon fire. Lieutenant Colborne of the 20th, who was wounded during the battle, would write back home:

> Since we have been here the 1st Battalion of the 20th have had the honour of occupying the advanced post of the whole army, consequently we have been but a few yards from the enemy for this last fortnight. Our picquets have had frequent skirmishes; but on the 10th September the enemy made an attack on the whole line, advancing on the right and left as a diversion, but making their real attack on our battalion. Three large columns advanced on us in very good order with riflemen in front, who spread themselves on all sides in a few minutes, and came within eight or nine yards, picking out the officers to fire at. The grenadiers were advanced about a quarter of a mile in front of the battalion and defended the post until all their ammunition was expended, firing more than a hundred rounds. At this time a company in our rear, defending a bridge, was obliged to retire, the officer of the artillery being wounded and having no ammunition remaining; we then retreated with difficulty. The enemy passed the bridge and pressed on us. Part of the 1st and 2nd Battalions charged and drove them back; we then charged them twice in a village which they had taken; they retreated immediately, leaving heaps of dead and

---

12 Letter of 11 September 1799 from J.S. Bruce to Dumonceau (NA 2.21.056 Collectie 130 Dumonceau, inventarisnummer 2).
13 A.F. Meyer, Dagboek van den luitenant-generaal jonkheer Adriaan Frans Meyer, geboren 1768 (NIMH, Handschriften, 511, inv.58), p.18.

wounded on the field. Our army being so much scattered no regiment could come to our assistance till the enemy had retired. The action began between four and five, and ended about twelve. Sir Ralf was very much pleased with the conduct of the regiment; indeed, it was impossible for them to behave better. Six officers of the 1st Battalion were wounded out of eighteen who were engaged. The wounded are removed to this place [Den Helder]. I hope in a few days to join the regiment again. The bullet took me on the side of my head just above the temple, but fortunately I had my hat on sideways, which prevented the ball from entering the skull; there is no fracture. I have been bled twice and find myself greatly relieved.[14]

The regimental history of the same regiment provides additional information:

They pressed the attack with so much determination that at one time it was feared that they would force their way into the entrenchments, but Colonel Smyth seeing the danger, stood upon the parapet (supported by some of his men, as the blood was flowing from a wound in his leg) and shouted in tones that could be heard above the din of battle, "Twentieth, remember Minden." The Grenadier company had at this time defended an outpost for three hours, till their ammunition was expended, and finding that the artillery which had to defend a bridge on their right had retired [i.e. the bridge at the Zijpe Sluices attacked by the French – see below], they had no alternative but to fall back. The enemy crossed this bridge, and then it was that the 1st battalion supported by the 2nd, charged, and with General Abercromby at their head, drove the enemy back. Following this, both battalions charged the enemy twice, as they endeavoured to establish themselves in a village. Leaving their killed and wounded in heaps, the French and Dutch retreated.[15]

The Batavians took also heavy fire from the British batteries along the Westfriesche Zeedijk. The 2/6e Halve Brigade suffered in particular, and the loss of many officers and NCOs caused disorder; the battalion panicked and routed. This rout caused panic among other troops and nearly all Batavian troops that were not in the village itself ran. After re-forming the fugitives and restoring order, the Batavians again captured part of Krabbendam and deployed a battery of two guns, but could not advance any further. The British fired from behind the cover of the Westfriesche Zeedijk at the Batavians, who were not able to cross the canal in front of this dike and had no room to deploy. This decided the outcome of the battle. At 3:00 p.m. Dumonceau ordered the retreat. The Batavians were not pursued. Losses were 86 men killed, 427 wounded and 294 missing. Dumonceau's after action report describes the engagement as follows:

On 9 September in the evening the *général-en-chef* gave the order to attack with the whole division on the 10th at daybreak 3:45 a.m., the enemy in his Zijpe position from Eenigenburg up to Krabbendam. The *lieutenant-generaal* accordingly ordered

---

14 Letter of 13 September from Lieutenant Colborne to Rev. T. Bargus, Moore Smith, *Life of John Colborne*, pp.14-15.
15 Smyth, *Lancashire Fusiliers*, pp.189-191.

the *Generaal-Major* Bonhomme to direct the attack of his brigade at the great Zijpe dike, between Krabbendam and Eenigenburg, marching over Tuitgenhorn and Warmenhuizen, while *Colonel* Bruce was ordered to attack the post of Krabbendam frontally. Approaching the great Zijpe dike at the point indicated between Krabbendam and Eenigenburg, the general-major encountered some difficulties, especially, as the road specified in the order did not exist; he could therefore only begin his attack at 5:00 a.m., and was forced to act against Eenigenburg, encountering the enemy at Tuitgenhorn were his advance guard dislodged an enemy post and took two prisoners. This column on leaving Tuitgenhorn approached the enemy to within cannon shot, we fired at him with two pieces of light artillery, while the *jager* acted in their skirmisher role, part of the 2e Bataljon Jagers from the division of *Generaal* Daendels had joined the force.

Generaal-Major Bonhomme ordered to charge the dike, but his advance guard, being nearly 50 paces from the ditch of the dike, was received by such a heavy canister fire and musketry that she was obliged to retreat; the ground did not allow the column to deploy. Having rallied in part, the *generaal-major* tried to charge a second time, but the 1st and 2nd battalions of the 7e Halve Brigade employed here were also forced to retreat. We once again rallied the troops, but not seeing the possibility of a successful attack, the *generaal-major* took up position backwards; the two artillery pieces were deployed, and the *jager* continued to act as skirmishers. This position was held as long as it was required by *Lieutenant-Generaal* Daendels, to cover the retreat of his division which retreated from St. Maarten. At 3:00 p.m. the *generaal-major* effected his retreat. The loss of this brigade both killed and wounded and missing, amounts to nearly 460 heads, among which are 15 officers.

The brigade of *Colonel* Bruce only arrived at 7:00 a.m.; encumbered by an infinite number of cars at the Friesche gate of Alkmaar which had caused the delay. The *lieutenant-generaal* saw himself compelled to begin the frontal attack against Krabbendam with a detachment of about 100 men, taken from the brigade of *Generaal-Major* Bonhomme and during this attack remained present in person. He ordered to advance a howitzer (the only artillery that was present that moment), supported by the above detachment and a hussar company. This small force advanced under the command of *Adjudant-Generaal* Vichery and following the example of this officer they attacked the enemy, though stronger in numbers, and which did not venture out of his entrenchments. Finally, one hour later the 2nd battalion of the 6e Halve Brigade arrived, and was followed at some distance by the rest of the brigade, we were waiting for so impatiently; at the head of the column marched 200 *jager* of the 3e Bataljon, which barely arrived received the order to attack, which they did with such impetuosity on the right and left on the first entrenchments of the enemy, that he was forced to abandon them. The brave Major Tulleken, who commanded these *jager*, had his head carried away by a cannonball. This position taken, the enemy threw himself with great haste in his second line, which he had constructed in the corner of the Zijpe dike, and was forced to abandon his weapons and baggage, we made many prisoners in this village. At the moment we were about to force the enemy out of his last position, an unexpected accident was the cause of diminishing expectations. Part of the 2nd battalion of the 6e Halve

Brigade fled, without having any reason, although the battalion, encouraged by his brave chief, *Lieutenant-Colonel* Anthing rallied quickly to its brighter honour and at the expense of the enemy. This disorder that took place under the eyes of the entire column of the braves, who were in the position that was just won yet this time undoubtedly the cause of consternation, by which everyone retreated. However we managed to rally the troops; *Colonel* Bruce, *Adjudant-Generaal* Vichery and the citizen Clement, ADC of the *général-en-chef*, at the head of the grenadiers of the 2e Halve Brigade restored the situation; we advanced again and established us again in Krabbendam. The artillery that was well served managed to deploy 2 pieces; but our success was limited; because the enemy perceiving our disorder had had time to recover and resumed the confidence necessary for his defence. We remained in this position until 3:00 p.m., then the lieutenant-general ordered the retreat, which was executed in such good order, that the enemy did not dare pursue us.

The loss of the brigade commanded by *Colonel* Bruce amounts in killed, wounded and missing 477 heads, among which there are 23 officers. This loss so great should be mainly attributed to the lay-out of the terrain; a wide canal on the left, meadows cut by ditches to our right, and the inability to deploy, forced us to attack in column on a long dike, while the battalions of the enemy were drawn up in battle in the bend of the dike from Krabbendam to Eenigenburg, from where he was able to direct his fire on the single point of our attack.[16]

The French Division (Vandamme)

At 2:00 a.m. the main part of *Général de Division* Vandamme's division debouched from the wooded area south of Schoorl where they had concentrated for the attack. They were partially formed up in three columns, proceed by troopers of the 16e Chasseurs à Cheval, the remainder of which was held in reserve to exploit any success. The French would attack the British positions behind the Schoorlsche Zeedijk, from the North Sea coast at Petten to the Kanaal van Alkmaar. The left column had to advance from Kamp along the Zanddijk to push the British out of Petten. It consisted of a battalion of the 54e Demi-Brigade led by *Général de Brigade* Gouvion. These troops took with them some 'portable bridges', to cross the numerous ditches. The centre column had to advance from Groet along the Slaperdijk and consisted of the 3/42e Demi-Brigade and a battalion of the 49e Demi-Brigade. They were under the direct command of *Général de Division* Vandamme and also accompanied by *Généraux de Brigade* David and Fuzier. The right column consisted of the 1/ and 2/42e Demi-Brigade supported by two cannon, led by *Chef de Brigade* Aubrée, and had to advance along the Kanaal van Alkmaar in the direction of Krabbendam.

The French columns pressed forward vigorously but the British outposts, including a picket of 50 men of the 3rd Foot Guards, commanded by Lieutenant Lord John Campbell, managed to hold on for about 20 minutes before they were forced back. Facing a bayonet charge and fearing to be surrounded they fell back running, following the roads on the

---

16 After action report of *Lieutenant-Generaal* Dumonceau, in Krayenhoff, *Geschiedkundige*, Appendix VIIIb, pp.55-59.

Krabbendam. Schoorlsche Zeedijk facing the direction of Zijpe Sluices. (Author photo)

Zanddijk and Slaperdijk back to the British main line. The villages Kamp and Groet were captured by the French and their columns proceeded to the main British defence line at the Schoorlsche Zeedijk. At this moment, according to Gachot, Burrard harangued his guardsmen: 'No retreat, because if you yield the terrain, the result would be a disaster! Today England has its eyes on you'.[17] The British guards were ready to receive the French attack and, advancing further, Gouvion's column on the Zanddijk was met by a withering fire. In front also from the cannon of a battery and in the flank by the fire from the frigate *Shannon* and the two gun-vessels anchored near Petten, as reported by a Batavian eyewitness: 'In the afternoon we saw a British warship firing full broadsides at the land, the French had a huge number of wounded'.[18] Finally the French had to retreat with heavy loss. They were not pursued.

In the centre the French advance along the Slaperdijk was preceded by an advance guard led by *Adjudant-Général* Rostollant. Pushing back the British outposts the French quickly reached the forty metres wide canal. There was neither the time nor the materials to construct some means of crossing this canal, therefore the French relied on the information that the canal was shallow and could be crossed. Vandamme ordered the battalion of the

---

17 Gachot, *Brune en Hollande*, pp.234-235.
18 Letter of a Batavian soldier of 12 September 1799 in J.K., '3 Brieven van het oorlogsterrein 1799 en 1800' in *De Navorscher* (Amsterdam: C.L.G. Veldt, 1909), p.577.

49e Demi-Brigade to deploy in skirmish order, to outflank the entrenchments on the head of the Slaperdijk and to engage the defenders. After some time he attacked frontally with his grenadiers, of whom several jumped into the canal trying to wade or swim to the other side under cover of fire of the skirmishers. Most of them drowned, or were killed or wounded. About what happened next sources differ, illustrating the chaos ensuing in the darkness. The following account is the most probable. *Capitaine* Delenteigne, whose company was next, did not want his men to suffer the same fate. Despite the intense musketry from the dike he jumped in the water and probed the depth of the canal, concluding that it was much too deep to wade through. At other places the French met the same fate and finally they had to retreat from the intense musketry and grapeshot, not able to cross the canal.[19] A regimental history has another interpretation:

> Amidst of the engagement, *Capitaine* Delenteigne was fighting on a dike, and his company was held down by the enemy who occupied the opposite bank of the Krabbendam canal; despite the grapeshot and musketry, this brave officer threw himself in the canal that separated them from the English to probe, to reconnoitre if it was fordable, then finished, he gave the order to march forward and dislodged the enemy from their positions. The Demi-Brigade suffered serious losses in this battle.[20]

Gachot tells yet another version of the incident, writing that 'unnecessarily, *Capitaine* Delenteigne and 30 officers threw themselves in and swam across to destroy the palisades on the right bank.'[21]

Despite not being able to cross the canal Vandamme continued feeding troops into the battle. Their advance restricted to the Slaperdijk, the dense column was time and again received by a devastating crossfire from the batteries covering the access and the musketry from behind the Schoorlsche Zeedijk. The battle continued for a few hours and in all 10 subsequent attacks were repulsed by the British.[22] The French suffered heavy losses: 3/42e Demi-Brigade lost no less than 400 men. *Général de Brigade* David, leading the column from the front, was mortally wounded, receiving a musket ball through his throat. A corporal with two soldiers tried to take him back behind the lines when a cannonball struck the corporal in the chest, killing him instantly, in addition taking away an arm from David.[23] Finally the French troops retreated out of range and at 10:00 a.m. fell back to their starting positions. They were for a short distance pursued by MacDonald's brigade.

Chef de Brigade Aubrée advanced along the west side of the Kanaal van Alkmaar. His aim was to capture the bridge at the Zijpe Sluices, leading to the windmill of Krabbendam and from there to support Dumonceau in his attack on the village itself. Despite of the fire of two cannon covering the bridge, the French stormed over it and managed to dislodge the British

---

19   Franz Joseph Adolph Schneidawind, Geschichte des Krieges in Holland im Jahr 1799, zwischen Franzosen und Holländer einer, und Engländer und Russen anderer Seits (Darmstadt: Carl Wilhelm Lebke, 1845), pp.109-110.
20   [Francis Louis Picard], *Histoire du 42e Régiment d'Infanterie* (Montbéliard: H. Barbier, 1875), p.311.
21   Gachot, *Brune en Hollande*, p.235.
22   Gachot, *Brune en Hollande*, p.235.
23   Schneidawind, Geschichte des Krieges in Holland, pp.110-111.

THE BATTLE OF ZIJPE, 10 SEPTEMBER   193

Zijpe Sluices. (Author photo)

from the windmill. Continuing their attack, both cannon were also captured. They were preparing to attack Krabbendam from the west when news was received about the retreat of Dumonceau's Batavian troops, putting the French in jeopardy. With a threatened right flank the French retreated hastily, even abandoning their wounded. Vandamme's division rallied at the foot of the dunes, facing north to fend off a possible British pursuit or counter-attack. Kamp, Groet, and Schoorl remained occupied.

Aftermath

The Franco-Batavians lost 1,759 men: French losses were *Général de Brigade* David, 3 officers and 36 others killed; 36 officers and 713 others wounded. Batavian losses were eight officers and 89 others killed; 32 officers and 466 others wounded; 375 missing.[24] About 300 of these missing Batavians would change sides and join the Dutch army raised by the Hereditary

---

24   Official French returns of 16 September by *Adjudant-Général* Dardenne, in report of *10 September 1799 from Dardenne to the Uitvoerend Bewind* in *Besluiten der Eerste Kamer van het Vertegenwoordigend Lichaam des Bataafschen Volks*. September 1799, 16 September 1799.

Prince of Orange. The British lost a total of 203 men: 37 dead, 147 wounded and 19 made prisoner or missing (the latter all from the 20th Foot). Among the wounded were Major General Moore, Lieutenant Colonel Smyth and Major Ross from the 1/20th Foot and 11 more officers.[25] Abercromby wrote in his after action report about the engagement:

> Having fully considered the position which the British troops had occupied on the 1st inst., and having in view the certainty of speedy and powerful reinforcements, I determined to remain until then on the defensive. From the information which we had received we were apprised of the enemy's intention to attack us, and we were daily improving the advantages of our situation. Yesterday morning at daybreak the enemy commenced an attack on our centre and right, from St. Martin's to Petten, in three columns, and apparently with their whole force. The column on the right, composed of Dutch troops, and under the command of Gen. Daendels, directed its attack on the village of St. Martin's. The centre column of the enemy, under the orders of Gen. de Monceau, likewise composed of Dutch troops, marched on to Crabbendam, and Zyper Sluys. The left column of the enemy, composed of French, directed itself on the position occupied by Major Gen. Burrard, commanding the second brigade of Guards.
>
> The enemy advanced, particularly on their left and centre, with great intrepidity, and penetrated with the heads of their columns to within a hundred yards of the post occupied by the British troops. They were, however, everywhere repulsed, owing to the strength of our position, and the determined courage of the troops. About ten o'clock the enemy retired towards Alkmaar, leaving behind them many dead and some wounded men, with one piece of cannon, a number of waggons, pontoons, and portable bridges. Col. M'Donald with the reserve pursued them for some time and quickened their retreat.
>
> It is impossible for me to do full justice to the good conduct of the troops. Col. Spencer, who commanded in the village of St. Martin's, defended his post with great spirit and judgment. Major Gen. Moore, who commanded on his right, and who was wounded, though I am happy to say slightly, was no less judicious in the management of the troops under his command. The two battalions of the 20th regiment, posted opposite to Crabbendam and Zyper Sluys did credit to the high reputation which that regiment has always borne. Lieut. Col. Smyth of that corps, who had the particular charge of that post, received a severe wound in his leg, which will deprive us for a time of his services. The two brigades of guards repulsed with great vigour the column of French which had advanced to attack them, and where the slaughter of the enemy was great. I continue to receive every mark of zeal and intelligence from the Officers composing the Staff this army. It is difficult to state with any precision the loss of the enemy, but it cannot be computed at less than eight hundred or one thousand men; and on our side it does not exceed, in killed, wounded, and missing, two hundred men.[26]

---

25 Official British returns in Anon., *Campaign in Holland*, Appendix No.7, p.80; Anon., *The History of the Campaign of 1799, in Holland*, pp.317-319.
26 Dispatch of 11 September 1799 from Abercromby to Henry Dundas in the *London Chronicle*, 17 September 1799.

Already surprised by the fighting capabilities of the Batavians during his landing on 27 August, Abercromby was again impressed by the vigour by which he was attacked by the French as well as the Batavians. At one moment during the battle he apparently panicked a bit when ordering Mitchell to clear the roadstead. As stated above, the attack justified his decision to remain on the defence until his reinforcements arrived. Regarding the Franco-Batavians, in name of Brune, *Adjudant-Général* Dardenne wrote the following after action report which was send to the Batavian *Uitvoerend Bewind* already that same day:

> As soon as the *Général en Chef* was able to unite an army, roughly equal to that of the enemy, he decided to attack, according to your desire. This morning at four o'clock the army, in accordance to his orders, marched against the enemy in three Columns. The right wing, commanded by *Lieutenant-Generaal* Daendels, was responsible for attacking from Eenigenburg until St. Maarten; the centre Column the orders of *Lieut. Gen.* Dumonceau, connected with its right wing on the left of *Gen.* Daendels, and with the left below Krabbendam, on the right bank of the canal that leads from Alkmaar to the Zijpe. A French Column, seven thousand men strong, under the orders of *Général de Division* van Damme, connected on its right on the left side of the said Canal, extending his left towards the sea. The enemy was entrenched behind the Dike of the Zijpe, and had established batteries along the Dike and ahead of his frontline. By the force of the attack he was, initially, forced to abandon his outposts and to retreat behind the Dike. The French forced them to yield Kamp; many times they have charged to overpower the enemy in their last entrenchments, but despite the fearless courage they showed, the enemy fire, entrenched behind the dike and behind the canal below Zypsluis up to Petten, were obstacles that could not be tackled with French heroism. Several tried to swim across the canal. About thirty drowned with their weapons in their hands. We were not able not to notice that fresh conscripts were among these troops; everybody desired to attack the enemy. They remained master of the battlefield, occupying Kamp and Slaperdijk; they had about 650 wounded, among which is *Général de Brigade* David, who is mortally wounded, and many officers, of which 22 from two Battalions of the 42e Demi-Brigade. The Columns of the right wing and centre did not have more luck; they resumed the position they occupied before the battle: the number of injured is 450. The number of killed French and Batavians is not known to me yet. The Batavians Generals will, without doubt, provide a detailed report to the Minister of War. As the English did not leave their entrenchments we cannot estimate their loss; but it is believed to be quite considerable. The General-in-Chief gives praise to the conduct of the Batavian *jager*, Cavalry and Artillery.[27]

There is not a word in Dardenne's after action report about the panics and subsequent routs that took place among the Batavian troops. This was reason for Brune to send an additional letter to the *Uitvoerend Bewind* on the 11th, probably also sent as an excuse for the failure:

---

27 Report of *10 September 1799 from Dardenne to the Uitvoerend Bewind* in *Besluiten der Eerste Kamer van het Vertegenwoordigend Lichaam des Bataafschen Volks*. September 1799, 11 September 1799. An English translation is in the *London Chronicle*, 28 September 1799.

The *Chef d'Etat-Major* has given you an account of the attack we made yesterday against the enemy. The day would have been decisive for us if all units would have done equally well their duty. Anyway we held the positions we had before the battle, and even captured some closer to the enemy positions. There are units that indeed conducted very well, and braves whose names deserve to be known: as soon as the *Généraux de Division* have sent me their reports, I will let you know those that are entitled to praise and encouragement; cowards will be removed from the Army, and then I hope our efforts against the enemy will be crowned with more decisive results.[28]

The battle had been a clear defeat for the Franco-Batavians. They lost 1,759 men against only two hundred British. Brune had only one chance to throw the British back into the sea before their reinforcements, including the feared Russians, would arrive. A second attack in the short term was not possible; the troops were exhausted, a number of units had taken heavy losses, ammunition was low. The British on the other hand now knew the strength of their positions. They could use the cover of the Schoorlsche and Westfriesche Zeedijk while the attackers had to advance across open ground and saw their charges limited to a few access points because of the terrain intersected by numerous canals and ditches. All movement had to be made along the roads. Cavalry was of no use and as the artillery from the attackers had to deploy on the same roads, their line of fire blocked by their own advancing infantry. Although because of the strong British position the chances for a Franco-Batavian victory were very small beforehand, a number of facts can be summed up that made a victory even more unlikely. First of all, the French troops and Dumonceau's division were still exhausted from their march to the front line just one or two days before the battle occurred. Otherwise they could have been given time some time to concentrate closer to their starting positions. Bruce could also have potentially concentrated his brigade at Koedijk instead of south of Alkmaar, which would have enabled him to attack on time. The few days' respite would also have enabled the officers to acquaint themselves with the terrain; to reconnoitre the roads they had to advance on; to find positions to support the attacks with artillery and to prevent the mistake in the marching orders that had caused the confusion among the Batavian troops. That would have enabled Daendels to concentrate on his attack at Eenigenburg and in the direction of St. Maarten rather than having to intervene in the centre. Finally, there would have been time to prepare the crossing of the canals in front of the Schoorlsche and Westfriesche Zeedijk, by means of bridging materials and other preparations.

---

28 Letter of 11 September 1799 from Brune to the *Uitvoerend Bewind* in *Besluiten der Eerste Kamer. September 1799*, 12 September 1799.

11

The Russians Arrive

The Franco-Batavians Consolidate

The morale of the Batavian troops was low after their defeat. Already during the battle panics occurred as described in the previous chapter. In the evening of 10 September, a sergeant of the 1e Bataljon Jagers located at the village of Broek yelled that the British were attacking, after which a great panic followed, with men yelling that they were surrounded and British cavalry cutting down everyone. Five thousand men, nearly the whole of Daendels' division, took flight. It was only at St. Pancras, the headquarters of Daendels, that the rout of most of them could be stopped by the 3/5e Halve Brigade. With order restored the troops were brought back to their positions. Some fugitives made it to Alkmaar and they spread the panic to the train, drivers joining the rout as far as Haarlem. At Haarlem after the panic, some two hundred deserters of various units were discovered, among them some officers. In addition, on the 11th, the pay chest from the 3/2e Regiment Zware Cavalerie was discovered, together with many other goods stolen in the confusion.[1]

What was the real cause of the panic? The 2/1e Halve Brigade received the order to retreat too late. So when they retreated the other troops had already occupied their defensive positions again and did not expect more friendly troops to arrive from the side of the enemy. The sergeant of the outpost where the battalion arrived mistook the troops in the fading light, with their red facings on cuffs and collars, for a British battalion and he immediately fell back on his supports, calling out that the British attacked and that they had to fall back immediately. At these supports two sutlers were present who spread the word of the attack as far as Alkmaar, causing the panic.[2] The sergeant of the outpost was shot in front of the troop, because of the fact that he did not properly identify the advancing troops and retreated without firing any shots at all. Brune was furious about the panics that had taken place in both Batavian divisions, during and after the battle, writing to Daendels that same evening:

---

1 W.A. van Rappard, 'De Haarlemmer in zorg en angst', *Haerlem Jaarboek 1983* (Haarlem: Schuyt & Co C.V., 1984), pp.67-68.
2 N.L. Hoevenaar, *Militair dagboek van kolonel N.L. Hoevenaar, geb. 22 mei 1772, lopende over de veldtochten in Frankrijk, Brabant, Oostenrijk, Pruysche, Zweeds Pommeren, Spanje en Holland tot aan het Franse Keizerrijk*, p.15.

Citizen General. I ask you to tell me as soon as possible, if you can answer for your troops. I authorize you to shoot on the spot the motor of the disorder. I require this from you. I also require you to make known to me the instigators of the infamous lie of an attack by the enemy, which has disrupted your troops... Send away the officers and replace them with brave NCOs or soldiers. Your division will no longer be accommodated in the cities. You will determine an encampment at your previous position; you will stand your ground; you will entrench your encampment by cutting field channels, by making steps and redoubts. It is only by severity and military conduct that the evils spread by cowardice and treason can be stopped. I know your feelings. I expect you will express absolute determination. You will arrange that the food is distributed in the camp. When marching against the enemy, anything that is not ambulance must be at the rear in Alkmaar.[3]

These events and the panics and subsequent routs that occurred during the battle did not do much good for the Batavian reputation and the opinion Brune had of them. Brune wrote to his chief of staff Dardenne:

General Dardenne will go to the Batavian *Uitvoerend Bewind* to obtain:
(1) that all the appointments I have made, I shall make of officers, be confirmed by the patents which the Minister of War will be charged to dispatch so that they may take the oath to the colours;
2) that all the officers whom I shall send back are no longer employed;
3) that 3,000 national guards be sent to me to be organized by me, and that the others will return to protect the public tranquillity in towns other than their own;
(4) to explain to the *Uitvoerend Bewind* that the proposal to destroy the National Guards is a proposal of the Orangist Committee, and that the notes of my espionage show that the Committee has done everything possible to dissolve them, with the twofold aim of demoralize the volunteers, to make them believe that the people were returning from hatred to the Stadtholder, and appeal to them to lay down their arms;
5) that the known Orangists be arrested and taken hostage at 's Hertogenbosch;
6) that I be given a state of the supply of fortified places;
7) that the regiments of Waldeck and Saxe-Gotha be assimilated into the other national troops, and that their recruitment suffers no delay;
8) a declaration that I will defend this country to the last extremity, but that the government, on its side, must set a great example on the Orangists, to testify that it approves of the rigorous conduct which I propose to hold, and which I hope will save the Batavian liberty.
P. S. Let him give me knowledge of the means of the Minister of Marine to defend the Zuiderzee. It has been proposed to burn the English fleet. What did he do in fact, what will he do? I request the company of pontoneers.[4]

---

3   Letter of 10 September from Brune to Daendels, in Koolemans Beijnen, 'Krijgsgeschiedkundige studie', 1891, p.566.
4   Letter of 11 September 1799 from Brune to Dardenne in D.H. Delprat, 'Journal concernant les évenements politiques de notre patrie depuis 1798-1807 redigé par Daniel Delprat', in *Bijdragen en Mededeelingen van het Historisch*

The Batavian Government agreed with the greater part of Brune's demands, ordering beside the already existing *Gewapende Burgermacht* the forming of the Bataafsch Legioen of 3,000 men (see Chapter 3). On 22 September the pontoneer company arrived in Alkmaar.

After the battle of 10 September both armies remained at their previous positions without much fighting; there was only some exchange of gunfire. A few days later some fighting occurred at Warmenhuizen. *Lieutenant-Generaal* Dumonceau judged the British outpost at Warmenhuizen of about 100 men to be too close to his positions and a threat. The British position was very strong however, because of the demolition of the bridge in front of them. During the night of 14-15 September two companies of the 4e Bataljon Jager and two grenadier companies of 6e Halve-Brigade, commanded by the *Capitein* Goudoever of the *jager*, attacked the British. Covered by the fire of the *jager* the grenadiers repaired the bridge and stormed over it. The British did not wait for them to arrive and retreated to their own lines. Batavian losses were one man killed and three wounded, the British lost two men killed and three wounded. A small feat of arms but it did help to restore Batavian morale. Another fact boosting morale was the knowledge that substantial French reinforcements were finally marching to the Batavian Republic, although mostly raw conscripts. Batavian minister of war Pijman was informed that:

> About 12,500 men will arrive successively from France, marching to the Batavian Republic; and that these, as they have arrived in Rotterdam, will be embarked for Haarlem. These troops, including 3,500 men to complete the various units, and who will be clothed; further march with them a detachment of gunners, six artillery pieces, seven caissons and 35,000 cartridges. Of these 12,500 men, 1,500 are cavalry.[5]

Brune realised that for the moment he was in no position to attack. The Franco-Batavian troops improved their defences to await the inevitable Anglo-Russian advance. The main defences were along the line Oud-Karspel–Schoorldam–Groet–Kamp. The 1e Bataafsche Divisie (Daendels, 6,892 men) was positioned on the right flank and had to defend the approaches to the south along the Langendijk. Therefore, Daendels ordered the construction of a redoubt in front of the village Oud-Karspel. The redoubt was armed with 14 guns. Daendels' proposition to extend the defences to the east was rejected.[6] The town of Medemblik had no garrison, Enkhuizen just 150 unreliable armed citizens commanded by *Capitein* Egenberger, and Hoorn also had no garrison, although precautions were taken and the considerable magazines emptied and their contents brought behind the Franco-Batavian lines.

In the centre stood the 2e Bataafsche Divisie (Dumonceau, 6,660 men) on the east side of the Kanaal van Alkmaar. His forward troops were at Schoorldam where a bridge crossed the canal. His headquarters and his main force were at Koedijk were the French *Chef de*

    Genootschap ('s Gravenhage : Martinus Nijhoff, 1892), pp.186-188.
5 Letter of 13 September 1799 from Dardenne to the Batavian minister of war Pijman, in: *Besluiten der Eerste Kamer van het Vertegenwoordigend Lichaam des Bataafschen Volks. September 1799*, 13 September 1799.
6 Van Sypesteijn, 'Krijgskundige Beschouwingen over den Veldtogt van 1799 in Noord-Holland', in *Nieuwe Spectator* (Nijmegen: J.F. Thieme, 1854), p.141.

"Field bakery", by Joannes Bemme after a drawing of Dirk Langendijk. (Rijksmuseum, RP-P-1912-306)

Brigade Saint-Julien, *commandant en chef le génie*, had constructed a floating bridge across the Kanaal van Alkmaar to enable communications between the Batavians and the French. On the west side this bridge was protected by two entrenchments. On the east bank, half way the road to Krabbendam, an entrenchment with two cannon protected the bridge.

On the Franco-Batavian left flank, between the North Sea and the Kanaal van Alkmaar, the French Division commanded by *Général de Division* Vandamme (now 9,935 men) was deployed, occupying forward posts at Kamp and Groet and the main force at Schoorl, Bergen, Alkmaar and Egmond aan Zee. Brune had his headquarters in Alkmaar, with a reserve consisting of the 49e Demi-Brigade (3 battalions), the 3/60e Demi-Brigade and four squadrons of the 10e Dragons. South of Alkmaar the artillery park was situated. With his chief of staff *Général de Brigade* Dardenne being ill, his secretary Vern was charged with transmitting orders to the commanding generals, 150 *chasseurs à cheval* being assigned to that task. Total Franco-Batavian strength was about 23,500 men.[7]

The Defence of Amsterdam

The Batavians feared an attack on Amsterdam most of all, but not only the Batavians: it was also a concern for the French, illustrated by a letter from the French ambassador Florent-Guiot to Talleyrand:

---

7   For the composition of the Franco-Batavian army see Appendix XIII.

I fear even more that the English in North Holland will arm a flotilla of light ships to attack Amsterdam by the Zuiderzee. Its inhabitants are generally well disposed; but it is certain that some bombs directed at a city as populous and with all their riches in the magazines they would be determined to surrender. This would be the *coup de grâce* for the Batavian government; it would have no money, no credit, nor resources; and the next day he would be unable to pay the loan from the army. His embarrassment is already very large in this respect, because despite its design and in this critical situation nobody pays his ordinary and extraordinary taxes.[8]

So not surprisingly after the British landings and the capture of the Batavian fleet, leaving the Zuiderzee wide open for the British navy, many measures were taken to reinforce the defences of Amsterdam on the sea-side and to the north. On 1 September, just one day after their arrival in Haarlem, the corps of citizen artillery of the *Gewapende Burgermacht* of Amsterdam was recalled. *Generaal-Major* van Guèricke was appointed commander of Amsterdam when he fell in disgrace after his behaviour during the British landing. The very able *Lieutenant-Colonel* Krayenhoff of the engineers had on 31 August been send to Amsterdam by Daendels with orders to take all measures for defence that were necessary. With great zeal Krayenhoff went to work. Batteries were constructed to defend all accesses to Amsterdam. The entrance of the Ij, the inlet from the Zuiderzee north of Amsterdam giving access to the city, was defended by two batteries: the one on the north side armed with six 18pdr cannon, four mortars and two howitzers; the one on the south side armed with eight 18pdr howitzers, two mortars and two howitzers. To protect these batteries against an attack from the land-side, additional batteries were constructed on the dikes leading to these batteries. Beside both batteries three ships were moored in the entrance: the ship of the line *Bato* (74 guns), with a crew of 250 men and armed with 34x 24pdr cannon; a hulk with a crew of 120 men, armed with eighteen 18pdr and 12pdr cannon and a howker (a 20 metre long fishing boat with one pole mast, converted into a gun platform) with a crew of 100 men and armed with eighteen 12pdr cannon. Beside these ships, on 26 September the following smaller ships were also present to support the batteries and bigger ships and to operate in shallow waters when necessary: the gunboat *Helhond* (30 men, four cannon); the schooner *Zwerver* (24 men, six cannon); 16 converted fishing boats, with crews of 20 men and armed with four 4pdr or 5pdr cannon; 19 barges with crews of 10-12 men and armed with a 24pdr cannon; three fishing trawlers with crews of 24-80 men and armed with two 30pdr and two 4pdr cannon; two fire ships and an explosion ship or hellburner. The following days this flotilla was augmented with 10 additional barges and 14 armed fishing trawlers. Also arriving were four French gunboats from Flushing, which moved from there through the inland canals. More than enough artillery to arm the boats and batteries was available. To find reliable men to crew these ships was more difficult; in the end some French officers, 200 sailors and 60 gunners came from Flushing to crew the boats and operate the batteries.

To the west of Amsterdam additional batteries were constructed and inundations prepared. On the north side extensive inundations were executed, flooding parts of the

---

8   Letter of 6 September 1799 from Florent-Guiot to Talleyrand in Gachot, *Brune en Hollande*, p.243.

"View of the Ij", anonymous. (Noord-Hollands Archief, NL-HlmNHA_359_000369_M)

Beemster and Purmer polders. All avenues of access, the roads on the dikes leading trough the inundations, were protected by batteries with numerous guns. This was the position to which Daendels would retreat after the battle of 2 October (see Chapter 15). Inhabitants of the cities and villages were pressed to construct all the necessary batteries.[9] To reinforce the defences of Amsterdam even further, or even to undertake offensive actions on the Zuiderzee and the Waddenzee, a French flotilla consisting of 70 gunboats was ordered from Dunkirk using the inland canals in Belgium and the Batavian Republic. On 18 October this flotilla arrived in Amsterdam, but due to the armistice they would remain there and return a few days later.[10]

Anglo-Russian Reinforcements

In contrast with the Franco-Batavians the British were in high spirits. They had executed a landing on a defended coast and won a battle, inflicting heavy casualties for few losses. They held a major harbour and the promised Russian army had finally arrived, although there had been some delay as the Russian ships had sailed to England first, as reported in the *London Chronicle*:

---

9   J.C. de Jonge, *Geschiedenis van het Nederlandsche Zeewezen* (Zwolle: Van Hoogstraten en Gorter, 1869), Vol.V, pp.492-495; Krayenhoff, *Geschiedkundige*, pp.273-297; Colenbrander, *Gedenkstukken*, Vol.III, p.418.
10 Krayenhoff, *Geschiedkundige*, Appendix XVIIIe, p.141.

An Officer came to London yesterday with information, that eight or nine sail of the Russian fleet had arrived in Yarmouth Roads. They had unfortunately missed the several dispatch vessels which had been sent in quest of them, with orders to proceed directly to the Texel. The wind, on the departure of the Messenger, blew straight on shore, which rendered the sailing of the Russian fleet from Yarmouth Roads impracticable.'[11]

The British trust in the outcome was also illustrated by the *London Chronicle*, although at some points the truth was stretched a bit:

> During the action between 3 and 400 Dutchmen deserted to the British standard, and many more were attempting to do so, but were fired upon by the French. The second division of the Russians was in sight when the Circe left the Helder, and the Duke of York was preparing to land from the Amethyst frigate. If the enemy were repulsed by Sir Ralph Abercromby alone, how much more will our superiority be established by the junction of the Russians, which would immediately take place, and the large reinforcements from the Downs and Yarmouth that have lately sailed? Under these considerations there can be but little cause to doubt that our army has by this time taken Alkmaar, and that all the country North of Amsterdam would fall in a few days afterwards. The military force, or the fortifications of the enemy in that quarter, could oppose but a slight resistance. Admiral Mitchell was preparing to aid the army, by assailing Amsterdam from sea; but when our troops approach the place it will most probably surrender, to avoid the horrors of an attack. It is doubtful whether the enemy, inferior as they are, will oppose our progress to that city through the several strong passes by which it is defended; perhaps they will reserve themselves to prevent our passing the rivers and entering Brabant. It is also stated in the private letters which have been received that the gallant Gen. Moore is only wounded in the little finger, one-half of which he has lost… Five hundred stand of arms were taken. The Militia Volunteers, who are mostly formed into particular battalions, behaved with extraordinary gallantry. In one instance they actually repulsed the French grenadiers. The general result of this engagement gives the best hopes that the attempt to rescue Holland from the French will be attended with complete success.[12]

On 13 September, as reported, York arrived in Holland with the frigate *Amethyst*. He took over command from Abercromby:

> The arrival of the Duke of York and nearly all the reinforcements both Russian and British, enables us to undertake with every prospect of success immediate operations. We are now occupied in disembarking the troops and stores, and everything is ordered forward. I believe it was essentially necessary that the Duke of York

---

11   *London Chronicle*, 9 September 1799.
12   *London Chronicle*, 17 September 1799.

should take the command the moment that we became a combined army. I am not certain that the Russian general would have liked to obey any other officer. The Hereditary Prince of Orange is here with us. He is modest and unassuming; his manners are not popular, and he does not yield readily to the friendships of his countrymen, whose sincerity he perhaps has good reason to suspect. The Duke of York will now carry on the correspondence with you, and I shall only write you occasionally.[13]

Indeed from that moment on strong reinforcements arrived: On the 11th the 2nd Division of the Russian army had arrived before Texel: eight infantry battalions, a hussar squadron and 107 Cossacks, artillery with a total of 56 guns and a pioneer company; 7,300 men commanded by Lieutenant General Zherebtsov. With them had also sailed the commander in chief of the Russian troops, Lieutenant General Hermann. Because of the strong wind and the heavy surf disembarkation could only take place on the 13th, the Russian troops being landed by British boats. The soldiers were exhausted from their unaccustomed journey crammed into the ships' holds, even worse because of the bad weather the transport ships had encountered. After their landing they immediately received their arms and had to parade past the Duke of York and the Hereditary Prince of Orange. Nevertheless the Prince was impressed by the Russians, writing to his mother:

The Russian troops are very nice men, there are full of grenadiers, who have 2 or 3 medals; they have a very martial air, but are horribly ragged. General Hermann seems to be a clever man and a good soldier, with an excellent way of speaking and a real soldier.[14]

The medals mentioned here were also 'astonishing to their British allies, as at that time no British medals were conferred on private soldiers'.[15] The British soldiers would have more surprises as described by one of their officers:

At the period of the embarkation of the Russians I had some business to do at the Helder, and on my ride down I observed a party of them in a bivouac near the sandhills: it had been washing-day with them, and in order to procure a current of air to dry their linen, they had pulled down the two side walls of a small house that had been used as a temporary shed for cattle, where their chemises were flapping in the wind. Near this laundry of new invention cookery was in progress, and I had the curiosity to peep into the cauldron hanging over a wood fire: it contained in the boiling water the head of a bullock or cow, with the hair peeling off by the force of the hot water; its mouth was stuffed full of grass, and it had all the look of imploring the pity of the bystanders; one of the assistant cooks had just made a successful

---

13 Letter in English of 16 September 1799 from Abercromby to Henry Dundas in Colenbrander, *Gedenkstukken*, Vol.III, pp.400-401.
14 Koolemans Beijnen, *De Erfprins van Oranje in Noord-Holland*, p.26.
15 Moore Smith, *The Life of John Colborne*, p.17.

attack on the wheels of a tumbril, from which he returned with a good handful of cart grease, to serve a relish after the delicate soup in the camp kettle.[16]

A British soldier of the Light Infantry Battalion also saw the Russian cooks at work, recording that:

> The regiment which we saw on this occasion had with it, I should think, full half as many followers as soldiers, some of whom carried immensely large copper kettles; others the provisions, and others the officers' baggage; in short, these were the scullions, the cooks, and, as it were, the beasts of burden of the regiment; but this was a bad system, for it increased by one half the number of mouths to fill, and must have been attended with the worst consequences when provisions were scarce.[17]

After the parade the Russians immediately continued with a long and fatiguing march to their assigned positions in the Zijpe, behind the Schoorlsche Zeedijk between Petten and Krabbendam. Again the soldiers were to suffer, especially from the lack of fresh water. On the morning of the 14th they arrived at their assigned positions. On that same day the 1st Division of the Russian army, which initially sailed to Yarmouth, arrived also: eight infantry battalions, hussars, Cossacks and artillery with eight guns, commanded by Major General Essen (5,484 men in all). Next day disembarking started with the boats of the Russian ships on which the troops had been embarked. Because of the heavy surf it would take three days to complete, the last Russian soldiers setting foot on land on the 17th. As a result they were force marched to Petten, arriving there in the evening of the 18th and they would have to go into battle the next day.

Two Russian rowing frigates, the *Sviatoi Konstantin* and *Sviatoi Nikolai*, built for operating in the shallow waters of the Baltic, were believed to be useful in Holland as well. It was already ordered before sailing from Reval that they had to be re-armed with a full complement of cannon to operate in cooperation with the British smaller warships.[18] They would take no part in any action although they could have been of some use in the shallow waters of the Zuiderzee.

Between 14 and 17 September the 3rd British Division, containing the 7th, 8th and 9th Brigades, commanded by Lieutenant General Dundas, arrived: 11 infantry battalions, the 7th Light Dragoons, and artillery. Arriving with them were 1,730 additional men of flank companies to oppose the Franco-Batavian light infantrymen and 342 men of the horse artillery to aid in the speedy advance of the artillery pieces. A total of 9,839 men.[19] They immediately marched to their assigned positions in the Zijpe:

---

16 Anon. [Lieutenant Colonel Fletcher Wilkie], 'Recollections of the British army, in the early campaigns of the Revolutionary War' in *The United Service Journal and Naval and Military Magazine*, Part I (London, Henry Colburn, 1836), p.323.
17 William Surtees, *Twenty-five years in the Rifle Brigade* (Edinburgh & London: William Blackwood & T. Cadell, 1833), p.9.
18 Miliutin, *Geschichte des Krieges*, Vol.IV, p.277.
19 Embarkation return of the Seventh, Eighth, and Ninth Brigades in Anon., *The History of the Campaign of 1799, in Holland*, p.322.

Zijpe polder seen from the Westfriesche Zeedijk between Eenigenburg and St. Maarten. (Author photo)

Having disembarked at the Texel we were marched up to the town of Schaagenbrug. The men were quartered in the churches, and the officers billeted in the private houses, where we were received with much civility. Schaagen is a pretty, neat-looking place, and like most Dutch towns, has a canal with trees planted along, and the houses, with their gables towards the street, are painted in all sorts of gaudy colours.[20]

Surtees, with the light infantry, recorded that his battalion

[M]oved forward to the town of Schagen, and took up our quarters in the church. I thought this extremely odd, as I had been accustomed to view so sacred an edifice with more reverence than to suppose they would quarter soldiers in it; but we were stowed in it as thick as we could well be, and made the best of our quarters; some taking the chancel, others the vestry, and some the body of the church; nay, some even took up their lodging in the reading-desk and pulpit.[21]

---

20   Anon., 'Recollections of the British army', p.185.
21   Surtees, *Rifle Brigade*, p.9.

Total Anglo-Russian strength was now about 35,000 men. The 69th Foot was detached from the 3rd Brigade and encamped near Den Helder at Huisduinen, remaining there as a rearguard during the whole campaign. Marines occupied the arsenal at the Nieuwe Diep and the islands Texel and Wieringen.[22] York was pleased with the state of things, writing to Henry Dundas:

> I have to acquaint you with my arrival at this place yesterday evening, having sailed from Deal on board the Amethyst frigate, on Monday morning the 9th instant. Upon coming on shore, I had great satisfaction in witnessing the disembarkation of eight battalions of Russian auxiliary troops, consisting of 7000 men, under the command of lieutenant-general D'Herman, which had arrived from Revel in the course of the preceding day and yesterday morning. I afterwards saw these troops upon their march towards the position occupied by the British near Schagen; and I have great pleasure in assuring you, that, from their appearance in every respect, the most happy consequences may be expected from their co-operation with his majesty's arms in this country: lieutenant-general D'Herman seems to enter most heartily into our views, and I form very sanguine hopes of receiving essential assistance from his zeal and experience.
>
> I understand that Sir Ralph Abercrombie has made you acquainted with his having repulsed the enemy in an attack made upon him on Tuesday last. I proceed to join him at his quarters at Schagen immediately. I have had the pleasure to meet the hereditary prince of Orange here. His serene highness is occupied in arranging into corps a large body of deserters from the Batavian army, and volunteers from the crews of the Dutch ships of war which have proceeded to England. Every assistance shall be given to his serene highness, to render these corps an efficient addition to our force.[23]

Naval Operations

On 9 September Vice Admiral Mitchell ordered the *Arrow* (Sloop 28, Captain Portlock) and the *Wolverine* (Gun-brig 12, Captain Bolton) to sail to the island of Vlieland and to attack the Batavian ships that had been sighted there. On the 12th they spotted the *Draak* (6th Rate 24, *Capitein-Lieutenant* van Esch) and the *Gier* (Gun-brig 16, *Capitein-Lieutenant* Nicolaï Connio – an officer of Italian origin). The *Wolverine* engaged the *Gier* which surrendered after a single shot fired. The *Draak* was engaged by the *Arrow* and after 15 minutes this ship also struck its colours. Following up their success, on 15 September Portlock and his crews took the island Vlieland. In the harbour they captured the *Dolfijn* (6th Rate 24), which was taken into British service as the *Dolphin*. Captain Portlock reported:

---

22   For the composition of the Anglo-Russian army see Appendix XI.
23   Letter of 14 September from the Duke of York to Hendry Dundas in Walsh, *Narrative*, p.110.

We anchored on the edge of the Flack or Flat, abreast of Wieringen: at this anchorage I found it necessary to lighten the ship, which was very speedily done, bringing her from twelve feet eight inches to twelve feet, and on the day following we turned over the Flack, carrying shoal water from one side to the other. On the morning of the 12th inst. we weighed again, and proceeded on for the Fly Island [Vlieland], on approaching which we saw a ship and brig at anchor in the narrow passage leading from the Fly Island towards Harlingen: it was soon perceived they were vessels of force, and bearing the Batavian Republic colours; we approached, the British and ancient Dutch colours flying together, until within half gunshot of the brig, she being the nearest to us, without either of them changing their colours: the Dutch colours were then hauled down, and I made the signal to engage the enemy as coming up with them, meaning the Wolverene to engage the brig and to pass on to the ship myself. Captain Bolton anchored his ship in the most masterly and gallant manner, and just in the position I could have wished, which was on his weather quarter, at a quarter of a cable distance, and so as to have enabled me, had it been necessary, to give the enemy a broadside in passing, without annoying the Wolverene, and after heaving on his spring until his broadside bore on the brig, fired one shot just to try his disposition, upon which the enemy fired three guns to leeward and hauled down his colours.

I made the signal for the Wolverene to take charge of the prize, and desired the Officer sent on board to send her pilot to conduct the Arrow to the ship, (my Dutch pilots having declined the charge) and requested of Captain Bolton to follow me to the Jetting Passage, where the ship lay, and then pushed on towards her. We had to turn to windward towards the enemy against a strong lee tide, which retarded our progress much; she lay with springs on her cables, and her broadside opposed directly to our approach, and for twenty minutes before we could bring a gun to bear with effect on her, annoyed us very much, and cut us up a good deal in the hull, sails, and rigging; but after bringing the ship up by the stern and head in a very narrow passage at about a quarter of a cable from him, the contest became smart, but was short, for she struck in about fifteen minutes after we commenced our fire upon her, and just before the Wolverene (which was pressing in the most gallant manner to my aid) came up. I sent my first Lieut. to take possession of her, and found her to be the Batavian Republic guard-ship De Draak, commanded by Captain-Lieutenant Van Esch, mounting 24 guns, 16 of them long Dutch eighteen-pounders, two long English thirty-two pounders, six fifty pound howitzers, and 180 men. From the howitzers I rather suppose Langridge was fired,[24] as several pieces of iron were picked up in the ship after the action was over… On my going on board the Draak I found that she had been built for a sheer hulk, and converted into a guard ship, extremely old; her masts and rigging very much cut, and the vessel altogether unfit for his Majesty's service, determined me to destroy her. I therefore directed Capt. Bolton to perform that duty, which he did effectually by burning

---

24 Langrage: Bag or case of any junk, especially bolts and nails but also old musket balls, rocks, gravel, etc., fired to injure enemy crews or to damage sails and rigging.

her. This service performed, we weighed and proceeded towards the Fly Island, at which place we anchored on the 15th instant. I immediately sent Capt. Bolton to take possession of the Batavian Republican ship the Dolphin, riding at anchor close to the town of the Fly. She had on our anchoring hoisted the Orange colours, and the same step was taken on the island. A person came off from the municipality, desiring him to surrender the island to the Government of the Prince of Orange; and I have the honour to request you will be pleased to direct some persons to be sent as soon as convenient to take upon themselves the arrangement and management of civil affairs in the island. The Island of Scheling [Terschelling] has not yet adopted the same step. I shall therefore; if it meets your approbation, take the necessary steps to induce them to do it.

To the Captains and Officers I have given paroles, which measure I hope will meet your wishes. The prisoners from the ship and brig, amounting to about two hundred and thirty, I have put on board the Dolphin until I know your pleasure respecting them (I think they will mostly volunteer for the Prince's service; the command of which ship I have given (until your pleasure is known), to Lieut McDougal of the Wolverene… I have given 1st Lieutenant Gilmour the temporary command of the Batavian Republican brig Gier, and shall send her round to the Texel as soon as possible. She mounts fourteen long Dutch twelve pounders, with a complement of eighty-men. She is a most complete vessel, quite new, copper bottomed, well found, and never yet at sea, and in every respect fit for his Majesty's service, only wanting men. I mean to take four of her guns out for the purpose of arming four schoots to act hereabouts, either on the defensive or offensive.[25]

As a result of the loss of their ships *Capitein-Lieutenant* van Esch was degraded and *Capitein-Lieutenant* Connio shot by the Batavian government for their supposed lack of resistance. On 19 September a British warship approached the North Sea coast between Zandvoort and Noordwijk aan Zee. A boat with eight men rowed to the beach, cut down the telegraph pole and spiked the signal gun. It is not clear if this action was directly related to the Anglo-Russian attack on the Franco-Batavian positions on the same day, in order to disturb communications.

The Dutch Corps on the Island of Texel

As described, as a result of the Franco-Batavian attack at the Zijpe position on 10 September, Abercromby ordered the roadstead of the Texel to be prepared for an emergency re-embarkation of his army. The Batavian ships had to sail for Great Britain immediately. As a result the disembarkation of the Dutch volunteers from their ships had been complete chaos. The volunteers were put on all kinds of small vessels and boats without food or other necessities and came ashore on the island of Texel:

25 *Naval Chronicle*, Vol.III, pp.70-71.

The English officers did not permit us to make preparations for our so-called volunteers, until after we had helped them to put the ships under sail. While the ships were already sailing away with considerable speed, such an amount of men fell in our vessels, that we had to abandon the ships without being able to take with us any food, even had to cut the ropes, in order not to be overwhelmed until we sank. Everything happened in such chaos, that until now we do not know how many men we have because darkness had already fallen. We estimate to have about 3,000 men.'[26]

The few officers – only 11 were present at the moment – did their utmost to make preparations for the sailors which were near to mutiny. All public buildings and churches were requisitioned. After that the men were provided with a drop and some money (sailors 1 Dutch Guilder, corporals fl. 1.50, sergeants fl. 2) and order was more or less restored. Command of Texel was given to *Lieutenant-Colonel* van Panhuys. Of course the population of Texel was not happy having to accommodate the 3,000 men and sent a commission to the Prince of Orange with their complaints. The Prince promised them relief in a couple of days. *Lieutenant ter Zee* van Braam proposed to make ready the frigates *Heldin, Minerva, Valk* and *Venus*, which lay anchored in the Nieuwe Diep. On the first frigate, 250 sailors could be placed, 190 each on the other ones without the marines which could be employed on Texel to maintain order among the sailors. Van Braam offered to prepare these frigates so that they could anchor at the roadstead of Texel and, in case of a retreat, could be used to transport Dutch officers and men to Great Britain. This proposal was discussed with Vice Admiral Mitchell, who promised his full cooperation, ordering the British captain having command in the Nieuwe Diep to provide all the support he could. It was added however that a British frigate would join the four Dutch ones, its captain having command of this flotilla. By order of 12 September *Lieutenant ter Zee* Van Braam received command of the *Heldin* and the *Lieutenants ter Zee* Fagel of the *Minerva*, Martinius of the *Valk*, and Twent of the *Venus*.[27]

The Hereditary Prince of Orange had plans that were even far more reaching. He worked out a proposal to send away part of the sailors to Great Britain. As it was not possible to use them in Holland by lack of officers, they would be of more use on the Dutch ships that had sailed there. Secondly, a corps of about 1,200 men was to be formed on the island of Wieringen, out of the deserted Batavian soldiers, the marines, and those sailors that could handle a musket; an additional two hundred sailors and artillerymen would serve the cannon, giving the corps a total of 1,400 men. This corps could be used for diversions along the Zuiderzee coast. It would also relieve the pressure on Texel and save food. Initially Vice Admiral Mitchell objected, not willing to send away transport ships with the Dutch sailors to Great Britain while they might be needed in case of a retreat of Abercromby's army. However, when the transport fleet came in sight that brought the Russians this urgency was removed. Next, Abercromby was asked for permission and indeed promised to deliver

---

26 Letter of 2:00 a.m., 11 September 1799 from *Lieutenant ter Zee* van Braam to the Hereditary Prince of Orange in Koolemans Beijnen, *De Erfprins van Oranje in Noord-Holland*, pp.116-118.
27 Koolemans Beijnen, *De Erfprins van Oranje in Noord-Holland*, pp.23-24, 120-121.

THE FRANCO-BATAVIANS CONSOLIDATE 211

the muskets for the Dutch corps. He added however that the Dutch frigates would only be equipped if their draught would permit their use on the Zuiderzee.

However it was not to be this way. The 800 sailors needed to crew the four Dutch frigates could not be found, all 3,000 of them refusing, stating that they were prepared to serve on land but not at sea again. In addition *Lieutenant-Colonel* van Panhuys still needed the two hundred marines to maintain order amongst the sailors on Texel. In the end only three hundred Batavian deserters were transported to Wieringen, commanded by *Major* van der Hoop.[28]

On 15 September some of the officers sent from Lingen to Great Britain finally arrived in Holland. Not all though, as it was the opinion in Great Britain that the Prince of Orange and the Duke of York would first have to decide were the officers could be used best. Especially useful was the arrival of *Generaal-Major* Bentinck who was ordered to take command of all Dutch men on Texel and in Holland. On the island of Texel there were at this moment about 2,800 sailors and 350 deserters present. They still lacked food, although discipline was better by now after five sailors had been severely punished for opposing their officers. Fifty Dutch sailors were sent over to Den Helder to do labour in the warehouses. New problems occurred when after the Battle of Bergen (19 September) about 1,000 Batavian prisoners of war and deserters arrived. With no room for them in Den Helder nor on Texel, these Batavians were imprisoned for the moment on several ships at the roadstead. *Generaal-Major* Bentinck was ordered to verify how many were on these ships and how many would be willing to serve in the Dutch corps of the Prince of Orange.

---

28 Koolemans Beijnen, *De Erfprins van Oranje in Noord-Holland*, pp.24-27, 121.

12

The Battle of Bergen, 19 September

The Anglo-Russian Plan of Attack

The weather was bad during the first weeks of September. Constant north-western winds brought much rain and cold. The low grounds in this part of Holland were already wet under normal conditions but now they became a marsh and fields flooded. The canals were not able to drain all this water and overflowed; this situation deteriorated quickly when more and more windmills, which should have served to remove the water out of the polders, were destroyed during the fighting. Most Anglo-Russians soldiers lacked protection from the weather. Those that were lucky found shelter in the farmhouses and barns in the Zijpe, but most had to bivouac right behind the front line, in the open along the Schoorlsche and Westfriesche Zeedijk. The troops were also suffering from shortage of supplies. The number of vehicles was much too small and the quality of the roads much too bad to move all needed supplies from Den Helder to the front line. Bringing the supplies with ships through the Zuiderzee to Oude-Sluis was not always possible, due to bad weather. Even when the supplies arrived the Russian soldiers could not get used to the British food.

The Russian artillery, cavalry and senior officers were provided with British horses as had been agreed; only the Cossacks brought their own horses with them. The British did their best to find enough horses, even buying or requisitioning as many as they could in Holland itself, but the Russian staff officers, the adjutants and even part of the Life Guard Hussars would remain without mounts. Although the Russian artillery was provided with enough horses, it turned out that the gunners were used to work with weak and old draught horses, not the fine British and Frisian ones they received now. Most Russians were afraid to come near them and as a result most of the Russian artillery would have to be manhandled in the upcoming battle.[1]

The continuous bad weather, the suffering of his soldiers and the knowledge that French reinforcements were constantly marching to Holland forced York to act as soon as possible. Therefore he decided to attack on 19 September, although the Russians were still not recovered fully from their sea journey, had been force marched to the front, and the commanders did not have the time to get acquainted with the terrain. One source states that York was

---

1   Ritter, *Een Russisch verhaal*, p.22.

Approaching lane from Schoorl to Bergen at the curve near the dunes. (Author photo)

inclined to postpone the attack a day to enable the Russians to recover but that the Russian commander-in-chief Hermann deemed that this was not necessary.[2] Together with Major General Essen, Hermann climbed up the windmill at Krabbendam to observe the terrain their soldiers had to cross; visibility, though, was no more than about 2,000 metres. That was all the preparation made by the Russians for the upcoming battle.

York decided that the attack would start at daybreak and would be made in four columns.[3] The Russian Commander in Chief, Lieutenant General Hermann, commanded the First or Right Column. It was to consist of about 9,000 Russians (Preliminary Attack Force, Advance Guard to which the British horse artillery was attached, 1st and 2nd Lines) with the British 9th Brigade (Manners) of 2,500 men in reserve. The First Column would engage the French commanded by Vandamme. York's ADC Captain Taylor would accompany Hermann to act as a liaison with the British. The Advance Guard, forming the right wing, had to move from Petten along the coast following the Zanddijk and gain the dunes at Camperdown, and was then to attack the villages Kamp and Groet from the rear and flank, while the Preliminary Attack Force would capture the battery at the end of the Slaperdijk. With these objectives

---

2   Anon., *History of the Campaign of 1799*, pp.98-99.
3   See Appendix XII for the Anglo-Russian order of battle.

taken the remainder of the column would advance along the Slaperdijk and make contact with the right wing. The main force consisting of the 1st and 2nd Line commanded by Lieutenant General Zherebtsov would then advance through Groet and Schoorl to Bergen, covered on their right by the Advance Guard. A force of 20 Cossacks would reconnoitre in front of the advancing Russians. Manners' 9th Brigade would remain somewhat behind as a reserve.

The terrain between the Schoorlsche Zeedijk and the villages Kamp and Groet was flat and open, bordered on the right by the North Sea and the Zanddijk protecting the country against the sea, and cut by the Slaperdijk leading to Groet. South of Kamp and Groet were extensive dunes, for the greater part covered with brushwood and further east also with trees. From Groet a road followed the edge of the dunes, with numerous bends, leading to Schoorl and on to Bergen. The terrain east of this road was covered with gardens, hedges, and trees. Bergen was a fairly extensive village, bordered to the north and west by dunes covered with thick brushwood and trees. To reach the centre of Bergen from the direction of Schoorl a wide and straight avenue had to be followed, about 1,000 metres long. Bergen consisted of about 90 brick houses, arranged around a rectangular square with eight streets leading from it. The gardens had many hedges and strong fences. In the centre of this square stood the Protestant church, built of brick. Half of this church was destroyed in 1574 during the war against Spain but the ruined walls were still standing. South-west of Bergen stood a manor house called Het Hof, situated in a park with straight lanes, forming a strong defensive position.

The Second Column under the command of Lieutenant General Dundas consisted of a Russian Brigade of about 2,000 men commanded by Major-General Sedmoratzki: three battalions, a hundred *jégerski* and a few cannon. These were positioned in Krabbendam to support the attack on Warmenhuizen. The Second Column consisted further of both British guards brigades and Prince William's 8th Brigade, about 4,500 men. The guards would attack the village Warmenhuizen through the villages Eenigenburg and Haringkarspel. The 1st Guards Brigade and both squadrons of the 11th Light Dragoons would then cross the Kanaal van Alkmaar using a pontoon bridge and advance to the village Schoorldam from the west. There they would have to take up positions, while the 2nd Guards Brigade and the Russians attacked Schoorldam from the east. Alternatively they would have to advance south in the direction of the village St. Pancras. The 8th Brigade would leave one battalion at the village St. Maarten and one battalion near Schoorldam. The Duke of York and the Hereditary Prince of Orange would accompany this column. The advance along the Kanaal van Alkmaar would be supported by three gunboats on the canal, armed with 12pdr carronades and commanded by Captain Sir Home Popham and Captain Godfrey of the Royal Navy.[4]

The Third Column was commanded by Lieutenant General Pulteney and would consist of Coote's 3rd and Don's 5th British Brigades of about 5,000 men. Major General Don would advance through Dirkshorn to Daendels' position at Oud-Karspel and attack this village frontally. Coote would move through Schagen and the Heer-Hugowaard and outflank Daendels'

---

4   A 'carronade' is an iron gun with a short smoothbore barrel, used as a short-range weapon. It could fire roundshot as well as grape and canister.

Bergen, church ruins 1. (Author photo)

Bergen, church ruins 2. (Author photo)

Straight avenue from the curve at the dunes to Bergen. (Photo by John Grooteman)

position at Oud-Karspel. If Oud-Karspel was captured, Don would have to advance in the direction of Schoorldam to support the Second Column, while Coote would move south and keep in contact with the Left Column by way of patrols. Coote would have to leave an infantry battalion as a reserve near the village Kalverdijk. It was known that this was the strongest position of the Franco-Batavian army, nevertheless, it was believed that Pulteney would be able to force back the Batavians, to keep them busy and to cover the left flank of Dundas' column. Pulteney would also have to open communications with Abercromby.

The Left Column, commanded by Lieutenant General Abercromby, would consist of 9,000 British: the Advance Guard (Knox), Moore's 4th, Cavan's 6th and Chatham's 7th Brigade and the Reserve (MacDonald). This column had to advance on the 18th from the villages Winkel and Aartswoude between the Schermer polder and the Zuiderzee to the city of Hoorn. On the 19th they had to outflank the Batavian positions and to advance to the town of Purmerend as quickly as possible. If the attack on the right wing did succeed, the Left Column would be able to advance further south without any danger. In this way this column would outflank all the Franco-Batavian positions and force them to retreat.

First or Right Column

Around 1:00 a.m. the Russian columns were formed. York had ordered daybreak as the time for the simultaneous attack of all columns. As may be clear this could be interpreted in many different ways. So, the attacks of the various columns were made at different times. First to start at 2:30 a.m., while it began to rain again, Major General Suthoff advanced with the *jégerski* and the Combined Grenadier Battalion 'Ossipov', followed by the remainder of the Advance Guard. One hour later Lieutenant General Hermann marched with the main force. Suthoff advanced with his troops from Petten along the Zanddijk and stormed the village of Kamp. The French here were completely taken by surprise by what in fact was a night attack as it was still completely dark, and Kamp was captured without fighting. Lieutenant Colonel Baklanowski advanced along the Slaperdijk in column of divisions on both flanks covered by the *jégerski* in skirmish order, where his Preliminary Attack Force immediately stormed the battery covering the dike, which was abandoned before their arrival. Continuing with their impetuous advance the village of Groet, defended by the 1/54e Demi-Brigade was also quickly taken, the Russians capturing a field gun at its entrance.[5] The French troops that were holding the forward defences in the line Kamp–Groet–Schoorl, were the 3/48e Demi-Brigade, 54e Demi-Brigade (3 battalions, *Chef de Brigade* Varé), a squadron each of the 5e and 16e Chasseurs à Cheval and 1/8e Artillerie Légère (six cannon), commanded by *Adjudant-Général* Rostollant. These had been completely taken by surprise by the unexpected attack and did not resist, some men dispersing into the dunes and the remainder retreating in disorder in the direction of Schoorl and the Kanaal van Alkmaar. Arriving at Schoorl, Rostollant re-formed his units, ably aided by his *adjoint* Martcolle, and deployed in a new defensive position with the three battalions of the 54e Demi-Brigade. His artillery, consisting of two 4pdr and six 3pdr cannon, took up positions to the left of the village.

---

5   Ritter, *Een Russisch verhaal*, p.23.

Another battery consisting of two 12pdr and two 4pdr cannon covered the approaches to the bridge at Schoorldam. The 3/48e Demi-Brigade and both squadrons of the Chasseurs à Cheval formed the reserve. Because of the darkness and the difficult terrain the Russian troops were in great disorder. The 2nd Line mingled with the 1st Line and this mass bumped into and mingled with the Advance Guard. They had to march in the dark along a narrow road with an unknown enemy of unknown strength all around. They could not recognise their own troops; officers lost their units; and, although they suffered only minor casualties from enemy fire, they lost many more from their own:

> Many Russians fell through the bullets of their own comrades: it happened that in the darkness of the night a murderous fire was being held between two Russian regiments; indeed, even after daylight had come, it still occurred; the Russian regiments, which had come to Holland on various ships, had never before seen each other, and only met on the battlefield. As they were distinguished by the very different colours of their collars and turnbacks, they often regarded an unknown Russian regiment in the distance as a hostile one. Only the grenadiers differed visibly from the enemy troops by their peculiar caps.[6]

Despite their disorder the Russians rashly continued their advance to Schoorl as one compact mass and, arriving within range, they discharged their muskets at the French. The latter replied, their artillery firing canister at close range and inflicting heavy casualties. The fight continued for some hours, Russian officers forcing their infantry forward again and again. Finally the 54e Demi-Brigade, losing *Chef de Bataillon* Gaillard of the 1st battalion who was killed, could not withstand the pressure any longer and the French had to yield the village to the Russians at about 7:30 a.m. Rostollant ordered *Chef de Brigade* Varé to retreat to the east with the 1/54e Demi-Brigade, the 3/48e Demi-Brigade, the squadron of the 5e Chasseurs à Cheval and both 12pdr cannon. He had to protect the bridge at Schoorldam and especially the floating bridge at Koedijk to maintain communications with Dumonceau. Six companies of the 3/48e Demi-Brigade occupied Schoorldam joining the *jager* of the Batavian 4e Bataljon Jagers already present. Varé used the cover of hedges and bushes to deploy his skirmishers and these maintained a heavy fire on the Russians who were advancing to Bergen, inflicting many casualties. Rostollant retreated with both remaining battalions of the 54e Demi-Brigade and the artillery to Bergen, fired at by the British horse artillery. The squadron of the 16e Chasseurs à Cheval, commanded by *Capitaine* Raulet, covered his retreat, skirmishing with the Cossacks.

The Russians of Suthoff's Advance Guard meanwhile had advanced southwest into the dunes after taking the village of Kamp. They mistook the Russians on the road to Schoorl for the French because of the heavy firing in their direction (from the fighting between the French skirmishers and the Russians column on the road to Bergen) and also opened fire on the unfortunate Russian column. This column suffered heavy casualties but were still advancing slowly, firing left and right and without any order, in the direction of the village of Bergen. Rostollant continued his fighting retreat to Bergen, with the 1/8e Artillerie

---

6 Based on Dubiansky's account in Miliutin, *Geschichte des Krieges*, Vol.V, pp.38, 45-46.

Légère deploying seven cannon on the road alternately firing at the advancing Russians and retreating to a new position. On an open field just east of Schoorl Major General Essen managed to re-form the mass of Russian infantry in companies, of the Benkendorf and Zherebtsov Grenadiers and the Fersen musketeers. Having regained some order the Russians resumed their advance along the edge of the dunes on the road to Bergen, preceded by Suthoff's *jégerski* in skirmish order. The Russians failed however to occupy Schoorl in strength, maybe trusting that they would be followed by Manners' brigade.

Continuing along the road to Bergen again the Russian infantry was met by a withering fire from the French and suffered heavy casualties. By now the Russians had lost nearly a third of their effective strength, with bodies piling up along the road and the blood flowing into the ditches.[7] This was too much for the *jégerski,* who broke and fled into the wooded dunes on their right. The Arbénev Musketeers found themselves leading the advance and undauntedly they pressed on, pushing back the French. Having arrived close to Bergen the 3/54e Demi-Brigade had to withstand a bayonet attack by the Arbénev Musketeers, only to be saved by the timely arrival of the grenadier company of the 72e Demi-Brigade, commanded by *Capitaine* Neller, which although counting only 37 men sufficed to defeat the attack.

At Bergen *Général de Brigade* Gouvion did not expect the Russians at all. Rostollant had not thought about sending him any news about the Russian attack and at Bergen the French could not hear the firing because of the strong southwest wind. So he only realised that the Russians were coming when Rostollant's disordered battalions streamed back, followed closely by the advancing Russians:

> I was informed yesterday 7:00 a.m. that the advanced guard was attacked. The 42nd was in an instant under arms. A battalion was send to come to the aid of the advance guard, part of which was falling back to Bergen in disorder when a Russian column, taking advantage of the success it had already achieved, appeared on the dunes and seemed to want to turn our troops. The excellent dispositions of *Chef de Brigade* Aubrée and the firmness of his Demi-Brigade managed to halt the enemy, already master of part of the village. They gave time to the reserve to arrive and two battalions of the 54e to rally.[8]

Hastily Gouvion organised the troops he had available; the 42e Demi-Brigade (3 battalions, *Chef de Brigade* Aubrée), the grenadier company of the 72e Demi-Brigade (*Capitaine* Neller), and some artillery, to which Rostollant's retreating troops were added. First, the grenadiers of the 72e Demi-Brigade were send forward to cover the retreat of Rostollant's troops, saving the 3/54e Demi-Brigade as described. Then he deployed 2/ and 3/54e Demi-Brigade in front of Bergen. The 1/42e Demi-Brigade was placed at the manor house Het Hof. In the centre of Bergen, half of 3/42 Demi-Brigade and the grenadier company of the 72e Demi-Brigade were placed. The other half of 3/42e Demi-Brigade was positioned just west of the village. The 2/42 Demi-Brigade occupied the redoubt near Sanegeest windmill, east

---

7   Gachot, *Brune en Hollande*, p.254.
8   Report of 20 September 1799 from Gouvion to Vandamme, in Gachot, *Brune en Hollande*, p.255.

Bergen, town hall. (Author photo)

Bergen, Sterkenhuis, the oldest house of Bergen. (Author photo)

of Bergen. To arrive at Bergen the Russians had to advance some 800 paces along a straight avenue. Just to the north-east of Bergen, covering this avenue and not far from the before mentioned redoubt, five guns of the 1/8 Artillerie Légère (*Capitaine* Leroux) deployed, covered by both squadrons of *chasseurs à cheval* reinforced with some Batavian hussars. Skirmishers deployed on both sides of the avenue.

When the first Russians arrived, the Benkendorf Grenadiers, heavy fire at close range from the battery in front and the skirmishers on both flanks stopped them. Hermann had to wait for the arrival of his own artillery to be able to make any further progress. It took over forty minutes before three guns arrived, because of the disorder and all the wounded soldiers lying on the road – sometimes the guns riding right over them – and the weariness of the horses, which had been pulling the guns for a considerable distance. After the arrival of these guns, and having fired at the village Bergen and the French positions for some time, Hermann resumed the attack, which was supported by Lieutenant General Zherebtsov who was advancing on his right along the dunes with three grenadier battalions, forcing back the 2/54e Demi-Brigade deployed here. Around 8:00 a.m. the Russian infantry penetrated into the village and the French were pushed out house after house. Finally the French had to retreat south and Bergen was captured by the Russians. A Russian pursuit was ambushed by elements of the 42e Demi-Brigade, led by *Chef de Brigade* Aubrée who was covering the French retreat, and the Russians were thrown back into the village with a loss of 150 men. For the moment the fighting at Bergen slackened.

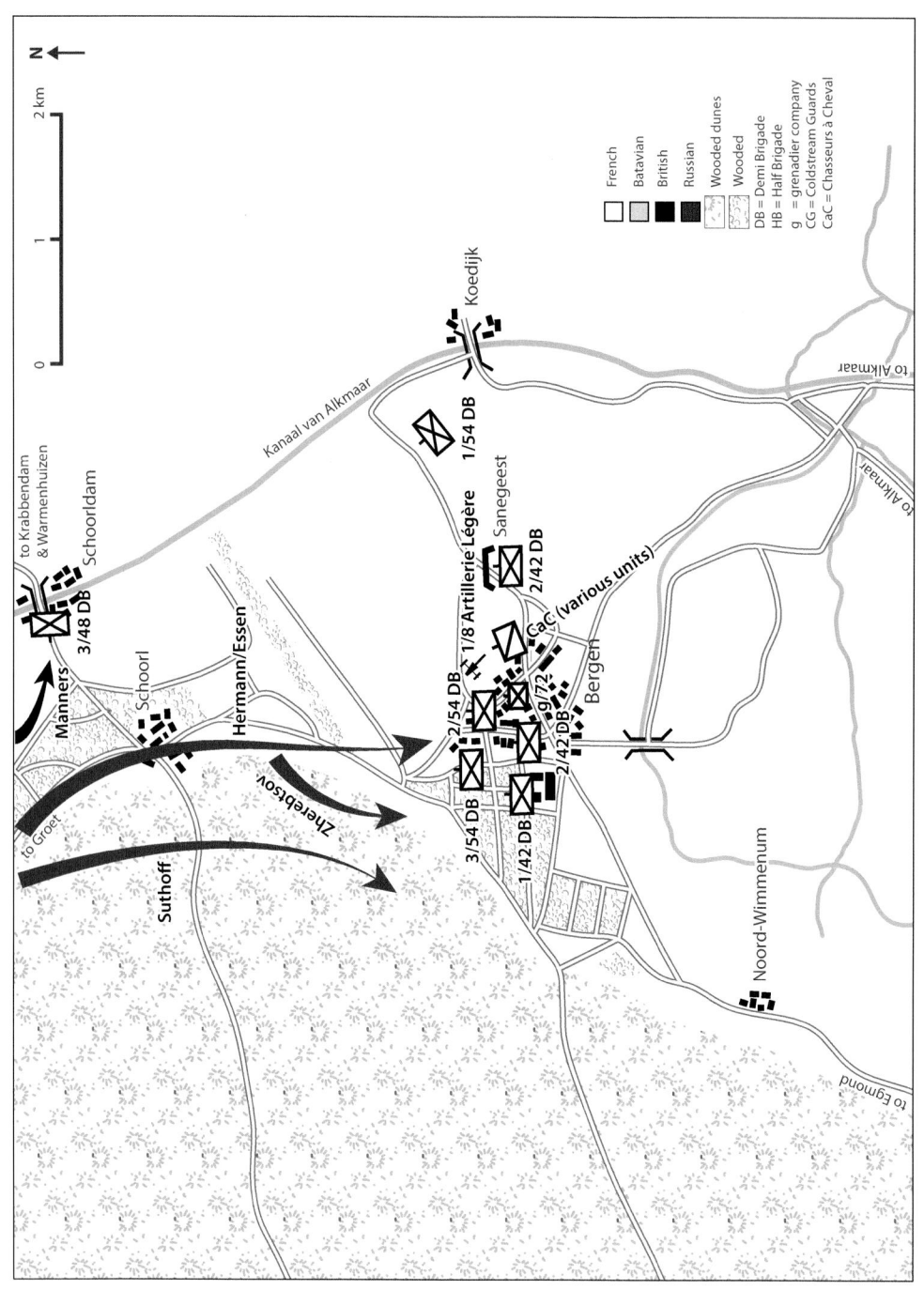

Map 7a The fighting around Bergen Phase 1, c. 8:00-9:00 a.m.

Inside Bergen all order was gone and the disordered Russian troops, who had already been fighting and advancing under fire for many hours, started plundering. Before the battle the Russian soldiers had been provided with double rations of rum; one ration they could drink at the start of the battle, the other one was to celebrate the victory afterwards. As can be imagined most of the soldiers drank both rations at the start, a fact that was one of the causes of the disorder and plunders that took place.[9] Hermann was informed about the arrival of fresh French troops from the south and realised it would not be long before the French would counter-attack. Accordingly, he feverishly tried to rally his troops and to make them ready for the defence while he waited for the arrival of the reserve, Manners' 9th Brigade. Major General Manners had initially received the order from Hermann to follow the Russian main force. Advancing along the Slaperdijk, however, Manners' brigade encountered behind Groet some of the French troops who had been retreating in the direction of the Kanaal of Alkmaar and attacked them. Because these French were retreating in the direction of Schoorldam he decided to follow them, as described by a lieutenant of the 1/9th Foot:

> At ten o'clock at night the two battalions of the 9th marched, according to orders, towards the villages of Schorel and Schoreldam, where the French had intrenched themselves, and arrived at the post occupied by the Russians, close to the village above-named, at about two o'clock in the morning of the 19th, after a march of about fourteen miles. Here we halted. At daybreak, about 3 a.m., the Russians began the attack upon the village of Schorel, and after a pretty obstinate resistance drove the enemy from thence. The two battalions of the 9th advanced gradually in the rear of the Russians, joined by the 56th Regiment, under the command of Major-General Manners, being the brigade destined to the Reserve of the Russians that day. About 6 a.m. the 9th and 56th Regiments mounted the sandhills behind the village of Schorel in order to drive from thence any enemy that might remain in that part. Having met with none we descended from the hills, and everything seemed again perfectly quiet. We marched through the village of Schorel and marched on to the plain when the enemy opened a very heavy fire of musketry and grape upon us. The Russians were now gone off in different directions, and consequently the brigade, consisting of the two battalions of the 9th and the 56th Regiments was at this time engaged alone; the two battalions of the 9th being each about 600 men, and the 56th Regiment about the same number. For about two hours the heaviest fire of musketry possible was kept up on both sides, the British advancing by degrees, but not very regularly; the plain being intersected every twenty yards nearly with small canals, many of which could not be passed without wading through, being too wide to leap, and at the same time very deep. At length the British advanced with the bayonet. The enemy were unwilling to stand the charge, and retreated very precipitately through Schoreldam, which they were obliged to evacuate, the English still advancing, but in the greatest disorder; for being very much fatigued by the night march, and still more so by the former part of the action, most of the

---

9   Ritter, *Een Russisch verhaal*, pp 22, 25; Miliutin, *Geschichte des Krieges*, Vol.V, p.46.

> troops were scarcely able to walk. We were therefore ordered not to advance any farther, but to form in the plain between Schorel and Schoreldam, where the action had commenced.[10]

Except for the French troops that had retreated from Schoorl in this direction, Manners' brigade was opposed by six companies of the Batavian Combined Grenadiers commanded by *Major* Bruce, as well as *Lieutenant-Colonel* Trip with part of the 4e Battalion Jagers. One of these *jager* related: 'Here we were met by an English battalion, which stood on the field on the right side, greeting us with such a fierce volley fire that only few *jager* managed to reach Schoorl, and *Lieutenant-Colonel* Trip returned to Schoorldam with the remainder'.[11] As a result Manners' brigade became embroiled in combat and could not be of any use for Hermann for the next hours, which would have serious consequences.

With much trouble Hermann managed to rally some of the disordered troops in Bergen and made them ready for the inevitable French counterattack. He placed a battalion of the Fersen Musketeers in front of the church and a grenadier battalion in a street a little to the right. A hundred *jégerski* deployed at the southern end of the village. The remainder took up positions between the houses to cover the approaches. The infantry had almost used all of their cartridges and many Russian soldiers were totally without them. To remedy this, Hermann's liaison with the British, Captain Taylor, was ordered to find Major General Manners to bring up his brigade and to send cartridges as soon as possible. Major General Essen was ordered to take up position with his four battalions of the 1st Line and his four regimental guns between the Kanaal van Alkmaar and Bergen. Lieutenant General Zherebtsov had to occupy the terrain between Bergen and the dunes.

Gouvion had reported the loss of Bergen to Brune. Brune, who did not leave his headquarters in Alkmaar during the whole day, ordered his reserve; the 49e Demi-Brigade (3 battalions) led by the just-promoted *Chef de Brigade* Bardet, 3/60e Demi-Brigade, 10e Dragons (4 squadrons) and some artillery, to advance to Bergen. It is not clear if this happened by order of Brune or that it was a more or less a natural reaction to adapt to the kind of terrain the battle was fought on, but the French abandoned the usual organisation and instead generals received command of a sector to defend, with the necessary troops assigned. Vandamme was charged with the attack on Bergen with all troops available. The following troops would participate in the attack:

> From the south-west, Rostollant with:
> 42e Demi-Brigade (1 battalion)
> 49e Demi-Brigade (1 battalion)
> Artillery (4 guns)
>
> From the south, Vandamme with:
> 42e Demi-Brigade (2 battalions)

---

10 Francis Culling Carr-Gomm (ed.), *Letters and Journals of Field-Marshall Sir William Maynard Gomm, G.C.B.* (London: John Murray, 1881), pp.36-37.
11 Anon., 'Teregtwijzing op J. Bosscha's Heldendaden te land, en wel inzonderheid betreffende hetgene in het eerste Stuk van het derde Deel voorkomt, omtrent de Jagers van Trip', *Militaire Spectator*, 1844, p.195.

Wooded dunes north of Bergen. (Author photo)

49e Demi-Brigade (2 battalions)
72e Demi-Brigade (grenadier company)
10e Dragons (200 men)
5e Chasseurs à Cheval (detachment)
Artillerie Légère & à Pied (6 4pdr cannon, 4 howitzers)

From the south-east, Gouvion with:
3/48e Demi-Brigade
1/ and 3/6e Halve Brigade (Batavian)[12]
10e Dragons (2 squadrons)
5e Chasseurs à Cheval (1 squadron)
16e Chasseurs à Cheval (1 squadron)
1e Compagnie Rijdende Artillerie (Batavian, 4 guns)
Artillery (4 guns)

---

12 The French had been reinforced by a Batavian force which had crossed the Kanaal van Alkmaar at Koedijk, consisting of the 1/ and 3/6e Halve Brigade, some hussars and four guns of the 1e Compagnie Rijdende Artillerie, under the command of *Lieutenant-Colonel* Carteret.

The reserve was formed by the 54e Demi-Brigade (three battalions) which was allowed to recover from the intense fighting it had seen earlier, and about 150 cavalry (including Batavian hussars), while the 3/60e Demi-Brigade covered the road to Alkmaar. One battalion of the 54e Demi-Brigade was placed at the dunes close to the manor house Het Hof, while both other battalions of the 54e Demi-Brigade were placed behind Gouvion's units. Rostollant was able to give Vandamme a fairly accurate report of the dispositions of the Russians and when all troops were in position a simultaneous attack at around 9:00 a.m. followed. The French troops were ordered to attack the village from three sides while both Batavian battalions moved around it on the east side to cut off the Russian retreat. Vandamme's troops attacked first. The Russians inside Bergen were still too much disordered to receive his attack effectively and after some fierce fighting, during which the *jégerski* distinguished themselves, the French entered the village. Heavy house-to-house fighting ensued. The Fersen Musketeers retreated to the cemetery of the Protestant church, allowing Vandamme to deploy a battery of six 4pdr cannon on a crossroads just inside the village covered by a platoon of dragoons, which opened fire at close range with canister along the avenue leading to the centre of the village. Gachot describes what happened:

> This bold move accomplished, the soldiers of the 49th, passing the canon, advanced while singing *La Marseillaise* in the streets, braving the musketry coming from the houses, slaughtered the Cossacks which had dismounted in order to plunder, expelling several companies from these houses and halted fifty paces from the Arbénev Musketeers which were drawn up six ranks deep across the avenue, covering the entrance to the Protestant cemetery, high ground on which the Russian artillery was deployed. In front of such men resolved to oppose a desperate resistance, to avoid too much loss, the French soldiers took shelter in ditches, behind the trees, behind the corners of the buildings, leaving the enemy exhausting his ammunition and waiting patiently until the enveloping columns might enter on their turn.[13]

Gouvion on the east flank had deployed the troops under his command facing west between the Catholic church of Bergen and the right angle of the woods of Schoorl. On his right he charged *Adjutant-Général* Clément to lead the Batavian infantry. In the centre he deployed two howitzers and six 4pdr cannon. On the left he deployed the 3/48e Demi-Brigade and his cavalry. The artillery immediately opened fire at Essen's battalions which had deployed in an open area located near the woods. The four Russian regimental guns tried to reply but they were soon disabled. Essen ordered his infantry, which had no cartridges left, to form a huge square, presenting an ideal target for the Franco-Batavian artillery, which killed and wounded many Russians. This left them no other option than to retreat into the woods in disorder, not able to support the Russians in Bergen any longer and so exposing their right flank. Essen tried to rally his battalions back on the road leading to Schoorl. Gouvion ordered a battalion of the 42e Demi-Brigade and the squadron of the 5e Chasseurs à Cheval to guard against them, while he redeployed his artillery on both sides of the road between Schoorl and Bergen facing Bergen, his infantry forming a line behind the guns.

---

13   Gachot, *Brune en Hollande*, p.259.

Wooded area east of Bergen. Close to the manor house Het Hof. (Author photo)

"Battle of Bergen", by Pieter Gerardus van Os. (Rijksmuseum, RP-P-1914-4345)

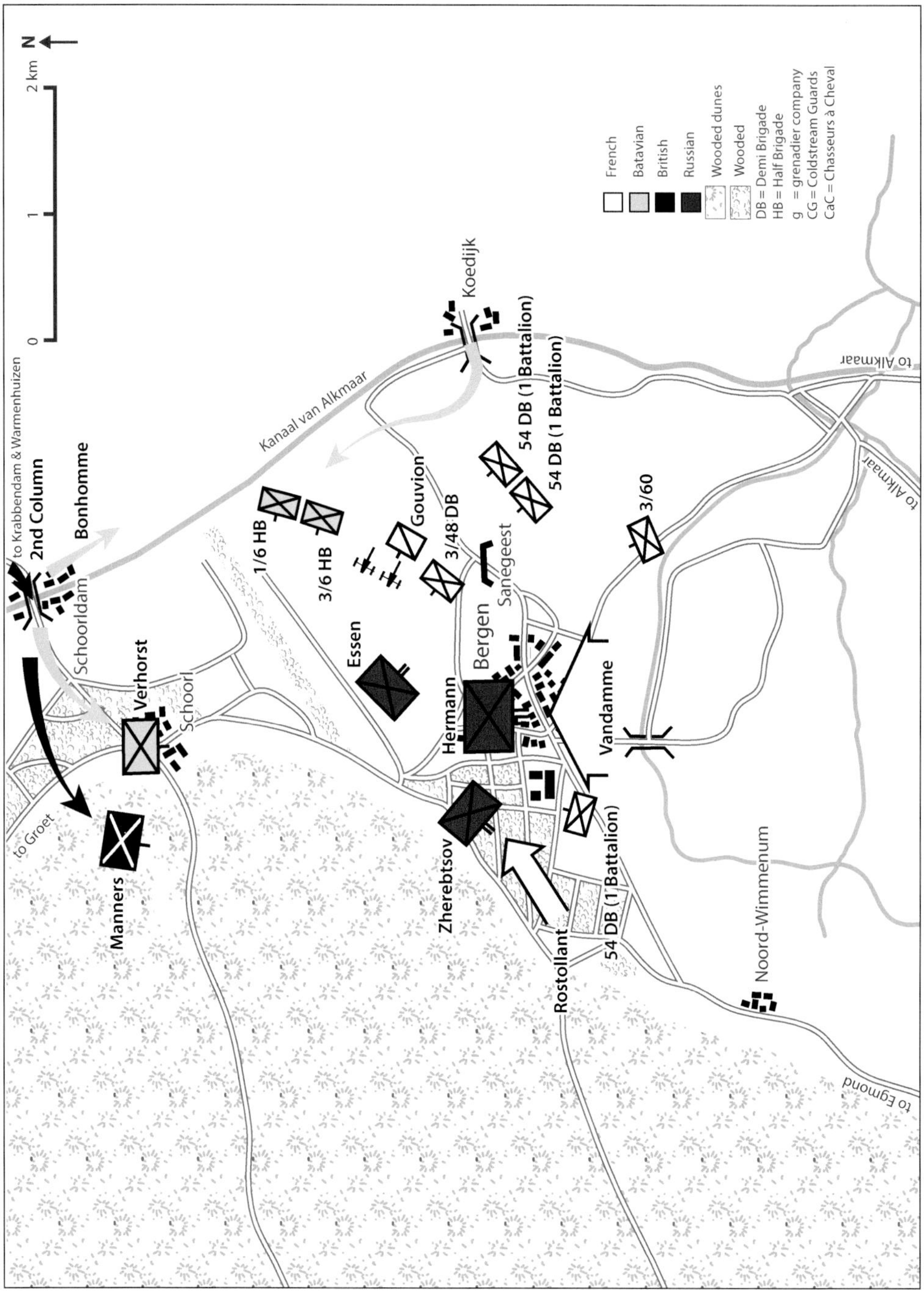

228 **THE SECRET EXPEDITION**

Map 7b The fighting around Bergen Phase 2, c. 9:00–10:00 a.m.

THE BATTLE OF BERGEN, 19 SEPTEMBER 229

"Bitter close quarter combat", by Jacob de Vos after a drawing of Dirk Langendijk. (Noord-Hollands Archief,NL-HlmNHA_480_000429_M)

Inside Bergen, Hermann was still ignorant of Essen's defeat and the fact that he had nearly been cut off. He was still positioning his troops, with Major General Arbénev deploying his own and the Fersen Musketeers in the side-streets of the main avenues leading from the centre of the town to Alkmaar and Schoorl. In the centre, behind the Protestant church, the combined grenadier battalions were concentrated. The cannon were loaded with canister. As described, the Russian musketeers opened a heavy fire at Vandamme's infantry that had penetrated the village, expending their last cartridges. Next the Combined Grenadier Battalion 'Strick' was ordered to drive the French out of the village with a bayonet attack. But as soon as they appeared on the avenue to Alkmaar, they were met by a barrage of canister of the French cannon, mowing down whole platoons. Lieutenant Colonel Strick was badly wounded in his leg and his decimated battalion fell back in disorder, blocking the advance of other battalions. Lieutenant General Zherebtsov was mortally wounded by a canister ball while reforming the troops and would die the next day.

At about the same time, Rostollant and Gouvion entered the village from the north and east, taking Hermann by surprise as he had not expected an attack from that side. In vain the Fersen Musketeers tried to stop the French but they were received by heavy musketry. Not able to reply due to lack of cartridges they fell back. Heavy hand to hand fighting ensued but gradually the Russians were pushed back, despite their heroism, battalions falling apart. Split in two, one part, accompanied by Hermann, tried to break out in the direction of the manor house Het Hof, but this move was blocked by Rostollant. At about 10:30 a.m. the Russians in Bergen completely broke and groups of soldiers and individuals desperately

"Capture of Hermann", by Jacob Ernst Marcus after Dirk Langendijk. (Rijksmuseum, RP-P-OB-67.852)

tried to cut their way out in an effort to reach their own lines again through the dunes. Many Russians could not escape and were taken prisoner. The Russian commander in chief Hermann also tried to escape through the dunes together with a mass of routing soldiers, mostly without cartridges. While he was in the process of reforming the soldiers that had followed him, the 10e Dragons prepared to charge. Hermann tried to form square but with only two sides ready he received a bayonet charge by the 42e Demi-Brigade, while at the same time the dragoons attacked from the other side. The incomplete square was broken instantly and Hermann and most of his staff were taken prisoner as they tried to escape. Another body of Russians were surrounded at the Protestant church but still continued the fight, using their bayonets, musket butts, and even stones, having been told that the French would execute them all on the guillotine:

> The British had persuaded the Russians that if they were captured by the French, they would be immediately led to the guillotine, it is for this reason that those unfortunate if captured, they were seen wearing their hands at their collars and praying to the French not to be guillotined. We offered them, instead, bread and meat for their consolation.[14]

14 Letter of 20 September 1799 from Citizen Galdi, representative of the Cisalpine Republic in The Hague, to Serbelloni in Milan, quoted in Gachot, *Brune en Hollande*, pp.261-262; *Besluiten der Eerste Kamer. September 1799*, 20 September 1799.

THE BATTLE OF BERGEN, 19 SEPTEMBER

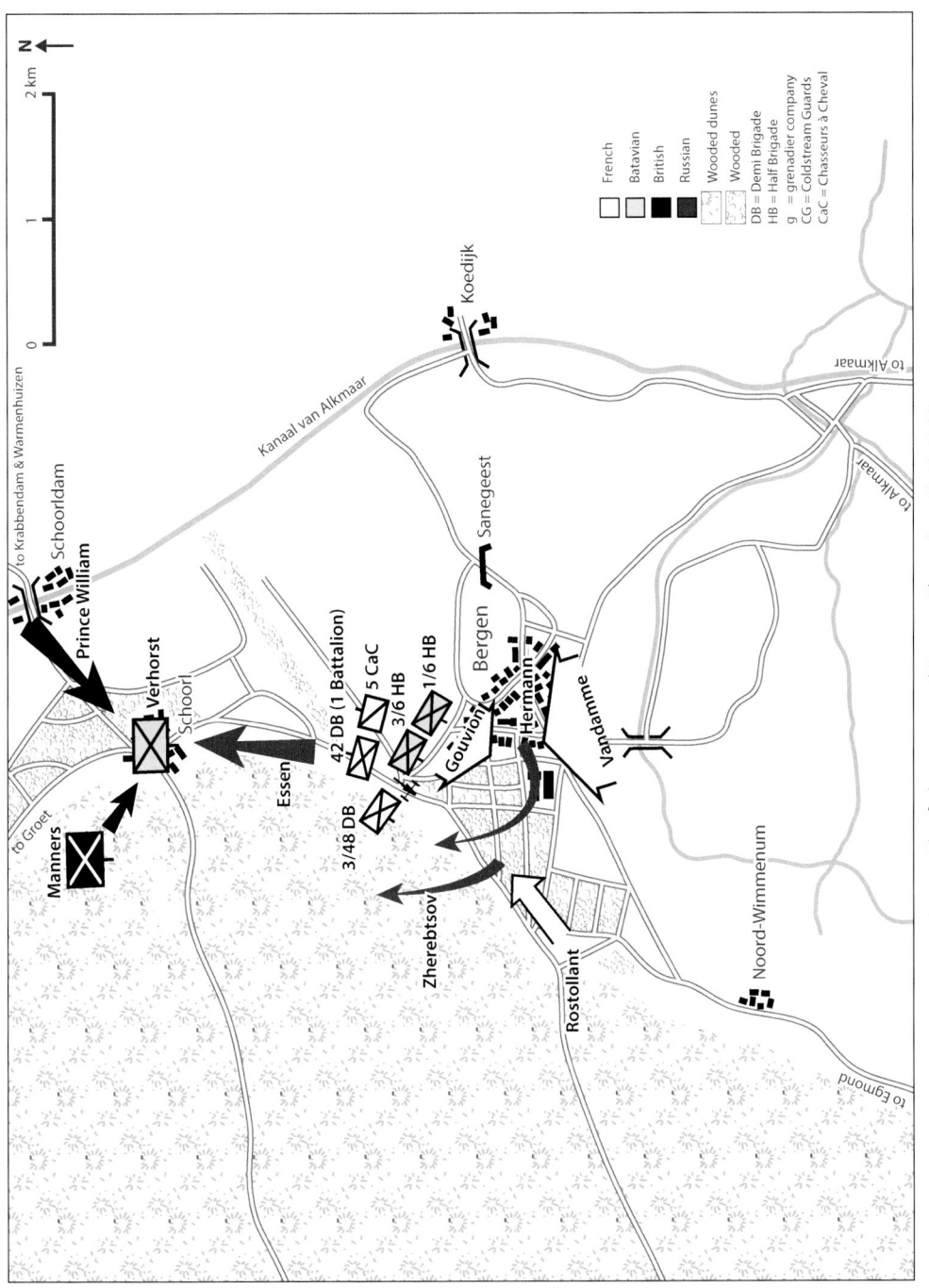

Map 7c The fighting around Bergen Phase 3, c. 10:00-11:00 a.m.

Enraged by their desperate resistance the French soldiers at first gave no pardon and many Russians were killed trying to surrender. After some time fighting ceased and the rage made room for compassion. The Protestant church was turned into a hospital. The Russian soldiers, nearly starving, received bread and water. Around 11:00 a.m. the 90e Demi-Brigade arrived in Bergen, serving as a reserve. A company of the 5e Chasseurs à Cheval was send along the road to Schoorl, followed by a strong infantry column. On their left flank Rostollant advanced with the 42e Demi-Brigade along the dunes. On the right, *Général de Brigade* Simon advanced with the 3/48e Demi-Brigade, the aforementioned Batavian troops, and the bulk of the cavalry, between the wooded area near Schoorl and the Kanaal van Alkmaar.

Second Column

The Second Column, commanded by Lieutenant General Dundas and accompanied by York himself, began the advance at daylight at 5:00 a.m., more than two hours later than the Right Column. They directed their advance against Warmenhuizen following the road from Krabbendam, occupied by the advance guard of the 2e Bataafsche Divisie (Dumonceau). *Lieutenant-Generaal* Dumonceau was at his headquarters at the village of Koedijk close to the floating bridge across the Kanaal van Alkmaar. Four 6pdr cannon protected this bridge. At 5:00 a.m. he received the news of the Russian attack and the French retreat on the Franco-Batavian left wing. He ordered *Colonel* Bruce to assemble his 2nd Brigade near the floating bridge while he hastened to Schoorldam in person. Holding Schoorldam was important because of the presence of the bridge across the Kanaal van Alkmaar. When Dumonceau arrived he observed that the Anglo-Russians were already debouching from the village of Krabbendam and advancing in the direction of the village of Warmenhuizen. He could hear from the musketry that the enemy had already advanced behind his position on the left wing on the other side of the Kanaal van Alkmaar; chances were real that he would lose Schoorldam. His first care was to prevent his troops at Warmenhuizen from being cut off and he also decided to attack the enemy on his left wing, to release some pressure of the obviously hard pressed French troops.

The troops positioned on the road between Schoorldam and Warmenhuizen were the 1/ and 2/7e Halve Brigade, two companies of the 4e Battalion Jagers and five field guns, all commanded by *Lieutenant-Colonel* Verhorst. Verhorst, hearing the noise of the fighting in the direction of Groet and later also at Schoorl, had ordered four companies of the 7e Halve Brigade and some men of the 4e Bataljon Jagers commanded by *Major* Broman, to occupy Warmenhuizen. It was not before long that he noticed the advance of the three Russian battalions of Major General Sedmoratzki, who led his troops straight through the pastures to Warmenhuizen. When Broman received at 7:00 a.m. the order from Dumonceau to withdraw on Schoorldam it was too late, for the troops at Warmenhuizen had already been cut off by the 1st Foot Guards, which had advanced from the north from the direction of the village Tuitgenhorn. Completely surrounded, *Major* Broman had no other choice then to surrender with his troops; the Anglo-Russians captured 500 prisoners and the three guns. *Lieutenant-Colonel* Verhorst succeeded in retreating to Schoorldam with the remainder of his troops and two field guns. To delay the Anglo-Russians he destroyed all bridges behind him. Because of this, it took the latter two hours to advance the two kilometres to reach Schoorldam.

At Schoorldam in the meantime *Lieutenant-Generaal* Dumonceau had ordered *Major* Bruce to cross the Kanaal van Alkmaar with his Combined Grenadiers, to join the French troops commanded by *Chef de Brigade* Varé who had retreated east from Schoorl and to cooperate in the counterattack in the direction of Schoorl. In addition, *Lieutenant-Colonel* Carteret was ordered to cross the floating bridge at Koedijk with the 1/ and 3/6e Halve Brigade, some hussars, and four guns of the 1e Compagnie Rijdende Artillerie and to advance on Bergen from the east. Upon the arrival of *Lieutenant-Colonel* Verhorst with his troops, Dumonceau ordered *Lieutenant-Colonel* Trip with the remainder of the 4e Bataljon Jagers, and *Capitein* van Geen with 50 volunteers of the 1/7e Halve Brigade to support *Major* Bruce. While giving these orders Dumonceau was hit by a bullet in the chest. After passing over the command of his division to *Generaal-Major* Bonhomme he had to leave the field. Probably this passing of command was the cause of a misinterpretation of orders: instead of only fifty men, Verhorst left Schoorldam with 1/ and 2/7e Halve Brigade and the *jager*, and in cooperation with the French the Franco-Batavians had no trouble recapturing Schoorl which was left virtually undefended by the Russians. In the centre, it appears that some units retreated in disorder after the wounding of Dumonceau. The fact that Bonhomme never made an after-action report adds to the obscurity of what happened. There are indications that Brune ordered *Lieutenant-Colonel* Martuschewitz, commander of the Batavian artillery, to go to the Batavian division to restore order. It appears that although Bonhomme had nominal command, the division was in fact commanded by Martuschewitz. Before things were sorted out though Schoorldam was nearly abandoned by the Batavians. Small luck that *Lieutenant-Colonel* Verhorst had ordered the engineer *Lieutenant* Everts to demolish the bridge after he had crossed, in which Everts succeeded but was killed in the process.

After the capture of Warmenhuizen, the British 1/3rd Foot Guards and 2/5th Foot were detached to march east, to make contact with Lieutenant General Pulteney's Third Column. Then Schoorldam was attacked from two sides; from the west by Manners' brigade and from the north by the remainder of the Second Column. Because of the destroyed bridges, it took some time for the Second Column to gather materials in order to cross the ditches and canals by all means possible. Therefore it was not until 9:00 a.m. that Schoorldam was reached and the attack could commence. With few Batavian troops present it took little time to capture the village. Again some prisoners were taken. The Duke of York immediately ordered the repair of the bridge at Schoorldam by Sedmoratzki's pioneers under cover of the British gunboats, which took about an hour. Just when the bridge was repaired around 10:30 a.m. Captain Taylor arrived, bringing York the news of the Russian predicament and requesting immediate support. York however was not ready to venture into the woods of Schoorl without knowing what he was getting into and with Franco-Batavian troops in Schoorl. Therefore he ordered Sedmoratzki, the 1st Guards Brigade, and both battalions of the 35th Foot, under the command of Major General Prince William, to cross the canal, join Manners' brigade and to form a line from Schoorldam to Schoorl. These troops now attacked the Franco-Batavian troops in Schoorl from the north and east, while Essen's Russians from the Right Column streaming back from Bergen came in from the south, a lieutenant in Manners' brigade relating:

> We remained here [deployed between Schoorl and Schoorldam] about half an hour, when we received intelligence that the enemy were at that time in the very same

part of the sandhills behind Schorel where we had been searching for them before we entered into the action on the plain, so that they could never have been driven completely from the sandhills, but must have been in some part of them even at the time we were searching for them. Upon this intelligence we were obliged to march against them immediately, notwithstanding our fatigue, to prevent being cut off, for they were then getting in our rear. We got up the hills as quickly as possible, and the enemy immediately opened a fire upon us from all sides. The enemy's riflemen had got into the woods about Schorel, and by that means fired upon our officers and men on the hills without being themselves seen or exposed.

The Russians were now returned to our assistance, but our numbers were even then far inferior to those of the enemy, who were now stronger than ever. Had our numbers been known, it is generally believed that we should have been made prisoners, but we were so dispersed about the hills that it was impossible for the enemy to judge of our strength. For about two hours and a half an unceasing fire of musketry was kept up. The enemy had several pieces of cannon upon the hills, with which they played upon us during the whole time. By this time it was nearly one o'clock. Great numbers of our men began to want ammunition. We were ordered to descend from the hills and rally once more, determining to make another vigorous attempt to drive the enemy from the woods and hills. H.R.H. Prince William of Gloucester had now joined us with the 1st battalion of the 35th Regiment. A battalion of the Guards also arrived and advanced upon the sandhills. The 2nd battalion of the 9th, the 1st battalion of the 35th, and the 56th Regiment, after having formed a continued line, began a vigorous fire upon the enemy in the woods, and in a short time drove them a considerable distance along the hills and woods. The Guards lost great numbers upon the hills. Small parties of the Russians were still with us upon the hills.[15]

The Franco-Batavian troops at Schoorl, heavily outnumbered and completely surrounded, had no option then but to surrender, and were taken prisoner. Schoorl was captured by the Anglo-Russians for a second time. Attempts to rally the Russians, who had expended all their ammunition, had no effect. The only formed troops between the Zijpe and the enemy was a weak screen of British troops. Some moments later, French troops pursuing the Russians from Bergen arrived. Schoorl was abandoned by the Anglo-Russians without any fighting, the troops streaming back in disorder. *Général de Brigade* Simon tried to cut them off by turning their left flank, moving between Schoorl and Schoorldam, but his advance was stopped by the British gunboats on the Kanaal van Alkmaar forcing Simon to dodge west to take cover in the wooded area around Schoorl. From here he observed five Anglo-Russian battalions which tried to deploy to stop the French advance. Before these were ready they were attacked by a battalion of the 42e Demi-Brigade and 45 troopers of the 5e Chasseurs à Cheval led by *Lieutenant* Denain and after a short fight were routed. The French took about 300 prisoners of which 27 were British; six guns, four caissons and 24 horses.[16]

---

15 Carr-Gomm, *Letters and Journals of Sir William Maynard Gomm*, pp.37-38.
16 Gachot, *Brune en Hollande*, pp.262-263.

THE BATTLE OF BERGEN, 19 SEPTEMBER

"The Franco-Batavians attacking the Anglo-Russians near Schoorl", C. v.d. Voort van Zijp. (Noord-Hollands Archief, NL-HlmNHA_480_000497_K)

West of Schoorl, two British battalions (apparently a battalion of the 9th and one of the 35th) tried to take up defensive positions in the dunes but these were quickly pushed back by Rostollant moving though the dunes, the British losing about 150 men killed or wounded. Both battalions retreated to Petten together with a detachment of the 7th Light Dragoons:

> The firing continued till four o'clock, great slaughter being made on both sides. The enemy had now been able to make a stand for the space of about two hours. Nearly the whole of our ammunition was now exhausted, and numbers of our troops being absolutely useless from the excessive fatigues of the day, at about 4:30 p.m. a general retreat was made. While we were retiring a body of the enemy's Hussars came up with the rear of the 9th Regiment (for we happened to be hindmost of those who retreated on that side). They cut down and took prisoners a few stragglers, but advanced no farther, being unwilling to encounter our Dragoons. The whole of the army took up their former position as soon as possible… In the beginning of the action the Russians behaved with the greatest intrepidity, but in the latter part, being very much weakened and fatigued, they for the most part quitted the field, and for a long time the 9th and 56th were the only regiments that faced the

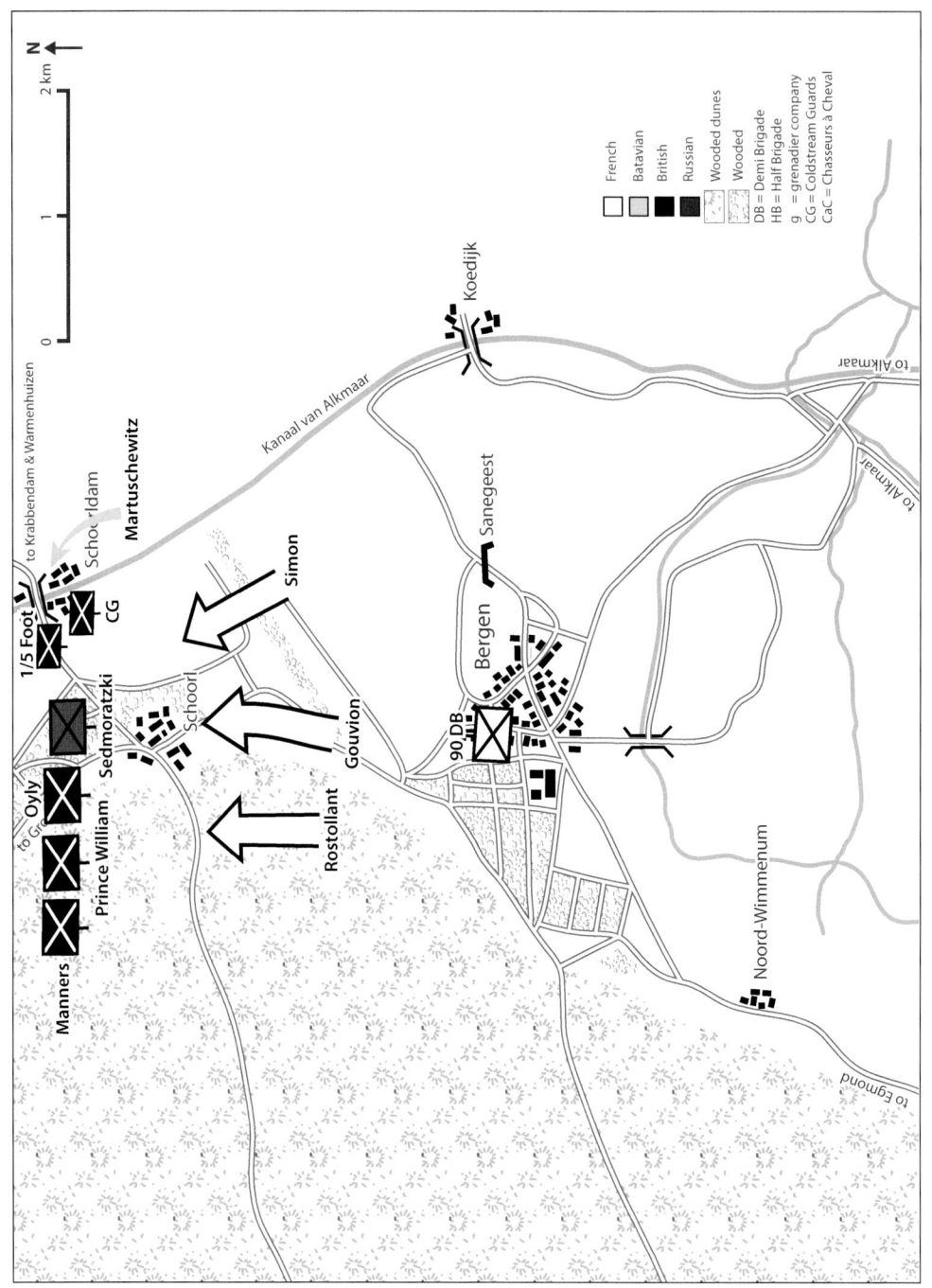

Map 7d The fighting around Bergen Phase 4, c. 11:00 a.m.–2:00 p.m.

enemy… Part of the 9th returned to their quarters at Grotskerk the same night. The remainder went only as far as Petten that night.[17]

By 2:00 p.m. nearly all Russian troops that had managed to escape were back in the Zijpe. They were followed by the British infantry which, seeing the Russian debacle and being pressed by the victorious French, also lost order. The only British troops that had remained at Schoorldam were the Coldstream Guards and the 1/5th Foot, commanded by Lieutenant General Dundas in person. The three gunboats in the Kanaal Van Alkmaar or the Koedijkervaart – sources differ as to which – supported them. With this feeble force Dundas was unable to undertake any offensive action and he had to limit himself to the defence of the bridge at Schoorldam. The Batavian troops facing their position were commanded by *Lieutenant-Colonel* Martuschewitz. Without artillery support the 2/6e Halve Brigade, commanded by *Lieutenant-Colonel* Anthing, was ordered to retake Schoorldam from the British. Anthing's after action report related how:

> The undersigned *Lieutenant-Colonel*, commander of the 2nd battalion of the 6th ½ Brigade had received orders on 19 September (around noon about one o'clock) to push the enemy out of the village of Schoorldam. We attacked them with the bayonet (having no cannon with us) and had the luck to force the enemy to retire from the village, along the road across the bridge behind the retrenchments abandoned by our troops, and behind the dike. The undersigned tried to dispel them from there as well, however several attacks were repelled by the fierce fire which took away complete ranks, in a way that it seemed we had to give away for the superior force, having to leave the village to the enemy again. The *Lieutenant-Colonel* [Anthing] again succeeded to advance to the bridge, however the enemy fire, from behind, as from the houses on the left, and from behind the dike, inflicted so many dead and wounded that he again had to retreat.
>
> Now the undersigned took the colours in person, placed himself at the head of the 1st platoon and encouraged his men to follow him once again; everyone marched again against the enemy, drums beating. However the flagpole was shot through and the pole was now too short for the colours to be seen by all the men. *Adjudant-Major* Visscher, who was still mounted, asked permission to carry the colours and to hold them high so that the whole battalion could see it. This was granted by undersigned, on the promise of the *Adjudant-Major* not to ride faster than the men could march. Crossing the bridge, the reinforced enemy opened a fierce fire, killing the brave *Adjudant-Major* Visscher on his horse with the colours in his hand; the colour was dragged towards the enemy by the horse, but it was retrieved by the brave *Sergeant* Westerheide of my battalion in a hail of bullets. After a few minutes I again attacked but in vain; *Cadet* Van Wartum who carried the colours this time was killed here, as well as *Captain* Cammartin and some NCOs; at this moment over half of my battalion was out of action, by the loss of dead and wounded as well

---

17 Carr-Gomm, *Letters and Journals of Sir William Maynard Gomm*, pp.38-40. Grotskerk is the Grote Kerk, the main church in Schagen.

as bringing behind the latter. At that moment I received the order from *Adjudant-General* Vichery to retreat behind the houses on this side of the bridge until the cannon arrived.[18]

In this way, the 2/6e Halve Brigade erased the shame of their behaviour in the battle of Zijpe.

Around 3:00 or 4:00 p.m. two guns of the 1e Compagnie Rijdende Artillerie, commanded by *Onder-Lieutenant* Straube arrived and advanced together with *jager* of the 3e and 4e Bataljon Jagers. The artillery opened fire on the British at Schoorldam, setting fire to some of the houses. Their artillery was silenced and abandoning two guns the British pulled back out of the fire of the Batavian horse artillery, allowing the *jager* to penetrate into the village. After about an hour the British retreated back to their Zijpe position. Warmenhuizen was again occupied by the Batavians; *jager* and grenadiers of the *Voorhoede* commanded by *Capitein* Arensma. To prevent an attack on the Zijpe positions before the defence was ready, the British set fire to the houses in Krabbendam and 'at half past seven Krabbendam was burned to the ground'.[19] Around 4:00 p.m. all Anglo-Russian units were back in their Zijpe positions.

Third Column

At daybreak the troops of Lieutenant General Pulteney also began their advance. At 2:00 a.m. Coote's 3rd Brigade marched through the village of Schagen, arriving at 5:00 a.m. at Nieudorper Verlaat. Here they found the bridge demolished which caused some delay. Coote left the 85th Foot in reserve at Nieudorp while a cavalry patrol was send south in the direction of Rustenburg. Advancing further, the 27th Foot and a 6pdr cannon were deployed at a crossroads. With the remainder of his brigade, Coote advanced along a dike in the direction of Oud-Karspel, the light companies of his brigade, commanded by Major Knight, clearing the woods on his left. Arriving near Oud-Karspel Coote saw his advance stopped by a broad canal, about 15 metres wide: all the bridges across the canal had been removed. On the other side of the canal Daendels had deployed some infantry supported by artillery. Coote's troops started to collect materials from a nearby house to prepare a crossing of the canal.[20]

Don's 5th Brigade in the meantime had advanced through the village Dirkshorn to Oud-Karspel accompanied by Pulteney himself. The light dragoons remained in reserve. Pulteney ordered the 2/17th Foot to occupy the village of Kalverdijk to act also as a reserve. He continued his advance to Oud-Karspel with the remainder of his brigade. His advance had to take place along a dike, the Langendijk, which was so narrow that only eight men could move abreast. Around 5:30 a.m. he arrived at the redoubt constructed by Daendels in front of the village Oud-Karspel. Although the redoubt formed a very strong position, its field of fire was limited to only about 80 metres because of the ring-dike around Bleekmeer

---

18 After action report of *Lieutenant-Colonel* Anthing, quoted in J. Fox, 'De brug van Schoorldam onder vijandelijk vuur', in *Holland* (Haarlem: Historische Vereniging Holland, 1978), pp.329-330.
19 Albert Kaan Kz., *Journaal van 1799*, p.5.
20 Major H. Everard, *History of Tho's Farrington's Regiment, subsequently designated the 29th (Worcestershire) Foot 1694 to 1891* (Worcester: Littlebury & Company, 1891), p.238.

in front of it. Brushing away the *jager* in front of the redoubt, Pulteney ordered an immediate attack that was made with much vigour. Inside the redoubt at the same moment the change of the guards took place. *Colonel* Crass, present here, commanded therefore not only the *jager* and the artillery but also two whole infantry battalions. In co-operation with the French *Adjudant-Général* Durutte, added by Brune to Daendels' staff, Crass positioned the infantry behind the parapets and let the British advance to within thirty paces. At this distance the British were received by overwhelming musketry and canister and had to retreat after suffering heavy losses. They found cover behind the ring-dike and in a cornfield. After restoring order Pulteney ordered forward his own artillery and an artillery-duel followed, in which the British came of worst. Despite the losses suffered, the Batavian artillery kept up the fight, managed to disable two British guns and to set the caissons on fire. Pulteney ordered a second and a third attack but both attacks were beaten off with heavy losses, although on Franco-Batavian side *Adjudant-Général* Durutte was slightly wounded.

It was clear now for Pulteney and Don that they had to wait for the advance of Coote who could attack the Batavian position in the right flank and back. Pulteney did not stay idle though: Reinforced by the 1/3rd Foot Guards and 2/5th Foot, he ordered Don to take the Guards and four companies of the 40th Foot in an effort to outflank the Batavian position on their left through the heavily ditched terrain. Colonel Spencer was ordered to maintain fire on the Batavian positions with part of 1/17th Foot, the 1/40th Foot and additional companies of light infantry, and to attack the Batavians if a good opportunity would occur. Time now was 10:00 a.m.

Daendels, receiving news of Dumonceau being wounded and receiving a request from *Generaal-Major* Bonhomme for reinforcements, ordered at around 10:00 a.m. *Generaal-Major* Van Zuylen van Nyevelt to take with him 1/and 3/4e Halve Brigade, the Regiment Dragonders (except for three platoons) and four guns of the horse artillery to reinforce Bonhomme.[21] These reinforcements would arrive too late in the centre though to have any effect.

Daendels, informed about the advance of British troops in the direction of the city of Hoorn (the British Left Column) ordered a battalion to occupy the village Schermerhorn and another battalion to the towns of Purmerend and Monnikendam to secure his rear. After taking these precautions he moved in person to the redoubt in front of Oud-Karspel. Arriving there he noticed that the British artillery was silenced. Only some sporadic musketry made clear there were still some British troops in front of the redoubt. On his left flank there was no sign of the outflanking British troops; Don had ordered his troops to lie down in the corn. At that moment he received another request from Bonhomme: his troops were attacking the British and to aid these attacks he requested Daendels to support him by advancing also. Receiving also a request from Durutte and *Colonel* Crass to attack, a company of grenadiers was ordered to undertake a sally and to capture the two disabled guns that were left behind by the British. This sally proved to be disastrous: as soon the grenadiers reached the open terrain in front of the redoubt, Don ordered his troops to raise and to attack the grenadiers in the flank, while at the same time Colonel Spencer attacked them frontally. The grenadiers, attacked so unexpectedly, took flight back into the redoubt. In doing so they masked the fire of their own artillery. A caisson exploded inside

---

21 van Es, *De Veldtocht in Noord-Holland*, p.14.

the redoubt, killing a great number of the gunners serving the cannon. Making use of the resulting disorder the British troops entered the redoubt together with the routing grenadiers. The Batavians now had no chance left to stop them and Daendels ordered the retreat, leaving behind his artillery.

The Batavians did not get the chance to rally, closely pursued as they were by the British, suffering heavy loss from their musket fire. Only at the end of the Langendijk, at the village of Broek, could the British advance be stopped by the grenadier company of the 1/1e Halve Brigade and three grenadier companies of the 4e Halve Brigade, commanded by *Lieutenant-Colonel* Nicolson and *Major* Storm de Grave. The result of the quick British advance along the Langendijk was that the Batavian troops that had been placed at the side of the Langendijk behind the circular canal to watch Coote were cut off and all taken prisoner. In total the British in this attack took 42 officers and 1,314 others prisoner and captured 18 guns in the redoubt and along the Langendijk, complete with ammunition caissons and horses.

At Broek it turned out that the Batavian troops were in such a strong position that Pulteney did not think it possible to attack without reinforcements. Therefore he tried to get Coote with his brigade across the circular canal. This took much time: because of the absence of bridging material the crossing had to be done by boats that first had to be found and brought to the crossing point. While the crossing was taking place Pulteney received the message of the defeat of the Right and Second Columns and the order to retreat to the Zijpe position. Late in the afternoon Pulteney retreated with his troops also.

Until that moment the Franco-Batavian position was precarious. Although on the left wing the battle was won by the Franco-Batavians, the British now occupied the Langendijk all the way to Broek, piercing the Franco-Batavian lines. Because of this danger, and because Brune was angered by Daendels' defeat, he was ordered to recapture his lost position immediately. Daendels attacked with the grenadiers of the 1/1e Halve Brigade, which by chance coincided with Pulteney's retreat. The grenadiers were in hot pursuit of the retreating British who lost about a hundred men and four officers as prisoners. The Batavians recovered all their lost artillery, although the British had tried to disable them as much as they could or had turned them over in the ditches on both sides of the road. In addition they captured a field ambulance and the two disabled British guns left behind in front of the redoubt, the British having no time or horses to take the guns with them.

Left Column

The Left, or 4th, Column consisted of 9,000 British under Lieutenant General Abercromby. They started their march from Winkel and Aartswoude on the 18th at 6:00 p.m. under a heavy rain, which continued all night. They had to follow a narrow paved causeway for fourteen miles, with a strip of deep mud on both sides and then broad ditches filled with water up to the brim:

> We moved off as it became dark, but such was the state of the roads that it became the most trying and distressing march that I believe ever troops undertook; the roads were literally knee deep in mud in most places, while every now and then they were rendered nearly impassable, both by the enemy having broken down

the bridges over the innumerable canals and dikes which intersect this country, and these canals in many places having overflowed their banks. None but those who have experienced this or something similar, can form an idea of the fatigue attending a night march in such a country, where the column is large… During this march, I remember, when the road was extremely deep, someone on the right of my section called out that there was an excellent path a little beyond him; when one poor fellow moved in that direction, but had not made many steps, till souse he went into a deep canal. Whether the man who called out had been actually deceived by the smooth surface of the water, which appeared in the dark like a nice level road; or whether he did it through mischief, I know not, but the poor simpleton who followed his advice paid dearly for his curiosity, being with some difficulty extricated from his uncomfortable situation.[22]

They did not meet any resistance on their way to the city of Hoorn because there were no Franco-Batavian troops posted east of Daendels' position. Also Hoorn had no garrison although by chance there were Batavian soldiers present: on the 16th and 17th, Daendels had sent a detachment of the 2e Regiment Zware Cavalerie, commanded by *Ritmeester* Sterke, as well as 150 men of the 3/7e Halve Brigade commanded by *Capitein* Thomson, to reconnoitre in the direction of Hoorn. The cavalry had already left but the infantry was still present. Arriving in front of Hoorn, two envoys with a trumpeter were sent to the north-gate, asking the commander to come out to receive a verbal message from Abercromby. *Major* van der Mey, commander of the city, tried to gain time because he knew he had no chance to hold the city with the few men he had at his disposal. The least he could do was to try to save the infantry and gain time to let them escape to Monnikendam. After the third demand of the envoys, he opened the north-gate and walked out to meet them. With the gate nearly open a British column stormed inside, overpowered the guard and took *Major* van der Mey prisoner and with him the infantry. Hoorn was filled with troops, stared at by the amazed civilians.

Abercromby entered the city and took possession of Hoorn in name of the King of Britain and the Hereditary Prince of Orange. After the capture of Hoorn Abercromby continued his advance in the direction of the town of Purmerend. He found that all the bridges had been removed and the roads destroyed in many places. An attempt to advance in the direction of the village of Schermerhorn failed also for the same reason. The Batavian engineers had done their job very well. So Abercromby was compelled to stay where he was and had to wait for news from the other three columns. In the evening of the 19th he received the order to evacuate Hoorn again and to retreat to the Zijpe positions. He started his retreat the next morning at 8:00 a.m., leaving behind the 55th Foot in Hoorn, but just having departed the city it started to rain again:

> We had not started on our return above half an hour when the rain fell in torrents, making the road, which was previously scarce passable, one mass of mud. Our newly enlisted heroes did not like this at all; many of them fell out in the dark, and

---

22 Surtees, *Twenty-five years in the Rifle Brigade*, pp.10-12.

we had to make several halts to pick up the stragglers. We could hear the words now and then: "D—d bad sort of soldiering this! I wish the man had his ten guineas again!" and other phrases of discontent. However, they were obliged to bundle along, half asleep and half awake. On one occasion there was a false alarm of the enemy: the men were ordered to fix bayonets, the adjutant shouted out, "Keep your places—form two deep!" when a fellow called out, "We are too deep already—we are knee-deep." At length, soon after daylight, we reached our cantonment, bringing but a small proportion of our mighty men with us. The company to which I was attached had about fifteen old soldiers, six Irish rebels taken at Vinegar Hill; the remainder of 110 being the militia aforesaid. When we reached our quarters we had two Serjeants and eighteen rank and file, six of which were the boys from Vinegar Hill, who were indeed the best soldiers of the batch during the campaign.[23]

It was not before the 22nd that the last British troops left Hoorn. On the 24th Hoorn was occupied again by a battalion of the 22e Demi-Brigade and the 10e Dragons, commanded by *Chef de Brigade* Bardet.

Aftermath

The routing Russians could not be stopped at the Zijpe position and ran further to the north. Most of the British skeleton battalions also returned to their positions in great disorder and shaken. The battalions were without proper command and did not think of defending the Zijpe. There was every chance that the pursuing enemy could capture the Anglo-Russian defence lines without trouble. York and his staff officers managed by the greatest of efforts to bring some troops together for the defence, among these the 3/1st Foot Guards. After a while the British could show some force and after some skirmishing the French withdrew, but it had been a near run thing. The battle of 19 September had been bloody. Both armies suffered heavy loss but Anglo-Russian losses were higher than those of the Franco-Batavians; the Russians especially suffered many casualties.

The Batavian army had suffered major losses. Total Batavian losses were 2,905 men. Daendels' 1e Bataafsche Divisie lost five officers and 20 others killed; 19 officers and 95 others wounded; 42 officers and 1,314 others missing, including two battalion commanders, the *Lieutenant-Colonels* Sels of the 3/4e Halve Brigade and Faure of the 2/5e Halve Brigade. Dumonceau's 2e Bataafsche Divisie lost six officers and 66 others killed; 12 officers and 216 others wounded, including Dumonceau himself, *Colonel* Gilquin commander of the Voorhoede, *Lieutenant-Colonel* Lambrechts and *Major* Bruce commanding the Combined Grenadiers; 39 officers and 1,013 others missing. The Batavian artillery park, which had provided the artillery crews for the guns in the redoubt in front of the village Oud-Karspel, had three officers and 55 others missing.[24] Of course, the major part of the missing men

---

23 Anon., 'Recollections of the British army', p.186.
24 Official returns of 22 September 1799 by *Generaal-Major* Boecop, *Chef van den Etat Major Generaal der Bataafsche Armee* in J. Bosscha, *Neerlands Heldendaden te Land, van de Vroegste Tijden af tot op Onze Dagen* (Leeuwarden, G.T.N. Suringar, 1873), Appendix I, pp.618-624.

had been taken prisoner by the Anglo-Russians. 1,052 of these would desert and join the Dutch army in Holland that was raised by the Hereditary Prince of Orange: 'The English took 2,000 prisoners, I saw them pass by with nearly 60 Batavian officers. The prisoners are well-intentioned and there are many arriving here with an orange cockade on the hat. Many joined us, 60 of them are French.'[25] The French lost less troops then the Batavians, 836 men: 815 dead and wounded, 21 that were taken prisoner.[26] The commander of the 1/54 Demi-Brigade, *Chef de Bataillon* Gaillard, had been killed. Total Franco-Batavian loss was 3,741 men out of about 23,500, a loss of 16 percent.

British returns of losses are not complete: of the 1/35th Foot, 350 rank and file could not exactly be accounted for, owing to the nature of the battle and the regiment having been sent to Den Helder immediately after the battle, to escort the Franco-Batavian prisoners. Of the 35th nearly 100 men were supposed to be killed, the remainder wounded or missing. Except for the 35th Foot total British losses were 1,067 men: six officers, 123 others and four sailors killed, including Lieutenant Colonel Morris of the 1/Coldstream Guards; 38 officers, 386 others and seven sailors wounded, including the Lieutenant Colonels Wynyard, Cook, Dawkins and Cunningham of the guards, Lieutenant Colonels Stephenson and Oswald; 503 men missing. The sailors killed and wounded were from the crews of the gunboats on the Kanaal van Alkmaar.[27] Many of the wounded had to be left behind and were taken prisoner by the Franco-Batavians. Total Russian losses were 3,067 men: 43 officers and 1,749 others killed or missing, including the Russian commander in chief Lieutenant General Hermann von Fersen taken prisoner and Lieutenant General Zherebtsov killed; 50 officers and 1,225 men wounded, including Major General Suthoff.[28] Total Anglo-Russian loss was about 4,500 men out of about 35,000, a loss of 13 percent.

Again the Anglo-Russians suffered much from the Franco-Batavian riflemen: 'Scarcely any of our officers escaped without some slight hurt, and many were killed'.[29] Another account of a sergeant of the 9th Foot about the effective fire from his enemy:

> The balls came whistling about us like hail as we advanced. First came one, and knocked away the hilt of my sword; then came another, and cracked off the iron head of my halberd …Then smack came another, whack through my canteen, and spilt all my brandy… By and bye, half-a-dozen of balls or so went through the blanket I carried on my shoulders… I stopped to take a musket from a dead Russian for my own defence… I was just in the act of biting off the end of my third cartridge to fire again, when a musket ball took me in the left cheek, and knocked me over as flat as a sixpence on the ground.[30]

---

25 Letter of 25 September 1799 from Count Bentinck van Rhoon to Hendrik Fagel in Colenbrander, *Gedenkstukken*, Vol. III, p.1074. According to Dubiansky, '2,000 Batavians of the party of Orange changed sides on the battlefield'. This is not confirmed by other reports: Ritter, *Een Russisch verhaal*, p.29.
26 Gachot, *Brune en Hollande*, p.269.
27 Official British returns in Anon., *Campaign in Holland*, Appendix No.8, pp.81-82; Anon., *The History of the Campaign of 1799, in Holland*, pp.332-335.
28 Official returns of 24 September 1799 by Major General Essen in Miliutin, *Geschichte des Krieges*, Vol.V, pp.283-284.
29 Carr-Gomm, *Letters and Journals of Sir William Maynard Gomm*, p.40.
30 Account of Sergeant Archy Stewart in Thomas Dick Lauder, *Legendary Tales of the Highlands* (London: Henry Colburn, 1841), Vol.I, pp.55-57.

The Battle of Bergen had been a clear defeat for the Anglo-Russians. Over all, York's battle plan had many faults. The Russian troops had no time to recover fully from their long journey at sea and the officers had no time to acquaint themselves and to reconnoitre the terrain and roads they had to advance on. Their artillery was not able to keep up for the reasons already described, exposing the Russian infantry to the destructive fire of the superior Franco-Batavian guns. The British brigade that was assigned to the Russian column was not present when needed: it appears that Major General Manners was not at ease with the strange army unknown to him and indeed used the first opportunity to join the British troops of the Second Column. There is a possible other explanation, stated by Gachot:

> In the morning, at time they should have take up arms, the brigade Manners demanded bread and coffee. Without supplies it refused to fight. At 6:15 a.m. the commissariat distributed biscuits and jenever. Then it was learned that Kamp and Groet were in Hermann's power. Always ready to change his plans, the Duke of York decided that he should not support the Russians which had such a beautiful momentum; he ordered Manners to follow Dundas and Sedmoratzki on the right bank of the Kanaal van Alkmaar, to help them to seize the bridge at Schoorldam. Dundas, refusing to listen to the complaints of his hungry soldiers, had started a 5:00 a.m. After conferring with the commander in chief, who was to follow his column, he indicated that the brigades Oyley, Burrard and [Prince William of] Gloucester had to march straight to Warmenhuizen, occupy it at any price and then support the left, to Eenigenburg to assist Pulteney's action. To their right, Sedmoratzki and Manners were to follow the road to Schoorldam.[31]

Gachot thus explains the absence of Manners, as well as giving a reason for its late start. No other source has been located confirming this.

What also surprises is that Dundas or York never threatened the Batavian centre at Koedijk and the floating bridge situated there, allowing the Batavians to reinforce the French fighting the Russians at their convenience. Victory would further depend on Abercromby being able to execute his march around the Franco-Batavian flank, forcing them to retreat. York should have reconnoitred the roads in the direction of Hoorn and Purmerend and obtained information about the removal of the bridges and demolishing of the roads. This would not have been difficult given the fact that the Franco-Batavians had virtually no troops placed there. Now the column of Abercromby, consisting of the best British units, made a useless move on the far left wing of the Anglo-Russian army and could not take part in the battle. Major General Moore's opinion was equally harsh in his diary about sending Abercromby to Hoorn, as well as about Pulteney's retreat from Langendijk:

> The detaching of Sir Ralph with so large a body of men so late as the evening before the general attack was ill imagined. Such a body, taking advantage of the first successes of the Russians, might have decided the day. It should have been detached, if at all, at least ten days earlier. Had that been done and the bridges and

---

31 Gachot, *Brune en Hollande*, pp.263-264.

roads upon the flank of the enemy been repaired, the detachment might have given him jealousy; but even as it was, this body might still have profited by the advantages gained by Sir James Pulteney, and at least have made it possible to retain Oude Karspel. I can impute the retiring from thence to panic only. The enemy immediately reoccupied it, and have again strengthened themselves.[32]

Abercromby did not show his usual vigour on this occasion, although given the bad quality of the roads, the obstacles met and the exhaustion of his troops it would have been an enormous task to have an effect on the outcome of the battle. Still, he could have tried to threaten the Franco-Batavian line of retreat or at least threaten the Batavian flank as soon battle was commenced. As it was now, the Anglo-Russians charged head-on at the strongest part of the Franco-Batavian lines, the Russians trying to break through by sheer force. They were also not aided by the fact that their attacks did not take place simultaneously. 'Daybreak' (which in fact was at 5:00 a.m.) is not a very definitive moment to define the time of attack, something which easy could have been prevented by York by setting a specific time, although it is also clear that the Russians started their attack too early.

Looking at all these facts, there are enough reasons for the Russians to have come to believe that they had been abandoned by their allies and that the loss of the battle was mainly due to the actions – or, rather, the inactivity – of the British. Major General Essen wrote to Tsar Paul about the battle:

> On the eighth, between three and four o'clock in the morning before dawn we broke up into three columns, attacking the enemy with the usual Yours Imperial Majesty's own bravery, threw him out of his three entrenchments, took some batteries with the bayonets, and took possession of three captured villages, as well as the little town of Bergen. All this occurred at a distance of about two miles. Fourteen enemy guns, a thousand prisoners and over two thousand fallen enemies were sufficient proof of the extraordinary bravery and zeal of Your Majesty's troops; but the soldiers, who had not yet fully recovered from the troublesome sea journey, were so exhausted by these efforts that they were unable to fulfil the orders of their brave leader to penetrate further, which was also because of the lack of artillery, Since the horses were not yet preserved, only a small part could be used. In addition, each gun was only pulled by two horses. After we had used all the artillery ammunition and cartridges, we had to advance against a numerous enemy, which directed almost all his forces against us. As we were on the right flank of those allies who should have attacked with us at the same time were delayed by two hours for unknown reasons, which made victory over the enemy much more difficult. After the troops had dwindled out of fatigue, and only had their bayonets left for their defence, they began to retreat in disorder. On this disordered retreat, those guns which had been taken from the enemy and a part of our own guns, of which the horses had been slaughtered, and of which the gun carriages had been shattered, were abandoned. The commander in chief Lieutenant-General Hermann was

---

32 Maurice (ed.), *Diary of Sir John Moore*, Vol.I, p.350.

taken prisoner; Lieutenant-General Zherebtsov has fallen, Major-General Suthoff was wounded.

As I commanded from the beginning to the end of the battle on the front, and by the unhappy event of becoming the oldest, I took over the command, collected and restored the troops, and then returned to our former advantageous position in a way that the enemy did not dare to pursue us. In general, our loss of dead, prisoners, and wounded amounts to 3,000 men; The enemy has suffered a much greater loss. As much as this misfortune is close to my heart, I cannot help but to report to Your Imperial Majesty that many of the staff and senior officers showed unprecedented bravery, especially Major-General Sedmoratzki, who, by Lieutenant-General Hermann detached to the Duke of York on the left flank with his regiment and the Comb. Gren. Battalion Ericsson, defeated the enemy everywhere, capturing 700 prisoners as well as three guns, and delivered them to the allies. On the whole, more than 3,000 enemies were captured by us and the English.[33]

Beside all this, the French as well as the Batavians fought again hard and coordinated well; they supported each other and managed to win a clear victory. Although the wounding of *Lieutenant-Generaal* Dumonceau caused confusion and Daendels' counterattack on Pulteney's troops which caused unnecessary loss was a clear mistake, the Franco-Batavians re-formed after every setback and counterattacked. At once all previous distrust was forgotten. Relations between the French and Batavians were much improved and morale was high. The glory of the victory was increased by the capture of seven Russian colours and the Russian commander in chief Hermann.[34] Also captured were 20 cannon, six howitzers, twenty ammunition-caissons, 24 transport wagons, 200 horses and 4,000 muskets. Also shown by the French was an extreme flexibility in the assignment of units to generals. Whenever the tactical situation demanded it, units were shifted from one commander to another and Batavian units were intermingled with French ones, fighting side by side. Units just arriving on the battlefield marched straight into battle, without any fuss about who commanded what unit. There also seemed to be no seniority problem, brigade and division generals fighting side by side against a common enemy.

---

33 Report of 20 September 1799 by Major-General Essen to Tsar Paul in Miliutin, *Geschichte des Krieges*, Vol.V, pp.284-285.

34 There is confusion about the number of colours that were taken. Of the colours that were taken, one was lost by the Benkendorf Grenadiers and another one by the Arbénev Musketeers. According to Miliutin, *Geschichte des Krieges*, Vol.V, p.45, the Russians lost only two colours and fifteen guns. The difference in numbers could be caused by the fact that each regiment had one 'white colour' and an additional nine 'coloured flags' for each company, so probably the Russians only counted the loss of their white colours while the French counted all of them. Brune sent the seven colours to Paris. After complaints by the Batavian government, three colours were handed over to the Batavians.

13

Distrust and Doubt

The Anglo-Russian troops

Only with difficulty did the Anglo-Russians manage in the aftermath of the Battle of Bergen to get enough units into order to form a proper defence of the Zijpe position, especially in the absence of Abercromby's column which still had to return from Hoorn. All units were placed in the frontline of the Zijpe position as soon as they were back in some shape. The Russian Colonel Dubiansky describes an incident happening the same evening after their defeat:

> The wound that I had received, did not prevent me remaining in service. I had to defend my battery. After letting my battalion take up its position I was, just like the [British] officer of the artillery, prepared to defend it with my last drop of blood. In the distance we observed a dense column coming towards us. The gunners were ready with the fuse in their hand. The column closed in. The Englishman watched them through his spyglass. "They are ours!", he called; "They are ours!" he handed me his spyglass and continued: "Look for yourself, Mr colonel!" Indeed I distinguished in the distance red cloaks, and soon an officer approached at the gallop. It was a French negotiator, sent to our battery with some captured English marauders. I was not allowed to let anyone approach my post from the enemy's side and the Frenchman, not wanting to wait on the open dike any longer, rode away. At that moment hundred fifty women stood before my battery, which came from an English packet and had followed their husbands. These foragers of a new kind were supplied with such huge amounts of foodstuff that they looked like bales covered with red cloth. I learned that similar heroines had showed themselves at other batteries. About ours we were very satisfied, because they sold us for little money the Alkmaar cheese and the fresh bread they had with them, stuff we did not taste for a long time.[1]

---

1   Ritter, *Een Russisch verhaal van den veldtocht in Noord-Holland in 1799*, p.35.

Not all Anglo-Russian marauders were so harmless. The Franco-Batavians had to hunt down Russian soldiers who were cut off from their own troops in the debacle at Bergen. They robbed, plundered, raped and killed the unfortunate inhabitants, and would rather starve to death instead of surrendering:

> The Russians are horrible folk and have hardly any clothes on them. They still look 80 percent worse than the nastiest French I ever saw. They are cruel and plunderous and have bayoneted children with their long bayonets in Schoorldam and committed horrific atrocities to women and girls.[2]

Although the above might be a bit exaggerated, up until this day the memory of their behaviour lives on in this part of the Netherlands. The behaviour of the British troops also worsened: until then there was only the requisitioning, but from the 23rd on reports of stealing and plunder of cattle and goods are reported. Clearly morale was sinking.

Abercromby was still neutral in his opinion of the Russians, still supported the battle plan, and did not blame anyone for the loss of the battle, as he related to Henry Dundas:

> You will receive with this an account of an action that took place yesterday between the allied army under the command of the Duke of York and the troops of the French and Batavian Republics. As it was not my lot to have any share in it, I shall not enter into any detail. The plan of attack was, I am persuaded, the best that could be devised; it was laid by H. R. H. before general d'Hermann, myself and general Dundas, and it met with our united approbation. General d'Hermann declared that it contained all his ideas, and I heard of no difference of opinion on the subject. I think it necessary to say so much, as general d'Hermann, who had a great share in the execution of the plan, is prisoner, and cannot write to his court on this subject. The event of a battle is at all times doubtful, but in this country the difficulties that an attacking army has to surmount are not to be equalled in any country in Europe… From the knowledge I have of the ground, as much was done and as great advantages were gained as could have been expected. Victory was already in our hands, when, from one of those unfortunate accidents to which the best generals are exposed, it was lost. Having only returned to head quarters this morning at two o'clock, I know nothing of our loss, or of that of the Russians. Some of the best brigades of the army, and who had no share in the action, are fresh. Our numbers are not much diminished, and we are ready to try another attack. The same plan must be followed nearly, I hope with better success, and free from the circumstances which prevented its being more complete yesterday.[3]

---

2   Letter from J.C.C. den Beer Poortugael to his wife, 21 September 1799 in J.C.C. den Beer Poortugael, 'Levensbericht van Diederic Jacob den Beer Poortugael' in *Jaarboek van de Maatschappij der Nederlandsche Letterkunde, 1880 – Bijlage tot de Handelingen van 1880* (Leiden: E.J. Brill, 1880), p.39.
3   Letter in English of 20 September 1799 from Abercromby to Henry Dundas in Colenbrander, *Gedenkstukken*, Vol.III, pp.402-403.

Old farmhouse in Dirkshorn, a model to be found in the whole of North Holland in 1799. (Author photo)

Despite Abercromby's opinion, already there was friction between the British and the Russians: Most British held the opinion that the reckless advance and the bad behaviour of the Russian troops in Bergen was the cause of their defeat. In a secret report to Henry Dundas about the outcome of the battle, York wrote:

> I have as much as possible avoided in my dispatch saying anything against the behaviour of the Russian troops, knowing of what consequence it is to keep the Emperor in good humour, but it is owing to their conduct only that we were obliged to give up the advantages which we had gained. I do the Russians full justice for bravery, but their discipline is terrible. General Hermann, though a willing, well-disposed, and in some degree well-informed man, kept up no discipline; he was likewise very anxious to make himself a name in Russia, and to be as much beloved by the soldiers as Suwarow is said to be; and certainly, I am convinced that the affection and confidence that the officers and soldiers had in him was one of the principal causes of their retreating upon his being taken. I am very glad to be able to inform you, however, that the Russians are beginning to recover themselves, and are exceedingly ashamed of their conduct.[4]

---

4   Quoted in English from the secret report of 20 September 1799 from York to Henry Dundas in Colenbrander, *Gedenkstukken*, Vol.III, p.1070.

The Russians believed that the British had abandoned them: 'General Hermann curses the English for their perfidy; he accuses them of having abandoned his brave troops and being the cause they were almost destroyed. He says that for 40 hours they remained without food'.[5] The Russian officers taken prisoner by the Franco-Batavians shared Hermann's opinion:

> The troops of Paul 1st seem to have adapted a very bad opinion of those of George III and their commanding general H.R.H. the Duke of York. An English officer brought here was taken in the room of captured officers. They refused to receive him and testified by some pretty humiliating gestures their contempt and indignation. These officers threatened the English with the wrath of the Emperor of all the Russias.[6]

Moore, never hesitating to write down his opinion in his diary, recorded just before the battle of 2 October would take place:

> A body of a thousand British were to act in the sand-hills upon the right of the Russians. General Dundas's column, instead of acting upon both sides of the Alkmaar Canal, on the left of the Russians, are now to move in their rear, to act as a second line and reserve to them, extending to the right through the sand-hills, and endeavour to communicate with the column under Sir Ralph. The Russian General, Herman, who at first commanded them, despised all assistance, held everybody cheap, and certainly had too much boast and pretension for a man of sense. His action fell short of his talk as much as it generally does with men of that description. He displayed nothing but personal courage, and was at last taken prisoner, as some suspect purposely to cover his misconduct. The present Commander of the Russians [Major General Essen] seems as cautious as the other was imprudent. Whether he is too much so for the bold undertakings our situation requires will be seen hereafter.[7]

About 60 years after the battle, the Russian Lieutenant Colonel Miliutin pointed out the differences between British and Russian tactics on that day:

> The English troops were very slow and deliberate in their advance, totally opposite to the rapid and careless advance of the Russians. As we have seen, Hermann's column had advanced blindly in the dark, without any signposts, without general staff officers, without the slightest material for building bridges; the English columns, on the other hand, did not advance until daybreak; they had guides leading the columns, were only gradually pushing forward, build bridges across the

---

5 Letter of 20 September 1799 from citizen Galdi, representative of the Cisalpine Republic in The Hague, to Serbelloni in Milan in Gachot, *Brune en Hollande*, pp.261-262.
6 Letter of 19 September from Brune's secretary Vern in Alkmaar to the French ambassador Florent-Guiot, quoted in Gachot, *Brune en Hollande*, p.263.
7 Maurice (ed.), *Diary of Sir John Moore*, Vol.I, pp.352-353.

canals and made the roads passable for the artillery; every step was deliberate. They also had to deal with bad Batavian troops, while the Russians fought against belligerent and brave Frenchmen. Dundas did not arrive at the village of Schoorldam until 9 o'clock when Hermann was already in Bergen.[8]

The accusations and mistrust between the British and Russians, which were the result of the battle of the 19th, would hamper all Anglo-Russian operations from now on. The only thing they could be proud of was the Russian capture of two colours and a gun. The allied defeat would also mean that the campaign in Holland would be prolonged, already late in season with even higher chances on bad weather with all its negative effects. Beside that the weather was already extremely worse and after the battle a fierce storm prevented all military operations on both sides. For the first time there was doubt if the campaign would succeed in its purpose, reinstating the Stadtholder and with him the Dutch Republic. As such this battle would become the turning point and decide the outcome of the campaign. This doubt is also illustrated in Moore's diary, where he recorded on 28 September:

> The natural strength of this country is such that without a general rising of the people in our favour it is vain to hope to conquer it. Government would have done well to have withdrawn the army after the destruction of the Dutch fleet, making that the object of the expedition. The arrival of the Duke of York with the strong reinforcements makes it necessary for the honour of our country and for our own as soldiers that we should make another attempt to force the enemy. If we are successful we shall probably be able to secure winter quarters in North Holland. If we are beaten we shall have no option but to re-embark.[9]

The Russian troops had received heavy loss and some units were so depleted that they could not be used any longer as an effective fighting force during the upcoming battles. For example, the Combined Grenadier Battalion 'Strick' was down from 627 to 256 men and the Combined Grenadier Battalion 'Osipov' had out of 643 only 329 men left. The Benkendorf Grenadiers (2 battalions) were down from 1,516 to 750 men and the Arbénev Musketeers (2 battalions) down from 1,546 to 908 men. The Anglo-Russians were on the 24th, 25th and 27th reinforced with the last Russian troops that still had to arrive, commanded by Major General Emmé:[10]

---

8   Miliutin, *Geschichte des Krieges*, Vol.V, pp.40-41.
9   Maurice, *The Diary of Sir John Moore*, Vol.I, pp.350-351.
10 These were transported on the following British ships, arriving from Reval at Elsinore roads on 9 and 10 September: *Blonde* (170), the ex-East Indiaman *Calcutta* (700) and the transport ships *Walter Boyd* (550) and *Minerva* (470). The numbers in brackets are the number of troops transported according to the Batavian newspaper *Nouvelles Politiques* (27 September 1799). This same newspaper states that there were four additional Swedish transports, not giving the names of the specific ships, only the name of their captains and the number of men transported: The Captains Ornberg (450), Castegreen (403), Olon234 (270) and Martin (baggage only). It is also stated that these transports were escorted by the British warships *Espion* (5th Rate 36) and *Ranger* (Sloop 16), without having additional troops on board.

Unit	Battalions	Strength
Emmé Grenadiers	2 battalions	1,516
Comb. Grenadier Battalion 'Mitiouchin'	1 battalion	631
Comb. Grenadier Battalion 'Ogarev'	1 battalion	648

After the battle of the 19th also several detachments of the British battalions serving in Holland arrived, and in addition some artillery horses. These detachments had been on ships that were forced to return due to the stormy weather or had not been ready to sail with the rest. On the 25th three troops of the 15th Light Dragoons arrived in transports. One or two days later the sloop *Camilla* (6th Rate 20) arrived with the rifle company of the 6/60th Foot, consisting of 110 German and other foreign recruits. They had embarked at Cowes on the Isle of Wight on 13 September, sailing immediately for Holland to make up for the lack of light infantry and counter the substantial loss of officers by the fire of the Batavian *jager* and the French skirmishers. The riflemen joined Colonel MacDonald's Reserve. Over in Great Britain the light infantry companies of the guards were ordered to prepare for foreign service as well.[11] Total Anglo-Russian strength was now nearly 40,000.

The Franco-Batavian troops

The Franco-Batavians were elated about their victory, unexpected by many. Especially the defeat of the Russians was a resounding success. After the battle most of the wounded were transported to Alkmaar or even further to Haarlem, where barges were used to serve as crude hospitals. But this was still not enough to take care of the huge amount of wounded soldiers. Beside Amsterdam, an additional French hospital was set up in Utrecht. Wounded were sent to Leiden, Woerden, Rotterdam, and Breda. The prisoners were also send to Haarlem: on 20 September nearly a thousand arrived escorted by French *chasseurs a cheval* and soldiers of the *Gewapende Burgermacht*: 642 Russian soldiers were put in the Janskerk (St. John's Church); 298 British soldiers on the attic of the Vleeshal (meat-hall); and 27 officers, 19 Russian and eight British, were lodged in the 'Gouden Leeuw'. On the 22nd more prisoners arrived: 54 Russians, 42 British and six British and Russian officers.[12] By order of Brune the Russian prisoners were paraded in all the big cities of the Batavian Republic and in Paris, to show everyone that the Franco-Batavians were able to defeat the Russians despite their qualities: 'All prisoners that were not wounded left for the interior on the *quatrième, cinquième et sixième jours complémentaire* [20, 21 and 22 September]; they were led through Haarlem, Amsterdam, Utrecht and 's-Hertogenbosch to convince the unbelievers', an eye-witness in Amsterdam commenting: 'The unfortunate prisoners gave us a spectacle like bears'.[13] On their arrival in Utrecht the whole population watched the spectacle when at 12:30 p.m. the convoy arrived in the city:

---

11   *London Chronicle*, 27 September 1799.
12   Anon., *Geschiedkundig Gedenkstuk van het Voorgevallene binnen Haarlem in de Laatste Helft van het Jaar MDCCIC* (Haarlem: A. Loosjes Pz., 1803), pp.160-164.
13   Gachot, *Brune en Hollande*, pp.270-271.

1. Half company citizen-cavalrymen from Amsterdam;
2. Escort of French dragoons;
3. Two platoons *Gewapende Burgermacht* of Amsterdam;
4. Four mail coaches with Russian officers;
5. Escort of French dragoons;
6. About 700 Russian infantry;
7. Escort of French dragoons;
8. Two platoons *Gewapende Burgermacht* of Amsterdam;
9. A mail coach with British officers;
10. Over 100 British infantry;
11. 13 farmers' wagons with sick and exhausted soldiers;
12. Half company citizen-cavalrymen from Amsterdam.

"Anglo-Russian prisoners brought in", anonymous. (Noord-Hollands Archief, NL-HlmNHA_53001376_K)

Next day the convoy continued to 's Hertogenbosch with the citizens and *Gewapende Burgermacht* replaced by those of Utrecht.[14]

On 16 October 800 Russians were marched through Paris. Until this battle the Russians were respected as the best army in the world, especially after Suvorov's successes in Italy and in the Alps. This completely changed, not only in France and the Batavian Republic, as illustrated by Robert Jackson's treatise. In his 1804 edition, the view of the Russian army is

---

14 Hendr. Keetell, 'Aanteekeningen betreffende de Bat. Omwenteling voornamelijk binnen Utrecht. Door een ooggetuige' in *De Navorscher* (Utrecht: C. Snoek Wz., 1902), pp.468-471.

still positive but also contains some criticism, giving an explanation about what went wrong during this battle:

> The Russian soldiers frequently expend their ammunition without an adequate object; for their military operation partakes of the nature of the operation of a machine; or the shackles of fear give way, the native character develops in the midst of strong causes and the artificial fabric rushes headlong into disorganization and ruin. The illustrations are numerous; for instances abound, where Russian troops, after expending ammunition without object, have given themselves up to slaughter without resistance; or where, throwing off the shackles of restraint, they have run into every wildness of insubordination, drunkenness and plunder, even in the midst of battle... The Russian arms have attained a high fame among military nations; but, if causes be referred to the true source, it will probably be found, that the whole of their fame is not the fruit of their mechanical discipline. The causes of success are various. The Russian soldier, the slave of military authority, reduced apparently to an automaton, in the common routine of duty, still retaining a quality of his native barbarity, is greedy of the spoils of the enemy. Covetousness is thus a motive which urges him forward... Suwarrow, who is considered as a buffoon by the multitude, was in reality a genius in war; for he knew how to create enthusiasm in the mind and thereby support action, when the exertions of the animal body, as actuated by the supposed impulse of mechanical armies had become feeble. He impressed the credulous with an opinion that he was inspired; hence the simple and otherwise torpid Russian, moved by this impulse, felt himself strong and proved himself to be invincible. By means of this impression, the Russians were led to perform acts of boldness and to persevere in difficulties, which would have been insurmountable to a mechanical force, acting solely by the external impulse of fear, the assumed principle of the customary tactic. It may hence be concluded and the fact appears to have been frequently confirmed in practice, that it is to the enthusiasm of the Russian soldiery, as impressed by a religious sentiment, or devotion to the will and confidence in the supernatural powers of Suwarrow, that the most brilliant successes of that people are chiefly to be ascribed; for, it is here, as in other cases, that effect arises from influence of example, operating upon the mind and inspiring the congenial sentiment of an ennobling passion, rather than from an effect of a mechanical routine of duty, resulting from a discipline, originating in an impression of fear, forced to persevere in its routine, by an impression of constraint... The celerity of manual movement and the exact correspondence in time, with which it performs its exercises and manoeuvres, cannot perhaps be exceeded. It appears capable of throwing out a greater quantity of fire, in a given time, in proportion to numbers, than any other army perhaps in Europe. Its columns, arranged in order of battle, are compact and firm; the movement is rapid and while the scene of action admits of union and rapid movement, it may be reckoned irresistible; for it has superior weight and it is vigorously impelled forwards by an impulse threatening the rear. But, as the movement is mechanical, depending on the efficiency of complex causes, it is easily deranged; and when deranged, it is not easily rectified, for its motives of action are adventitious and external. In such a

case, a skilful enemy, refusing close action, suffers this blind machine to expend, or play off the measure of its charge without an adequate object; for individually it has no intellectual discretion. When this is done, the action is silent, the instrument comparatively harmless; and the power being exhausted, the fabric is prepared for an easy destruction.[15]

In 1824, a 2nd edition of the Jackson's *Systematic View* appeared, in which he added his view on the Russian actions during the 1799 expedition in Holland:

> When Russians begin to fire, they would appear to fire without interval and without aim, until they sweep the field by showers of bullets, obtain possession of it by the intimidation of noise, or until they expend their ammunition, exhaust their power and become comparatively harmless. The Russian soldier is not allowed the exercise of his intellectual discretion. He is supposed to act by order and by order only; consequently, if he have no order to advance to a given point, or to retire upon a given position, he stands still, according to the letter of his discipline, to be slaughtered on the spot; for his life is devoted to obedience… A detachment of the Russian army was joined in that year with a British force for the re-establishment of the stadtholder. The number of the detachment amounted to about seventeen thousand men apparently well selected for service; indeed, in so far as the eye can judge, an army of elite. The sharpshooters seemed to have been well drilled to their duty. The Kalmuck and Cossack were not numerous, but they were choice troops of the kind. The infantry were healthy and physically strong; so imposing in aspect that, if an estimate were to be made by appearance, that is, closeness and compactness of force, they might have been thought to be capable of walking over the enemy, or over any troops in Europe, as over a stubble-field. The Russians were sent into action soon after they landed. They moved on with a rapidity which astonished; and, as they advanced, they threw out a fire that was tremendous by its noise, but otherwise harmless: it was chiefly expended on the sand hills. Having met with little opposition, they penetrated to Bergen, entered the town, found liquor and drank to excess: they were soon intoxicated, ungovernable, mutinous, or dead drunk. The enemy, who had wisely given way to the torrent, halted and watched, returned in force and, enveloping the town, made the Russians prisoners. Whether the Russians were led into the snare by design, or fell into it by accident, is not distinctly known; but this at least is known, that it is a snare which is always before them and always available for their destruction by an intelligent enemy. The Russian was so humbled by the disaster at Bergen, that, in all the subsequent affairs in Holland, he seemed to be an unwilling actor. In advancing to the field, the soldiers dropped off occasionally from the advancing lines; even officers assumed the retrograde. One general literally ran away; another, wounded, as it were by the first fire, retired. It is common and allowable that wounded persons retire from action; but the person in question

---

15   Robert Jackson, *A Systematic View of the Formation, Discipline and Economy of Armies* 1st edition (London: John Stockdale, 1804), pp.78-81.

was wounded in such a manner that it was scarcely possible to suppose he had been wounded by the ball of an enemy's musket. The general who ran away was cashiered by the Emperor Paul in a passion; but the manner in which he was treated by his brother officers after his disgrace, affords a striking example of the trivial light in which military cowardice is regarded in Russia. Instead of being shunned and despised, the person alluded to walked at large as if nothing had happened to him; he was even regaled by his brother officers, prior to his departure for Russia, with a fete of honour as if he had returned from a victory. It is not meant to insinuate, in stating this fact, that the Russian officers are generally deficient in courage: it is clear that they have not the same feeling respecting it that officers have in the west of Europe.[16]

Beside the clear victory believed to be won, the Franco-Batavian army was reinforced by a steady stream of French units. Already during the battle of the 19th the 2/22e Demi-Brigade arrived in Alkmaar. On the 20th and the following days more French reinforcements arrived. On 1 October the 2/72e Demi-Brigade arrived. The French were now 13,444 strong.[17] With Brune's chief of staff Dardenne being ill, *Général de Brigade* Rostollant was appointed chief of staff.[18] Gouvion was promoted to *général de division* on the 19th on the field of battle, Aubrée becoming *général de brigade*. Total Franco-Batavian strength was now about 22,000 men. Six Batavian battalions had received such heavy losses that they had to be removed from the army temporarily.[19] Among these battalions were 1/ and 2/7e Halve Brigade and 3/4 Halve Brigade. Other battalions also had lost many men; for example after the Battle of Bergen, the 2e Bataljon Jager had only 60 men left![20]

The Franco-Batavian positions, which were the same as before the battle of the 19th, were reinforced and prepared for a defence in depth. The initial defences were in the line Kamp–Groet–Schoorl–Schoorldam. The main defences were in the line Koedijk-Bergen. Behind these lines stood the bulk of the French troops to act according to the threat. To enhance the protection of the forward positions, French engineers entrenched the entrances to the villages Groet and Schoorl. Bergen, key of the French defences, was completely fortified.

---

16 Robert Jackson, *A Systematic View of the Formation, Discipline, and Economy of Armies*, 3rd edition (London: Parker, Furnivall, and Parker, 1845) [similar to the 2nd edition 1824], pp.178-179, 183.
17 See Appendix XVI.
18 Dardenne was a very able chief of staff, and had commanded French troops in North Holland from 1796 to 1797. Therefore he knew the terrain the campaign took place very well. Although Dardenne's illness was the official reason for his replacement (he would die of tuberculosis in 1802), apparently differences with Brune were the real cause, as explained in P.J. Blok & P.C. Molhuysen, *Nieuw Nederlandsch Biografisch Woordenboek*, Vol.7 (Leiden, A.W. Sijthoff, 1927), pp.356-360. After his replacement and despite his supposed illness, Dardenne was send to Belgium to promote the dispatch of reinforcements to North Holland.
19 Van Sypesteijn, 'Krijgskundige Beschouwingen over den Veldtogt van 1799 in Noord-Holland', in *Nieuwe Spectator* (Nijmegen: J.F. Thieme, 1854), p.203.
20 Letter from J.C.C. den Beer Poortugael to his wife, 21 September 1799, in: *Jaarboek van de Maatschappij der Nederlandsche Letterkunde, 1880 – Bijlage tot de handelingen van 1880* (Leiden: E.J. Brill, 1880), p.39. On 22 September, Brune send a letter to the *Uitvoerend Bewind* proposing to exchange the 2/3e Halve Brigade, part of the bodyguard of the Batavian Government, for the 3/4e Halve Brigade so that it could recuperate. The 2nd Chamber refused though: with the 3/4e Halve Brigade only 250-300 men strong the constitutional strength of the bodyguard of 700 men could not be reached.

DISTRUST AND DOUBT

"Russian Cossacks". (Noord-Hollands Archief, NL-HlmNHA_53001377_K)

Batavian engineers reinforced Schoorldam and Koedijk. Most of the work was done by peasants and citizens, pressed from the neighbouring farms and villages:

> One Saturday five riders rode through the Schermer and with cursing and yelling the farmers were forced to go to the Langendijk with their spade... In the evening at eleven o'clock we arrived on the spot and were immediately put to work. At the dike the clay must be transported and the specie deposited in the canal on either side. Thirteen hours long, the 'lazy farmers' are pressed in the rain and wind and without giving food to them, doing this wicked job. No wonder, our Jacob sights: "I would rather see death in this case". After having plodded all night, the next day the forced workers were chased to the church like dogs to rest on the blue gravestones with some straw as pillow. But already in the early morning of the next day their oppressors appeared again and chased them out with sticks. With teeth chattering they went to the assigned spot. Now holes have to be dug into the dike so that the polders can be inundated. First the Woudmeer suffered this fate where the cows are still in the field. This job finished, gun emplacements have to be made and some houses that are in the way are taken down. Meanwhile, the soldiers do not fail to provide themselves with food to which purpose they slaughter the cows in the field. Finally, the workers are also thought about. They are given a dry piece of bread of one and a half pounds a day. And all this labour

has to be done for the Gallo-Batavians, while the sympathy of the population goes to the English – certainly not to the Russians.[21]

Not all were keen to dig and some fled south, away from the frontline. On 27 September the Heerhugowaard and the Geestmer Polders were inundated, so the Anglo-Russians could only attack along the Langendijk, by way of Oud-Karspel. At this place the redoubt was strengthened and reinforced with other defences. The ring-dike around Bleekmeer, which had provided cover for Pulteney's troops, was levelled to the ground. Further back, the Purmer, Beemster, and Schermer polders were also inundated. From all these measures can be concluded that Brune had decided not to undertake any further attacks on the strong Anglo-Russian positions in the Zijpe but to prepare for another attack and concentrate on preventing any further Anglo-Russian advance. Besides that, Brune took in account the possibility that the Anglo-Russians would execute a second landing behind his defence lines. It was rumoured that the Anglo-Russians would leave 20,000 men in North Holland, and that the other troops would sail to Naarden to attack Amsterdam from the south.

However, there was more bothering the Franco-Batavians: the corpses of the many dead, especially Russian soldiers had to be disposed of. From 19 until 26 September, 38 men were employed in collecting and burying them. These were put in mass graves, allegedly one in the dunes at a place locally known from this moment on as 'Russenduin' and beneath the Russian memorial in Bergen. On 21 September, patrols swept the dunes and the wooded area near Bergen and Schoorl. They gathered many British and Russian soldiers, some wounded and others trying to hide, starving from hunger and thirst. A Batavian soldier gives a vivid description of what he saw:

> The number of Russian dead is unspeakable, near and behind Bergen the corpses lie 3 or 4 high on the roads, so full that the carriages cannot pass… The remaining Russians have been surrounded in the woods of Bergen by French and Batavian troops. One found a wounded Russian in the woods who ate the bark of a tree against his hunger. On the 20th another 100 Russians and English have been brought in, on the 21st another 60 and on the 22nd even more. The Russians taken prisoner are so bitter about the English that they spit fire from their eyes, that they have cheated them stating that the French would run as soon as they saw them and that they would march into Alkmaar. Where they arrived although in another way than they believed.[22]

Naval Operations

Initially, Vice Admiral Mitchell did not embark on any ambitious activities in the Zuiderzee, although there was no serious Batavian opposition to be expected after the surrender of the Batavian fleet and the capture of the vessels in the Nieuwe Diep and on the Wadden Sea. The

---

21 R.P. Goettsch, 'Merkwaardigheden uit een achttiende-eeuws handschrift', in: *West-Frieslands Oud en Nieuw* (Hoorn: Drukkerij 'West-Friesland', 1971), pp.92-93.
22 Letter of a Batavian soldier of 23 September 1799 in J.K., '3 Brieven van het oorlogsterrein 1799 en 1800' in *De Navorscher* (Amsterdam: C.L.G. Veldt, 1909), p.578.

Zuiderzee lay completely open and the British had safe roadsteads for their ships. Mitchell decided only to act in concert with the army: without knowing York's plans, it would be of no use to embark on adventures in the Zuiderzee. Unfortunately, this also included the longed for support for the Orangists in the east. On 17 September 11 British warships anchored before Enkhuizen, commanded by Captain Dundas of the *Juno* (5th Rate 32). On the 21st, Mitchell joined them on the *Babet* (6th Rate 20, Captain Mainwaring) to lead the naval operations in the Zuiderzee in person. The following days more ships joined and a squadron of warships with small draught was formed.[23] Mitchell's report describes in detail what took place over the next days:

> The weather having moderated on the 21st inst. I shifted my flag to the Babet: though blowing a gale of wind the day before, Capt. Mainwaring, by his great exertions, had lightened her sufficiently for the pilot to take charge, and the Captains of the bomb vessels made equal exertions for the same purpose, having lightened their respective ships to 12 feet 8 inches; I left the Isis, Melpomene, and Juno with yards and top-masts struck, having taken all the seamen and marines that could be spared from them, with Sir C. Hamilton, Captains Dundas and Oughton, and a proper number of officers in large schuyts to assist me in the expedition; about ten we weighed in the Babet, accompanied by the four bombs, L'Espiegle and Speedwell brigs, and Lady Ann lugger, and Prince William armed ship. We fortunately had a fair wind, which raised the tide considerably over the flats, though in many parts we had only 12 feet 6 inches. On our approaching Medenblic at noon, I made the signals for the Dart and Gun brigs to weigh and join me; and at three P.M. I anchored with the squadron off Enkhausen [Enkhuizen], and a boat came off with four men wearing Orange cockades; in consequence of which I went on shore attended by the Captains; we were received by all the inhabitants with every testimony of joy at their deliverance from their former tyrannical government, and in the highest degree expressive of their loyalty and attachment to the House of Orange.
>
> I proceeded to the Stadthouse, and having summoned all the old and faithful Burgomasters, who had not taken the oath to the Batavian Republic, I instantly reinstated them, until his Highness the Hereditary Prince of Orange's instructions were received; to whom, and to his Royal Highness the Duke of York, I immediately sent an express, and at the same moment summoned before me and dissolved the Municipality, amidst the joyful acclamations of the inhabitants around the Stadthouse, part of them at the same time cutting down the tree of liberty, which they instantly burned; all of which was done in the most loyal, quiet, and regular manner.
>
> 1 have detached Capt. Boorder, in the Espiegle, with the Speedwell, to scour the coast from Steveren to Lemmer; but previous to his going on that service I sent him to Steveren, to bring me intelligence of the disposition of the inhabitants, he returned yesterday morning with the pleasing information of their having hoisted the Orange colours, and most of the neighbouring towns had done the same, and the

---

23 For a list of all British warships present on the Zuiderzee see Appendix XIV.

inhabitants joyfully complying with the same terms at Enkhausen and Medenblic; I have likewise detached the Dart, with two gun brigs to cut off the communication with Amsterdam and the towns in East Friesland, that have not returned to their allegiance. Our appearance in the Zuyder Zee with such an unexpected force has had a most wonderful and happy effect, and given the greatest confidence to those well disposed to the House of Orange. I shall not lose a moment's time in moving forward, when the wind and tide will permit, to complete, as far as lays in my power, what is finally entrusted to my charge.[24]

In the harbour of Enkhuizen two merchant ships were taken. At Medemblik at the marine wharf, two frigates the *Enkhuizen* (24 guns) and *'t Zeepaard* (24 guns) were taken, although both were not seaworthy. Mitchell possessed now two good bases for further actions on the Zuiderzee.

On 28 September, the *Blanche* (5th Rate 32, Captain Ayscough) was wrecked near Texel when leaving for Great Britain escorting a convoy. Ayscough reported about the incident:

It is with great concern I have to state to you, that, agreeable to your orders, I got under weigh from the Mars Diep on the 27th instant, at one o'clock P.M. making several signals for the convoy to follow me, the wind then being at S.E. At 4 P.M. the Pilot, who had the charge and direction of the ship, got her on shore on the Middle in the Sculp Gat; we very shortly got her off, but at six we got on shore again, Kyck Duyn bearing S.S.E. about two miles. I then made the signal for having struck on a shoal, and repeated it several times. It being the top of high water, and finding it impossible to get her off, I struck lower yard- and top-gallant masts, started all the water but the ground tier, and got a stream-anchor out ready to heave her off when the flood made, which we succeeded in about 10 o'clock A.M. on the 28th, and came to with the small bower in four fathoms; at five in the morning we attempted to weigh, but the wind had shifted to S.W. and blew so strong that it was impossible, therefore we cut the cable, made sail, and steered the course the Pilot directed, which very shortly brought us up upon Dalrymple shoal; the Black Buoy bearing S. by W. one cable length. I then made the signal for boats with anchors and hawsers, likewise for schuits, it being my intention to get the guns and all the heavy things into them; but these plans were frustrated by the gale increasing, so much so that it was scarcely possible to stand the deck, the sea breaking over in on every side, and the ship having so much motion. About 11 o'clock I cut away my main-mast; and a little after, the ship broaching to, I cut away my mizen-mast, and rigged two boat-sails on the poop, to endeavour to steer her, having previously to this lost my rudder, and nothing left to steer the ship in case she drifted over the shoal. I continued repeating the signal for assistance until I saw that none could be afforded; several boats being overset, and many lives lost in attempting it. By this time the ship making three inches of water every minute, and gaining very last upon us, the officers and men almost ready to drop with fatigue, about four o'clock

---

24   Letter on 24 September 1799 from Vice Admiral Mitchell to Evan Nepean in *Naval Chronicle*, Vol.III, p.72.

P.M. on the 28th, she drifted off the shoal, having only the fore-mast standing, and the water in the cable tiers, I thought the only chance I had to save the ship's company's lives was to run her on shore; which I fortunately succeeded in, by backing and filling with the foresail and two boats sails abaft, the fore yard being lowered down almost to the gunwale. We hove every thing overboard we could to lighten the ship, excepting the guns, there being only eight and ten feet water alongside, and the ship's draught 17 feet 3 inches, they would have gone into her bottom, and nothing could have saved the people's lives. I beg leave to observe, that the Blanche is now alongside the Mould Head in the New Diep; from her being bilged, her stern-frame shook to pieces, and the water upon the main-deck, together with a number of other defects, I almost despair of her ever being put in condition to be sent home, and scarcely to be removed from where she is, as you will more fully observe from the Carpenter's report which accompanies this. Although the utmost endeavours of those who were sent to my assistance could avail nothing, so far as regarded the saving of the ship, yet I must speak of them with equal gratitude and regret: the Dortrecht's launch was overset, the Gunner and six men drowned; Mr. Davison, Master of the Romney, who had got on board, persevered in sounding a-head in the Blanche's boat until she overset, and it was with much hazard and difficulty that the people were saved; Mr. Hodgson, Master, and Mr. Corney, Gunner of the Savage, were very active and enterprizing, as well in lightening the ship as in their efforts to save the people who were overset.[25]

The *Blanche* would sink in the Nieuwe Diep just as it entered the harbour. As usual a court martial was held, on board of the *Expedition* in Sheerness harbour on 1 November, to inquire into the cause and circumstances of the loss of the *Blanche* and the conduct of Captain Ayscough, the officers, and crew on that occasion. It was concluded that: 'the ship was run on shore through the entire fault of the Pilot; that very peculiar exertions were made, and professional skill shown, by the Captain, officers, and company of the Blanche, to get her off, and afterwards to save the lives of the people and the stores, which redounds greatly to their credit. The captain, officers and crew most honourably acquitted.'[26]

The Capture of the Town of Lemmer

As described in Mitchell's report, many more towns at the Zuiderzee had showed their inclination, or their fear for the British, by hoisting the orange flag. On the East Side of the Zuiderzee one town refused to hoist the orange flag. This town was Lemmer, a small fishing town, almost surrounded by water. Captain Bolton of the *Wolverine* (gun-brig 12), who arrived before the town with a British naval squadron on 27 September, estimated the garrison at a 1,000 French infantry, although a few hundred at the most, including men of the *Gewapende Burgermacht*, is more likely. *Tweede Lieutenant* van Grutten commanded

---

25 Report of 29 September from Captain Ayscough to Captain Lawford of the *Romney* in the *Naval Chronicle*, Vol.II, pp.634-635.
26 *Naval Chronicle*, Vol.II, pp.537, 634.

the garrison, consisting at least of a detachment of the 2/4e Halve Brigade. On 28 September, Bolton decided to attack the town. His after-action report about the attack:

> On Friday morning, at six o'clock, I came to an anchor, with the Haughty and Piercer, close to L'Espiegle, distant about six miles from Lemmer; from Captain Boorder I received every information I could desire. Finding the enemy had a thousand regulars in the town, and desperately determined to defend it, I immediately gave directions for completing the flotilla which Captain Boorder, with his usual judgment, had begun. He had pressed two schoots; on board of each were put two of L'Espiegle's six-pounders, which, with the two flat bottom boats, and Isis's launch, formed a respectable armament. Being willing to spare the effusion of human blood, especially of innocent victims, on Saturday at day-light I sent Capt. Boorder on shore with the following letter: "Sir, Resistance on your part is in vain; I give you one hour to send away the women and children; at the expiration of that time, if the town is not surrendered to the British arms for the Prince of Orange, your soldiery shall be buried in its ruins."
>
> Soon after Captain Boorder's departure I weighed and stood in shore. About nine A.M. I observed him returning, and soon after a flag of truce came out of the harbour. Before Captain Boorder arrived, I noticed the gun-boats which had been moored across the harbour moving towards the canals; I instantly dispatched Lieutenant Simpson with a flag of truce to inform them, that I considered their removal, or any other military arrangement, as a breach of the armistice, and if persisted in I should instantly bombard the town: before he returned, the flag of truce came on board with the following letter: "I have received your summons; the Municipality request twenty-four hours to send to their proper authority to accede to your demands."
>
> I immediately replied as follows: "Sir, I have received your letter; and have the honour to inform you, that if the Prince's colours are not hoisted in half an hour after the receipt of this, I shall bombard the town." I dispatched the Dutch Officer, and informed him I was coming down into my disposition before the town. I found by Captain Boorder, that the north part of the pier was considerably reinforced by some eighteen-pounders, taken from the gun-boats, which made a little alteration in our disposition necessary; and I was much concerned to find my brave able Dutch pilot declare, that from the southerly winds the water was so low, the Wolverene could not get in. Finding it a regular oozy flat for two miles, I pushed through the mud until within musquet-shot of the shore. The gun-brigs passed ahead within pistol-shot of the pier; but both, as well as myself, were not in the most favourable position, completely aground; but seamen ought never to be at a loss. The enemy, notwithstanding the flag of truce, commenced a heavy fire, which in an instant was returned from every part of the squadron: the action continued nearly an hour, when the enemy flew from their quarters, the soldiers deserted the town, and the Piercer's boat's crew planted the British standard on the pier. I do not wonder at the strong opposition, as the troops were mostly French… To Captain Boorder I confided the arrangements on shore. The gale freshened fast, and it was necessary to preserve the Wolverene; with some difficulty her bow was hove round:

"British attack on Lemmer", by Reinier Vinkeles after a drawing of Dirk Langendijk. (Rijksmuseum, NL-HlmNHA_53001377_K)

the wind fortunately came round to the southward; and by starting all the water, with a heavy press of sail for two miles, I dragged her through the mud, steering by sails only into eleven feet water, where she now lies. All last night it blew excessively hard, the ship struck repeatedly, but using every means to lighten her, she rode it out tolerably well. This morning at ten o'clock I observed a body of the enemy advancing against the town along the northern causeway; I immediately sent to Captain Boorder to apprize him of the danger: in a little time the town was attacked on all sides, but very soon I had the satisfaction of seeing the enemy retreat. From the mast head I perceive the town is nearly surrounded by water, so that a few brave men, with a flotilla on the canal, can most effectually defend it. I have no doubt but a well-timed succour to these people would cause the whole province to throw off the French yoke.[27]

Other sources provide additional information not included in Bolton's report. After the engagement with two Batavian gunboats and some 18pdr guns on the pier which fired 36 shots, the gunboat *De Schrik* was burned and the gunboat *De Vernieler* sunk. *Tweede Lieutenant* van Grutten evacuated Lemmer with his men and the place was promptly occupied by the British. On 2 October a force of the Batavian *Gewapende Burgermacht*

---

27 *Naval Chronicle*, Vol.III, pp.137-138. Contrary to Bolton's claim the troops in Lemmer were Batavian, not French.

reconnoitred in the direction of Lemmer. They found out that near the Follegaster Bridge the British were throwing up a battery. The British, not prepared for an attack, were easily driven off and the Batavians captured an 18pdr cannon, taking it with them to the town of Joure. On the same day a second attack was made on this battery, which was occupied again by the British. Again the British had to retreat, suffering a loss of two men killed and five wounded. This time the Batavians took a 12pdr and a 6pdr cannon. During both actions the Batavians suffered no loss.

At this moment *Colonel* Gelderman, commander of the 3e Halve Brigade, arrived from North Holland to take over command, while *Colonel* Queysen arrived in Joure with part of the *Gewapende Burgermacht* of the north-eastern provinces. The Batavians decided to attack Lemmer with 400 men, mainly from the *Gewapende Burgermacht*, commanded by *Lieutenant-Colonel* Pacqué (commander of 2/4e Halve Brigade), and supported by two 6pdr guns and four gunboats. On the 11th at 5:00 a.m. the British garrison of Lemmer, consisting of 157 marines and sailors, was attacked from the north. The attack was led by a by a force of 26 *jager* with an officer of the 3e Bataljon Jagers. They had orders to capture a battery and to spike the 18-pdr cannon in it, to prevent it firing at the soldiers of the main attack. Unfortunately they advanced too far. Heavily outnumbered, two *jager* were killed and most of the remainder wounded and taken prisoner, only five escaping. Immediately after this had happened, the main force of the *Gewapende Burgermacht* attacked, fired at from three sides. They kept up the fight for over three hours but finally had to retreat again.[28] Batavian losses were 23 killed and about 30 wounded. The British suffered no losses. The latter engagement is described in the report from Captain Boorder:

> I have the honour to inform you, that at five o'clock this morning the enemy made a general attack on this town in four different parts. Their advanced party attempted to storm the North Battery. We soon got them between two fires; our tars with pikes surrounded them, and they immediately laid down their arms. Their force was one officer, one serjeant, one corporal, and 28 men, two of the latter killed. We had no sooner secured our prisoners than they attacked us with the remainder of their force, 670 in number. Our little army did wonders; for with sailors and marines our force was only 157. We fought them for four hours and a half, when the enemy gave way in all directions: I immediately ordered the marines to pursue them. Their breaking down a bridge prevented their colours and two field pieces from falling into our hands; but before this was effected the heavy fire from the marines had killed 18 of the enemy, and wounded about 20; and in their general attack they had five men killed, and nine wounded… It affords me great satisfaction to inform you we had not a man hurt.[29]

Bolton's opinion was that the eastern part of the Batavian Republic was ripe to revolt and he planned attacks on the cities Harlingen, Kampen and Stavoren. He sent word of his plans to Mitchell and asked for reinforcements, especially infantry. York told Mitchell that he could

---

28   van der Aa, *Geschiedenis van den Jongst-geëindigden Oorlog*, Vol.VIII, pp.213-218.
29   *Naval Chronicle*, Vol.III, p.141.

spare none. So Mitchell gave Bolton only the *Tigress* (Gun-brig 12) and *Plumper* (Gun-vessel 12) and ordered him to stop further operations. There was no point in taking coastal cities without the soldiers to defend them. In fact, no further operations of importance would be undertaken in the Zuiderzee. During the night of 13 October the British evacuated Lemmer again.

The Orangists in Holland

The Hereditary Prince of Orange was still doing his best to get British support for the Orangists along the eastern border of the Batavian Republic. Realizing that he had made no progress he was looking for other means. Besides that, the Duke of York had requested that the islands of Vlieland and Terschelling be occupied as soon as possible with 250 Dutch and two cannon each. The British would provide the cannon and ammunition. Therefore, on 24 September, the Prince of Orange established a new organisation for the Dutch navy and army corps. A Dutch naval squadron would be formed of six ships: the *Hector* (5th Rate 44, 300 men, *Capitein-Lieutenant* van Voss), the *Heldin* (5th Rate 32, 250 men, *Lieutenant ter Zee* van Braam), the *Minerva* (6th Rate 24, 190 men, *Lieutenant ter Zee* Twent), the *Valk* (6th Rate 24, 190 men, *Lieutenant ter Zee* Martinius), the *Venus* (6th Rate 24, 190 men, *Lieutenant ter Zee* van Spengler) and *'t Duifje* (6th Rate 18, 130 men, *Lieutenant ter Zee* Voss). In addition a guard ship would be made serviceable. For service on land a marine corps would be formed, consisting of an infantry battalion with six companies of 118 men each and an artillery company. If possible a pioneer company would be formed as well. Command of this corps was given to *Lieutenant-Colonel* Baron von Gross, receiving the order to prepare for the occupation of Vlieland and Terschelling with the marine corps.

Creating this new organisation turned out to be more difficult than anticipated. Regarding the navy, the mentioned frigates were in poor condition. When these on 25 September were handed over by Commodore Lawford (commander of the roadstead) and cleared by the British, *Lieutenant ter Zee* Twent recorded that:

> We found the ships in very poor condition; larders and barrels had been busted open or smashed to pieces. Peas, grits and other dry food was mixed up; the light sails had been cut, most of the cordage cut down, etc. …With 14 or 15 men, among which were a shipmaster, a boatswain, a cook, a butler and a boy, I managed to set up the rigging, after which on 28 September the old Dutch flag and pennant were hoisted. However, because of the lack of men, we could not bring over the frigate to the roadstead.[30]

Over the next days the Dutch naval officers struggled to make their ships seaworthy. In the meantime, *Generaal-Major* Bentinck was equally struggling to raise the marine corps. On 7 October the Prince of Orange in Alkmaar send a letter to Bentinck, requesting him to

---

30 F.E.M., 'Uit de nagelaten herinneringen van den Vice-Admiraal Jhr. Anthony Cornelis Twent', *Marineblad* (Helder: C. de Boer Jr., 1905), p.345.

report about the progress and how many small vessels would be available to transport the corps and sailors in case it was decided to cross the Zuiderzee. An answer was not needed anymore: after the battle of Castricum (6 October) the Anglo-Russian army retreated to the Zijpe positions and on the 8th, the Prince of Orange would be back in Den Helder again.[31]

After the Battle of Zijpe (10 September), *Major* van der Hoop was sent to the island Wieringen with about 300 Batavian deserters. On 25 September, finally, *Colonel* van Rechteren Limpurg arrived with 70 officers that had been sent from Lingen to Great Britain.[32] That same evening Van Rechteren Limpurg went to Wieringen with about 30 officers. On the 26th, he organised the deserters present there into two infantry battalions of four companies each and an artillery company. The Duke of York provided muskets, sabres, and cartridges out of the weaponry collected after the Battle of Bergen. Nevertheless much that was needed was not available. The men could not be provided with proper uniform pieces; most arrived without shoes, stockings and shirts. This was especially a problem because of the continuous bad weather. With only few houses on the island at the most 1,300 men could be lodged on Wieringen. That number was soon to be reached: every day, newly recruited prisoners of war and deserters arrived from Den Helder and the number of companies per battalion was raised from four to six, of 108 men each.

Then there was the pending occupation of Vlieland and Terschelling. It turned out that *Lieutenant-Colonel* Baron von Gross had made no progress, not wanting to be sent to some islands were no honour could be gained. He sent several letters to the Prince of Orange, summing up all kinds of concerns respecting the occupation of Vlieland and Terschelling. On 4 October the Prince of Orange received yet another extensive document with the title: 'Main considerations regarding the occupation of the islands of Vlieland and Terschelling'. Baron von Gross went even further, on the 10th producing a wild plan titled 'Project of an expedition to Friesland and Groningen'. In this plan he proposed to concentrate the 2e Regiment Waldeck, the 5e Bataljon Waldeck and a Batavian *jager* battalion (all in Batavian service but according to von Gross 'dedicated to the good cause'); the British regiment at Den Helder (69th Foot) which was of no use there; the Russian hussars, useless at the moment without horses which they could procure in Friesland; and two newly-organised Dutch regiments; one raised from the men at Wieringen, the other from the Dutch present in Den Helder and surroundings, including an artillery company and *jager*; for an expedition to Groningen and Friesland. Yet even that was not enough for him: Baron von Gross also presented a piece with the title 'Remarks on the situation of the British army in North Holland in mid-October 1799', containing an indirect disapproval of the measures taken by the British commander in chief and his opinion how to act to be victorious. There is no evidence that the Duke of York ever received this piece; probably it was taken care of by the Dutch so that that York never did. So Baron von Gross was very busy with writing, but not with the things he was ordered to do: in the end no Dutch troops would occupy Vlieland and Terschelling.[33]

Finding manpower was no problem for the Orangists at the moment. Provisions and equipment was more difficult, with already so many troops compressed in such a small and

---

31 Koolemans Beijnen, *De Erfprins van Oranje in Noord-Holland*, pp.61-63.
32 See Chapter 9 and Appendix XVIII.
33 Koolemans Beijnen, *De Erfprins van Oranje in Noord-Holland*, pp.66-70, 140-143.

for the most part barren region. After the battles of 10 and 19 September many prisoners of war and deserters became available. On 28 September the Hereditary Prince of Orange wrote to his mother: 'The Batavians are just waiting for the opportunity to cross over to our side. Desertion amongst them is very high, they arrive every day and that by droves'. Robert Fagel wrote to his brother on 30 September: 'There are now 3,000 Batavian deserters present, increasing with 20 to 30 men every day'.[34] On the 25th, the same day the Orangist officers had arrived, the Prince of Orange sent a letter to the Duke of York, outlining his plans and the aid he needed from the British. This letter and the reply of the Duke of York the next day, give a good insight in the opinions both had on these matters:

1. Among the marines and sailors who are on the island of Texel, I propose to choose those most suitable to bear arms and to be used on land and form an infantry battalion, an artillery company and a pioneer company, if found feasible.
   Reply: 'Fully approved'

2. The rest of the crew can hardly be employed for military purposes on land, and of which it is good to use them for a period of time aboard vessels first. Save the opportunity to use them effectively on land, they would be destined to equip these vessels that are on the Nieuwe Diep, and that with a little effort and in a short time would be able to make them seaworthy; Hector of 44, Heldin of 32, Valk of 26, Minerva of 26, Venus of 26, and Duifje of 18. The Count Rhoon believes that by talking to the crews, and giving them some benefits, they can be persuaded to embark, however they do not seem to be inclined so at the moment.
   Reply: 'I cannot decide on this matter without further instructions from the British government, for which it is necessary that I communicate with them at the first opportunity'

3. The marine battalion, and the artillery company that would occupy the islands of Vlieland and Terschelling, are still impossible to transport to there, given the absolute lack of transport ships. However there will not be a moment of time lost in occupying the islands as soon as it is feasible, also noting that the necessary artillery to maintain possession of these islands lacks entirely, so that the undersigned would like to pray Your Royal Highness in this matter to order the commander of artillery in Den Helder, to provide the necessary cannon, and if possible a couple of howitzers with ammunition in proportion to this object, to the disposal of General Bentinck.
   Reply: 'I will give the order without delay'

4. The undersigned has the honour to inform Your Royal Highness that we have started to move our troops from Den Helder to Wieringen. But as we are

---

34 Koolemans Beijnen, *De Erfprins van Oranje in Noord-Holland*, p.70.

having only few vessels to use for this purpose, it is not possible to perform this transfer promptly. As soon as possible however, we will put ashore most of the troops that are still on the ships, and orders were given to go to Medemblik, Enkhuizen and Hoorn to search for all vessels that are still required and bring them to Den Helder to use them to transport troops.
Reply: 'Fully approved'

5. The island of Wieringen is not as significant to be able to place all our troops, even after having deducted those intended to go to Vlieland and Terschelling, and the desire of undersigned would be to occupy the island of Texel as well from the moment it will be evacuated by the sailors; I also propose to send some troops to Schokland and Urk in the Zuiderzee, as the officers have arrived from England, enabling the troops to be organized.
Reply: 'Also approved'

6. The first intention of the British government, which was communicated by Mr. Grenville when the undersigned was in Lingen, was to form 3 Dutch infantry regiments. But as there are among the soldiers who have joined us, many artillerymen and *jager*, which can be more useful by using them the way in which they have been until now, I take the liberty to request the approval of Your Royal Highness if it would be better for their service to raise a few companies or a battalion of *jager*, also a few companies or artillery battalions, all calculated after the number of men of these two arms that are at our disposal, and train the rest as infantry battalions or regiments according to the number of men available. By this arrangement, maintenance costs of the Dutch troops corps will to be honest increased a little, but it will be in proportion to the value that would result in forming body of able *jager* and artillerymen. In case that Your Royal Highness approves this proposal, I will honour Him by submitting calculations of the training and maintenance costs of these troops and further requests permission to add a pioneer company, which in a country like this, and for our armies, could especially be a major benefit.
Reply: '*Jager* and artillery strike me as a great advantage; the formation of a pioneering company also seems necessary to me in this country. I shall be delighted to receive the calculation of training costs and maintenance of these troops'.

7. The weapons, swords, cartridges etc. which were captured from the Batavian army during the day of the 19th are of no use to the English army and could be perfectly well used by our troops. That is why I pray His Royal Highness to order that all these items are delivered to the General Bentinck to arm the Dutch soldiers; otherwise the mentioned general would need to search for these himself, even when they are here or nearby.

8. The body of troops that will be formed on the field, which can go up to about 3000 men, independent of the crews of six ships, as proposed above, it is still

desirable that the artillery commander in Den Helder be authorized to provide as many muskets that will be necessary to complete the arming of troops and artillery and ammunition required.'
Reply to 7. and 8.: 'I will give orders to Major-General Farrington, commander of the artillery, to collect and provide to and to deliver to General Bentinck the weapons, swords, pouches etc. which were taken from the enemy, and the same order will be given to the provision of the required ammunition, artillery and muskets'.

9. Finally, as the undersigned is in the process of employing officers and others which cannot be included in the organization of the corps, and for the salaries which there is therefore no money, such as adjutants, engineers, commissioners etc., I take the liberty to ask His Royal Highness to submit to him in time a list with a proposal for a salary grant them so that He can approve.
Reply: 'As soon as His Royal Highness send me the list of officers not included in the organization of the corps with the proposal of the salary to grant them, I will not fail Him to communicate the answers I have about it'.[35]

In return, also on the 25th, the Duke of York asked the Prince of Orange for as much men as possible to aid the British Captain Finlay at the work on the entrenchments of Den Helder. This request was passed on to *Colonel* Bentinck, who assigned *Capitein* van Meurs, *Lieutenant* van Tuyll van Serooskerken and *Lieutenant* Schummelketel to this task. However, it proved difficult to find quarters for these men, as Den Helder was already full of all sorts of personnel and wounded and the British quartermaster-general had only tents available. So it was fortunate that, because of the bad weather, instead of the needed 500 men initially only 100 could be fetched from Texel, later augmented by more. On 3 October *Colonel* Bentinck reported: 'On the island of Wieringen there are (including *jager* and artillerymen) already 1,115 men; in Helder for labour over 460 and another 200 on the ships'.[36] Lack of equipment was still a huge problem. Measures were taken to remedy this by the Dutch as well as by the British. On 1 October, the Duke of York appointed Lieutenant Colonel Sontag as British commissioner with the Dutch, to mediate in all requests regarding equipment and finances for the Dutch troops. Luckily, relief came when on 2 October a victorious battle was fought, which was hoped would be decisive for the campaign. The Franco-Batavian army retreated south and occupied a new defence line from Beverwijk to Purmerend. The greater part of North Holland was now occupied by the Anglo-Russian army, including a number of cities: Alkmaar, Medemblik, Enkhuizen and Hoorn.

---

35 Letter of the Prince of Orange to the Duke of York, 25 September 1799 in Koolemans Beijnen, *De Erfprins van Oranje in Noord-Holland*, pp.143-147.
36 Koolemans Beijnen, *De Erfprins van Oranje in Noord-Holland*, pp.71-73.

14

The Battle of Alkmaar, Egmont op Zee, or 2nd Battle of Bergen 2 October

The Anglo-Russian Battle Plan

After the battle of the 19th no offensive operations were possible for some days due to severe and incessant storms, with heavy rain, rendering the roads impassable and flooding the fields. Even more, for nearly two weeks York did nothing, although it must have been clear to him that time was in favour of the Franco-Batavians. In addition, because of the late season and the continuous bad weather it became more and more difficult for the British Royal Navy to supply the army. Many soldiers became unfit for battle by sickness and the lack of good shelter. At last, York decided to attack the Franco-Batavian positions again on 29 September, but although at daylight the troops were put in motion, due to very bad weather and the muddy terrain, as well as the high tide with heavy surf making the beach impassable, the troops were recalled. The attack had to be delayed until 1 October, the birthday of Tsar Paul. Then yet again the attack had to be delayed because of bad weather and the attack would finally take place on the 2nd.

Just as in the battle of the 19th, the attack was to be made in four columns.[1] Lieutenant General Abercromby commanded the First Column, on the right wing. It consisted of the 1st Guards Brigade, Moore's 4th and Cavan's 6th Brigades, and MacDonald's Advance Guard. The Advance Guard was reinforced with three hundred Russian *jégerski* and the rifle company of the 6/60th Foot, to fight the French skirmishers. MacDonald would initially lead the advance and, after driving off the French at Kamp, would have to move into the dunes, advance at the same level as Abercromby's main column on the beach and protect its flank. Total strength of Abercromby's command was about 7,900 infantry, 900 cavalry, foot artillery, and the British horse artillery. Abercromby had to advance along the North Sea beach to the village of Egmond aan Zee and from there to the village of Egmond op de Hoef, to turn the French flank and to cut off their retreat. Attached to Abercromby was naval aide-de-camp Captain Daniel, commanding a party of sailors with the task of:

---

1   See Appendix XV for the Anglo-Russian order of battle.

gaining information respecting the sluices; making observations on the tides, so as to enable a brigade to advance along the sands during the absence of the sea; directing a party of seamen in the erection and destruction of bridges as occasion required; removing wounded men from the field of battle; burying the slain; arming fishing-boats to cover the advance of the army along the coast, and others to carry despatches.[2]

Major General Essen commanded the Second Column. It was to consist of 8,000 Russians. The battalions were accompanied by their regimental guns.[3] The remaining Russian troops, the Fersen Musketeers (2 battalions, 1,094 men) and the Arbénev Musketeers (2 battalions except the grenadier companies, 908 men) which had suffered heavy loss during the battle of the 19th, remained behind to defend the Zijpe position in order not to leave this position defenceless as had happened during the battle of Bergen. The Advance Guard (Emmé) and the Brigade Arbénev had to follow the same road that Hermann had taken on the 19th; along the Slaperdijk in the direction of Schoorl and Bergen over Groet. Their left flank would be protected by the Brigade Gladkov which had to advance along a narrow footpath between the Zijper sluices and the Slaperdijk. The Brigade Sedmoratzki had to cover the left flank of these troops and had to advance from Zijpe Sluices along the Kanaal van Alkmaar. This brigade then had to attack the village Schoorldam from the west and to support the attack on Bergen. The Russian task was to pin down the enemy so that they could be cut off by Abercromby. Major General Knox was attached to this column as liaison.

Lieutenant General Dundas commanded the Third Column. It was to consist of the Burrard's 2nd Guards Brigade, Coote's 3rd and Chatham's 7th Brigades. Strength was 6,130 infantry, 158 light dragoons and 17 guns. This column was split in its separate brigades and each of them received separate orders. Coote's 3rd Brigade started from the village of Petten and had to follow Abercromby's Advance Guard, circumnavigate the village of Kamp through the dunes and clear the road to the village of Groet. In this way they first supported the Russians from the Second Column in their advance to Groet and then they had to protect their right flank. Chatham's 7th Brigade, together with the light dragoons, had to follow the Russian Brigade Sedmoratzki, starting also from the Zijpe Sluices, and then move to the right to join the left wing of Essen's Second Column and support him in the capture of Bergen. In addition this brigade had to maintain contact with Abercromby's troops. Burrard's 2nd Guards Brigade started from the villages of Tuitgenhorn and Krabbendam and had to advance along the north-east bank of the Kanaal van Alkmaar in the direction of Schoorldam. They had to attack Schoorldam from the east, simultaneously with Sedmoratzki's brigade. Seven gunboats on the Kanaal van Alkmaar would support this

---

2 John Marshall, *Royal Naval Biography; or, memoirs of the Services of all the Flag-Officers, Superannuated Rear-Admirals, Retired-Captains, Post-Captains, and Commanders, Whose Names appeared on the Admiralty List of Sea Officers at the commencement of the year 1823, or who have since been promoted* (London: Longman, Hurst, Rees, Orme, Brown, and Green, 1825), Vol.II, Part II, p.664.
3 Miliutin, *Geschichte des Krieges*, Vol.V, p.290. Strengths as on 24 September. It has proven impossible to find detailed information about the Russian artillery. Total strength of the artillery was as follows: Field Artillery; 425 men with eight 12pdr and eight 6pdr cannon, eight 24pdr unicorns: Regimental Artillery; 246 men with nine 6pdr and five 3pdr cannon, five 12pdr and five 8pdr unicorns.

Location of the French positions on the beach at Egmond aan Zee facing north. (Author photo)

attack, again commanded by Captain Popham.[4] Burrard also had to maintain contact with the Fourth Column.

Lieutenant General Pulteney commanded the Fourth Column. This column consisted of Don's 5th, Prince William's 8th, and Manners' 9th Brigades, to which 200 grenadiers of the Arbénev Musketeers were added to act as an advance guard. This was done by special request of York as he believed that the mere sight of the Russians would have a demoralising effect on the Franco-Batavians. Strength was 6,930 infantry and 250 light dragoons. Pulteney's orders were to cover the left flank of the Anglo-Russian army, to threaten Daendels' 1e Bataafsche Divisie positioned along the Langendijk, and to prevent in this way Daendels from reinforcing the left wing of the Franco-Batavian army. Pulteney was free to use his troops in any other way, if he believed the situation made it necessary or when he would see an opportunity.

The plan of attack shows that York had learned from his earlier mistakes. This time nearly all his available troops, 31,000 men, attacked concentrated on a small front, with both flanks effectively covered (on their right by the North Sea, on their left by the Kanaal van Alkmaar and Pulteney's column) and able to support each other. There were no detours which could weaken his strength. If Abercromby would fulfil his task well he would be able to cut off the retreat of the Franco-Batavians and destroy them. In this way, finally a decisive victory could be gained. The Russians were positioned in the allied centre so that they would be closely

---

4   Of these gunboats, three were armed with 18pdr and four with 24pdr cannon. These boats would fight for about ten hours and fired about a hundred rounds each. Three of the gunboats were sunk by enemy fire during the course of the battle, but only Lieutenant Rowed and two sailors were wounded.

supported by the British; they would have no reasons to complain about being abandoned. In addition however, this was done because of the British distrust of the Russians after their disorderly retreat during the previous battle. The infantry would also be supported by sufficient artillery this time. Because of the Franco-Batavian measures taken at Oud-Karspel and the Langendijk, which also had levelled the ring-dike around the Bleekmeer which had provided cover for Pulteney on the 19th, it was clear for York that it was impossible to attack this position with any hope of a positive result. Pulteney's only task was to keep Daendels busy without taking risk or suffering heavy loss and to protect the Anglo-Russian flank.

Nevertheless, to be victorious the Russians as well as Abercromby had to fulfil their assigned task, as pointed out by Major General Moore in his diary:

> The whole evidently depended upon the success of Sir Ralph Abercromby's column. The others, till such time as he had forced the enemy and turned their flank, were merely to keep them in play and prevent their detaching to reinforce their left. It was, however, very necessary for the Russian columns to advance pretty boldly towards Bergen in order to enable Sir Ralph to advance with safety.[5]

To make sure that the Russians would not make the same mistakes as on the 19th, Major General Essen also made his dispositions for the upcoming battle, with his own general orders including the following:

> The columns will attack the enemy with bravery, defeat him, knock him down and pursue him, wherever you will encounter them, putting him to flight. Wherever the terrain permits, the columns will deploy and attack in front, while backwards of the first line a strong reserve with artillery will be deployed, so that not all troops together will be sent into the fire and in case of any mishaps a regroup can take place. These reserves are not allowed to move from the spot. It is ordered not to fire without any purpose and the infantry is assigned to attack from their rearward position [*wird die Infanterie angewiesen von rückwärts anzugreifen*]. The artillery has to be used in front of the column or on the flanks, according to the situation of the terrain; one has to use the heights and to try to use the artillery from above. Nobody is allowed to leave his post. The officers are responsible for order and the battalion and column commanders will have to severely punish those, who are guilty in not complying with this, and register those who distinguish themselves for their deserved reward. During their march the columns have to keep direction to the right, which means that every column has to regulate its advance to that of the one to the right of it, so that they are able to support each other whenever necessary. The attack on posts, entrenchments, batteries etc. should be executed in such a way that the men are divided and used gradually, so that the whole force is not sent into the fire all together and making it possible to renew the attack time and again with fresh troops and increased force… The commanders of the columns will have to take care that the march will not be hasty, in order not to attack the enemy with

---

5   Maurice (ed.), *Diary of Sir John Moore*, Vol.I, p.353.

tired troops. When reaching woods or close bushes or such, one will move in front or to the side of it, so that this point can be cleared with canister first and when no *jégerski* are available sending single platoons to the right and left, which will dissolve and protect the flanks of their column… Every column will be followed by the necessary material to bridge the canals. All carpenters will have to march at the head of the columns and are commanded by a pioneer officer; the superfluous train soldiers will find themselves with the material for the crossings which follows every column. The entrenchment tools have to be brought to the assembly points, from there they will be loaded on wagons to follow the columns as well.[6]

The Battle

At 6:00 a.m., three signal shots were fired and at the third shot all columns started their advance. The column that advanced along the Zanddijk and the Slaperdijk was supported by artillery fire from the batteries in the Zijpe position on both sides of these dikes. The first to meet the full force of the Anglo-Russian attack was French *Général de Brigade* Simon commanding the French Advance Guard, consisting of the 54e Demi-Brigade (3 battalions), 3/60e Demi-Brigade, 16e Chasseurs à Cheval, and 4/4 Artillerie Légère. Abercromby began his attack with MacDonald's Advance Guard supported by some troopers of the 7th Light Dragoons leading the advance. MacDonald attacked the village of Kamp and easily succeeded in expelling the 3/60e Demi-Brigade deployed here which retreated skirmishing through the dunes in the direction of Schoorl. Abercromby's main column moved south along the beach as planned, with the infantry in column of companies from the right at half distance. The artillery was on the right, between the infantry and the sea, opposite the proper intervals in the infantry column. The cavalry was also on the right. To close the gap caused by the retreat of 3/60 Demi-Brigade, Gouvion reacted by ordering *Général de Brigade* Aubrée to send 3/48e Demi-Brigade and 2 battalions of the 49e Demi-Brigade into the dunes between the beach and Schoorl. After capturing Kamp, MacDonald apparently followed 3/60e Demi-Brigade and as such veering to the left instead of covering Abercromby's flank as planned. This would bring Abercromby's column into trouble as will be described later.

Coote's 3rd Brigade, which had followed the Advance Guard, turned left at Kamp and followed the road to the village Groet. Brushing aside the 1/54e Demi-Brigade they cleared the road for the Russians and captured Groet. The Russians had until that moment halted on the Slaperdijk firing at the French defences at Groet with their artillery. With Groet cleared they resumed their advance. Arriving at this village, however, Essen refused to advance any further until Coote with his brigade had occupied the dunes to the right of the road to Schoorl so as to effectively protect his flank. Despite of not having received orders to do so Coote complied, in co-operation with MacDonald, in order to get the Russians advancing again. Inside the dunes there were numerous engagements between British and French troops, as described by Private Surtees of the 56th Foot:

---

6   Miliutin, *Geschichte des Krieges*, Vol.V, pp.291-293.

High dunes along the beach at Egmond aan Zee facing north. (Author photo)

After the fight had fairly commenced, we kept but little order, owing partly to the want of discipline and experience in our people, and partly to the nature of the ground, which was rugged and uneven in the extreme, being one continued range of sand-hills, with hollows more or less deep between them; and partly it may be attributed to the ardour of our young men, who pressed on perhaps too rapidly. We continued to advance, and never once made a retrograde movement, the enemy regularly retiring from height to height on our approach; but they had greatly the advantage over us in point of shooting, their balls doing much more execution than ours; indeed it cannot be wondered at, for they were all riflemen, trained to fire with precision, and armed with a weapon which seldom fails its object if truly pointed; while we were (what shall I say) totally ignorant of that most essential part of a soldier's duty. They consequently suffered little from our fire; but we could not believe this, and tried to persuade ourselves they had either buried their dead in the sand before we came up to them or carried them off as they retreated; but experience has since taught me to know that we then must have done them little harm.[7]

---

7   Surtees, *Twenty-five years in the Rifle Brigade*, pp.16-17.

Meanwhile Sedmoratzki's Russian brigade and Burrard's 2nd Guards Brigade, with Chatham's 7th Brigade in reserve, had started to advance south along both sides of the Kanaal van Alkmaar, supported by Popham's gunboats. The first attack by Sedmoratzki on a French battery obstructing his advance failed. Popham closed in with his gunboats and a fierce cannonade followed, during which some of the gunboats were sunk by the French fire. With a second attack Sedmoratzki managed to take the battery. Burrard's 2nd Guards Brigade had advanced on the east side of the Kanaal van Alkmaar remaining in line with Sedmoratzki's, maintaining contact with Pulteney's Fourth Column during his advance by way of some infantry detachments.

Upon discovering the advance of Sedmoratzki's brigade and Essen's column, *Général de Brigade* Simon withdrew his outposts. He deployed his troops between the villages of Schoorl and Schoorldam at the Kanaal van Alkmaar on a prepared line with artillery in field works at strategic points, his left wing resting on the dunes and his right wing protected by the canal. In front of Schoorl he deployed his grenadiers in skirmishing order. The village itself was occupied by the 3/60e Demi-Brigade with the 16e Chasseurs à Cheval in the rear. The horse artillery deployed on both sides of the village. Further to the east on the terrain between Schoorl and the canal the three battalions of the 54e Demi-Brigade deployed. On the other side of the canal, the Batavians blocked Burrard's advance in a formidable position at Schoorldam, their left flank protected by the canal, their right by the inundated terrain. This position was defended by units of the 2e Bataafsche Divisie (commanded by *Generaal-Major* Bonhomme, Dumonceau having still not recovered from his wounds). Vandamme ordered *Général de Brigade* Barbou, aided by *Adjudant-Général* Maison to reinforce Simon's Advance Guard with two battalions of the 42e Demi-Brigade and the 1/8e Artillerie Légère; to cover its retreat in the direction of Bergen when necessary. It would take these troops some time to get in position though.

According to Gachot, Major General Burrard in the meanwhile had decided not to attack the formable Batavian position at Schoorldam frontally but to cross the Kanaal van Alkmaar instead, joining Sedmoratzki's Russians. His guards charged the French positions on this side of the canal. The French artillery opened fire with canister on the advancing guardsmen of Burrard's Guards Brigade at 300 metres, inflicting heavy loss and stopping them short. A second discharge forced them back, the guards veering to their left somewhat out of range, waiting for a chance to resume their advance with more chance of success.[8] Their place was immediately taken by Semoratzki's Russians but their attack also failed. On their right, opposite Schoorl, the space was filled with Essen's arriving Russians, deploying into line, but then Essen was reluctant to advance any further, demanding that the dunes on his right flank had to be cleared from the enemy first. Fulfilling this task, Coote still managed to make progress although he was slowed down by the difficult terrain, the dunes covered with brushwood and trees. Nevertheless, after a while he was already advancing west of Schoorl, but still Essen did not stir.

---

8   Gachot, *Brune en Hollande*, p.278. Gachot's account is doubtful and cannot be confirmed by other sources. The official return of British losses gives no losses for Burrard's 2nd Guards Brigade, which in itself is also doubtful though.

THE BATTLE OF ALKMAAR, EGMONT OP ZEE 277

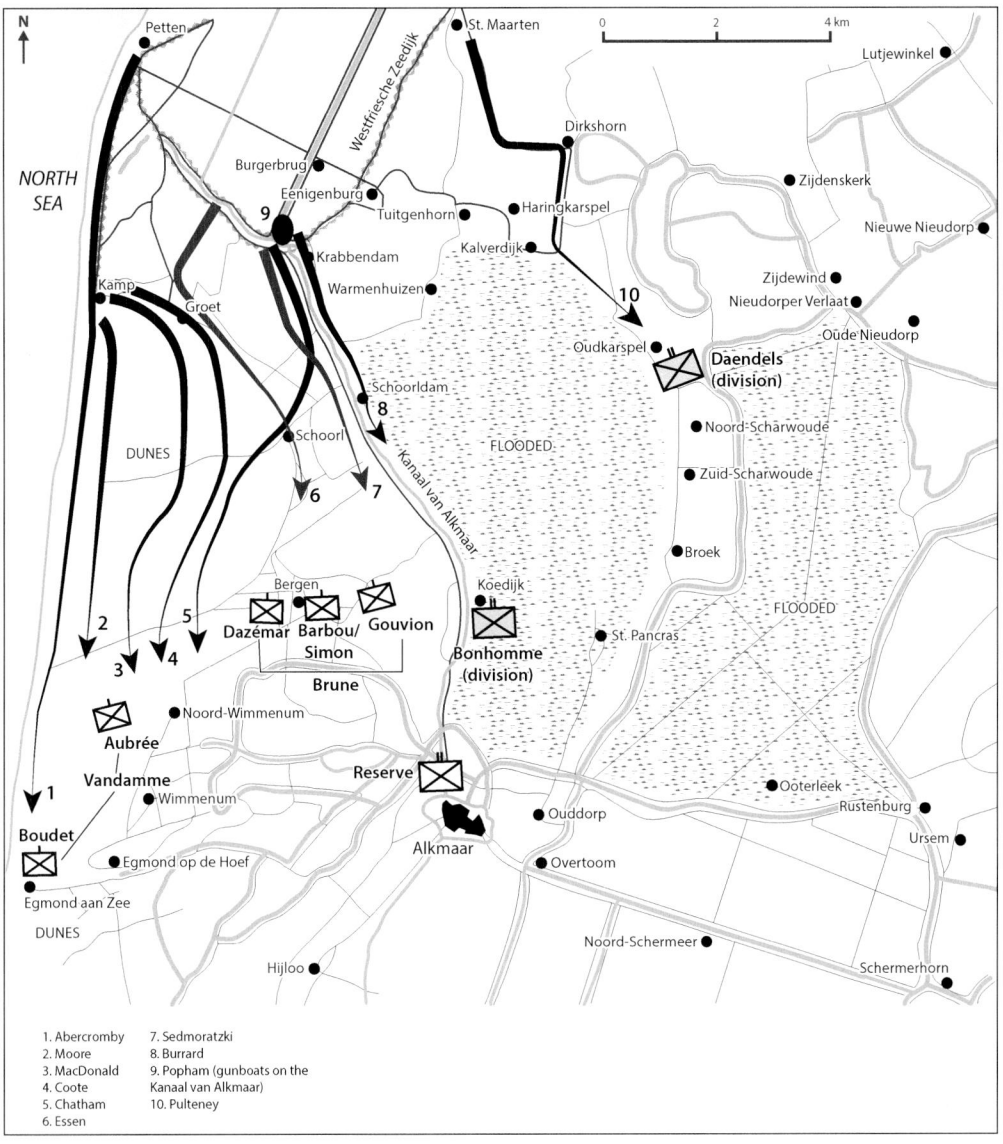

1. Abercromby
2. Moore
3. MacDonald
4. Coote
5. Chatham
6. Essen
7. Sedmoratzki
8. Burrard
9. Popham (gunboats on the Kanaal van Alkmaar)
10. Pulteney

Map 8 The Battle of Alkmaar.

Major General Sedmoratzki showed much more energy then Essen and was still trying to advance west of the Kanaal van Alkmaar, but because of the terrain, intersected by many ditches, his progress was hampered as well, as Surtees relates:

> Soon after this, there were some tremendous volleys of musketry heard on our left, apparently down in the plain below us. I, with one or two others, now inclined a little towards the left, in order to have a peep at the troops there, so hotly opposed to each other, in doing which, we still kept our line in front of the enemy's skirmishers. We found it was the Russian army endeavouring to force their way towards the village of Bergen, the scene of their former disaster; but they were most distressingly retarded by the innumerable canals or ditches, by which the country was so intersected, and which were generally impassable by fording. On some occasions I could perceive, when they had found an entrance into an enclosure, and had fought their way to the farther side of it, they were obliged to retrace their steps, and get out by the same way by which they had entered, the enemy all this while pouring into them a close and destructive fire. This appeared to me to be most trying to their patience, and very disheartening; but they bore it with great steadiness.[9]

Because of the intersected terrain the Russian artillery could hardly advance and was of no use to the Russians. At around 11:00 a.m., having undertaken several attacks and supported by Chatham's brigade, Sedmoratzki finally succeeded in dislodging the French from their position in front of him, the greater part of the 54e Demi-Brigade opposing him, led by *Chef de Brigade* Varé, falling back across the bridge over the Kanaal van Alkmaar at Schoorldam joining the Batavian defenders at Schoorldam. Their retreat forced Simon to fall back at Schoorl as well. Retreating by echelons into the shelter of the wooded area south of Schoorl, the village was set on fire to cover their retreat. Their retreat coincided with the arrival of *Général de Brigade* Barbou. To cover the French retreat, Barbou occupied with the 42 Demi-Brigade two farmsteads from which they were only dislodged at about 12:30 p.m., after having repulsed five successive Russian assaults. *Adjudant-Général* Maison was severely wounded during the intensive fighting. Covered by the 3/60e Demi-Brigade, Barbou finally retreated, taking direction to the dunes just west of Bergen.

Burrard had in the meantime returned to the east side of the Kanaal van Alkmaar. Apparently he was in no hurry to return to the fire again, as his advance was slow, his guardsmen passing slowly the numerous ditches and canals. Around noon he arrived close to Schoorldam, when at that same moment Gouvion recalled Varé with his 54e Demi-Brigade to Bergen while the Batavians left Schoorldam and retreated to an even more formidable position at Koedijk to remain in line with the French army. Without fighting, Burrard's guards captured Schoorldam and the bridge there. Leaving Schoorldam to Sedmoratzki's Russians, Burrard did not advance any further but placed himself to the right of Pulteney's column, not taking any further part in the battle.

The Russian main column at Schoorl advanced somewhat further south but then Essen again halted his troops. Apparently he had no stomach for attacking the now completely

---

9   Surtees, *Twenty-five years in the Rifle Brigade*, p.18.

fortified village of Bergen again and he limited his actions for the remainder of the day to cannonading of the Franco-Batavian positions around Bergen and at Koedijk on the other side of the Kanaal van Alkmaar. On the other hand, he believed he had fulfilled his task for the day; to pin down the enemy so that they could be cut off by Abercromby. This gave the French the time to redeploy their troops behind their prepared defences. They formed a new defensive line from Koedijk across the fields to Bergen, the village reinforced with artillery in field works covering all approaches and the roads blocked by abatis. From Bergen on the defence line continued to a dominating position in the dunes to the coast, and from there through the dunes to the North Sea beach. In person Brune, accompanied by Rostollant, resumed command of all French troops around Bergen while Vandamme commanded all troops on the beach and in the dunes. As on 19 September, Brune again decided to abandon the usual organisation and instead his generals received command of a sector to defend, with the necessary troops assigned. The French defence line was as follows:

- *Général de Division* Gouvion defended two redoubts east of Bergen with 3/48e and 3/60e Demi-Brigades and four 8pdr cannon;
- *Généraux de Brigade* Barbou and Simon defended the fortifications at Bergen with two battalions of the 42e Demi-Brigade, 54e Demi-Brigade (3 battalions) and five guns;
- West of Bergen, at the foot of the dunes a 'Grand Battery' of fourteen guns was deployed at a strategic point with excellent field of fire;
- *Adjudant-Général* Dazémar defended the sector between Bergen and the dunes with a battalion of the 42e Demi-Brigade and 49e Demi-Brigade (2 battalions);
- *Général de Brigade* Aubrée defended the dunes between Bergen and the North Sea beach with the 90e Demi-Brigade (3 battalions) and a battalion of the 49e Demi-Brigade;
- *Général de Division* Boudet , who had just arrived with the army, defended the beach with the 72e Demi-Brigade (two battalions) which had come up from Alkmaar. *Général de Brigade* Saint-Martin, commander in chief of artillery, was ordered to send additional artillery from the artillery park to support Boudet but it would take some time to arrive.

A substantial part of the French army was held in reserve around Alkmaar. The artillery park was also south of Alkmaar. The dragoons of the 10e Dragons were used to supply the infantry with ammunition as the expenditure was high and the caissons had difficulties reaching the troops through the loose sand.

The dunes on this part of the coast were about 100 metres high. At the east side they were very steep and planted with very thick brushwood, on the sea-side the slopes were much shallower. York believed that a decision could not be reached before the French were dislodged from the dunes. To achieve this Coote was ordered to continue his advance south through the left part of the dunes. Coote immediately advanced with the 85th Foot in front on his right wing which was hotly engaged. Because of the extent of the dunes, the regiments became separated by great intervals. Major General the Earl of Chatham was ordered to march along the rear of the stationary Russians to support Coote with his 7th Brigade. Arriving there, he advanced with the single battalion of the 31st Foot on Coote's left wing along the edge of the dunes, while the three battalions of the 4th Foot came in line with the 85th Foot on Coote's right wing. Coote's 29th Foot was ordered to dislodge a French force

"French infantry defending a farm", by Dirk Langendijk. (Noord-Hollands Archief, NL-HlmNHA_480_000636_K)

that had deployed on a high dune near Bergen. Supported by the light companies of the 2nd (Queen's) and 27th Foot they charged, driving the enemy back into thick brushwood at the foot of the dune.[10] Now the whole British line advanced, the three battalions of the 4th in line with the 85th in front and connected with the remainder of Coote's battalions in oblique formation. In this way they succeeded in dispelling the French from the dominating part of the dunes west of Bergen and to drive them back to the environs of Noord-Wimmenum, cutting off direct communications between the French troops around Bergen and those around the beach. Surtees again provides an eyewitness account:

> Meantime, our own heavy troops were advancing on the right by the sea-beach, where was a plain of sand, of perhaps from 100 to 200 yards in breadth; the sandhills between the two wings, as I said before, being swept by us, assisted by a small corps of Russian riflemen. We moved on till we got a little in advance of the Russian army, (which, from the obstacles they had to contend with, did not make very rapid progress,) and immediately over the village of Bergen, which stood on the plain, close under the sand hills. Here, the enemy being in possession of considerable field-works, plied us pretty plenteously with shells from their howitzers, (their guns

---

10 Everard, *29th (Worcestershire) Foot*, p.240.

Dunes north of Egmond aan Zee. (Author photo)

they could not elevate sufficiently to reach us,) but from which we suffered very little; for our people being much extended, and the sand being deep, the bursting of the shells was attended with very little mischief.[11]

The moment was there to undertake an attack on Bergen, but Major General Essen again refused to comply with York's orders, still following his original orders to the letter by pinning down the enemy while Abercromby turned their flank. Both brigades under Lieutenant General Dundas (Coote's 3rd and Chatham's 7th) were too weak to undertake this attack on their own and to occupy the dunes at the same time. In addition they lacked the necessary artillery, which was unable to follow the infantry into the dunes. Therefore the British had no choice other than to remain in the dunes and maintain their previous position. The refusal of Essen to attack is not mentioned in York's after action report, probably for political reasons and because the Russian was, after all, complying with his original orders. There is no doubt of this fact though, Essen's refusal being mentioned in various contemporary sources.

Brune, who already had made good use of the Russian hesitation by arranging his troops in its defensive line, was able to shift some infantry to the left and around 4:00 p.m. ordered

---

11 Surtees, *Twenty-five years in the Rifle Brigade*, pp.18-19.

to charge the British in the dunes with two columns in an effort to throw them back and to restore communications. One column, consisting of two battalions of the 42e Demi-Brigade led by *Général de Brigade* Simon, charged the 85th Foot with the bayonet; the other one, consisting of the 54e Demi-Brigade led by *Général de Brigade* Barbou and supported by two squadrons of *chasseurs à cheval*, charged the 27th Foot. Three companies of the 27th counterattacked while at the same moment Major General MacDonald arrived on the right flank of the attacking French and, seeing the time was right, attacked the French in their flank. Supported by the 29th Foot he succeeded in throwing the French out of the dunes into the open terrain south of Bergen. Upon observing the counter charge of the 27th, it is said that Chatham exclaimed: 'Twenty-seventh, you have done more than my whole brigade!'[12] During this advance, MacDonald's battalions advanced too far and came into trouble:

> During the general advance, which took place shortly before this, the reserve, which had moved forwards too rapidly, found themselves far in advance of the corps on their right and left; and as a formidable column of French appeared right in their front, Colonel Macdonald deemed it prudent to fall back a little. He therefore directed the 55th to cover the retirement of the other three battalions, which they succeeded in doing, and were themselves filing off to the rear when the enemy advanced, covered with a cloud of skirmishers. A party of these, we are told, succeeded in getting to within thirty or forty yards of the regiment, and annoyed it very much with their fire; and to disperse them, Major Lumsden, the commanding officer of the 55th, ordered one of the companies to form up and drive them off with the bayonet, which they soon did, but the gallant Major fell shot through the heart before this was accomplished. Sir Ralph, not having yet cleared the French from his immediate front, Colonel Macdonald, with the 23rd and 55th Regiments, was now sent to his assistance.[13]

So MacDonald left the grenadiers and light infantry battalions in line with those already present, the British now having eleven battalions deployed in line. Opposing this formidable force the French were not able to undertake another effort to dislodge them from the dunes but they still held on to Bergen. With the 23rd Royal Welsh Fusiliers and the 55th Foot, MacDonald advanced to the southwest to fulfil his task of protecting the left flank of Abercromby's troops advancing along the beach, but it would take considerable time for him to arrive, leaving Abercromby exposed. In the meantime, Abercromby had advanced along the beach with Moore's brigade in front and was already past Bergen. The French had dispersed skirmishers in the dunes which kept up a constant fire on the advancing British. Especially the 25th Foot suffered heavily, many of the officers shot down by the French skirmishers. Abercromby himself had two horses killed under him. The French 90e Demi-Brigade (three raw battalions) and a battalion of the 49e Demi-Brigade, under the command of the *Généraux* Boudet and Fuzier, tried to block the British advance, but heavily

---

12 Anon., *The Campaign in Holland, 1799*, p.48.
13 George Noakes, *A Historical Account of the Services of the 34th & 55th Regiments, the linked Line Battalions in the 2nd or Cumberland & Westmorland Sub-District Brigade, from the Periods of their Formation until the Present Time* (Carlisle: C. Thurnam and Sons, 1875), pp.47-48.

outnumbered they had to give way in disorder. They also received gunfire from British warships on the North Sea which, although not very effective, was nerve-wracking for the French soldiers. *Général de Brigade* Aubrée restored order again, restocked with cartridges and together with the battalion of the 49e Demi-Brigade, the French soldiers went forward again. The absence of MacDonald's brigade, which should have covered the left flank, had serious consequences and compelled Abercromby to send Moore with the 25th Foot and the 79th Highlanders into the dunes to drive off the French skirmishers. Soon Moore had to fight his way through the dunes, dislodging the French from several positions, as these retreated when Moore's infantry advanced, opposing them when the terrain was favourable:

> As we continued to advance, the sand-hills increased in breadth, which required additional troops to fill up the line of communication across them; we who remained upon the beach, saw nothing that was doing in the interior of the sand-hills, and as the firing there was only musketry, the roar of the sea upon the beach prevented us from hearing it, except when it was close to us. We had frequent and long pauses, waiting for the movements of others. There was a great deal of bloodshed in the interior of the sand-hills, by the continued skirmishing, and detached attacks upon particular points. These sand-hills were admirably adapted for this mode of warfare; the enemy would have been much more easily driven out of trenches; for the sand-hills were the same as a succession of trenches, so that when the enemy saw our troops advancing, they continued to fire upon us until they saw that we were just near enough to allow them time safely to retire to the next range of hills.[14]

The British suffered serious losses during this confused fighting, Moore received a shot through the thigh but remained in command: as it would turn out, for two more hours. The 1st (Royal) and 49th Foot were ordered to enter the dunes as well to reinforce both battalions there, Lieutenant Colonel Brock commanding the 49th relating:

> It is impossible to give you an adequate idea of the nature of the ground, which I can only compare to the sea in a storm. On my getting to the left of the 79th, I found that its flank was already turned, and that the ground which we were to occupy did not afford the least shelter: my determination was instantly taken. I had gone on horseback to view the ground, and on my return to the regiment, which I met advancing, I found the left actually engaged with the enemy, who had advanced much beyond our left. I, however, continued advancing with six companies, and left Colonel Sheaffe with the other four to cover our left: the instant I came up to the 79th, I ordered a charge, which I assure you was executed with the utmost gallantry, though not in the greatest order, as the nature of the ground admitted of none. The enemy, however, gave way on every side, and our loss would have been very trifling had the 79th charged straightforward; but unfortunately it followed the course the 49th had taken, thereby leaving our right entirely exposed. I detached Lord Aylmer

---

14 Anon., *Narrative of a Private Soldier*, p.44.

with the grenadiers, who, after charging different times, totally cleared our right. The 25th then advanced, and behaved with the greatest good conduct.[15]

Later also three companies of the 92nd Highlanders were sent into the dunes, followed by the Guards Grenadier Battalion. A description of the terrain and the difficulties met by the British troops fighting here are accurately described by one of the participants in this battle:

> The Army, having been put in order after the affair I have alluded to, and the weather having "looked up" for a few hours, was put in movement very early on the 2nd of October, and the heads of the columns on the right where the principal attack was made, were in front of the sand-hills of Camperdown, with the sea-dyke of Petten on their right, about day-break in the morning: and the advance immediately took place, and the Cavalry and Artillery keeping along the beach on the right, the tide having sufficiently ebbed for that purpose. This sandy district, which extends from the north, gradually widens in approaching Bergen, and may be about from three to four miles in breadth, again tapering off towards Egmont-op-Zee, and is, in longitudinal extent, about ten miles, the whole of it formed by sand blown up on the land in high westerly gales. We have nothing in England to compare to this tract… And as far as external appearance goes, these sands may assimilate to the comparison, with this difference, that they are constantly changing their forms: in some places the wreaths of sand assumed the shape of the sloping side of a huge billow, ending in a long fringe-like ridge, overhanging on the other side a descent as perpendicular as the nature of sand would admit; in other places were to be found small heaps, like inverted cones, placed apparently in regular rows, while in occasional spots would be found small level plains of sand surrounded on all sides by these many-shaped hillocks. The line of hills as it sloped towards the level country was partly covered with long slips of scrubby wood or coppice; affording shelter for such troops as the enemy might please to keep in concealment. Through all this region it was impracticable to bring up Artillery, even the Hussar horses of the French that were opposed to us were frequently up to their shoulders in the loose sand, and the difficulty of even moving infantry in any shape was very great. Taking into consideration the want of cohesion amongst our new levies, this was perhaps an advantage, as they blundered along as well as the more disciplined regiments on their right, but the movements were little better than those of a mob. The only chance of getting these heroes into any shape was to promise them a charge, when they would scramble up the sand-hills more like the rush of a flock of sheep than a charge of infantry, and we were perfectly surprised to see the French give way to such a scrambling attack. However, fortunately they were not much better than ourselves in the way of discipline, being from the last levy of the conscription and not half drilled. We could see, during the day, the Officers plying the men with canteens of gin, and three parts of their wounded, and the prisoners we took, were drunk.[16]

---

15 Letter of 26 November 1799 from Lieutenant Colonel Brock to his brother in Ferdinand Brock Tupper, *The Life and Correspondence of Major-General Sir Isaac Brock* (London: Simpkin, Marshall & Co., 1847), pp.12-13.
16 Anon., 'Recollections of the British army', pp.186-187.

On the beach Abercromby's column continued to move forward according to the progress Moore made in the dunes. But this turned out to be slow, as Moore's advance was much hampered by the French resistance – as illustrated – and it took hours before Abercromby was within a few kilometres of Egmond-Aan-Zee, were he observed a fresh French corps advancing fast. The French were of course aware of the danger of Abercromby's advance. *Général de Division* Vandamme received reinforcements, including some Batavian troops; Bonhomme had to send three infantry battalions, the Regiment Huzaren and the 1e Compagnie Rijdende Artillerie. Two of these battalions, commanded by Colonel Bruce, moved into the dunes to reinforce the French who, fighting here already for a long time, were running low on cartridges. Daendels also had to send troops; two infantry battalions, the Regiment Dragonders and part of the 2e Compagnie Rijdende Artillerie; clearly Brune did not underestimate the consequences of a British advance along the beach. However, because of the distance the Batavian reinforcements had to cover most of them arrived too late. Only four cannon of the 1e Compagnie Rijdende Artillerie and the Regiment Huzaren, which received the order to reinforce Vandamme at 5:00 p.m., took part in the battle.

Vandamme took up a strong position in front of the village Egmond aan Zee: The infantry, consisting of a battalion of the 49e Demi-Brigade, the 72e Demi-Brigade (2 battalions) and the 90e Demi-Brigade (3 battalions) were deployed in the dunes. The artillery, including the four Batavian cannon, was deployed across the beach, behind a barricade of two fishing boats loaded with sand across the beach covered by the cavalry:

> The [Batavian] horse artillery under orders of *Capitein* Cordes, is above all praise. There is no braver artillery. At all opportunities it has proved his ability, especially on 2 October at Egmond aan Zee, the gunners manoeuvring up to their knees in the sea, throwing out a withering fire. I dare to say that the company on this day was of great service to the French column.[17]

In this position Vandamme waited for the arrival of the British. Coming into range the British were welcomed by heavy artillery fire and musketry from the dunes and again the British advance stopped:

> Towards the afternoon we drew near a place called Egmont, a small fishing town among the sand-hills, near to where the battle of Camperdown was fought. Here the enemy had drawn a number of fishing sloops and schuyts upon the beach, in two lines, leaving intervals between them, for their troops to pass. These formed a cover to their columns from our shot, and concealed their cavalry from our view. During the action they had received a reinforcement which they pushed along the sand-hills close to the beach. The line across these, owing to their increased breadth, now occupied all the regiments of our division but ourselves. The enemy began to press hard upon the troops that were near us, and so posted themselves as to annoy us who were standing upon the beach; we were a considerable time exposed to this,

---

17 Report of 1 November 1799 from *Lieutenant-Generaal* Dumonceau to the Batavian Minister of War in J.W. van Sypesteijn, *Geschiedenis van het Regiment Hollandsche Hussaren* ('s Gravenhage & Amsterdam: Gebroeders van Cleef, 1849), p.34.

and had a number both of officers and men wounded, amongst which was Lord Huntly, our Colonel, and a son of Sir Ralph Abercrombie, who was at that time an ensign in the regiment.[18]

Moore had his horse killed under him and finally had to hand over command after being hit again the moment his troops were pressed hard, as he describes the events in the dunes in his diary:

> My brigade, as a consequence of five hours' constant movement and action in so broken a country, were dispersed and infinitely fatigued, and from the absence of some of the regiments which had not been able to keep up on the left, the enemy had struck upon the flank of the 25th Regiment, which was the most forward. The fire was extremely galling. Three companies of the 92nd Regiment were sent to their support; but, coming incautiously into so hot a fire, they suffered prodigiously, and the whole began to give way. I sent my aide-de-camp, Captain Anderson, for the rest of the 92nd, which, though belonging to my brigade, had till then continued with the column upon the beach; but, before they could come up, in spite of every effort to oppose them, the enemy advanced briskly, and my men were forced back. I saw myself on the point of being surrounded, when, turning round to get back, I was knocked down by a shot, which entered behind my ear and came out at my cheek under my left eye. Just before I received this shot I saw the impossibility of rallying or stopping my men under such hot fire. They were falling in numbers in every direction, and I had given up the point, and had just determined in my own mind to let them go a certain distance to the rear and then to rally and bring them back. I was much stunned by the shot, and thinking my wound mortal, I made no effort to rise. A soldier, however, raised me and assisted me in getting off. Being unequal to further exertion I was led to the rear, where my wounds were dressed; after which I was put upon my horse, and, my groom leading him, I was conveyed back to my quarters in the Ragge Wey... Before I left the field I had the satisfaction of learning that, when the 92nd were brought up, those who had been retiring returned to the charge, attacked the enemy with great spirit, and repulsed them with slaughter, but not without great loss on our part. The killed and wounded of my brigade amounted to 44 officers and something more than 600 non-commissioned officers and men.[19]

As a result of his injuries Moore was shipped back to Great Britain, on the same frigate *Amethyst* that had brought York to Holland. For him the campaign would be over. Not so for Abercromby and his column, who were still fighting hard. The remaining companies of 92nd Regiment of Foot were ordered to push back the French from the dunes along the beach:

---

18   Anon., *Narrative of a Private Soldier*, p.45.
19   Maurice (ed.), *Diary of Sir John Moore*, Vol.I, pp.355-356.

> The remaining six companies were then ordered to form in three divisions, and march forward along the beach, and then to wheel to our left, and charge the enemy. I was in the front division. We marched forward, and passed a number of the enemy's troops, and came to a place where there was a more than ordinary opening, and the sand rose pretty high, in the form of a semicircle; into this opening we wheeled, and were instantly exposed to a fire upon both our flanks and front. This staggered us, and we began to fire upon the enemy, in place of pushing instantly forward to that part of the height that was on our right, driving the enemy from it, and taking up a position there; from which we could have done them more harm, and not have been so much exposed ourselves. We continued to stand still and fire for a few seconds, and then began to move forward, firing as we advanced; the other two divisions had wheeled into various openings in the sand hills in our rear, at the same time that we did. They were strongly opposed by the enemy, who were very superior in number; but hearing the firing of our division in their rear, the enemy who opposed them began to retreat into the interior of the sand-hills; those who opposed us did the same, and we continued to pursue them; but the action soon became on both sides quite irregular; for the sand hills separated us into parties, so that the one party frequently did not see what the other was doing, and, in some instances, parties of our troops came suddenly upon parties of the enemy… For three quarters of an hour we maintained a furious action, and drove the enemy to a considerable distance; but so many had been killed, and wounded, and scattered, that the officers could no longer collect any great number into one body. We then began to retreat: the enemy turned upon us, and we lost a number of men by their fire during the retreat. Our previous advance had exhausted our bodily strength, and we were much in want of water. I was very thirsty, and began to grow very weak.[20]

The British suffered heavy losses but despite that and heavy fighting that lasted until dark, the British 6th Brigade commanded by Major General Hely-Hutchinson managed to force back the French on the village of Egmond aan Zee. During this intense fighting, *Chef de Brigade* Mercier of the 72e Demi-Brigade was mortally wounded while leading a counterattack. However, the battle was not over yet. Vandamme made use of the falling darkness to surprise the British with an attack of two squadrons of 16e Chasseurs à Cheval. Their charge succeeded and the gunners of the British horse artillery were forced to abandon their guns which were taken. The 15th Light Dragoons, led by Colonel Paget, counterattacked and retook the lost guns, as recorded by one of the watching infantry:

> During the time that we were engaged in the interior of the sand-hills, the enemy, seeing no infantry on the beach to protect our guns, sent out his cavalry, from their cover at Egmont, to seize them. Our cavalry had gone into the chasm of the sand-hills, that were next the beach, a little in the rear, to shelter themselves from the fire of the enemy's cannon. They formed upon the beach, and sprung forward to

---

20 Anon., *Narrative of a Private Soldier*, pp.46-47.

meet the enemy, who had, by this time, reached the guns. They charged the enemy briskly, and drove them back with considerable loss, and pursued them close to Egmont.[21]

Another account describes this feat of arms in more detail:

> It was at this time that the Chestnut Troop received its baptism of fire. By some oversight on the part of the General, or possibly owing to ignorance as to the powers of this new weapon Horse Artillery, Major Judgson's Troop had been advanced to a dangerous distance, and left with an inadequate escort. General Vandamme observed this, and, placing himself at the head of his Cavalry, swept down upon the guns. The scene which followed was an exciting one. Taken by surprise, the gunners did not lose their presence of mind, but fired into the advancing cavalry until they were in their midst; and then, with any weapons they could lay hands on, they struggled with the troopers, who, in immense numbers, surrounded them, and sabred them at their guns. According to one account, only two of the guns were carried off by the cavalry when they retired; according to another, the whole were captured. Be it as it may, the prize was not left long undisputed, for Lord Paget, placing himself at the head of the 15th Light Dragoons now the 15th (King's) Hussars charged the enemy's cavalry, pursuing them for over a mile; and, assisted by the explosion of one of the captive limbers, succeeded in recovering all the guns.[22]

In their turn the British cavalry was attacked by the Batavian Regiment Huzaren which, commanded by *Colonel* Quaita and supported by the musketry from the dunes, halted the attack of the light dragoons and drove them back. Despite the fading light fighting raged on, with heated exchanges of musketry in the dunes. Lieutenant Colborne of the 20th Foot recollected:

> At that time we had so little baggage, and there was so much difficulty in getting things, that we all wore our large cloaks strapped on to us. I had mine slung across my shoulders. I was standing with an old Scotch officer, a friend of mine, Captain Walker of the 20th, as the enemy were firing from a hill opposite to us, when a shot hit me, at least on the cloak, and when I took it off I found it had gone through and through every fold. Captain Walker said, 'Ah! I see they are determined to have you yet.' Captain Powlett, of the 20th, received a wound in his head, and putting up his hand, exclaimed, 'I'm done for!' on which I took the command of the [light] company. At this battle a militia officer named Musket, a very fierce-looking man, his face covered with black whiskers, &c., took fright almost at the first shot, set spurs to his horse, galloped for his life to the Helder, embarked for England, and was never afterwards heard of. Innumerable were the jokes and epigrams made in

---

21 Anon., *Narrative of a Private Soldier*, p.48.
22 Duncan, *History of the Royal Regiment of Artillery*, Vol.II, p.100.

the army on this occasion. Colonel Mac-Donald declared that the captain of the ship, seeing an officer arrive at full gallop, thought he was the bearer of despatches, and sent a boat off for him.[23]

Abercromby was not able to advance any further because of the darkness and against an enemy of unknown strength. In addition his flank was not secure and the reports he received did not confirm that the Russians had been successful on his left. Abercromby decided to remain where he was, taking measures to secure his position against a French attack. As a result his men spent an uneasy night at the edge of the dunes, suffering from the cold.

The Fourth Column, commanded by Lieutenant General Pulteney, had made three successive attacks on the Batavian redoubt in front of the village of Oudkarspel. Not surprisingly the British did not make any impression on Daendels, who had entrenched his troops very strongly, and understandably this time they did not make the same mistake as in the previous battle to try to counterattack. Pulteney kept the Batavians under fire, but this did not prevent Daendels from sending two infantry battalions, the Regiment Dragonders and part of the 2e Compagnie Rijdende Artillerie to reinforce the Franco-Batavians left wing as described. This left him with three infantry battalions and a *jager* battalion, more than enough to defend this position. At this stage it became too dark to fight. The Russians retreated somewhat and took up positions between Schoorldam and Schoorl.

A restless night followed with both sides remaining under arms. The British held the positions they ended up in when darkness fell, which meant that especially the British troops in the dunes and on the beach suffered from thirst: having fought for hours, biting off the top of the salty cartridges, their water bottles were already empty around noon and there was no water to be found to refill them. Eating their rations of salt meat did not help either. Some relief came when during the night a heavy shower of rain came down:

> In the early part of the day, the weather had been quite warm and, with the exercise, occasioned the men to have frequent recourse to their canteens, which were emptied before the middle of the day. There was hardly a moment for them to snatch a mouthful of food from their haversacks, and that being salt, added much to the sensation of thirst, which in the evening became extremely painful, the country we were in being as arid as an African desert. When halted for the night, the men tried to dig wells in the sand, and in one or two places succeeded in getting a few drops; but the rush was so great as to endanger some of their lives, without procuring the relief desired ; and we were obliged to lie down in all the agony of extreme thirst. We had not, however, been long in a recumbent position, when the rain began to descend in torrents; a visit of this kind, after such a day of fatigue, would have been regarded, under other circumstances, as a matter of small comfort, it was now looked on as a blessing; many lay with their mouths open to catch some drops of the descending shower, and when their clothes and blankets became saturated with the wet, they were wrung out into their hats and the water was drunk with avidity.[24]

---

23 Moore Smith, *Life of John Colborne*, pp.18-19.
24 Anon., 'Recollections of the British Army', pp.187-188.

The French artillery at Egmond aan Zee kept firing at the British during most of the night. Now and then fighting flared up, especially in the wooded terrain west of Bergen where French troops and the flank companies of Coote's 3rd Brigade frequently clashed. Finally at 11:00 p.m. firing ceased.

On the French side Vandamme believed his position to be untenable. The British could easily outflank him now that they controlled the dunes. Therefore, before dawn, Vandamme retreated: according to some sources, without permission by Brune.[25]

Aftermath

Again a bloody battle had been fought, with heavy losses on both sides. This time the French lost more than the Batavians as the main Anglo-Russian thrust was directed at the French positions at Bergen, the dunes, and the beach. Ascertaining Franco-Batavian loss for this battle is difficult as there are no official French returns known, nor from Bonhomme's 2e Bataafsche Divisie. Daendels stated that he lost only 15 wounded at the redoubt in Haringkarspel, not including the troops send to reinforce the French. According to Gachot, the French lost 1,069 men, the 1e Bataafsche Divisie 93 men and the 2e Bataafsche Divisie 470 men and seven guns.[26] *Adjudant-Général* Maison was wounded, as was *Chef de Brigade* Mercier of the 72e Demi-Brigade whose legs were pierced by a musket ball, and *Chef de Brigade* Grillot of the 90e Demi-Brigade. Mercier would die of his wounds four days later. York estimated the Franco-Batavian losses at 4,000 men. Again, the French showed an extreme flexibility in the assignment of units to specific tasks and commanding generals. Again seniority was no issue, *généraux de brigade* commanding multiple demi-brigades while *Général de Divison* Gouvion came to the aid of a subordinate general in person at the head of a single battalion. This flexibility, again shown during the upcoming battle, even with Batavian units mixing with French ones, contributed greatly to the success of the Franco-Batavian army.

The Anglo-Russian army lost about 2,000 men with the British losing the most, 1,535 men: 11 officers and 226 others killed; 71 officers and 1,034 others wounded, including Major General Moore, Colonels Alan Cameron of the 79th Highlanders and the Marquis of Huntly of the 92nd Highlanders, Lieutenant Colonels Erskine, Ross, and Sontag; 5 officers and 188 others missing or taken prisoner.[27] Among them were 23 men killed out of 110 of the rifle company of the 6/60th Foot, proving they had seen some hard fighting this day in their effort to protect the British troops against the fire of the Franco-Batavian *jager*. Major General Knox received command of Moore's 4th Brigade. The Russians lost 467 men: 2

---

25 Van Sypesteijn, 'Krijgskundige beschouwingen over den Veldtogt van 1799 in Noord-Holland', in: *Nieuwe Spectator* (Nijmegen: J.F. Thieme, 1854), pp.214-215, 221.
26 Gachot, *Brune en Hollande*, p.282.
27 Official British returns of 6 October 1799 in Anon., *Campaign in Holland*, Appendix No.9, p.83-86 & Walsh, *Narrative*, pp.130-131; Anon., *The History of the Campaign of 1799, in Holland*, pp.377-383. On the 3rd 107 British soldiers and six officers taken prisoner arrived in Haarlem.

officers and 77 others killed, missing or taken prisoner; 16 officers and 372 others wounded, including Major General Emmé.[28]

The Duke of York wrote a short after action report to Henry Dundas, on the 6th followed by a more detailed report which is too extended to provide here. Brune wrote the following after action report to the French minister of war, also explaining the reasons for his retreat:

> The retreat from Alkmaar to Beverwijk took place without us losing neither men, nor guns, nor equipment. The battle of two days ago lasted from five in the morning until eight at night. At ten, they still fired muskets at us. The enemy began the attack against the front of Vandamme's division, to our right the forces did not act and in the centre a corps that, after capturing Warmenhuizen and Shoreldam, outposts of Dumonceau's division, reinforced the many troops that attacked our left composed of French. The terrain was hotly contested. While a strong column with difficulty advanced from dune to dune, another column had reached the beach. At night the enemy had cut off communications between Bergen and Egmont and threatened to cut off those between Alkmaar and Bergen. The fatigue of the soldier, and while I could not know the dispositions in the minds of the soldiers, becoming it known to me that the enemy had the superiority in numbers, if we would attack the next day, fatigue could cause a real setback. I ordered that, in the case of a vigorous attack, a slow retreat in good order would be executed to Beverwick. Yesterday morning, according to general reports that the enemy had prepared for a new attack, the retreat began, and ended today without any loss. I did leave open the gates of Alkmaar, in order to preserve this city of the barbarity of the Anglo-Russians. They burned without reason the village Coedick [Koedijk]. The loss of the enemy in killed and wounded is very considerable. Among the prisoners we have made, there are Russian grenadiers, Don Cossacks and Highlanders of Scotland. I received two battalions from *général* Tilly after the affair; which I was waiting for a long time now: I am told that the others follow. This piecemeal arrival make me lose great benefits, perhaps even a complete victory. But we must act in the position where we are; and I hope that when the reinforcements arrive, we will promptly make up for the lost time.[29]

York's plan to defeat the Franco-Batavians was well designed this time. That the Anglo-Russian attack did not succeed as planned, notwithstanding the subsequent retreat of the Franco-Batavian army, was due to a number of reasons. The Russians were moving too cautiously and gave the French the liberty to support threatened parts of their defences, especially in the dunes. If there was still a bit left of the reputation of the Russian soldier, this had totally disappeared now, for example Rostollant wrote: 'Yesterday we have done

---

28 Official returns of October 1799 by Major-General Essen as listed in Miliutin, *Geschichte des Krieges*, Vol.V, pp.293-294. According to the British returns though, the Russians lost 595 men: 4 officers and 168 others killed, missing or taken prisoner; 20 officers and 403 others wounded.
29 Letter of 4 October 1799 from Brune to the French minister of war Milet de Mureau, in: L. Bourgoin, *Esquisse Historique sur le Maréchal Brune* (Paris: Rousseau, 1840), Vol.I, pp.351-353.

much harm to the enemy. The Russians did not show up'.[30] By advancing too slowly, and later refusing to advance any further, they deprived Abercromby of his reserves and of the cover for his left wing, forcing him to send into the dunes troops needed to force through the French lines along the beach. Abercromby had to execute the main thrust and a speedy advance would have forced the French to retreat and cut them off. Of course there were reasons to protect the flank of his advance, but as it happened the French troops had the time to retreat and to take up new positions. They even had the time to reinforce their left wing with units from the centre and the right. It would have been better if Pulteney had had fewer troops assigned to him and instead had been added to Abercromby's column. Since an attack on Daendels' redoubt was now impossible, Pulteney's 7,000 men were ineffective. Finally, British naval forces could have been used more effectively, by using gun vessels to make Vandamme's position on the beach untenable.

---

30 Letter of 3 October 1799 from Rostollant to the Batavian Minister of War Pijman, quoted in Gachot, *Brune en Hollande*, p.282.

15

The Battle of Castricum (or 2nd Battle of Egmond op Zee) 6 October

The Tables are Turned

So again a decisive battle had not been fought. Although the Franco-Batavians retreated as a result, they managed to execute their retreat undisturbed and with their troops intact. Meanwhile, the distance between York's troops and Den Helder had now become too great to supply the troops sufficiently. The area they occupied had been denuded of supplies by the opposing army. The weather was wet and deteriorating and most of the soldiers had to sleep without cover. Furthermore, chances of taking Amsterdam were diminishing every day, the city having been turned into an impregnable fortress by *Lieutenant-Colonel* Krayenhoff as described in Chapter 11. The morale of the Franco-Batavian troops was very high. Despite their retreat they did not think themselves beaten. In every combat it was clear that they were more than a match for the British and especially for the Russians who had lost their reputation completely after the last battle. They were acquainted with the terrain and supplied with the most urgent things needed. Very capable and experienced officers led the French and the Batavian troops, something that was not always the case with their opponents.

Opinions about the Franco-Batavian commander-in-chief Brune differed, but all the subordinate commanders were prepared to act on their own initiative when the situation demanded it. Of course they were secure in the knowledge that if something did go terribly wrong, Brune would be the first to be blamed. The British had also some very capable subordinate commanders but their efforts came often to no effect because of the mistakes of the high command, the friction between the British and Russians, and last, but not least, the unfamiliar terrain they had to fight on. What was needed in this kind of terrain, was commanders who did not look over their shoulders too often, who dared to take decisions, and who could act independently. On every occasion, the Anglo-Russian troops were divided into separate columns and issued with detailed orders, lacking the flexibility to react to the ever-changing tactical and strategic situation. Beside this the soldiers had already been fighting for nearly five weeks in extremely bad weather even for that time of the year, mostly in mud up to their ankles or knees, without a dry place to sleep and without enough food and other supplies. Many soldiers at this time wore rags and were barefooted. Hundreds fell sick every day and there was no place where they could be nursed properly.

In contrast to the high morale of the Franco-Batavian army the Batavian government was in poor spirits; the enemy occupied most of North Holland and the damage done to this province was extensive. Vast tracts had been flooded and made unusable for agriculture by salt water. Whole villages had been burned and were nothing more than ruins. Dikes, canals, windmills, bridges, and roads were destroyed. Brune did not take much notice of the Batavian government's pleas; the Batavian Republic was still nothing more than a French satellite and above all Brune acted according to the orders he received from Paris, with Brune reporting to the French minister of war and pro forma to the Batavian government. The Batavians could only decide matters that did not conflict with French interests. Although Brune too had his problems, he was continuously reinforced by French troops from Belgium and Northern France so his losses were quickly replaced. On 3, 4, and 5 October the 51e Demi-Brigade (2 additional battalions) and 12 companies of the 98e Demi-Brigade arrived. Despite the losses suffered during the battle of the 2nd, on 3 October the French were 15,142 men strong, 1,698 more than before the battle.[1] As had turned out during the previous battle, the French army had become too large to be effectively controlled by Vandamme alone. Which had forced Brune to take over effective command of the French troops around Bergen in person, while Vandamme commanded those at Egmond. Therefore, Brune decided to split the French into two divisions: the 1er Division was commanded by *Général de Division* Boudet, the 2e Division by *Général de Division* Gouvion. *Général de Brigade* Fuzier stood at Beverwijk with a reserve of two demi-brigades. Commander-in-Chief of the French troops became *Général de Division* Vandamme.

Despite the reinforcements, Brune had already ordered preparations in case for a necessary retreat further south. Schoonhoven and Gorinchem were put into a state of defence; the artillery park would be moved from Haarlem to Heusden; Bergen op Zoom and Breda would receive strong garrisons; Brune would move his headquarters to 's Hertogenbosch. In these positions he would await the arrival of further French reinforcements in case the Anglo-Russians were able to defeat him and advance further south.[2] On 3 October all detached French soldiers doing guard duty and occupying posts in the Batavian Republic were ordered to join the army immediately, their place to be taken over by members of the *Gewapende Burgermacht*.

Dispositions

The retreat of the left wing under Vandamme and the advance of Abercromby along the beach made the remaining Franco-Batavian position untenable. Even without Vandamme's retreat, the Franco-Batavians' previous positions had become vulnerable with Abercromby having advanced as far as Egmond aan Zee. So already that same evening Brune issued orders for the retreat of his whole army which started at 3:00 a.m. next day, his retreat covered by *Général de Division* Gouvion with a French brigade west of Bergen and *Generaal-Major* Bonhomme with the 2e Bataafsche Divisie between Bergen and Koedijk. Shrouded in fog, and with

---

1   See Appendix XVI.
2   Krayenhoff, *Geschiedkundige*, p.306.

THE BATTLE OF CASTRICUM

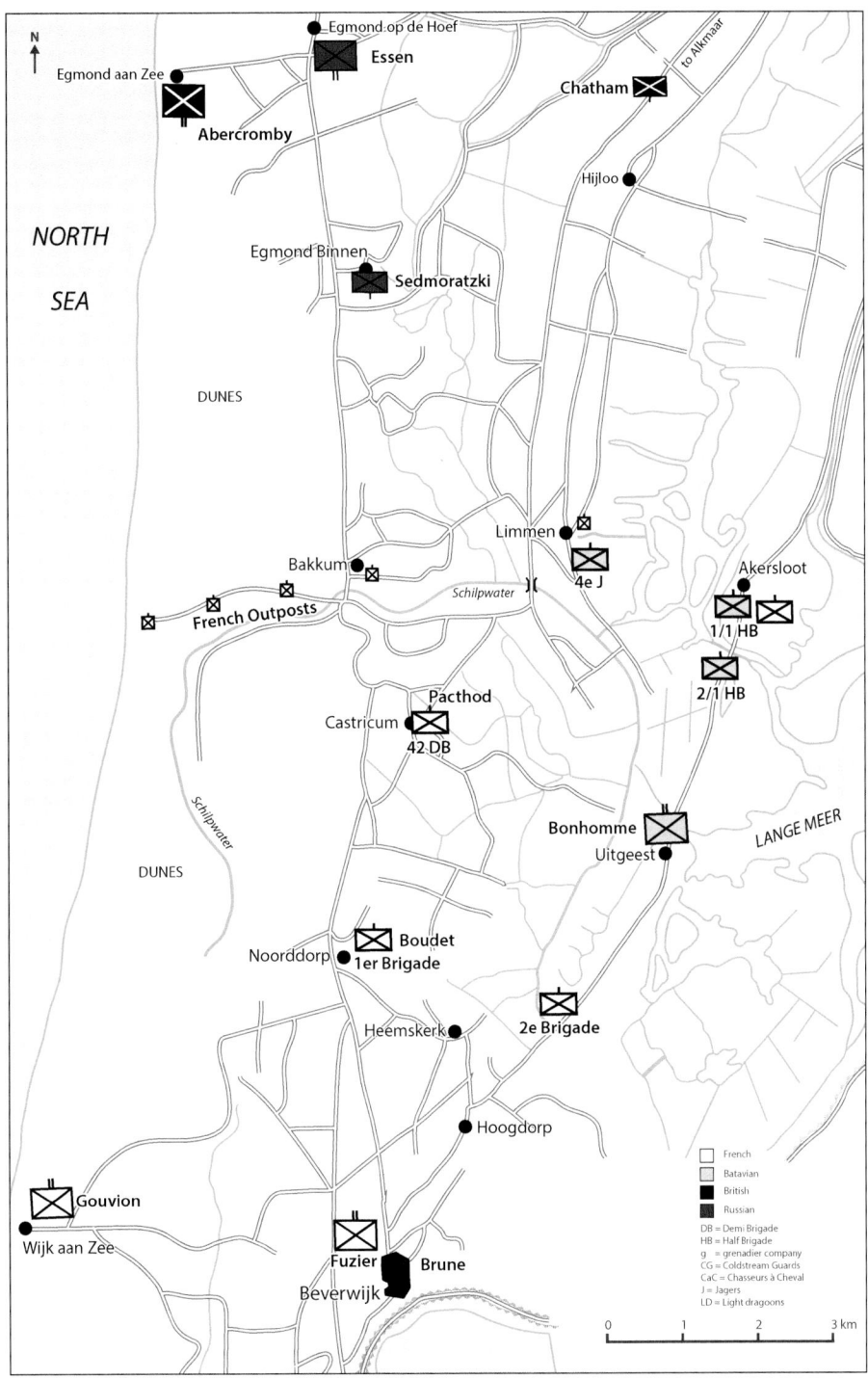

Map 9a The Battle of Castricum: positions before the battle.

the wheels of the gun carriages covered with straw, the retreat took place undisturbed, the Franco-Batavians leaving nothing behind that could be of any use to the Anglo-Russians. Next morning both brigades covering the retreat also pulled back, together with Daendels' Batavians at Oud-Karspel who started his retreat at 9:00 a.m. Daendels' 1e Bataafsche Divisie retreated to a prepared line roughly from the towns of Purmerend and Monnikendam. The terrain in front of his position was already completely inundated for the defence of Amsterdam and was only passable along four roads on top of dikes protected by six batteries armed with 62 cannon, creating a nearly unapproachable position easy to defend. To occupy this position 4,000 men were sufficient. The remainder of the Franco-Batavian army, about 20,000 men, had to defend the left wing and was positioned for a defence in depth. They were placed in a line of about seven kilometres long, between the Lange Meer and the North Sea, with the village of Castricum in the centre. The 2e Bataafsche Divisie (Bonhomme, 3,200 men) occupied the terrain just west of the Lange Meer, around the village of Uitgeest. From the French division Boudet, the 1er Brigade was at the village Noorddorp and the 2e Brigade near the villages of Heemskerk and Uitgeest, the Batavian 1/ and 2/1e Halve Brigade were attached to Boudet's division and on outpost duty around Akersloot. Gouvion's division, reinforced with the Batavian Regiment Huzaren, were near the village Wijk-aan-Zee, in the dunes and Castricum. Of this division, *Général de Brigade* Pacthod with the 42e Demi-Brigade occupied the village of Castricum with outposts at Limmen and Bakkum. On the beach the French soldiers started constructing entrenchments. The Batavian 4e Bataljon Jagers was on outpost duty in Limmen, and Gouvion had also outposts in the Dunes. The Franco-Batavian artillery train and reserve; two demi-brigades commanded by *Général de Brigade* Fuzier, were at Beverwijk. Here was also Brune's headquarters.

The impact of Brune's arrival in this small town was gigantic, as described by a member of its Municipality:

> On this day [3 October] headquarters and the complete artillery train entered. Nobody not having experienced it can have an idea: 20,000 Dutch as well as French soldiers, on foot and mounted, was the number which had to be put in less than 400 houses. One wanted to burden the workers and poor with having to quarter only 10 men, but this was nothing and some received 30 or even 40 soldiers. Many were forced to give up their house with everything in it completely. The empty houses were requisitioned by the generals and officers and seized. The country seats, mostly abandoned, were occupied and full of soldiers. The Reformed, Catholic, Lutheran and Mennonite churches were transformed in barracks and hospitals. The terrains for the cannon, ammunition and baggage wagons came on the lands especially at the southern end of the Breestraat until the Schulpen… Here everywhere great fires were lit. The fences and the wood in the forests all around was cut and dragged away to feed these fires and to make tents or huts. The country seats included. In the artillery parks the most expensive horses lay dead, the land was driven completely useless. Impossible requisitions were made on the Municipality. One was forced to appoint a commission which had to go from house to house to fulfil the requested requisitions for the generals and other officers. While the empty houses and country seats were mostly without furniture, as most people had already brought these to safety, making the task for the commission an impossible one. This caused

Typical terrain north of Bakkum. (Author photo)

as a result terrible threats with some French, regarding this unwillingness from the Municipality, while their requisitions could not be met by far.[3]

A similar account was given by a teacher from Beverwijk:

> Then on 3 October, came here in the morning unexpected the headquarters of the French and Batavian army of the general en chef Brune with both artillery parks, the French and Dutch... Because of this the whole place was crowded with soldiers, as well as the villages Heemskerk, Noorddorp, Heemskerkerduijn, Wijk aan het Duin and Wijk aan Zee. All houses ran full of people however a great part had to camp in open air. The weather was unfavourable, it rained hard constantly; this caused that those who could not be lodged in houses had to make tents the best they could, for which they broke off and cut wood and branches from the trees everywhere, searching for hay and straw to lie and rest on. Lacking all necessities and already under the open air for several days, suffering many inconveniences and

---

3   Anon., *Dagverhaal der doormarcheerende troepen, Inkwartieringen en in garnizoen Liggende Militairen in de Steede Beverwijk, sedert October 1787 tot op het Sluiten van de Vreede in den Jaare 1802*, in J. van Venetien e.a., *"Dagverhaal der doormarcheerende troepen" – Beverwijk in de ban van de Fransen (1787-1802)* (Beverwijk: Historisch Genootschap Midden-Kennemerland en Museum Kennemerland, 1999), pp.57-58.

having to fight the enemy constantly, they were exhausted, hungry and thirsty. It was for us citizens impossible to care for them properly. So they made themselves master of everything they could lay their hands on, causing much misery. Not because of everything they needed, but mostly because of everything they took, damaged etc., especially the fruits of the gardens and the land, hay, straw, oats and other cereals, as well as wood, etc.[4]

The Franco-Batavian positions were reinforced with artillery batteries armed with 37 cannon and eight howitzers. Their retreat was not interfered with by the Anglo-Russians, as York would later justify:

The exhausted state of the troops, from the almost unparalleled difficulties and fatigues which they had to encounter, prevented me from taking that advantage of the enemy's retreat to Beverwyck and Wyck-op-Zee, which, in any other country, and under any other circumstances, would have been the consequences of the operations of the army upon the 2d.[5]

The Anglo-Russians were slow to follow up on the Franco-Batavian retreat. Prince William advanced to Schermerhorn following Daendels. According to a British source Prince William captured three field guns which Daendels had abandoned on the road during his retreat.[6] Lieutenant General Pulteney occupied Oud-Karspel and Langendijk. Major General Burrard advanced to Koedijk. The Russians passed Bergen and took up positions near the village Egmond op de Hoef. The Russian advance guard under Major General Sedmoratzki advanced further forward to the village of Egmond-Binnen. In their rear Bergen was occupied by the 85th Foot.

According to the same British source already mentioned above, a patrol of the 18th Light Dragoons, commanded by Captain Harcourt, captured a strong picket belonging to the rearguard of the French army. Then they followed up their success and entered the city Alkmaar, which had been evacuated by the Franco-Batavians.[7] A Batavian source tells a somewhat different story although it is not sure this refers to the same incident: two hundred British light dragoons performed a reconnaissance in force. They surprised a French infantry picket of the 49e Demi-Brigade and charged them in a very unfavourable defensive position. Fortunately for the French the dragoons were attacked by a squadron of the Batavian hussars, commanded by *Colonel* de Quaita. Their attack broke the light dragoons instantly and the British were pursued back to their own lines, the Franco-Batavians capturing an officer and 30 troopers.

On 4 October the Anglo-Russians moved forward and occupied positions in the line Egmond-Alkmaar-Hoorn: Lieutenant General Abercromby around the village Egmond

---

4   Broer Schermer, *Verslag van het voorgevallene te Beverwijk van den 3e tot de 9e October 1799*. Published J. van Venetien e.a., *"Dagverhaal der doormarcheerende troepen" – Beverwijk in de ban van de Fransen (1787-1802)* (Beverwijk: Historisch Genootschap Midden-Kennemerland en Museum Kennemerland, 1999), p.65.
5   York's after action report dated 6 October in: Walsh, *Narrative*, p.128.
6   Anon., *Campaign in Holland*, p.52.
7   Anon., *Campaign in Holland*, p.53.

aan Zee, with Moore's 4th Brigade (now commanded by Major General Knox), Hely-Hutchinson's 6th Brigade, MacDonald's Advance Guard, and the Cavalry Brigade (Paget). Between Hijloo and Alkmaar was Chatham's 7th Brigade and a squadron of the 11th Light Dragoons. Chatham was replaced under the orders of Abercromby, where he was before the battle of 2 October, to replace d'Oyly's 1st Guards Brigade. Coote's 3rd Brigade stood further back around Bergen. Between Egmond aan Zee and Alkmaar stood the Russian main force, commanded by Major-General Essen. This included all Russian troops except for the Brigade Sedmoratzki, which was deployed at Egmond Binnen with forward outposts. The left of the Anglo-Russian position was protected along the line Ouddorp–Rustenburg–Schermerhorn by Lieutenant General Pulteney with Don's 5th Brigade and Manner's 9th Brigade, their outposts in Schermerhorn and Avenhorn. Prince William's 8th Brigade was positioned at Hoorn, occupying this city: because of the distance his troops had to cover and the bad state of the roads, he did not reach these positions before morning of the 5th. York had his headquarters in Alkmaar with both guards brigades (d'Oyly's and Burrard's) in reserve.

Despite their advance and the capture of the city Alkmaar the situation of the Anglo-Russian army was still far from good. It soon turned out that the country could not provide the necessary provisions and therefore everything had to be brought forward from Den Helder, a substantial distance over roads that were rendered all but impassable by the constant heavy rain and the overflowing of the numerous ditches and canals. Sickness began to take its toll and it is estimated that because of this, the casualties in battle, and the need to detach troops to the towns and cities along the Zuiderzee, effective strength had dwindled to 27,000 effectives. There were numerous clashes between patrols from both sides. The Anglo-Russians made many reconnaissance's, probing for weak spots in the Franco-Batavian defences, as illustrated by Dubiansky:

> On 25 September [Russian calendar, i.e. 6 October] at daybreak, our Ural Cossacks, on patrol, ran into some French, exchanged a few shots and routed them. The Cossacks on their light horses pursued the French, riding on Flemish horses, and ran into an ambush of skirmishers in the gardens and orchards of Castricum. Received by rifle fire they had to take flight themselves for the mounted chasseurs, without losing a single man though.[8]

The Occupation of Alkmaar

Alkmaar was the first major city captured by the Anglo-Russian army and therefore was of strategic and political importance. It was a city of considerable size and strength situated in a fertile plain. It was encompassed with a thick wall, faced with brick, about three miles in circumference and strengthened with bastions at regular intervals, outside of which was a broad and deep fosse, always full of water. The town was intersected with canals whose

---

8 Diary of Colonel Dubiansky in Ritter, *Een Russisch verhaal*, p.38. According to Dubiansky, this incident started the Battle of Castricum.

quays were lined with large warehouses. The houses were built in the old style; very few of them dated from after 1600. The town was surrounded by groves of fine tall trees, with broad avenues leading to the ramparts in radiated directions. The intervals were laid out in gardens, ornamented with a variety of summer-houses in the Chinese style. In the morning of 4 October, various British units entered the city, in the afternoon followed by yet another British battalion. There was no opposition from the Franco-Batavians and the British found the gates thrown wide open. They were welcomed by a display of Orange flags from the citizens and by the chimes of the cathedral tinkling 'God save the King'. Also on this occasion several Dutch soldiers went over to join the Prince of Orange. A total of 2,800 men occupied barracks and hospitals only hours before cleared by the Franco-Batavians, the officers billeted with the citizens. They were followed by numerous women and children, followers of the British army, glad to be out of the mud and inside a proper city. According to eye-witnesses the soldiers, undoubtedly happy that they were finally out of the cold and mud, behaved themselves very well, paying for everything they needed. They even wore orange ribbons, the citizens were requested to do the same. Orange flags were hoisted from the towers. Around 4:00 p.m. the municipality was gathered in the name of the Duke of York. On his behalf, Baron van Heerdt appeared, declaring the municipally dismissed, at the same time requesting them to remain in office until a new municipality had been formed. After that the British garrison commander ordered the municipality to deliver 5,000 loafs of bread of three English pounds each; 1,000 bags of oats of 150 pounds each; 1,000 bottles of brandy, 200 carts each with a team of two horses, and 60,000 pounds of good quality hay.

The Prince of Orange appointed *Capitein-Ingenieur* de Veye as town-major: 'in order to have an officer present who can speak with foreigners, and will be responsible for all matters to be taken care of here, such as deserters, prisoners, weapons etc'.[9] In the afternoon the Duke of York and the Prince of Orange arrived in the city, without any ceremony. Between 4:00 and 5:00 p.m. some British sloops and gunboats passed through the city, moving south. On the 5th numerous British troops passed through the city to the south, a few hundred remained behind to be billeted with the civilians. The municipality received yet another written requisition: to deliver twenty barges with accompanying crew and a delivery of 10,000 loaves of bread each day for a week. Complying with this requisition was impossible though: for over a month, Alkmaar and its neighbourhood had to provide provisions for the Franco-Batavian army and the stocks were completely exhausted. An additional requisitioning on the 6th, of 8,000 rations of oats of 14 pounds and for the next day 15,000 loaves of bread instead of 10,000 could of course also not be met: all the supplies left were 82 bags of oats and no hay. That same day, at 9:30 a.m. divine service was to be held in the Dutch language attended by the Prince of Orange himself. Two hours later, another divine service was to be held which would be attended by the Duke of York. He did not show up however, as on that same day the Battle of Castricum was fought. He would remain in Alkmaar at his headquarters to direct what started as some outpost skirmishing and would become a general battle. As a result the Duke of York decided to retreat to his strong defensive Zijpe position. Next day on the 7th, the British commander requisitioned all barges and boats,

---

9 Letter of the Hereditary Prince of Orange to the Stadtholder on 6 October 1799 in Koolemans Beijnen, *De Erfprins van Oranje in Noord-Holland*, p.78.

supposedly to fetch provisions from the Zijpe. Although prisoners were still brought in from the previous battle and word was that the battle had been won by the British, this turned out to be otherwise as these vessels were loaded with soldiers, wives, luggage and provisions. In the evening they sailed north, followed by the departure of the sloops and gunboats. According to some sources at 2:00 p.m. the Duke of York and the Prince of Orange left the city, although it was more probably around 5:00 p.m. In any case the British retreat continued during the night, next morning around 8:00 a.m. the last British troops left Alkmaar. One hour later the first French cavalry arrived.

The Battle of Castricum

Neither side intended the battle that was fought on 6 October. York had decided to fight a final decisive battle, probably on 7 October, but to gain the right starting positions on the 6th he attacked the Franco-Batavian outposts at the villages of Bakkum, Limmen, and Akersloot which were blocking the roads to the south. Possession of these villages would enable him to start the attack closer to the Franco-Batavian positions and by using the roads rather than travelling cross-country, his troops would be less tired on arrival. The attempt to take these outposts would escalate to a complete battle, with both sides feeding in more and more troops.

At about 7:00 a.m. Burrard's 2nd Guards Brigade attacked the outpost at the village Limmen. Arriving at Limmen, the British had no trouble in pushing back the outnumbered Batavian 4e Bataljon Jagers. Another part of Burrard's brigade advanced to the village of Akersloot. The advance guard was formed by three companies of the 1st Foot Guards and a company of the Coldstream Guards, commanded by Colonel Cléphane. This village was occupied by the Batavian 1/1e Halve Brigade, a French battalion, and a cavalry squadron, under the command of the Batavian *Lieutenant-Colonel* Nicolson, who related:

> They reconnoitred an enemy patrol, followed by about 4,000 men, which immediately engaged the outposts, pushing them back on the picket in reserve, which managed to hold up the enemy to enable a French battalion, as well as that of the *Lieutenant-Colonel* Nicolson, to deploy in order of battle. The fighting became quickly general, but lasted not longer than five minutes when the French routed, except its brave officers, some NCOs and a few privates, doing all in their power to rally the routing troops. But despite their efforts, with hitting and striking, were all in vain to stop them. Contrary the brave Batavian battalion, abandoned by its brothers in arms, only retreating in good order after a full hour of fighting, nearly surrounded by the much superior enemy, with a loss of 150 men.[10]

Slowly pulling back to the hamlet of Dorregeest south of Akersloot and the sluice there, Nicolson continued an orderly retreat, destroying all the bridges behind him.

---

10 Report of *Colonel* Nicolson in van der Aa, *Geschiedenis van de jongst-geëindigden oorlog*, Vol.VIII, pp.300-301. Although it is not known which French battalion routed, most probably it was a battalion of the 90e Demi-Brigade which was in Boudet's division and consisted mainly of conscripts.

Brune ordered *Général de Division* Boudet to pull back his outposts and to join the 2e Bataafsche Divisie at Uitgeest. The British consolidated their positions at Dorregeest and started throwing up batteries near the sluice. Coote's 3rd Brigade came up from Bergen, passed Alkmaar and deployed at Limmen to support Burrard. Captain Popham's gunboats took up positions to support the British infantry in case of a Franco-Batavian counterattack. A local source reports 12 to 16 Franco-Batavians killed, who were buried on the spot in gardens and in the field; some wounded, and approximately 70 men taken prisoner by the British and send back to Alkmaar. Akersloot was plundered by British soldiers.[11] About the same time Sedmoratzki left the village of Egmond-Binnen and attacked *Général de Brigade* Pacthod's outposts occupied by the 42e Demi-Brigade at the village of Bakkum and in the dunes and drove them back with ease. Sedmoratzki's force consisted of:

	Battalions	Strength
1st *Jégerski* of Suthoff	1	c.300
Benkendorf Grenadiers	2	719
Sedmoratzki Musketeers	2	1,208
Comb. Grenadier Battalion 'Ericsson'	1	422
Life-*Sotnia* of the Ural Cossacks	detachment	30
Company Artillery of Major Bastian	1 company (7 guns)	

Sedmoratzki's orders were to take the outposts and then to stop his advance, but, elated by the ease with which the French were pushed back, the Russians continued their advance, proceeded by the Cossacks. Just north of Castricum a bridge crossed the Schilpwater, a small and marshy stream. At this point the French had placed a cannon and a howitzer. Undauntedly the Cossacks charged across the bridge on their small horses yelling wild cries, received by canister at close range which emptied 15 saddles. Despite their loss the Cossacks continued, forcing the gunners to retreat. This allowed the Russian pioneers to construct a supporting bridge across the Schilpwater, enabling the Russian infantry to cross the stream quickly and to deploy on the other side. The Russian artillery followed the road and deployed, at about 11:00 a.m. starting to cannonade Castricum which was barely visible for the gunners because of the number of elm trees in front of them.[12]

Next the village was attacked by some Russian *jégerski*, both battalions of the Benkendorf Grenadiers and the Combined Grenadier Battalion 'Ericsson'. Castricum was defended by *Général de Brigade* Pacthod with the 42e Demi-Brigade (3 battalions) and some guns of the 12/7e Artillerie à Pied. They received the Russians with heavy fire from the loopholed walls and roofs of the houses and the first Russian attack failed. The Russian infantry immediately charged again and penetrated into the village. Heavy house-to-house fighting followed with both sides making no prisoners. '*La furia francese* answered the Muskovite savagery'.[13] Running out of cartridges the soldiers continued the slaughter with bayonets, musket butts,

---

11 Municipaliteit van Akersloot, *Voor de Nakomelingschap*, written report, origin unknown. Photocopy in possession of the author. Transcription in *De Groene Valck* (Vereniging "Oud-Akersloot", 1985), pp.6-8.
12 Gachot, *Brune en Hollande*, p.290.
13 Gachot, *Brune en Hollande*, p.291.

"Battle of Castricum", by Joannes Bemme after a drawing of Dirk Langendijk. (Rijksmuseum, RP-P-OB-86.744)

and knives. Upon receiving the message that a Russian battalion supported by *jégerski* had already turned his flank by way of the dunes – it was the Combined Grenadier Battalion 'Ericsson' – and was threatening to cut him off, Pacthod believed it advisable to evacuate his position at Castricum and to retreat in the direction of Noorddorp, rallying his battalions at the foot of the dunes.

Sedmoratzki occupied Castricum and his artillery was deployed at the southern entrance of the village. The village itself was occupied by the Sedmoratzki Musketeers and the *jégerski*. The Benkendorf Grenadiers and the Combined Grenadier Battalion 'Ericsson' took up positions to the west of the village. By now the action had become much more than an outpost skirmish and the whole Franco-Batavian army was alarmed and deployed in order of battle. *Général de Division* Boudet was ordered to deploy between the villages of Noorddorp and Heemskerk and to block any further Russian advance. Batavian horse artillery deployed and replied to the gunfire from British artillery deployed at Limmen. With news of British troops also advancing along the beach, *Général de Division* Gouvion also deployed his division in the dunes and on the beach as will be described later.

Major General Essen in the meantime had concentrated the Russian main force at Egmond-Binnen, not being aware of the fighting that took place at Castricum because of the strong northern wind. When Essen heard of Sedmoratzki's gains he decided to reinforce him with the Combined Grenadier Battalions 'Ogarev' (490), 'Ossipov' (300), 'Strick' (225) and six guns, commanded by Colonel Dubiansky. The remaining Russian units remained in reserve near Egmond-Binnen under the command of Major General Arbénev. After some

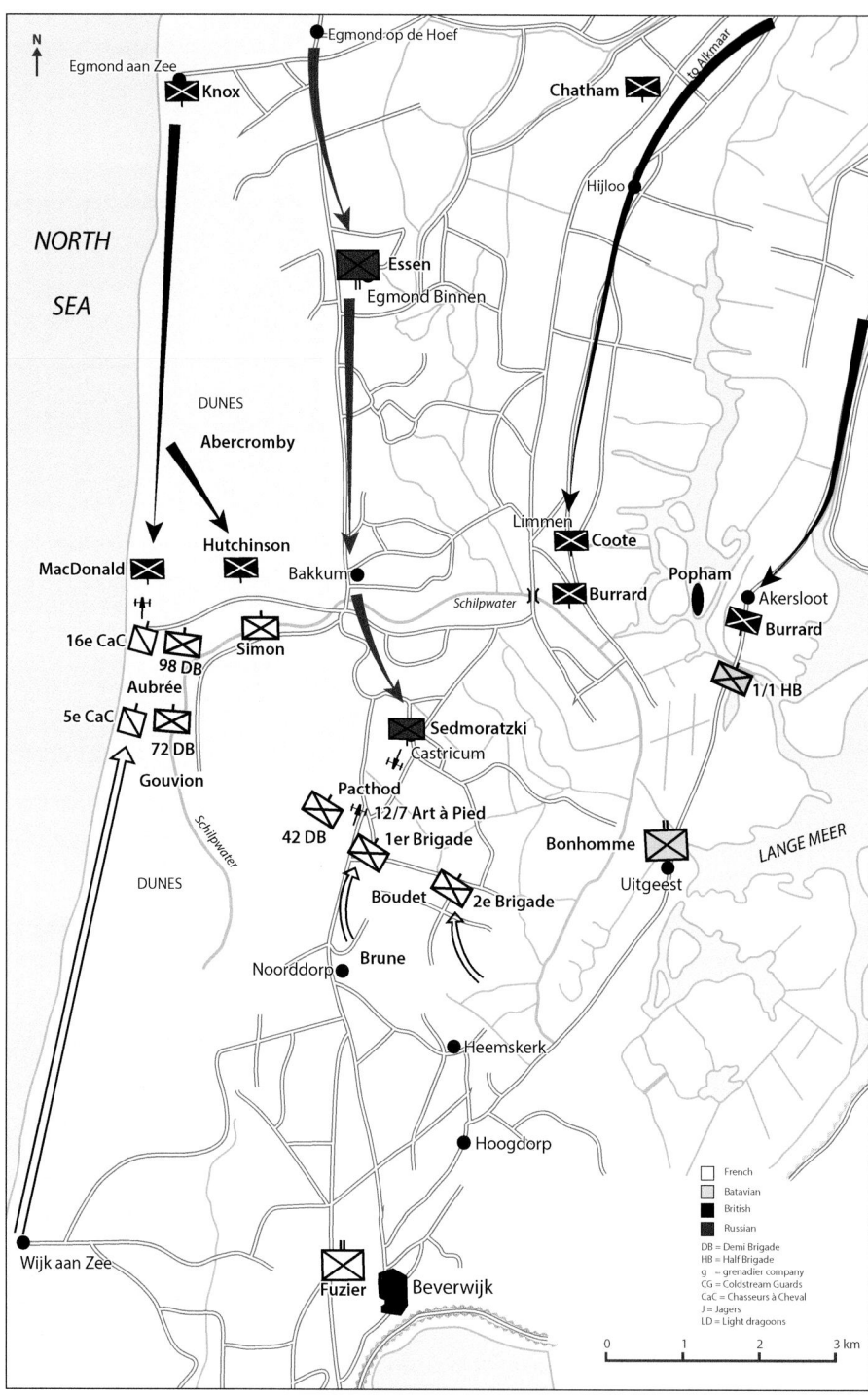

Map 9b The Battle of Castricum, Phase 1: c.7:00–12:00 a.m.

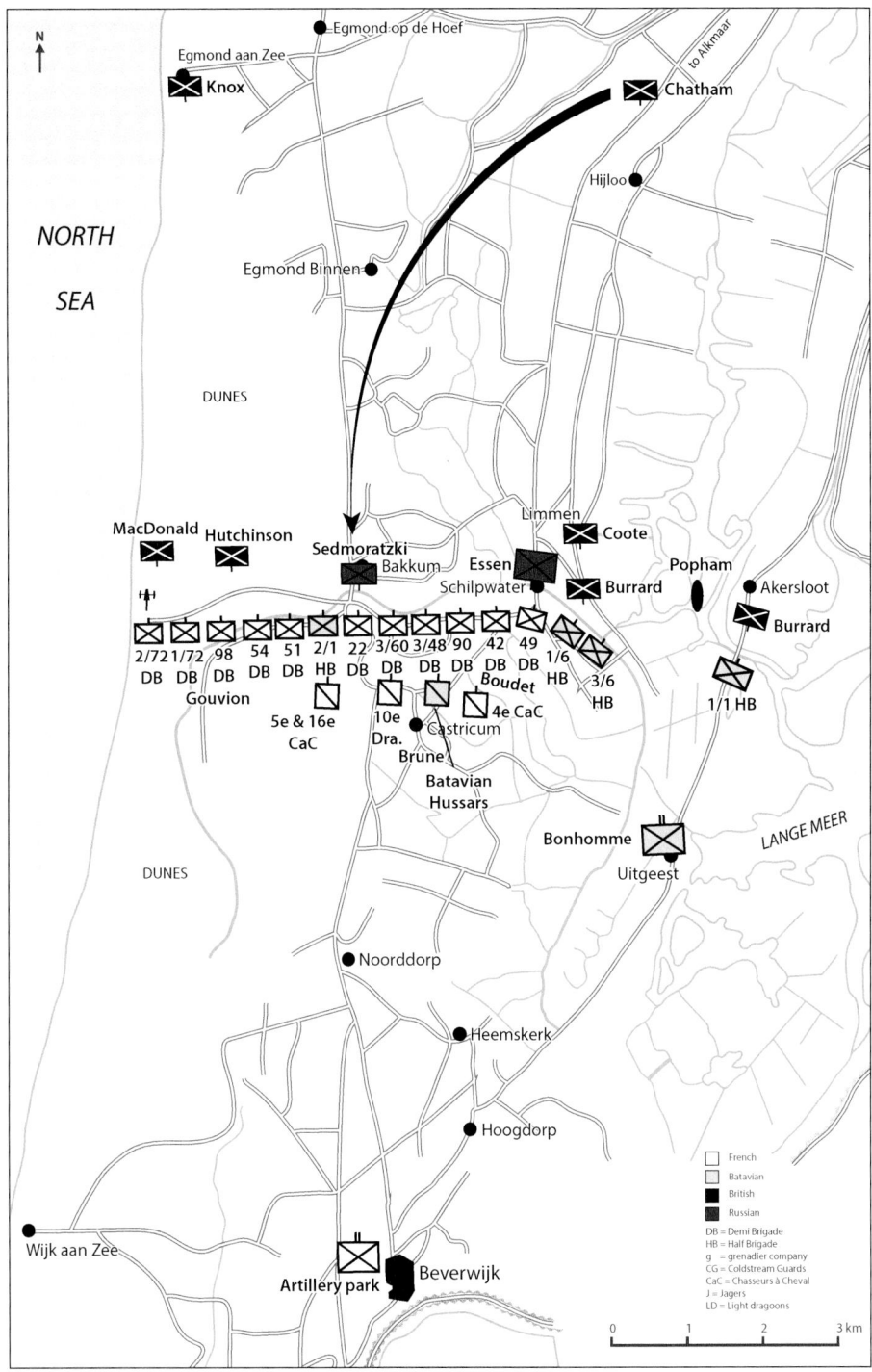

Map 9c The Battle of Castricum, Phase 2: c.12:00–5:00 p.m.

"Cavalry engagement", by Dirk Langendijk. (Noord-Hollands Archief, NL-HlmNHA_480_000902_M)

time the Emmé Grenadiers (1,435) and the Zherebtsov Grenadiers (1,059) received orders to advance as well.[14]

Général de Brigade Pacthod in the meantime pulled back from Castricum, his retreat covered by the Batavian Regiment Huzaren, which repulsed an attack of two hundred British light dragoons. He took up a new position with his infantry in the dunes south of Castricum and the 12/7e Artillerie à Pied and 1/8e Artillerie Légère (*Capitaine* Leroux) on the road to the village of Noorddorp, in such a way that they could fire at anything on the road to Castricum, the edge of the dunes and the terrain to the north-east of his position. There the French held their ground against a number of subsequent Russian attacks until they were reinforced by five battalions (French and Batavian, including the 2/1e Halve Brigade commanded by *Major* Achenbach which had retreated from the direction of Akersloot), accompanied by Vandamme, Boudet, and Brune himself. More reinforcements followed but the five battalions already arrived were estimated to be sufficient to counterattack the Russians in Castricum. The French attack was a complete success and they retook Castricum, the Russians losing their artillery after the horses had been killed and most of the gunners put out of action. There was heavy fighting around Castricum and in the dunes. At that moment Colonel Dubiansky arrived with the Russian reinforcements. While the Combined Grenadier Battalion 'Ogarev' covered their right, both other combined grenadier battalions, supported by the Benkendorf Grenadiers, took Castricum again, retaking also the lost guns. These guns went into action again, reinforced by another

---

14 The above strengths of the Russian units are the strengths of 24 September, with the losses suffered on 2 October deducted.

four guns commanded by Lieutenant Rjabikov. The Franco-Batavians had now formed an extensive battle line of battalions in the dunes and in front of Castricum. There was heavy fighting all along the line and the Russian Lieutenant Colonel Ogarev was wounded leading his grenadiers. Neither side was able to make any progress and finally fire slackened by lack of ammunition on both sides. By then Brune had ordered Boudet to march his 2nd Brigade, consisting of the 48e Demi-Brigade (3e battalion and 2 grenadier companies) and the 90e Demi-Brigade (3 battalions) from Heemskerk to Uitgeest, to unite with the 2e Bataafsche Divisie (Bonhomme). Not being needed here he was ordered to advance in the direction of Castricum. After picking up two squadrons of the 4e Chasseurs à Cheval on his way, Boudet ran into a strong Russian force, taking it in its flank by surprise. Confused fighting followed between isolated farms and ditches and finally the Russians were thrown back to Castricum.

At about 3:00 p.m. another Russian force – Probably both grenadier regiments of Emmé and Zherebtsov – advanced into the terrain east of Castricum, threatening Bonhomme's Batavian troops at Uitgeest. This movement was much hampered by the terrain which was intersected by many ditches. Brune suspected that because of this manoeuvre, the Russians opposite him and in the dunes had to be weakened. To keep the Russians east of Castricum busy he ordered a battalion of the 42e Demi-Brigade and the 1/ and 3/6e Halve Brigade under the command of *Lieutenant-Colonel* Carteret to engage them. This effectively prevented any Russian advance on this part of the battlefield. Then Brune ordered his infantry in the dunes to charge the opposing Russians with the bayonet. The Russians, lacking ammunition, did not wait for them and retreated in disorder, running out of the dunes in great disorder and trying to rally in the low fields between Castricum and Bakkum. The British militiamen had to cope with yet another new experience:

> It was somewhat trying to young and unformed soldiers to see this broken and ill-shapen mass approach, like a migration of land-crabs, and followed up by an elated and noisy enemy; but to do our big fellows justice, they did not quail at the sight, but, covering themselves in the sand, they showed fight. They were at least conversant with the mysteries of priming and loading, and rattled away in very good style. But when from the approach of the enemy in such force it was found necessary to retire, there was no small difficulty in keeping them in hand, and preventing what ought to have been an orderly retreat of pickets becoming a disorderly rout. One fellow, when embayed amongst sand-hills that rendered the enemy invisible, fired off his piece in their direction in the air; and being asked his reason for so doing, said, he thought it might hit somebody. An officer threw up the muzzle of another man's firelock who had taken deliberate aim at a Russian, within forty yards; and on asking if he did not know that it was a Russian and a friend, the reply was, he did not care; he was sure he was not an Englishman, and he would have a slap at him, from which he was only induced to desist, by the officer's sword threatening him with a like compliment.[15]

---

15 Anon., 'Recollections of the British army', p.190.

Brune advanced his troops from the west in the direction of Castricum. In front of this village Colonel Dubiansky had taken up positions with five Russian battalions, with two more Russian battalions under Sedmoratzki inside the village itself. The Russians in front of the village had to be dislodged first to retake Castricum. Before Brune could give orders to achieve this, the Russians were attacked by the 2/1e Halve Brigade, as its commanding officer *Major* Achenbach had already received the order from Vandamme to attack the Russians in front of Castricum. The Batavians performed this task very well: they advanced in line in perfect order, without firing, until they had reached a distance that their fire would have a maximum effect. At this distance, a volley was fired with a telling effect on the Russians. Although they outnumbered the single Batavian battalion heavily, the Russian infantry broke and routed.[16]

With the way cleared for an attack on Castricum itself, Pacthod was ordered forward with some companies of the 42e and 49e Demi-Brigades, followed closely by three battalions commanded by Brune in person. After heavy house to house fighting Castricum was retaken. Sedmoratzki lost his artillery again to the Franco-Batavian troops and Dubiansky was taken prisoner, relating:

> Who knows the Russian soldier, knows that he cannot remain in place idle after repeated success. My grenadiers saw the enemy taking flight into the dunes and it was impossible for them not to pursue them so to speak straight to hell. I was only able to keep the 1st company in line and gradually they served as a rally point. The "assembly" was blown and I advanced the grenadiers in the direction of Castricum, to try to unite them with my other battalions. Zeal carried us away though to a kilometre in front of Castricum, were at once I observed a full regiment of enemy dragoons on my right wing and in front of me a 6,000 men strong French column, of two brigades, under the command of Brune in person. While advancing from dune to dune my exhausted grenadiers had to climb steep slopes time and again. At once a French officer appeared at the head of my column, walking straight into my hands. But behind him on a height appeared a platoon of French line infantry, and so we suddenly encountered the enemy. The unexpected always causes a moment of hesitation. Such was the case with the French officer and me. He was a head taller than me, and grabbed me by my silver medals, while I grabbed him at his chest. I had my sword in the hand, but he was unarmed and shouted "pardon"! The French platoon on the height took aim but did not fire though. My grenadiers came running, and when I would not have yelled to them: "Halt, children; this is my prisoner" our mutual deeds of valour would have been covered by the sand of the dunes. We both found ourselves soon in the midst of my grenadiers, but the French descended quickly from their dune and now a struggle occurred, during which nor my orders, nor the orders of the French officer were listened to. A moment later we were surrounded by the French grenadiers, which aimed at me. Now it was the turn of the French officer to yell to his soldiers: "Spare my comrade, he has saved my life

---

16   Van Sypesteijn, 'Krijgskundige Beschouwingen over den Veldtogt van 1799 in Noord-Holland', *De Nieuwe Spectator, Krijgs- en Geschiedkundig Tijdschrift voor Neerlands land- en Zeemacht* (Nijmegen: J.F. Thieme, 1853), p.482.

"Cavalry fight", by Dirk Langendijk. (Noord-Hollands Archief, NL-HlmNHA_480_000597_G)

and is now our prisoner". In this way he saved my life and repaid the service which I did to him a moment before.[17]

Général de Brigade Barbou was ordered to pursue the Russians with the 10e Dragons along the edge of the dunes, but while achieving this he was attacked in his flank by a squadron of the 11th Light Dragoons, commanded by Major Cummings, which was concealed in the dunes. The surprised French cavalry immediately broke and retreated in disorder, its commander Godard severely wounded. The disorder spread to some of the exhausted French units following, but as the British cavalry did not pursue this had no bad consequences for the French. Pacthod pursued the Russians in the direction of Limmen with the 49e Demi-Brigade. At the Schilpwater he had to end his pursuit because the retreating Russians had destroyed the bridge over it. Two Russian guns and three hundred infantry made it impracticable for the Franco-Batavians to force a crossing and Pacthod had to content himself with busying the Russians with skirmishing fire.

---

17 Diary of Colonel Dubiansky in Ritter, *Een Russisch verhaal*, p.41.

For the moment most of the fighting ceased, both sides recovering from the previous fighting while reinforcements marched to take their place in the frontline. The Franco-Batavians were supplied with cartridges, for which again good use was made by the cavalry to reach the infantry in the difficult terrain. Brune reorganised the troops at his disposal. Again he abandoned the formal structure of his army and assigned his generals to specific sectors of the defence line, with units assigned to them accordingly. At the foot of the dunes the 51e Demi-Brigade (2 battalions), the 2/1e Halve Brigade, and both squadrons of the 5e and 16e Chasseurs à Cheval had to occupy the gap between Gouvion's division in the dunes and Brune's remaining forces. Between this force and Castricum stood the next units in line: the 22e Demi-Brigade (2 battalions), 3/60e Demi-Brigade, 3/48e Demi-Brigade and the 90e Demi-Brigade (3 battalions). Behind this line stood the 10e Dragons as a reserve. In front of Castricum stood the 42e Demi-Brigade (3 battalions) and the 49e Demi-Brigade (3 battalions). To the east of Castricum stood the 1/ and 3/6e Halve Brigade, while further to Uitgeest the terrain was covered by the Batavian division of Bonhomme. Brune's reserve was formed by the 4e Chasseurs à Cheval and the Batavian Regiment Huzaren.

Essen felt himself too weak to attack again with the troops at his disposal and asked Abercromby for support. Abercromby hesitated, as battle orders were lacking. MacDonald's Advance Guard and Hely-Hutchinson's 6th Brigade had been committed as will be described, opposed by a full French division. Only Knox's (formerly Moore's) 4th Brigade, which had suffered heavy losses on 2 October, as well as the cavalry, remained in reserve on the beach. Abercromby knew from his previous experience that the beach proved excellent terrain for a swift attack and a quick advance; in the event the French would undertake such an attack they would form a threat to the complete Anglo-Russian army which could be cut off from Den Helder. However, after repeated requests from Essen he decided to reinforce him with the four battalions of Chatham's 7th Brigade, under his personal command.

Knox's 4th Brigade remained in reserve at Egmond aan Zee and was not engaged. At the same time Abercromby ordered Major General Coote to advance from Limmen to Castricum with two infantry battalions and some guns. These battalions were probably the 27th and 85th Foot as these units had the most severe losses, 17 respectively 25 men missing after the battle. Missing men were common when the battlefield was in the hands of the enemy after the battle, which was the case with the terrain around Castricum. By 5:00 p.m., Chatham's battalions arrived on the scene.[18] On his arrival Abercromby found the Russian infantry tired, disordered and lacking ammunition but the arrival of the British infantry raised spirits again. He deployed Chatham's brigade to attack the Franco-Batavians west of Castricum through the dunes, enabling the Russians to attack from the direction of Limmen supported by Coote's battalions and artillery. At 5:00 p.m. Abercromby started his advance from the direction of Bakkum, in co-operation with the Russians who had repaired the bridge across the Schilpwater. Again heavy fighting ensued. The Franco-Batavian troops, exhausted by the daylong battle and lacking ammunition, could not resist the renewed attack and were pushed out of Castricum again, retreating west into the dunes. After being rallied by Boudet and Fuzier the Franco-Batavians counterattacked but they could not stop

---

18   Gachot, *Brune en Hollande*, p.293.

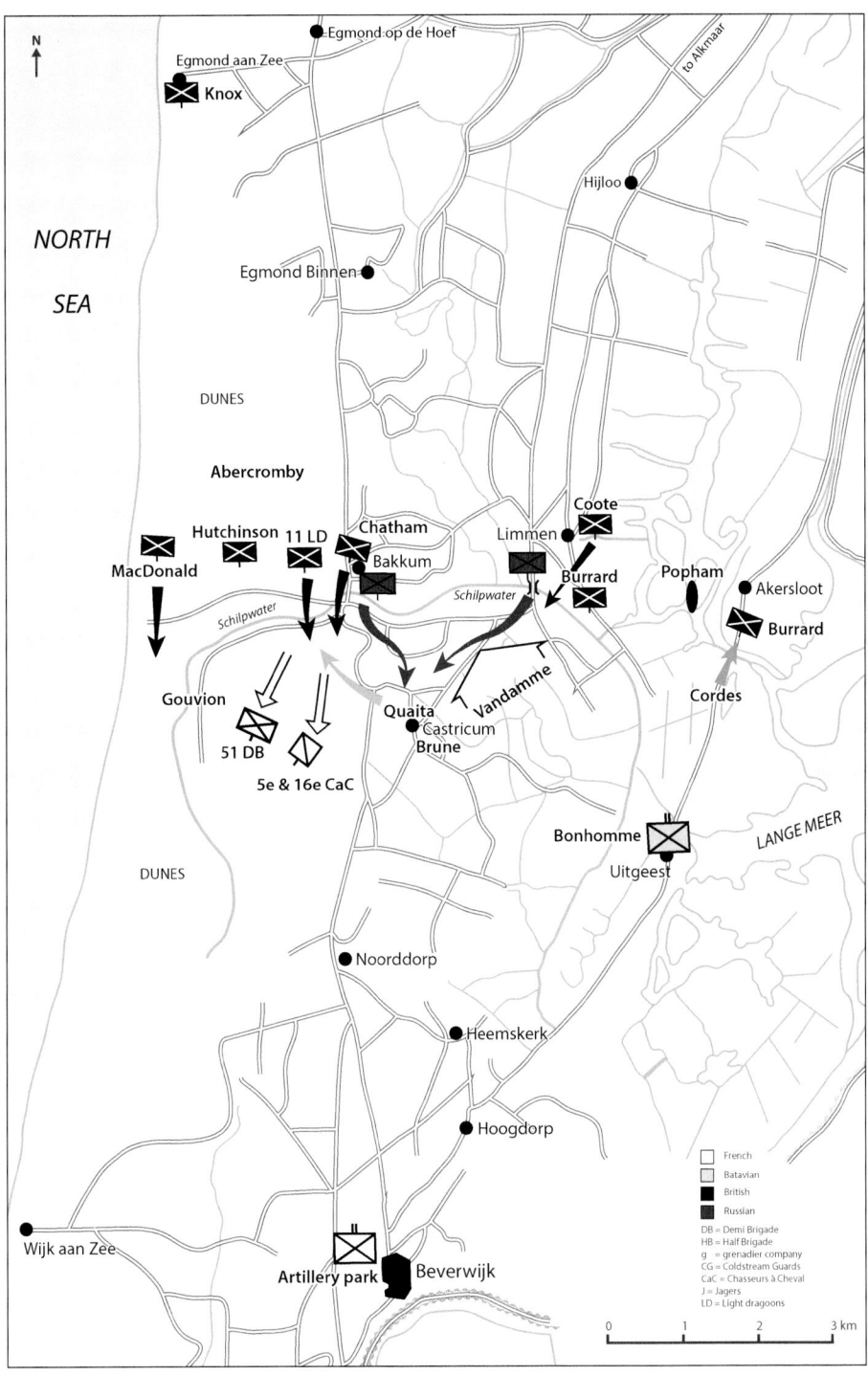

Map 9d The Battle of Castricum, Phase 3: c.5:00-7:00 p.m.

the advance of the Anglo-Russians. The troops were entangled in close combat in the dunes and the situation became very confused with various units mingling with each other.

The after action report of *Major* Achenbach, commanding the 2/1e Halve Brigade, describes the fighting west of Castricum:

> A short while later I received information of the commander of the left wing [Durutte] that they enemy had entered the woods at the foot of the dunes with a substantial force. So I let my men penetrate into the woods with the bayonet, to drive them from there. The attack was executed with such vigour that the enemy had to abandon the woods, after a great part of his people had been massacred and 18 men had been taken prisoner by ours. These were transported to the French Division and surrendered to them. At that moment the French skirmishers, forward on the right, moved backwards, my right wing also starting to retreat with them. By the encouragements and courage of my brave officers I brought them back into the fire. The French *chasseurs à cheval* brought me cartridges to supply my men. The grenadiers and a company deployed forward behind a house, opening a steady fire on the enemy gunners on the dunes, silencing them with their fire, while the two detached companies in the dunes and the skirmishers on the right wing made several prisoners which were surrendered to the French troops. In this position I held my ground against the superior enemy; I constantly fetched cartridges and encouraged the battalion, until night fell, when I had used up nearly all cartridges and the enemy abandoned his position… The muskets are very worn out, obliging me to send them to Haarlem for repairs.[19]

The Batavian battalion would lose 126 men that day. Although the above account does not mention if the Batavians fought against Russian or British troops these could have been Chatham's 7th Brigade.

The fighting continued along the whole line. Two squadrons of the 11th Light Dragoons, led by Captain Sleigh, started turning the left wing of the Franco-Batavian line at Castricum, defeating the 5e and 16e Chasseurs à Cheval. The 51e Demi-Brigade panicked and routed. The situation looked grave for the exhausted Franco-Batavians. At this critical moment the initiative of a Batavian officer, who already had distinguished himself during various actions prior to this one, saved the day. *Colonel* de Quaita, commander of the Batavian Regiment Huzaren, some hours before had received the order from Brune to use his regiment at the time and in a way he believed was best. At this moment De Quaita judged the time to act had come. He ordered his regiment to charge the British cavalry. At the same time he inspired the infantry to attack, by ordering the infantry to stop firing and attack the enemy with the bayonet: *'La cavalerie ne-tirez plus, en avant enfants de la patrie, battez la charge aux baïonnettes, pas de charge!'*[20] This proved to be the turning point. The charge of the Batavian hussars was supported by the French 10e Dragons and the 4e Chasseurs à Cheval and was

---

19 Report of 8 October 1799 from *Major* Achenbach to *General-Major* Bonhomme in Van der Aa, *Geschiedenis van de jongst-geëindigden oorlog*, Vol.VIII, pp.306-308. The bayonet attack was led by *Capitein* Pfeiffer, *Eerste Lieutenant* Roodeman with the grenadiers silencing the cannon.
20 According to some French historians Brune led the charge of the Batavian hussars in person. Not confirmed by eyewitness reports this is highly unlikely and seems something to enhance Brune's service record.

a complete success. The British light dragoons, with their horses blown from their previous charge, also exhausted from a day of marching and fighting through loose sand and mud, could not resist the charge of the Batavian hussars, and they broke when the 4e Chasseurs à Cheval hit them in the flank, leaving behind some prisoners. Next the Franco-Batavian cavalry wheeled to the right and fell on the flank of Chatham's battalions surprising them between two groves. At the same moment, Vandamme charged the Anglo-Russians before him with the 42e and 49e Demi-Brigade in the direction of Bakkum; Fuzier charged the Russian right with the 90e Demi-Brigade, while Pacthod drove the Russians before him in the direction of Limmen, engaging Coote's 3rd Brigade positioned there. Caught between the cavalry and infantry Chatham's inexperienced soldiers broke, trying to find refuge in the dunes to the northwest were the cavalry would have difficulties to follow. The exception was for a large part of the 4th Foot, presumably the 2nd Battalion, which was cut off by *Chef de Bataillon* Alexandre Aubrée of the 42e Demi-Brigade:

> I remember the report to have reached us that on the right we had suffered considerable loss, and that a whole battalion of one regiment, one of the strongest in the army had been surrounded, and made prisoners by the enemy's cavalry.[21]

One source states that Aubrée (brother of *Général de Brigade* Aubrée), greatly outnumbered, believed he would have to surrender, but making use of the darkness he bluffed the British in to surrendering their arms instead.[22] This bluff is not confirmed though. Again, Castricum was retaken and many prisoners were made. At Bakkum, Essen managed to deploy three of his battalions covering the rout of his Russians and stopping the pursuit. The darkness ended the fighting.[23]

The battle of the 6th had started at Limmen and Akersloot with the British capturing the Franco-Batavian outposts there. During the day there was no fighting here. In the evening the British outposts in front of Akersloot were counterattacked by a small Batavian force under the command of *Capitein* Cordes of the Batavian horse artillery. He had received permission from *Colonel* Gilquin to make a reconnaissance in force with a volunteer force, consisting of 50 infantry, 40 troopers of the 1e Regiment Zware Cavalerie and 16 gunners on horseback of his own 1e Compagnie Rijdende Artillerie. He sent forward an advance guard of three gunners which he followed with 33 infantry and the horse, while the remainder of the infantry advanced in skirmishing order to his right to dislodge the enemy from some brushwood and the forward houses. The British infantry opened fire at the advancing Batavians, but afraid of being cut off, retreated into Akersloot after noticing the advance of the cavalry. There the British took up defensive positions; two battalions forming the centre, their left covered by a squadron of light dragoons and on their right, behind a drawbridge, a 6pdr cannon and a

---

21 Francis Maule, *Memoirs of the Principal Events in the Campaigns of North Holland and Egypt* (London: F.C. and J. Rivington, 1816), p.40.
22 Anon., *Mémoires Historiques sur la Campagne du Général en Chef Brune en Batavie, Du 5 Fructudor an 7, au 9 Frimaire an 8; Rédigés par un Officier de son État-Major* (Paris : Chez Favre, An IX), p.79. A biography on Chatham has recently been written by Jacqueline Reiter, *The Late Lord – The Life of John Pitt 2nd Earl of Chatham* (Barnsley, Pen & Sword Books Limited, 2017).
23 Gachot, *Brune en Hollande*, pp.295-296.

howitzer. Cordes noticed that the British infantry was unsteady and after asking Gilquin to support him with an infantry battalion he slowly advanced. However, Gilquin did not send any support and therefore the Batavians had to retreat again. While the infantry deployed in the centre, Cordes positioned the cavalry and his gunners to the left behind some cover, in such a way that they would be able to take a British infantry attack in the flank. This plan worked beyond expectation; the British advanced with an infantry battalion to attack the Batavian infantry and were promptly attacked in the flank by *Capitein* Cordes. The British had no time to fire before the Batavians were at them but managed to form a loose line behind a ditch. Despite this obstacle they were fiercely attacked by the Batavians, who jumped across the ditch with their horses, or even on foot when the horse refused to jump. The British battalion instantly broke and routed back to Akersloot, with many men throwing away their muskets in the process. The pursuing Batavians captured 10 prisoners. Because it became dark now and afraid of being cut off by enemy cavalry, Cordes retreated to Uitgeest and the fighting ended. Batavian losses were only four wounded horses.[24]

The Fighting on the Beach and in the Dunes

What had happened on the beach in the meantime? *Général de Division* Gouvion, who had been ordered to take up positions in the dunes and on the beach to stop a possible advance of the British, had already received news about the fighting between the Anglo-Russians and Boudet's troops. At 8:00 a.m. he ordered *Général de Brigade* Simon to advance into the dunes with his brigade, to watch for Anglo-Russian movements and to maintain in contact with the Franco-Batavian centre. *Général de Brigade* Aubrée was ordered to take up position on the beach with the 16e Chasseurs à Cheval and the artillery west of Bakkum and to attack the British if they would advance along the beach. Gouvion himself remained in reserve with both battalions of the 72e Demi-Brigade and the 5e Chasseurs à Cheval. Not much later Abercromby's Advance Guard (MacDonald) advanced along the beach, trying to keep in line with the advance of the Russians, They were preceded by the four squadrons of the 11th Regiment of Light Dragoons and four cannon, covered on their left flank by a force of skirmishers moving along the edge of the dunes. To halt their advance Gouvion ordered Aubrée to advance a squadron of the 16e Chasseurs à Cheval. Covered by these he deployed a battery across the beach, consisting of six guns of the 4/4e Artillerie Légère commanded by *Capitaine* Couturier and a division of the Batavian 1e Compagnie Rijdende Artillerie (2 guns). Another squadron of the 16e Chasseurs à Cheval and one and a half battalion of the 98e Demi-Brigade supported them. The British cavalry could only see the advanced squadron of the *chasseurs à cheval* and immediately charged them. After coming within canister range, the *chasseurs à cheval* unmasked the artillery battery, which opened fire at the British light dragoons and inflicted heavy casualties. The British had to retreat and pursued by the French cavalry they retreated as far as the village Egmond aan Zee, were they finally rallied behind MacDonald's infantry. The French cavalry did not engage these troops but retreated orderly to their former position. Now MacDonald's infantry advanced, with the Light Infantry Battalion and

---

24 van Es, *De Veldtocht in Noord-Holland 1799*, pp.19-24.

Grenadier Battalion in front, while Hely-Hutchinson's 6th Brigade was sent into the dunes to cover his flank. In their turn MacDonald's infantry was attacked fiercely by the French. They did not stand this ordeal for long and had to retreat:

> We maintained the action as well as our limited means permitted, and for a while kept tolerable order; but as the fight became hotter, and the disparity of force more apparent, I regret to say, our young troops fell into considerable disorder and confusion. This giving the enemy greater confidence, of course he availed himself of it, and attacked us with redoubled impetuosity; and, I lament to say, our dismayed and disheartened young soldiers fell from one degree of confusion to another, till at length all order seemed entirely lost amongst us; and what was at first a rather regular retreat, became at last a disorderly flight; for wherever an attempt was made to check the ardour of the enemy, the immense inequality of force they possessed soon completely overthrew the few that stood; and many were the brave fellows, both officers and men, who fell in this unequal contest, without their having the slightest chance of successfully opposing our impetuous foe. The flight now became more like a race than any thing else, and I imagine they drove us not less than three or four miles without giving us time to breathe; but when we had reached within about a mile of the village we had left in the morning, we perceived some regiments advancing to our succour; among them was the 23d, which advanced in line, and showed so good and steady a front as quite delighted us.[25]

Général de Brigade Aubrée deployed the 98e Demi-Brigade in skirmishing order into the dunes, to engage the British skirmishers that tried to turn his flank. In the dunes the French were fiercely attacked by British infantry. Pressed hard *Général de Brigade* Simon came into serious trouble. Because of the terrain fighting was very confused. This confusion is described in the regimental history of the 20th Foot, part of Hely-Hutchinson's 6th Brigade:

> Both battalions marched from their quarters about two o'clock and advanced in line. Some of the companies charged into the enemy's line and were mixed with a French corps at the close of the evening, indeed Captain Chalmers had for a short time a French General in his hands. It was a confused battle, fought without intention or object. Heavy rain fell throughout the day and this, together with the difficult country, made it impossible for anyone to direct what has well called an off hand engagement, contested with great obstinacy and ended only by the darkness.[26]

Général de Brigade Simon with three battalions of the 54e Demi-Brigade, and the 98e Demi-Brigade were attacked and the former nearly cut off by Hely-Hutchinson's 6th Brigade. Simon was desperately trying to extricate his infantry. Gouvion, receiving the news of the peril his subordinate was in, committed his reserve. Joining *Général de Brigade* Aubrée west of Bakkum he left six companies of the 2/72e Demi-Brigade in position to keep the British on the beach in

---

25   Surtees, *Twenty-five years in the Rifle Brigade*, pp.25-26.
26   Smyth, *Lancashire Fusiliers*, p.195.

check and to protect his artillery and moved into the dunes with the remainder of his troops. There he encountered four British battalions that had deployed on a small level plain in the dunes, half way between the village Bakkum and the beach. To engage these troops he ordered the grenadiers of the 72e Demi-Brigade to deploy in skirmish order in the dunes to the right of the plain. He positioned the 1/72e Demi-Brigade in line at the edge of the plain, the left covered by two companies of the 2/72e Demi-Brigade in skirmishing order. After the arrival of the grenadiers at their designated position he advanced into the plain with his infantry line and opened a heavy platoon-fire on the surprised British. Supported by the grenadiers on his right and by the skirmishers on his left the British were nearly surrounded and suffered heavy losses. This gave *Général de Brigade* Simon the chance to extricate his troops and both sides retreated and reformed, observing each other. This situation would last until 6:00 p.m. when the British again advanced, with most of their troops moving along the beach. Initially the Franco-Batavian artillery managed to stop their advance but when the ammunition ran out Gouvion thought it advisable to retreat. The British light dragoons attacked the rearguard, consisting of some companies of the 72e Demi-Brigade, but their attack was beaten off by well-directed fire. Darkness made an end to the fighting and the British retreated to Egmond aan Zee.

Aftermath

The left wing of the Anglo-Russian army, commanded by Lieutenant General Pulteney, was not committed to the battle. He also would not have had a chance against the fortified positions of Daendels. Brune had ordered Daendels to send most of his troops to Beverwijk and the only troops left were three infantry battalions and the 2e Bataljon Jagers. Despite this small force Daendels was sure he could defend his position which, as already described, was made unassailable by the inundations.

The Franco-Batavians retook all the positions they had lost except for their outposts at Bakkum, Limmen, and Akersloot which were still occupied by the Anglo-Russians. On both sides victory was claimed, in fact the only result of the battle was more dead and wounded. Strategically the battle was a Franco-Batavian victory, the Anglo-Russians being unable to break through the Franco-Batavian defences. Brune did not fail to claim victory as well as the credits for it, writing to the Batavian Government:

> I had foreseen that the position, which we had taken up backwards, would cause the enemy to make the wrong judgment, and today he attacked us. One has fought since 7 o'clock in the morning until 8 o'clock in the evening. The enemy has been driven back and pursued to Egmond. We have captured 11 pieces, 1500 Russians and English are prisoner. The amount of dead is considerable, mainly among the Russians. The Batavian generals Bonhomme and Vichery have distinguished themselves. I have to give deserved praise to the National Guards of Rotterdam, which have been in the fire like veteran soldiers.[27]

---

27 Letter of 7 October 1799 from General Brune to the *Uitvoerend Bewind*, in *Besluiten der Eerste Kamer van het Vertegenwoordigend Lichaam des Bataafschen Volks. October 1799*.

The Batavians lost a total of 242 men: nine men dead, 56 wounded and 177 missing. The French lost 156 men: 1,114 men killed or wounded and 42 taken prisoner. Total Franco-Batavian losses were 1,398 men.[28] Total British losses were 1,439 men: four officers and 89 others killed, including the Lieutenant Colonels Bainbridge and Dickson; 35 officers and 699 others wounded, including Major General Hely-Hutchinson, Major General Chatham, Colonel Maitland of the 1st Foot Guards, and Lieutenant Colonel Hodgson; 19 officers and 593 others missing or taken prisoner, including Lieutenant Colonel Lake of the 1st Foot Guards and Lieutenant Colonel Cholmondeley. Chatham's 7th Brigade alone, supporting the Russians around Castricum, lost 31 killed, 213 wounded and 385 missing, a total of 626: this amounted to 44 percent of total British losses.[29] Russian losses were 1,118 men and eight guns: nine officers and 374 others dead or missing, with Colonel Dubiansky taken prisoner; 26 officers and 709 others wounded, including Colonel Gladki.[30] Total Anglo-Russian losses were 2,557 men and 11 guns.[31]

That the battle of the 6th was not intended by York can be read between the lines of his after action report of 7 October, which also tells us nothing about a certain plan or order of battle:

> The enemy, after the action of the 2d, having taken up the position between Beverwick and Wyck-op-Zee, I determined to endeavour to force him thence before he had an opportunity of strengthening by works the short and very defensible line which he occupied and to oblige him still further to retire before he could be joined by the reinforcements which I had information were upon their march. Preparatory, therefore, to a general forward movement, I ordered the advanced posts which the army took up on the 3d inst. in front of this place, of Egmont-op-te-Hooff and Egmont-op-Zee, to be pushed forward, which operation took place yesterday morning. At first little opposition was shown and we succeeded in taking possession of the villages of Schermerhoorn, Acher Sloot, Limmen, Baccum and of a position on the Sand-Hills near Wyck-op-Zee: the column of Russian troops under the command of major-general D'Essen, in endeavouring to gain a height in front of their intended advanced post at Baccum (which was material to the security of that point), was vigorously opposed and afterwards attacked by a strong body of the enemy, which obliged general Sir Ralph Abercrombie to move up in support with the reserve of his corps. The enemy on their part advanced their whole force; the action became general along the whole line from Limmen to the sea and

---

28 Gachot, *Brune en Hollande*, p.296
29 Official British returns of 9 October 1799 in Anon., *Campaign in Holland*, Appendix No.11, pp.87-89; Walsh, *Narrative*, pp.135-136; Anon., *The History of the Campaign of 1799, in Holland*, pp.391-395.
30 Official returns of 7 October 1799 by Major-General Essen as listed in Miliutin, *Geschichte des Krieges*, Vol.V, pp.297-298.
31 According to Gachot, *Brune en Hollande*, p.296, the Franco-Batavians took an additional 900 Russians prisoner, but this is highly improbable. 351 prisoners arrived in Haarlem (249 British and 79 Russian soldiers, as well as 17 British and six Russian officers). They were accompanied by about a hundred British woman and children who had followed their men taken prisoner. On the 9th these were separated from their men and sent back to the Anglo-Russian army, the cause of heartbreaking scenes making a huge impression on the citizens of Haarlem (Anon., *Geschiedkundig Gedenkstuk van het Voorgevallene binnen Haarlem*), pp.214-215.

was maintained with great obstinacy on both sides until night, when the enemy retired, leaving us masters of the field of battle. The conflict however has, I am concerned to state, been so severe and has been attended with as serious a loss (in proportion to the numbers engaged) as any of those which have been fought by the brave troops composing this army since their arrival in Holland. The gallantry they displayed and the perseverance with which they supported the fatigues of this day, rival their former exertions.

The corps engaged were:

> Major-general D'Oyley's brigade of guards.
> Major-general Burrard's brigade.
> Major-general Earl Chatham's brigade.
> Major-general Coote's brigade.
> Major-general the earl of Cavan's brigade, commanded by major-general Hutchinson.
> The reserve under the command of colonel Macdonald.
> Part of the 7th and 11th dragoons.
> And seven battalions of Russians.

To General Sir Ralph Abercrombie and the other general-officers in command of the brigades before-mentioned, as also to colonel Macdonald, my warmest acknowledgments are due, for their spirited and judicious exertions during this affair; nor ought I to omit the praise due to colonel Clephane, commanding four companies of the 3d and one of the Coldstream regiments of guards, who, by a spirited charge, drove two battalions of the enemy from the post of Acher Sloot, making two hundred prisoners. I have sincerely to regret, that, in the course of the action, major-general Hutchinson received a musket-shot wound in the thigh, which, however, is not serious. I have not yet received any reports of the killed and wounded, but I am apprehensive that the number of British is not less than five hundred and that the loss of the Russian troops, as far as I can understand, amounts to twelve hundred men. I shall, as early as circumstances possibly admit, transmit particular returns. The loss of the enemy upon this occasion has been very great; and, in addition to their killed and wounded, five hundred prisoners fell into our hands.[32]

In his after action report, Major-General Essen put the blame of the defeat with the British and on Abercromby specifically:

> Major-General Sedmoratzki advanced bravely at eight o'clock in the morning, and soon gained the desired success. The English column however, which had

---

32 Dispatch of 7 October 1799 from the Duke of York to Henry Dundas in Walsh, *Narrative*, pp.132-133. The mentioned village of Schermerhorn was situated east of Alkmaar just in front of Lieutenant General Pulteney's positions, 11 kilometres in front of the Franco-Batavian defence line and not occupied by them. It was captured without opposition or British losses.

been assigned to cover our right flank, did not move from the spot. The battle was very heated on both sides; one fought with the bayonet. At about two o'clock the numerical superior enemy, recognizing the importance of the heights occupied by us, was fighting with all his forces, while he turned our right flank, which he found not covered. I sent for the English general, who finally arrived with his column at four o'clock in the afternoon. At six o'clock, the enemy was put to flight with heavy losses, but we had also lost many people in the meantime.[33]

As described the British were far from inactive and their losses, which were more severe than those of the Russians show that the British were hotly engaged as well. York was, at least officially, more positive about the Russians, writing to the Tsar:

I can not applaud enough the excellent achievements of the Russian troops, although their ferocity has unexpectedly led them into a general struggle against considerably superior forces, and therefore they could not be supported in time.[34]

The Orangist Military Forces in Holland

The Franco-Batavian retreat after the battle of Alkmaar had brought the Dutch in high spirits. On 4 October, *Colonel* Bentinck requested orders from the Prince of Orange to go to Medemblik with a group of reliable man, to requisition everything that was needed from there. The plans of the Prince of Orange went even further. On the 5th he ordered *Colonel* Bentinck to bring all soldiers of Dutch origin he could find from Den Helder to Medemblik, in addition all those on Wieringen. These men would form the core of the 'New Army of the State', initially to consist of five infantry battalions, a *jager* battalion, two artillery companies, a pioneer company, and a cavalry corps. The Prince of Orange was in his orders especially elated about the prospect of having his own cavalry: 'We also have now the beginning of cavalry, some hussars with their horses crossed to serve with us'. These were in fact only seven men though; a corporal and six hussars.[35]

On the 7th, the day after the Battle of Castricum, for most of the day the Prince of Orange was convinced that the Anglo-Russian army had won another victory, as proven by a series of letters he wrote that morning. Firstly a letter to Baron d'Yvoy, 'The number of Batavian deserters increases every day: yesterday, when we won the outposts of Limmen, Bakkum and Akersloot, we had about 250. I doubt the enemy would offer much resistance when he was pursued'; and to *Generaal-Major* Bentinck, 'We had the advantage'; and to Van der Spiegel, 'I hope things will soon be able to conduct here, to establish communications with Germany and to revolutionise the land provinces'. It has to be seen if the amount of Batavian deserters reflected any aversion of the population against the Batavian Republic. Sir Ralph Abercromby remarked on this matter in a letter to Henry Dundas on the 8th that: 'It is indeed true, that many Dutch soldiers have deserted, most of whom are deserters by

---

33 Report of 7 October 1799 from Major-General Essen to Tsar Paul in Miliutin, *Geschichte des Krieges*, Vol.V, p.297.
34 Letter of 8 October 1799 from York to Tsar Paul in Miliutin, *Geschichte des Krieges*, Vol.V, p.66.
35 Koolemans Beijnen, *De Erfprins van Oranje in Noord-Holland*, pp.81–82.

profession, Germans, Belgians and Austrians'.[36] The letter above to Van der Spiegel was finished in an entirely different way though. While in the process of writing the letter, the Prince of Orange was called to the Duke of York. Arriving there he was told that the Duke, after having conferred with his lieutenant generals, would retreat to the Zijpe position. The Prince saw all his plans fall to pieces and reinstatement of his father the Stadtholder as head of State of a new Dutch nation as well. Of course he desperately objected, but to no avail. As a result his letter to Van der Spiegel was on 9 October finished with: 'What will come now, heaven knows. I have moved to Den Helder, and I will wait for the circumstances to unfold and await orders from England'.[37]

---

36 Koolemans Beijnen, *De Erfprins van Oranje in Noord-Holland*, p.108.
37 Koolemans Beijnen, *De Erfprins van Oranje in Noord-Holland*, pp.83-84.

16

The Armistice

In all five battles together the British alone had lost 512 dead, 2,571 wounded and 1,307 missing. These figures do not include the sick.[1] The Russians had lost 4,653 men and an additional 2,576 Russians were sick.[2] At Castricum the British again suffered a substantial loss of officers attributed to the light infantry and riflemen of the Franco-Batavians, for example by Lieutenant Steevens of the 20th Foot:

> I was Lieutenant of grenadiers at the time I was wounded, but had command of a battalion company; and Ensign Favell and myself, who were the only officers of that company, were both wounded before a single man of the company were hit, which was a proof that we were picked off by the French riflemen, numbers of which they had in front of their Army; we, unfortunately, had but few in front of ours, and they, I believe, belonged to the 60th Rifles. The riflemen the enemy had gave them a great advantage over us, and in consequence of their having so many light troops many of our officers were picked off by them, and the proportion of killed and wounded officers was very great; but we are wiser now, and can show as good a front as the enemy whenever we have an opportunity to cope with them. Note: The marked difference between the uniforms of the officers and privates at that time also accounted for so many of the former being easily distinguished and picked off.[3]

After the Battle of Castricum the Anglo-Russian soldiers had a tiring night, remaining under arms in their position during the night. Firing continued for a long time as described by Walsh:

> Evening now set in, accompanied with deluges of rain, yet still the engagement continued with changeable success, but with unabating obstinacy. Even the darkness of the night, combined with the severity of the weather, did not terminate it. The fire of the small arms was incessant, and became quite vivid, running along the undulating line of the hills, and extending in various directions into the plain,

---

1 Returns of 7 October 1799 in Koolemans Beijnen, *De Erfprins van Oranje in Noord-Holland*, p.156.
2 Miliutin, *Geschichte des Krieges*, Vol.V, p.67.
3 Steevens, *Reminiscences*, pp.10-11.

whilst the gloomy horizon was every now and then illuminated by the flashes of the cannon, and the curved train of fire of the shells. At length, about ten o'clock at night, the firing entirely ceased, the enemy everywhere retired, and the allied army was left in undisturbed possession of the scene of action.[4]

Next morning the Anglo-Russian army was in a dangerous position, the various corps dispersed and without any order or supports. Again the rain came down heavily. Exposed in the open, arms and ammunition were spoiled and the uniforms drenched. Luckily for the Anglo-Russians, the Franco-Batavians had also suffered from the battle and the bad weather, and had expended most of their ammunition. Therefore although morale was high they were in no position to attack. So on the 7th no fighting occurred as both armies recovered from the intense fighting the previous day. The Franco-Batavians returned to their former positions. To improve communications between Daendels and the remainder of the Franco-Batavian army, six companies of the 7e Halve Brigade were ordered to occupy the villages Krommeniedijk and Knollendam.

Major General Don's Mission

During the morning of the 6th and despite the raging battle, Daendels was so sure of the strength of his positions that he decided to pay a visit to Brune, following the part of his division that had been ordered to Beverwijk, giving temporary command to *Generaal-Major* Van Zuylen van Nyevelt at Purmerend. Some hours later around 11:00 a.m., a British officer approached the outposts, demanding to enter as a special envoy to His Royal Highness the Duke of York with a mission to the Batavian Government. Owing to the extensive flooding it took a long time to receive the permission from *Generaal-Major* Van Zuylen van Nyevelt. Once obtained, the British representative, being Major General Don, was led through the floods without a blindfold and saw all the preparations that were made to stop any Anglo-Russian attack. Being brought before Van Zuylen van Nyevelt, Don was told that it was not customary to appear as a negotiator in the middle of a battle! Don assured him that at the time he left Alkmaar, there were no plans for an attack on the Franco-Batavians. However, he could give no reason for the fact that he did not return to the Anglo-Russian lines upon hearing the noise of battle. Don was embarrassed by his predicament and wanted to return to York, however, he was placed under guard until Daendels would return. On his arrival Daendels found a pack of proclamations on Don and immediately declared him if not a spy, at least his prisoner of war by right. As a prisoner he was send to Brune's headquarters. Brune agreed to Daendels view and Don was duly send to the citadel of Lille, not to be released before the Peace of Amiens. What Don's mission was never became clear; probably York had send him to negotiate about a possible evacuation of Holland by the Anglo-Russians and it was the unexpected battle which caused confusion.

---

4   Walsh, *Narrative*, p.75.

The Retreat

The battle of 6 October had brought nothing for the Anglo-Russians except further loss. The Franco-Batavian positions were strong and their army was by now more than a match for the Anglo-Russians, with French reinforcements arriving every day. After the Battle of Castricum York considered it impossible to win the campaign. His army was demoralised by their sufferings and their fatigue, having fought five consecutive battles without reaching a decisive result. He even considered himself too weak to hold his positions: only about 17,000 Anglo-Russians were still capable of fighting and there were not enough artillery rounds and cartridges left to fight another battle. In addition, he received intelligence about the latest reinforcements of the Franco-Batavian army, estimated at 6,000 men. York decided to fall back on his old positions at the Zijpe.

There is a fair amount of confusion as to when, how, and in what circumstances York decided to retreat. In any case, the Anglo-Russian retreat was unexpected by many. According to York, the direct cause was the outcome of the battle of 6 October which, although not a clear defeat in any case was no victory for the Anglo-Russian army. After the battle York requested advice from the Lieutenant Generals Abercromby, Dundas, Hulse, and Pulteney, about the current situation. They replied: 'That therefore we should return to the position of the Zijpe which we quitted and there await a more favourable change of circumstances'.[5] During the morning of the 7th York wrote to the Secretary of War Dundas, that it would most probably be necessary to follow the above advice. On the 8th, after the retreat had taken place, he again wrote from his headquarters in Schagerbrug to Dundas:

> You will perceive by the date of this letter that I have been under the painful necessity of doing what I mentioned to you in my letter, that I was afraid I should be obliged to do, I mean to resume my former position here. Soon after I had written to you, Sir Ralph Abercromby, Lieutenant-General Dundas and Sir James Pulteney came to me and represented to me in the strongest manner the absolute necessity of taking this step.[6]

That same day, Abercromby also wrote a letter to Dundas, explaining the bad circumstances the Anglo-Russian army was in:

> I do not imagine you have been for some time very sanguine in your hopes of our succeeding in the conquest of Holland. The grounds on which this great undertaking were founded have failed. We have found no cooperation in the country, and the French have found the means of sending a powerful force to maintain their authority on the Batavian Republic. It is indeed true that many Dutch soldiers have deserted, most of whom are deserters by profession: Germans, Poles, and Austrians. Every action, whether successful or otherwise, has proved an accession of force to the enemy: we have lost men, they have been able to supply their

---

5   Letter of 7 October 1799 of the four mentioned generals to the Duke of York. Letter in English in Koolemans Beijnen, *De Erfprins van Oranje in Noord-Holland in 1799*, pp.153-156. For the complete text see Appendix XX.
6   Quoted in English in Koolemans Beijnen, *De Erfprins van Oranje in Noord-Holland*, p.91.

loss. We are certainly 10,000 men fewer in our effective strength since the 1st of September; the French with all their loss, which has been considerable, are more than 10,000 stronger than on the 1st of last month, and not a day passes that does not bring them some reinforcement. It is a well known fact that military operations in Holland cease in November: the moisture of the country will not allow troops to encamp, and the badness of the roads puts a stop to all land carriage. With the advantage of water carriage, I do not know that the troops have actually had the means of immediately receiving four days supplies in advance, that is to say that we have not had with the army sufficient magazines to furnish this supply.

It must be considered that this is not a corn country; that every species of grain must come by sea; that our getting possession of Haarlem did not give us a port, and that until we got Amsterdam the Zuyder Zee was not to us of much benefit; our only direct communication remained the Helder. With regard to Amsterdam, I believe the most sanguine person could scarcely persuade himself that we could get that important place unless the French chose to evacuate Holland. As to reinforcements from England, I have been one of those who did not wish for them. If with such an army as the Duke had, we could not carry the point, I should have been sorry if the remaining land force had been wasted here. We are not under any kind of uneasiness on our own account: we are conscious that we have done our duty, and the troops in every attack have maintained their national character, and in general have been victorious. Were we however to sustain a severe check, I much doubt if their discipline would have been able to prevent a total dissolution of the army. This is a melancholy fact, and is the natural consequence of young soldiers and unexperienced officers, all powerful when they attack, but without resource if beaten. These considerations and many others have of late occurred to all those who think in the army, and I have been one of those who have ventured to suggest the real situation to H.R.H., who will no doubt state our situation better than I can do. I scarcely believe there is a difference of opinion amongst us, and all those whose rank entitles them to be consulted are unanimous in approving of the measures which have been taken since the affair of the 2d. What your decision with regard to us will be, I know not, but you will probably not keep all of us in this corner, nor do I see that much can be done in Friesland or Groningen, which is a country full as difficult as the province of Holland.[7]

The next day, York sent a second and more comprehensive letter to Dundas:

I have already acquainted you with the result of the action of the 6th inst. which terminated successfully to the allied arms, and at the same time pointed out the necessity of the movement which produced this affair. From the prisoners taken upon the 6th inst. I learnt the certainty of the enemy having been reinforced since the action of the 2d by two Demi-Brigades, amounting to about six thousand infantry, and of their

---

[7] Letter in English of 8 October 1799 from Abercromby to Henry Dundas in Colenbrander, *Gedenkstukken*, Vol.III, pp.428-429.

having strengthened the position of Beverwick, and fortified strongly in the rear of its point, which it would still be necessary to carry before Haarlem could be attacked. It ought also to be stated, that the enemy had retired a large force upon Purmerend, in an almost inaccessible position, covered by an inundated country, and the debouches from which were strongly fortified and in the hands of the enemy: and further, that as our army advanced, this corps was placed in our rear. But such obstacles would have been overcome, had not the state of the weather, the ruined condition of the roads, and total want of the necessary supplies arising from the above causes, presented difficulties which required the most serious consideration.

Having maturely weighed the circumstances in which the army was thus placed, and having felt it my duty, on a point of so much importance, to consult with general Sir Ralph Abercrombie and the lieutenant-generals of this army, I could not but consider (and their opinion was unanimous on the subject) that it would be for the benefit of the general cause to withdraw the troops from their advanced position, in order to wait his majesty's further instructions. I must request you will again represent to his majesty the distinguished conduct of his army, which, while acting under the pressure of uncommon difficulties, never for a moment ceased to be actuated by the noblest feelings for the success of the public cause, and the honour of the British arms. As there are many points resulting from our present situation upon which you may require particular information, and such details as cannot be brought within the compass of a letter, I have thought it necessary to charge my secretary, colonel Brownrigg, with this dispatch, who will be able to explain fully all matters relating to this army. I transmit a return of killed, wounded, and missing, of his majesty's and the Russian troops in the action of the 6th instant. I most heartily lament that it has again been so serious, and that so many brave and valuable men have fallen.[8]

Apparently, the mentioned officers were convinced that the campaign had been lost. But they were not the only ones, their view shared with many others: 'On our side sickness had set in, provisions became scarce, the season advanced and still continuing its character of unremitted wet. We could gain nothing by advancing; and the armistice, under all the circumstances, was the wisest step that could have been taken'.[9] News about the situation in Holland had not became public in Great Britain though. Newspapers were on 12 October still writing about reinforcements being sent:

We hear that not only the light infantry battalions of the guards are to be sent off to Holland without delay, but also a strong reinforcement of cavalry, and four additional regiments of infantry. The guards will number 1200 men; the cavalry will consist of 14 squadrons of heavy horse, which will be employed to keep the line of advanced posts, which by the late victory is become very extensive, occupying a space of 21 miles in front. With the above reinforcements, it is intended to send 150

---

8 Letter of 9 October 1799 from the Duke of York to Henry Dundas, in Walsh, *Narrative*, pp.133-134.
9 Anon., 'Recollections of the British army', p.191.

large row-boats, which are to carry one long three pounder in the bow, to be rowed by 12 picked seamen, and to carry 24 infantry, who are to be attached to each boat. This addition to our naval forces cannot fail to be of the greatest advantage. The boats are to be employed in the Lake of Haerlem and in the canals.

La Pomone of 44 guns, Capt. R.C. Reynolds, is now under weigh, for the Texel, with the ships Castle, Henrietta, Ralph Nicholson, Northumberland, Kitty, Mary, and Prince Royal, with thirteen others, names unknown transports, having on board 800 artillery and baggage-horses, for the use of the Russian army in Holland. Fourteen transport vessels are going into Ramsgate harbour, to take in 500 horses more which completes the full number intended for the service of the expedition.[10]

Of course the horses would arrive much too late. The events leading to some kind of armistice were as follows. Around noon on the 7th, a meeting took place between French, Batavian, and British officers in a smithy in Limmen. Russians officers were not present and were also not consulted about a possible armistice. What was discussed on this meeting is not known, nor the contents of the armistice, but apparently it seems that the French had informed the British about the continuous arrival of reinforcements. As already described this was no bragging. To recall: on 1 October the 2/72e Demi-Brigade arrived; on the 3rd, 4th, and 5th two battalions of the 51e Demi-Brigade; also on the 3rd, 12 companies of the 98e Demi-Brigade. On the 7th, still more units had already entered the Batavian republic, on their way to the theatre of war: the 1/ and 3/21e Demi-Brigade, three battalions of the 4e Demi-Brigade, and more on their way. This information was used to show to the British that chances to force the Franco-Batavian lines and to win the campaign were low.

So, apparently, the proposal for an armistice came from the French. An indication for this comes from Sir Ralph Abercromby in a letter to his family:

> I wrote to you on the signing of the Convention. What could tempt the French to agree to it, I cannot conceive. One-half of this Army must have fallen into their hands, with all our artillery, stores, etc. It would have overset the Ministry, so great would have been the indignation of the nation, however ill directed. I am sure they ought to thank the Duke of York for listening to the advice which he got on this occasion. Whether our conduct is approved or not, is to me a matter of indifference, being conscious that we were in the right. The first hint came from the French Army, which was taken up by the Duke's Etat-Major; when proposed by them to me, I desired them to put it down in writing. I heartily concurred with them, and desired them to carry it to Lord Chatham, which was done.[11]

It is not clear if or what kind of armistice was closed between the French and British officers in that smithy in Limmen. The only description we have of this event, copied in local accounts by others but not described by national historians, is from Pastor Bommers of Castricum in his notes about the events of 6 and 7 October:

---

10   Letter of 31 October in *London Chronicle*, 12 October 1799.
11   James Lord Dunfermline, *Lieutenant-General Sir Ralph Abercromby K.B. 1793-1801. A Memoir by his Son* (Edinburgh: Edmonston and Douglas, 1861), pp.200-201.

But on Monday [7 October], a quarter before noon, a wagon left from Castricum with seven officers of the Highest Rank, on the road from the English outposts being blindfolded there to the house of citizen Frederik Zinniger, blacksmith [in Limmen]. The English commander had already given him the order to make fire and to prepare a table and chairs, as he did. The wagon arrived, the officers came into his house one by one, the blindfolds were taken off and they sat near the fire. The English were still working on the batteries. The named officers ate some breakfast and drank a glass of wine or liquor, and were talking heatedly. By the way the house, and the doors of the house were occupied by sentries, though the blacksmith and his son were and remained in the same room, but they did not understand a word. A quarter before two everything was over, the officers, of which apparently four French and three Dutch, were brought back to the wagon one by one and blindfolded, and following the road brought back again to Castricum. Some time later an Englishman came through the English outposts at the roads until near the outpost of the French at the boundary stone between Castricum and Limmen, waving a white cloth, among his head. The French outpost went and came with the Englishman and his entourage, and received from the English three or four boxes or briefcases. Crelis Schrama has seen it; what was inside it does one not know, but certainly no rotten nuts. This is, until now, a secret, as well as the retreat of the whole English army, Monday 7 October in the evening and during the night to North-Holland.[12]

As a result of the secret armistice, which according to local legend was signed on the anvil of the smithy in Limmen, the Anglo-Russian retreat started on 7 October at 2:00 p.m. during heavy downpours, all the way back to its former position in the Zijpe, behind the Westfriesche Zeedijk, and because morale was low it was disorderly and hasty. The retreat took place with much confusion under incessant rain. Battalions chose what they believed was the best way to their assigned position in the Zijpe, many soldiers lost their unit and straggled along. The retreat is described by Walsh:

> About seven o'clock in the evening a very unexpected order was issued, for the troops to fall in, and the different brigades immediately to form. It was pitchy dark, and the clouds descended in cataracts. In this situation the arrangements were at length effected; but with how much difficulty and confusion may be easily conceived. About ten o'clock at night the whole army was in full retreat. The right wing faced towards Petten, and marched along the strand close to the tide. The rest of the army retired by Alkmaar. Fires had been previously lighted on the heights, at the advanced picquets, to deceive the enemy... Indeed, a general consciousness of our critical situation operated as a bond of union, which kept the whole army in some order, until they arrived at their own lines. But then, the line of march was entirely broke up, by the different regiments attempting to move off, in

---

12 Nicolaas Bommer, 'Korte Beschrijvinge Van Den Slag Of Batailje Op Den Zesden October, Zijnde Ook Castricummer-Kermes 1799 Voorgevallen', in: M. Kramer, 'De slag bij Castricum 6 en 7 Oct. 1799', *Vragen van den Dag* (Amsterdam: S.L. van Looy, 1905), pp.467-468.

various directions, towards their respective stations. In the disorder which ensued, numbers were thrown out, who found it impossible to recover their different corps during the remainder of the march. The intense darkness was still accompanied by deluges of rain. There was no sure footing; all was quagmire; but the firmest bottom, and, on the whole, the safest way, lay through pools of water, though it was impossible to guess whether the next step would be up to the knees or the neck. Notwithstanding so many difficulties and dangers, the greater part of the troops arrived safely at their different quarters in the evening of the 8th; and those who were thrown behind dropped in the ensuing day. The medium length of this harassing march (from Egmont to Schagen) was about thirty miles.[13]

Despite the armistice the Anglo-Russians were pursued by the Franco-Batavians, although they were not pushed very hard. Maule relating:

On the 7th of October, at the earliest dawn, the brigade were under arms, and marched immediately, taking the sea-shore. The movement was retrograde. The security which this route afforded, was evident; but we were dreadfully harassed by the deep and heavy sands. The baggage horses were frequently seen rolling over with their oppressive and heavy burthens, and no inconsiderable number of them as well as men, fell into the hands of the enemy's hussars, who followed close upon us, and seized upon every weary straggler. The weather and elements seemed to conspire against us, and continued hostile during the whole of the retreat. A powerful corps of cavalry hung upon our rear. These very troops had, a few hours before, covered the retreat of their own columns. No sooner, however, did they perceive the unexpected retrograde movement of the combined army, than they instantly changed their route.[14]

In all their hurry two complete field hospitals including the wounded and sick were left behind and captured by the Franco-Batavian cavalry which was leading the pursuit, because as soon as the Anglo-Russian retreat became known to Brune he had ordered the advance. The hospitals contained 216 Russians and about 50 British; Lieutenant Steevens of the 20th Foot was one of the wounded left behind at Egmond aan Zee, recollecting:

I was amongst the number, being very severely wounded [in the leg], and afterwards taken prisoner by the French cavalry at Egmont-op-Zee on the morning of the 8th; our Army having commenced their retreat on the evening of the 7th, leaving their own wounded behind, as well as the wounded prisoners... The wounded of course passed an anxious night on the 7th, expecting the enemy to enter the town every moment. As soon as daylight appeared in galloped the French cavalry, sword in hand. One came into the room where I was lying, attended by my servant, Private Thomas Lamb, who was taken prisoner with me, as, when I was

---

13 Walsh, *Narrative*, pp.84-86.
14 Maule, *Memoirs*, pp.40-41.

left behind at Egmont-op-Zee, he would not leave me, but was determined to share my fate. Immediately the Frenchman saw me he said "Qui etes vous"? I answered "Un officier Anglais"; he then said "Les officiers sont braves, mais les soldats ne le sont pas," and taking up my canteen drank part of its contents, which consisted of either white brandy or hollands; he then left the room; others came in, amongst whom was a French officer; I was glad to see him, as I expected to be well used, and I found it to be the case, for the French officers treated us prisoners with the greatest humanity and attention.

Soon after the French entered Egmont-op-Zee preparations were made to remove the wounded out of the town towards the rear. Poor Favell and I were put into the same open Dutch wagon, and were taken that night to Alkmaar, where we were put into a hospital for the night. Here our wounds were dressed (I mean Favell's and mine, for my servant was not wounded). There were a great many Dutch females in the hospital, making bandages and assisting the wounded; some appeared to be ladies, for there were Dutch officers and men, as well as French and English, in the hospital. The French General (Le Brun) promised that my servant should remain with me, but it was not attended to, and poor Tom Lamb was put into prison with the other soldiers who were taken, and I heard nothing of him for many months … We were about a week or ten days reaching Breda; we were laid generally in our clothes upon mattresses, sometimes being carried into an inn. We suffered much from the jolting of the wagons, and at one time we were obliged to halt for a day or so to recruit our strength, for it was very fatiguing travelling so many days in open wagons, without our clothes being taken off, and the surgeons were fearful and apprehensive lest some of us should be thrown into a fever. The journey to Breda was very harassing, the wounded being conveyed in boats by canal, as well as in wagons… One day the French soldiers were carrying me through the streets with other wounded English officers, and a party of Dutch insulted us by hooting, etc. The French soldiers immediately drove them off with the butt-end of their muskets, and no doubt would have floored a few of them if they had not made themselves scarce. The French always behaved well to us, but the Dutch were very boorish and uncivil.[15]

The French troops advanced north on a broad front, from Egmond aan Zee to Alkmaar, although much hampered by the bad state of the roads. On 8 October the Franco-Batavians entered Alkmaar again. The French *chasseurs à cheval* captured about 600 stragglers and three to four hundred women and children. The latter would be sent to Amsterdam, but released three days later, after having being kindly treated and provided with new clothes by the citizens. That same day in the afternoon the French advanced guard was the first to arrive in front of the Zijpe position and were stopped by the Anglo-Russians at Petten and Krabbendam. *Lieutenant-Colonel* Collaert, commanding an advance guard of Batavian hussars, pursued the British to the village of Petten. *Lieutenant-Generaal* Dumonceau, recovered from his wound, resumed command of the 2e Bataafsche Divisie on 9 October

---

15 Steevens, *Reminiscences*, pp.10-16.

and ordered *Colonel* Bruce to take the village Dirkshorn with his brigade. An advance guard was formed of the 3/2e Halve Brigade and 50 troopers of the 1e Regiment Zware Cavalerie, which reached the village of Oud-Karspel without opposition. From there a reconnaissance in force was made to Dirkshorn. This Batavian force was commanded by *Major* Meyer and consisted of some infantry skirmishers and 20 cavalrymen supported by a 6pdr cannon (*Eerste Lieutenant* Spies). Arriving at Dirkshorn they encountered an outpost at a small bridge, consisting of about 250 infantry from the British 17th Foot and 20 light dragoons. The outpost was attacked immediately and after the Batavians had been reinforced, they retreated to St. Maarten. Dirkshorn was taken by the Batavians. The British lost an officer and 16 soldiers which were captured. Batavian losses were three dead and 18 wounded.[16]

Generaal-Major Bonhomme at the same time was ordered by Dumonceau to capture Nieudorper Verlaat, occupied by about 1,000 British infantry of the 35th Foot with two 6pdr cannon and a howitzer from Prince William's 8th Brigade. The 2/1e Halve Brigade commanded by *Major* Achenbach, which had distinguished itself at Castricum on the 6th, was ordered to execute the attack across the bridge over the canal, but was repulsed by the British, commanded by Prince William in person, who had deployed behind the dike on the other side of the canal. Achenbach lost two officers and 65 others and the Batavians had to retreat. Next day, the British were pushed out of this position when Daendels approached the village from the east and on the 11th Nieudorper Verlaat was occupied by a Batavian force consisting of grenadiers, *jager*, hussars and a few guns of the horse artillery, commanded by *Lieutenant-Colonel* Collaert. On the 10th the French captured Warmenhuizen and attacked Tuitgenhorn and Haringkarspel, but these attacks failed. Next day, the French attacked again and this time remained in possession of both villages.

Daendels in the meantime had received on 8 October the order to leave his positions behind the inundations and take the city of Hoorn. The only troops at his disposal were the 2/1e Halve Brigade and three more infantry battalions, the 2e Bataljon Jagers, and a few guns of the 2e Compagnie Rijdende Artillerie, the remainder of his troops still not having returned from reinforcing the Franco-Batavian centre on the 6th. The execution of this order was difficult, because of the demolition of bridges and roads and the flooding of the area. Only on the 9th, after a long and hard night march, a column from Monnikendam and another one from Purmerend succeeded in reaching Hoorn in the afternoon.

On the 10th, Daendels received the order advance further and to take the village of Winkel on the Zuiderzee, which was occupied by the rear guard of the British 8th Brigade (Prince William) consisting of both battalions of the 5th Foot. Advancing to the village Opmeer, the advance guard consisting of the 2e Bataljon Jagers was attacked by a squadron of the 18th Light Dragoons (Lieutenant Colonel Stewart) supported by infantry. The light dragoons were driven off with musketry by the Batavian *jager*, which had deployed in skirmishing order on both sides of the road where the light dragoons could not reach them. The British lost an officer, 19 troopers and 13 horses, their infantry lost 10 men. The remainder of the squadron and the supporting infantry retreated to the village Aartswoude, only to be

---

16 A.F. Meyer, *Dagboek van den luitenant-generaal jonkheer Adriaan Frans Meyer, geboren 1768* (NIMH, Handschriften, 511, inv.58), pp.21-22.

attacked again by the Batavians and had to fall back to a redoubt constructed on the sea-dike behind the village. The redoubt was armed with two cannon and in front of it the dike had been cut. At 3:00 p.m. Daendels arrived in front of this position with his infantry and *jager*, his advance delayed by the bad state of the roads. Despite the lateness of the hour and the exhaustion of the troops Daendels decided to make an immediate attack on the British positions. The attack would be made in three columns. One column would undertake a frontal attack on the redoubt while both other columns would try to cross the Langereis Canal somewhat further in order to cut the British off. The latter attacks would be very difficult, because the British had destroyed all the bridges across the canal, had taken cover behind the dike on the other side, and were supported by artillery as well.

With much effort the Batavians managed to deploy a howitzer of the 2e Compagnie Rijdende Artillerie on top of the sea dike and opened fire, while the infantry attacked the British defending the cutting and then the redoubt behind it. After the howitzer had thrown some shells into the redoubt the British ran and abandoned it, the Batavians quickly occupying the redoubt. After the construction of some bridges across the cutting more Batavian infantry advanced, outflanking the British behind the Langereis canal and causing them to retreat. Now more bridges were thrown across the canal and the remainder of Daendels' division crossed. Threatened by superior numbers the British troops evacuated Winkel which was then occupied by Daendels at 8:00 p.m., taking six men prisoner. The whole Anglo-Russian army had now retreated back in their original positions in the Zijpe. The regimental history of the 5th Foot describes the above incident, although their opponents were not the French but Daendels' Batavians:

> On the 10th of October the posts occupied by the two battalions of the Fifth, in front of the village of Winkle, were attacked by the enemy in great strength. The French troops had succeeded in forcing a passage over a canal which covered the village, when Colonel Bligh, who commanded the first battalion, perceiving that if the advance of the enemy was not checked, the remainder of the brigade was in danger of being cut off, planted the colours of the Fifth on the top of the dyke, and kept his ground till he had secured and covered the retreat of the brigade; the second battalion, under Lieutenant-Colonel Talbot, in the mean time maintaining its positions till ordered to retreat by Prince William, who on this occasion, issued the following general order: "Prince William desires Colonel Bligh and the first battalion of the Fifth Regiment will accept his thanks, for the gallant manner in which they attacked the enemy when he was passing the canal opposite Winkle; and Lieutenant-Colonels Talbot and Lindsay, of the second battalion of the Fifth, for their exertions on the 10th instant".[17]

With ample news about the battle of 6 October, the British newspapers presented the combat at Winkel as a resounding British victory, attributed to Prince William:

---

17 General order of 12 October 1799 from Prince William in: Richard Cannon, *Historical Record of the Fifth Regiment of Foot, or Northumberland Fusiliers* (London: W. Clowes and Sons, 1838), pp.57-58.

Aartswoude facing south-east. (Author photo)

Aartswoude facing in the direction of Kolhorn. (Author photo)

The detachment of the enemy, with which Prince William of Gloucester had lately to contend, is said to have amounted to no less than 6000 men, under the command of Gen. Daendels. With his little division of 1100 men, consisting chiefly of the 35th foot, his Highness is said to have first repelled the attack of his assailant, but a reinforcement coming up, he was forced to abandon the advanced post of Winkle, and to fall back to Golhorn. His Highness, it is abided, had a horse shot under him, but he lost only one man killed and nine wounded, including Col. Stewart. The enemy's loss is stated at 100 men, including a General Officer. Prince William displayed the utmost gallantry on the occasion. This partial affair, we understand, took place on the 10th or 12th inst. The enemy had six pieces of cannon; the English only two. No pursuit was attempted by the Republicans.[18]

This report was followed a few days later by an eyewitness account:

Extract of a Letter from an Officer, dated Oude Sluys, Oct. 14. "Our brigade at Winkle was attacked by the main body of the French army on the 8th [10th]. We were in a very severe action for an hour, and the 1st battalion of the 5th regiment was lucky enough to cover the retreat of the 35th, and second battalion of the 5th, and saved their cannon, viz. four pieces. Only two hundred and fifty of the 1st battalion of the 5th advanced against a body of 5000 French and Dutch, and four pieces of cannon, commanded by Gen. Daendels."[19]

It was decided to declare the battle at Winkel, in fact nothing more than a rearguard skirmish, a victory to boost the morale of the demoralised British troops. As well as presenting for home consumption a retreat in which the British could hold their heads high. The truth was different though, as various locals which had no love for the Batavians either reported. For example in the following letter an inhabitant of Nieuwe Nieudorp describes the retreat of the British:

Thursday 10 October was a bad day, as a battle was fought between Langedijk and the [Nieudorper] Verlaat until finally the cannon stood on the road near the tavern and the water was between the Dutch and the English. Then the English took flight as quick as they could, sick, wounded, baggage great and small. Even madam [the wife of a British colonel] on her horse crying: "Put away the Orange, away the Orange"! So that Nieuwe Nieudorp was soon emptied by the English. To our luck we believed, but the sorrow came next. We had to watch how they took with them the cattle from the land, even the dairy cows. There are farmers of whom they took twenty dairy cows and sheep, countless! On one day over three thousand cows passed Winkel, all stolen by the English.[20]

18 *London Chronicle*, 19 October 1799.
19 *London Chronicle*, 24 October 1799.
20 Letter from Mrs M. Koog-Koeman in H.J. Calkoen, 'Ooggetuige-verslag van de woelige dagen te Nieuwe Niedorp, October 1799' in *De Speelwagen*, Vol.6 (1953), pp.163-166.

On the 11th Daendels advanced to the village of Lutjewinkel and there joined units of Dumonceau's division. Supported by the 2/1e Halve Brigade, Dumonceau attacked the village of Nieudorper Verlaat again, this time forcing the British to retreat. British losses were 50 men killed or wounded and 16 men captured. On that same day Daendels ordered *Generaal-Major* Van Zuylen van Nyevelt to garrison the cities of Enkhuizen and Medemblik. British sailors were still busy emptying the stores in these cities and the arrival of the Batavian troops prevented the already-started plundering of the civilian houses, and they were just in time, aided by the citizens, to douse the fires that had been set in the naval magazines and aboard the two frigates that had been captured here previously. A letter from Vice-Admiral Mitchell to the municipality and inhabitants, on leaving Enkhuizen:

> Previous to my quitting this place, I wish to express my feelings, to convince you, that it is entirely owing to the smallness of my forces, that I do not remain to make a needless defence against superior numbers. Convinced of your agreeing with me in this point, I have thought proper, after the tidings received from Hoorn and Medemblyk, rather to evacuate the town than expose it to the vengeance of our enemies.
>
> It is with great concern I state, that the laws of war oblige me to destroy your armed shipping in this port, &c.; yet I find the consolation that none of the buildings of your city will receive the least injury, &c. I hope that the Members of your Provisional Regency, established by my express orders, will not suffer the least molestation; but, should I hear that any of them have been injured, I shall return with my fleet to bombard the town, until not one stone remains upon another.[21]

On the 12th, finally the remainder of Daendels division arrived and he advanced his lines somewhat more forward, to Lutjewinkel and Boerensluis. Here the troops entrenched themselves to be able to resist any Anglo-Russian attack. At the end of the day Daendels' troops were deployed as follows:[22]

Winkel/Boerensluis:	1/3e Halve Brigade
	1/5e Halve Brigade
	2e Compagnie Rijdende Artillerie
	Regiment Dragonders (2 squadrons)
Canterbrug:	1/4e Halve Brigade
Lutjewinkel:	1e Bataljon Jagers
	2e Bataljon Jagers
	4e Halve Brigade (3 grenadier companies)
Nieuwe Nieudorp:	1e Halve Brigade (3 battalions)
	Regiment Dragonders (2 squadrons)
Oude Nieudorp:	2e Regiment Zware Cavalerie
Hoorn:	3/4e Halve Brigade
Medemblik:	2/5e Halve Brigade
Enkhuizen:	3/5e Halve Brigade

21 *Naval Chronicle*, Vol.II, p.536.
22 Krayenhoff, *Geschiedkundige*, Appendix XVIIa, pp.123-124.

At Boerensluis a battery was constructed armed with eight guns. Dumonceau's troops were positioned along the line Tuitgenhorn–Haringkarspel–Dirkshorn. His connection with Daendels' troops was protected by a strong detachment at the village of Zijdenskerk, commanded by *Lieutenant-Colonel* Collaert, consisting of six grenadier companies, part of the 3e Bataljon Jagers, a hussar squadron and a division of the 1e Compagnie Rijdende Artillerie. French positions were in the line Kamp–Groet–Schoorl–Schoorldam–Warmenhuizen. The Franco-Batavian army had captured over 1,400 prisoners since the moment the Anglo-Russian retreat started, including the wounded that had been abandoned.[23]

From the ease of the Franco-Batavian advance it becomes clear that the Anglo-Russian morale was very low. Rumours of negotiations were strong and the situation of the Anglo-Russians army was bad. Many soldiers had lost or thrown away their weapons. The Anglo-Russians were enclosed in the Zijpe, a region which was by now mainly one of mud, barren dunes and beaches, and no shelter for the many sick and wounded. The still healthy soldiers had to fight daily against the rains. Another letter from Abercromby to Dundas on 12 October describes the perilous situation:

> After the action of the 2d and 6th we began to feel our real situation: without supplies of any kind we could not advance into a country much exhausted, and naturally barren. We are now with only ten days supply of bread, with a growing scarcety of every article of consumption. We cannot by any exertion extricate ourselves, and we must wait patiently till you can cross us off. It will require some address on our part to get the troops on shipboard, and it will not be without the loss of stores and artillery. I beg you may not consider the Helder as a port to be held, in the first place the works ordered are not yet finished, and in itself it has no advantages. The Texel island may receive a certain portion of troops for a certain time, and it may possibly furnish the means of keeping a squadron in the Zuyder Zee. The Duke of York is desirous that I should write you a few lines on this disappointing subject.[24]

Meanwhile, conflicts between British and Russians were running high. Supplying all the troops was difficult, with stormy beaches and the weather deteriorating even further. Against all this misery stood an enemy that was becoming stronger every day, with more than enough supplies, fighting partially in their own country. Not surprisingly discipline was declining and much stealing and plundering took place: the British and Russian soldiers did not hesitate to kill resisting inhabitants. York in the meantime, having moved his headquarters from Alkmaar to Schagerbrug in the Zijpe again, had issued on his arrival on 8 October the following General Order to his army:

> His Royal Highness the Commander-in-Chief desires the troops will accept his best thanks for the persevering bravery and good order which have so eminently distinguished their conduct during the whole period from the 2nd to the 8th past, although suffering from the inclemency of the weather and precarious supplies,

---

23 Vonk, *Geschiedenis der Landing*, Vol.II, p.103.
24 Letter in English of 12 October 1799 from Abercromby to Henry Dundas in Colenbrander, *Gedenkstukken*, Vol.III, p.430.

necessarily originating out of the situation of the army. From the former of these two causes, His Royal Highness has found it necessary to withdraw the troops from a situation where they must have been continually exposed to insupportable hardships, and which no efforts of an enemy twice beaten could have effected.[25]

York now had the difficult task to bring the English army safely back to Great Britain. Even with the port of Den Helder at his disposal, this would be very difficult, if not impossible, when hard pressed by the Franco-Batavians. As outlined by Walsh, York had two options:

> To render safe and effective this resolution, there were left to choose but two practicable expedients – either to flood the country in front of our lines, and to fortify the heights that command the Helder, in order to cover the embarkation, or to negotiate an armistice with the enemy. The command of the waters of the Ocean and of the Zuider Zee was certainly in our power; by possessing the sluices at Colhorn, Oude-Sluys, and Petten: but to take advantage of this power would be to destroy the country, and involve the unoffending inhabitants in irretrievable ruin, for whose protection and security the expedition was undertaken. So calamitous an expedient was never executed by the enemy, either to protect Alkmaar, or to cover his own retreat. This desperate measure, therefore, was so utterly repugnant to the feelings and sentiments of his royal highness the commander in chief, and so contrary to the well-known generous and liberal mode of warfare exercised by a British army, that nothing but the most urgent plea of self-preservation could induce its adoption. At, the same time, it must be acknowledged, that it would be extremely hazardous to trust entirely to any works thrown up on the heights of Heuysden [Huisduinen], or round the Helder; for should the enemy once succeed in forcing those works, he would entirely command the embarkation. Induced by such motives, the negotiation for an armistice was preferred.[26]

So according to Walsh, York's care for the inhabitants was high on his mind. The facts show a different picture though. First, York used the threat to inundate the whole of North-Holland in his letter to General Brune to force him to agree with a treaty:

> It depends upon us either to await the period when a favourable change of weather and of circumstances may enable us to renew offensive operations, or to withdraw our army by degrees, and without risk from this country, retaining possession of such detached points as might be judged most favourable for annoying the enemy, or for securing real advantages to ourselves. In the event of our recurring to this last-mentioned measure, it will become our duty to neglect no means which can contribute to the preservation of the brave troops entrusted to our care, and for this purpose (however distressing, however ruinous to the inhabitants and to the country, the alternative may be) we shall be compelled to avail ourselves of those

---

25 General Order issued by the Duke of York in his headquarters, Schagerbrug 8 October 1799, in Anon., *The Campaign in Holland, 1799*, p.90.
26 Walsh, *Narrative*, pp.87-88.

dreadful expedients which it is in our power to adopt. Having perfectly at our disposal the sea-dykes, both towards the Ocean and the Zuider Zee, as well as the interior dykes, we should in that case be reduced to the terrible necessity of inundating the whole country of North Holland, and of adding to this calamity every destructive evil which must necessarily result from an attempt to force or interrupt our retreat.[27]

Secondly York was not only threatening to do so, local reports describe the Anglo-Russian preparations for the inundations:

On the 16th [October] something of great importance happened here [Wieringerwaard], the English dug 2 holes in our Northern Dike being the one 28 feet wide and the depth of the daily tide, only leaving a dam of 6 feet wide and 8 feet high in the middle of the hole. To be able in case of a retreat to inundate our polder in an instant. So that over here everyone has to be prepared to flee… On the 28th we tried to repair the dike, but the English prevented this… On 7 November again we tried to repair our sea dike, but on the 8th the labourers were chased away by an officer with some soldiers and so we had to remain even longer in these dangerous circumstances. Luckily we had daily southern winds and low water as a result. Because a small north-western storm for sure would have flooded our whole polder. On the 9th, our dike council send a committee to the Duke of York still in his headquarters in the Zijpe, to request permission to repair our dike. Luckily they succeeded in their undertaking and they became consent from the said Duke. Immediately as many people as possible were put to work, so that the dike was repaired in a short time.[28]

Finally, a British vindication of the decisions taken concludes:

If there be any circumstance which national policy may blame, it is at least one in favour of which HUMANITY pleads in the strongest manner. The sacrifice of the innocent inhabitants of a very considerable portion of North Holland, might have saved all convention on our part, we might have embarked in safety, and even destroyed the Helder batteries, had the Russians completed, entirely, what they had very nearly accomplished. The great sea dyke, which would have laid the country under water for a considerable length, and the entire breadth of the peninsula, the ridge of sand hills excepted, was very nearly cut through, when orders came from head quarters to desist, by which the lives of many thousands would have been sacrificed, men, women, and infants. It is not permitted to condemn such an act, it is even scarcely allowable to weigh it in too nice a balance; we must all join and "Plead with angels, trumpet-tongued, against. The deep damnation, of their taking off". The disagreeable, the mortifying part of the business is then defended, by what

---

27   Letter from the Duke of York to General Brune on 15 October 1799, in Walsh, *Narrative*, p.143.
28   Albert Kaan Kz., *Journaal van 1799* (NL-WpDStvA-C1746; NL-WpDStvA-C2423), pp.7-9. As the Duke of York had left for Great Britain on 31 October it is not clear who gave the permission to repair the dike.

speaks louder to an English ear, than any argument; and I hope no Briton would wish that twenty thousand innocent people should have been drowned, and the English name become a reproach, rather than sit down with the honour of preferring the cause of humanity to that of interest.[29]

York's threat was understandable, though, considering the situation he was in, illustrated by a letter of 17 October published in the *London Chronicle*:

The main army are retired within the Zype, our right wing is covered by Petten, and our left by Oude Sluys. Schagen is our advanced post, outside the great canal, which we have strongly fortified. Gen. Coote's brigade composes the garrison. Schagenburgh, two miles in the rear, immediately on the canal, is head-quarters. Our great park of artillery is at the Helder, and our heavy ordnance is now embarking. We are incessantly busy in throwing up works all round this place; they extend some miles along the sand hills, as far as the signal post, where we first landed. Numbers of Dutch deserters are employed in this service. They are now embarking the crews of Admiral Story's fleet on board transports for the Isle of Wight. We are in hourly expectation of the return of Col. Brownrigg, with orders for our re-embarkation. The 9th foot arrived here yesterday, and, with the 69th, are encamped outside the place. The garrison is composed of 2000 Russians, and part of the 35th regiment. The enemy, ever active and vigilant, press closely all round us. Our situation is undoubtedly critical; and, although we have collected all the cattle of this part of the country, every article of consumption is exorbitantly dear. Our losses in the recent actions were very great, and there are at present not fewer than 5000 sick and wounded in the hospital and hospital ships at this place.[30]

The Treaty

On 13 October, Brune informed Daendels and Dumonceau that he was engaged in secret negotiations with York. No government participated in these negotiations and the completion of the treaty took place under very obscure conditions, being a sole achievement of Brune. On the Anglo-Russian side, the Russians were also not involved. The treaty, which was closed in Alkmaar on 18 October, was a shame for the Franco-Batavian troops, who had given all for a cause that at least part of them believed in. It gave the Anglo-Russians a free retreat and handed over the Batavian fleet to them as well – something even Abercromby could not understand as already described. The Duke of York dispatched his aide, Lieutenant Colonel Clinton, to Henry Dundas with the news of the treaty that he had closed:

---

29 Anon., *The Dutch Expedition vindicated; with Brief Observations on the Emigrants* (London: John Stockdale, 1799), pp.14-15.
30 *London Chronicle*, 24 October 1799.

In my late communications I have represented to you the circumstances under which I found it expedient to withdraw the army from its forward position in front of Alkmaar, within that which it at present occupies, and which I trust will have appeared to his majesty sufficient to warrant the measure. The season of the year, which has already assumed here the aspect of winter, gave me, from day to day, additional reason to apprehend that any attempt towards a prosecution of the campaign in this country could not be attended with decisive advantages, whilst the impossibility of covering the troops in the narrow district of the country in our possession during the winter, and the precarious state of supplies to be expected in that season, added to the conviction I felt, that the most advisable measure to be pursued was to remove with the army to England, an operation which, although it might have exposed the army to some loss in its execution, I judged in my mind preferable to any other which could be adopted. Under this impression, and considering that serious loss might ensue from delay, I have been induced to conclude an armistice, in conjunction with vice-admiral Mitchel, with general Brune, commanding the French and Batavian armies, of which the conditions are inclosed, and which, although they provide for delivering up a large number of prisoners of war, now in our hands, yet I trust will not be thought by his majesty an inadequate compensation for many valuable lives which must have been lost, after the object which has hitherto directed them no longer promised success; and when the only means which presented themselves of ensuring a secure retreat were those of resorting to the destructive measure of inundation from the sea, which, as it would have involved the inhabitants in the northern parts of this province in ruin for a series of years, must have been highly repugnant to the feelings, as well as contrary to the character and practice of the British nation. I rest confident that the motives which I have here detailed will excuse me to his majesty for having acted without waiting for previous instructions from home, and that I shall have the satisfaction of knowing that my conduct in this respect has met with his majesty's gracious approbation.

Articles agreed upon between major-general Knox, duly authorised by his royal highness the duke of York, commander in chief of the combined English and Russian army, and citizen Rostollant, general of brigade and adjutant-general, duly authorised by citizen Brune, general and commander in chief of the French and Batavian army.

Art. I. From the date of this convention all hostilities shall cease between the two armies.

Art. II. The line of demarcation between the said armies shall be the line of their respective out-posts, as they now exist.

Art. III. The continuation of all works, offensive and defensive, shall be suspended on both sides, and no new ones shall be undertaken.

Art. IV. The mounted batteries taken possession of at the Helder, or at other positions within the line, now occupied by the combined English and Russian army, shall be restored in the state in which they were taken, or (in case of improvement) in their present state, and all the Dutch artillery taken therein shall be preserved.

Art. V. The combined English and Russian army shall embark as soon as possible, and shall evacuate the territory, coasts, islands, and internal navigation of the Dutch republic, by the 30th of November, 1799, without committing any devastation, by inundations, cutting the dykes, or otherways injuring the sources of navigation.

Art. VI. Any ships of war, or other vessels, which may arrive with reinforcements for the combined British and Russian army shall not land the same, and shall be sent away as soon as possible.

Art. VII. General Brune shall be at liberty to send an officer within the lines of the Zype and to the Helder, to report to him the state of the batteries and the progress of the embarkation. His royal highness the duke of York shall be equally at liberty to send, an officer within the French and Batavian lines, to satisfy himself that no new works, are carried on on their side. An officer of rank and distinction shall be sent from each army respectively, to guarantee the execution of this convention.

Art. VIII. Eight thousand prisoners of war, French and Batavians, taken before the present campaign, and now detained in England, shall be restored, without conditions, to their respective countries. The proportion and choice of such prisoners for each to be determined between the two republics. Major-general Knox shall remain with the French army to guarantee the execution of this article.

Art. IX. The cartel agreed upon between the two armies, for the exchange of the prisoners taken during the present campaign, shall continue in full force till it shall be carried into complete execution; and it is further agreed that the Dutch admiral De Winter shall be considered as exchanged.

Concluded at Alkmaar, the 18th of October, 1799, by the undersigned general-officers, furnished with full powers to this effect.[31]

Except for one article, the treaty was closed on York's terms. The Batavian fleet remained in British hands and to compensate for this 8,000 Franco-Batavian prisoners would be released. In short, the Anglo-Russians had achieved an unconditional retreat. No payment of war costs or damage done to the Batavian Republic, no restitution of Batavian colonies and no restitution of the Batavian fleet, which was a *condition sine qua non* of the Batavian Government. All this, despite the fact that the Anglo-Russians were beaten and with their backs to the wall. Many in the Batavian Republic held the opinion that Brune was a traitor to both the Batavians and the French, and to the Republican cause. Also it was said Brune had been bribed. Although there is no hard evidence for this, he at least received a gift from York of some beautiful horses. Furthermore at least one local source, already cited in this chapter, mentions the British handing over to the French 'three or four boxes or briefcases'. In any case, it was again made clear that the Batavian Republic was only a French satellite and that it was the French deciding on important matters.

On 18 October the Anglo-Russian army was informed about the treaty with a circular letter to the senior officers:

31 Dispatch of 20 October 1799 from the Duke of York to Henry Dundas in Walsh, *Narrative*, pp.138-140.

I am commanded by his Royal Highness the Commander in Chief to signify, that a suspension of arms has been agreed upon by the two armies, in consequence of which hostilities are to cease, all field works are to be suspended, and such measures as might have been required for the purpose of defence, and which tend to distress the country, are not now to be pursued. The posts now held are to be maintained; no intercourse is to be allowed with the enemy, and you are held responsible, that the same vigilance in respect of duty shall exist as heretofore.[32]

On that same day, the public in Great Britain finally became aware that something went wrong in Holland:

The last dispatches received from Holland are said to bring an account of a partial action having taken place between the advanced guard of the British army, commanded by his Highness Prince William of Gloucester, and the enemy, the latter having attempted to surprize and cut off the English division, consisting of 1100 men, in which however they completely failed. His Highness made in the first instance a most spirited resistance to the attack of the enemy, and finding that they were greatly superior in numbers, he brought off his whole party in three columns with very little loss. The Hon. Col. Stewart, brother to Lord Castlereagh, was wounded in this affair, and several other Officers. It is supposed this affair took place on Sunday or Monday last. The reports respecting the future measures to be adopted by the army in Holland, are much at variance; some stating that the whole of the troops will be immediately withdrawn; others, that the Helder, Point and the Texel Island, commanding the navigation of the Zuyder Zee, will be strongly fortified and garrisoned through the winter. A great number of men of war, and ships *armé en flute*, have sailed from different ports to the Texel, to bring away our troops from Holland.[33]

When the news became known, the treaty and subsequent retreat were turned in something positive:

This measure is certainly the result of the severe and unseasonable weather, from the effects of which the country of North Holland has been almost entirely inundated, the positions excepted which the British troops occupy, and which are the most elevated of the whole country. It is a measure however that we cannot but rejoice in, as such troops as are to be withdrawn will be able to re-embark for this country without inconvenience or loss.[34]

Of course the opportunity to retreat with the army intact was reason enough to rejoice. On 22 October the Anglo-Russians started re-embarking. On 31 October York embarked for Great Britain, handing over command of the remaining Anglo-Russian troops to Lieutenant General

---

32 Circular letter of 18 October 1799 from Deputy-Adjutant-General Hope, published in the *London Chronicle*, 24 October 1799.
33 *London Chronicle*, 18 October 1799.
34 *London Chronicle*, 24 October 1799.

Pulteney. On 3 November about three quarters of the Anglo-Russian army had sailed but then weather deteriorated and heavy storms prevented nearly all further embarkations until the 9th.

These storms would also be the cause that some British soldiers would never see their homeland again. A disaster took place when the frigate *Valk* foundered in a storm on 10 November near the island of Ameland. On 27 October the 23rd Royal Welsh Fusiliers received orders to march from Kolhorn to Den Helder to embark for England. Next day, fishing boats brought them to the frigates with Dutch crews (see Chapter 13). Some companies of the 23rd, including the grenadiers, embarked on the *Valk*, commanded by the Dutch *Lieutenant ter Zee* Martinius. Scheduled to leave with the morning tide, their departure was delayed when receiving orders to embark more men of the 23rd, coming from another Dutch frigate *Venus* which turned out to be in such a bad state that passage to England on this ship was impossible. For this reason the *Valk* left later that day, arriving 30 miles from Yarmouth when darkness fell. With fading light and without a pilot, and none of his crew knowing the local situation, *Lieutenant ter Zee* Martinius did not find it safe to try to enter the harbour. On 1 November at 5:00 a.m. the strongly increasing wind turned south-west, the *Valk* drifting to the western end of the Dogger Bank. From 3 to 5 November a heavy gale carried the ship far away, west of Norway. On the 6th, the gale lost strength and the *Valk* again set course to England. It would never come that far: at 3:00 a.m. in the early morning of the 10th, the ship ran aground seven miles from the Batavian island of Ameland.

With the wind raising again, the inexperienced crew and soldiers had no chance and in the surf the ship quickly broke to pieces. Of the 444 passengers and crew; 285 British soldiers of the 23rd Royal Welsh Fusiliers,[35] the Dutch crew of 120, 15 British women and 10 children, 12 Dutch women and children as well as Captain Darcie and his wife, only 25 were saved: 20 men of the 23rd and five of the Dutch crew. All others drowned. Initially the many bodies were buried in mass graves in the dunes near Hollum village, on Ameland island, much to the displeasure of the locals of Ballum village, who dug them up again and gave them a proper burial on the churchyard. On 15 November the survivors were brought to Den Helder in a fishing boat.[36] From there they finally managed to reach England, as reported in the *Naval Chronicle*:

> Portsmouth: The Pelter gun brig, Lieutenant John Walsh (second) Commander, from the Texel, having been ashore on the Dutch coast, was sent on Wednesday into this harbour for refitting, having lost her anchors, cables, and false keel. She has brought Lieutenant Hill, of the Welsh Fusileers. He was one of the twenty-five persons, and the only officer, saved out of 529 that were on board the Voolk, a Dutch frigate wrecked in the night of the 10th instant, on the island of Ameland. Among the above passengers were three companies of the said regiment. Lieutenant Hogart, who had got safe on a piece of the wreck, died instantly in a state of delirium, caused by excess of joy, after exclaiming, "Thank God, my Lads, we are once again safe on shore!"[37]

---

35 Some sources mention 370 men of the 23rd Royal Welsh Fusiliers. It is possible this number is correct (and concurs with the number mentioned in the *Naval Chronicle*) and that the additional men came from the *Venus*.
36 Diary of Cornelis Pieter Sorgdrager and a report by the surviving British officer Lieutenant Hill, both quoted in Epke van der Geest et al., *Wat gebeurde er in 1799 bij de Engelsmanduun?* (Ameland: De Ouwe Pôlle, 1999), pp.7, 11-20.
37 *Naval Chronicle*, Vol.II, p.546.

"Re-embarkation of the Anglo-Russian army", by Dirk Langendijk. (Rijksmuseum, RP-P-1908-2473)

The embarkation slowly continued and Pulteney embarked on 18 November. That afternoon, the first Franco-Batavian unit, the 1/3e Halve Brigade commanded by *Lieutenant-Colonel* Abbema, arrived near Den Helder and encamped at Huisduinen. On 19 November the last members of the Anglo-Russian army left Batavian soil and on the 20th Pulteney reported from the cutter *Swan*:

> I have from time to time reported to you, for the information of his royal highness the commander in chief, the progress which had been made in the embarkation and departure of the British and Russian troops which were left under my command in the province of North Holland; and I am now happy to acquaint you, that the last of them embarked yesterday morning, when, the wind being fair, the whole of the ships of war and transports remaining in the Texel left that port. Everything belonging to the army was brought off, excepting a small proportion of damaged provisions, a few waggons, and above 300 draft horses of little value, for which there was no tonnage; of these the latter alone were saleable; but they bore so small a price, that I thought it better to distribute the whole to the magistrates of the different villages in and near which the army had been cantoned, to be delivered to any of the inhabitants who might have suffered from the inevitable consequences of war. Several large Dutch Indiamen, and other ships, which it was impossible for us to remove in their present state, but which might have been fitted out as ships of war by the enemy, were completely disabled and rendered useless for any further purpose, through the exertions of a detachment of seamen, under the direction of Captain Bovar. The desire of complying most strictly with the articles of the.

agreement entered into between his royal highness and general Brune prevented their being blown up, which could not have been done without endangering the navigation of the Nieuwe Diep. Vice-admiral Dickson, as well as myself, made it our study to comply in this, as in every other instance, with the articles of the agreement; and I must do the French general the justice to say, that he seemed actuated by the same spirit. Previous to quitting the Helder, I had, in obedience to his royal highness's instructions, discharged every just demand of the inhabitants of the country which has been occupied by the army; and I was happy to find that very few claims were brought forward beyond those which it was in my power to satisfy. The embarkation of the troops, difficult from the multiplicity of the arrangements required, and sometimes arduous from the state of the weather, was carried on with the utmost zeal and activity by Vice-admiral Dickson, and the officers and seamen under his command. I feel particularly indebted to Captain Lawford, of his majesty's ship Romney, who was left on shore, and had the immediate direction of the embarkation, for his exertions and his attention to every branch of his majesty's service, and to Captain Woodriffe, principal agent of the transport service, for his great zeal in the execution of the duties of that situation.[38]

Three British schooners remained, cruising off the Texel, to give all arriving British ships warning that the Anglo-Russians had evacuated Holland. If nevertheless a British ship would enter the harbour accidentally, it was agreed upon that it would be allowed to depart again until the end of the month of November.

Naval Actions

On 6 October, Vice-Admiral Mitchell ordered Campbell, commander of the *Dart*, to take the *Cracker* (gunvessel 12), *Defender* (gunvessel 12), *Hasty* (gunvessel 12) and the launch from the *Isis* and to advance in the direction of Amsterdam. On the 7th he reached Marken island, near the mouth of the IJ. There he captured some gunboats and three schuyts, armed with four carronades each. Apparently these ships were hailed in Dutch by the British boats. The Batavian crews, thinking it was Batavians approaching, were surprised and the ships captured without any fighting. Among these was the *Helhond* (4 guns, *Eerste Lieutenant* Eilbracht). Campbell's report about this engagement:

> I beg to inform you, that I yesterday sailed from Urk, with the Hasty, Defender, and Cracker brigs, and Isis schuyt; and having reached this place by four A.M. I proceeded with the boats to attempt cutting out the Dutch gunboats lying on or near the Pampus, and am happy to say, succeeded in getting possession of four without the loss of a man. They each mount four long guns or carronades, and have between twenty and thirty men; one of them built on purpose for a gun-vessel,

---

38 Letter of 20 November 1799 from Lieutenant-General Pulteney to Lieutenant Colonel Alexander Hope in Walsh, *Narrative*, pp.141-142.

and quite new, carrying two long eighteen-pounders in her bow, and two eighteen-pounder carronades on her broadside; the rest are schuyts.

I beg to recommend to your notice Messrs. Hall and Winter, Midshipmen, for their spirited behaviour on this occasion, as also all the seamen engaged, for their alacrity in boarding, and good conduct after having gained possession. I have sent the Defender with charge of the gun-boats.[39]

The gun-vessel in the report was the *Helhond* already mentioned. It would be taken into British service as the gun-brig *Contest* (two 32pdr carronades, three 24pdr cannon). Before Campbell could move any closer to Amsterdam, he received orders from Mitchell to retreat after the news of York's defeat at Castricum. This was the closest the Anglo-Russians would come to Amsterdam during this campaign.

On 8 October Captain Winthrop of the *Circe* (6th Rate 28) discovered the Batavian gunboat *Lynx* (10 guns, *Capitein-Lieutenant* Pool) and the schooner *Perseus* (6 guns, *Capitein-Lieutenant* Westerholt), anchored under the batteries of Delfzijl. The *Perseus* was especially built to be used as privateer. That night, a party with boats was sent to seize the Batavian ships. Not expecting an attack both ships were easily captured.[40] Winthrop's report about the capture:

Being detained here by contrary winds, which deprived me of the pleasure of acting with you in the Zuyder Zee, I proceeded to reconnoitre the port of Delfzel, where I discovered a sloop of war and a schooner lying within musket-shot of the batteries; and conceiving it practicable to carry them by a *coup-de-main*, I gave the necessary orders for that purpose, but the weather proving tempestuous nothing could be effected until eight at night. Delfzel being distant 20 miles from the Circe, the boats proceeded with the first of the tide, and arrived there just as the moon went down; at which time I ordered the attack to be made by Lieut. Maughan upon the ship, and Lieutenant Powle upon the schooner, who boarded and carried them in a most gallant manner, and I am happy to say without any loss, notwithstanding the enemy's guns were loaded, primed, and the matches lighted. The name of the ship is the Lynx, of 12 guns, eight and twelve-pounders, and 75 men; that of the schooner, the Perseus, mounting eight four-pounders, and 40 men.[41]

The hired cutters *Hawke* (12, Lieutenant Buckle) and *Nancy* (6, Lieutenant Kilkardy) shared in the prize money. Probably members of their crews and their boats participated in the attack, at least Lieutenant Buckle did.

On 9 October the British suffered a painful loss when the frigate *Lutine* was wrecked in a storm near Vlieland:

Oct. 12. It is with extreme concern we relate, that intelligence was on Saturday received at the Admiralty, from Admiral Mitchell, communicating the total loss

---

39 Letter of 7 October 1799 from Commander Campbell to Vice-Admiral Mitchell in the *Naval Chronicle*, Vol.III, p.141.
40 de Jonge, *Geschiedenis van het Nederlandsche Zeewezen*, Vol.V, pp.502-503.
41 Letter of 11 October 1799 from R. Winthrop to Vice-Admiral Mitchell in the *Naval Chronicle*, Vol.III, p.142.

of La Lutine, of 32 guns, Captain Skynner, on the outward bank of the Fly Island Passage, on the night of the ninth instant, in a heavy gale at N. N.W. La Lutine had, on the same morning, sailed from Yarmouth Roads with several passengers and an immense quantity of treasure, for the Texel; but a strong lee tide rendered every effort of Captain Skynner to avoid the threatened danger unavailable and it was alike impossible, during the night, to receive any assistance either from the Arrow, Captain Portlock, which was in company, or the shore, from whence several schoots were in readiness to go to her. When the dawn broke, la Lutine was in vain looked for, she had gone to pieces and all on board unfortunately perished, except two men, who were picked up [by *l'Espiègle*] and one of whom has since died from due fatigue he had encountered. The survivor is Mr. Schabrack, a notary public. In the annals of our naval history, there has scarcely ever happened a loss attended with so much calamity, both of a public as well as private nature. We learn, from good authority, that there was Six Hundred Thousand Pounds sterling in specie on board the Lutine, which had been shipped by individual merchants in this country for relief of different commercial houses in Hamburgh. There were also several merchants on board.[42]

After the armistice had been closed, on 12 October Mitchell's ships started their retreat out of the Zuiderzee to Den Helder and Lemmer was also evacuated. But despite hostilities had ended, bad weather was still the cause of losses. On 14 October, the *Nassau* (originally 3rd Rate 64, became a 36 gun troopship in 1797) was wrecked at the Batavian coast, losing 42 of its crew. A letter from an officer describes the incident:

I am sorry to inform you that the Nassau struck on a sand bank, called the Kicks, off the Texel, at twelve o'clock on Thursday evening the 14th inst. We fired guns as a signal of distress all night, but to no purpose, as it blew such a gale of wind, and the breakers were so high, that it was impossible any vessel could come to our assistance. At day-light all our hopes vanished, and death in all its dismal forms appeared. All hands were employed making a raft to save our lives, when, about eleven o'clock in the afternoon, we saw a brig making all sail possible towards us, but she could not venture within a mile and a half of the Nassau, and it continued blowing so hard, that it was impossible for a boat to venture out. However, hope began to revive in us, and we sat down on the quarter deck, about twelve o clock, and forced down a few mouthfuls of mutton, and a glass or two of wine.

I think I shall never forget the serious countenances of all present at this repast. We sat upon the quarter deck, as the water had driven us from every other part, and even there the sea washed over us. About three o'clock we hoisted out one of the boats, and the Captain of Marines, Purser, and a Midshipman, along with the boat's crew, went in her to try if they could make the brig; but alas! they hall not gone above ten yards from the ship, when the boat upset, and all hands perished.

---

42 Copied from the *London Gazette* in the *Naval Chronicle*, Vol.II, pp.441-442. An interesting book looking at all aspects of the loss of the ship and its gold and the mysteries surrounding it, although in Dutch, is Bert Huiskes, Gerald de Weerdt e.a., *De Lutine 1799-1999, de raadselachtige ondergang van een schip vol goud* (Bussum: THOTH, 1999).

After that accident happened, there was not a word to be heard in the ship: all hands again desponded, till about five o'clock, when the wind began ran moderate, and the brig sent her boats to and fro, loaded with our people; and about six o'clock in the evening I had the good fortune to get into one of the boats, and was put safe on board the brig. – I had hardly got on board when it again blew a hurricane, which prevented any more boats going to the assistance of the rest; 205 had by this time been placed in safety in the brig, from the Nassau. Next morning, however, there were a good number of boats, which came to assist the rest of the men and officers, and had the good fortune to save all except about 100, who perished before any assistance could be given, and by the upsetting of the Nassau's boats. We arrived here yesterday forenoon in the Jealous brig, and in all probability shall remain here until after the trial of the Captain. There was not a single person who saved any of his property except what was on his back.[43]

The court martial would conclude that 'H.M. ship Nassau was lost through gross ignorance and inattention of Captain Tripp, and that he did not set a good example to those under his command: and for such a conduct he was sentenced to be dismissed from the service as unfit and unworthy, and rendered incapable of serving his Majesty, his heirs or successors'.[44]

The Orangists in Holland

The evacuation of Holland by the Anglo-Russian forces left the Orangists in dire straits. On 15 October the Stadtholder wrote to the Secretary of War Henry Dundas to request the British Government for aid for the 6 or 7,000 Dutch sailors and soldiers, and all others that had declared in favour of the House of Orange, in case the British army would evacuate Holland entirely. It was clear that these Dutch could not hold out on the islands of Texel and Wieringen, even more so since they were without any food. Already some days earlier, the Hereditary Prince of Orange had asked the Duke of York if it was possible to take the Dutch to Great Britain for a month, to rest and equip them for future use. York replied that regrettably this was not possible, as the Bill of Rights prevented the landing of foreign troops in Great Britain without the consent of Parliament. The Prince of Orange again outlined the predicament the Dutch were in and requested to send them to the Isle of Wight, which was treated as not covered by the Bill of Rights and on which island various foreign troops had been allowed before. To this the Duke agreed, replying on the 13th to the Prince of Orange that:

> I send by this opportunity orders to Captain Popham, or in his absence to Captain Lawford to embark with all possible speed the Dutch troops and to sail them to Yarmouth with the exception of 6 or 700 men more robust which I have to pray Your Royal Highness kindly to leave them at Den Helder under the leadership of

---

43 *Naval Chronicle*, II, p.537.
44 Hamilton & Laughton (eds.), *Recollections of James Anthony Gardner*, p.213.

the most intelligent officers and ordering them to do service as pioneers. I see no difficulty as to the number and they will be most useful. I will undertake further to order Lieutenant-Colonel Sontag to confer with the naval officers and to do everything in his power to hasten the implementation of the arrangements made, and he also will receive the order to accompany the Dutch troops to be shipped. I intend to send a letter tonight to England to inform the government about which I was forced to do, and to request them to decide, before the arrival of these troops at Yarmouth, about the way in which they will be disposed of for the moment.[45]

Probably there were more reasons for York to agree to the evacuation of the Dutch: apparently there were only provisions left for eleven more days and the continuous bad weather and the lateness of the season made shipping and therefore supplying the army more dangerous every day. In any case, the Hereditary Prince of Orange was very satisfied with this solution for the Dutch and on 13 October *Lieutenant-Colonel* Panhuys was ordered to fulfil the request of the pioneers, to which purpose 520 sailors and 80 marines were send to Den Helder. These were employed to construct entrenchments to cover a possible embarkation of the Anglo-Russian army. On the 17th, orders from the Prince of Orange went out for the embarkation of the Dutch on various ships. *Lieutenant-Colonel* Panhuys received orders to embark the men on Texel on barges and to transport them to the *Calcutta* (600), *Adventure* (400), *Blonde* (350), *Niger* (400) and also the *Experiment*, *Ulysses*, and *Ceres*. These men were the remaining sailors and the Dutch Marine corps of 342 men in five companies, less the men working at the entrenchments around Den Helder as described; the other half of the sailors formed the crews of the *Hector, Heldin, Valk, Minerva* and *Venus* (see Chapter 13). *'t Duifje* could not be made seaworthy in time and had to be left behind, the sailors divided over the other ships. At the same time, *Colonel* van Rechteren Limpurg at Wieringen received also orders to embark his soldiers on barges. They were to be transported to the roadstead of Texel to embark on the *Weymouth* (1st Battalion, *Colonel* van Rechteren) and the *Alkmaar* (600 men of the 2nd Battalion, *Lieutenant-Colonel* von Schwartz). The *Hector* was used to transport the sick and part of the women. In total, 3,600 to 3,800 Dutch embarked for transport.

On 18 October, the Prince of Orange received a letter from the Duke of York, with news that was not completely unexpected:

> I will not lose a moment to inform Your Royal Highness, that I just concluded with the enemy a suspension of hostilities, and as I wish to share with Your Royal Highness the rather detailed armistice and all that is relevant, I hope Your Royal Highness will do me the honour of dining here tomorrow.[46]

On 21 October 1799 the Hereditary Prince of Orange embarked for Great Britain. He would have to wait until 1813 to set foot on Dutch soil again.

---

45 Quoted in French in Koolemans Beijnen, *De Erfprins van Oranje in Noord-Holland*, pp.94-96.
46 Quoted in French in Koolemans Beijnen, *De Erfprins van Oranje in Noord-Holland*, p.103.

17

The End of the Campaign

The Russian Troops

The evacuation from Holland was not easy, despite the harbour of Den Helder could be used. Weather was still bad with strong winds and frequent storms. The Russian squadron commanded by Rear Admiral Chichagov was again used to transport the Russians but only four ships were able to sail before 29 October (*Alexsandr Nevskii, Venus, Arkhangel Rafail*, and the store-ship *Minerva*). The other Russian ships tried to sail on the 30th but were not able to reach the open sea and forced to anchor again, except for the *Iona*. This ship was caught in a heavy storm and forced to enter a Scottish harbour with severe damage, needing six months of repairs before it was able to sail again. The soldiers on board sailed to Portsmouth on two British ships, while the sick were brought to the hospital in Edinburgh.[1]

Some of the troops that had embarked in Den Helder had to be disembarked again, not able to remain on the ships, packed together and suffering from lack of provisions and fresh water. One of the British ships transporting Russian troops, the frigate *Espion* armed *en flute*, was wrecked on 15 November on the Goodwin Sands. Luckily the Russians that were on board, as well as its crew, were saved by boats from Deal and Ramsgate. Next day weather cleared and finally the ships were able to sail again. As no foreign troops were allowed on British soil, it was first proposed to send the Russians to Ireland, but its Governor Lord Cornwallis objected, writing to the Prime Minister that: 'the revengeful Tory magistrates might call upon the Russian troops to help in scouring the country and hunting down the rebels, and writes that, "unacquainted with our language and the nature of our Government, these troops would give loose to their natural ferocity and a scene of indiscriminate plunder must ensue".'[2] So after their arrival in Great Britain it was decided to send the Russian troops to Guernsey and Jersey, close to the French coast ready for another invasion next year.

On Guernsey and Jersey everything was prepared to receive the Russians:

---

1   Miliutin, *Geschichte des Krieges*, Vol.V, p.304.
2   Quoted in Joan Stevens, 'Further light on the Russians in Jersey', *Annual Bulletin of the Société Jersiaise*, (Jersey: Guernsey Press Co. Ltd., 1968), p.328; Charles Ross, *Correspondence of Charles, First Marquis Cornwallis* (London: John Murray, 1859),Vol. III, pp. 137-138.

> Three hundred English carpenters debarked yesterday, for the purpose of erecting temporary barracks to lodge the Russians. The States of the Island, with a liberality which reflects high honour upon them, have ceded the General Hospital; which alone can contain about 1000 men. The Wallace, Argyle, Limerick, and Banffshire fencibles will leave us, to make room for our Northern auxiliaries; the Wexford militia and the Royal garrison battalion alone will remain.[3]

At their arrival many Russians were or became sick from the hardships suffered during the campaign and measures had to be taken to care for them: 'The *Britannia* is fitting up as a convalescent ship for the Russian troops, who are very sickly. The *Portland* is also fitting for them as an hospital ship.'[4] After having been evacuated from Holland the Russian troops, those being wounded or sick, had been disembarked all along the English coast and it took some time before they had all been brought over to Guernsey and Jersey. For that purpose they were collected at Portsmouth to embark there:

> His Excellency Count de Woronzoff, Minister Plenipotentiary from the Court of Petersburgh, and Commander in Chief of the Russian troops in this country, set off on Saturday last for Portsmouth. The different corps of these troops distributed along our coasts are to meet there, and be reviewed by his Excellency, previous to their receiving instructions for their departure to the islands of Jersey and Guernsey. The whole of the Russian troops upon the British territory amounts to about 14,000 men. The second in command under the Count de Woronzoff, is Major Gen. D'Essen. Gen. Bauer, who was to have superseded Gen. D'Essen, has returned to Germany, where that brave and intelligent Officer, together with Gen. Rosenberg, will command the army that was under the orders of Suwarrow and Korsakoff.[5]

This does not reflect the hardships the Russian soldiers had to went through before they set foot on the Channel Islands. Luckily, the historian Clara Tucker has looked into this matter:

> Russian sick and wounded ended up at Yarmouth, Portsmouth. Sheerness, Gosport, and even Edinburgh. Able-bodied troops were not put ashore in England; some of the sick and wounded were. Others were sent to special hospital ships. Since few men, including the officers, could speak English, the confusion must have been considerable. Many of the troops arrived from Holland in ships too large for the harbours of Jersey and Guernsey and had to await special transports to take them to winter quarters. There was still some question as to whether all the Russian men had been located and accounted for when the troops were finally assembled for the return home. An idea of the delays and discomforts experienced by the Russians can be obtained from the scattered records on the squadron of the Russian Counter-Admiral Breyer. On October 9th General Essen's troops were reported aboard Breyer's ships off the Netherlands. They arrived at Spithead on

---

3 *London Chronicle*, 23 November 1799.
4 *London Chronicle*, 17 December 1799.
5 *London Chronicle*, 23 December 1799.

November 20th. Early in December a tally of Russian sick and wounded was made by Dr. Johnson, who had been chosen by the Sick and Hurt Board to supervise their care. His records show that Breyer had 2,860 troops and 1,809 seamen crowded into his seven ships. Some 260 were medical cases, and Johnson feared that the filthy conditions and overcrowding on the ships would lead to more illness. In January Vorontsov complained to the British government that these same troops were still awaiting transport to the Islands and urged that they be taken there promptly. Bad weather delayed their transfer even longer. There is a report dated March 7, 1800 which simply states that the transport Neptune went aground while disembarking troops at Guernsey. Since the Neptune is listed as one of Breyer's ships, it is possible that some Russians had remained on shipboard almost six months.[6]

On Jersey, 6,505 Russians were landed on Jersey and about the same number on Guernsey. Fear initially struck the islanders when they learned about the arrival of the Russians, but that turned out less worse than expected, as described in her diary by Mary Dumaresq:

After the unfortunate expedition to Holland, temporary barracks were built in this Island and in Guernsey to receive about twelve thousand Russians, who had acted with our troops in Holland, and whom the lateness of the season prevented from returning to their own country. Barracks were got ready in a very short time to receive near seven thousand in Jersey and upwards of five thousand in Guernsey. Various reports had been circulated with regard to the behaviour of these troops in Holland, and of their manner & discipline. We were led to expect a great deal of plundering from them, with manners very rough and unpolished. People in general were extremely apprehensive of their arrival. The lower classes in particular expected nothing better than a set of savages who were to plunder them, eat their children and commit all sorts of depredations…

The latter end of November a part of the "Régiment de Paul" arrived. The Russians continued arriving until the end of January 1800; after which time the Russian garrison consisted of Major-General Kapsovitch, Commander-in-Chief; the "Régiment de Paul", consisting of two battalions of Grenadiers, commanded by Major-General Emmé, quartered in St. Helier; Major-General Zovalischen's regiment of Grenadiers, quartered at Belle Vue, which had lost a number of men in Holland; Major-General Mamaouf's Regiment of Grenadiers, a young regiment, quartered in the new barracks in St. Aubin's bay; Major-General Sutoff's regiment of Chasseurs, almost cut up in Holland, quartered at Grouville; the remains of a battalion of Hussars, who were a part of the Czar's guard, commanded by Col. Gladcoff; Colonel Lindsforth's battalion of Infantry; Colonel Erickson's battalion and Major Osimoff's, all quartered at Grouville. About forty Cossacks from the borders of the Don, who were also a part of the Emperor's guard, and about the same number of Cossacks, with long beards, from the borders of Tartary, near the

---

6   Clara J. Tucker, 'Russians in the Channel Islands' in *Annual Bulletin of the Société Jersiaise* (Jersey: Bigwoods Printers Ltd., 1974), pp.259-260.

River Kral. The Russians and Cossacks altogether amounted to upwards of 6000 men…

The Russians had not been in Jersey six weeks before the inhabitants discovered how very much they had been deceived in the behaviour they were led to expect from them: instead of men rough and uncivilized, as prejudice had painted them, the most polite and gentle manners were observable in them… I never heard a word in the mouth of a Russian that was either rude or indelicate. As to their morals, we had little opportunity to know them. They have however left no debt unpaid, and although they were great favourites with the fair sex, I have not heard of their having left any one to mourn the loss of her reputation… The inhabitants got very soon acquainted with the Russian officers. Their very strict discipline, the good order in which they kept their men, their universal desire to please, their very great fear of offending against any of our laws or customs, gained for them the esteem and good will of every one… There were no complaints whatever against the men, unless it were at first some few thefts of firewood, of which they did not know the value, and which they thought they might make free with as in their own country.[7]

Although Mary Dumaresq was very positive about the behaviour of the Russian soldiers, Philippa Marett was not, although she shows understanding:

To our good Jersey people, who in 1799 were more shut out of the world than they are now, the sight of these soldiers, especially of the Cossacks with their strange manners and costumes, must have been a revelation; and if report speaks true not altogether a pleasant one: for food being scarce, the Russian troops who were half starved used to prowl about and lay hands on whatever they could seize, even it is said committing highway robberies on the people returning provision-laden from the markets. Their love of tallow was so great that they went round begging for candle ends, which they greedily devoured; and woe to the tradesman who unwittingly displayed packets of these dainties outside his shop, the temptation was too great! It is recorded too that on one occasion the town of St. Aubin's was left in total darkness the Russians having drunk up all the oil from the lamps. Perhaps in consequence of this uncritical gormandizing it is said that the officers ill treated the men fearfully, and that their cries could be heard some way off.[8]

As it was, the participation in the campaign in Holland turned out to be without positive gains for the Russians, as the capture of the Batavian fleet was only profitable for the British. Of the 17,000 men that had sailed from Reval, in January 1800 only 10,539 effectives and 3,308 sick remained.[9] The reputation of the Russians was significantly damaged

---

7 Mary Dumaresc, 'Account of the stay in Jersey of Russian troops. 1799-1800' in *Annual Bulletin of the Société Jersiaise* (Jersey: Labey et Fils, 1914), pp.417-420, 424. Mary was the wife of Lieutenant General Le Couteur, who was assistant quartermaster-general on Jersey during the Russian stay.
8 Philippa L. Marett, 'The Russians in Jersey' in *Jersey Ladies'College Magazine* (1892), pp.9-10. Marett lived on Jersey and collected information and anecdotes about the Russians on Jersey.
9 Miliutin, *Geschichte des Krieges*, Vol.V, p.73.

by their behaviour in Holland and stood in sharp contrast with those of Suvorov's troops in the Alps. The effect was even bigger because of the articles in the newspapers and public opinion fed by these earlier victories. Tsar Paul was enraged by the negative reports about the conduct of his troops, perceiving it as an personal insult. Although Major General Essen was promoted to lieutenant general and the Major Generals Emmé and Kaptsevich received the Order of St. Anna, the Russian commander-in-chief Hermann was dismissed from military service by Tsar Paul, as well as Major General Arbénev, but these would not be the only ones punished. Nearly the whole corps that fought in Holland suffered:

> Because of violation of order, discipline and subordination the regiments of Zavalishin [Benkendorf], Mamaev [Zherebtsov], Sedmoratzki, Vyazmitinov [Arbénev] and Fersen, as well as Grenadier Battalion Ogarev, Ericsson, Weliashev [Strick], Osipov, Mitiouchin and Lindfors [Timofeyev] is forbidden the beating of the Grenadier march; The regiment Zavalishin, which lost its colours, will not be replaced.[10]

When this became known in London, January 1800, the Duke of York immediately wrote to Count Vorontsov, the Russian ambassador in London, declaring that a number of Russian regiments had showed much order and bravery during the various encounters with the enemy:

> With sincere regret I have heard that His Majesty the Russian Emperor, on the basis of very superficial and inaccurate reports, expressed his displeasure to the whole Corps of His Majesty which took part in the expedition to Holland. I regard it as a duty and a pleasure to have full justice done to many regiments who, in the various battles, were as distinguished by bravery as by order. The Musketeer Regiment Sedmoratzki and the comb. Gren.-Bat. Ericsson seized during the battle of September 19 the village of Warmenhuizen, and captured about 700 prisoners and 3 guns. In the battle of 2 October, the three mentioned battalions captured two batteries at the Canal of Alkmaar and pushed the enemy back. In the last battle, on 6 October, they took possession of the village of Bakkum and made many prisoners. The Musketeer Regiment Fersen, at the battle of 19 September, was detached to the right column together with English troops and has fought excellent. The comb. Gren.-Bat. Ogarev and Mitiouchin as well as the Gren.-Bat. Emmé were disembarked in Helder later than the rest of the troops and joined the army only after the unfortunate battle of 19 September; they have distinguished themselves particularly in the following battles of 2 and 6 October. I myself was a witness of the bravery and order with which these units fought against the enemy; on every occasion they were worthy of my pride. Therefore I am very sorry to hear that Your Majesty's disgrace also extends to these troops, and I am convinced that this would not have been the case if His Majesty would have received accurate reports of their conduct. I would turn directly to the Emperor, if I did not fear to bother

---

10   Most Highest Order of Tsar Paul of 4 November 1799 in Miliutin, *Geschichte des Krieges*, Vol.V, p.73.

His Majesty. But as I know how much he loves his troops, and how much he can do to the merit of justice, I turn to Your Highness, the commander in chief of all the Russian troops here, in the conviction that you feel like I wholly feel, how painful it must be for meritorious people, who were fulfilling their duty with honour, to have indulged in the displeasure of their Lord and Emperor. I am convinced that you consider it your duty to respect the just attention of His Royal Majesty to turn to those who deserve the same.[11]

Vorontsov immediately forwarded York's letter to the Tsar, accompanied by a letter of his own, confirming what York stated and recommending the Benkendorf Grenadiers to the Tsar's favourable consideration since the regiment, having lost one of his colours to the enemy, had attempted to make up for the loss by capturing a colour belonging to the enemy:

After Lieutenant-General Essen, in his relation to Your Imperial Majesty of the unfortunate battle of 19 September, did not mention those regiments and battalions which were disordered and which, Your Most Gracious Emperor, deprived many of these of beating of the Grenadier march, I must suppose that General Essen wrote to you in private, or that he send someone to Petersburg to report to your Imperial Majesty personally, and that all the regiments and battalions without difference were represented as if the same were in disorder. The commanders of these have given me their account, especially Major-General Sedmoratzki, whose regiment as well as Battalion Ericsson not only did not break the proper order, but distinguished himself in an excellent manner; As well as Colonel Baklanovski, who commanded the Regiment Fersen which, during the affair, did not even fight with our troops, but stood with the English on the right flank where the regiment fought bravely and maintained order, discipline, and subordination. The regiment of Major-General Emmé and the comb. Battalions Ogarev and Mitiouchin took no part in the unfortunate battle; these arrived later and disembarked in Helder later than the other troops, and joined the corps only three or four days afterwards. As I have not been an eye-witness of these events, I decided to make all sorts of inquiries about this before I would report to my Most Gracious Emperor... On this occasion I cannot fail to report Your Imperial Majesty to the fact that the regiment Zavalishin, formerly Benkendorf, had made good the loss of his colours by taking one of the enemy, which is now kept with the regiment. As to the loss of its own colours, I can report to Your Majesty that during the battle of 19 September the regiment was stationed at the most dangerous point, and suffered considerably more than all the others; but it only lost its colours when the ensign, Schegolowitz, during the severest and desperate attack of the enemy, saw that it would be impossible to save it. Ordered to do so by Ensign Boggowut, who was with the colours, he tore them off the pole, wrapped it round his body, and thus remained, together with

---

11 Letter in German, translated from French of 22 January 1800 from the Duke of York to Count Vorontsov in Miliutin, *Geschichte des Krieges*, Vol.V, pp.305-306.

Ensign Boggowut, on the field of battle. The remaining nine colours belonging to the regiment are all full of holes.[12]

As a result of the above letters Tsar Paul reconsidered his orders and the punishment for the above mentioned regiments was revoked. The Benkendorf Grenadiers received new colours. This would not save all the Russian units that participated. The Arbénev Musketeers, which also lost a colour, was included in the Most Highest Order of Tsar Paul of 20 April 1800, together with the regiments that had lost a colour during the Battle of Zurich. These all would receive no replacement colours. The 1st *Jégerski* of Suthoff became the scapegoat of the failure, especially for routing during their advance on Bergen and for not being able to hold off the French skirmishers and Batavian *jager*. As a result the regiment was disbanded on its return to Russia on 8 March 1800. Although Essen had recently been promoted he soon fell in disgrace for his continuously complaining about the British; already during the campaign but also after the retreat. Although there were grounds for Essen's complaints, because of this he became a real threat for the Anglo-Russian relations and on 10 November he was dismissed and replaced by General Golenishchev-Kutuzov.

During the winter the Russians remained on Guernsey and Jersey, recovering from their hardships in Holland, while negotiations were taking place for a new invasion. This time the attack would take place on France itself, the Russians would be transported by Russian ships to land between the mouth of the Rivers Loire and Garonne. Informed by a deserter the French were already aware of this threat for a long time:

> In another ten days all the Anglo-Russians are gone. The Russians will disembark on Jersey and Guernsey; in the close proximity of the provinces of Brittany and Normandy, it may well be that the English will put them ashore to join the Chouans. This wild race that is not good in war for their plunder, murder, etc., could easily act in these parts and increase their number. I invite you, citizen minister to not ignore the information I give you. They are likely to fix your attention and that of the Directory.[13]

The plan was that the British would land at a different location and together they would support the Royalists and when possible advance into the interior of France. The reason that there would be no combined army this time, was that the Tsar did not want to place his troops under the command of British senior officers again. In addition he did not want the Duke of York to have any role in the upcoming campaign.[14] Of course this was cause for disagreement, and Anglo-Russian relations quickly deteriorated. First, the alliance with the Austrians was broken and Tsar Paul pulled back his troops. Next, more and more evidence came to the light that Essen's accusations of the British had not been entirely without grounds and that indeed the British did not provide for the Russians as they should have, at

---

12　Letter of 26 January 1800 from the Russian Ambassador Vorontsov to Tsar Paul in Miliutin, *Geschichte des Krieges*, V, pp.306-308.
13　Letter of 31 October from Rostollant to the French minister of war Dubois-Crancé, in Gachot, *Brune en Hollande*, p.308.
14　Miliutin, *Geschichte des Krieges*, V, pp.139-140.

Russian memorial at Bergen. (Author photo)

Plaque on the Russian memorial at Bergen. (Author photo)

least in Tsar Paul's opinion, and that the British treated the Russians with disdain. One of the incidents took place on the ship *Diadem* transporting Russians:

> Captain Abernibesov of the Musketeer Regiment Sedmoratzki reported that during the passage from Holland to England the English sailors of the ship Diadem were offensive to the Russian soldiers by their impudent behaviour, and that Captain Dawson himself, on the other hand, took not only no measures, but the sailors by his forbearance made more insults. After hearing this, Vorontsov complained to the British Government; Captain Dawson was immediately put to justice, recognized as guilty, and relieved from the command of his ship. The other officers were also punished according to their guilt. General Sedmoratzki believed that his regiment was fully satisfied for the insult that had been done, and later interceded to pardon Dawson. The English admiralty however, did not consider it possible to alter the verdict of the court martial.[15]

Although the Russians were satisfied for now there were other problems. As described, the departure for the Channel Islands took time, only on 5 January 1800 did the first transports

---

15 Report of 22 January 1800 from Count Vorontsov in: Miliutin, *Geschichte des Krieges*, Vol.V, pp.395-396. Dawson would, however, receive command of the *Asia* (3rd Rate 64) in 1801.

leave for Guernsey and Jersey. On these islands the soldiers lacked a lot of necessities. According to Vorontsov: 'They lacked everything; they wore their garments, which had been completely torn, far above the appointed duration; some of them had already been wearing them for a whole year'.[16] On top of all these troubles a disagreement arose about the payment of the subsidies, as according to the British Ministry the Russians did not provide the amount of men that had been agreed upon. This meant the end of the Anglo-Russian military cooperation and in March Count Vorontsov received the order from the Tsar to return to Russia with the complete army and navy. In April Vorontsov himself was recalled. It took some time to fetch the Russians army, totalling 12,834 men, from the islands. At Portsmouth they embarked on the Russian warships and hired British merchants. Sailing home in five different squadrons, the first squadron sailed on 17 June and arrived in Reval on 4 July. The fifth squadron sailed on 31 July, arriving in Reval on 14 September.[17] So ended the Russian participation in the invasion of Holland.

The French Forces in the Batavian Republic During the Invasion

Opinions differ about the quality of Brune as a commander in battle. Nevertheless, studying the campaign shows that it was in fact impossible in this kind of terrain to fight a proper battle: weather and terrain conditions were bad, visibility very limited, and therefore command and control difficult. Each battle turned in a whole series of isolated combats. Brune understood this very well and during the battles of Bergen, Alkmaar, and Castricum he abandoned the formal structure of his army and assigned his generals to specific sectors of the defence line, with units assigned to them accordingly. In this way he was able to assign the necessary amount of troops to a specific part of the line, while his generals, able to act on their own and authorised to make the necessary decisions, could exercise close control on their troops, inspiring them by their personal example. This enabled Brune also to mix more experienced Batavian units with his raw French Demi-Brigades, giving him a huge advantage over the Anglo-Russians, not accustomed to, and untrained in, this kind of war. If the Anglo-Russians attacked on a broad front and managed to push back the Franco-Batavians, the whole line could retreat to a new and prepared defence line, with the terrain in North Holland providing many defensible positions. If the attack took place at one or more specific points along the defence line, Franco-Batavian troops were automatically in position (and commanded) to undertake an immediate attack on the flanks of the penetration. This happened, for example, with the Russians at Bergen on 19 September, Abercromby's flank on the beach on 2 October, and again the Russians at Castricum on 6 October. In addition, Brune made good use of the capabilities of his artillery, especially his horse artillery which inflicting heavy casualties on the Anglo-Russians. The 1/8e Artillerie Légère distinguished itself time and again, especially during the battle of Bergen, its commander *Capitaine* Leroux receiving honourable mentioning in Brune's after action report. He also made good use of his light infantry capabilities, especially in this kind of terrain, outclassing the

---

16 Quoted in Miliutin, *Geschichte des Krieges*, Vol.V, pp.156.
17 Miliutin, *Geschichte des Krieges*, Vol.V, pp.402-403.

Anglo-Russians on every occasion. It can be concluded that the Franco-Batavians possessed the flexibility to adapt to the tactics needed in this terrain whereas the Anglo-Russians did not, this fact alone virtually removing the chance of a successful Anglo-Russian campaign from the start.

During the campaign in Holland the Franco-Batavian troops received substantial reinforcements as described in the previous chapters, resulting in numerous reorganisations. The month before the Anglo-Russian invasion the French troops in the Batavian Republic were organised as follows:

Division	Commander	Strength	Location
1er Division	*Général de Brigade* Gouvion	3,756	's Hertogenbosch, Utrecht.
2e Division	*Général de Division* Reubell	5,336	South Holland.
3e Division	*Général de Division* Desjardin	9,321	Zeeland.
Total		18,413[18]	

These were not all available to be used against the invasion as it was necessary to garrison the numerous Batavian cities, fortresses, ports and other strategic points. After the landing had taken place, Gouvion with the 1st Division moved to North-Holland, gradually reinforced with units from both other Divisions. Comparison of Appendix V with Appendix XVI shows that the greater part of the French battle-worthy troops present in the Batavian Republic moved to the front. Command of this enlarged division was initially given to *Général de Division* Vandamme, who was singled out by the French minister of war to provide Brune with an experienced second in command. Assigned to him were *Généraux de Brigade* Gouvion, Barbou, Fuzier, and David. The 2e Division in South Holland, effectively commanded by *Adjudant-Général* Dazémar, with *Général de Brigade* Prévost second in command consisted of only 1,600 infantry in depots as well as 720 cavalry and 178 gunners. Desjardin was still in command of the 3e Division in Zeeland, consisting of 4,330 infantry (mainly depots), 620 men of the 16e Chasseurs à Cheval, and 420 gunners. Assigned to him were *Généraux de Brigade* Rivaud and Osten. As further reinforcements arrived at the front from the Army of the Rhine and from Belgium, Vandamme's division was split in two. The divisions were numbered 1er (Boudet), 2e (Gouvion) and later also the 3e (Morlot). *Général de Division* Vandamme commanded this French Corps with Brune remaining commander in chief of all Franco-Batavian forces in the Batavian Republic. The old 2e and 3e Division became temporarily the 4e and 5e Divisions. These weakened divisions were gradually reinforced again with units from the Armée du Rhin and National Guard battalions from Belgium and northern France, counting together at the end of the campaign about 11,000 men. The French order of battle of 22 November 1799, after the closing of the campaign (see Appendix XVII) is different from the previous orders of battle as experienced units were immediately sent to the front in Germany. With the French field army disbanded, the 4e and 5e Divisions again became the 2e and 3e Divisions. Some units, having received heavy losses during the campaign, disappeared altogether and new units are listed as they marched to the Batavian Republic during the campaign.

18 Strength of 4 July 1799. For details see Appendix V.

Plunder

Sources differ greatly about the extent that plundering and other disorders took place and by whom. Of course this subject was widely used for propaganda purposes. That plunder took place is however not denied and it is also not surprising when taking in regard the lack of provisions suffered by the Anglo-Russians in particular. After the arrival of the Russians and the Battle of Bergen on 19 September, plundering became more common. Miliutin treats this aspect in depth in his work, not trying to clear his own Russians from the blame, but explaining why it took place and stating that not only the Russians but also the British troops behaved just as bad, maybe even worse: 'They even complained to each other of the violation of discipline and plundering during the battle. The allied troops, who suffered a great lack of food, thought themselves justified on the battlefield and even the women who had followed the English troops to Holland eagerly assisted.'[19] According to the same Miliutin, Russian eye witnesses assured that the English returned from the battle with a lot of loot. There is also a British account of what happened after the battle of 2 October, mentioning British as well as Russians:

> The following morning I was sent with a piquet to bring in stragglers, who had found their way to a village on the skirts of the sandy range, when a curious scene was presented: the troughs which had been set out with milk for the pigs had been drained in an instant by the first visitors from the bivouac; in one house we found two fellows very quietly ripping up the bed ticken in a farmer's house in search of plunder, while in the garden was a large party in actual combat with two hives of bees, which they had turned out of their houses; at the opposite side of the way was the post-office, where some of our gentry, addicted to letters, had made sure of their fortunes, and everything that felt like a double letter was broken open, but as none of the enclosures looked anything like "Abraham Newland", they were dispersed to the winds of heaven: in one house that had been gutted by a party of Russians, another party of their countrymen made their appearance, and finding nothing left but a harmless Dutch clock ticking behind the door, they took it down, pulled it in pieces, and divided the works.[20]

Locals also reported plunder by the British and Russians:

> On the 23rd and 24th [September], we heard no shooting and the English, which were quartered in Kolhorn and Barsingerhorn came from there and alarmed the inhabitants at the Kreijl and in our Polder [Wieringerwaard] and took the cows

---

19 Miliutin, *Geschichte des Krieges*, Vol.V, p.46. A Batavian account describing the most horrible scenes although reliability is questionable: Anon., *Dag-verhaal wegens de Landing der Engelsche en Russische Troupen; Ongehoorde Wreedheden door Dezelve Gepleegt, en Eindelijk de Schandelijke Aftogt. Alles met Egte Bewyzen Gestaafd*, pp.27-30, 43. An in-depth dissertation of plunder by Russians and its use in propaganda is H.J. Broersma, *De grenzen van het beeld – Het Nederlandse beeld van de Russische soldaten tijdens de Engels-Russische Invasie in Noord-Holland in 1799* (Unpublished dissertation, Rijks Universiteit Groningen, 1996).
20 Anon., 'Recollections of the British army', p.188.

and sheep from the land and gave for a small part a little money but many were absolutely stolen. On the 25th in the afternoon the cows from Teunis Coorn from the Zijpe were brought to Kornelis Horn here saying the bringer that over there the Russians fetched the cows and sheeps from the land and slaughtered so that on the land no cattle was safe... On the 9th [October] passed a party of English troops dragoons and soldiers which had with them about 400 sheep and a host of cows which had all been stolen by them.[21]

On the Franco-Batavian side, in his report directly after the Battle of Bergen Brune already mentions plundering by the Anglo-Russians: 'The Anglo-Russians have committed the greatest excesses in the villages they occupied during the action. The poor Batavian peasants were massacred or burned in their homes with women and children. Many villages are still on fire. The English especially distinguished themselves by their cruelty.'[22] It is true that many villages were set on fire during the Anglo-Russian retreat to the Zijpe position, by both sides, by accident or on purpose. That there were good grounds for the news about the plundering by Anglo-Russian soldiers will be illustrated by eye-witness accounts. In any case, the Batavian government used this news immediately for their propaganda, pointing out that this was what the 'liberators' brought the Batavian people. That the propaganda worked is shown by the description of the events after 19 September in the previous chapters; support for the Orangist cause dried up and in every city along the Zuiderzee occupied by the British navy they were met with apathy or even contempt.

Still, rumours of especially bad behaviour of Russian soldiers were so strong that Count Vorontsov believed it necessary in a letter of 14 October to urge Essen to do his utmost to maintain order among his troops in England and later on Guernsey and Jersey. Essen's reaction offended Tsar Paul: 'One might think that Count Vorontsov was talking about some band of robbers. It is however true that during the battle some people dispersed and committed atrocities; but they were only looking for cattle for slaughter and were punished for this.'[23] True or not, a few months later Count Vorontsov remarked:

> Essen had scarcely taken over command from Hermann, when he did all things in a manner as if he tried to effect a division between the Russians and the English on purpose: he sent out a few rumours, allowed the soldiers to sell the provisions received from the British; he did not address subordination; his troops plundered in Holland, but were not punished for their crude and indecent conduct.[24]

Not only the Anglo-Russians plundered though, as there are also numerous reports about the French and Batavians. The French in those revolutionary days were used to living of the land, and when there were not enough provisions available, even in befriended countries,

---

21 Albert Kaan Kz., *Journaal van 1799*, p.6.
22 Letter of 19 September 1799 from Brune to the French minister of war Milet de Mureau in: Krayenhoff, *Geschiedkundige Beschouwing van den Oorlog op het Grondgebied der Bataafsche Republiek in 1799*, Appendix Xc, p.80.
23 Quoted in Miliutin, *Geschichte des Krieges*, Vol.V, p.315.
24 Letter of 19 December 1799 from Count Vorontsov to Count Kushelev, in: Miliutin, *Geschichte des Krieges*, Vol.V, pp.318-319.

not surprisingly they fell into their old habits. There is a letter from the French ambassador Florent-Guiot to the French minister of foreign affairs, stating that after the Battle of Alkmaar supplies were directed to Amsterdam and by oversight were not transported further forward to the army. Also that the Anglo-Russians captured 10,000 rations of bread and 14,000 of flesh in Alkmaar.[25] What is stated in this letter, written a few weeks later in an extreme political context, is not confirmed by French, Dutch, nor local sources. Nevertheless, based on this letter in a recent book about the campaign it is concluded that the French troops were starving, a fact having a great impact on the Battle of Castricum.[26] Certainly they would have been hungry, but all soldiers on both sides during this campaign were hungry most of the time and also very resourceful in finding means to eat, as illustrated in many contemporary accounts.

One of the most extensive descriptions of plunder is given by Pastor Bommer of Castricum of the fighting that took place on 6 October and what happened in Castricum before, during and after the battle:

> The Russians were on the Bleekveld before I knew it; some English came into my house, the horse were deployed on the Kerkstraat on the road before the church gate, before and near the houses of J. Glorie, Jacob Molenaar and Maarten Knaap. Some requested for some refreshments and something to drink; they gave them some cups with coffee and soup. They asked what they should pay us for what they had consumed, shook our hands and thanked us friendly. The English and Russians did not plunder here in Castricum, but the French definitely did for four days before the arrival of the English. Yes, our Dutch troops were not above plundering as well and together with the French they excelled in plundering, stealing and robbing above the English and Russians, although these were blamed… In that same house a daughter was shot by a Russian, who had sought refuge with her parents and other children in the cellar, the Russian thinking that French had fled into the cellar. The girl is buried in the dunes near her father's house, without coffin… Tuesday 8 October, when the French were still busy plundering, breaking in, stealing cattle, robbing and slaughtering, the trumpet blew and the army of the French and Batavians left head over heels through Castricum, north, to hunt down the English and to pursue them, which some time later embarked with the Russians, to go to England from here, and the French with the Batavians returned.
>
> It is by the way amazing that there are people outside and south of Castricum, purporting that the English and Russians robbed and plundered in Castricum, but not the French and some Batavians. But even if the English and Russians would have acted as is being said, that they did so at other places from where they retired as well, this could be reconciled as they came as enemies. But the French and our Batavians ate the bread of our land, received their pay from our country. To remain with the French for a moment; what did they do in Brabant, Flanders, the country around Liège, Switzerland, Italy and other places?

---

25 Letter in French of 18 October 1799 from Florent Guiot to Reinhard in Colenbrander, *Gedenkstukken*, Vol.III, p.104.
26 Philip Ball, *A Waste of Blood & Treasure* (Barnsley: Pen & Sword Books Limited, 2017), pp.139-140, 147.

Would these people without religion have forgotten their greedy nature after they had come to our country five years ago? No, when they came and were here they still had that same nature. There is clear and real proof of this. 1799, on Thursday 3 October the French came in Castricum from North Holland. The outposts were also here, and already that same evening they started to steal, destroy and plunder, as well as on Friday the 4th, the 5th and Sunday, the 6th, early, yes the night before the battle.

The plundering is irregular; the best objects of some had already been put away; al that the French found not put away, left behind and abandoned by the fled citizens, was for them "French freedom"… The French chasseurs with their green coats (horse) and then the dragoons were the first to start with robbing, plundering and destroying and then also some of the Batavians. In the Kerkbuurt the houses of Mr Joachim Neuwhout, van Veen, bailiff and secretary here, as well as those of reverend Fabritius, the houses of Pieter Janz. Schavemaker, the widow of Jan Jacobz. Kuys, bakers and shopkeepers, were all in a terrible shape. Wheat, rye, groceries and equipment, everything gone, and destroyed, other houses somewhat less but still bad enough. Baker Schavemaker managed to save his money in a peculiar way. When the soldiers arrived he threw his purse in the chimney. There it fell on a plank, covered with soot. The money was not found, but he had to watch the grain swept with brooms from his attic on to the road where it partially served as food for the horses, partially trampled. From the dunes up to Bakkum, Noord-Bakkum and the gathering place for the shells, also some houses were miserable; on the Noordend and Oosterbuurt in general not so worse. From Pieter Duyneveld, churchwarden of our community the catholic funds of about 1,000 guilders were stolen and lost.

On Sunday 6 October, after the battle, our same French returned to Castricum after the retreat of the English and Russians and remained until the afternoon of 8 October. During that time they did nothing else then destroy, rob and slaughter cattle. About that time the alarm was raised, and all French and Batavian troops, from here and the surrounding places, had to leave altogether from here north, to pursue the English and Russians retiring north from Akersloot, Limmen and the Egmonds. Otherwise it would have been even worse here. So the French have plundered here for about six days. Because of the alarm raised, Jan Glorie managed to keep two cows which had been taken by the French to slaughter them. And Jan Glorie has defended himself so bravely in his house against the French robbers that, with all their violence, were not able to enter two rooms of his house, and have not been inside these… The amount of stolen Edam and Leidse cheese is innumerable. And the cheeses still too young and in the salt were cut in half with sabres and destroyed. Butter barrels with butter, recently churned butter, unspeakable much was robbed. Around the house of Miss Nieuwhout van Veen, the new house, were the officers were billeted is much found after their departure. The French soldiers cooked the cabbages in pure butter, without water. Being cooked it was not edible and they threw it away: destroyers and squanderers. Cooked flesh, bacon and hams, everything they discovered was taken away. Chickens, ducks, eggs, beehives, honey, wine, beer, jenever, brandy, cream and milk, everything was to their liking and fell in their hands. Copper kettles, farmer's milk kettles, and pans of ceramic, pewter spoons, dishes, plates, pots, steel forks were taken away, asked to borrow to be never returned, so that some citizens were not able to cook food, some of them released from that task as they had nothing left to cook as well. Silver chatelaines, headpieces and silver locks, and braces cut off from prayer books, as well as all other silver and gold and money robbed. Beds, sheets, pillows, pillowcases, blankets, table-cloths, napkins, coats, men's and women's clothing, shoes, silver clasps etc., unimaginable amounts. Hay, oats, straw and peas, beans, apples, pears, potatoes, wood and peat. Carts, carioles, wagons, yes the iron of the wheels, buckets and barrels, were of their liking. There are also horses gone. This and much more from 3 October until the 8th ditto 1799 only in Castricum, so one can calculate from here how much worse it must have been in Bergen and further to the north...

After the English and Russians had embarked and had returned to England, the French and Batavians returned. The French then, who previously had no baggage carts, passed through Castricum on 2 November, to the south, with many stolen carts, stage wagons, carriages and carts fully loaded with robbed goods, and the French train soldiers being the biggest robbers, and the soldiers with full backpacks to Haarlem. On these vehicles lay the all kinds of visible goods, like a glass greenhouse, copper kettles, ceramics, etc. Nice and clean English horses, for the French, were loaded with great robbed treasures...

Now I have to report some about the French brigades billeted in and which have pestered and plagued the Egmonds, Bakkum and part of Castricum, until they also left for Haarlem on 22 November. These soldiers came nearly every day, sometimes with complete troops, also along the edge of the dunes with their muskets, accompanied by some civilians of Egmond aan Zee serving as guides, digging up the potatoes from the land of the farmer's, robbing them from their equipment and stealing potatoes already dug up. They broke into houses, took all kinds of goods and destroyed what they left behind. They came with troops and dug the rabbits out of the dunes, from the Egmonds up to Castricum and all the way to Heemskerk, so that no rabbit was to be found anymore, except for some stray ones left in the woods... While digging up rabbits two of them, a French soldier and a deserted Dutch soldier, have been suffocated in the holes by falling sand and found dead... They, the French soldiers, have also torn down and robbed the lead of the house of Mr Akerlaaken, and the lead of the chimneys of other houses, as well as the crampirons from the walls, standing and flat fire pits, seeds, peas, beans, apples, copper kettles, pewter and ironwork, potatoes etc.[27]

There are more reports about the bad behaviour of the Batavian troops, for example from a grenadier of the Bataafsch Legioen:

---

[27] Nicolaas Bommer, 'Korte Beschrijvinge Van Den Slag Of Batailje Op Den Zesden October, Zijnde Ook Castricummer-Kermes 1799 Voorgevallen' in M. Kramer, 'De Slag bij Castricum 6 en 7 Oct. 1799', *Vragen van den Dag* (Amsterdam: S.L. van Looy, 1905), pp.466, 468-473.

> The house of the pastor in Winkel was completely ruined; the house looked more like an irregular horse stable then the house of a human. The Scots had treated him very well, but the English had spared nothing except his library, were he had put away his most valued possessions and his linen; but when our own people had wreaked havoc (according to the pastor), nothing was spared: while his linen was stolen, the most excellent beds were sliced open, cartridges were made from his most valuable books! So that this truly honest man is completely ruined! He told me which battalion it was, and the name of the lieutenant-colonel commanding it.[28]

To conclude, the report of the Municipality of Akersloot describes how on both sides soldiers plundered:

> The English troops were lodged with the citizens at Sluijs and Startingh and committed many acts of atrocities against the defenceless locals, extorting money in the meanest manner. Everyone they engaged suffered, and many citizens left their houses to escape the violence and fled to Schermer and Woude. Their abandoned houses were plundered and robbed… This happened on 6 and 7 October 1799, on the 7th they had nearly completed their work and nearly all locals had fled, only few remained in their houses. In the evening a great consternation occurred and the English packed their own and robbed goods, stole another twenty horses, five wagons and a carriage, and abandoned the village at 2:00 a.m.… After the departure of the English the Batavian army advanced, and the division of General Daendels moved through Akersloot, that same and the next day, plundering all that had remained from the houses that were still not occupied by their inhabitants.[29]

The Captured Batavian ships

The Batavian ships captured during the invasion in Holland can be divided into three categories. In the first category are the ships captured on the Wadden Sea and Zuiderzee. These were regarded by the British as prizes and treated as such, with some of the best ships taken into service of the British Royal Navy. In the second category are the ships captured in the Nieuwe Diep when Den Helder was occupied by the British. These ships were also regarded as prizes. The British took the best ships captured in the Nieuwe Diep, leaving those not seaworthy. Even the sheer hulk was taken. The *Broederschap* had sunk in the harbour as well as the British *Blanche*. The latter was for the most part demolished, providing firewood for the British bakeries. The ships left behind were completely plundered and severely damaged. This was done on purpose by a detachment of British sailors as described in the previous chapter and as a result most of these would never sail again. *Lieutenant-Colonel* Krayenhoff, overseeing the Anglo-Russian embarkation as defined in the treaty, reported as follows:

---

28 Anon., *Eenige Berichten omtrent den Veldtocht der Gewapende Groningers, naar Noord-Holland*, pp.39-40.
29 Municipaliteit van Akersloot, *Voor de Nakomelingschap*, pp.3-4.

> Regarding the Nieuwe Diep harbour; the most useful ships have already been taken away, namely the *Heldin*, the *Hector*, the *Venus*, the *Minerva*, the *Valk* and the hulk: being commanded by the following exiled Dutch naval officers F. Thom, van Braam, Vos, Spengler , Twent, Martinius, of the hulk we do not know by who it is commanded now. The ships still present at this place are the *Alarm, Constitutie, Sebilla, Drechterland, Gouda, 't Duifje* and the *Unie*, several of which are still being rigged, to leave with the rest. The *Broederschap* has sunk transversal of the Nieuwe Werk…; a Russian forty-four is sunk at the mouth of the said port, against the mould head and is being demolished, in order to provide fuel to the bakeries.[30]

Of the ships mentioned by Krayenhoff, the *Valk* would founder at Ameland (see Chapter 16). Six others indeed sailed to Great Britain and were regarded prize: 'Proceeds of the Dutch hulks, Drotchterland and Broederschap; and of the ships, Helder, Venus, Minerva, and Hector, taken in the New Diep, Holland, 28 August, 1799'.[31] About the latter four frigates a dispute raised, the British declaring they belonged to Great Britain by right for being captured. March 1800 it was arranged with the Stadtholder that these frigates indeed belonged to the British. Prize money was paid to the crews of the British ships that had participated in their capture as well as the British land forces. Of the ships mentioned by Krayenhoff as still being rigged only the *Drechterland* would sail to Great Britain with the remainder not seaworthy, Krayenhoff reporting again on 19 November:

> All the ships in the port of the Nieuwe Diep, including the hulk, have been taken. *'t Duifje*, the *Unie, Sibilla Antoinetta, Constitutie, Gouda*, the *Alarm*, and the *Verwachting*, as well as the flute *Vreden Lust* are left behind, but all being plundered and damaged. Some of them had powder and other fuels scattered, with the purpose of sacrificing them to the flames.[32]

That these ships were not seaworthy and would remain at the Nieuwe Diep, is also illustrated by a report to the Batavian government about the salvage of the *Broederschap*. David de Ridder had been contracted to salvage the *Broederschap* which had sunk in the waterway of the Nieuwe Diep. Already after a few weeks by a masterly disposition of the ships *Constitutie*

---

30 Letter of 3 November 1799 from Krayenhoff to the Batavian Naval Minister in: Krayenhoff, *Geschiedkundige Beschouwing*, Appendix XXIIb, pp.154-155. The 'Russian forty-four' was in fact the British *Blanche* (see Chapter 13), confirmed by Krayenhoff in Appendix XXIII, p.164.
31 *Steele's Prize Pay Lists*, 2nd edition corrected till 1805, p.116. The 'Drotchterland' was the *Drechterland*. The 'Broederschap' was not the *Broederschap* which, as described, had sunk in the Nieuwe Diep but the sheer hulk. There is confusion about the names *Heldin* and *Helder*. Apparently, initially the *Heldin* was mistakenly named *Helder*. Realising the mistake in 1800 the *Heldin* was taken into British service with its original name.
32 Letter of 19 November 1799 from Krayenhoff to the Batavian Naval Minister in Krayenhoff, *Geschiedkundige Beschouwing*, Appendix XXIIe, p.160. Colledge mentions the *Alarm* also captured and renamed *Helder* (J.J. Colledge, *Ships of the Royal Navy: An Historical Index. Vol. I Major Ships* (Newton Abbot: David & Charles, 1969), pp.30, 262. The *Alarm* was however left behind as referred to by Krayenhoff, confirmed by a decree of the Batavian government of 12 March 1802, authorising the breaking up of the frigate *Alarm*, as well as taking out of service the flute *Vredelust* used as lodgings for labourers. Also ordering to convert the *Gouda* and *'t Duifje* into corvettes (*Besluiten van het Staats-bewind der Bataafsche Republiek*, 12 Maart 1802). The *Alarm* is not mentioned in *Steele's Prize Pay Lists* either.

and *Gouda* he managed to raise the *Broederschap*, sealed its leaks and drained some water, when on 9 November 1800 a heavy storm tore the *Verwachting* and *Sibilla Antoinetta* loose from their moorings. Driven forward by the storm and the current, both ships rammed the *Constitutie* and *Gouda* and tore the whole side out of the *Broederschap*, sinking it again.

There remains the fate of *Schout-bij-Nacht* Story's fleet that surrendered at the Vlieter. As described these ships sailed to Great Britain on 10 September to clear the roads of Texel for an emergency evacuation of the British troops, their arrival being reported in the *London Chronicle*:

> We have the satisfaction to announce the arrival in Ozely Bay, on the Suffolk Coast, of twelve sail of Dutch men of war, principally line of battle. These ships left the Texel on Tuesday last, bound to the Nore, under the command of Capt. Cobb, of the Glatton, accompanied by the Veteran, Ardent, Belliqueux, Monmouth, Overyssel, and two Russian ships. Previous to their departure many of the Dutch sailors were inclinable to be refractory, and absolutely refused to assist in getting up the ships anchors; however, a detachment of our gallant tars were soon distributed on board the respective ships, and Admiral Mitchell judged it necessary to send a sufficient force to see them safe to the Nore. The Washington is a remarkable fine ship, of 74 guns, was never before at sea, and sails faster than any ship in the fleet. The Ambuscade Dutch frigate, of 32 guns, came over with the above ships, but proceeded to Yarmouth Roads. Prior to the ships before mentioned leaving the Texel, the Marines were landed from all the English ships to do garrison duty, to enable the regular troops to join the main army… Such of the Dutch sailors who declared for the Stadtholder, were drafted out of the respective ships before the fleet sailed.[33]

Among the marines landed at Den Helder were also 180 Russians. The Batavian ships that sailed to Great Britain had the Batavian flags (the Republican sign cut out) flying beneath the British flag and were sailed by British prize crews, except for the *Washington* and *Beschermer*. Both ships were regarded as being captured by the Russian ships participating in the capture and were sailed by Russian prize crews. They would be ceded to Great Britain later in 1799. The *Washington* was renamed *Prinses van Oranje* by the Orangists, taken over by the British as *Princess of Orange*. The two Russian ships mentioned accompanying the Batavian fleet were the *Mstislav* and *Retvizan*, of which the latter had been grounded when advancing on the Batavian fleet in the Vlieter and badly needed repairs. The stay of the surrendered ships at the Nore was not completely without incident though:

> On Monday last, paroles were brought down here from London, for such of the Dutch Captains as were on board the ships lately taken near the Helder; and all of them, except one, have already departed for town. The Dutch ships make every fine appearance; their sides, which are painted black and yellow, are considerably above the level of the water; they have a pendant flying at the main-top-gallant-mast and

---

33 Letter from Harwich of 12 September 1799 in the *London Chronicle*, 14 September 1799.

an English ensign at the stern. There are some Dutch sailors still on board of them. A party of these fellows, to the number of fifty or sixty, some time ago attempted to seize a small vessel near this place, and make their escape; but they were soon discovered and compelled to abandon their project.[34]

After their arrival in Great Britain these ships remained in port. On 11 March 1800 the 'Convention between his Britannic Majesty, and his Serene Highness the Prince of Orange, respecting the Dutch Ships of War which surrendered to Vice Admiral Mitchell, in the Vlieter, on the 30th of August, 1799'[35] was signed. Among other things, it stipulated that:

- His Serene Highness engages; on behalf of the lawful Government of the Republic of the United Provinces, to furnish the ships mentioned in the margin [One of 60 guns, 450 men; one of 44 guns, 350 men; one of 36 guns, 250 men; one of 18 guns, 100 men: Total 1,150 men], completely officered, manned and victualled, to be employed under his Majesty's orders, in the European seas only and for the advantage of the common cause, during the present war, or until the lawful Government of the Republic shall be re-established therein and shall reclaim those ships. His Serene Highness is to be at liberty to employ any Dutch seamen, now on board of the said ships, or on board of the *Hector*, or on board of the *Heldin*, or on board of the *Venus*, or on board of the *Minerva*; or any other Dutch seamen well affected to the lawful Government of the United Provinces and who may be disposed to serve in the manner and on the terms now proposed;
- His Serene Highness agrees to place at the disposal of his Majesty the ships mentioned in the annexed schedule [containing all twelve ships captured in the Vlieter], in the state in which they now are, to be employed as his Majesty shall judge proper and for the benefit of the common cause, within the European seas, during the war, or until the lawful Government of the Republic shall be re-established therein and shall reclaim those ships;
- His Majesty engages that the said ships and sloop shall, at the conclusion of the present war, be delivered up to his Serene Highness on the behalf of the lawful Government of the United Provinces, provided that at that period the said government shall be re-established in those provinces and that the same shall be delivered from the power of the French.

The four ships mentioned that were to receive Dutch crews were initially the *Leyden* but this was changed to the *Gelderland* (3rd rate 68, *Capitein* Tulleken), *Amphitrite* (5th Rate 40, *Capitein* May), *Embuscade* (5th Rate 32, *Capitein* W. van Voss) and *Galathée* (Sloop 16, *Lieutenant ter Zee* Spengler, later *Capitein-Lieutenant* F.T. van Braam). The core of their crews was formed from the crews of the former Dutch-crewed frigates, augmented with sailors from the Isle of Wight and prison ships. June 1800 they were joined by a detachment of 150 infantry of the Dutch Brigade commanded by *Capitein* von Rappard, to be

---

34 Report from Sheerness of 24 October 1799, in the *Naval Chronicle*, Vol.II, p.535.
35 William Woodfall, *An Impartial Report of the Debates that Occur in the two Houses of Parliament* (London: T. Chapman, 1800), Vol.III, Appendix pp.45-48.

used as marines. The ships remained in port until May 1801, when, after having been idle for eighteen months, they were placed under the orders of Admiral Gardner, to be used to transport troops between Ireland and the Isle of Wight, Guernsey, and Jersey. Later they cruised along the French coast together with British ships but they never were engaged in battle.

With the Peace of Amiens in 1802, on 25 May the Dutch squadron was disbanded and most of the Dutch crews and officers returned to the Batavian Republic where they received amnesty. Although the Batavian fleet was treated differently, the British crews of the warships participating in the Secret Expedition as well as the British land forces would receive prize money in 1802. With the Battle of Camperdown and the surrender of the fleet at the Vlieter, the Dutch/Batavian navy had received a blow from which it never again would recover. From this moment on, the Netherlands ceased to exist as a naval superpower.

In the Batavian Republic, all captains that were in command when Story's fleet surrendered, were sentenced by a council of war. The *Capiteins* Van Braam, Van Capellen, and Kolff were sentenced to death, but these captains had already gone in exile and escaped their execution. Story also took the wise decision not to return in the Batavian Republic after his surrender and went in exile as well.[36]

The Dutch Brigade

On 6 November 1799 nearly all Dutch men that had been evacuated from Holland had arrived on the Isle of Wight. On 17 November strength of the military contingent on the Isle of Wight was 2,030 infantry, 294 *jager*, 34 cavalry and 138 artillery, a total of 2,496 men. This did not include the sailors and marines. These troops were to be the core of the Dutch Brigade that was to be raised. The basis for this brigade was laid down in a 'Convention between His Britannic Majesty and His Serene Highness the Prince of Orange, for receiving the Dutch troops into His Majesty's Service'.[37] The convention closed on 18 January 1800 and signed by the Hereditary Prince of Orange and Grenville, consisted of thirty-six terms, stipulating among other things that:

- Formation of the Corps. These troops to be formed into four regiments of infantry, one regiment of chasseurs, four companies of artillery and one company of pioneers;
- These troops to take the oath of allegiance to his Majesty and to serve in any part of Europe his Majesty may think proper for the term of seven years and to sign an engagement accordingly and be liable to the same regulations of war as his Majesty's British troops;
- Whenever it shall be judged proper to complete or augment this corps by recruits from the continent, the Hereditary Prince of Orange, or whoever under his Serene Highness's authority may undertake to furnish such recruits, only to enlist men who have been in

---

36 de Jonge, *Geschiedenis van het Nederlandsche Zeewezen*, Vol.V, pp.479-481.
37 Woodfall, *An Impartial Report*, Vol.III, Appendix pp.37-41.

the service of Holland, or who are natural born subjects of the United Provinces, or belong to the Hereditary States of the Prince of Orange;
- The officers commissions to bear date from the day on which this capitulation shall be signed; and the officers belonging to the corps who shall be in England to receive British pay from the 24th October 1799;
- In the event of the lawful government of the United Provinces being restored, or his Serene Highness the Stadtholder, or the Hereditary Prince of Orange being so situated in virtue of any arrangements which may have received the concurrence of his Majesty, as to be able to maintain and employ these troops on the continent of Europe, they are to be held at his Serene Highness's disposal, on his transmitting a requisition to the Commander in Chief for the time being, three months previous to the time at which the troops are to quit his majesty's service;
- The officers formerly in the service of Holland and now receiving an allowance from Great Britain, to be among the first person placed in this corps;
- The Hereditary Prince of Orange, with the approbation of his Serene Highness the Stadtholder, to be considered as proprietor of the whole of the corps;
- The Dutch troops to be allowed to wear blue uniforms and the officers to wear the English sash with the old Dutch sword knot.

The Dutch that had been evacuated from Holland were reinforced by exiles from Germany and a few hundred soldiers originating from Nassau who had deserted from the Batavian Republic. They were thoroughly trained on the Isle of Wight and in August each regiment received two colours: the ancient Dutch colour and a British colour. Plans to send the Dutch Brigade to Portugal were cancelled. In December 1800 the Dutch were sent to Ireland to help maintain order. Returning in 1801 they guarded Jersey, Guernsey and the Isle of Wight against a French invasion. With the Peace of Amiens in 1802, on 12 July the Dutch Brigade was disbanded and with British transports the Dutch soldiers and officers returned to the Batavian Republic where they received amnesty.

Conclusion

After much fighting the Batavian Republic had been saved, although not without loss. The damage done to the countryside was extensive. Dikes, roads, bridges, and windmills had to be repaired, villages rebuilt, and the countryside cleaned up. Great parts of the country had been flooded which had to made dry again. But morale was as high as ever. The Batavian army had shown that they were willing to fight for their country and that they were up to that task. The loss of the Batavian fleet was of course severe, but it never would have been a match for the superior British Royal Navy. Its removal, however, meant that yet another British squadron was now free to operate on the French coast or in the Mediterranean. Moreover, proverbially Dutch to the end, many were glad the fleet was not there any longer, so that it would cost no money! Only Napoleon would regret the loss later; possession of the Batavian fleet would have helped him greatly in his efforts to invade Britain. The Batavian Government realised that they had nothing to say in matters which were of interest to France. However, in internal affairs, their position was again secure.

"The Bond Street Battalion" (imposters impersonating wounded soldiers of the 1799 campaign in Holland), by John Cawse. (Rijksmuseum, RP-P-1911-747)

During this campaign the co-operation between the Batavian and French troops was remarkably good and would stay this way until the very end of Napoleon's reign. In this way, it will surprise no one that the Batavian (and later Dutch) troops behaved well as a French ally in the campaigns that were to come and after the annexation of 1810. So well, indeed, that Napoleon even integrated part of the Dutch army in his own Imperial Guard.

The British showed that they were very good soldiers fighting bravely, even with many of them coming from the militia. On their return home, British Parliament had thanked Vice Admiral Mitchell, Lieutenant General Abercromby, and other officers for their efforts. They believed the honours well deserved: although the expedition on land had failed, the Batavian fleet had been captured and the British troops preserved to fight another day. The main reason for the failure of the expedition was in their opinion the refusal of the inhabitants of the Batavian Republic to support the Anglo-Russian army and to rise against the Batavian government and the French. Public opinion and that of the opposition was completely the opposite. Overlooking the success in capturing the Batavian fleet, they condemned the disappointing results of the expedition, the loss in both men and money and the way the campaign had been conducted.[38] The impact of the retreat was even bigger because the newspapers had time and again told them how well the campaign was going

---

38 Anon., *The Campaign in Holland*, p.70.

"Opening the Sluices or the Secret Expedition" (depicting the unexpected Franco-Batavian resistance) by John Cawse. (Rijksmuseum, RP-P-1981-43)

on, already illustrated before and as described by Lieutenant Gardner of the *Blonde* which participated in bringing the Russians to Holland:

> On our arrival at the Texel the whole were immediately landed, and were soon after in action, and the most of those we had on board put *hors de combat* by the next day. Poor Peter Glebhoff, who had been sharpening his spear at the grinding stone a few days before the landing, and vowing to sacrifice every Frenchman he met with, was one of the first that fell… I was several times on shore and saw the numerous wagons of wounded soldiers from the scene of action which by no means corresponded with the accounts given in our Gazettes… I had two cousins, captains in the 17th regiment of foot – one of them (Knight) was killed just as I was going to see him.[39]

The Russians lost the high opinion that the British and the rest of the world had of them. The problem was not so much the soldiers, but the officers and NCOs, who were not capable of keeping the troops disciplined and to lead them. This was one of the main causes that in the coming years many foreign officers would continue to serve in the Russian army.

Finally in Great Britain, it was realised that much of the loss suffered was due to the tactics the Franco-Batavians used, especially the effective Franco-Batavian skirmishers and riflemen and that a new arm was needed to counter this threat:

> To profit by disaster, and learn lessons from an enemy, may be said to constitute one of the first qualities of a general. In this respect, the royal commander of the combined army was not deficient. Observing the superiority of the French system, and feeling for the loss which it produced in his ranks, he resolved to introduce, when occasion offered, the rifle practice into the British service. This establishment accordingly took place immediately after the conclusion of the present expedition, and selections from different regiments being made by the officers of the second brigade of the Royals, the new Rifle corps was placed under Colonel Coote Manningham of the 41st, as the chief, and Lieutenant Colonel William Stewart of the 67th regiment, as the second in command.[40]

This unit would in due course become the famous 95th Rifles.

---

39 Hamilton & Laughton (eds.), *Recollections of James Anthony Gardner*, pp.207-208.
40 John Watkins, *A Biographical Memoir of his Late Royal Highness Frederick, Duke of York and Albany* (London: Henry Fisher, Son, and Co., 1827), pp.364-365.

Appendix I

Convention closed between Great Britain and Russia on 22 June 1799[1]

Convention between his Britannic Majesty, and the Emperor of all the Russias, signed at St. Petersburgh, 22d (11th) June, 1799.[2]

In the Name of the Most Holy and Indivisible Trinity.
His Majesty the King of Great Britain, and his Majesty the Emperor of all the Russias, in consequence of the friendship and the ties of intimate alliance which exist between them, and of their common and sincere co-operation in the present war against the French, having constantly in their view to use every means in their power most effectually to distress the enemy, have judged that the expulsion of the French from the Seven United Provinces, and the deliverance of the latter from the yoke under which they have so long groaned, were objects worthy of their particular consideration; and wishing, at the same time, to give effect, as far as possible, to a design of that importance, their said Majesties have resolved to conclude with each other a Convention relative to this plan, and to the most proper means of carrying it into the most speedy execution. For this purpose, they have named, as their Plenipotentiaries, to wit, his Majesty the King of Great Britain, Sir Charles Whitworth, his Envoy Extraordinary and Minister Plenipotentiary to the Imperial Court of Russia, Knight of the Order of the Bath; and his Majesty the Emperor of all the Russias, the Count of Kotschoubey, his Vice-Chancellor, actual Privy Counsellor, actual Chamberlain, Knight of the order of St. Alexander Newsky, Commander of that of St. John of Jerusalem, and Great Cross of the Order of St. Vladimir of the Second Class; and the Count of Rostopsin, his actual Privy Counsellor, Member of the College of Foreign Affairs, Director-General of the Posts, Knight of the Order of St. Alexander Newsky and of St. Anne of the First Class, Great Chancellor and Great Cross of that of St. John of Jerusalem; who, after having reciprocally communicated to each other their full powers, have agreed upon the following Articles:

---

[1] Anon., *A Collection of State Papers Relative to the War against France. Now carrying on by Great Britain and the Several other European Powers* (London: S. Gosnell, 1800), pp.x-xv.
[2] 11 June according to the Russian calendar.

Article I. His Majesty the King of Great Britain, thinking that the object above announced cannot be better attained than by the aid of a body of Russian troops, his Imperial Majesty, notwithstanding the efforts which he has already made, and the difficulties of his employing an additional body of forces to act at a distance from his dominions, has nevertheless, in consequence of his constant solicitude in savour of the good cause, consented to furnish seventeen battalions of infantry, two companies of artillery, one company of pioneers, and one squadron of hussars, making in all 17,593 men, to be destined for the said expedition to Holland. But as that number of troops, according to the plan proposed by his Britannic Majesty, is not sufficient, and as it has been judged that 30,000 men would be necessary for that purpose, his said Majesty will, on his side, furnish 13,000 men of English troops, or at least 8,000 men, if that smaller number should be deemed sufficient, and amongst whom there shall be a proportion of cavalry sufficient for the services of such an army.

II. This corps of troops, of 17,593 men, together with the necessary artillery, shall assemble at Revel, in order that they may be from thence conveyed to their destination, either in English or other vessels freighted by his Britannic Majesty.

III. In order to enable his Majesty the Emperor of all the Russias to afford to the common cause this additional and efficacious succour, his Majesty the King of Great Britain engages to furnish the undermentioned subsidies, upon the condition that his Imperial Majesty of all the Russias shall have a right to recall, into his dominions, the above-mentioned corps of troops, if, through any unforeseen event, such subsidies should not be regularly furnished to him.

IV. The amount and the nature of those pecuniary succours have been settled and regulated in the following manner: 1st. In order to enable his Imperial Majesty to assemble and expedite this corps as soon and as well equipped as possible, his Majesty the King of Great Britain engages, as soon as he shall receive advice that the above-mentioned troops have reached the place of their rendezvous, that is to say, at Revel; and that it shall be declared that they are ready to embark (whether the transports be arrived or not), to pay for the first and most urgent expenses, the sum of 88,000 l. sterling, dividing the payments into two parts, to wit, that 44,000 l. sterling be paid immediately after it shall have been declared, either by the Commander in Chief of that corps to the English Commissary, or by the Ministry of his Imperial Majesty to the Minister of his Britannic Majesty resident at St. Petersburgh, that the said corps is ready; and that the second payment, completing the sum total of 88,000 l. sterling, shall take place three months afterwards and at the commencement of the fourth. Secondly, his Majesty the King of Great Britain engages, in like manner, to furnish to his Majesty the Emperor of all the Russias, a subsidy of 44,000 l. sterling per month, to be computed from the day on which the above-mentioned corps of troops shall be ready. This subsidy shall be paid at the commencement of each month, and destined for the appointments and the entertainment of the troops. It shall be continued until they shall return into Russian ports, in English or other vessels, freighted by his Britannic majesty.

V. If this corps of Russian troops should meet with difficulties in procuring, during the expedition to which it is destined, or in case of its wintering, as shall be hereafter mentioned, in

England, or during the voyages it shall have to make, its necessary subsistence, by means of the measures which the Russian Commanders or Commissaries may take for that purpose, his Britannic Majesty, upon the requisition of the Minister of his Majesty the Emperor of all the Russias, residing at his Court, shall furnish whatever may be necessary to the Russian troops; and an exact account shall be kept of all the provisions and other articles so delivered, in order that their value may be afterwards deducted from the subsidy, such provisions and other articles being valued at the price paid for them by his Majesty for his own troops.

VI. As the transport of the horses necessary for the Officers, the artillery, and the baggage, would require a great many vessels, and as that arrangement would lead to many other inconveniences, and more particularly to that of delay, prejudicial to the above-mentioned expedition, his Britannic Majesty engages to furnish, at his own expense, the necessary number of horses, according to the statement which shall be delivered, and to have them conveyed to the place where the Russian troops are to act: his said Majesty will in like manner, maintain them at his own expense during the whole time these troops shall be employed, and until they shall be re-embarked, in order to return to the ports of Russia. His Britannic Majesty will then dispose of them in such a manner as he shall judge proper.

VII. In case that the Russian troops, after having terminated in Holland the projected expedition, or in consequence of its being deferred through any unforeseen circumstances, should not be able to return into the ports of his Imperial Majesty during the favourable season, his Majesty the King of Great Britain engages to receive them into his own dominions, to provide them there with good quarters, and all other advantages, until the troops shall be able to return on the opening of the navigation, or shall be employed upon some other destination, which shall be previously settled between their royal and imperial majesties.

VIII. As the principal object of the employment of this corps of or troops is a sudden, attack to be made on Holland, by means of which his Britannic Majesty hopes to produce there a favourable change; as, besides, no fixed term for the continuance of the subsidies is stipulated, whilst on the other hand the said troops, after their return to Russia, must be reconducted to their ordinary quarters, mostly at a great distance; and as the marches which they will have to make will require considerable expences, his Majesty the King of Great Britain hereby engages to make good this charge by a payment of subsidies for two months, to be computed from the day of the arrival of those troops in Russian ports. In like manner his Majesty the Emperor of all the Russias, without fixing any term, reserves to himself the right of causing the said corps of troops to return into his dominions, in the spring of the next year, 1800; or if any hostile aggression upon Russia, or any other important event, should render it necessary: in these two cases, the above-mentioned engagement of his Britannic Majesty, concerning the payment of two months subsidy, shall equally take place.

IX. As it is understood that the expedition to Holland, which has given rise to the present convention, is to be effected in common by Russian and English troops, each party shall follow, relative to the employment and to the command of the troops, literally, the Treaty of Defensive Alliance concluded between the two High Contracting Parties, the 7th (18th) of February in the year 1795. In like manner, if any difficulties should arise either between the

Commanders of the respective forces, or otherwise, which may regard the above-mentioned troops of his Majesty the Emperor of all the Russias, the solution of such difficulties shall be looked for in the stipulations of the said Treaty of the year 1795, or otherwise in that concluded with the Court of Vienna, the 3d (14th) of July 1792.

X. The present Convention shall be ratified by his Majesty the King of Great-Britain, and by his Majesty the Emperor of all the Russias; and the ratifications shall be exchanged here in the space of two months, to be computed from the day of its signature, or sooner, if it can be done.

In witness whereof, we, the undersigned, furnished with full powers by his Majesty the King of Great Britain, and by his Majesty the Emperor of all the Russias, have, in their names, signed the present Convention, and have affixed thereto the seal of our arms.
   Done at St. Petersburgh, 22d (11th) of June 1799.
   (L.S.) Le Comte de Kotschoubey.
   (L. S.) Le Comte de Rostopsin.
   (L.S.) Charles Whitworth.

Separate Articles

I. Although it be stated in Article II. of the Convention concluded this day, that the corps of Russian troops, forming 17,593 men, destined for the expedition to Holland, shall be conveyed to its destination in English or other vessels freighted by his Majesty the King of Great Britain; nevertheless, in order so much the more to facilitate this important enterprise, his Majesty the Emperor of all the Russias consents to furnish six ships, five frigates, and two transport vessels, which, being *armée en flutes*, will receive on board as many troops as they shall be able to contain, whilst the remainder of the said corps shall be embarked on board of English or other transport vessels, freighted by his Britannic Majesty.

II. His Majesty the Emperor of all the Russias will lend these ships and frigates upon the following conditions: 1, There shall be paid by England, upon their quitting the port of Cronstadt, in order to go to the place of rendezvous, which is Revel, the sum of 58,917 l. 10s. sterling, as a subsidy for the expences of equipment,. &c. for three months, to be computed from the day, as it is above stated, of their departure from Cronstadt. 2dly, After the expiration of these three months, his Britannic Majesty shall continue the same subsidies, that is to say, of 19,642 l. 10s. sterling a month, which shall be paid at the commencement of each month. 3dly, Independently of this pecuniary succour, his Britannic Majesty shall provide for the subsistence of the crews; and the Officers and sailors shall be treated on the same footing as are the English Officers and sailors in time of war, and as are the Russian Officers and sailors, who are at present in the squadron of his Imperial Majesty, which is united to the English squadron. 4thly, All these stipulations shall have full and entire effect until the return of the above-mentioned ships and frigates into Russian ports.

III. If it should happen, contrary to all expectation, that those six ships, five frigates, and two transport vessels, should not be able, through some unforeseen event, to return to Russia before the close of the present campaign, his Britannic Majesty engages to admit them into the ports of England, where they shall receive every possible assistance, both for necessary repairs, and for the accommodation of the crews and Officers.

IV. As the six ships, five frigates, and two transports, above-mentioned, having been originally intended for another destination, were furnished with provisions for three months, his Britannic Majesty, instead of furnishing them in kind, as it is stated in the second article, engages to pay, according to an estimate which shall be made, the value of these provisions. With regard to the Officers, his Majesty the King of Great Britain will adopt the same principle as has been followed until the present time, respecting the Officers of the Russian squadron which is joined to the naval forces of England. That shall serve as a rule for indemnifying them for the preparations which they may have made for the campaign, such as it had been originally intended to take place.

These separate articles shall be considered as forming part of the Convention above-mentioned, as being inserted therein word for word; and it shall be ratified, and the ratification exchanged in the same manner.

In witness whereof, we, the undersigned, furnished with powers of his Majesty the King of Great Britain, and of his Majesty the Emperor of all the Russias, have, in their name, signed the present separate articles, and have affixed thereto the seal of our arms.
  Done at St. Petersburgh, 22d (11th) of June 1799.
  (L.S.) Le Comte de Kotschoubey.
  (L. S.) Le Comte de Rostopsin.
  (L.S.) Charles Whitworth.

Appendix II

The Escort Squadron under the Command of Vice Admiral Andrew Mitchell

Name	Class	Commander
Isis (Flagship)	4th Rate 50	Captain Oughton
Belliqueux[1]	3rd Rate 64	Captain Bulteel
Monmouth	3rd Rate 64	Captain Hart
Overyssel	3rd Rate 64	Captain Bazely
Romney	4th Rate 50	Captain Lawford
Melpomene	5th Rate 38	Captain Hamilton
Proselyte	5th Rate 32	Captain Fowke
Shannon	5th Rate 32	Captain Pater
Circe	6th Rate 28	Captain Winthrop
Babet	6th Rate 20	Captain Mainwaring
Arrow[2]	Sloop 28	Commander Portlock
Zebra	Sloop 18	Commander Sparke
Cynthia	Sloop 18	Commander Malbon
Dart	Sloop 18	Commander Campbell
Hornet	Sloop 16	Commander Nash
Piercer	Gun-vessel 16	Lieutenant Menzies
Fury	Bomb 16	Commander Curry
Otter	Brig-sloop 14	Commander McKinley
Rosario	Brig-sloop 14	Commander Carthew
Speedwell	Brig-sloop 14	Lieutenant Reddy
Pelter	Gun-vessel 14	Lieutenant Walsh
Swinger	Gun-vessel 14	Lieutenant Lucas
Teaser	Gun-vessel 14	Lieutenant Robins
Tigress	Gun-brig 12	Lieutenant Atkins
Wolverine	Gun-brig 12	Commander Bolton

1. On his way to Holland, Mitchell encountered the *Glatton* 4th Rate 56 and exchanged it for the *Belliqueux* because this ship had a smaller draft.
2. Built for 20 guns, this ship was modified to carry 28 32pdr carronades.

Adder	Gun-vessel 12	Lieutenant Joyce
Attack	Gun-vessel 12	Lieutenant James
Bouncer	Gun-vessel 12	Lieutenant Bamber
Contest	Gun-vessel 12	Lieutenant Short
Cracker	Gun-vessel 12	Lieutenant Atkinson
Defender	Gun-vessel 12	Lieutenant Leavy
Eling	Gun-vessel 12	Lieutenant Peake
Force	Gun-vessel 12	Lieutenant Tokely
Furnace	Gun-vessel 12	Lieutenant Suckling
Gallant	Gun-vessel 12	Lieutenant Lyall
Griper	Gun-vessel 12	Lieutenant Simpson
Hasty	Gun-vessel 12	Lieutenant Carlton
Haughty	Gun-vessel 12	Lieutenant Davies
Plumper	Gun-vessel 12	Lieutenant Barreté
Trial	Cutter 12	Lieutenant Dowsing
Discovery	Bomb 10	Commander Dick
Hecla	Bomb 10	Commander Bover
Tartarus	Bomb 8	Commander Hand

Appendix III

Ships Transporting the Russian Army from the Baltic

The Russian squadron commanded by Rear Admiral Pavel Chichagov, transporting the 2nd Russian Division from Reval[1]

Name	Class	Captain	Transporting:	Men
Alexsandr Nevskii	3rd Rate 74	Scott	1/Sedmoratzki Musketeers	949
Iona	3rd Rate 66	Piatzov	2/Sedmoratzki Musketeers, 40 life hussars	978
Sviatoi Ianuarii	3rd Rate 66	Ignatief (Sr)	1/Arbénev Musketeers	948
Mikhail	3rd Rate 66	Pasinkov	2/Arbénev Musketeers	939
Panteleimon[2]	3rd Rate 66	Nolkovskoi	Comb. Gren. Bat. 'Ogarev'	739
Emgeiten	3rd Rate 66	Ignatief (Jr)	Comb. Gren. Bat. 'Strick'	739
Venus	5th Rate 44	Gasper	Comb. Gren. Bat. 'Ossipov' (part)	539
Arkhangel Rafail	5th Rate 44	Boyle	1st *Jégerski* of Suthoff (1 bat)	406
Revel[3]	38/46	Malagen	Comb. Gren. Bat. 'Timofeyev' (part)	739
Sviatoi Konstantin	Rowing frigate 34	Kazenkov	Comb. Gren. Bat. 'Timofeyev' (part)	

1. Composed of various sources, unfortunately there are still some discrepancies in this list. The major point that is unclear is that of the Combined Grenadier Battalions 'Ogarev' and 'Timofeyev' two different battalions are listed. The indicated amount of men is taken from the official lists; other contemporary sources sometimes mention different numbers.
2. Had to return to port after the departure in Reval.
3. Departed Reval with troops for Holland but was forced to return because of a leak.

Name	Class	Captain	Transporting:	Men
Sviatoi Nikolai	Rowing frigate 34	Rose	Artillery company with guns, stores, etc.	240
Neptune	Store-ship	Dunn	Comb. Gren. Bat. 'Ossipov' (part)	200
Minerva	Store-ship	Ogilvie	Artillery with stores, etc.	80
Gleb	3rd Rate 74	Demidov	Emmé Grenadiers	750

The British transport ships commanded by Captain Ferris, transporting the 1st and 3rd Russian Division from Reval

Name	Class	Captain	Transporting:	Men
Inflexible	3rd Rate 64	Ferris	Comb. Gren. Bat. 'Ericcson', 20 hussars	739
Experiment	5th Rate 44	Saville	1st *Jégerski* of Suthoff (1 bat)	455
Coromandel	4th Rate 56	Mortimer	Benkendorf Grenadiers (part)	800
Dictator	3rd Rate 64	Hardy	Benkendorf Grenadiers (part), 58 hussars	728
Expedition	5th Rate 44	Livingston	Benkendorf Grenadiers (part)	403
Diadem	3rd Rate 64	Dawson	Fersen Musketeers (part)	770
Brakel	4th Rate 54	Walker	Fersen Musketeers (part)	753
Hebe	5th Rate 38	Birchall	Fersen Musketeers (part)	360
Wassenaar	3rd Rate 64	Craven	Zherebtsov Grenadiers (part)	650
Romulus	5th Rate 36	Culverhouse	Zherebtsov Grenadiers (part)	350
Tromp	4th Rate 60	Worsley	Zherebtsov Grenadiers (part)	650
Alkmaar	4th Rate 54	Burdon	Comb. Gren. Bat. 'Timofeyev'	650
Ulysses	5th Rate 44	Pressland	Comb. Gren. Bat. 'Ogarev'	650
Blonde	5th Rate 32	Dobree	Com. Gren. Bat. 'Mitiouchin', Emmé's Grenadiers (part), 380 convalescents of the 1st Division.	730
Niger	5th Rate 32	Larmour	idem (350)	
Espion	5th Rate 36	Rose	idem (350)	
Calcutta	24 guns	Anderson	idem (ex-E. Indiaman *Warley*, 300)	
Weymouth	26 guns	Ryder	(ex-E. Indiaman *Earl Mansfield*, 300)	
Walter Boyd	Store ship	Meers	idem (650)	
Minerva	Store ship	Pearson	idem (650)	
Levant	Transport ship		(471 men, artillery)	

Name	Class	Captain	Transporting:	Men
Contents Increan	Transport ship		(60 men, 36 horses)	
Dolphin	Transport ship		(50 men, 36 horses)	
Amphion	Transport ship		(450)	
St. Nicholas	Transport ship		(baggage)	
Christiana Juliana	Transport ship		(330)	
Five Sisters	Transport ship		(12 men, artillery)	
Charles	Transport ship		(258 men)	
Frau Helena	Transport ship		(40 men, 36 horses)	
Bargo	Transport ship		(300 men)	

Captain Popham sailed with the 1st Division of the British transport fleet to Reval on 12 July, arriving on 27 and 28 July. The 2nd Division of British transports arrived in Reval on 10 and 11 August. The Russian squadron, under Rear Admiral Chichagov, sailed from Reval 29 July and arrived at Elsinore 20 August and sailed again for Den Helder 28 August. The squadron under Captain Ferris sailed from Reval 17 August, and arrived at Elsinore on 13 September.

Appendix IV

British Invasion Force under the Command of Abercromby, 27 August 1799

Commander in chief: Lieutenant General Sir Ralph Abercromby
Deputy Adjutant-General: Lieutenant Colonel John Hope
Assistant Adjutant-General: Lieutenant Colonel Alexander Hope
Deputy Quartermaster-General: Lieutenant Colonel Anstruther
Commander of the artillery: Lieutenant Colonel Whitworth
Commander of the engineers: Lieutenant Colonel Hay

Southern Division (Lieutenant General Pulteney)
3rd Brigade (Major General Coote) (3,520)
2nd (Queen's) Foot	632	Lieutenant Colonel Jones
27th Foot	904	Lieutenant Colonel Graham
29th Foot	664	Lieutenant Colonel Enys
69th Foot	660	Lieutenant Colonel Atkinson
85th Foot	660	Lieutenant Colonel Ross
Flank companies (detached)		Major Ramsay

5th Brigade / Reserve (Colonel MacDonald) (1,406)
23rd Royal Welsh Fusiliers	934	Lieutenant Colonel R.W. Talbot
55th Foot	472	Major Lumsden

Northern Division (Lieutenant General Abercromby)
1st (Guards) Brigade (Major General d'Oyly) (1,996)
Grenadier Battalion Guards	992	Colonel Wynyard
3/1st Foot Guards	1,004	Colonel A. Maitland

2nd (Guards) Brigade (Major General Burrard) (1,984)
1/Coldstream Guards	1,005	Colonel Finch
1/3rd Foot Guards	979	Colonel Barnett

4th Brigade (Major General Moore) (3,086)

2/1st (Royal) Foot	717	Lieutenant Colonel Lumsdaine
25th Foot	534	Lieutenant Colonel Wright
49th Foot	501	Lieutenant Colonel Brock
79th Highlanders	506	Colonel A. Cameron
92nd Highlanders	828	Col. Marquis of Huntly

After the initial landings, these troops would be reinforced with the cavalry and artillery:

18th Light Dragoons	193	(2 squadrons, Lieutenant Colonel Stewart)
Artillery	456	(10 guns)
Driver Corps	176	(200 horses)
Pioneers	100	

Appendix V

French troops stationed in the Batavian Republic (4 July 1799)[1]

Général en chef: *Général de Division* Brune
Chef de l'Etat-Major: *Général de Brigade* Dardenne
Commandant en chef l'artillerie: *Général de Brigade* Seroux
Commandant en chef le génie: *Chef de Brigade* Saint-Julien

Unit	Strength	Commander
1er Division (*Général de Brigade* Gouvion, 3,756 men, HQ Utrecht)		
Général de Brigade Barbou		
42e Demi-Brigade		*Chef de Brigade* Aubrée
2e Bataillon	835	
3e Bataillon (incl. depot)	1,129	
3/72e Demi-Brigade (incl. depot)	1,385	*Chef de Brigade* Mercier
5e Chasseurs à Cheval (depot)	407	
2e Division (*Général de Division* Reubell, 5,336 men, HQ The Hague)		
Général de Brigade Prévost		
1/42e Demi-Brigade	752	
54e Demi-Brigade		*Chef de Brigade* Varé
1er Bataillon	786	*Chef de Bataillon* Gaillard
2e Bataillon	743	

1 The effective strength of the French troops in the Batavian Republic is difficult to ascertain because of the ever changing situation with French units departing and other troops and conscripts added again. A number of Batavian historians did not hesitate to state that the required 25,000 French were not present by far, with only 8,000 French able to take the field in August 1799 as the lowest number given (Krayenhoff, Knoop). Koolemans Beijnen was regarded as giving the most reliable number at 17,890. However, Koolemans Beijnen made a miscalculation, putting the most reliable number of French troops present on 4 July 1799 at 18,413 men, including the depots. This number differs not much from the number stated by the French chief of staff, *Général de Brigade* Dardenne on 29 July: 18,702 men. G.J.W. Koolemans Beijnen, 'Krijgsgeschiedkundige studie over de verdediging der Bataafsche Republiek in 1799' in *Militaire Spectator* (1891), pp.185-200.

3e Bataillon (incl. depot)	1,144	
3/60e Demi-Brigade (incl. depot)	1,113	
11e Chasseurs à Cheval (depot)	406	
16e Chasseurs à Cheval	119	
1/8e Artillerie Légère	83	
12/7e Artillerie à Pied	54	
Escouades d'artillerie à pied	136	

3e Division (*Général de Division* Desjardin, 9,321 men, HQ Bergen op Zoom)
Généraux de Brigade Osten and Rivaud

15e Demi-Brigade		*Chef de Brigade* Faure
1er Bataillon	938	
2e Bataillon	857	
3e Bataillon (incl. depot)	1,088	
48e Demi-Brigade		*Chef de Brigade* Arnaud
1er Bataillon	833	
2e Bataillon	572	
3e Bataillon (incl. depot)	1,119	
49e Demi-Brigade		*Chef de Brigade* Paradis
1er Bataillon	263	
2e Bataillon	978	
3e Bataillon (incl. depot)	827	
16e Chasseurs à Cheval	797	*Chef d'Escadron* Koenig
4/4e Artillerie Légère (half company)	38	*Capitaine* Couturier
7 & 15/6e Artillerie à Pied	186	
16/6e Artillerie à Pied	77	
5e/7e Artillerie à Pied	92	
Escouades d'artillerie à pied	656[2]	

---

[2] It is unknown which escouades were attached to which division and what their formation was. The following foot artillery units were present: 6e Artillerie à Pied:1er cie; 5e escouade, 2e cie; 1er escouade, 5e cie; complete (i.e. 5 escouades), 7e cie; 1er, 2e, 3e escouades, 15e cie; 1er, 2e, 3e, 5e escouade, 16e cie; 1er, 2e, 3e, 4e escouades: 7e Artillerie à Pied: 4e cie, 5e cie and 6e cie complete, 12e cie; 1er, 3e, 4e and half of the 5e escouades.

Appendix VI

The Batavian Fleet at the Roads of Texel, 27 August 1799

Name	Class	Commander
Washington (flagship)	3rd Rate 74	*Capitein* van Capellen
Admiraal de Ruijter	3rd Rate 68	*Capitein* Huys
Cerberus	3rd Rate 68	*Capitein* de Jong van Rodenburgh
Gelderland	3rd Rate 68	*Capitein-Lieutenant* Waldeck
Leyden	3rd Rate 68	*Capitein* van Braam
Utrecht	3rd Rate 68	*Capitein* Kolff
Batavier	4th Rate 56	*Capitein* van Senden
Beschermer	4th Rate 54	*Capitein* Eilbracht
Mars	5th Rate 44	*Capitein* Bock
Amphitrite	5th Rate 40	*Capitein* Schutter
Embuscade	5th Rate 32	*Capitein* Rivery
Galathée	Sloop 16	*Eerste Lieutenant ter Zee* Droop

The crews totalled 4,380 men.

Appendix VII

Composition of the 1e Bataafsche Divisie (Daendels) before the British landing

Unit	Strength	Commander	Dislocation
1e Bataafsche Divisie (*Lieutenant-Generaal* Daendels)			HQ Schagerbrug
1e Brigade (*Generaal-Major* van Guèricke)			HQ Den Helder
2e Bataljon Jagers	674	*Lt-Colonel* Chassé	Keeten & Zijpe
5e Halve Brigade		*Colonel* Crass	Wieringerwaard
1e Bataljon	618	*Lt-Colonel* Lycklama à Nijeholt	
2e Bataljon	600	*Lt-Colonel* Herbig	
3e Bataljon	583	*Lt-Colonel* van Sandick	
7e Halve Brigade		*Colonel* Gilquin	Den Helder
1e Bataljon	617	*Lt-Colonel* Verhorst	
2e Bataljon	534	*Lt-Colonel* Lambrechts	
3e Bataljon	664	*Lt-Colonel* Zeebis	
1e Regiment Zware Cavalerie (4 sq)	411	*Colonel* du Ry	Den Helder & Schagen
2e Compagnie Rijdende Artillerie (4x 6pdr cannon, 2x 24pdr how)	149	*Capitein* d'Anguerand	't Zand
Compagnie Artillerie te Voet (6x 6pdr cannon)			't Zand

Unit	Strength	Commander	Dislocation
2e Brigade (*Generaal-Major* van Zuylen van Nyevelt)			HQ Haarlem
1e Bataljon Jagers	741	*Lt-Colonel* Luck	Calandsoog
1e Halve Brigade		*Colonel* Rietvelt	
1e Bataljon	579	*Lt-Colonel* Nicolson	Haarlem
2e Bataljon	590	*Lt-Colonel* Step	Haarlem
3e Bataljon	865	*Lt-Colonel* van Till	Alkmaar
1/3e Halve Brigade	604	*Lt-Colonel* Abbema	Petten, Kamp, Groet
1/4e Halve Brigade	740	*Lt-Colonel* Pitcairn	Koedijk, Warmenhuizen
3/6e Halve Brigade	686	*Lt-Colonel* Carteret	Bergen
2e Regiment Zware Cavalerie (2½ sq)	169	*Colonel* Mascheck	Schagerbrug
Regiment Dragonders (4 squadrons)	488	*Colonel* Broux	Schagerbrug
Compagnie Artillerie te Voet (6x 6pdr cannon)			Burgerbrug

Appendix VIII

Composition of the Anglo-Russian North Sea fleet, commanded by Admiral Adam Duncan

Name	Class	Commander
British Squadron		
Kent (flagship)	3rd Rate 74	Captain Hope
Ganges	3rd Rate 74	Captain M'Douall
America	3rd Rate 64	Captain Smith
Ardent	3rd Rate 64	Captain Bertie
Veteran	3rd Rate 64	Captain Dickson
Glatton	4th Rate 54	Captain Cobb
Latona	5th Rate 38	Captain Sotheron
Juno	5th Rate 32	Captain G. Dundas
Russian Squadron (Rear-Admiral Makarov)		
Elisaveta	3rd Rate 74	Rear-Admiral Makarov
Vsevolod	3rd Rate 74	Captain Grevnitz
Mstislav	3rd Rate 74	Captain Moller
Boleslav	3rd Rate 66	
Evropa	3rd Rate 66	
Retvizan	3rd Rate 64	Captain Greig
Aleksei	3rd Rate 74	
Sviatoi Pyotr	3rd Rate 74	
Schastlivyi	5th Rate 44	Captain Roundling
Riga	5th Rate 38	Captain Ogilvie?
Dispatch	Cutter (18)	Captain Kosliotsov

Appendix IX

Order of Battle of the Anglo-Russian Fleet engaging the Dutch Fleet, 30 August 1799

Name	Class	Commander	
Isis	4th Rate 50	Captain Oughton	(Flagship)
Mstislav	3rd Rate 74	Captain Moller	Russian
Retvizan	3rd Rate 64	Captain Greig	Russian
America	3rd Rate 64	Captain Smith	
Ardent	3rd Rate 64	Captain Bertie	
Belliqueux	3rd Rate 64	Captain Bulteel	
Monmouth	3rd Rate 64	Captain Hart	
Overyssel	3rd Rate 64	Captain Bazely	
Veteran	3rd Rate 64	Captain Dickson	
Glatton	4th Rate 54	Captain Cobb	
Romney	4th Rate 50	Captain Lawford	
Latona	5th Rate 38	Captain Sotheron	
Melpomene	5th Rate 38	Captain Hamilton	
Lutine	5th Rate 32	Captain Skynner	
Juno	5th Rate 32	Captain G. Dundas	
Shannon	5th Rate 32	Captain Pater	
Babet	6th Rate 20	Captain Mainwaring	
Tisiphoné	Sloop 20	Commander Grant	
Arrow	Sloop 20	Commander Portlock	
Victor	Sloop 18	Captain Rennie	
Dart	Sloop 18	Captain Ragget	
Pylades	Sloop 16	Commander Mackenzie	

Appendix X

Composition of the Franco-Batavian Army in Holland on 9 September 1799

Right Wing – 1e Bataafsche Divisie (*Lieutenant-Generaal* Daendels) HQ St. Pancras
Adjudant Generaal: *Lieutenant-Colonel* van Uslar
Capitein Adjoint: *Capitein* Grabner
                    Capitein Hespe
                    Capitein Villers
Aide-de-Camp: *Lieutenant-Colonel* Rouget (French, attached)
                    Capitein van Römer

Unit	Commander	Location
Voorhoede (*Colonel* Crass)		
1e Bataljon Jagers	*Majoor* Roussel	Oud-Karspel
2e Bataljon Jagers	*Lt-Colonel* Chassé	Noordscherwoude
1e Brigade (*Colonel* Rietvelt)		
1/1e Halve Brigade	*Lt-Colonel* Nicolson	Zuidscherwoude
2/1e Halve Brigade	*Lt-Colonel* Step	Broek
3/1e Halve Brigade	*Lt-Colonel* van Till	Broek
Bataljon Grenadiers		Broek
2e Compagnie Rijdende Artillerie	*Capitein* d'Anguerand	St. Pancras
Regiment Dragonders (4 squadrons)	*Colonel* Broux	St. Pancras
Pioneers with bridges (1 company)		St. Pancras
2e Brigade (*Generaal-Major* van Zuylen van Nijevelt)		
1/3e Halve Brigade	*Lt-Colonel* Abbema	Ouddorp
1/4e Halve Brigade	*Lt-Colonel* C. Pitcairn	Ouddorp
3/4e Halve Brigade	*Lt-Colonel* Sels	Ouddorp

3/5e Halve Brigade	*Lt-Colonel* van Sandick	St. Pancras
2e Regiment Zware Cavalerie
  (2½ squadrons)	*Colonel* Mascheck	St. Pancras

Centre – 2e Bataafsche Divisie (*Lieutenant-Generaal* Dumonceau) HQ Alkmaar

Adjudant Generaal:	*Colonel* l'Olivier	
	Lieutenant-Colonel Vichery	
Capitein Adjoint:	*Lieutenant* Nahuys	
	Lieutenant Beekman	
Aide-de-Camp:	*Ritmeester* Cornets de Groot	
	Capitein Muysken	

Unit	Commander	Location
Voorhoede (*Colonel* Gilquin)		
4e Bataljon Jagers	*Lt-Colonel* Trip	Schoorldam
Bataljon Grenadiers		
(6 companies)	*Major* Bruce	Schoorldam
Regiment Huzaren		
(1 squadron, 114)		Schoorldam
1e Compagnie Rijdende		
Artillerie (2x 6pdr)	*Lieutenant* Straube	Schoorldam
1e Brigade (*Generaal-Major* Bonhomme)		
1/6e Halve Brigade	*Lt-Colonel* Jaussaud de Vedelen	Koedijk
3/6e Halve Brigade	*Lt-Colonel* Carteret	Koedijk
1/7e Halve Brigade	*Lt-Colonel* Verhorst	Koedijk
2/7e Halve Brigade	*Lt-Colonel* Lambrechts	Koedijk
3/7e Halve Brigade	*Lt-Colonel* Zeebis	Koedijk
Regiment Huzaren		
(3 squadrons, 372)	*Colonel* de Quaita	Koedijk
1e Compagnie Rijdende		
Artillerie (2x 6pdr)	*Capitein* Cordes	Koedijk
2e Brigade (*Colonel* Bruce)		
1/2e Halve Brigade	*Lt-Colonel* Montanus	
2/2e Halve Brigade	*Lt-Colonel* van Hasselt	Koedijk
3/2e Halve Brigade	*Lt-Colonel* J. Pitcairn	Koedijk
2/6e Halve Brigade	*Lt-Colonel* Anthing	Koedijk
1e Regiment Zware		
Cavalerie (3½ sq)	*Colonel* du Ry	Koedijk
Achterhoede (*Major* Tulleken)		
3e Bataljon Jagers	*Major* Tulleken	Alkmaar

Combined grenadiers
  (3 companies 2e HB)   *Capitein* MacPherson   Alkmaar
1e Regiment Zware
  Cavalerie (1 company)   Alkmaar
1e Compagnie Rijdende
  Artillerie (2x 6pdr)   Alkmaar

Also present were three foot artillery companies (18x 6pdr guns), under the command of *Lieutenant-Colonel* Martuschewitz.

Left Wing – French Division (*Général de Division* Vandamme)

Unit	Strength	
Infantry		
42e Demi-Brigade (3 battalions)	2,350	*Chef de Brigade* Aubrée
49e Demi-Brigade (2 battalions)	1,357	*Chef de Brigade* Paradis
54e Demi-Brigade (3 battalions)	2,376	*Chef de Brigade* Varé
3/60e Demi-Brigade (1 battalion)	621	
3/72e Demi-Brigade		
(1 grenadier company)	81	*Capitaine* Neller
Cavalry		
5e Chasseurs à Cheval		
(1 squadron)	89	*Lieutenant* Denain
16e Chasseurs à Cheval		
(1 squadron)	170	*Capitaine* Raulet
Artillery (*Général de Brigade* St. Martin)		
4/4e Artillerie Légère	36	*Capitaine* Couturier
1/8e Artillerie Légère	67	*Capitaine* Leroux
5/6e Artillerie à Pied (2x 4pdr)	33	
12/7e Artillerie à Pied	46	
Total:	7,226	

Appendix XI

Composition of the Anglo-Russian army on 18 September 1799

Commander in Chief of the combined Anglo-Russian army in Holland: York, Frederick August, Duke of York and Albany

British Army:[1]
Deputy Quartermaster-General: Lieutenant Colonel Anstruther
Commander of the artillery: Major General Farrington

Unit	Commander
Advance Guard[2] (Major-General Knox) (1,730)	
Battalion Grenadiers	Lieutenant Colonel Baylis
Battalion Light Infantry	Lieutenant Colonel Shairpe
1st Division (Lieutenant General Abercromby)	
1st Brigade (Major General d'Oyly)	
Grenadier Battalion Guards	Colonel Wynyard
3/1st Foot Guards	Colonel A. Maitland
2nd Brigade (Major General Burrard)	
1/Coldstream Guards	Colonel Finch
1/3rd Foot Guards	Colonel Barnett
3rd Brigade (Major General Coote)	
2nd (Queen's) Foot	Lieutenant Colonel Jones
27th Foot	Captain Warren (?)
29th Regiment of Foot	Lieutenant Colonel Enys
85th Regiment of Foot	Lieutenant Colonel Ross
4th Brigade (Major General Moore)	
2/1st (Royal) Foot	Lieutenant Colonel Lumsdaine

1 Exact strengths, except for the units just arrived from Great Britain and the documented strength of the Russian units, are unknown.
2 Composed of the flank companies of six infantry regiments.

25th Foot   Lieutenant Colonel Wright
49th Foot   Lieutenant Colonel Brock
79th Highlanders   Colonel A. Cameron
92nd Highlanders   Col. Marquis of Huntly

2nd Division (Lieutenant General Pulteney)
5th Brigade (Major General Don)
1/17th Foot   Lieutenant Colonel Stovin
2/17th Foot   Lieutenant Colonel Tinling
1/40th Foot   Colonel Spencer
2/40th Foot   Lieutenant Colonel Browne
6th Brigade (Major General the Earl of Cavan)
1/20th Foot   Major Power
2/20th Foot   Lieutenant Colonel Clephane
63rd Foot   Lieutenant Colonel Brereton
Reserve (Colonel MacDonald)
23rd Royal Welsh Fusiliers   Lieutenant Colonel R.W. Talbot
55th Regiment of Foot   Major Lumsden

3rd Division (Lieutenant General Dundas)
7th Brigade (Major General the Earl of Chatham) (2,469)
1/4th King's Regiment of Foot   594   Lieutenant Colonel Hodgson
2/4th King's Regiment of Foot   541   Lieutenant Colonel Cholmondeley
3/4th King's Regiment of Foot   540   Lieutenant Colonel Dickson
31st Regiment of Foot   794
8th Brigade (Major General Prince William) (1,466)
1/5th Foot   386   Lieutenant Colonel Stephenson
2/5th Foot   466   Lieutenant Colonel Talbot
2/35th Foot   607   Lieutenant Colonel Oswald
2/35th Foot   614   Major MacAlister
9th Brigade (Major General Manners) (1,923)
1/9th Foot   624   Lieutenant Colonel de Berniere
2/9th Foot   625   Lieutenant Colonel Crewe
56th Foot   676

Artillery
3rd & 4th Marching Battalions   474   8 companies
Battalion guns   348
Horse artillerymen   342

Cavalry Brigade (Colonel Paget) (1,200)
7th Light Dragoons (4 squadrons)   540 Colonel Paget
11th Light Dragoons (4 squadrons) 540 Lieutenant Colonel Childers
18th Light Dragoons (2 squadrons) 160 Lieutenant Colonel Stewart
A Troop, Royal Horse Artillery   185 Major Judgson

Garrison at Den Helder:
69th Foot
Marines (including 180 Russians)

Russian Army[3]
Lieutenant General Hermann von Fersen, Commander in Chief of the Russian troops
Major General Kaptsevich, commander of the artillery

Unit	Battalions	Strength
1st Division (Major General Essen I)		
Brigade Arbénev (Major General Arbénev)		
1st *Jégerski* of Suthoff	1	368
Arbénev Musketeers	2	1,546
Comb. Grenadier Battalion 'Strick'	1	627
Regimental artillery		142
Field artillery (Battalion Durnov, 8 guns)	1 company	222
Brigade Sedmoratzki (Major General Sedmoratzki)		
Sedmoratzki Musketeers	2	1,576
Comb. Grenadier Battalion 'Osipov'	1	643
Comb. Grenadier Battalion 'Timofeyev'	1	633
Regimental artillery		123
Cavalry		
Life Guard Hussars of Colonel Gladkov	1 squadron	45
Life Guard Don Cossacks	1 squadron	25
Company Pioneers of Captain Dreyer	detachment	54
2nd Division (Lieutenant General Zherebtsov)		
Brigade Suthoff (Major General Suthoff)		
1st *Jégerski* of Suthoff	1	376
Benkendorf Grenadiers	2	1,516
Fersen Musketeers	2	1,542
Regimental artillery		144
Field artillery (Battalion Durnov, 8 guns)	1 company	101
Brigade Emmé (Major General Emmé)		
Zherebtsov Grenadiers	2	1,551
Comb. Grenadier Bat. 'Ericsson'	1	622
Regimental artillery		177
Field artillery (Battalion Kaptsevich, 8 guns)	1 company	305

3   Miliutin, *Geschichte des Krieges*, Vol.V, pp.275-276. Strengths given are the effective strengths including non-combatants. Each infantry battalion was accompanied by regimental artillery; usually one gun for each *jégerski* battalion, two guns for each grenadier or musketeer battalion. According to Miliutin the Russian regimental artillery had a total of 36 guns.

Cavalry

Life Guard Hussars of Lt-Col Sladkov	1 squadron	76
Life Guard Don Cossacks	1 squadron	35
Life-*Sotnia* of the Ural Cossacks	1 squadron	62
Company Pioneers of Captain Dreyer	1 company	125

Appendix XII

Anglo-Russian Order of Battle, 19 September 1799

Commander in Chief of the combined Anglo-Russian army in Holland: Frederick August, Duke of York and Albany

Unit		Strength[1]	
First or Right Column (Lieutenant General Hermann)			
Preliminary Attack Force (Lieutenant Colonel Baklanowski)			
1st *Jégerski* of Suthoff	1 company	*100*	(Captain Murawief)
Fersen Musketeers	2 battalions	1,542	
7th Light Dragoons	1 squadron	*150*	(British)
Regimental artillery	4 guns		
Advance Guard (Major General Suthoff)			
1st *Jégerski* of Suthoff	1 battalion	*400*	
Comb. Grenadier Battalion 'Ossipov'	1 battalion	643	
Cossacks	detachment	20	
7th Light Dragoons	1 squadron	*150*	(British)
Pioneers of Dreyer	½ company	56	
A Troop, Royal Horse Artillery	4 guns		(British)
1st Line (Major General Essen)			
Zherebtsov Grenadiers	2 battalions	1,551	
Benkendorf Grenadiers	2 battalions	1,516	
Regimental artillery	4 guns		
2nd Line (Major General Arbénev)			
Arbénev Musketeers	2 battalions	1,546	
Comb. Grenadier Battalion 'Strick'	1 battalion	627	
Comb. Grenadier Battalion 'Timofeyev'	1 battalion	633	
Regimental artillery	4 guns		

1   Italics are estimated strengths.

Reserve; British 9th Brigade (Major General Manners)
9th Foot	2 battalions	1,249
56th Foot	1 battalion	676

British marching artillery	2x 6pdr cannon		
7th Light Dragoons	2 squadrons	*200*	(British, Colonel Paget)
Russian field artillery	10 guns		

Second Column (Lieutenant General Dundas)
Russian Brigade (Major General Sedmoratzki)
1st *Jégerski* of Suthoff	1 company	100
Sedmoratski Musketeers	2 battalion	1,576
Comb. Grenadier Battalion 'Ericsson'	1 battalion	622
Pioneers of Dreyer	½ company	56
Regimental artillery	4 guns	

1st Brigade (Major General D'Oyly)
Grenadier Battalion Guards	1 battalion
3/1st Foot Guards	1 battalion

2nd Brigade (Major General Burrard)
1/Coldstream Guards	1 battalion
1/3rd Foot Guards	1 battalion

8th Brigade (Major General Prince William)
5th Foot	2 battalions	852
35th Foot	2 battalions	1,221
11th Light Dragoons	2 squadrons	*270*
Marching artillery	4x 12pdr and 4x 6pdr cannon, 4x howitzers	

Third Column (Lieutenant General Pulteney)
3rd Brigade (Major General Coote)[2]
2nd (Queen's) Foot	1 battalion
27th Foot	1 battalion
29th Foot	1 battalion
85th Foot	1 battalion

5th Brigade (Major General Don)
17th Foot	2 battalions
40th Foot	2 battalions

11th Light Dragoons	2 squadrons	*270*
Marching artillery	6x 6pdr cannon, 2x howitzers	

---

2 A troop of the 11th Light Dragoons, two 6pdr cannon and a howitzer were attached to Coote's Brigade.

Left Column (Lieutenant General Abercromby)
Advance Guard (Major General Knox)   1,730
Battalion Grenadiers   1 battalion
Battalion Light Infantry   1 battalion
4th Brigade (Major General Moore)
2/1st (Royal) Foot   1 battalion
25th Foot   1 battalion
49th Foot   1 battalion
79th Highlanders   1 battalion
92nd Highlanders   1 battalion
6th Brigade (Major General the Earl of Cavan)
20th Foot   2 battalions
63rd Foot   1 battalion
Reserve (Colonel MacDonald)
23rd Royal Welsh Fusiliers   1 battalion
55th Foot   1 battalion
7th Brigade (Major General the Earl of Chatham)
4th Foot   3 battalions   1,675
31st Foot   1 battalion   794

18th Light Dragoons   2 squadrons   160
Marching artillery   4x 12pdr and 4x 6pdr cannon, 4x howitzers

Appendix XIII

Dispositions of the Franco-Batavian Army on 18 September 1799

Général en Chef: *Général de Division* Brune
Chef de l'etat-major: *Génèral de Brigade* Dardenne

FRENCH ARMY (9,935)[1]

Commandant en chef: *Général de Division* Vandamme
Commandant en chef l'artillerie: *Général de Brigade* Seroux
Commandant en chef le génie: *Chef de Brigade* Saint-Julien

Unit	Strength	Location
Avant-garde (Rostollant)		Kamp, Groet, Schoorl
3/48e Demi-Brigade (1 bat + gren. coy)	740	
54e Demi-Brigade (3 battalions, Varé)	2,306	
5e Chasseurs à Cheval (1 sq, Denain)	87	
16e Chasseurs à Cheval (1 sq, Raulet)	175	
Artillery (6 3pdr, 4 4pdr, 2 12pdr cannon)		
Brigade Gouvion		
42e Demi-Brigade (3 battalions, Aubrée)	1,835	Bergen
90e Demi-Brigade (2 battalions, Grillot)	1,370	Egmond aan Zee
3/72e Demi-Brigade (1 gren coy, Neller)	37	Bergen
Artillery		
Reserve (Brune)		Alkmaar
49e Demi-Brigade (3 battalions, Bardet)	2,130	
3/60e Demi-Brigade (1 battalion)	587	

1 Gachot, *Brune en Hollande*, pp.265-266. The artillery consisted of the 4/4e Artillerie Légère (1 escouade) and 1/8e Artillerie Légère (2 escouades); 98 men and the 6/6e Artillerie à Pied & 6/8e Artillerie à Pied (5 escouades, 83 men).

10e Dragons (4 squadrons, Godard)	487	
Artillery park		

BATAVIAN ARMY

1e Divisie (*Lieutenant-Generaal* Daendels) (6,892) — HQ St. Pancras
Voorhoede (*Colonel* Crass)

1e Bataljon Jagers	483	Oud-Karspel
2e Bataljon Jagers	489	Noordscherwoude

1e Brigade (*Colonel* Rietvelt) — HQ Zuidscherwoude

Comb. grenadiers/4e Halve Brigade (3 coys)	299	Zuidscherwoude
1/1e Halve Brigade	571	Zuidscherwoude
2/1e Halve Brigade	669	Broek
3/1e Halve Brigade	700	Broek
2e Compagnie Rijdende Artillerie	154	St. Pancras
Regiment Dragonders (4 squadrons)	492	St. Pancras

2e Brigade (*Generaal-Major* van Zuylen van Nijevelt) — HQ Ouddorp

1/4e Halve Brigade	678	Ouddorp
3/4e Halve Brigade	498	Ouddorp
2e Regiment Zware Cavalerie (2½ squadron)	198	Ouddorp
1/5e Halve Brigade (Lyclama à Nijeholt)	529	St. Pancras
2/5e Halve Brigade (Faure)	457	St. Pancras
3/5e Halve Brigade	481	St. Pancras

Foot artillery[2] (3 companies)	194	

2e Divisie (*Lieutenant-Generaal* Dumonceau) (6,660) — HQ Alkmaar
Voorhoede (*Colonel* Gilquin)

4e Bataljon Jagers	511	Schoorldam
Battalion Grenadiers (6 companies, D. Bruce)	489	Schoorldam
Regiment Huzaren (1 squadron)	114	Schoorldam
1e Compagnie Rijdende Artillerie (2 guns)	60	Schoorldam

1e Brigade (*Generaal-Major* Bonhomme) — HQ Koedijk

1/6e Halve Brigade	509	Koedijk
3/6e Halve Brigade	550	Koedijk
1/7e Halve Brigade	502	Koedijk
2/7e Halve Brigade	375	Koedijk
Regiment Huzaren (3 squadrons)	372	Hijloo
1e Compagnie Rijdende Artillerie (2 guns)	88	Hijloo

---

2 Serving seventeen 6pdr cannon and three 24pdr howitzers.

2e Brigade (*Colonel* Bruce)   Koedijk (HQ)

3e Bataljon Jagers	298	Koedijk
Combined grenadiers (3 companies)	208	Koedijk
1/2e Halve Brigade	474	Koedijk
2/2e Halve Brigade	421	Koedijk
3/2e Halve Brigade	449	Koedijk
2/6e Halve Brigade	582	Koedijk
1e Compagnie Rijdende Artillerie (2 guns)	12	Koedijk
1e Regiment Zware Cavalerie (4 squadrons)	434	Alkmaar/Schermeer
Foot artillery[3] (2 companies)	212	

Artillery Park: 216 men with nine 12pdr, seven 6pdr, and four 3pdr cannon and sixteen 24pdr howitzers.

---

[3] Serving two 12pdr and fourteen 6pdr cannon.

Appendix XIV

British ships present on the Zuiderzee on 23 September 1799

Name	Class	Commander	Remarks
At the Vlieter:			
Isis	4th Rate 50	Captain Oughton	
Melpomene	5th Rate 38	Captain Hamilton	
Juno	5th Rate 32	Captain Dundas	
Near Vlieland:			
Arrow	Sloop 20	Commander Portlock	
Wolverine	Gun-brig 12	Commander Bolton	
Pelter	Gun-vessel 14	Lieutenant Walsh	
Swinger	Gun-vessel 14	Lieutenant Lucas	
At Enkhuizen:			
Babet	6th Rate 20	Captain Mainwaring	Flagship
Zebra	Sloop 18	Commander Sparke	
Fury	Bomb 16	Commander Curry	
Piercer	Gun-vessel 16	Lieutenant Menzies	
Otter	Brig-sloop 14	Commander McKinley	
Rosario	Brig-sloop 14	Commander Carthew	
Teaser	Gun-vessel 14	Lieutenant Robins	
Tigress	Gun-brig 12	Lieutenant Atkins	
Adder	Gun-vessel 12	Lieutenant Joyce	
Attack	Gun-vessel 12	Lieutenant James	
Cracker	Gun-vessel 12	Lieutenant Atkinson	
Eling	Gun-vessel 12	Lieutenant Peake	
Force	Gun-vessel 12	Lieutenant Tokely	
Furnace	Gun-vessel 12	Lieutenant Suckling	Guard ship
Gallant	Gun-vessel 12	Lieutenant Lyall	
Haughty	Gun-vessel 12	Lieutenant Davies	

Plumper	Gun-vessel 12	Lieutenant Barreté	
Hecla	Bomb 10	Commander Bover	
Tartarus	Bomb 8	Commander Hand	
Lady Ann	Lugger 14	Lieutenant Wright	
Prince William	Armed vessel	Commander Clayton	Hired; 14 24pdr carronades

Some large armed schuyts

Near Kolhorn (guarding Oude-Sluis):

Bouncer	Gun-vessel 12	Lieutenant Bamber	Guard ship

Cruising on the Zuiderzee (to cut off communications between Amsterdam and Friesland):

Dart	Sloop 18	Commander Campbell	
Espiegle	Brig-sloop 14	Commander Boorder	From 2/9 Commander Slade
Speedwell	Brig-sloop 14	Lieutenant Reddy	
Defender	Gun-vessel 12	Lieutenant Leavy	
Hasty	Gun-vessel 12	Lieutenant Carlton	

Appendix XV

Anglo-Russian Order of Battle, 2 October 1799

Frederick August, Duke of York and Albany, Commander in Chief of the combined Anglo-Russian army in Holland

Unit **Strength**[1]

First Column (Lieutenant General Abercromby)
1st (Guards) Brigade (Major General D'Oyly)
Grenadier Battalion Guards	1 battalion	Colonel Wynyard
3/1st Foot Guards	1 battalion	Colonel A. Maitland

4th Brigade (Major General Moore)
2/1st Royal Foot	1 battalion	Lieutenant Colonel Lumsdaine
25th Foot	1 battalion	Lieutenant Colonel Wright
49th Foot	1 battalion	Lieutenant Colonel Brock
79th Highlanders	1 battalion	Colonel A. Cameron
92nd Highlanders	1 battalion	Colonel Marquis of Huntly

6th Brigade (Major General Hely-Hutchinson)[2]
1/20th Foot	1 battalion	Major Power[3]
2/20th Foot	1 battalions	Lieutenant Colonel Clephane
63rd Foot	1 battalion	Lieutenant Colonel Brereton

Advance Guard/Reserve (Colonel MacDonald)
23rd Royal Welsh Fusiliers	1 battalion		Lieutenant Colonel R.W. Talbot
55th Foot	1 battalion		Major Lumsden
Battalion Grenadiers	1 battalion		Lieutenant Colonel Baylis
Battalion Light Infantry	1 battalion		Lieutenant Colonel Shairpe
6/60th Royal American Regiment	rifle company	110	Lieutenant de Mangon
1st *Jégerski* of Suthoff		300	

---

1   Italics are estimated strengths.
2   The Earl of Cavan's former brigade was commanded by Major General Hely-Hutchinson: Cavan received a blow from a horse, fracturing his leg, just before the battle.
3   On 3 October, Lieutenant Colonel Bainbridge resumed command of the 1st battalion.

Cavalry Brigade (Colonel Lord Paget)
7th Light Dragoons	4 squadrons	Colonel Paget
11th Light Dragoons	3 squadrons	Lieutenant Colonel Childers
15th Light Dragoons	3 troops	Lieutenant Colonel Erskine

Artillery
A Troop, Royal Horse Artillery		Major Judgson
Marching artillery (4x 6pdr and 2x 12pdr cannon, 4x howitzers)		Lieutenant Colonel Whitworth
Party of Sailors		Captain Daniel RN

Second Column (Major General Essen)
Advance Guard (Major General Emmé)
1st *Jégerski* of Suthoff	detachment[4]	100
Comb. Grenadier Battalion 'Mitiouchin'	1 battalion	631
Comb. Grenadier Battalion 'Ossipov'[5]	1 battalion	585
Comb. Grenadier Battalion 'Ogarev'	1 battalion	583
Cossacks	detachment	*30*
Pioneers	detachment	50
Artillery (6 guns, two of them 12pdr guns)	company	

Brigade Arbénev (Major Generals Arbénev & Kaptsevich)
Zherebtsov Grenadiers	2 battalions	1,100
Emmé Grenadiers	2 battalions	1,516
Artillery (8 guns)	company	

Brigade Gladkov (Colonel Gladkov)
Benkendorf Grenadiers	2 battalions	750
Comb. Grenadier Battalion 'Timofeyev'	2 companies	*200*
Pioneers	detachment	25
Artillery (3 guns)		

Brigade Sedmoratzki (Major General Sedmoratzki, Lieutenant Colonel Timofeyev)
Sedmoratzki Musketeers	2 battalions	1,248
Comb. Grenadier Battalion 'Ericsson'	1 battalion	447
Comb. Grenadier Battalion 'Timofeyev'	2 companies	*200*
Pioneers	detachment	50
Artillery (7 guns)		

---

4 Total strength of the 1st *Jégerski* of Suthoff was 496 men.
5 Augmented with the remaining men of the Combined Grenadier Battalion 'Strick'.

Cavalry
Life Guard Hussars
  (Lt Colonel Sladkov) 2 squadrons 128

Third Column (Lieutenant General Dundas)
2nd (Guards) Brigade (Major General Burrard)
1/Coldstream Guards	1 battalion	Colonel Finch
1/3rd Foot Guards	1 battalion	Colonel Barnett

3rd Brigade (Major General Coote)
2nd (Queen's) Foot	1 battalion	Lieutenant Colonel Jones
27th Foot	1 battalion	Captain Warren (?)
29th Foot	1 battalion	Lieutenant Colonel Enys
85th Foot	1 battalion	Lieutenant Colonel Ross

7th Brigade (Major General the Earl of Chatham)
1/4th (King's) Foot	1 battalion	Lieutenant Colonel Hodgson
2/4th (King's) Foot	1 battalion	Lieutenant Colonel Cholmondeley
3/4th (King's) Foot	1 battalion	Lieutenant Colonel Dickson
31st Foot	1 battalion	Lieutenant Colonel McMurdo

11th Light Dragoons	1 squadron	158	Captain Sleigh
Marching artillery: 17 guns			
(8x 6pdr and 5x 12pdr cannon, 4x howitzers)			Lieutenant Colonel John Smith

Fourth Column (Lieutenant General Pulteney)
Advance Guard
Arbénev Musketeers (grenadiers)   *200*

5th Brigade (Major General Don)
17th Foot	2 battalions
40th Foot	2 battalions

8th Brigade (Major General Prince William)
5th Foot	2 battalions
35th Foot	2 battalions

9th Brigade (Major General Manners)
9th Foot	2 battalions
56th Foot	1 battalion

Cavalry
18th Light Dragoons	2 squadrons	250	Lieutenant Colonel Stewart

Appendix XVI

French Troops Present in Holland, 1 and 3 October 1799[1]

Unit	1 October Units	13,444 Strength	3 October Units	15,142 Strength
Infantry				
22e Demi-Brigade	1 battalion	860	2 battalions	1,633
42e Demi-Brigade	3 battalions	1,685	3 battalions	1,623
3/48e Demi-Brigade	1 battalion	887	1 (+ 2 gren. coys.)	731
49e Demi-Brigade	3 battalions	1,904	3 battalions	1,728
51e Demi-Brigade	1 battalion	833	2 battalions	1,572
54e Demi-Brigade	3 battalions	1,925	3 battalions	1,839
3/60e Demi-Brigade	1 battalion	515	1 battalion	498
72e Demi-Brigade	2 (+ 1 gren. coy.)	1,214	2 (+ 1 gren. coy,)	1,131
90e Demi-Brigade	3 battalions	2,135	3 battalions	1,805
98e Demi-Brigade			1½ battalion	1,167
Cavalry				
10e Dragons	4 squadrons	465	4 squadrons	439
4e Chasseurs à Cheval	4 squadrons	542	4 squadrons	520
5e Chasseurs à Cheval	1 squadron	86	1 squadron	86
16e Chasseurs à Cheval	1½ squadron	210	1 squadron	161
Artillery				
Artillerie Légère	1½ company	101	1½ company	105
6e & 7e Artillerie à Pied	2 companies	82	2 companies	101

---

1 Gachot, *Brune en Hollande*, pp.275-276, 288.

Appendix XVII

Order of Battle of the French troops present in the Batavian Republic, 22 November 1799

Général en Chef: Brune
Chef de l'Etat-Major: *Général de Brigade* Rostollant
Commandant en chef de l'artillerie: *Général de Brigade* de Saint-Martin
Engineers: *Général de Brigade* Saint-Julien

Unit	Battalions	Strength
1er Division (*Général de Division* Gouvion)		
Généraux de Brigade: d'Hinnisdal, Aubrée, Durutte, Malher and Dazémar		
Infantry		
4e Demi-Brigade	3	2,103
20e Demi-Brigade	3	2,098
51e Demi-Brigade	3	2,412
66e Demi-Brigade	3	2,511
Cavalry		
10e Dragons	4 squadrons	673
1/4e Chasseurs à Cheval	1 squadron	125
Artillery		
11er Artillerie à Pied	10e Cie.	42
6e Artillerie à Pied	10e Cie.	157
7e Artillerie à Pied	10e Cie.	89
13e Artillerie à Pied	10e Cie.	28
2e Division (*Général de Division* Reubell)		
Généraux de Brigade: Prévost, Paradis, Simon, Fuzier and Dardenne		
Infantry		
49e Demi-Brigade	3	2,077
1er Batallion des Ardennes	1	880

1er Batallion du Nord[1]	1	699 |//
Cavalry		
4e Dragons	3 squadrons	321
Artillery		
7e Artillerie à Pied	1 company	89
4e Artillerie Légère	4e Cie	40
8e Artillerie Légère	1er Cie	67

3e Division (*Général de division* Desjardin)
Généraux de Brigade: Rivaud, Osten

Infantry		
15e Demi-Brigade	3	2,558
98e Demi-Brigade	3	2,034
49e Demi-Brigade (depot)	1 company	104
51e Demi-Brigade (depot)	detachment	23
96e Demi-Brigade (depot)	1 company	94
Cavalry		
16e Chasseurs à Cheval	4 squadrons	788
4e Dragons (depot)	4 squadrons	119
Artillery		
6e Artillerie à Pied	1 company	224
7e Artillerie à Pied	1 company	150
4e Artillerie Légère	4e Cie.	31

---

1 Both the 1e Battalion du Nord and the 1e Battalion des Ardennes were National Guard units.

Appendix XVIII

Officers sent to Holland to raise the 1st and 2nd Dutch Regiments[1]

1st Regiment
Colonel van Rechteren Limpurg
Lieutenant-Colonel van Schinne
Major Douglas
Capitein De Virieu
Capitein Morack
Capitein Colthoff
Capitein C.L. de Veye
Capitein Van Meurs

Lieutenant Van Oijen
Lieutenant Van Panhuys
Lieutenant Gillot
Lieutenant S. Balneavis
Lieutenant Werden
Lieutenant Aelmans
Lieutenant Lambrechts sr.
Lieutenant Beck
Lieutenant Eichholz sr.
Lieutenant Petersen
Lieutenant Schummelketel
Lieutenant Roodbeen
Lieutenant Streithorst
Vaandrig[2] Van Maanen
Vaandrig Kerckerink

2nd Regiment
Lieutenant-Colonel Van Mollem Bruyn
Lieutenant-Colonel Van Dopff
Major Detmers
Capitein Eymann sr.
Capitein W. Gordon
Capitein Barchon
Capitein De Backer
Capitein Schutter
Capitein Eymann jr.
Capitein De Quay

Lieutenant Sloet van de Grimberg
Lieutenant Sloet van Everlo
Lieutenant Westenbrinck
Lieutenant Van der Hoya Kymmell
Lieutenant Pompe van Meerdervoort
Lieutenant Van Triest
Lieutenant Meijer
Lieutenant Boudrie
Lieutenant Woerdenbach
Lieutenant Van Solingen
Lieutenant Hamel

Vaandrig F. Gordon
Vaandrig La Verdure

1 Koolemans Beijnen, *De Erfprins van Oranje te Lingen in 1799*, pp.82-83.
2 *Vaandrig* = Ensign

Vaandrig Van Puttkammer
Vaandrig Van Ingen
Vaandrig Lindenberg
Vaandrig Dietz
Vaandrig De Klerck

Adjutant Capitein Blancken
Adjutant Vaandrig van Borck
Kwartiermeester Hesselinck
Chirurgijn-Major Van Malsen
Chirurgijn-Major Esveldt

Artillery
Capitein Van Hoey van Oostee
Sous-Lieutenant I. Ramaer
Sous-Lieutenant P. Ramaer

Vaandrig Le Maitre
Vaandrig Hulsteijn
Vaandrig Eichholtz
Vaandrig Kamphuis
Vaandrig Cardole
Vaandrig Hartelief
Adjutant Vaandrig Van Hogenhuijsen
Adjutant Vaandrig Van Sisseren
Kwartiermeester Lieutenant Geselschap
Chirurgijn-Major Vermeulen
Chirurgijn-Major Sleurs

Appendix XIX

Plans for the Orangist Invasion of the Batavian Republic

a. The initial plan for the advance into the Batavian Republic from the east:

Commander in chief: van Heeckeren van Suideras
- From Ijselburg to the Geldersoor entrenchment at Westervoort: *Lieutenant-Colonel* Spengler with 70 men.
- From Wehl to Doesburg: *Major* Schuller with 100 men.
- From Bocholt to Zutphen: *Lieutenant-Colonel* Heemskerck with 100 men.
- From Bentheim to Deventer: *Colonel* van Dongen with 100 men.
- To raise the countryside around Zutphen: *Major* Hessberg with 25 men.

b. Detailed plan for the Orangist invasion of the Batavian Republic[1]

Strength of the Orangist invasion force on 23 September 1799:

	Officers	NCOs, soldiers, etc.	Farmers and civilians	Total
Major van der Graaff	159	5		164
Colonel van Dongen	42	34		76
Major de Petit	30	7		37
Lt-Col van Heemskerck	98	92	10	200
Lt-Col Spengler	89	34	30	153
Total:	**418**	**172**	**40**	**630**

General dispositions.
After a landing of our Allies has been effectuated on [date left open] across the Zuiderzee at the Veluwe, the officer corps in service of the State, with all haste placed under the orders

---

[1] Koolemans Beijnen, *De erfprins van Oranje in Noord-Holland in 1799*, pp.28-29, 121-125.

of His Highness Lieutenant General Prince Christiaan van Hessen-Darmstadt gathered, try to force the Ijssel, to make contact with the landed corps of our Allies, which will cause a part of the provinces of Gelderland and Overijssel to revolt; which will cut off the provinces of Friesland and Groningen, as well as the landscape of Drente, it is to be hoped that the revolutionary work will be undertaken, if it not will happen by itself.

For this expedition
No.1. Shall Lt-Col Spengler in Ijsselborg be ordered that he on [date left open] the officers, troops and inhabitants under his command, present at Elten, Rees, Emmerik and the surrounding areas, concentrate in Ijsselborg and marches with these on [date left open] to Breevoort, Grol and Borculo, were he has to be on [date left open]. He has to take with him the cannon (in case when it still is under negotiation, when it will arrive in time) and to try to transport it on carts secretly, as well as the weapons and ammunition, the cannon not to be assembled before having arrived on the territory of the State, at the same time distributing the weapons and ammunition, carrying on carts the remainder. The officers will leave behind their baggage. He will communicate this order to Admiral Rietveld, d'Yvoy and Van Lijnden, requesting d'Yvoy, to inform Mr Van Enghuizen as soon as possible.

No.2. Lt-Col van Heemskerck in Boekholt will be ordered, to march on [date left open] with his command from Boekholt to Winterswijk, Grol and Borculo; however the day before he will detach major van Hessberg to Borculo with a number of officers, to be chosen by himself, in order to occupy this place, before the various corps will enter Borculo.

He shall carry all muskets, weapons and ammunition in his possession, quietly to the territory of the State, his command will carry with them all remaining weapons and ammunition. While transmitting this order Mr van Suideras is also informed.

No.3. Major van Hessberg will be ordered, as soon as he arrives in Borculo, to occupy it in the military sense of the word, covering it against all surprises; he will mount as much of his officers as possible, adding horses through written requisitioning.

No.4. Colonel van Plettenberg is ordered, on [date left open] to go with Colonel van Dongen and his command over Enschedé and Haaksbergen to Borculo, were he should be on [date left open]. He shall quietly transport all muskets, weapons and ammunition on to the territory of the State, distributing them there, carrying with him the remainder to Borculo. As soon as the various corps have arrived in Borculo, the complete corps will be divided into two columns and put into formation. The former will be commanded by Colonel van Plettenberg and the latter by Colonel van Dongen.

No.5. Major Petit shall, with the officers under his command, on [date left open] go from Lingen to Bentheim, were he should arrive the day before the colonels Van Plettenberg and Van Dongen will march, to place himself under their command.

No.6. To Lt-Col van Heyden [von Heydte] to go together with some other officers from here (Lingen) to Borculo, were he shall have to arrive after Major Hessberg has occupied it, however before Colonel van Plettenberg will arrive there.

No.7. A verbal instruction to all senior officers, present in Lingen, and senior in rank to Major de Petit, where and when they will gather and arrive in Borculo.

No.8. The Major van de Graaf is ordered, to send all cavalry officers and cavalrymen in his command to Bentheim, where they will place themselves under the orders of Colonel van Plettenberg, and he shall follow these with 20 to 30 officers with their orderlies of the artillery and infantry, the former having to take with them the pistols and sabres quietly.

Also he has, before al muskets and carbines, when the necessary number for the remaining officers have been deducted, have been sent quietly to Bentheim to Colonel van Plettenberg; and the Colonels Van Crause, Van Burmania, which like himself are destined for Friesland and Groningen, it goes without saying that, beside those reconnoitring in their support, will not go to Bentheim.

Follows the general disposition of His Highness Lieutenant General Prince van Hessen-Darmstadt, after all corps have arrived in Borculo [not preserved].

Appendix XX

Letter of 7 October 1799 to the Duke of York, proposing the retreat to the Zijpe[1]

His Royal Highness the commander in chief having required from General Sir R. Abercromby, and from Lieutenant Generals Dundas and Sir James Pulteney their opinion on the measures to be adopted in the present state and situation of the army they humbly beg leave to offer,

That since the landing of the army in Holland it has sustained five considerable actions without being able to make any considerable progress in the country, or to obtain any permanent or strong situation.

That in the actions the army has suffered a diminution of between 9 and 10,000 men, and a very considerable proportion of officers, those naturally the best and bravest. While we cannot expect to repair our losses, the enemy have very considerably increased, and doubtless must daily receive other reinforcements.

That the nature of the country we have been endeavouring to penetrate is singularly difficult. The Sand Hills afford neither firing, water or cover. The marshy country is intersected with canals and ditches which cut off the communication between advancing columns, and movements are to be made only along dykes and roads broken up, and rendered difficult of access, and every where liable to the enfilade of canon.

Beside the lateness of the season, the unheard of series of stormy and rainy weather, which has taken place for these last three weeks, has rendered the roads almost impassable, has fatigued and extenuated the men from being constantly in movement and on the alert. For being obliged to act in extended and bad cantonments, which of all kinds of warfare is the most difficult and dangerous, we must be eternally on the Qui vive, and liable to surprise and misfortune.

The country is so low and so wet, that it does not allow of encamping troops (except perhaps in the Sand Hills, as already mentioned) and, if it did, we have no means of transporting tents or any one convenience that may in general be expected.

We had a large nominal army, formed of raw soldiers, hastily assembled, ill clothed, and a very great proportion of inexperienced officers, not provided with horses, carriages or those means of transport without which no progress can be made in an enemy's country.

---

1   Letter in English in Koolemans Beijnen, *De Erfprins van Oranje in Noord-Holland in 1799*, pp.153-156

The farther we advanced in our present direction, the faster our difficulties increase, and the farther we are removed from our only communication port and supplies; for no vessel for this fortnight past has been able to appear, or anchor on our flank near the coast.

With all the advantage that canal-navigation can give, we have never been able to have above two days bread in advance, and seldom that quantity. We are now at the extremity of such conveyance, and if we still advance, there is no prospect of carriages to bring up our necessary supplies.

We have no assistance, or encouragement from the country, no universal rising or declaration in our favour, which we were taught to expect; nor do we even obtain accurate or useful intelligence.

Our allies have entered on a scene of which they had no Idea and are not much inclined to share the rough and the smooth with us; they are not satisfied, nor have we reason to be satisfied with them. It is evident that no great cordiality or united effort can be expected in such a situation.

We gained a great advantage on the 2nd inst.; our pressing wants and difficulties made it impossible to follow up our blow, or to advance farther than we have done, and which is no position but a situation, requiring a constant alert.

The enemy is now in great force about Beverwijck prepared to resist. Should we succeed in driving him from Beverwijck, it is a post we could not exist in, or keep, with the French army still stronger placed in our front at Haarlem, the greater part of the Batavian army on our left and rear at Purmerend, and no means of bringing up our supplies from the state of the roads and want of carriages. Should we fail in our attempt, the most imminent danger must attent our retreat. Even this afternoon a very considerable and almost general action has taken place on our right, where the enemy have advanced in great force, and in which we have reaped no advantage, but have sustained a considerable loss.

From what we see, and from what we feel, and have experienced; from the state of the troops, the greater part of whom have been now four days under arms in the Sand Hills and other situations; from the want of present and the impossibility of bringing up future supplies; from the unparalleled inclemency of the season and weather; from the advantage of defence the enemy possesses, his growing numbers, and his absolute command of the resources of the country; from the almost impassable state of the roads and the country; from the diminished condition of our cavalry and horses of every description; from our being now in a situation which is not an advantageous military position, and from many other concurring unfavourable circumstances:

We are humbly of opinion, that however we might have given efficacy to a revolution in Holland, we are not at this moment equal to the conquest of the country or of remaining (even if it was an eligible one) in our present situation, and that any farther advance affords no prospect of decisive advantage, but on the contrary is pregnant with much difficulty and danger, should we fail. That therefore we should return to the position of the Zijpe which we quitted and there await a more favourable change of circumstances.

October 7th after midnight

P.S. Even to this hour there is no alteration in the tempestuous state of the weather.

(Signed) Ra Abercromby G.
David Dundas Lt. Gen.
Sam.l Hulse Lt. Gen.
Jas Pulteney Lt. Gen.

Bibliography

Books and Articles

Anon., *Dagverhaal der doormarcheerende troepen, Inkwartieringen en in garnizoen Liggende Militairen in de Steede Beverwijk, sedert October 1787 tot op het Sluiten van de Vreede in den Jaare 1802*, in J. van Venetien e.a., *"Dagverhaal der doormarcheerende troepen" – Beverwijk in de ban van de Fransen (1787-1802)* (Beverwijk: Historisch Genootschap Midden-Kennemerland en Museum Kennemerland, 1999).

Anon., *Dag-verhaal wegens de Landing der Engelsche en Russische Troupen; Ongehoorde Wreedheden door Dezelve Gepleegt, en Eindelijk de Schandelijke Aftogt. Alles met Egte Bewyzen Gestaafd* (Alkmaar: Molkman en Hand e.a., 1799).

Anon., *Eenige Berichten Omtrent den Veldtocht der Gewapende Groningers, naar Noord Holland. Behelzende; Een meenigte vreemde lotgevallen; armoede; gebrek aan klederen; onthouding van traktement en vyvres; slegte cazernering en weinige troost van huis enz. Door een Grenadier* (Groningen: A.F. Vos, 1799).

Anon., *Geschiedenis van den Gewapenden Inval der Uitgeweeken Nederlanderen, in het Departement van den Rhyn, in de Maand September 1799* (Arnhem: J.H. Moeleman junior & Comp., 1801).

Anon., *Geschiedenis van de Landing der Engelschen en Russen in 't Najaar van 1799. Benevens Anecdotes Omtrent de Bevelhebbers. Opgesteld door een Officier van den Generaal Brune* (Gouda: H.L. van Buma, 1801).

Anon., *Geschiedkundig Gedenkstuk van het Voorgevallene binnen Haarlem in de Laatste Helft van het Jaar MDCCIC* (Haarlem: A. Loosjes Pz., 1803).

Anon. [translated and annotated M. Mac-Carthy], *Histoire de la Campagne faite en 1799, en Hollande* (Paris: Plancher, 1818).

Anon., *Landungsgeschichte der Engländer und Russen in Holland, im Herbst 1799. Nebst Anekdoten über die Anführer, Verfaßt von einem Officier im Gefolge des Generals Brüne* (Hamburg: August Campe, 1800).

Anon., *Mémoires Historiques sur la Campagne du Général en Chef Brune en Batavie, Du 5 Fructudor an 7, au 9 Frimaire an 8; Rédigés par un Officier de son État-Major* (Paris: Chez Favre, An IX).

Anon., *Naamregister der Officieren van de Nationaale Armée, in Dienste der Bataafsche Republiq: Mitsgaders die der Duitsche Troupes, Volgens Capitulatie nog in Derzelver Dienst Zijnde. Voor den Jaare 1799* ('s Graavenhaage: J. Thierry en C. Mensing, 1799).

Anon., *Narrative of a Private Soldier in His Majesty's 92d Regiment of Foot* (Glasgow: University Press, 1820).

Anon. [Lieutenant Colonel Fletcher Wilkie], 'Recollections of the British army, in the early campaigns of the Revolutionary War' in *The United Service Journal and Naval and Military Magazine*, Part I (London: Henry Colburn, 1836) pp.181-191, 322-333.

Anon. *Steel's Prize Pay Lists, containing accounts of prize and head-money, paid, and now payable, for prizes taken or destroyed, during the last war*, new series corrected till 1805 (London: David Steel, 1805).

Anon. (Oud jager van Trip), 'Teregtwijzing op J. Bosscha's Heldendaden te land, en wel inzonderheid betreffende hetgene in het eerste Stuk van het derde Deel voorkomt, omtrent de Jagers van Trip', *De Militaire Spectator* (Breda: Broese & Comp., 1844) pp. 195-197.

Anon., *The Campaign in Holland, 1799. By a Subaltern* (London: W. Mitchell, 1861).

Anon., *The Dutch Expedition vindicated; with Brief Observations on the Emigrants. To which is added, a Postscript, Containing the Supplement to the Account of the Armistice Concluded between His Royal Highness the Duke of York and General Brune* (London: John Stockdale, 1799).

Anon., *The History of the Campaign of 1799, in Holland* (London: J. Barfield, 1801).

Anon., *Veldtocht van den Generaal Brune, in de Bataafsche Republiek, in het Jaar 1799. Beschreeven door een officier van zijn Etat-Major* (Haarlem: A. Loosjes, 1801).

Cornelis van der Aa, *De zoogenaamde verdediging van Willem Paschen Gtz. Drossaard van het Ampt Bredevoort. Aangaande zijne bedrijven ten jaare 1799, als commissaris van de Militaire Rechtbank, aan den proefsteen der waarheid, en des gezonden verstands getoetst* (Utrecht: Cornelis van der Aa, 1807).

Cornelis van der Aa, *Geschiedenis van het Leven, Character, en Lotgevallen van Wijlen Willem den Vijfden, Prinse van Oranje en Nassau. Uit Echte Bronnen en Bescheiden Bijeengebragt, en in eene Voegzame Orde Opgesteld* (Amsterdam: Johannes Allart, 1808).

Cornelis van der Aa, *Geschiedenis van den Jongst-geëindigden Oorlog, tot op het Sluiten van den Vrede te Amiëns. Bijzonder met Betrekking tot de Bataafsche Republiek* (Amsterdam: Johannes Allart, 1802 & 1806).

Philip Ball, *A Waste of Blood & Treasure* (Barnsley: Pen & Sword Books Limited, 2017).

F. de Bas, *Prins Frederik der Nederlanden en zijn Tijd* (Schiedam: H.A.M. Roelants, 1891).

J.C.C. den Beer Poortugael, 'Levensbericht van Diederic Jacob den Beer Poortugael' in *Jaarboek van de Maatschappij der Nederlandsche Letterkunde, 1880 – Bijlage tot de Handelingen van 1880* (Leiden: E.J. Brill, 1880) pp.3-42.

L.H.C. Beijens, *De Inval der Orangisten in Gelderland in September 1799*, reprint from *Bijdragen en Mededeelingen der Vereeniging "Gelre"* Vol. 1 (1898), pp.104-127.

P.J. Blok & P.C. Molhuysen, *Nieuw Nederlandsch Biografisch Woordenboek*, Vol 7 (Leiden: A.W. Sijthoff, 1927)

Nicolaas Bommer, 'Korte Beschrijvinge Van Den Slag Of Bataille Op Den Zesden October, Zijnde Ook Castricummer-Kermes 1799 Voorgevallen' in M. Kramer, 'De Slag bij Castricum 6 en 7 Oct. 1799', *Vragen van den Dag* (Amsterdam: S.L. van Looy, 1905) pp. 464-479.

J. Bosscha, *Neerlands Heldendaden te Land, van de Vroegste Tijden af tot op Onze Dagen* (Leeuwarden: G.T.N. Suringar, 1873).

L. Bourgoin, *Esquisse Historique sur le Maréchal Brune* (Paris: Rousseau, 1840).

(J. Brauw), *Mijne emigratie in Duitschland, Engeland en Ierland, in de jaren 1799-1802;met een verslag omtrent de Hollandsche Brigade in dienst van Groot-Brittannien, onder bevel van Z.D.H. den Heere Erf-Prins* (Utrecht: N. van der Monde, 1837).

Ferdinand Brock Tupper, *The Life and Correspondence of Major-General Sir Isaac Brock* (London: Simpkin, Marshall & Co., 1847).

H.J. Broersma, *De grenzen van het beeld – Het Nederlandse beeld van de Russische soldaten tijdens de Engels-Russische Invasie in Noord-Holland in 1799* (Unpublished dissertation, Rijks Universiteit Groningen, 1996).

Sir Henry Bunbury, *A Narrative of the Campaign in North Holland. 1799* (London: T. And W. Boone, 1849). Included in Lieut.-Gen. Sir Henry Bunbury, *Narratives of some Passages in the Great War with France, from 1799 to 1810* (London: Richard Bentley, 1854).

Lieut. Col. Sir John M. Burgoyne, *Regimental Records of the Bedfordshire Militia from 1759 to 1884* (London: W.H. Allen & Co., 1884).

Calkoen, H.J., 'Ooggetuige-verslag van de woelige dagen te Nieuwe Niedorp, October 1799', *De Speelwagen*, Vol.6 (1953) pp.163-166.

Jules du Camp, *Histoire de l'Armée et de tous les Régiments depuis les Premier Temps de la Monarchie Française Jusqu'à nos Jours* (Paris: A. Barbier, 1850).

Richard Cannon, *Historical Record of the Fifth Regiment of Foot, or Northumberland Fusiliers* (London: W. Clowes and Sons, 1838).

A. du Casse, *Le Général Vandamme et sa Correspondance* (Paris: Didier et Cie, 1870).

J.J. Colledge, *Ships of the Royal Navy: An Historical Index. Vol. I Major Ships* (Newton Abbot: David & Charles, 1969).

Mary Ellen Condon, *The Administration of the Transport Service During the War Against Revolutionary France, 1793-1802* (Unpublished dissertation, University College London, 1968).

Francis Culling Carr-Gomm (ed.), *Letters and Journals of Field-Marshal Sir William Maynard Gomm, G.C.B.* (London: John Murray, 1881).

H.T. Colenbrander, *Gedenkstukken der Algemeene Geschiedenis van Nederland van 1795 tot 1840* ('s-Gravenhage: Martinus Nijhoff, 1907).

H.W. Daendels, *Rapport des Opérations de la Division du Lieutenant-Général Daendels; Depuis le 22 Août, jusqu'à la capitulation de l'Armée Angloise et Russe, le 18 Octobre 1799. An 5* (La Haye: I. van Cleef, 1799).

H.W. Daendels, *Rapport Van De Operatien Der Divisie Van Den Lieutenant-Generaal Daendels; Zedert den 22 Augustus, tot de gesloten capitulatie met de Engelsche en Russische armée, den 18 October 1799, het 5de jaar* ('s Gravenhage: I. van Cleef, 1799).

D.H. Delprat, 'Journal concernant les évenements politiques de notre patrie depuis 1798-1807 redigé par Daniel Delprat', *Bijdragen en Mededeelingen van het Historisch Genootschap* ('s Gravenhage: Martinus Nijhoff, 1892).

Charles Dolly, 'Chronologie historique des armées de la République et de l'Empire', *Le Spectateur Militaire*, Vol. XLIX (Paris: M. Noirot, 1850) pp.5-30.

Mary Dumaresc, 'Account of the stay in Jersey of Russian troops. 1799-1800', *Annual Bulletin of the Société Jersiaise* (Jersey: Labey et Fils,1914) pp.416-424.

Mathieu Dumas, *Précis des Événemens et Opérations Historiques et Militaires, Des Armées Franco-Batave et Anglo-Russes, sous les ordres du Général Brune et du Duc d'York. Dans la Campagne de la Nord-Hollande* (Hambourg: F. Perthès, 1799).

Mathieu Dumas, *Geschied- en Krijgskundige Gebeurdnissen van de Landing der Engelschen en Russen, Gedurende den Veldtogt in Noord-Holland. 1799* (Den Haag: I. van Cleef, undated).
Major Francis Duncan, *History of the Royal Regiment of Artillery* (London: John Murray, 1879).
James Lord Dunfermline, *Lieutenant-General Sir Ralph Abercronby K.B. 1793-1801. A Memoir by his Son* (Edinburgh: Edmonston and Douglas, 1861).
A.W. Engelen, *Uit de Gedenkschriften van een Voornaam Nederlandsch Beambte* (Tiel: H.C.A. Campagne & zoon, 1882).
N.J.A.P.H. van Es, *De Veldtocht in Noord-Holland 1799* (Arnhem: Coers & Roest – G.J. Thieme, 1898).
Major H. Everard, *History of Tho's Farrington's Regiment, subsequently designated the 29th (Worcestershire) Foot 1694 to 1891* (Worcester: Littlebury & Company, 1891).
F.E.M., 'Uit de nagelaten herinneringen van den Vice-Admiraal Jhr. Anthony Cornelis Twent', *Marineblad* (Helder: C. de Boer Jr., 1905) pp. 203-217, 341-358.
R. Fell, *A Tour Through the Batavian Republic During the Latter Part of the Year 1800. Containing an Account of the Revolution and Recent Events in that Country* (London: R. Phillips, 1801).
J.W. Fortescue, *A History of the British Army*, Vol. IV Part 1 (London: MacMillan and Co. Limited, 1906).
J. Fox, 'De brug van Schoorldam onder vijandelijk vuur', *Holland* (Haarlem: Historische Vereniging Holland, 1978) pp.32-34, 329-330.
Édouard Gachot, *Jourdan en Allemagne et Brune en Hollande* (Paris: Didier Perrin et Cie, 1906).
Jhr. F.M.L. van Geen, *De Generaal van Geen, 1773-1846* ('s-Gravenhage: Blankwaardt & Schoonhoven, 1910).
Epke van der Geest et al, *Wat gebeurde er in 1799 bij de Engelsmanduun?* (Ameland: De Ouwe Pôlle, 1999).
Edward Gibson, Lord Ashbourne, *Pitt: some Chapters of his Life and Times* (London: Longmans, Green, & Co., 1898).
C.G.H. [Cornelis Gijsberti Hodenpijl], 'De Russische vaandels veroverd in den slag bij Bergen op 19 September 1799', *De Militaire Spectator* ('s Gravenhage: C. van Doorn & Zoon, 1899) pp.631-637.
H. en J.P. Gildemeester, F.W. Conrad, *Reis door Noord-Holland in 1800* (Edam: Kring van Vrienden van de Hondsbossche, 2000).
R.P. Goettsch, 'Merkwaardigheden uit een achttiende-eeuws handschrift', *West-Frieslands Oud en Nieuw* (Hoorn: Drukkerij 'West-Friesland', 1971) pp.90-93.
Colonel James J. Graham, *Memoir of General Graham with Notices of the Campaigns in which he was Engaged from 1779 to 1801* (Edinburgh: R. & R. Clark, 1862).
A.G. Freiherrn von Gross, *Handbuch für die Kriegsgeschichte der jahre 1792 bis 1808, enthaltend eine genaue Uebersicht aller Feldzüge und Landungen, welche in diesem Zeitraume Statt gefunden haben* (Amsterdam: Verlage des Kunst- und Industrie-Comptoirs, 1808).
Sir R. Vesey Hamilton & John Knox Laughton (eds.), *Recollections of James Anthony Gardner Commander R.N. (1775-1814)* (London: Navy Records Society, 1906).

Hermann Hüffer, 'Der Feldzug der Engländer und Russen in Holland im Herbst 1799 und die Stellung Preussens', *Historische Vierteljahrschrift* (Leipzig: B.G. Teubner, 1902) pp. 161- 195, 347-386, 523-527.

Hermann Hüffer, *Der Krieg des Jahres 1799 und die Zweite Koalition* (Gotha: Friedrich Andreas Perthes, 1905).

Bert Huiskes, Gerald de Weerdt e.a., *De Lutine 1799-1999, de raadselachtige ondergang van een schip vol goud* (Bussum: THOTH, 1999).

J.K. '3 Brieven van het oorlogsterrein 1799 en 1800', *De Navorscher, een middel tot gedachtenwisseling en letterkundig verkeer tusschen allen, die iets weten, iets te vragen hebben, of iets kunnen oplossen* (Amsterdam: C.L.G. Veldt, 1909) pp.576-578.

Robert Jackson, *A Systematic View of the Formation, Discipline, and Economy of Armies*, (London: 1st Edition, John Stockdale, 1804; 3rd Edition, Parker, Furnivall, and Parker, 1845).

Jhr. J.C. de Jonge, *Geschiedenis van het Nederlandsche Zeewezen* (Zwolle: Van Hoogstraten en Gorter, 1869).

Cornelius de Jong, *Verantwoording en Verdediging van Cornelius de Jong als Kapitein ter Zee Gecommandeert Hebbende 's Lands Schip Cerberus. Wegens zijn Gehouden Gedrag voor, bij en na de Overgave van 's Lands Eskader voor de Vlieter, onder de Ordres van de Gewezen Schout bij Nacht Samuel Story, den 30 Augustus 1799* (Haarlem: François Bohn, 1804).

Hendr. Keetell, 'Aanteekeningen betreffende de Bat. Omwenteling voornamelijk binnen Utrecht. Door een ooggetuige', *De Navorscher, een middel tot gedachtenwisseling en letterkundig verkeer tusschen allen, die iets weten, iets te vragen hebben, of iets kunnen oplossen* (Utrecht: C. Snoek Wz., 1902) pp.453-479.

Hendr. Keetell, 'Aanteekeningen betreffende de Bat. Omwenteling voornamelijk binnen Utrecht. Door een ooggetuige', *De Navorscher, een middel tot gedachtenwisseling en letterkundig verkeer tusschen allen, die iets weten, iets te vragen hebben, of iets kunnen oplossen* (Zaltbommel: H.J. van de Garde & Co., 1903) pp.65-81.

G.J.W. Koolemans Beijnen, *De Erfprins van Oranje in Noord-Holland in 1799*, reprint from *Bijdragen voor Vaderlandsche Geschiedenis en Oudheidkunde* ('s-Gravenhage: Martinus Nijhoff, 1910).

G.J.W. Koolemans Beijnen, *De Erfprins van Oranje te Lingen in 1799*, reprint from *Bijdragen voor Vaderlandsche Geschiedenis en Oudheidkunde*, ('s-Gravenhage: Martinus Nijhoff, 1907).

G.J.W. Koolemans Beijnen, 'De invloed van de Oranje-partij in Gelderland op het voornemen tot de landing der Engelschen en Russen in Noord-Holland in 1799', *Jaarboek van de Maatschappij der Nederlandse Letterkunde* (Leiden: E.J. Brill, 1900) pp.162-175.

G.J.W. Koolemans Beijnen, 'De twee zendingen van den generaal Don uit het Engelsche hoofdkwartier in Noord-Holland in 1799 naar 's-Gravenhage', *Jaarboek van de Maatschappij der Nederlandse Letterkunde* (Leiden: E.J. Brill, 1900) pp.130-160.

G.J.W. Koolemans Beijnen, 'Een niet in de archieven aanwezig staatsstuk betreffende den veldtocht in Noordholland in 1799', *De Militaire Spectator* (Utrecht: A.W. Bruna & Zoon, 1918) pp.641-655.

G.J.W. Koolemans Beijnen, 'Engelands bedoelingen bij het werkdadig optreden op het vasteland gedurende den tweeden coalitie-oorlog', *Jaarboek van de Maatschappij der Nederlandse Letterkunde* (Leiden: E.J. Brill, 1898) pp.124-164.

G.J.W. Koolemans Beijnen, 'Het terugtrekken van Daendels in 1799 uit de Zijpe naar den Schermer', *Jaarboek van de Maatschappij der Nederlandse Letterkunde* (Leiden: E.J. Brill, 1898) pp.181-220.

G.J.W. Koolemans Beijnen, 'Krijgsgeschiedkundige studie over de Verdediging der Bataafsche Republiek in 1799', reprint from *De Militaire Spectator* (Breda: Broese & Comp., 1891-1895).

G.J.W. Koolemans Beijnen, 'Nieuwe gegevens betreffende de bedoelingen van Engeland bij het werkdadig optreden op het vasteland gedurende den tweeden coalitie-oorlog, *Jaarboek van de Maatschappij der Nederlandse Letterkunde* (Leiden: E.J. Brill, 1899) pp.64-82.

G.J.W. Koolemans Beijnen, 'Oranje en de Roomsch-Katholieken in 1799', *Jaarboek van de Maatschappij der Nederlandse Letterkunde* (Leiden: E.J. Brill, 1904) pp.3-21.

Lieutenant-Generaal Baron Krayenhoff, *Geschiedkundige Beschouwing van den Oorlog op het Grondgebied der Bataafsche Republiek in 1799* (Nijmegen: J.C. Vieweg en Zoon, 1832).

Sir Thomas Dick Lauder, *Legendary Tales of the Highlands* (London: Henry Colburn, 1841).

Lombard de Langres, *Bijzonderheden uit de tijden der Omwenteling, gedeeltelijk ten onderwerp hebbende den toestand en de betrekkingen van Nederland in het jaar 1798*, ('s – Gravenhage & Amsterdam: De Gebroeders van Cleef, 1820).

Lombard de Langres, *Les souvenirs, ou recueil de faits particuliers et d'anecdotes secrètes, pour server a l'histoire de la Révolution* (Paris: Librairie de Gide Fils, 1819).

Piers Mackesy, *Statesmen at War: the Strategy of Overthrow, 1798-1799* (London and New York: Longman Group Ltd., 1974).

Hermine Manschot-Tijdink, 'Een allerneeteligst caracter', *Het leven van Judith van Dorth (1747-1799)* (Aalten: Fagus, 1999).

Philippa L. Marett, 'The Russians in Jersey', in: *Jersey Ladies' College Magazine*, (1892) pp. 8-11.

John Marshall, *Royal Naval Biography; or, memoirs of the Services of all the Flag-Officers, Superannuated Rear-Admirals, Retired-Captains, Post-Captains, and Commanders, Whose Names appeared on the Admiralty List of Sea Officers at the commencement of the year 1823, or who have since been promoted* (London: Longman, Hurst, Rees, Orme, Brown, and Green, 1825).

Major Francis Maule, *Memoirs of the Principal Events in the Campaigns of North Holland and Egypt* (London: F.C. and J. Rivington, 1816).

Major General Sir J.F. Maurice (ed.), *The Diary of Sir John Moore* (London: Edward Arnold, 1904).

Dr. I. Mendels, *Herman Willem Daendels, vóór zijne Benoeming tot Gouverneur-Generaal van Oost-Indië (1762-1807)* ('s-Gravenhage: Martinus Nijhoff, 1890).

Oberst Miliutin, *Geschichte des Krieges Rußlands mit Frankreich unter der Regierung Kaiser Paul's I. im Jahre 1799* (München: Jos. Lindauer'schen Buchhandlung, 1857-1858).

James Carrick Moore, *The Life of Lieutenant-General Sir John Moore, K.B.* (London: John Murray, 1833).

G.C. Moore Smith, *The Life of John Colborne, Field-Marshal Lord Seaton, Compiled from his Letters, Records of his Conversations, and Other Sources* (London: John Murray, 1903).

George Noakes, *A Historical Account of the Services of the 34th & 55th Regiments, the linked Line Battalions in the 2nd or Cumberland & Westmorland Sub-District Brigade, from the Periods of their Formation until the Present Time* (Carlisle: C. Thurnam and Sons, 1875).

A.B. Piechowiak, 'The Anglo-Russian Expedition to Holland in 1799', *The Slavonic and East European Review* (London: Athlone Press, 1963) pp.182-195.

P.Q.R., 'Inval der Oranje-emigranten in Overijssel', *De Navorscher, een middel tot gedachtenwisseling en letterkundig verkeer tusschen allen, die iets weten, iets te vragen hebben, of iets kunnen oplossen* (Amsterdam: Frederik Muller, 1854) pp. 232-233.

Willem Paschen, *Verdediging van Willem Paschen gtz. Drost van Breedevoort tegen Cornelis van der Aa, schrijver der Geschiedenis van den Jongst Geeindigden Oorlog* (Deventer: Gerrit Brouwer, 1807).

[Francis Louis Picard], *Histoire du 42e Régiment d'Infanterie* (Montbéliard: H. Barbier, 1875).

G.J. Pijman, *Bijdragen tot de Voornaamste Gebeurtenissen Voorgevallen in de Republiek der Vereenigde Nederlanden, Sedert het Jaar 1778, tot en met het Jaar 1807* (Utrecht: J.G. van Terveen, 1826).

W.A. van Rappard, 'De Haarlemmer in zorg en angst', *Haerlem Jaarboek 1983* (Haarlem: Schuyt & Co C.V., 1984) pp.54-73.

Paul P. Reese, *"The Ablest Man in the British Army": The Life and Career of General Sir John Hope* (Diss. Florida State University, 2007)

Jacqueline Reiter, *The Late Lord – The Life of John Pitt 2nd Earl of Chatham* (Barnsley, Pen & Sword Books Limited, 2017)

H.A. Ritter, *Een Russisch verhaal van den veldtocht in Noord-Holland in 1799* (Utrecht: A.W. Bruna & Zoon, 1914).

David Robinson, 'The 1799 Anglo-Russian Invasion of Holland: A Comparative View from the Press', *Napoleonic Scholarship. The Journal of the International Napoleonic Society*, No. 6, December 2015, http://www.napoleonicsociety.com/english/pdf/journal2015.pdf accessed 10 July 2018.

Charles Ross, *Correspondence of Charles, First Marquis Cornwallis* (London: John Murray, 1859).

v. S., 'Iets over de maatregelen welke na het jaar 1799 zijn genomen. Om eenen vijand het doen eener landing op de Noord-Hollandse kust te beletten enz.', *De Militaire Spectator* (Breda: Broese & Comp., 1856) pp.256-267, 319-326, 383-392.

Broer Schermer, *Verslag van het voorgevallene te Beverwijk van den 3e tot de 9e October 1799*. Published J. van Venetien e.a., *"Dagverhaal der doormarcheerende troepen" – Beverwijk in de ban van de Fransen (1787-1802)* (Beverwijk: Historisch Genootschap Midden-Kennemerland en Museum Kennemerland, 1999).

Franz Joseph Adolph Schneidawind, *Geschichte des Krieges in Holland im Jahr 1799, zwischen Franzosen und Holländer einer, und Engländer und Russen anderer Seits* (Darmstadt: Carl Wilhelm Lebke, 1845).

C.D.H. Schneider, 'Oorlog in het polderland. Een bijdrage tot de kennis der verdediging van Nederland', *De Gids*, Vol.4 (Amsterdam, P.N. van Kampen & Zoon, 1880) pp. 9-40.

Isaac Schomberg, *Naval Chronology; or, an Historical Summary of Naval & Maritime Events, from the Time of The Romans to the Treaty of Peace 1802* (London: T. Egerton, 1802).

Major B. Smyth, *A History of the Lancashire Fusiliers (Formerly XX Regiment)* (Dublin: The Sackville Press, 1903).

J.W. Staats Evers, *De Geldersche Achterhoek in 1799. Eene bijdrage tot den Patriottentijd* (Winterswijk: K.J.M. van Tiffelen, 1879).

Lieut,-Col. Chas. Steevens, *Reminiscences of my Military Life from 1795 to 1818* (Winchester: Warren & Son, 1878).

Joan Stevens, 'Further Light on the Russians in Jersey', *Annual Bulletin of the Société Jersiaise* (Jersey, Guernsey Press Co. Ltd., 1968) pp. 327-333.

Samuel Story, *Verantwoording van Samuel Story, Wegens zijn Gehouden Gedrag als Commandant van 's Lands Esquader, voor, op, en na den 30. Augustus 1799, Nevens zijne Wederlegging van de op den 16. Januari 1804 tegen hem Uitgesprokene Criminele Sententie* (Amsterdam: Johannes Allart, 1805).

William Surtees, *Twenty-five Years in the Rifle Brigade* (Edinburgh & London: William Blackwood & T. Cadell, 1833).

Robert Keith Sutcliffe, *Bringing Forward Shipping for Government Service: The Indispensable Role of the Transport Service, 1793 to 1815* (Unpublished dissertation, University of Greenwich, 2013).

Jhr. J.W. Van Sypesteijn, 'Iets over den Veldtogt in Noord-Holland, in het jaar 1799', *De Militaire Spectator* (Breda: Broese & Comp., 1855) pp.193-220, 405-408.

Jhr. J.W. van Sypesteijn, *Geschiedenis van het Regiment Hollandsche Hussaren, vroeger Regiment Hussaren van Heeckeren, vervolgens Regiment Bataafsche Hussaren en daarna 2de en 11de Regiment Hussaren* ('s Gravenhage & Amsterdam: Gebroeders van Cleef, 1849).

Jhr. J.W. van Sypesteijn, *Geschiedenis van het Regiment Nederlandsche Rijdende Artillerie* (Zaltbommel: Joh. Noman en Zoon, 1852).

Jhr. J.W. van Sypesteijn, *Het Leven en Karakter van Jean Baptiste Graaf Du Monceau, Oud-Maarschalk van Holland. Uit Oorspronkelijke Bescheiden Beschreven* (s Hertogenbosch: Gebroeders Muller, 1852).

Van Sypesteijn, 'Krijgskundige Beschouwingen over den Veldtogt van 1799 in Noord-Holland', *De Nieuwe Spectator, Krijgs- en Geschiedkundig Tijdschrift voor Neerlands land- en Zeemacht* (Nijmegen: J.F. Thieme, 1853) pp. 311-316, 399-425, 651-680 (1854) pp. 24-36, 65-85, 137-173, 201-222, 409-417, 473-501.

Clara J. Tucker, 'The Russians in the Channel Islands', *Annual Bulletin of the Société Jersiaise* (Jersey, Bigwoods Printers Ltd., 1974) pp. 258-263.

Mr. H.W. Tydeman, *Levensbijzonderheden van den Luitenant-Generaal Baron C.R.T. Krayenhoff; door hem Zelven in Schrift Gesteld, en op zijn Verlangen in het Licht Gegeven* (Nijmegen: C.A. Vieweg, 1844).

Geert van Uythoven, *Voorwaarts, Bataven! De Engels-Russische Invasie van 1799* (Zaltbommel: Europese Bibliotheek, 1999).

L.F. Th. Vogel & J.M.J.H. Lambooy, *Plantenga. Strategie en Krijgsgeschiedenis* (Breda: Militaire Academie, 1910).

L.C. Vonk, *Geschiedenis der Landing van het Engelsch-Russisch Leger in Noord-Holland; Alsmede der Krijgsbedrijven en Politieke Gebeurtenissen, zoo aldaar, als in Vriesland en Gelderland, in den Jare 1799* (Haarlem: François Bohn, 1801).

G.W. Vreede, *Geschiedenis der Diplomatie van de Bataafsche Republiek* (Utrecht: J.G. Broese, 1863-4).

A.J.B. Wace, 'A British officer on active service, 1799', in *The Annual of the British School at Athens* Vol.XXIII (London: MacMillan & Co., Ltd., 1919), pp.126-138.

Wagenaar, *Vaderlandsche Historie, Vervattende de Geschiedenissen der Vereenigde Nederlanden, Zints den Aanvang der Noord-Amerikaansche Onlusten, en den daar uit Gevolgden Oorlogen tusschen Engeland en Deezen Staat, tot den Tegenwoordigen Tijd* (Amsterdam: Johannes Allart, 1808).

E. Walsh, *A Narrative of the Expedition to Holland in the Autumn of the Year 1799* (London: G.G. and J. Robinson, 1800).

John Watkins, *A Biographical Memoir of his Late Royal Highness Frederick, Duke of York and Albany* (London: Henry Fisher, Son, and Co., 1827).

Commandant M.-H. Weil, *Un Agent Inconnu de la Coalition – Le Général de Stamford d'Après sa Correspondance Inédite (1793-1806)* (Paris: Payot & Cie., 1923).

Kolonel A.W.P. Weitzel, *Het Leven van den Ridmeester J.P. Weitzel* (Breda: Broese & Comp., 1871).

Coleman Osborne Williams III, *The Role of the British Navy in the Helder Campaign, 1799* (Unpublished dissertation, UMI, 1985).

A.A. IJske, 'Inval der Oranje-emigranten in Overijssel', *De Navorscher, een middel tot gedachtenwisseling en letterkundig verkeer tusschen allen, die iets weten, iets te vragen hebben, of iets kunnen oplossen* (Amsterdam: Frederik Muller, 1855), pp. 33-35.

Jan Zuurbier e.a., *De Lange Herfst van 1799. De Russisch-Engelse Invasie in Polder en Duin* (Castricum: Stichting Herdenking 1799, 1999).

Periodicals and Magazines

Le Courier de l'Empire, Journal Historique, Politique et Littéraire. Pour l'An de grace 1799 (Munich: François Hübschmann, 1799).

Nouvelles Politiques, publiées à Leyde (Leyden: Abraham Blussé, 1799).

Oeconomische Courant. Ter bevordering van nationale huishoudkunde, nyverheid, koophandel, zeevaart, fabrieken, trafieken, beoefenende konsten, landbouw, en alle andere middelen van bestaan (Amstedam: C. Covens, 1799).

The London Chronicle for the Year 1799, vol. LXXXV

The Naval Chronicle, vols. I, II, and III, (London: Bunney & Gold).

Sylvanus Urban (ed.), *The Gentleman's Magazine: and Historical Chronicle for the Year MDCCXCVIII* (London, John Nichols, 1798).

Parliamentary Proceedings and Decrees

A Collection of State Papers Relative to the War against France. Now carrying on by Great Britain and the Several other European Powers (London: S. Gosnell, 1800).

Articles convenus, pour régler le service, l'administration, l'équipement & la solde de 25000 hommes de Troupes Françaises, qui doivent rester dans les Provinces-Unies, conformément au traité de paix & d'alliance fait entre les deux Républiques (1795).

Besluiten der Eerste Kamer van het Vertegenwoordigend Lichaam des Bataafschen Volks. September 1799 (Den Haag: 's Lands Drukkery, 1799); *October 1799* (Den Haag: 's Lands Drukkery, 1799); *Juli 1801* (Den Haag: 's Lands Drukkery, 1801).

Besluiten van de Tweede Kamer en Decreeten van het Vertegenwoordigend Lichaam des Bataafschen Volks. Augustus 1799 (Den Haag: 's Lands Drukkery, 1799).

Besluiten van het Staats-bewind der Bataafsche Republiek (1802).

Dagverhaal der handelingen van het Vertegenwoordigend Lichaam des Bataafschen volks (De Haage: Swart en Comp., 1799).

Instructie voor de Colonellen der Gewapende Burgermacht, Gearresteerd bij het Uitvoerend Bewind der Bataafsche Republiek, Den 22 Mey 1799 (Den Haag: 's Lands Drukkery, 1799).

Naamlyst der Militaire Officieren, in Dienst van de Bataafsche Republiek (Den Haag: 's Lands Drukkery, 1797).

Proclamatie van het Uitvoerend Bewind der Bataafsche Republiek; Behelzende de Capitulatie, tusschen de Generaals en Chef der Bataafsche en Fransche en der Engelsche en Russische Arméen gesloten; Gearresteerd den 20 October 1799 (Den Haag: 's Lands Drukkery, 1799).

Proclamatie van het Uitvoerend Bewind der Bataafsche Republiek; Betreffende de invoering van het Reglement voor de Gewapende Burgermacht. Den 7. Mey 1799 (Den Haag: 's Lands Drukkery, 1799).

Proclamatie van het Uitvoerend Bewind der Bataafsche Republiek; Tot Aanwerving en Recrutering der Nationale Armée; Gearresteerd den 23 September 1799 (Den Haag: 's Lands Drukkery, 1799).

Publicatie van het Uitvoerend Bewind der Bataafsche Republiek; tegen het verzorgen van mond- of andere behoeften aan den vyand; Gearresteerd den 11 September 1799 (Den Haag: 's Lands Drukkery, 1799).

Publicatie van het Uitvoerend Bewind der Bataafsche Republiek; Uitnodigende tot Vrywillige Wapendienst; Gearresteerd den 25 Augustus 1799 (Den Haag: 's Lands Drukkery, 1799).

Publicatie van het Uitvoerend Bewind der Bataafsche Republiek, wegens het beleid der Justitie in plaatsen, in staat van beleg gesteld (Den Haag: 's Lands Drukkery, 1799).

The Parliamentary History of England, from the Earliest Period to the Year 1803, Vol. XXXIV (December 1798-March 1800) (London: T.C. Hansard, 1819).

The Senator: or, Parliamentary Chronicle. Containing an Impartial Register: Recording, with the utmost Accuracy, the Proceedings and Debates of the Houses of Lords and Commons. Being the Fourth Session in the Eighteenth Parliament of Great Britain: Held in the Year 1799, vol. XXIV (London: W. Stratford, undated).

B.C. Gournay (ed.), *Journal Militaire, Contenant: Tout ce qui est relatif à la Composition et à l'Administration de la Force Publique ; et enfin tout ce qui concerne les Militaires* (Paris: Bureau du Journal Militaire, An VIII).

William Woodfall, *An Impartial Report of the Debates that Occur in the Two Houses of Parliament* (London: T. Chapman, 1800).

Archival Sources

J.S. Bruce, Letter of 11 September 1799 from Bruce to Dumonceau (NA 2.21.056 Collectie 130 Dumonceau, inventarisnummer 2)[Nationaal Archief] online transcript available at: http://home.planet.nl/~awaan/html/bruce_aan_dumonceau_17_september_1799.html, accessed 30 June 2018.

N.L. Hoevenaar, *Militair dagboek van kolonel N.L. Hoevenaar, geb. 22 mei 1772, lopende over de veldtochten in Frankrijk, Brabant, Oostenrijk, Pruysche, Zweeds Pommeren, Spanje en Holland tot aan het Franse Keizerrijk* (NIMH, Handschriften, 511, inv.61) [Nederlands Instituut voor Militaire Historie]

G.J. Honig, *Dagboek van G.J. Honig* (GA Zaanstad, PA Honig koffer 10, doos 3, no.2) [Gemeentearchief Zaanstad]

Albert Kaan Kz., *Journaal van 1799* (NL-WpDStvA-C1746; NL-WpDStvA-C2423) [Documentatiecentrum Stelling van Amsterdam].

A.F. Meyer, *Dagboek van den luitenant-generaal jonkheer Adriaan Frans Meyer, geboren 1768* (NIMH, Handschriften, 511, inv.58)[Nederlands Instituut voor Militaire Historie]

Municipaliteit van Akersloot, *Voor de Nakomelingschap*, 9 Oktober 1799.[written report, origin unknown. Photocopy in possession of the author. Transcription in *De Groene Valck* (Vereniging "Oud-Akersloot", 1985) pp.6-8]

Index

INDEX OF PERSONS

Abbema, *Lieutenant Colonel* Johan Carel 39, 343
Abercromby, Lieutenant General Sir Ralph iii, 70-72, 74-75, 77-79, 80, 110, 119, 120-123, 125-126, 131, 134, 139-140, 143-145, 152-155, 164, 166-167, 175, 180, 187-188, 194-195, 203-204, 207, 209-210, 217, 240-241, 244-245, 247-250, 270-274, 279, 281-283, 285-286, 289, 292, 294, 298-299, 310, 314, 317-319, 323-326, 335, 338, 358, 371, 384, 396, 402, 408, 419-420, 424
Aberson, *Eerste Lieutenant* Willem Diederik 38
Achenbach, *Majoor* Bernard Philip 306, 308, 312, 330
Aller, Joost Jacob van 76, 110-111
Ampt, *Colonel* Carel George 50
Anderson, Captain James 182, 286
Anguerand, *Capitein* Nicolaas François d' 136, 182, 184, 389, 393
Anthing, *Lieutenant Colonel* Carl Heinrich Wilhelm 106, 190, 237-238
Arbénev, Major General Ivan Iosifovich 67, 219, 226, 229, 246, 251, 271-272, 303, 353, 355, 381, 398, 400, 409-410
Arensma, *Capitein* Johan Willem 238
Arentz, *Eerste Lieutenant* Georg Fredrik 137
Arnaud, *Chef de Brigade* Antoine 387
Atkins, Lieutenant John Wyat 379, 406
Atkinson, Lieutenant Thomas 380, 406
Atkinson, Lieutenant Colonel William 384
Aubrée, *Chef de Bataillon* Alexandre Charles Joseph 313
Aubrée, *Général de Brigade* René François Jean 190, 192, 219, 221, 256, 274, 279, 283, 313-315, 386, 395, 403, 412
Auckland, William Eden, 1st Baron 19
Ayscough, Captain John 260-261

Bainbridge, Lieutenant Colonel Philip 317, 408
Baklanowski, Lieutenant Colonel Mikhail Alekseevich 217, 354, 400
Bamber, Lieutenant William Richard 380, 407
Barbou d'Escourières, *Général de Brigade* Gabriel 180, 276, 278, 282, 309, 386
Bardet, *Chef de Brigade* Martial 224, 242
Barnett, Colonel Charles 384, 396, 410
Barreté, Lieutenant H.W. 380, 407
Baylis, Lieutenant Colonel John 396, 408
Bazely, Captain John 150
Beekman, *Lieutenant* D. 394
Beer Poortugael, *Capitein* Jacobus Catharinus Cornelis den 46, 248, 256
Bentinck, Count Charles 31, 33, 175
Bentinck, *Generaal-Major* Jean Charles 211, 265, 319
Bentinck tot Buckhorst, *Colonel* Berend Hendrik 175, 269, 319
Bernadotte, *Général de Division* Jean Baptiste Jules de 178-179
Berniere, Lieutenant Colonel Henry de 397
Bertie, Captain Thomas 106, 150
Birchall, Captain William 382
Blanchard, *Commissaire Ordonnateur en Chef* Edóuard Henri 110
Bligh, Captain William 106
Bock, *Capitein* David
Boecop, *Generaal-Major* Laurens Theodorus Johannes van 75, 107
Bolton, Commander William 207-208, 261
Bommers, Pastor Nicolaas 326
Bonaparte, Louis 176
Bonaparte, Napoleon 23-25, 370-371, 433

Bonhomme, *Generaal-Major* Henri Damasius 39, 107, 180, 182-185, 189, 233, 239, 276, 285, 290, 294, 296, 307, 310, 312, 316, 330, 394, 404
Boonacker, *Colonel* Adrianus 159
Boorder, Captain James 90-92, 95, 97, 96, 259, 262-264, 407

Boudet, *Général de Division* Jean 52, 279, 294, 302-303
Bourdeaux, Pierre Etienne 28, 102, 112
Bover, Commander Peter Turner 343, 380, 407
Braam, *Capitein* Aegidius van 125-127, 148-149, 163, 167, 366, 368-369, 388
Braam, *Capitein-Lieutenant* Frans Thomas van 368
Braam, *Vice-Admiraal* Jacob Pieter van 167
Brereton, Lieutenant Colonel Robert 397, 408
Breyer, Rear Admiral Karl Magnus (Evstafevič) von 81-82, 350
Brock, Lieutenant Colonel Isaac 283-284, 385, 397, 408
Broers, *Lieutenant* Pieter Rutger 94
Broman, *Major* Charles Frederik 323
Broux, *Colonel* Eduard 390, 393
Browne, Lieutenant Colonel Gore 397
Brownrigg, Major General Robert 126, 325, 338
Bruce, *Colonel* Stuart John 38, 185, 189-190, 232, 285, 330, 394, 405
Bruce, *Major* David 38, 137, 224, 233, 242, 394
Brune, *Général de Division* Guillaume Marie Anne viii, 24, 36, 40-41, 43, 46, 49, 52, 81, 88, 102-103, 107-109, 111, 113, 125, 129, 138, 155-160, 178-180, 184, 191-192, 195-201, 219, 224, 226, 230, 233, 235, 239-240, 243-244, 246, 250, 252, 256, 258, 276, 279, 281, 285, 290-294, 296-297, 301-302, 306-308, 310, 312-313, 316-317, 322, 328, 336-340, 344, 355, 358-359, 361, 386, 403, 411-412, 421-424
Buckle, Lieutenant Mathew 345
Bulteel, Captain Rowley 150
Burdon, Captain George 382
Burmania, *Colonel* Frans Laes van 418
Burrard, Major General Sir Harry 77, 132, 140, 143, 191, 194, 244, 271-272, 276, 278, 298-299, 301-302, 318, 384, 396, 401, 410
Bybel, *Lieutenant ter Zee* David 90, 94

Cameron, Colonel Alan 290
Cammartin, *Capitein* A.237
Campbell, Lieutenant Lord John 190
Campbell, Commander Patrick 344-345, 379, 407
Cantagrelle, *Chef de Brigade* Claude Gabriel 113
Capellen, *Capitein ter Zee* Theodorus Frederik van 87, 121-122, 125-127, 148-149
Carlton, Lieutenant William 380, 407
Carteret, *Lieutenant-Colonel* Antoine Benedict 225, 233, 307
Carthew, Commander James 379, 406
Castagnier, *Chef de Division* Jean Joseph 51
Cate, *Lieutenant-Colonel* Maximiliaan Theodorus ten 118, 138

Cavan, Major General Richard Ford William Lambart, Earl of 62, 145, 217, 270, 318, 397, 402, 408
Chanykov, Rear Admiral Pëtr Ivanovic 25, 81-82
Charpignon, *Chef de Bataillon* 113
Chassé, *Lieutenant-Colonel* David Hendrik 389, 393
Chatham, Major General Sir John Pitt, 2nd Earl of 62, 64, 74, 81, 153, 217, 271, 276, 278-279, 281-282, 299, 310, 312-313, 317-318, 326, 397, 402, 410, 427
Chichagov, Rear Admiral Pavel Vasilievich 82, 349, 381, 383
Childers, Lieutenant Colonel John Walbanke 397, 349
Cholmondeley, Lieutenant Colonel Thomas 317, 397, 410
Clark, *Adjudant-Major* Daniel Clark 38
Clayton, Commander Thomas Whitwronge 407
Clephane, Lieutenant Colonel David 301
Cobb, Captain Charles 86, 150, 154, 367, 391-392
Colborne, Lieutenant John 145, 160, 187-188, 288
Collaert, *Lieutenant-Colonel* Jean Marie Antoine Philippe de 185, 329-330, 335
Collier, Lieutenant George Ralph 121, 127, 150, 154
Connio, *Capitein-Lieutenant* Nicolaï 207, 209
Coote, Major General Sir Eyre 61-62, 75, 77, 132-136, 140, 214, 217, 238-240, 271, 274, 276, 279-281, 290, 299, 302, 310, 313, 318, 338, 373, 384, 396, 401, 410
Cordes, *Capitein* Hendrik Frederik 285, 313-314, 394
Cornelisse, *Capitein* Jacobus 146-147
Crass, *Colonel* Christiaan Louis 131, 136-137, 139, 183, 239, 389, 393, 404
Crause de Frens, *Colonel* Johan Willem Theodoor Philip 175
Craven, Captain Charles 382
Crewe, Lieutenant Colonel John 397
Culverhouse, Captain John 382
Curry, Commander Richard 379, 406

Daendels, *Lieutenant-Generaal* Herman Willem iii, vii, 13, 15, 21, 32-33, 36-37, 40-41, 88-89, 98, 105-109, 111, 113-114, 118, 125, 128-131, 134-138, 142-143, 145, 154-158, 160, 180, 182-185, 189, 194-199, 201-202, 214, 217, 238-242, 246, 272-273, 285, 289-290, 292, 296, 298, 316, 322, 330-331, 333-335, 338, 365, 389, 393, 404, 423, 426
Daniel, Captain William Henry 270, 409
Dardenne, *Général de Brigade* Charles Ambroise 39-40, 46, 49-51, 75-76, 103, 108, 193, 195, 198-200, 256, 386, 403, 412

David, *Général de Brigade* Jean Antoine 52, 192-193, 195
Davies, Lieutenant Peter 380, 406
Dawson, Captain John 76, 357, 382
Dazémar, *Adjudant-Général Chef de Brigade* Jean Jacques 48, 52, 277, 279, 359, 412
Desjardin, *Général de Division* Jacques Jardin dit 359, 387, 413
Detmers, *Major* Hendrik 414
Dick, Commander John 380
Dickson, Vice Admiral Archibald 87, 97, 106, 344
Dickson, Captain Archibald Collingwood 150, 391-392
Dickson, Lieutenant Colonel William 317, 397, 410
Dobree, Captain Daniel 382
Don, Major General George 62, 68, 140, 144-145, 153, 160, 178, 214, 217, 238-239, 272, 291, 299, 322, 351, 397-399, 401, 410, 425
Dongen, *Colonel* Anthoon Bernard Coenraad van 166-168, 416-417
Dopff, *Lieutenant-Colonel* Jean François Baron van 414
Dorth tot Holthuizen, freule Johanna Magdalena Catharina Judith van 162, 171-174, 176
Douglas, *Major* A. 414
Dowsing, Lieutenant Jackson 380
Dreyer, Captain 68, 398-399
Droop, *Eerste Lieutenant* Jan Joost 87
Dubiansky, *Colonel* Alexander Jakoblewitsch 83, 218, 243, 247, 299, 303, 306, 308-309, 317
Dumonceau, *Lieutenant-Generaal* Jean Baptiste 16, 36-37, 39, 41, 43, 75, 88, 90, 107-108, 111, 113-114, 121, 125, 159-160, 180, 183-185, 187-188, 190, 192-193, 195-196, 199, 218, 232-233, 239, 242, 246, 276, 285, 291, 329-330, 334-335, 338, 394, 404, 431
Duncan, Admiral Adam iii, 23, 25, 33, 63-65, 74, 86-87, 90, 92, 96, 101, 119, 121-122, 125, 131, 149, 288, 391, 424
Dundas, Captain George 259, 391-392, 406
Dundas, Henry 38, 60, 71-72, 75, 78, 120, 126-127, 139, 153, 164, 194, 204-205, 207, 214, 217, 232, 237, 244, 248-251, 259, 271, 281, 291, 318-319, 323-325, 335, 338, 340, 347, 397, 401, 410, 419-420
Dundas, Lieutenant General Sir David 205, 214, 232, 237, 271, 281, 397, 401, 410
Dunne, *Capitein* Johan Franc van 91
Durnov, Captain 68, 398
Durutte, *Général de Brigade* Pierre François Joseph 103, 180, 239
Dusseau, *Capitein-Lieutenant* Charles 92

Egenberger, *Capitein* Ludovicus Constance 199
Eilbracht, *Capitein* Jan Florens 388
Eilbracht, *Lieutenant ter Zee* Johan Philip 92, 344
Emmé, Major General Ivan Fedorovich 67, 251-252, 271, 291, 306-307, 353-354, 382, 398, 409
Enys, Lieutenant Colonel John 384, 396, 410
Erskine, Lieutenant Colonel James 290, 409
Esch, *Capitein-Lieutenant* Anthony van 207-209
Essen I, Major General Ivan Nikolayevich Magnus Gustav 82, 205, 213, 219, 224, 226, 229, 233, 243, 245-246, 250, 271, 273-274, 276, 278, 281, 291, 299, 303, 310, 313, 317-319, 350, 353-355, 361, 398, 400, 409
Everts, *Lieutenant* Everard 233

Fagel, *Lieutenant ter Zee* François Willem 210
Fagel, Hendrik 71, 243
Fagel, Jacob 175
Fagel, Robert 267
Farrington, Major General Anthony 269
Faure, *Lieutenant-Colonel* Librecht Alexander 242, 404
Faure, *Chef de Brigade* Jean Baptiste 387
Favauge, *Capitein* Clemens Alexander 137
Ferris, Captain Solomon 382-383
Finch, Colonel Edward 384, 396, 410
Finlay, Major John 145-146
Florent-Guiot, Guiot de Saint-Florent dit 200-201, 250, 362
Fowke, Captain George 379
Frederiks, *Capitein-Lieutenant* Luytje 92
Friedrich Wilhelm III 14-16, 26, 28-29, 80, 174
Fuzier, *Général de Brigade* Louis 52, 294, 296

Gardner, Admiral Alan 106, 369
Geen, *Capitein* Jozef Jacobus van 137-138, 233
Gelderman, *Colonel* Jan 39, 152, 264
Gilquin, *Colonel* Herman Jan 122, 125-126, 135, 137-138, 147, 242, 313, 389, 394, 404
Ginkel, *Lieutenant ter Zee* Jan van 91-94
Girault, Claude Joseph 46
Girod, *Général de Brigade* Victor Bonaventure, de Vienney 52, 172-173
Gladkov, Colonel Ivan Vasilievich 317, 351
Glebhoff, Captain Peter 84, 373
Gloucester, Major General HRH Prince William of 62, 169, 214, 233-234, 244, 259, 272, 298-299, 330-331, 333, 341, 397, 401, 407, 410
Godard, *Chef de Brigade* Jean Baptiste 309, 404
Goes van Dirxland, Maarten van der 28-29, 31, 102-103, 112
Golenishchev-Kutuzov, General Mikhail Illarionovich 355
Goudakker, *Capitein-Lieutenant* 90, 94
Goudoever, *Capitein* Hendrik van 199

INDEX   435

Gouvion, *Général de Division* Louis Jean Baptiste 75-76, 155, 158, 190-191, 219, 224-226, 229, 256, 274, 278-279, 290, 294, 296, 303, 310, 314-316, 359, 386, 403, 412
Graaf, *Major* Lodewijk Ernst van de 416, 418
Grabner, *Capitein* Johann Jacob 393
Graham, Lieutenant Colonel Samuel 132, 134, 136, 141, 384
Grant, Commander Charles 90
Greig, Captain Aleksey Samuilovich 391-392
Grenville, William Wyndham 1st Baron 19, 26, 35, 71, 81, 105, 122
Grenville, Thomas 28-29
Grevnitz, Captain 391
Grillot, *Chef de Brigade* Remy 290, 403
Gross, *Lieutenant-Colonel* Albrecht David Gabriel Baron von 265-266
Grutten, *Tweede Lieutenant* Pieter van 261, 263
Guèricke, *Generaal-Major* David van 113, 121, 131, 135, 137-138, 156, 201, 389

Haer, Bonifacius van der 176
Halkett, Captain Peter 86
Hall, Captain John 106
Hamilton, Captain Sir Charles 259
Hardy, Captain James 382
Hart, Captain George 150
Hasselt, *Lieutenant-Colonel* Johan Conrad van 394
Hatry, *Général de Division* Jacques Maurice 24
Haugwitz, Christian August Heinrich Curt von 28-29
Hay, Lieutenant Colonel Lewis 64, 136, 141, 384
Heeckeren van Suideras, August Robert van 170-171
Heemskerck van Beest, *Lieutenant-Colonel* Willem Sybrand van 168
Heerdt tot Eversberg, Timon Cornelis Baron van 300
Heilman, *Capitein* Louis Joseph van 136
Hely-Hutchinson, Major General John 287, 317, 408
Herbig, *Lieutenant-Colonel* Johan George 129, 134, 141
Hermann von Fersen, Lieutenant General Ivan Ivanowitch ii, vi, 67, 81-83, 204, 213, 217, 221, 223-224, 229-230, 243-246, 248-251, 271, 353, 361, 398, 400, 425
Hespe, *Capitein* Johannes Christiaan 393
Hessberg, *Major* P.A. Baron von 416-417
Hessen-Darmstadt, *Lieutenant-Generaal* Christiaan Lodewijk Prince van 152, 167
Heydte, *Lieutenant-Colonel* Wilhelm von 417
Hill, Lieutenant J.T.H. 342
Hinnisdal, *Général de Brigade* Louis Maximilien François Herman, de Fumal, d' 52, 412

Hodgson, Lieutenant Colonel John 317, 397, 410
Hoevenaar, *Eerste Lieutenant* Nicolaas Ludolph 182
Hogart, Lieutenant 342
Hooff, Joannes Franciscus Rudolphus van 31, 156
Hoop, *Major* Adriaan van der 211, 266
Hope, Lieutenant Colonel Alexander 384
Hope, Lieutenant Colonel John 141, 384
Hope, Captain William Johnstone 391
Hulse, Lieutenant General Samuel 323, 420
Humphreys, Lieutenant Salusbury Pryce 94
Huntly, Colonel George Duncan Gordon, 8th Marquis of 140, 286
Huys, *Capitein* Johan Nicolaas 388

Inglis, Captain John 106

Janssens, Jan Willem 47-48, 50-51, 103
Jaussaud de Vedelen, *Lieutenant-Colonel* Jean Marc Antoine 394
Johnson, Ambassador 110-112
Jones, Lieutenant Colonel Love Parry 384, 369, 410
Joubert, *Général de Division* Barthélemy Catherine 98
Jourdan, *Général de Division* Jean Baptiste 21, 24, 156, 424
Joyce, Lieutenant John 380, 406
Judgson, Major Thomas 288, 397, 409

Kamps, *Capitein* Franciscus Ludovicus Hubertus 45
Kaps, *Capitein* Wolter van 88
Kaptsevich, Major General Petr Mikhailovich 351, 353
Keiser, *Eerste Lieutenant* F.A. 39
Kellermann, *Général de Division* Francois Etienne Christophe 179
Kerkhofs, *Eerste Lieutenant* Servaas 91
Kilkardy, Lieutenant A. 90, 345
King, Captain Richard 85
Kniest, former *Eerste Lieutenant* J.H. 169
Knox, Major General John 62, 84, 217, 271, 290, 299, 310, 339-340, 396, 402, 424
Kolff, *Capitein* Dirk Hendrik 125, 149, 388, 396
Kosliotsov, Captain 391
Kotschoubey, Victor Pavlovitch, Count 374, 377-378
Krayenhoff, *Lieutenant-Colonel* Cornelis Rudolphus Theodorus 87, 125-126, 132, 138-139, 141, 143, 147, 149, 156-157, 160, 190, 201-202, 293-294, 334, 361, 365-366, 386, 426, 428

Lake, Major General Gerard 20
Lambrechts, *Lieutenant-Colonel* Jan Baptist 242
Larmour, Captain John 382

Laroche-Dubouscat, *Général de Brigade* Antoine 49
Lawford, Captain John 150, 261, 344, 347, 379, 392
Leavy, Lieutenant S.P. 380, 407
Lejeune, *Adjutant-Général* Louis François 113
Livingston, Captain Thomas 382
Lochteren Stakebrand, *Colonel* Johan Wilhelm Anthonius Jacobus van 46
Lombard de Langres, Vincent 33, 99-102, 426
Lucas, Lieutenant John 379, 406
Luck, *Lieutenant-Colonel* George Willem 134, 138, 141
Lumsdaine, Lieutenant-Colonel James 385, 396, 408
Lumsden, Major William 282, 384, 397, 408
Lyal, Lieutenant William 380, 406
Lyclama à Nijeholt, *Lieutenant-Colonel* Albertus 141, 404
Lynden van Hoevelaken, Jan Carel Elias van 166

MacAlister, Major Archibald 397
MacDonald, Colonel Donald 62, 77, 132, 135, 140-141, 192, 217, 252, 270, 274, 282-283, 299, 310, 314-315, 318, 384, 397, 402, 408
M'Doual, Captain Robert 106, 391
McKinley, Commander George 379, 406
McMurdo, Lieutenant Colonel Charles 410
Mackenzie, Commander Adam 90, 92, 95, 392
Mainwaring, Captain Jemmet 259, 379, 392, 406
Maison, *Adjutant-Général Chef de Brigade* Nicolas Joseph 276, 278, 290
Maitland, Colonel Augustus 317, 384, 396, 408
Maitland, Lieutenant Colonel Frederic 121-122, 126-127, 140
Makarov, Rear Admiral Michail Kontratevič 25-26, 391
Malbon, Commander Micajah 379
Malher, *Général de Brigade* Jean Pierre Firmin 113, 172
Manners, Major General Robert 62, 204, 213-214, 219, 223-224, 233, 244, 272, 351-352, 397, 401, 410
Manningham, Colonel Coote 373
Maren, *Lieutenant ter Zee* Antonij van 94
Martinius, *Lieutenant ter Zee* Dithmar Bernardus 74, 153, 265, 342
Martuschewitz, *Lieutenant-Colonel* George Alexander 233, 237, 395
Mascheck, *Colonel* Charles 390, 394
Massabeau, *Chef de Bataillon* Jean Baptiste Vincent 50, 113
Menzies, Lieutenant Duncan 379, 406
Mercier, *Chef de Brigade* Jean Claude 287, 290, 386
Meurs, *Capitein* A.M. van 269, 414
Meyer, *Major* Adriaan Frederik 330

Mitchell, Vice Admiral Andrew iii, 55, 74, 78, 106, 119-121, 139, 144, 147-154, 187, 195, 203, 207, 210, 258-261, 264-265, 334, 344-346, 367-368, 371, 379, 422
Mollem Bruyn, *Lieutenant-Colonel* David van 414
Moller, Captain Anton Vassilievitch 150
Montanus, *Lieutenant-Colonel* Anthonius 394
Mortimer, Captain John 382
Moore, Major General John 61, 63, 67, 70, 75, 79, 119, 131-133, 140-141, 143, 178, 182, 185, 194, 244, 273, 290, 385, 396, 402, 408
Morlot, *Général de Division* Antoine 52, 359
Mosse, Captain James Robert 106
Murray, Lieutenant Colonel John 141
Muysken, *Capitein* Nicolaas Jacob 394

Nahuys, *Lieutenant* F.W. 394
Nash, Commander John 379
Neller, *Capitaine* 219, 395
Nicolson, *Lieutenant-Colonel* James 38, 240, 301
Nierop, *Capitein* Meindert van 86
Noblet, *Capitein* S.C. 166
Nooy, *Eerste Lieutenant ter Zee* Jan 92

Olivier, *Colonel* Jean Baptiste Joseph l' 394
Orange, Stadtholder Willem V, Prince of 9, 12-15, 17-19, 33-34, 121-125, 127, 147, 150-154, 163, 209, 211, 262, 368-370
Orange, Willem Frederik, Hereditary Prince of 18, 74, 102, 107, 112, 124, 144, 151-154, 163-168, 171, 174-176, 194, 204, 207, 210-211, 214, 241, 243, 259, 265-267, 269, 300-301, 319-320, 347-348, 369-370
Osten, *Général de Brigade* Pierre Jacques 103, 108
Oswald, Lieutenant Colonel John 243, 397
Oughton, Captain James 150, 259
Oyly, Major General Francis d' 77, 132, 140, 299, 318, 384, 396, 401, 408

Pacque, *Lieutenant-Colonel* Johan Anthony 264
Pacthod, *Général de Brigade* Michel Marie 52, 296, 302-303, 306, 308-309, 313
Paddon, Captain George 147
Paget, Colonel Lord Henry William 287, 397, 401, 409
Panhuys, *Lieutenant-Colonel* Willem Benjamin van 152, 210-211, 348
Panin, Nikita Petrovich Count 28-29
Paradis, *Général de Brigade* Joseph 387, 395, 412
Paschen, Willem 171, 173-174, 422, 427
Pater, Captain Charles Dudley 379, 392
Paul I 25, 27, 30, 34-35, 66, 67, 70-71, 81-82, 163, 245-246, 270, 319, 353, 355, 357, 361, 374-378
Peake, Lieutenant William 380, 406
Pecheloche, *Chef de Bataillon* Nicolas Amand 113

Petit, *Major* L.F. de 416-418
Pijman, Gerrit Jan 28, 50, 88, 99, 107-109, 121, 125, 156, 199, 292, 427
Pitcairn, *Lieutenant-Colonel* Charles 393
Pitcairn, *Lieutenant-Colonel* Joseph 390, 394
Pitt, William 17, 56, 60, 75, 313, 424, 427
Plettenberg, *Colonel* Lodewijk Baron van 417-418
Pletz, *Capitein-Lieutenant* Barthelomeus 86
Pool, *Capitein-Lieutenant* Scipio Oudkerk 90, 345
Popham, Captain Sir Home Riggs 34-35, 82, 110, 214, 272, 276, 302, 347, 383
Portlock, Commander Nathaniel 207, 346
Powlett, Captain Henry 288
Praed, Lieutenant Bulkeley Macworth 85
Pressland, Captain Thomas 382
Prévost, *Général de Brigade* Pierre Dominique 172, 359, 386
Prey, *Capitein-Lieutenant* Johannes Zacharias 90
Pulteney, Lieutenant General Sir James Murray 131-132, 135-136, 140-141, 178, 214, 217, 233, 238-240, 244-246, 258, 272-273, 276, 278, 289, 292, 298-299, 316, 318, 323, 342-344, 384, 397, 401, 410, 419-420

Quaita, *Colonel* Maria Aloisius Barnabas Franciscus de 288, 298, 312, 394
Queysen, *Colonel* Philip Hendrik 264

Ragget, Captain Richard 392
Rappard, Willem Hendrik Karel von 368
Rechteren Limpurg, *Colonel* Frederik Lodewijk Christiaan Graaf van 266, 348, 414
Reddy, Lieutenant James 379, 407
Reinhold, Johan Godard 28
Rennie, Captain James 149, 392
Reubell, *Général de Division* Henri Thomas 52, 359, 386, 412
Reynolds, Captain Robert Carthew 326
Rietveld, *Schout bij Nacht* Hendrik 166
Rietvelt, *Colonel* Jacobus Gysbertus 38, 156, 390, 393, 404
Rij, Laurens van 105
Rittner, Abraham 113
Rivaud, *Général de Brigade* Jean 359, 387, 413
Rivery, *Capitein* Johan 87
Robins, Lieutenant Thomas Lowton 379, 406
Rodenburgh, *Capitein* Cornelius de Jong van 125-127, 148-149, 388
Römer, *Capitein* T.C.E. van 393
Ross, Lieutenant Colonel John 194
Rostollant, *Général de Brigade* Claude 191, 217-219, 224, 226, 229, 232, 235, 256, 279, 291-292, 339, 355, 403, 412
Rouget, *Lieutenant-Colonel* Claude Pierre 393

Roussel, *Majoor* Charles 393
Ry, *Colonel* Gerard du 389, 394
Ryder, Lieutenant Charles 382

Saint-Julien, *Général de Brigade* Jean Louis, Bancal de 199, 386, 403
Saint-Martin, *Général de Brigade* Nicolas Louis, Guériot de 279
Sandick, *Lieutenant-Colonel* Onno Zwier van 141, 389, 394
Saville, Captain John Griffin 382
Schack, *Eerste Lieutenant* Dirk Willem van 89
Schickhardt, *Lieutenant-Colonel* Jan Alexander 170-171
Schimmelpenninck van der Oye, Assuer Jacob 175
Schinne, *Lieutenant-Colonel* Abraham van 414
Schober, *Capitein-Adjoint* Christian Heinrich 137
Schoonman, *Colonel* Derk 169-170
Schummelketel, *Lieutenant* Abraham 269, 414
Schuller, *Major* C. 416
Schutter, *Capitein* Jacob Diederik 87, 388, 414
Schwartz, *Lieutenant-Colonel* Christoffer Bernard Julius von 348
Searle, Lieutenant Thomas 86-87, 92, 95
Sedmoratzki, Major General Aleksandr Karlovich 67, 214, 232-233, 244, 246, 271, 276, 278, 298-299, 302-303, 308, 318, 353-354, 357, 381, 398, 401, 409
Sels, *Lieutenant-Colonel* Adriaan 242
Senden, *Capitein* Wouter Hendrik van 149, 388
Seroux, *Général de Brigade* Jean Nicolas 386, 403
Shairpe, Lieutenant Colonel Gideon 396, 408
Short, Lieutenant John Ides 97, 380
Simon, *Général de Brigade* Edouard François 52, 232, 234, 274, 276, 282, 314-316
Simpson, Lieutenant John 262, 380
Skynner, Captain Lancelot 346, 392
Slade, Commander James 95
Sleigh, Captain James Wallace 312, 410
Smith, Captain John 106
Smith, Lieutenant Colonel John 182
Smollet, Lieutenant Colonel Alexander Telfer 141
Smyth, Lieutenant Colonel George 194
Sontag, Lieutenant Colonel John 74, 269, 348
Sotheron, Captain Frank 86, 94, 391-392
Soullain, *Chef de Bataillon* M. 113
Sparke, Commander Thomas 379, 406
Spencer, Colonel Brent 182, 239, 397
Spengler, *Lieutenant-Colonel* Johannes Gerardus 265
Spengler, *Lieutenant ter Zee* Willem August van 153, 168-169, 265, 366, 368
Spiegel, Laurens Pieter van 319-320
Spies, *Eerste Lieutenant* Johannes Nicolaas 330
Spoors, Jacobus 31, 33, 88, 91, 105-106, 111, 120-121, 147, 149

Stamford, Henry Guillaume de 102, 112
Steevens, Lieutenant Charles 59, 321, 328
Step, *Lieutenant-Colonel* Nicolaas Jacobus 38, 390, 393
Stephenson, Lieutenant Colonel Charles 243, 397
Sterke, *Ritmeester* Nicolaas 241
Stewart, Lieutenant Colonel Charles William Vane 330, 333, 341, 385, 397, 410
Stewart, Lieutenant Colonel William 373
Storm de Grave, *Major* Adriaan Willem 240
Story, *Schout-bij-Nacht* Samuel 47, 78, 88, 120-122, 125-127, 138, 147-153, 174, 179, 298, 338, 367, 369, 425, 428, 434
Stovin, Lieutenant Colonel Richard 397
Straube, *Onder-Lieutenant* Pieter Josephus 184, 238
Suckling, Lieutenant Maurice William 380, 406
Surtees, Private William 205-206, 241, 274-275, 278, 280-281, 315, 428
Suthoff, Major General Ivan Efimovich 67, 217-219, 243, 246, 302, 355, 381-382, 398, 400-401, 408-409
Suvorov, Field Marshal Aleksandr Vasilevich 24, 27, 35, 249, 253-254, 350, 353

Talbot, Lieutenant Colonel Richard Wogan 384, 397, 408
Talbot, Lieutenant Colonel Thomas 331, 397
Talleyrand-Périgord, Charles Maurice de 98, 102, 200-201
Tate, Rear Admiral George 26, 106
Temple, Commander John 90
Thomson, *Capitein* Robert 38, 241
Till, *Lieutenant-Colonel* Gerhard Cazyn van 38, 390, 393
Tilly, *Général de Division* Jacques Louis François Delaistre, comte de 52, 179
Tinling, Lieutenant Colonel David Latimer 397
Tokely, Lieutenant Joseph 380, 406
Trip, *Lieutenant-Colonel* Scato Hendrik Burs 224, 233
Tripp, Captain George 347
Tulleken, *Major* Daniel 189, 394
Tulleken, *Capitein ter Zee* Jan 368
Tuyll van Serooskerken, *Ritmeester* Diederik Jacob van 175
Tuyll van Serooskerken, *Lieutenant* Willem Reinout van 269
Twent, *Lieutenant ter Zee* Anthony Cornelis 147, 265
Twiss, Lieutenant Colonel William 141

Ushakov, Rear Admiral Fyodor Fiodorovich 24-26
Uslar, *Lieutenant-Colonel* Willem van 393

Vandamme, *Général de Division* Dominique Joseph René 52, 158, 160, 180, 190-193, 200, 213, 219, 224, 226, 229, 276, 279, 285, 287-288, 290-292, 294, 306, 308, 313, 359, 395, 403, 423

Varé, *Chef de Brigade* Louis Prix 48, 217-218, 233, 278, 386, 395
Vedelen, *Lieutenant-Colonel* Jean Marc Antoine Jaussaud de 394
Verhorst, *Lieutenant-Colonel* Justinus 122, 137, 228, 231-233, 389, 394
Ver Huell, *Captain-Lieutenant ter Zee* Carel Hendrik 163
Verwoert, *Lieutenant* H.J. 269
Veye, *Capitein-Ingenieur* C.L. de 300
Vichery, *Lieutenant-Colonel* Louis Joseph 185, 394
Villantrois, *Chef d'Escadron* 113
Villers, *Capitein* L.R.J. 393
Virieu, *Capitein* W.C. de 414
Visscher, *Adjudant-Major* Teunis Kragt 137, 237
Vognitz, *Capitein* Johan Godefroy 168
Vorontsov, Semyon Romanovich 353-354, 357-358, 361
Voss, *Capitein-Lieutenant* Willem van 265

Waldeck, *Capitein-Lieutenant* Johan Hendrik 388
Walker, Captain James 288
Walsh, Lieutenant John 342
Westerholt, *Capitein-Lieutenant* Alexander Jan Augustus 345
Whitworth, Lieutenant Colonel Francis 384, 409
Whitworth, Sir Charles 26, 35, 71, 374, 377-378
Wiele, *Capitein* Pieter van der 137
Winter, *Vice-Admiraal* Jan Willem de 23, 37, 44, 47
Winthrop, Captain Robert 74, 90, 94, 121-122, 127, 143-144, 345, 379
Worsley, Captain Richard 382
Wright, Lieutenant Colonel Henry Addison 385, 397, 408
Wright, Lieutenant John 407
Wyck, *Major* Jan van der 137
Wynyard, Colonel Henry 243, 384, 396, 408

York and Albany, Field Marshal HRH Prince Frederick August, Duke of iv, 19-20, 25, 56, 58-60, 63, 70, 75, 78, 80-81, 175-176, 203-204, 207, 211-214, 217, 232-233, 242, 244-246, 248-251, 259, 264-267, 269-270, 272-273, 279, 281, 286, 290-291, 293, 298-301, 317-320, 322-326, 335-341, 345, 347-348, 353-355, 373, 396, 400, 408, 419, 422-423, 426, 429
Ysbrands, *Lieutenant ter Zee* John 84
Yvoy, Maximiliaan Louis van Hangest Baron d' 175, 319, 417

Zeebis, *Lieutenant-Colonel* Johannes 389, 394
Zherebtsov, Lieutenant General Petr Nikolaevich 67, 83, 204, 214, 221, 224, 229, 243, 398
Zuylen van Nyevelt, *Generaal-Major* Philip Julius van 89, 131, 136, 239, 322, 334, 390

GENERAL INDEX

Aachen 39
Aalten 171-172, 426
Aartswoude vi, 217, 240, 330, 332
Akersloot 296, 301-302, 306, 313-314, 316-319, 363, 365, 431
Alkmaar iii, vii, 40, 45, 113-114, 116, 125, 131, 155-158, 160, 180, 185, 189-190, 192, 194-200, 203, 214, 217, 223-226, 229, 232-234, 237, 243-244, 247, 250, 252, 256, 258, 265, 269-272, 276-279, 291, 298-302, 318-319, 322, 327, 329, 335-336, 338-340, 348, 353, 358, 362, 382, 390, 394-395, 403-405, 421
Altona 81
Ameland 70-71, 90, 92-94, 111, 159, 342, 366, 424
Amersfoort 13, 158
Amiens, Peace of 322, 369-370
Amsterdam 10, 14, 18, 21, 30-32, 54, 90-92, 100-101, 114, 116, 125, 156, 158-160, 168, 173, 191, 200-203, 252-253, 258, 260, 285, 293, 296, 324, 327, 329, 344-345, 362, 364, 407, 422, 424-429, 431
Ancona 25
Antwerp 12, 17, 179
Archangel 69, 105
Arnhem v, 158, 165, 169-173, 182, 421, 424
Artillery 18, 28, 30, 37, 40, 43-44, 47-48, 52-54, 56, 59, 63-64, 68, 76-77, 79-80, 83, 86, 89, 107, 114-115, 118, 125, 129, 131-132, 135-141, 158-159, 179-180, 183-190, 195-196, 199-201, 204-205, 212-213, 217-219, 221, 224-226, 233, 237-240, 242, 244-245, 247, 251-252, 265-271, 273-274, 276, 278-279, 281, 284-285, 287-288, 290, 294, 296-298, 302-303, 306, 308, 310, 313-314, 316, 319, 323, 326, 330-331, 335, 338-339, 358, 369, 375-376, 382-385, 387, 395-398, 400-405, 409-413, 415, 418, 424
Avenhorn 155, 158, 299

Bakkum vi, 296-297, 301-302, 307, 310, 313-316, 319, 353, 363-364
Baltic Sea iii, 26, 34, 69, 78, 82, 105, 111-112, 163, 205, 381
Barham Downs 58, 62, 72, 79
Batavian Army 22, 31, 36-44, 47, 107-108, 156-157, 207, 242, 268, 365, 370, 420; formations of: 1e Bataafsche Divisie iii, 36-37, 113, 125, 180, 182, 199, 242, 272, 290, 296, 389, 393; 2e Bataafsche Divisie 36, 113, 159, 180, 184, 199, 232, 242, 276, 290, 294, 296, 302, 307, 329, 394; units of: 1e Regiment Zware Cavalerie 43, 125, 131, 187, 313, 330, 389, 405; 2e Regiment Zware Cavalerie 43-44, 75, 159, 197, 241, 334, 390, 394, 404; Regiment Dragonders 43, 125, 136, 239, 285, 289, 334, 390, 393, 404; Regiment Huzaren 43, 285, 288, 296, 306, 310, 312, 394, 404; 1e Halve Brigade 37, 89, 125, 137, 156, 182, 184, 197, 240, 296, 301, 306, 308, 310, 312, 330, 334, 390, 393, 404; 2e Halve Brigade 40, 186-187, 330, 394, 405; 3e Halve Brigade 44, 137, 159, 256, 334, 343, 390, 393; 4e Halve Brigade 45, 93, 125, 137, 159, 239, 242, 256, 262, 264, 334, 390, 393, 404; 5e Halve Brigade 129, 131, 134, 136, 159, 197, 242, 334, 404; 6e Halve Brigade 38-39, 91, 94, 125, 137, 186-189, 225, 233, 237-238, 307, 310, 390, 394, 404-405; 7e Halve Brigade 38, 113, 131, 134-135, 146, 184, 189, 232-233, 241, 256, 322, 389, 394, 404; 1e Bataljon Jagers 113, 134, 141, 160, 197, 334, 390, 393, 404; 2e Bataljon Jagers 113, 129, 182-183, 189, 316, 330, 334, 389, 393, 404; 3e Bataljon Jagers 159, 187, 238, 264, 335, 394, 405; 4e Bataljon Jagers 184, 218, 232-233, 238, 296, 301, 394, 404; 1e Regiment Waldeck 42; 2e Regiment Waldeck 159, 266; 5e Bataljon Waldeck 42, 159; Regiment Saxen-Gotha 38, 42, 113, 159, 198; 1e Compagnie Rijdende Artillerie 225, 233, 238, 285, 313-314, 335, 404-405; 2e Compagnie Rijdende Artillerie 125, 131, 182, 185, 285, 289, 330-331, 334, 389, 404; 3e Artillerie Bataljon 91; Amsterdamsche Stadssoldaten 38, 42-43, 158-159, 172-173; Bataafsch Legioen 45-46, 199, 364; Bataafsch Mobiel Burger Corps 45; Compagnie Friesche Gardes 38, 42, 159; Compagnie Groninger Gardes 38, 42, 159; Corps der Genie 44; Corps Mineurs en Sappeurs 44
Batavian Navy iii, 23, 30, 32-33, 47, 74, 87, 101, 103, 114, 119-120, 122, 142-143, 147, 151-152, 159, 163, 167, 201, 258, 338, 340, 352, 367, 369-371, 388; Ships of: *Adder* 90, 93-94, 380, 406; *Admiraal de Ruijter* 104, 388; *Amphitrite* 87, 104, 368, 388; *Batavier* 104, 149, 388; *Beschermer* 104, 367, 388; *Broederschap* 116, 118, 144, 365-367; *Cerberus* 104, 388; *Constitutie* 116, 144, 366-367; *Draak* 92, 207-208; *'t Duifje* 144, 348, 366; *Embuscade* 87, 104, 368 388; *Furie* 85-86; *Galathée* 87, 104, 368, 388; *Gelderland* 104, 368, 388; *Gouda* 144, 366-367, 421; *Hector* 144, 265, 267, 348, 366, 368; *Heldin* 144, 210, 265, 267, 348, 366, 368; *Helhond* 92, 201, 344-345; *Leyden* 104, 163, 368, 388; *Lynx* 90, 345; *Mars* 104, 388; *Minerva* 144, 210, 251, 265, 267, 348-349, 366, 368, 382; *Utrecht* 104, 388; *Valk* 74, 144, 210, 265, 267, 342, 348, 366; *Venus* 144, 210, 265,

267, 342, 348-349, 366, 368, 381; *Vos* 91, 93, 229, 366, 421; *Washington* 121-122, 126-127, 148-149, 153-154, 367, 388; *Weerwraak* 94-95
Batavian Republic iii-iv, vii-viii, 9, 22-25, 29-31, 34, 37, 39, 43, 45-54, 65, 70-75, 84, 86, 98-103, 106-109, 113, 116, 119, 128, 152-153, 162-163, 165-166, 168, 171, 173-176, 178-180, 199, 202, 208, 252-253, 259, 264-265, 294, 319, 323, 326, 340, 358-359, 369-371, 386, 412, 416, 424
Battery 'De Unie' 116
Battery 'De Revolutie' 116, 118
Belgium 9, 15-17, 21, 27, 49, 179, 202, 256, 294, 359
Bergen op Zoom 22, 37, 51, 103, 108-109, 294, 387
Beverwijk 116, 157-158, 269, 291, 294, 296-298, 316-317, 322, 325, 421, 427
Biesbosch 20
Black Sea 25
Bleekmeer 238, 258, 273
Bleekveld 362
Boerensluis 334-335
Bois-le-Duc; see 's Hertogenbosch
Borculo 170-173, 417-418
Bornholm 83
Brabant 10, 16, 21, 32, 71-72, 80, 197, 203, 362, 431
Breda 16, 20-21, 37, 41, 50, 108-109, 113, 179, 252, 294, 329, 422, 426-429
Bredevoort 171, 174, 422
Breestraat 296
Breewijd 87-88
Bremen 101, 113
Brill 164
British Army; Formations of: 3rd Division 205; 1st Guards Brigade 77, 135, 137, 141, 177, 214, 233, 270, 299; 2nd Guards Brigade 77, 177, 214, 271, 276, 301; 3rd Brigade 43, 61-62, 77, 132, 134, 207, 238, 271, 274, 290, 299, 302, 313, 384, 396, 401, 410; 4th Brigade 43, 61, 77, 131, 178, 290, 299, 310, 385, 396, 402, 408; 5th Brigade 43, 62, 144, 178, 238, 299, 384, 397, 401, 410; 6th Brigade 43, 62, 145, 287, 299, 310, 315, 397, 402, 408; 7th Brigade 62, 142, 205, 217, 235, 271, 274, 276, 279, 281, 299-300, 310, 312, 317-319, 322-323, 326, 328, 344, 365, 376, 397, 400-402, 409-410, 420; 8th Brigade 62, 142, 205, 217, 235, 271, 274, 276, 279, 281, 299-300, 310, 312, 317-319, 322-323, 326, 328, 344, 365, 376, 397, 400-402, 409-410, 420; 9th Brigade 62, 142, 205, 217, 235, 271, 274, 276, 279, 281, 299-300, 310, 312, 317-319, 322-323, 326, 328, 344, 365, 376, 397, 400-402, 409-410, 420; Units of: 7th Light Dragoons 205, 235, 274, 397, 400-401, 409; 11th Light Dragoons 145, 214, 299, 309, 312, 397, 401, 409-410; 15th Light Dragoons 252, 287-288, 409; 18th Light Dragoons 77, 298, 330, 385,

397, 402, 410; 1st Foot Guards 20, 58, 61, 232, 242, 301, 317, 384, 396, 401, 408; Coldstream Guards 58, 61, 237, 243, 301, 384, 396, 401, 410; 3rd Foot Guards 58, 61, 141, 190, 233, 239, 384, 396, 401, 410; 1st (Royal) Foot 143, 408; 2nd (Queen's) Foot 61, 134, 140, 280, 384, 396, 401, 410; 4th (King's) Foot 58, 62, 158, 279-280, 313, 363; 5th Foot 58, 62, 233, 237, 239, 330-331, 397, 401, 410; 9th 58, 62, 153, 178, 207, 223, 234-235, 237, 243, 317, 330, 337-338, 342, 361, 397, 401, 410; 15th Foot 58; 16th Foot 58; 17th Foot 58, 62, 144, 238-239, 330, 397, 401, 410; 20th 40, 58-60, 62, 81, 83, 145, 147, 160, 178, 182, 187-188, 194, 256, 258, 288, 315, 321, 328, 343, 397, 402, 408; 23rd Royal Welsh Fusiliers 61-62, 140, 282, 342, 384, 397, 402, 408; 24th Foot 62, 94, 125, 179, 242, 251, 370; 25th 20, 61, 139, 178, 252, 267, 269, 282-284, 286, 361; 27th Foot 61, 90, 132, 134, 136, 139-140, 147, 154, 156, 159, 238, 260, 282, 310; 29th Foot 61, 133-134, 140, 282; 31st 62, 58, 81, 156, 279, 402, 410; 35th Foot 58, 62, 233-235, 243, 330, 333, 338, 397, 401, 410; 36th Foot 58; 40th Foot 58, 60, 62, 144, 182, 239, 397, 401, 410; 46th Foot 58; 49th Foot 61-62, 178, 226, 283; 52nd Foot 59; 55th Foot 62, 140-141, 241, 282, 397; 56th Foot 59, 62, 223, 234, 274, 397, 401, 410; 60th Foot 252, 270, 290, 321; 62nd Foot 59; 63rd Foot 59, 145, 397, 402, 408; 64th Foot 62; 69th 61-62, 207, 266, 338, 384, 398; 79th Highlanders 61, 178, 283, 290, 385, 397, 402, 408; 82nd Foot 59; 85th 61, 134, 140, 238, 279-280, 282, 298, 310; 92nd Highlanders 61, 141, 143, 178, 182, 284, 290, 385, 397, 402, 408; Light Infantry Battalion 205, 314; Royal Artillery 59, 141; Royal Engineers 64; 136, 141, 145; Royal Military Artificers 64; Royal Wagon Train 64, 72
British Royal Navy; Ships of: *Alkmaar* 348, 382; *America* 106, 148, 149, 391-392; *Ardent* 106, 150, 154, 367, 391-392; *Arrow* 207-208, 346, 379, 392, 406; *Attack* 380, 406; *Babet* 259, 379, 392, 406; *Belliqueux* 106, 150, 154, 367, 379, 392; *Blonde* 84, 251, 348, 373, 382; *Bouncer* 380, 407; *Brakel* 382; *Calcutta* 251, 348, 382; *Circe* 74, 90, 92, 121, 143, 203, 345, 379; *Contest* 97, 345, 380; *Coromandel* 112, 382; *Courier* 81, 84-87, 92, 94-97, 172, 429; *Cracker* 344, 380, 406; *Crash* 85, 90, 94-97; *Cynthia* 120, 152, 167, 379; *Dart* 259-260, 344, 379, 392, 407; *Defender* 344-345, 380, 407; *Diadem* 76, 83-84, 357, 382; *Dictator* 382; *Discovery* 380; *Eling*, 380, 406; *Espiegle* 90, 92, 94-95, 259, 262, 407; *Espion* 251, 349, 382; *Experiment* 348, 382; *Force* 380, 406;

Furnace 380, 406; *Fury* 379, 406; *Gallant* 380, 406; *Ganges* 106, 391; *Glatton* 86, 150, 154, 367, 379, 391-392; *Griper* 380; *Hasty* 344, 380, 407; *Haughty* 262, 380, 406; *Hebe* 382; *Hecla* 380, 407; *Hornet* 379; *Hyena* 92; *Inflexible* 83, 382; *Isis* 106, 120-121, 126, 150, 153, 259, 262, 344, 379, 392, 406; *Juno* 94-96, 150, 259, 391-392, 406; *Kent* 119, 128, 391; *Lady Ann* 259, 407; *Latona* 86, 94-96, 148-150, 391-392; *Lutine* 150, 345-346, 392, 425; *Melpomene* 61, 132, 150, 259, 379, 392, 406; *Monmouth* 86, 150, 154, 367, 379, 392; *Nancy* 90, 92, 94, 345; *Niger* 348, 382; *Otter* 90-91, 93, 379, 406; *Overyssel* 71-72, 154, 367, 379, 392; *Pelter* 342, 379, 406; *Piercer* 262, 379, 406; *Plumper* 265, 380, 407; *Prince William* 407; *Proselyte* 61, 379; *Pylades* 90, 92, 94, 96-97, 392; *Romney*150, 261, 344, 379, 392; *Romulus* 382; *Rosario* 379, 406; *Shannon* 150, 177, 191, 379, 392; *Sirius* 85-86; *Speedwell* 259, 379, 407; *Swinger* 379, 406; *Tartarus* 380, 407; *Teaser* 379, 406; *Tigress* 265, 379, 406; *Tisiphone* 90; *Trial* 380; *Tromp* 382; *Ulysses* 348, 382; *Undaunted* 94, 96; *Veteran* 106, 150, 154, 367, 391-392; *Wassenaar* 382; *Weymouth* 348, 382; *Wolverine* 207, 261, 379, 406; *Zebra* 379, 406; see also North Sea Fleet
Broek 197, 240, 393, 404
Brussels 16, 81, 179-180
Buitenveld 131, 138

Calandsoog iii, v, 115, 119, 133, 135, 137, 155, 390
Camperdown, Battle of 23, 25, 45, 47, 74, 100, 285, 369
Campo Formio, Treaty of 23-24
Canterbury 58-60, 72, 79
Castricum, Battle of iii, vi-vii, 266, 293, 295, 299-301, 303-305, 311, 319, 321, 323, 362
Coevorden 71, 159
Comité te Lande 40, 42
Congress of Rastatt 24
Copenhagen 82, 110-112
Crabbendam 160, 185-186, 194
Cronstadt 69, 110-112, 377

Deal 33, 56, 72, 75, 79, 95, 207-208, 251, 283, 349, 351
Delft 21, 37, 48, 109
Delfzijl 70, 90-91, 94, 113-114, 125, 159, 345
Den Haag; see Hague, The
Den Helder vii, 113, 116-119, 121-122, 125, 128, 131, 134-135, 137-139, 141-147, 152-153, 155-156, 167, 177, 188, 207, 211-212, 243, 266-269, 293, 299, 310, 319-320, 336, 342-343, 346-349, 365, 367, 383, 389, 398

Denmark 30, 85-86, 163
Deptford 76, 78
Deventer 30, 168, 174, 416, 427
Dinxperlo 168, 170, 173
Dirkshorn vi, 177, 182-184, 214, 238, 249, 330, 335
Doesburg 172, 416
Dokegat 94
Dordrecht 20, 74, 109
Dorregeest 301-302
Dover 79-80
Drenthe 10, 113
Dublin 55, 59, 428
Dunkirk 12, 89, 202

Edam 116, 363, 424
Eenigenburg v, 177-178, 180, 182-184, 188-190, 195-196, 206, 214, 244
Egmond aan Zee vi, 158, 200, 270, 272, 275, 281, 285, 287, 290, 294, 298-299, 310, 314, 316, 328-329, 364, 403
Egmond op de Hoef 270, 298
Egmont-op-Zee 284, 317, 328-329
Egypt 23-25, 136, 313, 426
Elsinore 76, 82-83, 110-111, 251, 383
Emden 30, 93, 152, 167
Emmerich 164, 166, 168
Ems 91, 93
Enkhuizen 114, 199, 259-260, 268-269, 334, 406

First Coalition 19, 21, 23, 33, 162
Flanders 21-22, 31, 55, 61, 72, 78, 103, 179, 362, 434
Flushing 22, 51, 102, 201
Fort Lillo 179
France viii, 9, 12-13, 15-17, 21, 23-25, 27-30, 32-34, 40, 71, 85, 100, 102-103, 128, 162-163, 165, 178, 199, 253, 294, 355, 359, 370, 374, 423, 429, 433
French Army; formations of: 1er Division 113, 294, 359, 386, 412; 2e Division 47, 52, 113, 294, 359, 386, 412; 3e Division 47, 113, 359, 387, 413 Armée de Hollande 20-21, 24, 109; Armée de Mayence 49-50; units of: 10e Dragons 200, 224-225, 230, 242, 279, 309-310, 312, 404, 411-412; 4e Chasseurs à Cheval 307, 310, 312-313, 411-412; 5e Chasseurs à Cheval 41, 49, 158, 217-218, 225-226, 232, 234, 310, 312, 314, 386, 395, 403, 411; 11e Chasseurs à Cheval 49; 16e Chasseurs à Cheval 41, 50, 190, 217-218, 225, 274, 276, 287, 310, 312, 314, 359, 387, 395, 403, 411, 413; 23e Chasseurs à Cheval 49; 1er Demi-Brigade 49; 8e Demi-Brigade 49; 21e Demi-Brigade 326; 22e Demi-Brigade 242, 256, 310, 411; 27e Demi-Brigade 53; 42e Demi-Brigade 50, 155, 157, 190, 192, 195, 219, 221, 224, 226, 230, 232, 234, 276, 279, 282, 296, 302,

307, 310, 313, 386, 395, 403, 411; 48e Demi-Brigade 49-50, 217-218, 225-226, 232, 274, 310, 313, 403, 411; 49e Demi-Brigade 49, 51, 190, 192, 200, 224-225, 274, 279, 282-283, 285, 298, 309-310, 313, 387, 395, 403, 411-413; 51e Demi-Brigade 294, 310, 312, 326, 411-413; 54e Demi-Brigade 48, 190, 217-219, 221, 226, 274, 276, 278-279, 282, 315, 386, 395, 403, 411; 60e Demi-Brigade 49, 157, 200, 224, 226, 274, 276, 278, 310, 387, 395, 403, 411; 68e Demi-Brigade 53; 70e Demi-Brigade 53; 72e Demi-Brigade 49, 155, 172, 219, 225, 256, 279, 285, 287, 290, 314-316, 326, 386, 395, 403, 411; 90e Demi-Brigade 53, 179, 232, 279, 282, 285, 290, 301, 307, 310, 313, 403, 411; 98e Demi-Brigade 53, 294, 314-315, 326, 411, 413; 1e Batallion des Ardennes 53; 1e Batallion du Nord 53; Légion Franche Étrangère 47; 4e Artillerie Légère 48-49, 314, 387, 395, 403; 7e Artillerie Légère 48; 8e Artillerie Légère 157, 217-218, 276, 306, 358, 387, 395, 403; 6e Artillerie à Pied 155, 395; 7e Artillerie à Pied 48, 302, 306, 387, 395

Friesche Gat 90-91
Friesland 10, 13-14, 32, 37, 43, 70-71, 93, 106, 111, 113, 153, 176, 258, 260, 266, 324, 407, 417-418, 424

Geertruidenberg 20-21
Gelderland 113, 153, 163, 175, 368, 388, 417, 422, 425, 428
Geldersoor 169, 416
Gelre 10, 13-14, 422
Gewapende Burgermacht v, 44-47, 88, 99, 107, 110, 158-159, 165, 167-170, 172-173, 201, 252, 261, 264, 294
Goeree 30, 71, 74-75, 111, 113, 120, 167
Golhorn 333
Goodwin Sands 349
Gorkum 14, 158
Gosport 350
Grave 22, 50, 108-109, 113, 172, 240, 312
Groenlo 171-172
Groet 158, 177, 190-191, 193, 199-200, 213-214, 217, 223, 232, 244, 256, 271, 274, 335, 390, 403
Groningen 10, 31-32, 37, 43, 45, 70-72, 93, 106, 111, 113-114, 127-128, 158-159, 176, 180, 266, 324, 360, 417-418, 421, 423
Groote Keeten 128-129, 135, 137-138
Guernsey 61, 349-351, 355, 358, 361, 369-370, 428

Haaks 86-88, 121
Haarlem 21, 45-46, 48, 113, 116, 125, 131, 155, 157-159, 169, 197, 199, 201, 238, 252, 290, 294, 312, 317, 324-325, 364, 390, 420-422, 424-425, 427-428
Hague, The 10, 13-14, 19-22, 31-33, 44, 46, 76, 99, 101, 107, 109, 113, 125, 159-160, 164, 230, 250, 386
Hamburg 28, 43, 81, 89, 101, 105-106, 111, 122, 346, 421
Hannover 55, 111
Haringkarspel 177, 182-183, 214, 290, 330, 335
Harlingen 153, 159, 208, 264
Harwich 79, 154, 367
Heemskerk 296-297, 303, 307, 364
Helder; see Den Helder
Hellevoetsluis 26, 75, 85, 113
Helvetic Republic 24
Hengelo 168
's Hertogenbosch 22, 37, 47, 108-109, 113, 180, 198, 253, 294
Het Hof v, 214, 219, 226-227, 229
Hijloo 299, 404
Holland i, iv, vi, viii, 10, 13-15, 21, 24, 26-27, 31-32, 37, 43, 45-48, 51-53, 55, 57-60, 62, 65-66, 68-69, 71-72, 74-75, 77, 79-82, 84-85, 100, 102, 108, 113-116, 119-120, 125, 127-128, 134-137, 141-142, 144, 146, 152-154, 157-160, 163-165, 167, 172, 175-176, 179-180, 182, 184-185, 192, 194, 197, 199, 201, 203-205, 210-212, 218, 238-239, 243, 247, 249, 251-252, 255-256, 258, 264-267, 269, 282, 286, 290, 294, 298, 300, 308, 313-314, 317-327, 336-337, 341, 343-344, 347-353, 355, 357-361, 363, 365-366, 369-371, 373, 375-377, 379, 381, 393, 396, 400, 408, 411, 414, 416, 419-429, 431, 434
Hollandsch Diep 21
Hoorn 113-114, 116, 152, 158, 199, 217, 239, 241-242, 244, 247, 258, 268-269, 298-299, 330, 334, 424
Huisduinen 125-126, 128-129, 136, 143, 147, 152, 207, 336, 343

Ij 158, 201-202, 344
Ijssel 30, 107, 417
Ionian Islands 24-25
Ireland 23, 35, 55, 61, 86, 105, 349, 369-370
Isle of Wight 105, 252, 338, 347, 368-370

Jersey 61-62, 349-352, 355, 358, 361, 369-370, 423, 426, 428

Kaaphoofd 116
Kamp 177, 190-191, 193, 195, 199-200, 213-214, 217-218, 244, 256, 270-271, 274, 335, 390, 403
Kanaal van Alkmaar 158, 180, 185, 190, 192, 199-200, 214, 217, 224-225, 232-234, 237, 243-244, 271-272, 276, 278-279

Kattegat 114
Kijkduin 116, 121, 128
Kleine Keeten 116, 128, 134
Klundert 21
Knollendam 158, 322
Koegras 115, 128-129, 131, 134-135, 137-138, 141, 156
Kolhorn vi, 332, 342, 360, 407
Krabbendam v, 177-178, 180, 182, 184-193, 195, 200, 205, 213-214, 232, 238, 271, 329
Kronstadt 25, 82
Lange Meer 296
Langendijk 199, 238, 240, 257-258, 272-273
Langereis Canal 331
Leeward Islands 55, 62
Leiden 13, 21, 46, 48, 89, 125, 156, 158-159, 163, 248, 252, 256, 422, 425-426
Lemmer vi, 259, 261-265, 346
Lichtenvoorde 171, 173
Liebrug 158
Liège 362
Lille 39, 322
Limmen 296, 301-303, 309-310, 313, 316-317, 319, 326-327, 363
Lingen 113, 152-153, 163-167, 175, 211, 266, 268, 414, 417-418, 425
London 17, 20, 25, 27, 55, 57-58, 60, 62-63, 66, 70-71, 76-79, 81-85, 89, 95, 101, 105, 107, 110, 122, 128, 136, 141-142, 145, 154, 163-164, 179-180, 194-195, 202-203, 205, 224, 243, 252, 255-256, 271, 284, 313, 326, 331, 333, 338, 341, 346, 350, 353, 367-368, 373-374, 422-430
Lübeck 101, 111-112

Maaslandssluis 74
Maastricht 16-17, 22, 52
Margate 72, 79-80
Marsdiep 116, 127, 131, 140, 149, 152, 260
Medemblik 114, 116, 140, 199, 259-260, 268-269, 319, 334
Meuse 21, 30, 71-72, 74-75, 109, 113-114, 119, 179
Middelburg 159
Monnikendam 116, 158, 239, 241, 296, 330

Nieudorper Verlaat 330, 334
Nieuwe Diep 32, 116, 118, 127, 143-144, 147, 207, 210, 258, 261, 267, 344, 365-366
Nieuwe Nieudorp 333-334
Nijkerk 153, 175
Nijmegen 13-15, 21, 50, 87, 113, 172, 199, 256, 290, 308, 426, 428
Noorddorp 296-297, 303, 306
Noordwijk 88-90, 209
Nore, The 23, 154, 367

North Sea iii, 25-26, 30, 65, 69, 74, 87, 90, 101, 105-106, 112, 115-116, 119, 138, 143-144, 154-155, 177, 190, 200, 209, 214, 270, 272, 279, 283, 296, 391
North Sea Fleet (British) iii, 25-26, 30, 65, 74, 87, 101, 119, 391

Oldenzaal 168
Oost-Egalement-Sloot 138, 154
Oostmahorn 91, 93
Orange, House of 15, 21, 26-27, 30, 32-34, 38, 71, 107, 123, 151, 162-163, 259-260, 347
Orangists iii, v, 9-10, 12-14, 33, 71, 107, 113, 147, 152, 162-176, 198, 259, 265-266, 347, 367
Oude Nieudorp 334
Oude Schild 147
Oude-Sluis 138, 146, 154, 333, 338, 407
Oud-Karspel 160, 199, 242, 245, 393, 404
Overflakkee 74
Overijssel 10, 71-72, 113, 150, 154, 168, 175, 367, 379, 392, 417, 427, 429

Paris 16-17, 24, 41, 52-53, 98, 110, 156, 179, 246, 252-253, 291, 294, 313, 421-424, 426, 429-430
Patriots iii, 9, 12-16, 18, 21-22, 98, 152, 162, 165, 167-171, 174, 176
Petten 115, 138, 154-155, 177, 180, 184, 190-191, 194-195, 205, 213, 217, 235, 237, 271, 284, 327, 329, 336, 338, 390
Portsmouth 79, 110, 342, 349-350, 358
Portugal 19, 61, 72, 105, 370
Prussia 12, 14-17, 19, 25-31, 80, 162-164, 174
Purmerend 116, 158, 217, 239, 241, 244, 269, 296, 322, 325, 330, 420

Ramsgate 72, 79-80, 326, 349
Rassemblement 162, 165
Reval 30, 34, 82-83, 112, 205, 207, 251, 352, 358, 375, 377, 381-383
Rhine 19, 22, 24, 30-31, 71-72, 74, 113, 119, 359
Roermond 16
Rotschensalm 82
Rotterdam 20, 45-46, 52, 74, 113, 158-159, 199, 252, 316
Rozenburg 74
Russia iii, 19, 24-25, 27-30, 34, 69, 81, 102, 112, 163-164, 249, 256, 355, 358, 374, 376, 378
Russian Army; Units of: Life Guard Don Cossacks 68, 398-399; Life Guard Hussars 68, 212, 398; Life-Sotnia of the Ural Cossacks 68, 302, 399; 1st Jégerski of Suthoff 66-68, 214, 217, 219, 224, 226, 270, 274, 302-303, 355, 381-382, 398, 400-401, 408-409; Benkendorf Grenadiers 67, 219, 221, 219, 246, 251,

302-303, 306, 353-355, 382, 398, 400, 409; Emmé Grenadiers 67; Zavalishin Grenadiers (ex-Benkendorf) 353-354; Zherebtsov Grenadiers 67; Arbénev Musketeers 219, 226, 246, 251, 271-272, 355, 381, 398, 400, 410; Fersen Musketeers 67, 83, 219, 224, 226, 229, 271, 382, 398, 400; Sedmoratzki Musketeers 67, 353, 357; Combined Grenadier Battalion Emmé 353; Combined Grenadier Battalion Ericsson 67, 353; Combined Grenadier Battalion Mitiouchin 67, 353; Combined Grenadier Battalion Ogarev 67, 252, 306, 353, 409; Combined Grenadier Battalion Ossipov 67, 217; Combined Grenadier Battalion Strick 67, 229, 251, 398, 400, 409; Combined Grenadier Battalion Timofeyev 67, 353, 381-2, 398, 400, 409; Battalion Kaptsevich (artillery) 68, 398; Pioneers 30, 68, 204, 233, 302, 398-401, 409

Russian Navy; Ships of: *Aleksei* 391; *Alexsandr Nevskii* 349; *Arkhangel Rafail* 82, 349; *Boleslav* 391; *Dispatch* 82, 391; *Elisaveta* 391; *Emgeiten* 82, 381; *Evropa* 391; *Gleb* 382; *Iona* 381; *Mikhail* 82, 381; *Mstislav* 367, 391-392; *Neptune* 82, 351, 382; *Panteleimon* 82, 381; *Retvizan* 367, 391-392; *Revel* 82, 381; *Riga* 391; *Schastlivyi* 391; *Sviatoi Ianuarii* 381; *Sviatoi Konstantin* 205; *Sviatoi Nikolai* 205; *Sviatoi Pyotr* 391; *Vsevolod* 391
Rustenburg 45, 238, 299

St. Domingo 59, 62
St. Helier 351
St. Maarten v, 178, 180, 182-184, 189, 195-196, 206, 214, 330
St. Martin 185, 194, 395
St. Pancras 197, 214, 393-394, 404
St. Petersburg 26, 34, 67, 71, 102, 110, 112, 163, 354
Schaagenbrug 206
Schagen 113, 177, 183, 206-207, 214, 238, 328, 338, 389
Scheldt 12, 15, 17, 22, 72, 80, 112, 179
Schermer 155-156, 257-258, 298, 365, 426-427
Schermerhorn 156, 239, 241, 298-299, 318
Scheysprong 169
Schiedam 74, 159, 422
Schiermonnikoog 90-91, 93-96
Schilpwater 302, 309-310
Schoorl v-vi, 115-116, 158, 190, 193, 200, 213-214, 217-219, 224, 226, 229, 232-235, 256, 258, 271, 274, 276, 278, 289, 335, 403
Schoorlsche Zeedijk 177, 180, 190-192, 205, 214
Schoreldam 223-224
Schouwen 111
Schulpegat Canal 116

Schulpen 296
Second Coalition iii, viii, 23, 25, 27, 29-30, 74, 81
Sheerness 97, 261, 350, 368
Slaperdijk 190-192, 213-214, 217, 223, 271, 274
Sluisdijk 118
Solingen 51, 414
Southampton 72, 78, 111
Steenbergen 20

Terschelling 93, 159, 209, 265-268
Texel iii, vii, 22-23, 26, 47, 74, 77, 82-83, 85-88, 92, 101, 103-104, 111, 113-114, 116, 118, 120-121, 125-128, 132, 143, 146-149, 152-154, 163-164, 167, 187, 203-204, 206-207, 209-211, 260, 267-269, 326, 335, 341-344, 346-348, 367, 373, 388
Transport Board 76, 81
Travemünde 111
Tuitgenhorn 180, 184, 189, 232, 271, 330, 335

Uitgeest 296, 302, 307, 310, 314
Uitvoerend Bewind 44, 86, 88, 91, 98-100, 102-103, 105-106, 108-109, 111, 156-157, 166, 193, 195-196, 198, 256, 316, 430
Unitarissen 98-99
Urk 268, 344
Utrecht 10, 13-14, 31-32, 37, 41, 47, 50, 71, 75-76, 84, 102, 113, 125, 149, 156-159, 169, 172-174, 252-253, 359, 386, 388, 422-423, 425, 427, 429

Veluwe 175, 416
Venlo 16, 22
Vijfsprong 118
Vlieland 88, 90, 93, 159, 207-208, 265-268, 345, 406
Vlieter 121, 147-149, 152, 367-369, 406
Voorne 30, 74-75, 113, 120, 167

Waal 71, 74
Wadden Islands 86, 93
Wadden Sea 65, 85-86, 90, 92-95, 106, 202, 258, 365
Walcheren 49, 71-72, 75, 80, 102-103, 108, 125
Warmenhuizen 177, 180, 184, 189, 199, 214, 232-233, 238, 244, 291, 330, 335, 353, 390
Wesel 29-30, 168, 171
West Indies 55-56, 59, 61-62, 79, 106, 434
Westfriesche Zeedijk v, 145, 153-154, 177-178, 180, 184, 186, 188, 196, 206, 212, 327
Wetzlar 30
Wexford 79, 350
Wieringen 207-208, 210-211, 266-269, 319, 347-348
Wieringerwaard 177, 337, 360, 389
Wijk aan het Duin 297

Wijk-aan-Zee 296
Willemstad 20-21, 75
Winkel 217, 240, 330-331, 333-334, 365
Winterswijk 168, 171, 173-174, 417, 428
Woerden 31-32, 50, 75, 252
Woolwich 78-79
Woudmeer 257
Wyck-op-Zee 298, 317

Yarmouth 78, 82-84, 86, 95, 97, 154, 203, 205, 342, 346-348, 350, 367

Zanddijk 128, 136, 190-191, 213-214, 217, 274
Zandvoort 90, 209
Zeeland 10, 13-14, 17, 22, 30, 47, 49, 92, 102-103, 105-106, 108, 111-114, 359
Zeeuws Vlaanderen 10
Zevenaar 169
Zijdenskerk 335
Zijpe Sluices 177-178, 188, 192, 271
Zijpe iv, vii, 113, 138-139, 145-146, 156, 177-178, 180-181, 187-189, 192, 195, 205, 209, 212, 234, 237-238, 240-242, 247, 258, 266, 271, 274, 301, 320, 323, 327, 329, 331, 335, 337, 361, 419-420
Zuiderzee iv, 30, 54, 65, 114, 138, 143, 153-154, 158-159, 167, 175-176, 198, 201-202, 205, 210-212, 217, 258-261, 265-266, 268, 299, 330, 346, 361, 406-407, 416
Zutphen 30, 37, 158, 165, 171-172, 176, 416
Zwolle 13, 30, 46, 138, 158, 166, 172, 202, 425

From Reason to Revolution – Warfare 1721-1815

http://www.helion.co.uk/published-by-helion/reason-to-revolution-1721-1815.html

The 'From Reason to Revolution' series covers the period of military history 1721–1815, an era in which fortress-based strategy and linear battles gave way to the nation-in-arms and the beginnings of total war.

This era saw the evolution and growth of light troops of all arms, and of increasingly flexible command systems to cope with the growing armies fielded by nations able to mobilise far greater proportions of their manpower than ever before. Many of these developments were fired by the great political upheavals of the era, with revolutions in America and France bringing about social change which in turn fed back into the military sphere as whole nations readied themselves for war. Only in the closing years of the period, as the reactionary powers began to regain the upper hand, did a military synthesis of the best of the old and the new become possible.

The series will examine the military and naval history of the period in a greater degree of detail than has hitherto been attempted, and has a very wide brief, with the intention of covering all aspects from the battles, campaigns, logistics, and tactics, to the personalities, armies, uniforms, and equipment.

Submissions

The publishers would be pleased to receive submissions for this series. Please contact series editor Andrew Bamford via email (andrewbamford@helion.co.uk), or in writing to Helion & Company Limited, Unit 8 Amherst Business Centre, Budbrooke Road, Warwick, CV34 5WE

Titles

No 1 *Lobositz to Leuthen: Horace St Paul and the Campaigns of the Austrian Army in the Seven Years War 1756-57* (Neil Cogswell)

No 2 *Glories to Useless Heroism: The Seven Years War in North America from the French journals of Comte Maurés de Malartic, 1755-1760* (William Raffle (ed.))

No 3 *Reminiscences 1808-1815 Under Wellington: The Peninsular and Waterloo Memoirs of William Hay* (Andrew Bamford (ed.))

No 4 *Far Distant Ships: The Royal Navy and the Blockade of Brest 1793-1815* (Quintin Barry)

No 5 *Godoy's Army: Spanish Regiments and Uniforms from the Estado Militar of 1800* (Charles Esdaile and Alan Perry)

No 6 *On Gladsmuir Shall the Battle Be! The Battle of Prestonpans 1745* (Arran Johnston)

No 7 *The French Army of the Orient 1798-1801: Napoleon's Beloved 'Egyptians'* (Yves Martin)

No 8 *The Autobiography, or Narrative of a Soldier: The Peninsular War Memoirs of William Brown of the 45th Foot* (Steve Brown (ed.))

No 9 *Recollections from the Ranks: Three Russian Soldiers' Autobiographies from the Napoleonic Wars* (Darrin Boland)

No 10 *By Fire and Bayonet: Grey's West Indies Campaign of 1794* (Steve Brown)

No 11 *Olmütz to Torgau: Horace St Paul and the Campaigns of the Austrian Army in the Seven Years War 1758-60* (Neil Cogswell)

No 12 *Murat's Army: The Army of the Kingdom of Naples 1806-1815* (Digby Smith)

No 13 *The Veteran or 40 Years' Service in the British Army: The Scurrilous Recollections of Paymaster John Harley 47th Foot – 1798-1838* (Gareth Glover (ed.))

No 14 *Narrative of the Eventful Life of Thomas Jackson: Militiaman and Coldstream Sergeant, 1803-15* (Eamonn O'Keeffe (ed.))

No.15 *For Orange and the States: The Army of the Dutch Republic 1713-1772 Part I: Infantry* (Marc Geerdinck-Schaftenaar)

No 16 *Men Who Are Determined to be Free: The American Assault on Stony Point, 15 July 1779* (David C. Bonk)

No 17 *Next to Wellington: General Sir George Murray: The Story of a Scottish Soldier and Statesman, Wellington's Quartermaster General* (John Harding-Edgar)

No 18 *Between Scylla and Charybdis: The Army of Elector Friedrich August of Saxony 1733-1763 Part I: Staff and Cavalry* (Marco Pagan)

No 19 *The Secret Expedition: The Anglo-Russian Invasion of Holland 1799* (Geert van Uythoven)

No 20 *'We Are Accustomed to do our Duty': German Auxiliaries with the British Army 1793-95* (Paul Demet)

No 21 *With the Guards in Flanders: The Diary of Captain Roger Morris 1793-95* (Peter Harington (ed.))

No 22 *The British Army in Egypt 1801: An Underrated Army Comes of Age* (Carole Divall)

No 23 *Better is the Proud Plaid: The Clothing, Weapons, and Accoutrements of the Jacobites in the '45* (Jenn Scott)

No 24 *The Lilies and the Thistle: French Troops in the Jacobite '45* (Andrew Bamford)

No 25 *A Light Infantryman With Wellington: The Letters of Captain George Ulrich Barlow 52nd and 69th Foot 1808-15* (Gareth Glover (ed.))

No 26 *Swiss Regiments in the Service of France 1798-1815: Uniforms, Organisation, Campaigns* (Stephen Ede-Borrett)

No 27 *For Orange and the States! The Army of the Dutch Republic 1713-1772: Part II: Cavalry and Specialist Troops* (Marc Geerdinck-Schaftenaar)

No 28 *Fashioning Regulation, Regulating Fashion: Uniforms and Dress of the British Army 1800-1815 Volume I* (Ben Townsend)

No 29 *Riflemen: The History of the 5th Battalion 60th (Royal American) Regiment, 1797-1818* (Robert Griffith)

No 30 *The Key to Lisbon: The Third French Invasion of Portugal, 1810-11* (Kenton White)

No 31 *Command and Leadership: Proceedings of the 2018 Helion & Company 'From Reason to Revolution' Conference* (Andrew Bamford (ed.))

No 32 *Waterloo After the Glory: Hospital Sketches and Reports on the Wounded After the Battle* (Michael Crumplin and Gareth Glover)

No 33 *Fluxes, Fevers, and Fighting Men: War and Disease in Ancien Regime Europe 1648-1789* (Pádraig Lenihan)

No 34 *'They Were Good Soldiers': African-Americans Serving in the Continental Army, 1775-1783* (John U. Rees)

No 35 *A Redcoat in America: The Diaries of Lieutenant William Bamford, 1757-1765 and 1776* (John B. Hattendorf (ed.))

No 36 *Between Scylla and Charybdis: The Army of Friedrich August II of Saxony, 1733-1763: Part II: Infantry and Artillery* (Marco Pagan)

No 37 *Québec Under Siege: French Eye-Witness Accounts from the Campaign of 1759* (Charles A. Mayhood (ed.))

No 38 *King George's Hangman: Henry Hawley and the Battle of Falkirk 1746* (Jonathan D. Oates)

No 39 *Zweybrücken in Command: The Reichsarmee in the Campaign of 1758* (Neil Cogswell)

No 40 *So Bloody a Day: The 16th Light Dragoons in the Waterloo Campaign* (David J. Blackmore)

No 41 *Northern Tars in Southern Waters: The Russian Fleet in the Mediterranean 1806-1810* (Vladimir Bogdanovich Bronevskiy / Darrin Boland)

No 42 *Royal Navy Officers of the Seven Years War: A Biographical Dictionary of Commissioned Officers 1748-1763* (Cy Harrison)

No 43 *All at Sea: Naval Support for the British Army During the American Revolutionary War* (John Dillon)

No 44 *Glory is Fleeting: New Scholarship on the Napoleonic Wars* (Andrew Bamford (ed.))

No 45 *Fashioning Regulation, Regulating Fashion: Uniforms and Dress of the British Army 1800-1815 Vol. II* (Ben Townsend)

No 46 *Revenge in the Name of Honour: The Royal Navy's Quest for Vengeance in the Single Ship Actions of the War of 1812* (Nicholas James Kaizer)

No 47 *They Fought With Extraordinary Bravery: The III German (Saxon) Army Corps in the Southern Netherlands 1814* (Geert van Uythoven)

No 48 *The Danish Army of the Napoleonic Wars 1801-1814, Organisation, Uniforms & Equipment: Volume 1: High Command, Line and Light Infantry* (David Wilson)

No 49 *Neither Up Nor Down: The British Army and the Flanders Campaign 1793-1895* (Phillip Ball)

No 50 *Guerra Fantástica: The Portuguese Army and the Seven Years War* (António Barrento)

No 51 *From Across the Sea: North Americans in Nelson's Navy* (Sean M. Heuvel and John A. Rodgaard)

No 52 *Rebellious Scots to Crush: The Military Response to the Jacobite '45* (Andrew Bamford (ed.))

No 53 *The Army of George II 1727-1760: The Soldiers who Forged an Empire* (Peter Brown)

No 54 *Wellington at Bay: The Battle of Villamuriel, 25 October 1812* (Garry David Wills)

No 55 *Life in the Red Coat: The British Soldier 1721-1815* (Andrew Bamford (ed.))

No 56 *Wellington's Favourite Engineer. John Burgoyne: Operations, Engineering, and the Making of a Field Marshal* (Mark S. Thompson)

No 57 *Scharnhorst: The Formative Years, 1755-1801* (Charles Edward White)

No 58 *At the Point of the Bayonet: The Peninsular War Battles of Arroyomolinos and Almaraz 1811-1812* (Robert Griffith)

No 59 *Sieges of the '45: Siege Warfare during the Jacobite Rebellion of 1745-1746* (Jonathan D. Oates)

No 60 *Austrian Cavalry of the Revolutionary and Napoleonic Wars, 1792–1815* (Enrico Acerbi, András K. Molnár)

No 61 *The Danish Army of the Napoleonic Wars 1801-1814, Organisation, Uniforms & Equipment: Volume 2: Cavalry and Artillery* (David Wilson)

No 62 *Napoleon's Stolen Army: How the Royal Navy Rescued a Spanish Army in the Baltic* (John Marsden)

No 63 *The Battle of the Chesapeake 1781: The Royal Navy and the Battle that Lost America* (Quintin Barry)

No 64 *Bullocks, Grain, and Good Madeira: The Maratha and Jat Campaigns 1803-1806 and the emergence of the Indian Army* (Joshua Provan)

No 65 *Sir James McGrigor: The Adventurous Life of Wellington's Chief Medical Officer* (Tom Scotland)

No 66 *Fashioning Regulation, Regulating Fashion: Uniforms and Dress of the British Army 1800-1815 Volume I* (Ben Townsend) (paperback edition)

No 67 *Fashioning Regulation, Regulating Fashion: Uniforms and Dress of the British Army 1800-1815 Volume II* (Ben Townsend) (paperback edition)

No 68 *The Secret Expedition: The Anglo-Russian Invasion of Holland 1799* (Geert van Uythoven) (paperback edition)

* indicates 'Falconet' format paperbacks, page size 248mm x 180 mm, with high visual content including colour plates; other titles are hardback monographs unless otherwise noted.